GW00402902

# CONTENTS

Published by Collins
*An imprint of* HarperCollins*Publishers*
77-85 Fulham Palace Road, Hammersmith, London
W6 8JB

The HarperCollins website address is:
www.**fire**and**water**.com

Copyright © HarperCollins*Publishers* Ltd 2001
Mapping © Bartholomew Ltd 1994, 1996, 1998, 1999, 2001

Collins® is a registered trademark of
HarperCollins*Publishers* Limited

Mapping generated from Bartholomew digital databases

Bartholomew website address is:
www.bartholomewmaps.com

London Underground Map by permission of London
Regional Transport LRT Registered User No. 00/3264

Printed in Italy          OM10944          UDC

ISBN 0 00 712810 X (spiral impression 007)
ISBN 0 00 712809 6 (paperback impression 006)
e-mail: roadcheck@harpercollins.co.uk

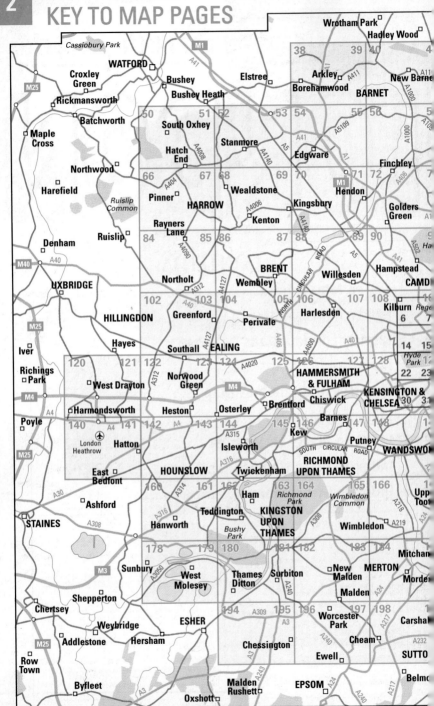

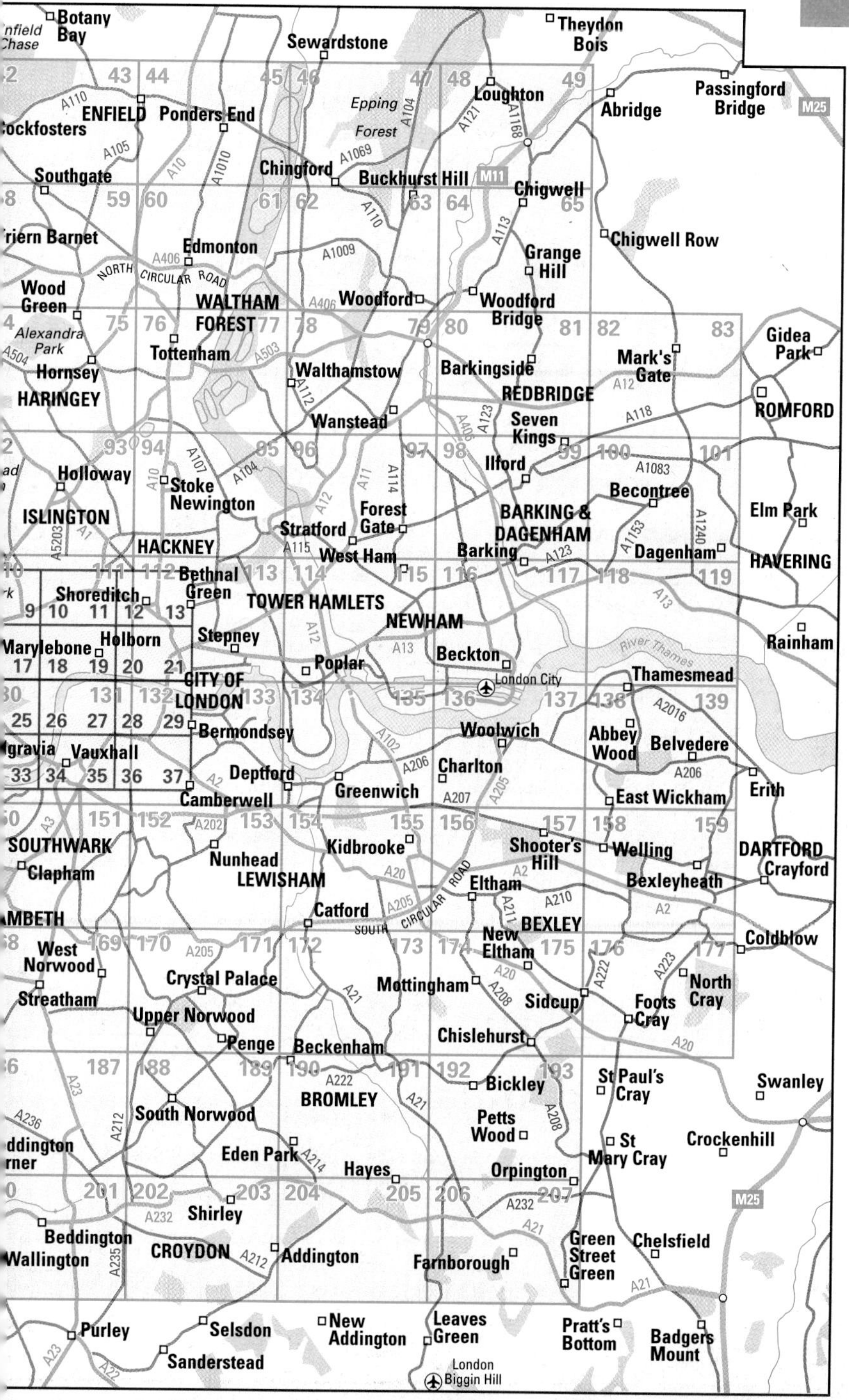

Botany Bay
nfield Chase
Sewardstone
Theydon Bois

2 | 43 | 44 | 45 | 46 | 47 | 48 | 49
Passingford Bridge
M25

ENFIELD  Ponders End
ockfosters
A110
A105
Epping Forest
A104
A121
A1168
Loughton
Abridge

Southgate
A10
A1010
Chingford
A1069
Buckhurst Hill
M11
Chigwell

8 | 59 | 60 | 61 | 62 | 63 | 64 | 65
riern Barnet
A110
A113
Chigwell Row

Edmonton
A1009
Grange Hill

Wood Green
NORTH CIRCULAR ROAD
A406
WALTHAM FOREST
A406
Woodford
Woodford Bridge

75 | 76 | 77 | 78 | 79 | 80 | 81 | 82 | 83
Alexandra Park
A504
Hornsey
Tottenham
A503
Walthamstow
Barkingside
Mark's Gate
A12
Gidea Park

HARINGEY
A112
Wanstead
REDBRIDGE
A118
ROMFORD

2 | 93 | 94 | 95 | 96 | 97 | 98 | 99 | 100 | 101
ad
Holloway
A10
A107
A104
A114
Seven Kings
A123
A1083
Elm Park

Stoke Newington
A12
A1
Forest Gate
Ilford
A406
Becontree
A1240

ISLINGTON
A5203
A1
HACKNEY
Stratford
A115
West Ham
Barking
BARKING & DAGENHAM
A123
A153
Dagenham
A13
HAVERING

Bethnal Green
Shoreditch
9 | 10 | 11 | 12 | 13 | 113 | 114 | 115 | 116 | 117 | 118 | 119
TOWER HAMLETS
NEWHAM
River Thames
Rainham

Marylebone  Holborn  Stepney
17 | 18 | 19 | 20 | 21
A12
A13
Beckton
Thamesmead

CITY OF LONDON
Poplar
London City
A2016
139

30 | 131 | 132 | 133 | 134 | 135 | 136 | 137 | 138
Bermondsey
Woolwich
Abbey Wood
Belvedere

25 | 26 | 27 | 28 | 29
A202
A206
Charlton
A206
Erith

gravia  Vauxhall  Deptford
33 | 34 | 35 | 36 | 37
Camberwell
Greenwich
A207
A205
East Wickham

Southwark
151 | 152 | 153 | 154 | 155 | 156 | 157 | 158 | 159
SOUTHWARK
Nunhead
Kidbrooke
Shooter's Hill
Welling
DARTFORD
Crayford

Clapham
LEWISHAM
A20
Eltham
A2
Bexleyheath
A2

MBETH
Catford
A205
SOUTH CIRCULAR ROAD
BEXLEY
Coldblow

8 | West Norwood | 169 | 170 | 171 | 172 | 173 | 174 | 175 | 176 | 177
New Eltham
A20

Streatham
Crystal Palace
A21
Mottingham
A208
Sidcup
Foots Cray
North Cray

Upper Norwood
Penge
Beckenham
Chislehurst

6 | 187 | 188 | 189 | 190 | 191 | 192 | 193
A236
A23
A212
BROMLEY
A21
Bickley
St Paul's Cray
Swanley

ddington rner
South Norwood
A214
Petts Wood
A208
St Mary Cray
Crockenhill

Eden Park
Hayes
Orpington

0 | 201 | 202 | 203 | 204 | 205 | 206 | 207
A232
A232
M25

Beddington
Shirley
A21
Green Street Green
Chelsfield

Wallington
A235
CROYDON
A212
Addington
Farnborough
A21

Purley
Selsdon
New Addington
Leaves Green
Pratt's Bottom
Badgers Mount

Sanderstead
A23
London Biggin Hill

**4**

# KEY TO CENTRAL MAP SYMBOLS

| | | | |
|---|---|---|---|
| **M4** Motorway | | Leisure & Tourism |
| Dual **A4** Primary Route | | Shopping |
| Dual **A40** 'A' Road | | Administration |
| **B504** 'B' Road | | Health & Welfare |
| Other Road | | Education |
| Street Market | | Industry & Commerce |
| Pedestrian Street | | Public Open Space |
| Access Restriction | | Park/Garden/Sports Ground |
| Track/Footpath | | Cemetery |
| One Way Street | | *POL* Police Station |
| Riverbus | | *Fire Sta* Fire Station |
| CITY Borough Boundary | | *PO* Post Office |
| EC2 Postal District Boundary | | Cinema |
| Main Railway Station | | Theatre |
| Other Railway Station | | Major Hotel |
| London Underground Station | | Embassy |
| DLR Docklands Light Railway Station | | + Church |
| Bus/Coach Station | | Mosque |
| P Car Park | | Synagogue |
| WC Public Toilet | | Mormon Other Place of Worship |
| i Tourist Information Centre | | |

The reference grid on this atlas coincides with the Ordnance Survey National Grid System. The grid interval is 250 metres.

A Grid Reference          8 Page Continuation Number

Scale 1:10,000 (6.3 inches to 1 mile)

# KEY TO MAIN MAP SYMBOLS

**5**

| | | | |
|---|---|---|---|
| M4 | Motorway | | Leisure & Tourism |
| Dual A4 | Primary Route | USA | Administration & Law Embassy |
| Dual A40 | 'A' Road | | Health & Welfare |
| B504 | 'B' Road | | Education |
| | Other Road | | Industry & Commerce |
| | Toll | | Cemetery |
| | Street Market | | Golf Course |
| | Pedestrian Street | | Public Open Space/Allotments |
| | Cycle Path | | Park/Garden/Sports Ground |
| ----- | Track/Footpath | | Wood/Forest |
| → | One Way Street | Pol | Police Station |
| --P-- | Pedestrian Ferry | Fire Sta | Fire Station |
| --V-- | Vehicle Ferry | PO | Post Office |
| | County/Borough Boundary | Lib | Library |
| | Postal District Boundary | ▲ | Youth Hostel |
| | Main Railway Station | □ | Tower Block |
| | Other Railway Station | i | Tourist Information Centre |
| | London Underground Station | Ⓗ | Heliport |
| DLR | Docklands Light Railway Station | WC | Public Toilet |
| | Tramway Station | + | Church |
| | Bus/Coach Station | ☾ | Mosque |
| P | Car Park | ✡ | Synagogue |

The reference grid on this atlas coincides with the Ordnance Survey National Grid System. The grid interval is 500 metres.

| A | Grid Reference | 24 | Page Continuation Number |
|---|---|---|---|

Scale 1:20,000 (3.2 inches to 1 mile)

| 25 | OS National Grid Kilometre Square |
|---|---|

0    0.25    0.50    0.75    1 kilometre

0         ¼        ½ mile

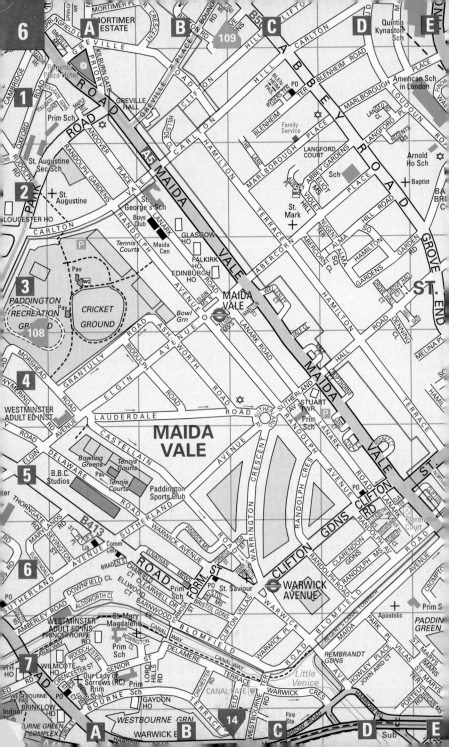

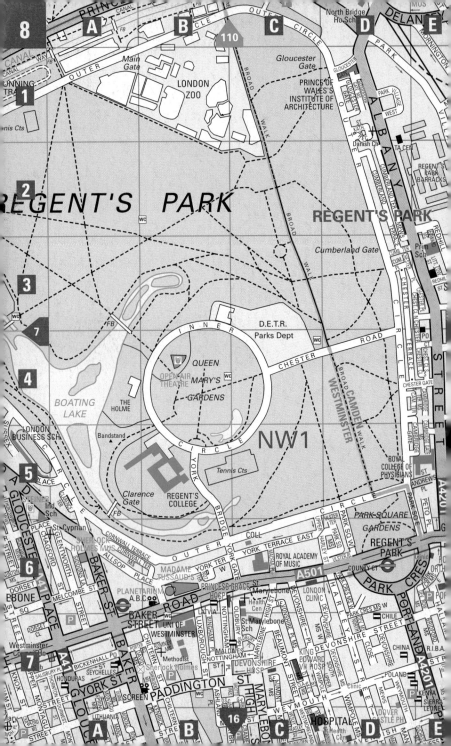

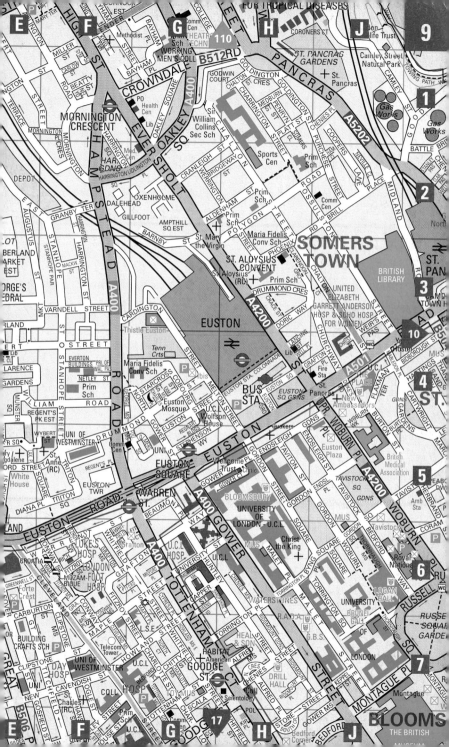

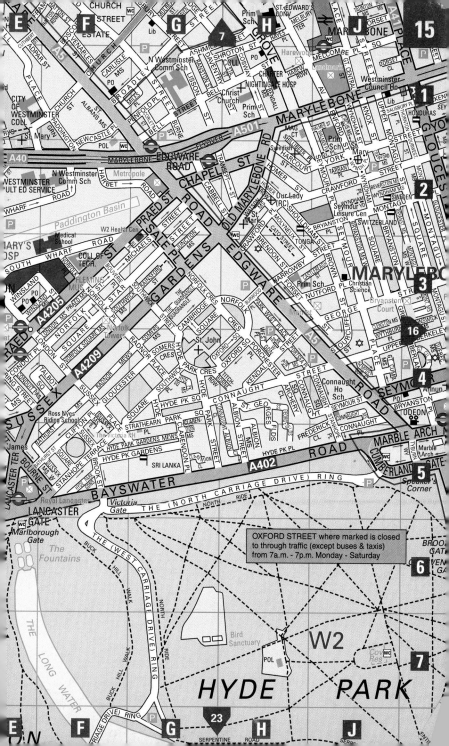

OXFORD STREET where marked is closed to through traffic (except buses & taxis) from 7a.m. - 7p.m. Monday - Saturday

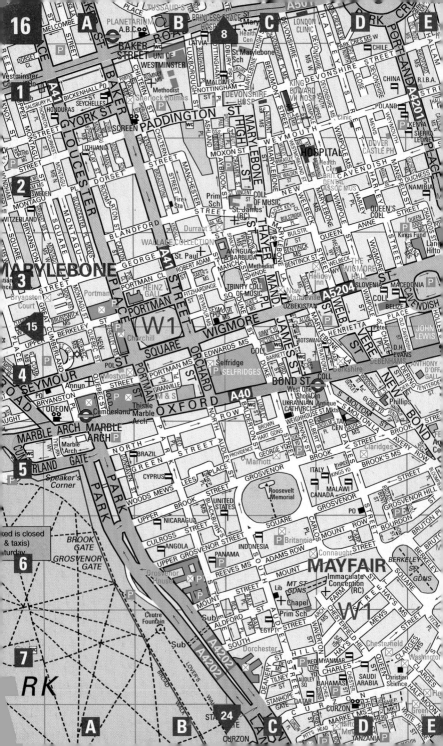

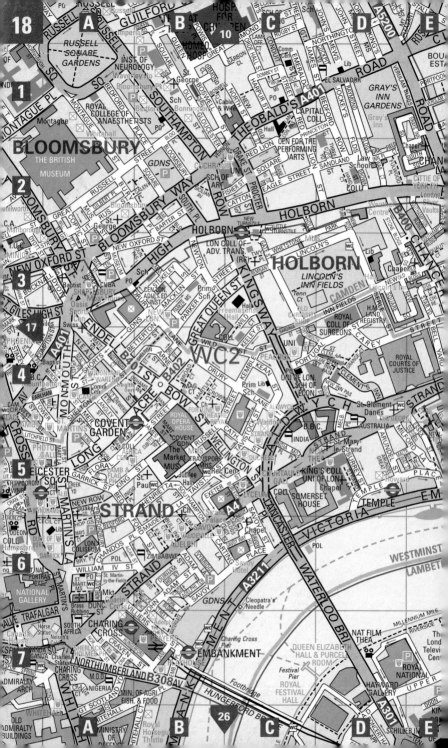

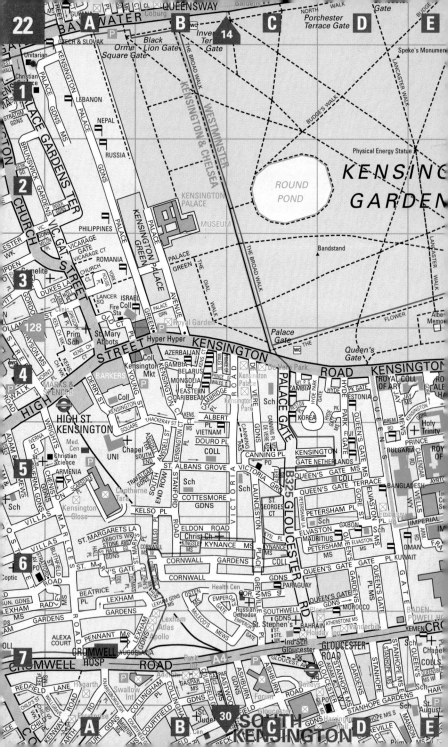

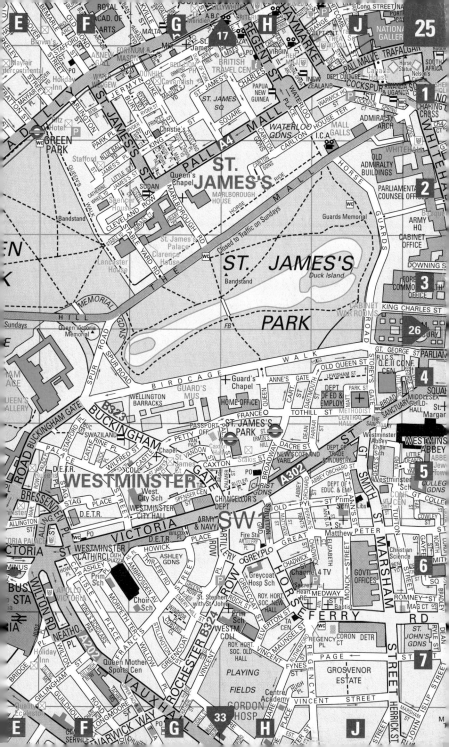

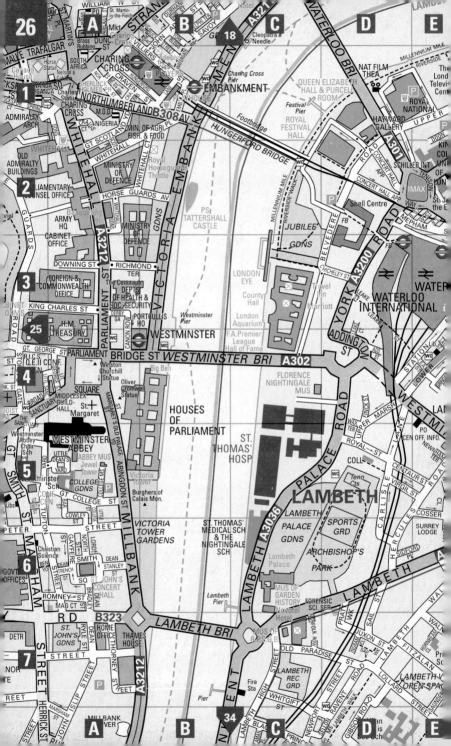

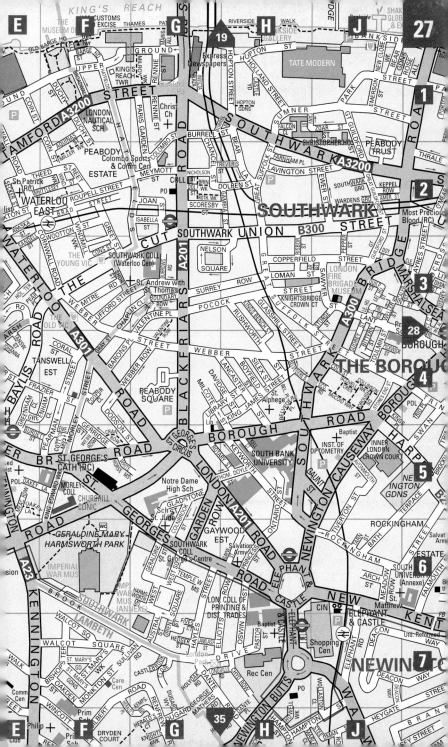

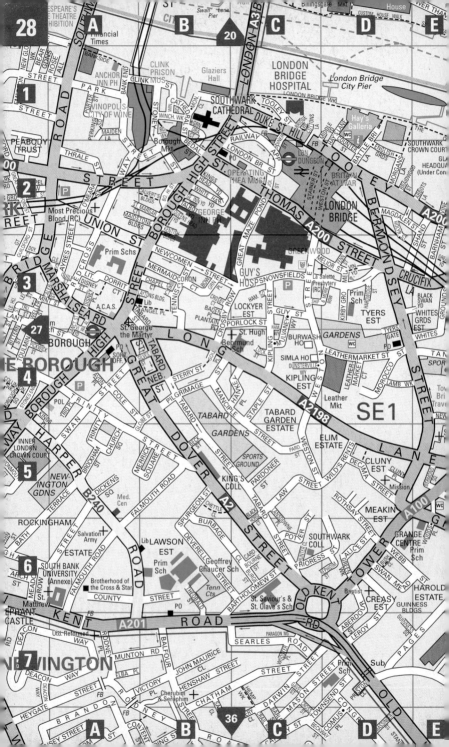

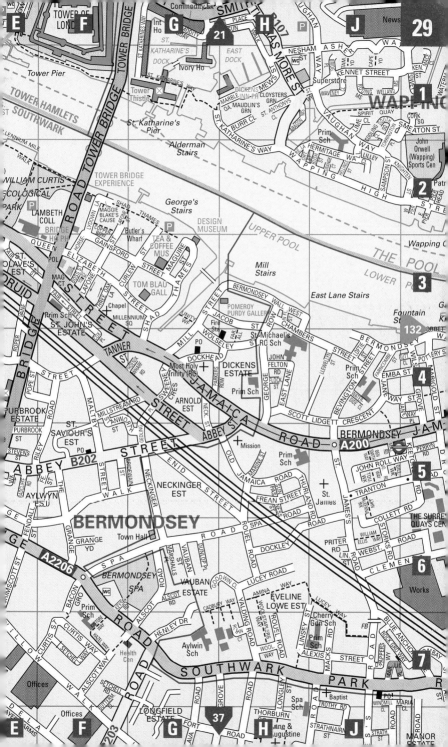

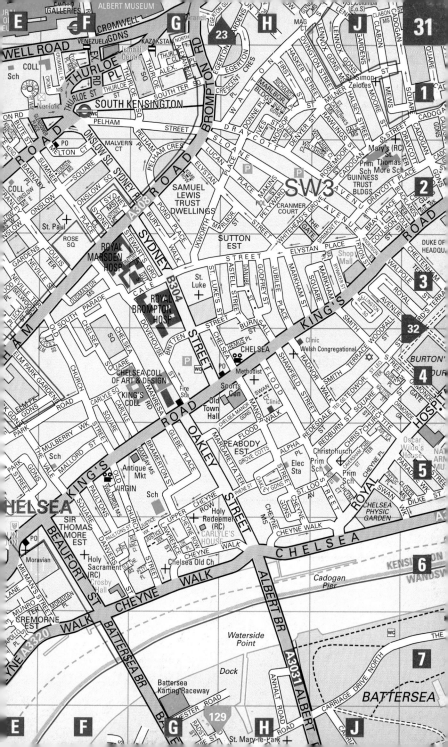

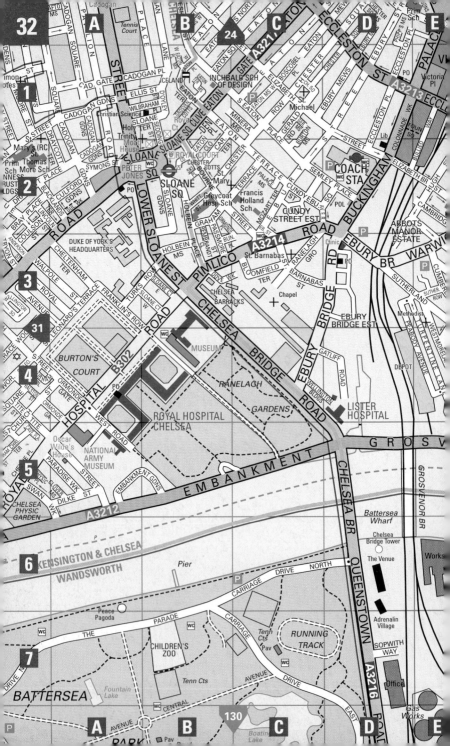

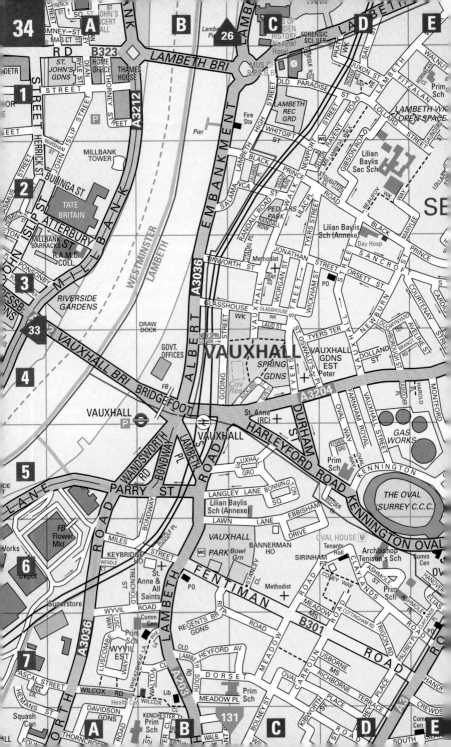

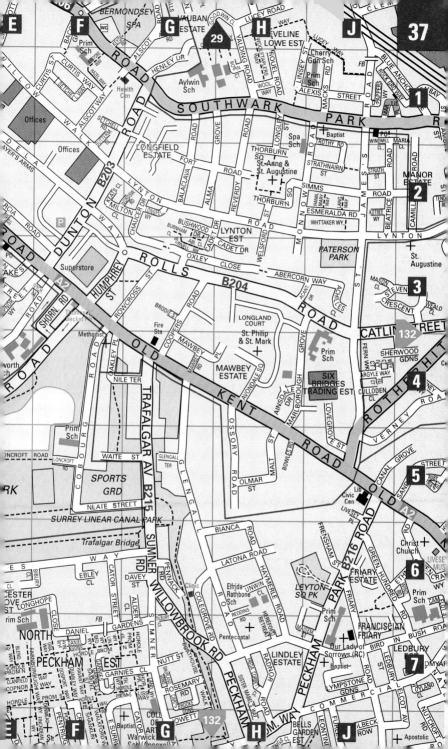

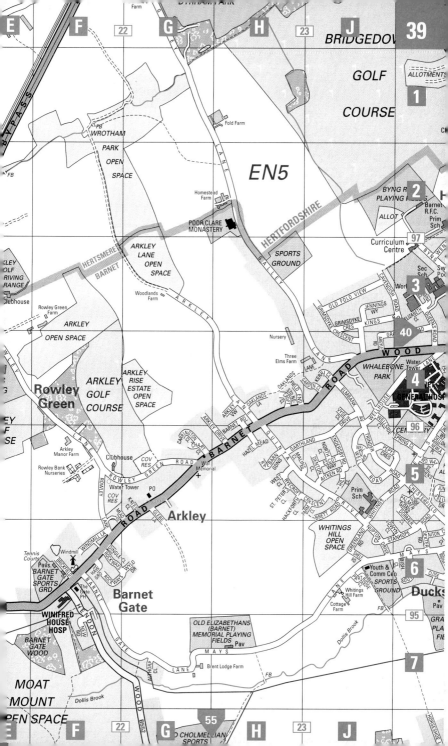

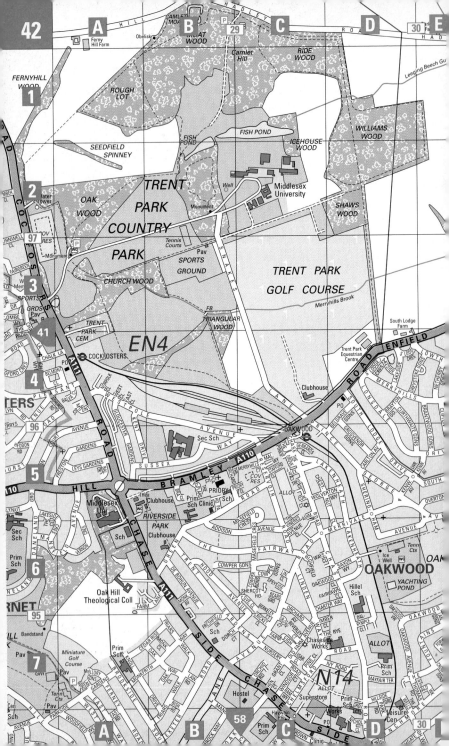

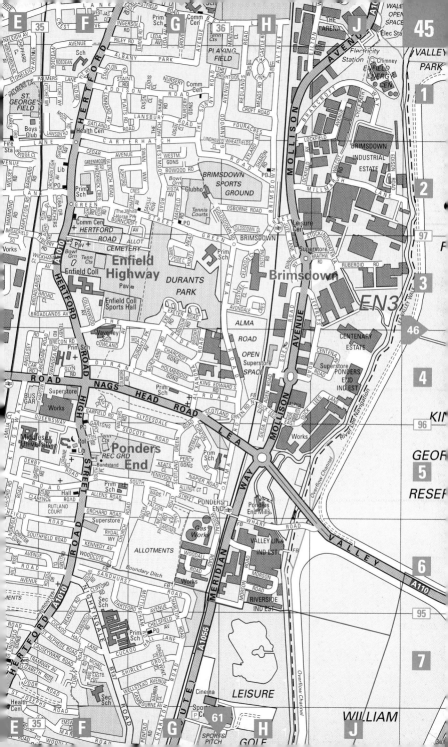

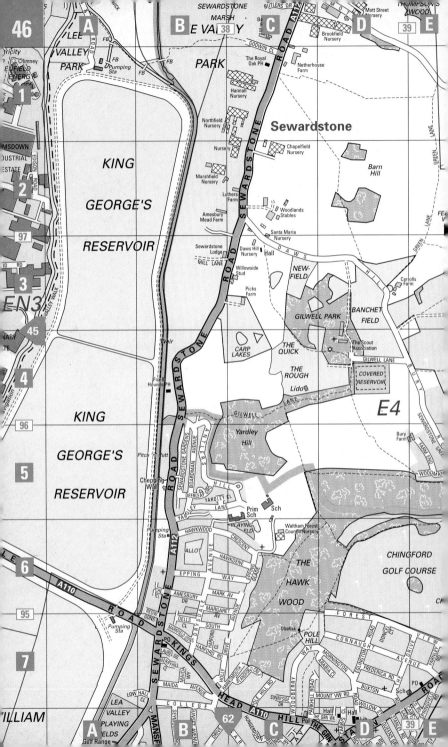

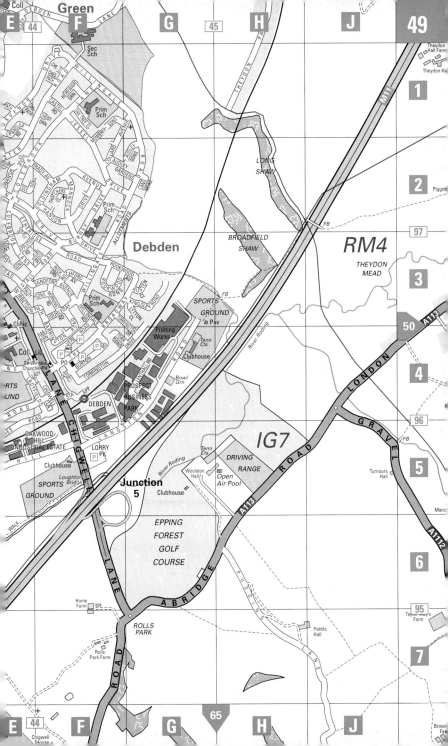

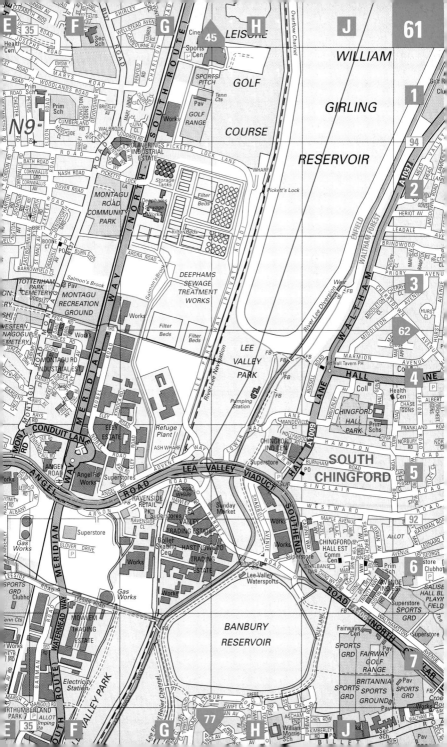

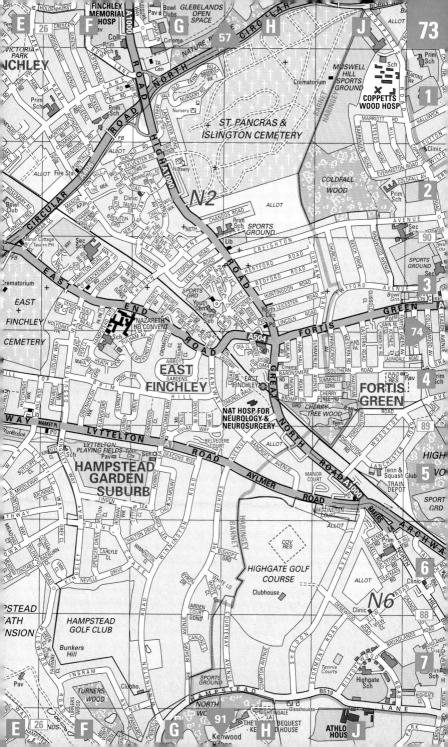

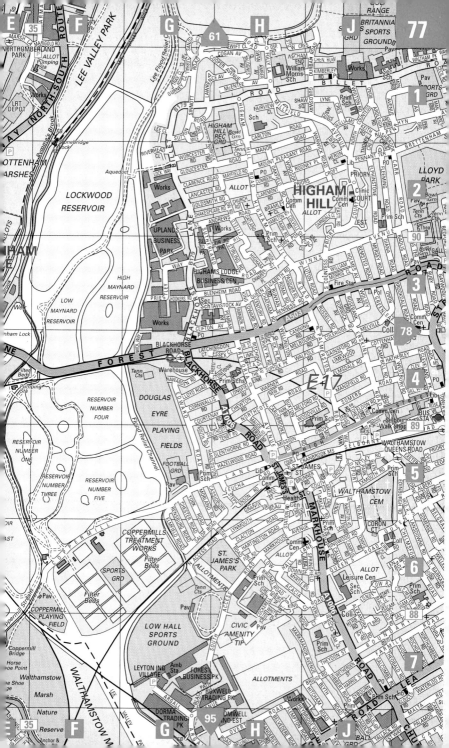

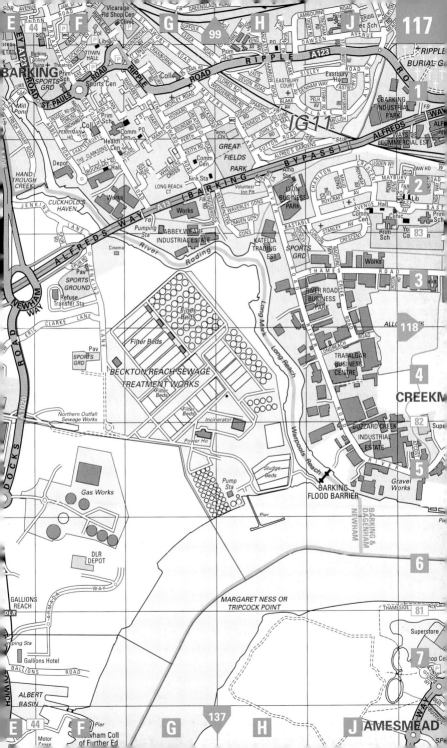

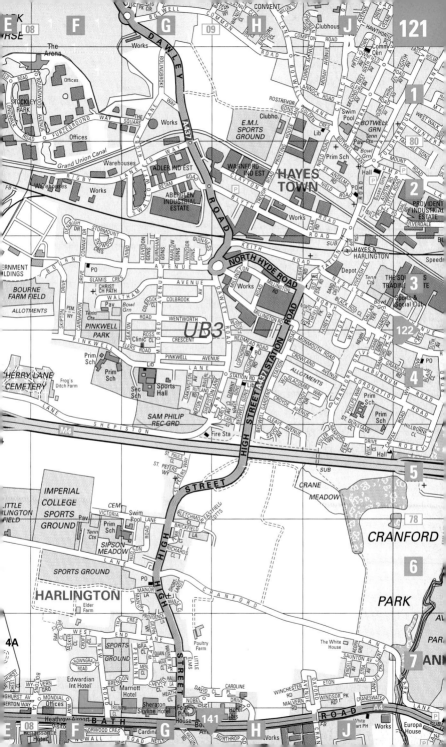

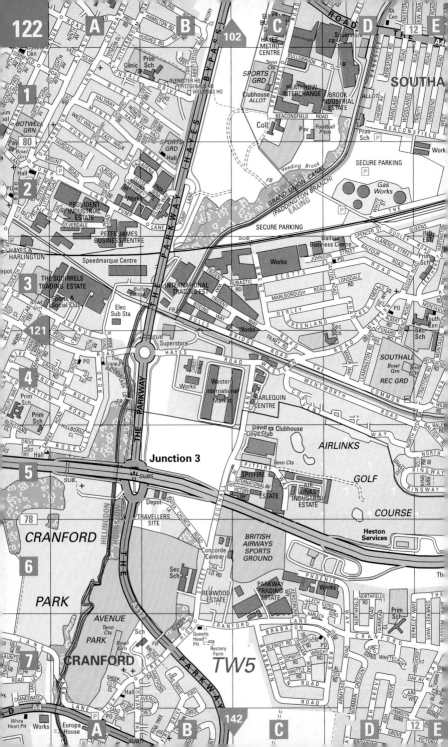

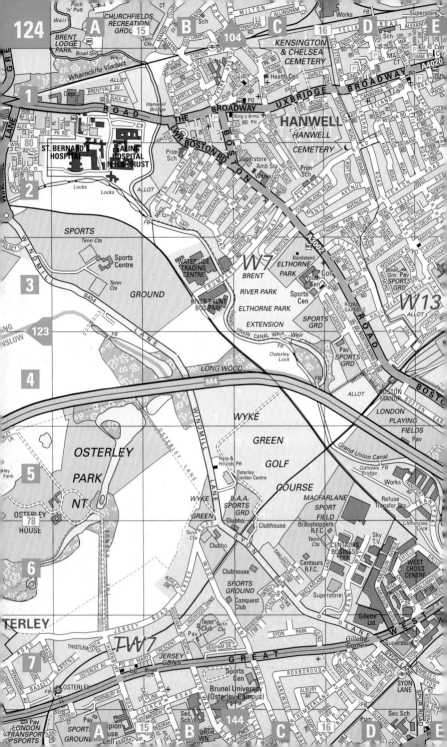

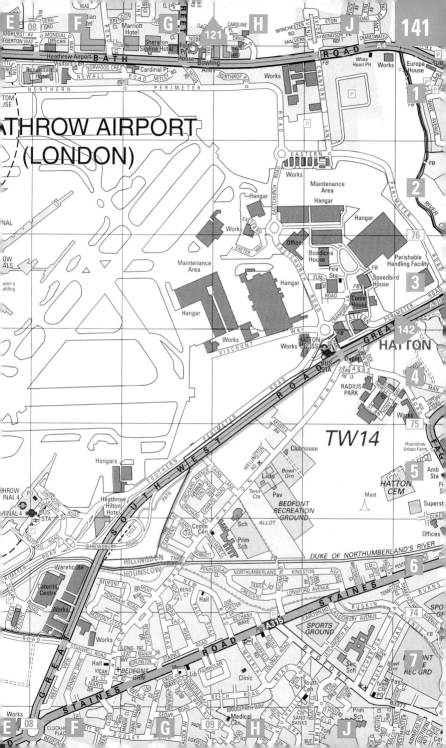

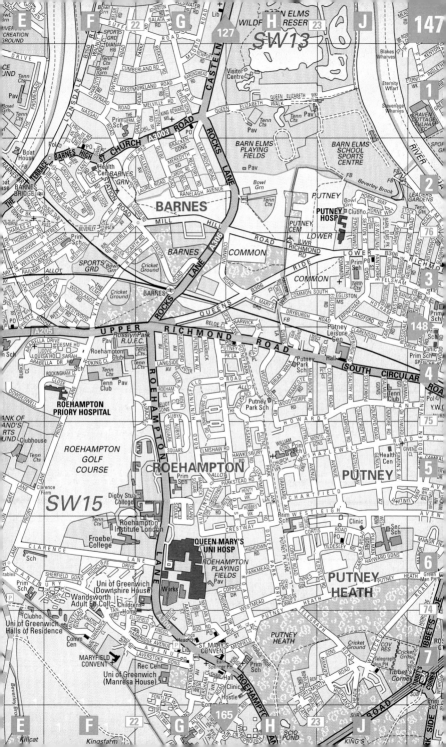

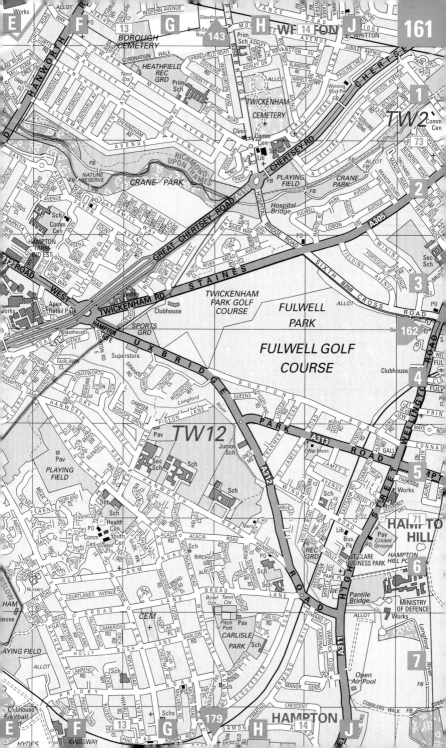

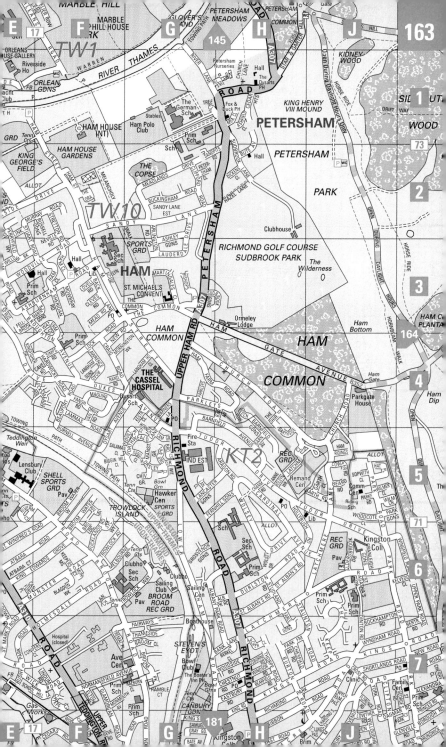

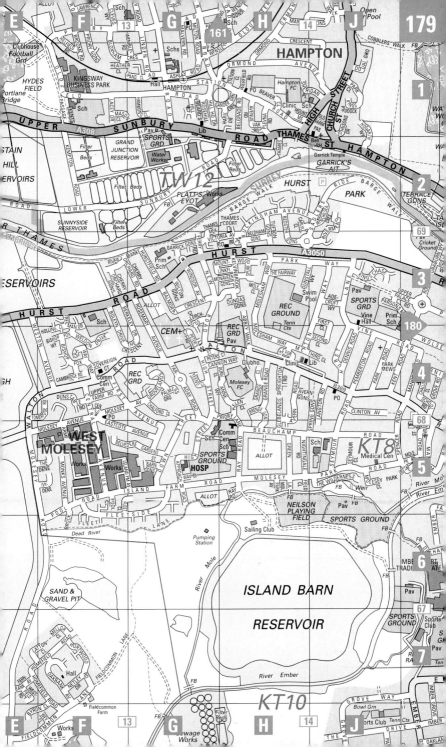

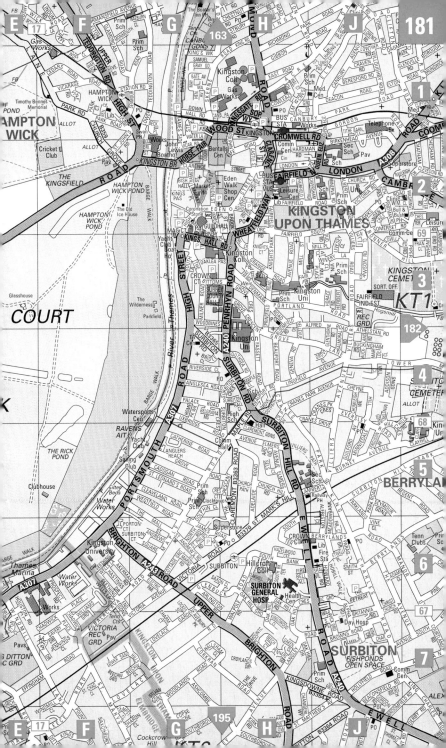

# WEST END THEATRES & CINEMAS

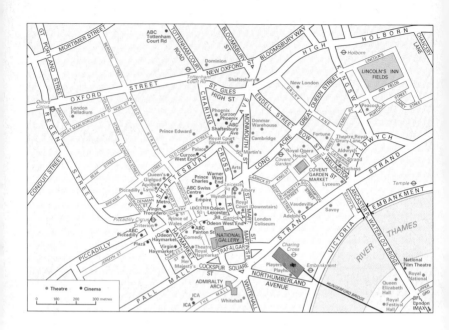

## THEATRES

Adelphi *020 7344 0055*
Albery *020 7369 1730*
Aldwych *020 7416 6003*
Apollo *020 7416 6022*
Arts *020 7836 2132*
Cambridge *020 7494 5054*
Comedy *020 7369 1731*
Criterion *020 7369 1747*
Dominion *020 7656 1888*
Donmar Warehouse
 *020 7369 1732*
Duchess *020 7494 5075*
Fortune *020 7836 2238*
Garrick *020 7494 5085*
Gielgud *020 7494 5065*
Her Majesty's *020 7494 5400*
ICA *020 7930 3647*

London Coliseum *020 7632 8300*
London Palladium *020 7494 5020*
Lyceum *020 7420 8191*
Lyric *020 7494 5045*
New London *020 7405 0072*
Palace *020 7434 0909*
Peacock *020 7314 8800*
Phoenix *020 7369 1733*
Piccadilly *020 7369 1734*
Players *020 7839 1134*
Playhouse *020 7839 4401*
Prince Edward *020 7734 8951*
Prince of Wales *020 7839 5987*
Queen Elizabeth Hall
 *020 7960 4242*
Queen's *020 7494 5041*
Royal Court Theatre Downstairs
 *020 7565 5000*

Royal Court Theatre Upstairs
 *020 7565 5000*
Royal Festival Hall *020 7960 4242*
Royal National *020 7452 3000*
Royal Opera House
 *020 7304 4000*
St. Martin's *020 7836 1443*
Savoy *020 7836 8888*
Shaftesbury *020 7379 5399*
Strand *020 7930 8800*
Theatre Royal, Drury Lane
 *020 7494 5550*
Theatre Royal, Haymarket
 *020 7930 8800*
Vaudeville *020 7836 9987*
Whitehall *020 7369 1735*
Wyndhams *020 7369 1736*

## CINEMAS

ABC Panton St *020 7930 0631*
ABC Piccadilly *020 7437 3561*
ABC ShaftesburyAvenue
 *020 7836 6279*
ABC Swiss Centre *020 7439 4470*
ABC Tottenham Court Rd
 *020 7636 6148*
BFI London IMAX *020 7902 1200*
Curzon Phoenix *020 7369 1721*
Curzon West End *020 7369 1722*

Empire *020 7437 1234*
ICA *020 7930 3647*
Metro *020 7437 0757*
National Film Theatre
 *020 7928 3232*
Odeon Haymarket *0426 915353*
Odeon Leicester Sq
 *020 8315 4215*
Odeon Mezzanine
(Odeon Leicester Sq)
 *020 8315 4215*

Odeon West End *020 8315 4221*
Plaza *020 7437 1234*
Prince Charles *020 7437 8181*
Virgin Haymarket *0870 907 0712*
Virgin Trocadero *0870 907 0716*
Warner West End *020 7437 4347*

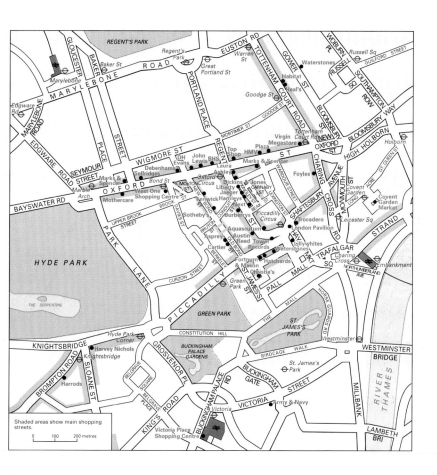

## SHOPS

Aquascutum *020 7734 6090*
Army & Navy *020 7834 1234*
Asprey *020 7493 6767*
Austin Reed *020 7734 6789*
BHS (Oxford St) *020 7629 2011*
Cartier *020 7493 6962*
Christie's *020 7839 9060*
Covent Garden Market
 *020 7836 9137*
DH Evans *020 7629 8800*
Debenhams *020 7580 3000*
Dickins & Jones *020 7734 7070*
Fenwick *020 7629 9161*
Fortnum & Mason *020 7734 8040*
Foyles *020 7437 5660*
Habitat (Tottenham Court Rd)
 *020 7631 3880*
Hamleys *020 7734 3161*
Harrods *020 7730 1234*

Harvey Nichols *020 7235 5000*
Hatchards *020 7439 9921*
Heal's *020 7636 1666*
HMV *020 7631 3423*
Jaeger *020 7200 4000*
John Lewis *020 7629 7711*
Laura Ashley (Regent St)
 *020 7355 1363*
Liberty *020 7734 1234*
Lillywhites *020 7930 3181*
London Pavilion *020 7437 1838*
Marks & Spencer (Marble Arch)
 *020 7935 7954*
Marks & Spencer (Oxford St)
 *020 7437 7722*
Mothercare *020 7580 1688*
Next (Regent St) *020 7434 2515*
Plaza on Oxford St
 *020 7637 8811*

Selfridges *020 7629 1234*
Sotheby's *020 7493 8080*
Top Shop & Top Man
 *020 7636 7700*
Tower Records *020 7439 2500*
Trocadero *020 7439 1791*
Victoria Place Shopping Centre
 *020 7931 8811*
Virgin Megastore *020 7580 5822*
Waterstones (Gower St)
 *020 7636 1577*
Waterstones (Piccadilly)
 *020 7851 2400*

# INDEX TO PLACES OF INTEREST

## General Abbreviations

| | | | | | |
|---|---|---|---|---|---|
| All. | Alley | Embk. | Embankment | Pav. | Pavilion |
| Allot. | Allotments | Est. | Estate | Pk. | Park |
| Amb. | Ambulance | Ex. | Exchange | Pl. | Place |
| App. | Approach | Exhib. | Exhibition | Pol. | Police |
| Arc. | Arcade | F.B. | Footbridge | Prec. | Precinct |
| Av./Ave. | Avenue | F.C. | Football Club | Prim. | Primary |
| Bdy. | Broadway | Fld./Flds. | Field/Fields | Prom. | Promenade |
| Bk. | Bank | Fm. | Farm | Pt. | Point |
| Bldgs. | Buildings | Gall. | Gallery | Quad. | Quadrant |
| Boul. | Boulevard | Gar. | Garage | R.C. | Roman Catholic |
| Bowl. | Bowling | Gdn./Gdns. | Garden/Gardens | Rd./Rds | Road/Roads |
| Br./Bri. | Bridge | Govt. | Government | Rec. | Recreation |
| C. of E. | Church of England | Gra. | Grange | Res. | Reservoir |
| Cath. | Cathedral | Grd./Grds. | Ground/Grounds | Ri. | Rise |
| Cem. | Cemetery | Grn./Grns. | Green/Greens | S. | South |
| Cen. | Central, Centre | Gro./Gros. | Grove/Groves | Sch. | School |
| Cft./Cfts. | Croft/Crofts | Gt. | Great | Sec. | Secondary |
| Ch. | Church | Ho./Hos. | House/Houses | Shop. | Shopping |
| Chyd. | Churchyard | Hosp. | Hospital | Sq. | Square |
| Cin. | Cinema | Hts. | Heights | St. | Saint |
| Circ. | Circus | Ind. | Industrial | St./Sts. | Street/Streets |
| Cl./Clo. | Close | Int. | International | Sta. | Station |
| Co. | County | Junct. | Junction | Sub. | Subway |
| Coll. | College | La./Las. | Lane/Lanes | Swim. | Swimming |
| Comm. | Community | Lib. | Library | T.A. | Territorial Army |
| Conv. | Convent | Lo. | Lodge | T.H. | Town Hall |
| Cor./Cors. | Corner/Corners | Lwr. | Lower | Tenn. | Tennis |
| Coron. | Coroners | Mag. | Magistrates | Ter. | Terrace |
| Cotts. | Cottages | Mans. | Mansions | Thea. | Theatre |
| Cov. | Covered | Mem. | Memorial | Trd. | Trading |
| Crem. | Crematorium | Mkt./Mkts | Market/Markets | Twr./Twrs. | Tower/Towers |
| Cres. | Crescent | Ms. | Mews | Uni. | University |
| Ct./Cts. | Court/Courts | Mt. | Mount | Vil. | Villa, Villas |
| Ctyd. | Courtyard | Mus. | Museum | Vw. | View |
| Dep. | Depot | N. | North | W. | West |
| Dev. | Development | N.T. | National Trust | Wd. | Wood |
| Dr. | Drive | Nat. | National | Wds. | Woods |
| Dws. | Dwellings | P.H. | Public House | Wf. | Wharf |
| E. | East | P.O. | Post Office | Wk. | Walk |
| Ed. | Education | Par. | Parade | Wks. | Works |
| Elec. | Electricity | Pas. | Passage | Yd. | Yard |

## Post Town Abbreviations

| | | | | | |
|---|---|---|---|---|---|
| Bark. | Barking | Har. | Harrow | Stai. | Staines |
| Barn. | Barnet | Hmptn. | Hampton | Stan. | Stanmore |
| Beck. | Beckenham | Houns. | Hounslow | Sthl. | Southall |
| Belv. | Belvedere | Ilf. | Ilford | Sun. | Sunbury-on-Thames |
| Bex. | Bexley | Islw. | Isleworth | | |
| Bexh. | Bexleyheath | Kes. | Keston | Surb. | Surbiton |
| Borwd. | Borehamwood | Kings.T. | Kingston upon Thames | Sutt. | Sutton |
| Brent. | Brentford | | | T.Ditt. | Thames Ditton |
| Brom. | Bromley | Loug. | Loughton | Tedd. | Teddington |
| Buck.H. | Buckhurst Hill | Mitch. | Mitcham | Th.Hth. | Thornton Heath |
| Cars. | Carshalton | Mord. | Morden | Twick. | Twickenham |
| Chess. | Chessington | N.Mal. | New Malden | Uxb. | Uxbridge |
| Chig. | Chigwell | Nthlt. | Northolt | W.Mol. | West Molesey |
| Chis. | Chislehurst | Nthwd. | Northwood | W.Wick. | West Wickham |
| Cob. | Cobham | Orp. | Orpington | Wall. | Wallington |
| Croy. | Croydon | Pnr. | Pinner | Walt. | Walton-on-Thames |
| Dag. | Dagenham | Pot.B. | Potters Bar | Wat. | Watford |
| Dart. | Dartford | Pur. | Purley | Wdf.Grn. | Woodford Green |
| E.Mol. | East Molesey | Rain. | Rainham | Well. | Welling |
| Edg. | Edgware | Rich. | Richmond | Wem. | Wembley |
| Enf. | Enfield | Rom. | Romford | West Dr. | West Drayton |
| Epp. | Epping | Ruis. | Ruislip | Wor.Pk. | Worcester Park |
| Felt. | Feltham | S.Croy. | South Croydon | | |
| Grnf. | Greenford | Sid. | Sidcup | | |

The street name and postal district or post town of an entry is followed by the page number and grid reference on which the name will be found, e.g. Abbey Road SW19 will be found on page 167 and in square F7.

All streets within the Central London enlarged scale section (pages 6-37) are shown in bold type when named in the index, e.g. **Abbey St. SE1** will be found on page **29** and in square **E5**.

This index contains some street names in standard text which are followed by another street named in italics. In these cases the street in standard text does not actually appear on the map due to insufficient space but can be located close to the street named in italics.

# A

A.C. Ct., T.Ditt. 180 D6
*Harvest La.*
Aaron Hill Rd. E6 116 D5
Abberley Ms. SW4 150 B3
*Cedars Rd.*
Abbess Cl. E6 116 B5
*Oliver Gdns.*
Abbess Cl. SW2 169 H1
Abbeville Rd. N8 74 D4
*Barrington Rd.*
Abbeville Rd. SW4 150 C6
Abbey Av., Wem. 105 H2
Abhey Cl., Hayes 122 A1
Abbey Cl., Nthlt. 103 F3
*Invicta Gro.*
Abbey Cl., Pnr. 66 B3
Abbey Cres., Belv. 139 G4
Abbey Dr. SW17 168 A5
**Abbey Gdns. NW8** **6 C2**
Abbey Gdns. NW8 109 F2
Abbey Gdns. SE16 132 D4
*Monnow Rd.*
Abbey Gdns. W6 128 B6
Abbey Gro. SE2 138 B4
Abbey Ind. Est., Wem. 105 J1
Abbey La. E15 114 C2
Abbey La., Beck. 172 A7
Abbey Ms. E17 78 A5
*Leamington Av.*
**Abbey Orchard St.** **25 J5**
**SW1**
Abbey Orchard St. 130 D3
SW1
Abbey Par. SW19 167 F7
*Merton High St.*
Abbey Par. W5 105 J3
*Hanger La.*
Abbey Pk., Beck. 172 A7
Abbey Retail Pk., Bark. 117 E7
Abbey Rd. E15 114 D1
**Abbey Rd. NW6** **6 C1**
Abbey Rd. NW6 90 E7
Abbey Rd. NW8 109 F2
Abbey Rd. NW10 106 B2
Abbey Rd. SE2 138 D4
Abbey Rd. SW19 167 F7
Abbey Rd., Bark. 117 F1
Abbey Rd., Belv. 138 D4
Abbey Rd., Bexh. 159 E4
Abbey Rd., Croy. 201 H3
Abbey Rd., Enf. 44 B5
Abbey Rd., Ilf. 81 G5
Abbey Rd. Est. NW8 109 E1
Abbey St. E13 115 G4
**Abbey St. SE1** **29 E5**
Abbey St. SE1 132 B3
Abbey Ter. SE2 138 C4
Abbey Vw. NW7 55 F3
Abbey Wk., W.Mol. 179 H3
Abbey Way SE2 138 D3
Abbey Wf. Ind. Est., 117 G2
Bark.
Abbey Wd. Rd. SE2 138 B4
Abbeydale Rd., Wem. 106 A4
Abbeyfield Est. SE16 133 F4
Abbeyfield Rd. SE16 133 F4
Abbeyfields Cl. NW10 106 A2
Abboyhill Rd., Sid. 176 E3
Abbot St. E8 94 C6
Abbots Cl. N1 93 J6
*Alwyne Rd.*
Abbots Cl., Orp. 207 F1
Abbots Cl., Ruis. 84 D3
Abbots Dr., Har. 85 G2
Abbots Gdns. N2 73 G4
**Abbots Gdns. W8** **22 A6**
Abbots Grn., Croy. 203 G6
**Abbots La. SE1** **28 E2**
**Abbots Manor Est.** **32 D2**
**SW1**
Abbots Manor Est. 130 D3
SW1
Abbots Pk. SW2 169 G1
Abbot's Pl. NW6 108 E1
Abbot's Rd. E6 116 A1
Abbots Rd., Edg. 54 C7
Abbots Ter. N8 74 E6
**Abbots Wk. W8** **22 A6**
Abbots Way, Beck. 189 H5
Abbotsbury Cl. E15 114 C2
Abbotsbury Cl. W14 128 C2
*Abbotsbury Rd.*
Abbotsbury Gdns., 66 C6
Pnr.
Abbotsbury Ms. SE15 153 F3
Abbotsbury Rd. W14 128 B2
Abbotsbury Rd., 205 F2
Brom.
Abbotsbury Rd., 184 E5
Mord.
Abbotsford Av. N15 75 J4

Abbotsford Gdns., 63 G7
Wdf.Grn.
Abbotsford Rd., Ilf. 100 A2
Abbotshade Rd. SE16 133 G1
Abbotshall Av. N14 58 C3
Abbotshall Rd. SE6 172 D1
Abbotsleigh Cl., Sutt. 198 E7
Abbotsleigh Rd. 168 C4
SW16
Abbotsmede Cl., 162 C2
Twick.
Abbotstone Rd. 147 J3
SW15
Abbotswell Rd. SE4 153 J5
Abbotswood Cl., 138/139 E3
Belv.
*Coptefield Dr.*
Abbotswood Gdns., 80 C3
Ilf.
Abbotswood Rd. 152 B4
SE22
Abbotswood Rd. 168 D3
SW16
Abbotswood Way, 122 B1
Hayes
Abbott Av. SW20 184 A2
Abbott Cl., Hmptn. 161 E6
Abbott Cl., Nthlt. 85 F6
Abbott Rd. E14 114 C5
Abbotts Cl. SE28 118 C7
Abbotts Cl., Rom. 83 H3
Abbotts Cres. E4 62 D4
Abbotts Cres., Enf. 43 H2
Abbotts Dr., Wem. 86 E2
Abbotts Pk. Rd. E10 78 C7
Abbotts Rd., Barn. 40 E4
Abbotts Rd., Mitch. 186 C4
Abbotts Rd., Sthl. 123 E1
Abbotts Rd., Sutt. 198 C3
Abbotts Wk., Bexh. 138 D7
**Abchurch La. EC4** **20 C5**
Abchurch La. EC4 112 A7
**Abchurch Yd. EC4** **20 B5**
Abdale Rd. W12 127 H1
Aberavon Rd. E3 113 H3
Abercairn Rd. SW16 168 C7
Aberconway Rd., 184 E3
Mord.
Abercorn Cl. NW7 56 B7
**Abercorn Cl. NW8** **6 C3**
Abercorn Cl. NW8 109 F3
Abercorn Cres., Har. 85 H1
Abercorn Gdns., Har. 69 G7
Abercorn Gdns., 82 B6
Rom.
**Abercorn Pl. NW8** **6 C3**
Abercorn Pl. NW8 109 F3
Abercorn Rd. NW7 56 B7
Abercorn Rd., Stan. 53 F7
**Abercorn Way SE1** **37 H3**
Abercorn Way SE1 132 D5
Abercrombie Dr., Enf. 44 D1
Abercrombie St. 149 H2
SW11
Aberdare Cl., W.Wick. 204 C2
Aberdare Gdns. NW6 91 E7
Aberdare Gdns. NW7 56 A7
Aberdare Rd., Enf. 45 F4
Aberdeen La. N5 93 H5
Aberdeen Par. N18 60/61 E5
*Angel Rd.*
Aberdeen Pk. N5 93 H5
Aberdeen Pk. Ms. N5 93 J4
**Aberdeen Pl. NW8** **6 E5**
Aberdeen Pl. NW8 109 G4
Aberdeen Rd. N5 93 J4
Aberdeen Rd. N18 60 E5
Aberdeen Rd. NW10 89 F5
Aberdeen Rd., Croy. 201 J4
Aberdeen Rd., Har. 68 C2
Aberdeen Sq. E14 133 J1
*Westferry Circ.*
Aberdeen Ter. SE3 154 D2
Aberdour Rd., Ilf. 100 B3
**Aberdour St. SE1** **36 D1**
Aberdour St. SE1 132 B4
Aberfeldy St. E14 114 C6
Aberford Gdns. SE18 156 B1
Aberford Rd., Borwd. 38 A2
Aberfoyle Rd. SW16 168 D6
Abergeldie Rd. SE12 155 H6
Aberglen Ind. Est., 121 G2
Hayes
Abernethy Rd. SE13 154 E4
Abersham Rd. E8 94 C5
Abery St. SE18 137 H4
Abingdon Cl. NW1 92 D6
*Camden Sq.*
**Abingdon Cl. SE1** **37 G3**
Abingdon Cl. SW19 167 F6
Abingdon Rd. N3 73 F2
Abingdon Rd. SW16 186 E2
Abingdon Rd. W8 128 D3
**Abingdon St. SW1** **26 A5**

Abingdon St. SW1 130 E3
Abingdon Vil. W8 128 D3
Abinger Cl., Bark. 100 A4
Abinger Cl., Brom. 192 B3
Abinger Cl., Wall. 200/201 E5
*Garden Cl.*
Abinger Gdns., Islw. 144 B3
Abinger Gro. SE8 133 J6
Abinger Ms. W9 108 D4
*Warlock Rd.*
Abinger Rd. W4 127 E3
Ablett St. SE16 133 F5
Abney Gdns. N16 94 C2
Aboyne Dr. SW20 183 G2
Aboyne Est. SW17 167 G3
Aboyne Rd. NW10 88 E3
Aboyne Rd. SW17 167 G3
Abridge Rd., Chig. 49 G6
Abridge Way, Bark. 118 B3
Abyssinia Cl. SW11 149 H4
*Cairns Rd.*
Acacia Av. N17 60 A7
Acacia Av., Brent. 124 E7
Acacia Av., Mitch. 186 B2
*Acacia Rd.*
Acacia Av., Ruis. 84 A1
Acacia Av., Wem. 87 H5
Acacia Cl. SE8 133 H4
Acacia Cl. SE20 188 D2
*Selby Rd.*
Acacia Cl., Orp. 193 G5
Acacia Cl., Stan. 52 B6
Acacia Dr., Sutt. 198 C1
**Acacia Gdns. NW8** **7 F1**
Acacia Gdns., 204 C2
W.Wick.
Acacia Gro. SE21 170 A2
Acacia Gro., N.Mal. 182 D3
Acacia Ms., West Dr. 120 A6
Acacia Pl. NW8 7 F1
Acacia Pl. NW8 109 G2
Acacia Rd. E11 97 E2
Acacia Rd. E17 77 H6
Acacia Rd. N22 75 G1
**Acacia Rd. NW8** **7 F1**
Acacia Rd. NW8 109 G2
Acacia Rd. SW16 187 E1
Acacia Rd. W3 106 C7
Acacia Rd., Beck. 189 J3
Acacia Rd., Enf. 44 A1
Acacia Rd., Hmptn. 161 G6
Acacia Rd., Mitch. 186 B2
Acacia Way, Sid. 175 J1
Academy Gdns., 202 C1
Croy.
Academy Gdns., 102 D2
Nthlt.
Academy Pl. SE18 156 C1
Academy Rd. SE18 156 C1
**Acanthus Dr. SE1** **37 H3**
Acanthus Dr. SE1 132 D5
Acanthus Rd. SW11 150 A3
Accommodation Rd. 72 C7
NW11
Acer Av., Hayes 102 E5
Acfold Rd. SW6 148 E1
**Achilles Cl. SE1** **37 J3**
Achilles Cl. SE1 132 D5
Achilles Rd. NW6 90 D5
Achilles St. SE14 133 H7
**Achilles Way W1** **24 C2**
Acklam Rd. W10 108 C5
Acklington Dr. NW9 70 E1
Ackmar Rd. SW6 148 D1
Ackroyd Dr. E3 113 J5
Ackroyd Rd. SE23 153 G7
Ackworth Cl. N9 45 F7
*Turin Rd.*
Acland Cl. SE18 137 G7
*Clothworkers Rd.*
Acland Cres. SE5 152 A4
Acland Rd. NW2 89 H6
Acock Gro., Nthlt. 85 H5
*Dorchester Rd.*
Acol Cres., Ruis. 84 B5
Acol Rd. NW6 90 D7
Aconbury Rd., Dag. 118 B1
Acorn Cl. E4 62 B5
*The Lawns*
Acorn Cl., Chis. 175 F5
Acorn Cl., Enf. 43 H1
Acorn Cl., Hmptn. 161 H6
Acorn Cl., Stan. 53 E7
Acorn Ct., Ilf. 81 H6
Acorn Gdns. SE19 188 C1
Acorn Gdns. W3 106 D5
Acorn Gro., Hayes 121 J7
Acorn Par. SE15 132/133 E7
*Carlton Gro.*
Acorn Wk. SE16 133 H1
Acorn Way SE23 171 G3
Acorn Way, Orp. 207 E4
Acorns, The, Chig. 65 H4

Acre Dr. SE22 152 D4
Acre La. SW2 150 E4
Acre La., Cars. 200 A4
Acre La., Wall. 200 A4
Acre Path, Nthlt. 84/85 E6
*Arnold Rd.*
Acre Rd. SW19 167 G6
Acre Rd., Dag. 101 H7
Acre Rd., Kings.T. 181 H1
Acris St. SW18 149 F5
Acton Cl. N9 60 D2
Acton Hill Ms. W3 126 B1
*Uxbridge Rd.*
Acton La. NW10 106 E2
Acton La. W3 126 C2
Acton La. W4 126 D3
Acton Ms. E8 112 C1
Acton Pk. Ind. Est. 126 D2
W3
**Acton St. WC1** **10 C4**
Acton St. WC1 111 F3
Acuba Rd. SW18 166 E2
Acworth Cl. N9 45 F7
*Turin Rd.*
Ada Gdns. E14 114 D6
Ada Gdns. E15 115 F1
Ada Pl. E2 112 D1
Ada Rd. SE5 132 B7
Ada Rd., Wem. 87 G3
Ada St. E8 112 E1
Adair Cl. SE25 188 E3
Adair Rd. W10 108 B4
Adair Twr. W10 108 B4
*Appleford Rd.*
**Adam & Eve Ct. W1** **17 G3**
Adam & Eve Ms. W8 128 D3
**Adam Ct. SW7** **30 D1**
Adam Pl. N16 94 C2
*Stoke Newington High St.*
Adam Rd. E4 61 J6
**Adam St. WC2** **18 B6**
Adam St. WC2 111 E7
Adam Wk. SW6 127 J7
Adams Cl. N3 56 D7
*Falkland Av.*
Adams Cl. NW9 88 B2
Adams Cl., Surb. 181 J6
**Adams Ct. EC2** **20 C3**
Adams Gdns. Est. 133 F2
SE16
*St. Marychurch St.*
Adams Pl. E14 134 B1
*North Colonnade*
Adams Pl. N7 93 F5
*George's Rd.*
Adams Rd. N17 76 B2
Adams Rd., Beck. 189 H5
**Adams Row W1** **16 C6**
Adams Row W1 110 A7
Adams Sq., Bexh. 158/159 E3
*Regency Way*
Adams Wk., Kings.T. 181 H2
Adams Way, Croy. 188 C6
Adamson Rd. E16 115 G6
Adamson Rd. NW3 91 G7
Adamsrill Cl., Enf. 44 A6
Adamsrill Rd. SE26 171 H4
Adare Wk. SW16 169 F3
Adastral Est. NW9 70 E1
Adcock Wk., Orp. 207 J4
*Borkwood Pk.*
Adderley Gdns. SE9 174 D4
Adderley Gro. SW11 150 A5
*Culmstock Rd.*
Adderley Rd., Har. 68 C1
Adderley St. E14 114 C6
Addington Ct. SW14 146 D3
Addington Dr. N12 57 F6
Addington Gro. SE26 171 H4
Addington Rd. E3 114 A3
Addington Rd. E16 115 E4
Addington Rd. N4 75 G6
Addington Rd., Croy. 201 G1
Addington Rd., 205 E2
W.Wick.
**Addington Sq. SE5** **36 A6**
Addington Sq. SE5 131 J6
**Addington St. SE1** **26 D4**
Addington Village 204 A5
Rd., Croy.
Addis Cl., Enf. 45 G1
Addiscombe Av. 188 D7
Croy.
Addiscombe Cl., Har. 69 F5
Addiscombe Ct. Rd., 202 B1
Croy.
Addiscombe Gro., 202 A2
Croy.
Addiscombe Rd., 202 B2
Croy.
Addison Av. N14 42 B6
Addison Av. W11 128 B1
Addison Av., Houns. 143 J1
Addison Br. Pl. W14 128 C4

Addison Cl., Nthwd. 66 A1
Addison Cl., Orp. 193 F6
Addison Cres. W14 128 B3
Addison Dr. SE12 155 H5
*Eltham Rd.*
Addison Gdns. W14 128 A3
Addison Gdns., Surb. 181 J4
Addison Gro. W4 127 E3
Addison Pl. W11 128 B1
Addison Pl., Sthl. 103 G7
*Longford Av.*
Addison Rd. E11 79 G6
Addison Rd. E17 78 B5
Addison Rd. SE25 188 D4
Addison Rd. W14 128 C3
Addison Rd., Brom. 191 J5
Addison Rd., Enf. 45 F1
Addison Rd., Ilf. 81 F1
Addison Rd., Tedd. 162 E6
Addison Way NW11 72 C4
Addison Way, Hayes 102 A6
Addison's Cl., Croy. 203 J2
**Addle Hill EC4 19 H5**
**Addle St. EC2 20 A2**
Adecroft Way, W.Mol. 179 J3
Adela Av., N.Mal. 183 H5
Adela St. W10 108 B4
*Kensal Rd.*
Adelaide Av. SE4 153 J4
Adelaide Cl., Stan. 52 D4
Adelaide Cotts. W7 124 C2
Adelaide Gdns., Rom. 82 E5
Adelaide Gro. W12 127 G1
Adelaide Rd. E10 96 C3
Adelaide Rd. NW3 91 G7
Adelaide Rd. SW18 148 D5
*Putney Br. Rd.*
Adelaide Rd. W13 124 D1
Adelaide Rd., Chis. 175 E5
Adelaide Rd., Houns. 142 E1
Adelaide Rd., Ilf. 99 E2
Adelaide Rd., Rich. 145 J4
Adelaide Rd., Sthl. 123 E4
Adelaide Rd., Surb. 181 H5
Adelaide Rd., Tedd. 162 C6
**Adelaide St. WC2 18 A6**
Adelaide Ter., Brent. 125 G5
Adelaide Wk. SW9 151 G4
*Sussex Wk.*
Adelina Gro. E1 113 F5
Adelina Ms. SW12 168 D1
*King's Av.*
**Adeline Pl. WC1 17 J2**
Adeline Pl. WC1 110 D5
Adeliza Cl., Bark. 98/99 E7
*North St.*
**Adelphi Ter. WC2 18 B6**
Aden Gro. N16 94 A4
Aden Rd., Enf. 45 H4
Aden Rd., Ilf. 81 E7
Aden Ter. N16 94 A4
Adeney Cl. W6 128 A6
Adenmore Rd. SE6 154 A7
Adie Rd. W6 127 J3
Adine Rd. E13 115 H4
Adler Ind. Est., Hayes 121 G2
**Adler St. E1 21 H3**
Adler St. E1 112 D6
Adley St. E5 95 H5
Adlington Cl. N18 60 B5
Admaston Rd. SE18 137 F7
Admiral Ct. NW4 71 G5
*Barton Cl.*
Admiral Pl. SE16 133 H1
Admiral Seymour Rd. SE9 156 C4
Admiral Sq. SW10 149 G1
Admiral St. SE8 154 A1
Admiral Wk. W9 108 D5
Admirals Cl. E18 79 H4
Admirals Wk. NW3 91 F3
Admirals Way E14 134 A2
Admiralty Cl. SE8 134 A7
*Reginald Sq.*
Admiralty Rd., Tedd. 162 C6
Adolf St. SE6 172 B4
Adolphus Rd. N4 93 H2
Adolphus St. SE8 133 J7
Adomar Rd., Dag. 100 D3
**Adpar St. W2 7 E6**
Adpar St. W2 109 G4
Adrian Av. NW2 89 H1
*North Circular Rd.*
**Adrian Ms. SW10 30 B5**
Adrian Ms. SW10 129 E6
Adrienne Av., Sthl. 103 F4
Advance Rd. SE27 169 J4
Advent Ct., Wdf.Grn. 63 F4
*Wood La.*
Advent Way N18 61 G5
Adys Rd. SE15 152 C3
Aerodrome Rd. NW4 71 F3
Aerodrome Rd. NW9 71 F2
Aerodrome Way, Houns. 122 C6
Aeroville NW9 71 E2
**Affleck St. N1 10 D2**
Afghan Rd. SW11 149 H2
Agamemnon Rd. NW6 90 C5
Agar Cl., Surb. 195 J2
Agar Gro. NW1 92 C7
Agar Gro. Est. NW1 92 D7
Agar Pl. NW1 92 C7
**Agar St. WC2 18 A6**
Agar St. WC2 110 E7
Agate Cl. E16 116 A6
Agate Rd. W6 127 J3
Agatha Cl. E1 132/133 E1
*Prusom St.*
Agaton Rd. SE9 175 F2
Agave Rd. NW2 89 J4
**Agdon St. EC1 11 G5**
Agdon St. EC1 111 H4
Agincourt Rd. NW3 91 J4
Agnes Av., Ilf. 98 E4
Agnes Cl. E6 116 D7
Agnes Gdns., Dag. 100 D4
Agnes Rd. W3 127 F1
Agnes St. E14 113 J6
Agnesfield Cl. N12 57 H6
Agnew Rd. SE23 153 G7
Agricola Ct. E3 113 J1
*Parnell Rd.*
Agricola Pl., Enf. 44 C5
Aidan Cl., Dag. 100 E4
Aileen Wk. E15 97 F7
Ailsa Av., Twick. 144 D5
Ailsa Rd., Twick. 145 E5
Ailsa St. E14 114 C5
Ainger Ms. NW3 91 J7
*Ainger Rd.*
Ainger Rd. NW3 91 J7
Ainsdale Cl., Orp. 207 G1
Ainsdale Cres., Pnr. 67 G3
**Ainsdale Dr. SE1 37 H4**
Ainsdale Dr. SE1 132 D5
Ainsdale Rd. W5 105 G4
Ainsdale Rd., Wat. 50 C3
Ainsley Av., Rom. 83 H6
Ainsley Cl. N9 60 B1
Ainsley St. E2 113 E3
Ainslie Wk. SW12 150 B7
Ainslie Wd. Cres. E4 62 B5
Ainslie Wd. Gdns. E4 62 B4
Ainslie Wd. Rd. E4 62 A5
Ainsty Est. SE16 133 G2
Ainsworth Cl. NW2 89 G3
Ainsworth Cl. SE15 152 B2
*Lyndhurst Gro.*
Ainsworth Rd. E9 95 F7
Ainsworth Rd., Croy. 201 H2
Ainsworth Way NW8 109 F1
Aintree Av. E6 116 B1
Aintree Cres., Ilf. 81 F2
Aintree Est. SW6 128 B7
*Dawes Rd.*
Aintree Rd., Grnf. 105 E2
Aintree St. SW6 128 B7
Air Links Ind. Est., Houns. 122 C5
**Air St. W1 17 G6**
Air St. W1 110 C7
Aird Ct., Hmptn. 179 F1
*Oldfield Rd.*
Airdrie Cl. N1 93 F7
Airdrie Cl., Hayes 102/103 E5
*Glencoe Rd.*
Airedale Av. W4 127 F4
Airedale Av. S. W4 127 F5
*Netheravon Rd. S.*
Airedale Rd. SW12 149 J7
Airedale Rd. W5 125 F3
Airlie Gdns. W8 128 D1
*Campden Hill Rd.*
Airlie Gdns., Ilf. 99 E1
Airport Roundabout E16 136 A1
*Connaught Br.*
Airthrie Rd., Ilf. 100 B2
Aisgill Av. W14 128 C5
Aisher Rd. SE28 118 C7
Aislibie Rd. SE12 155 E4
Aitken Cl. E8 112 D1
*Pownall Rd.*
Aitken Cl., Mitch. 185 J7
Aitken Rd. SE6 172 B2
Aitken Rd., Barn. 39 J5
Ajax Av. NW9 70 E3
Ajax Rd. NW6 90 D5
Akabusi Cl., Croy. 188 D6
Akehurst St. SW15 147 G6
Akenside Rd. NW3 91 G5
Akerman Rd. SW9 151 H2
Akerman Rd., Surb. 181 F6
Alabama St. SE18 137 G7
Alacross Rd. W5 125 F2
Alan Dr., Barn. 40 B6
Alan Gdns., Rom. 83 G7
Alan Hocken Way E15 114 E2
Alan Rd. SW19 166 B5
Alandale Dr., Pnr. 66 B2
Alander Ms. E17 78 C4
Alanthus Cl. SE12 155 F6
**Alaska St. SE1 27 E2**
Alba Cl., Hayes 102 D4
*Ramulis Dr.*
Alba Gdns. NW11 72 B6
Alba Pl. W11 108 C6
*Portobello Rd.*
Albacore Cres. SE13 154 B6
Alban Cres., Borwd. 38 B1
Alban Highwalk EC2 111 J5
*London Wall*
**Albany W1 17 F6**
Albany, The, Wdf.Grn. 63 F4
Albany Cl. N15 75 H4
Albany Cl. SW14 146 B4
Albany Cl., Bex. 158 C7
Albany Ct. E4 46 B6
*Chelwood Cl.*
**Albany Ctyd. W1 17 G6**
Albany Cres., Edg. 54 A7
Albany Cres., Esher 194 B6
Albany Mans. SW11 129 H7
Albany Ms. N1 93 G7
*Barnsbury Pk.*
**Albany Ms. SE5 36 A6**
Albany Ms., Brom. 173 G6
*Avondale Rd.*
Albany Ms., Kings.T. 163 G6
*Albany Pk. Rd.*
Albany Ms., Sutt. 198/199 E5
*Camden Rd.*
Albany Pk. Av., Enf. 45 F1
Albany Pk. Rd., Kings.T. 163 H6
Albany Pas., Rich. 145 J5
Albany Pl. N7 93 G4
*Benwell Rd.*
Albany Pl., Brent. 125 H6
*Albany Rd.*
Albany Rd. E10 78 A7
Albany Rd. E12 98 A4
Albany Rd. E17 77 J6
Albany Rd. N4 75 F6
Albany Rd. N18 61 E5
**Albany Rd. SE5 36 B6**
Albany Rd. SE5 132 A6
Albany Rd. SW19 166 E5
Albany Rd. W13 104 E7
Albany Rd., Belv. 139 F6
Albany Rd., Bex. 158 C7
Albany Rd., Brent. 125 G6
Albany Rd., Chis. 175 E5
Albany Rd., N.Mal. 182 D4
Albany Rd., Rich. 145 J5
*Albert Rd.*
Albany Rd., Rom. 83 F6
**Albany St. NW1 8 D1**
Albany St. NW1 110 B2
Albany Ter. NW1 110 B4
*Marylebone Rd.*
Albany Vw., Buck.H. 63 G1
Albatross St. SE18 137 H7
Albatross Way SE16 133 G2
Albemarle SW19 166 A2
Albemarle App., Ilf. 81 E6
Albemarle Av., Twick. 161 F1
Albemarle Gdns., Ilf. 81 E6
Albemarle Gdns., N.Mal. 182 D4
Albemarle Pk., Stan. 53 F5
*Marsh La.*
Albemarle Rd., Barn. 41 H7
Albemarle Rd., Beck. 190 B1
**Albemarle St. W1 17 E6**
Albemarle St. W1 110 B7
**Albemarle Way EC1 11 G6**
Alberon Gdns. NW11 72 C4
Albert Av. E4 62 A4
Albert Av. SW8 131 F7
**Albert Br. SW3 31 H6**
Albert Br. SW3 129 H6
**Albert Br. SW11 31 H6**
Albert Br. SW11 129 H6
**Albert Br. Rd. SW11 31 H7**
Albert Br. Rd. SW11 129 H7
Albert Carr Gdns. SW16 168 E5
Albert Cl. E9 112/113 E1
*Northiam St.*
Albert Cl. N22 74 D1
**Albert Ct. SW7 23 E4**
Albert Ct. SW7 129 G2
Albert Cres. E4 62 A4
Albert Dr. SW19 166 B2
**Albert Embk. SE1 34 B4**
Albert Embk. SE1 131 E5
Albert Gdns. E1 113 G6
**Albert Gate SW1 24 A3**
Albert Gate SW1 129 J2
Albert Gro. SW20 184 A1
**Albert Hall Mans. SW7 23 E4**
Albert Mans. SW11 149 J1
*Albert Br. Rd.*
Albert Ms. E14 113 H7
*Narrow St.*
**Albert Ms. W8 22 C5**
Albert Pl. N3 72 D1
Albert Pl. N17 76 C3
*High Rd.*
**Albert Pl. W8 22 B4**
Albert Pl. W8 129 E2
Albert Rd. E10 96 C2
Albert Rd. E16 136 B1
Albert Rd. E17 78 A5
Albert Rd. E18 79 H3
Albert Rd. N4 93 F1
Albert Rd. N15 76 B6
Albert Rd. N22 74 C1
Albert Rd. NW4 72 A4
Albert Rd. NW6 108 C2
Albert Rd. NW7 55 F5
Albert Rd. SE9 174 B3
Albert Rd. SE20 171 G7
Albert Rd. SE25 188 D4
Albert Rd. W5 105 E4
Albert Rd., Barn. 41 F4
Albert Rd., Belv. 139 F5
Albert Rd., Bex. 159 G6
Albert Rd., Brom. 192 A5
Albert Rd., Buck.H. 64 A2
Albert Rd., Dag. 101 G1
Albert Rd., Hmptn. 161 J5
Albert Rd., Har. 67 J3
Albert Rd., Hayes 121 H3
Albert Rd., Houns. 143 G4
Albert Rd., Ilf. 99 E3
Albert Rd., Kings.T. 181 J2
Albert Rd., Mitch. 185 J3
Albert Rd., N.Mal. 183 F4
Albert Rd., Rich. 145 H5
Albert Rd., Sthl. 122 D3
Albert Rd., Sutt. 199 G5
Albert Rd., Tedd. 162 C6
Albert Rd., Twick. 162 C1
Albert Rd., West Dr. 120 B1
Albert Rd. Est., Belv. 139 F5
Albert Sq. E15 97 E5
Albert Sq. SW8 131 F7
Albert St. N12 57 F5
Albert St. NW1 110 B1
Albert Ter. NW1 110 A1
Albert Ter. NW10 106 D1
Albert Ter., Buck.H. 64 A2
Albert Ter. Ms. NW1 110 A1
*Regents Pk. Rd.*
Albert Way SE15 132 E7
Alberta Av., Sutt. 198 B4
**Alberta Est. SE17 35 H3**
Alberta Est. SE17 131 H5
Alberta Rd., Enf. 44 C6
Alberta Rd., Erith 159 J1
**Alberta St. SE17 35 G3**
Alberta St. SE17 131 H5
Albion Av. N10 74 A1
Albion Av. SW8 150 D2
Albion Bldgs. EC1 111 J5
*Bartholomew Cl.*
**Albion Cl. W2 15 H5**
Albion Dr. E8 94 C7
Albion Est. SE16 133 G2
Albion Gdns. W6 127 H4
Albion Gro. N16 94 B4
Albion Hill SE13 154 B2
Albion Hill, Loug. 47 J5
Albion Ms. N1 111 G1
Albion Ms. NW6 90 C7
*Kilburn High Rd.*
**Albion Ms. W2 15 H4**
Albion Ms. W2 109 H6
Albion Ms. W6 127 H4
*Galena Rd.*
Albion Par. N16 94 A4
*Albion Rd.*
Albion Pk., Loug. 48 A5
**Albion Pl. EC1 19 G1**
Albion Pl. EC1 111 H5
Albion Pl. SE25 188 D3
*High St.*
Albion Pl. W6 127 H4
Albion Rd. E17 78 C3
Albion Rd. N16 94 A4
Albion Rd. N17 76 C2
Albion Rd., Bexh. 159 F4
Albion Rd., Houns. 143 G4
Albion Rd., Kings.T. 182 C1
Albion Rd., Sutt. 199 G6
Albion Rd., Twick. 162 B1
Albion Sq. E8 94 C7
Albion St. SE16 133 F2

**Albion St. W2 15 H4**
Albion St. W2 109 H6
Albion St., Croy. 201 H1
Albion Ter. E8 94 C7
Albion Vil. Rd. SE26 171 F3
**Albion Way EC1 19 J2**
Albion Way SE13 154 C4
Albion Way, Wem. 88 B3
*North End Rd.*
Albion Yd. E1 113 E5
Albrighton Rd. SE22 152 B3
Albuhera Cl., Enf. 43 G1
Albury Av., Bexh. 158 E2
Albury Av., Islw. 124 C7
Albury Cl., Hmptn. 161 G6
Albury Dr., Pnr. 50 D7
Albury Ms. E12 97 J1
Albury Rd., Chess. 195 H5
Albury St. SE8 134 A6
Albyfield, Brom. 192 C3
Albyn Rd. SE8 154 A1
Alcester Cres. E5 95 E2
Alcester Rd., Wall. 200 B4
Alcock Cl., Wall. 200 D7
Alcock Rd., Houns. 122 D7
Alconbury Rd. E5 94 D2
Alcorn Cl., Sutt. 198 D2
Alcott Cl. W7 104 C5
*Westcott Cres.*
Alcuin Ct., Stan. 53 F7
*Old Ch. La.*
Aldborough Rd., Dag. 101 J6
Aldborough Rd. N., Ilf. 81 J5
Aldborough Rd. S., Ilf. 99 H1
Aldbourne Rd. W12 127 F1
**Aldbridge St. SE17 36 E3**
Aldbridge St. SE17 132 B5
**Aldburgh Ms. W1 16 C3**
Aldbury Av., Wem. 88 B7
Aldbury Ms. N9 44 A7
Aldebert Ter. SW8 131 E7
Aldeburgh Cl. E5 94/95 E2
*Southwold Rd.*
Aldeburgh Pl., Wdf.Grn. 63 G4
Aldeburgh St. SE10 135 G5
Alden Av. E15 115 F3
**Aldenham St. NW1 9 G2**
Aldenham St. NW1 110 D2
Aldensley Rd. W6 127 H3
**Alder Cl. SE15 37 G6**
Alder Cl. SE15 132 C6
Alder Gro. NW2 89 H2
Alder Ms. N19 92 C2
*Bredgar Rd.*
Alder Rd. SW14 146 D3
Alder Rd., Sid. 175 J3
Alder Wk., Ilf. 99 F5
Alderbrook Rd. SW12 150 B6
Alderbury Rd. SW13 127 G6
Aldergrove Gdns., Houns. 142/143 E2
*Bath Rd.*
**Alderholt Way SE15 36 E7**
Alderman Av., Bark. 118 A3
Alderman Judge Mall, Kings.T. 181 H2
*Eden St.*
**Aldermanbury EC2 20 A3**
Aldermanbury EC2 111 J6
**Aldermanbury Sq. EC2 20 A2**
Aldermans Hill N13 58 E4
**Alderman's Wk. EC2 20 D2**
Aldermary Rd., Brom. 191 G1
Aldermoor Rd. SE6 171 J3
Alderney Av., Houns. 123 H7
Alderney Gdns., Nthlt. 85 F7
Alderney Rd. E1 113 G4
**Alderney St. SW1 32 E3**
Alderney St. SW1 130 B4
Alders, The N21 43 G6
Alders, The, Felt. 161 E4
Alders, The, Houns. 123 F6
Alders, The, W.Wick. 204 B1
Alders Av., Wdf.Grn. 62 E6
Alders Cl. E11 97 H2
*Aldersbrook Rd.*
Alders Cl. W5 125 G3
Alders Cl., Edg. 54 C5
Alders Gro., E.Mol. 180 A5
*Esher Rd.*
Alders Rd., Edg. 54 C5
Aldersbrook Av., Enf. 44 B2
Aldersbrook Dr., Kings.T. 163 J6
Aldersbrook La. E12 98 C3
Aldersbrook Rd. E11 97 H2
Aldersbrook Rd. E12 98 A3
Aldersey Gdns., Bark. 99 G6
Aldersford Cl. SE4 153 G5
**Aldersgate St. EC1 19 J3**
Aldersgate St. EC1 111 J5
Aldersgrove Av. SE9 173 J3
Aldershot Rd. NW6 108 C1
Aldersmead Av., Croy. 189 G6
Aldersmead Rd., Beck. 171 H7
Alderson Pl., Sthl. 123 J1
Alderson St. W10 108 B4
*Kensal Rd.*
Alderton Cl. NW10 88 D3
Alderton Cl., Loug. 48 D4
Alderton Cres. NW4 71 H5
Alderton Hall La., Loug. 48 D4
Alderton Hill, Loug. 48 B5
Alderton Ms., Loug. 48 D4
*Alderton Hall La.*
Alderton Ri., Loug. 48 D4
Alderton Rd. SE24 151 J3
Alderton Rd., Croy. 188 C7
Alderton Way NW4 71 H5
Alderton Way, Loug. 48 C5
Alderville Rd. SW6 148 C2
Alderwick Dr., Houns. 144 A3
Alderwood Rd. SE9 157 G6
**Aldford St. W1 24 B1**
Aldford St. W1 130 A1
**Aldgate EC3 21 F4**
Aldgate EC3 112 C6
**Aldgate Av. E1 21 F3**
**Aldgate High St. EC3 21 F4**
Aldgate High St. EC3 112 C6
Aldine Ct. W12 127 J1
*Aldine St.*
Aldine Pl. W12 127 J1
*Uxbridge Rd.*
Aldine St. W12 127 J2
Aldington Cl., Dag. 82 C7
Aldington Rd. SE18 136 A3
Aldis Ms. SW17 167 H5
*Aldis St.*
Aldis St. SW17 167 H5
Aldred Rd. NW6 90 D5
Aldren Rd. SW17 167 F3
Aldrich Gdns., Sutt. 198 C3
Aldrich Ter. SW18 167 F2
*Lidiard Rd.*
Aldriche Way E4 62 C6
Aldridge Av., Edg. 54 B3
Aldridge Av., Ruis. 84 D2
Aldridge Av., Stan. 69 H1
Aldridge Ri., N.Mal. 182 E7
Aldridge Rd. Vil. W11 108 C5
Aldridge Wk. N14 42 E7
Aldrington Rd. SW16 168 C5
**Aldsworth Cl. W9 6 A6**
Aldsworth Cl. W9 108 E4
Aldwick Cl. SE9 175 G3
Aldwick Rd., Croy. 201 F3
Aldworth Gro. SE13 154 C6
Aldworth Rd. E15 96 E7
**Aldwych WC2 18 C5**
Aldwych WC2 111 F7
Aldwych Av., Ilf. 81 F4
Alers Rd., Bexh. 158 D5
Alesia Cl. N22 58/59 E7
*Nightingale Rd.*
Alestan Beck Rd. E16 116 A6
*Fulmer Rd.*
**Alexa Ct. W8 30 A1**
Alexander Av. NW10 89 H7
Alexander Cl., Barn. 41 G4
Alexander Cl., Brom. 205 G1
Alexander Cl., Sid. 157 H5
Alexander Cl., Sthl. 123 J1
Alexander Cl., Twick. 162 C2
Alexander Evans Ms. SE23 171 G1
*Sunderland Rd.*
**Alexander Ms. W2 14 A3**
**Alexander Pl. SW7 31 G1**
Alexander Pl. SW7 129 H4
Alexander Rd. N19 92 E3
Alexander Rd., Bexh. 158 D2
Alexander Rd., Chis. 175 E5
**Alexander Sq. SW3 31 G1**
Alexander Sq. SW3 129 H4
Alexander St. W2 108 D6
Alexandra Av. N22 74 D1
Alexandra Av. SW11 150 A1
Alexandra Av. W4 126 D7
Alexandra Av., Har. 85 F1
Alexandra Av., Sthl. 103 F7
Alexandra Av., Sutt. 198 D3
Alexandra Cl., Har. 85 G3
*Alexandra Av.*
Alexandra Cotts. SE14 153 J1
Alexandra Ct. N14 42 C5
Alexandra Ct., Wem. 87 J4
Alexandra Cres., Brom. 173 F6
Alexandra Dr. SE19 170 B5
Alexandra Dr., Surb. 182 A7
Alexandra Gdns. N10 74 B4
Alexandra Gdns. W4 126 D7
Alexandra Gdns., Houns. 143 H2
Alexandra Gro. N4 93 H1
Alexandra Gro. N12 57 E5
Alexandra Ms. N2 73 J3
*Fortis Grn.*
Alexandra Ms. SW19 166 D6
*Alexandra Rd.*
Alexandra Palace N22 74 D2
Alexandra Palace Way N22 74 C3
Alexandra Pk. Rd. N10 74 B2
Alexandra Pk. Rd. N22 74 D2
Alexandra Pl. NW8 109 F1
Alexandra Pl. SE25 188 A5
Alexandra Pl., Croy. 202 B1
*Alexandra Rd.*
Alexandra Rd. E6 116 D3
Alexandra Rd. E10 96 C3
Alexandra Rd. E17 77 J6
Alexandra Rd. E18 79 H3
Alexandra Rd. N8 75 G3
Alexandra Rd. N9 44 E7
Alexandra Rd. N10 58 B7
Alexandra Rd. N15 76 A5
Alexandra Rd. NW4 72 A4
Alexandra Rd. NW8 91 F7
Alexandra Rd. SE26 171 G6
Alexandra Rd. SW14 146 D3
Alexandra Rd. SW19 166 C6
Alexandra Rd. W4 126 D2
Alexandra Rd., Brent. 125 G6
Alexandra Rd., Croy. 202 B1
Alexandra Rd., Enf. 45 G4
Alexandra Rd., Houns. 143 H2
Alexandra Rd., Kings.T. 164 A7
Alexandra Rd., Mitch. 167 H7
Alexandra Rd., Rich. 145 J2
Alexandra Rd. (Chadwell Heath), Rom. 82 D6
Alexandra Rd., T.Ditt. 180 C5
Alexandra Rd., Twick. 145 F6
Alexandra Sq., Mord. 184 D5
Alexandra St. E16 115 G5
Alexandra St. SE14 133 H7
Alexandra Wk. SE19 170 B5
Alexandria Rd. W13 104 D7
**Alexis St. SE16 37 H1**
Alexis St. SE16 132 D4
Alfearn Rd. E5 95 F4
Alford Grn., Croy. 204 D6
**Alford Pl. N1 12 A2**
Alford Rd. SW8 150 D1
Alfoxton Av. N15 75 H4
Alfred Cl. W4 126 D4
*Belmont Rd.*
Alfred Gdns., Sthl. 103 E7
**Alfred Ms. W1 17 H1**
Alfred Ms. W1 110 D5
**Alfred Pl. WC1 17 H1**
Alfred Pl. WC1 110 D5
Alfred Prior Ho. E12 98 D4
Alfred Rd. E15 97 F5
Alfred Rd. SE25 188 D5
Alfred Rd. W2 108 D5
Alfred Rd. W3 126 C1
Alfred Rd., Belv. 139 F5
Alfred Rd., Buck.H. 64 A2
Alfred Rd., Felt. 160 C2
Alfred Rd., Kings.T. 181 H3
Alfred Rd., Sutt. 199 F5
Alfred St. E3 113 J3
Alfreda St. SW11 150 B1
Alfred's Gdns., Bark. 117 H2
Alfreds Way, Bark. 117 F3
Alfreds Way Ind. Est., Bark. 118 A1
Alfreton Cl. SW19 166 A3
Alfriston Av., Croy. 187 E7
Alfriston Av., Har. 67 G6
Alfriston Cl., Surb. 181 J5
Alfriston Rd. SW11 149 J5
Algar Cl., Islw. 144 D3
*Algar Rd.*
Algar Cl., Stan. 52 C5
Algar Rd., Islw. 144 D3
Algarve Rd. SW18 167 E1
Algernon Rd. NW4 71 G6
Algernon Rd. NW6 108 D1
Algernon Rd. SE13 154 B4
Algers Cl., Loug. 48 A5
Algers Mead, Loug. 48 A5
Algers Rd., Loug. 48 A5
Algiers Rd. SE13 154 A4
Alibon Gdns., Dag. 101 G5
Alibon Rd., Dag. 101 G5
Alice Ct. SW15 148 C4
*Deodar Rd.*
Alice Gilliatt Ct. W14 128 C6
Alice La. E3 113 J1
Alice Ms., Tedd. 162 C5
*Luther Rd.*
**Alice St. SE1 28 D6**
Alice St. SE1 132 B3
Alice Thompson Cl. SE12 173 J2
Alice Walker Cl. SE24 151 H4
*Shakespeare Rd.*
Alice Way, Houns. 143 H4
Alicia Av., Har. 69 E4
Alicia Cl., Har. 69 F4
Alicia Gdns., Har. 69 F4
**Alie St. E1 21 G4**
Alie St. E1 112 C6
Alington Cres. NW9 88 C1
Alison Cl. E6 116 D6
Alison Cl., Croy. 203 G1
*Shirley Oaks Rd.*
Aliwal Rd. SW11 149 H4
Alkerden Rd. W4 127 E5
Alkham Rd. N16 94 C2
All Hallows Rd. N17 76 B1
All Saints Cl. N9 60 C2
All Saints Dr. SE3 155 E2
All Saints Ms., Har. 52 B6
All Saints Pas. SW18 148/149 E5
*Wandsworth High St.*
All Saints Rd. SW19 167 F7
All Saints Rd. W3 126 C3
All Saints Rd. W11 108 C5
All Saints Rd., Sutt. 199 E3
**All Saints St. N1 10 C1**
All Saints St. N1 111 F2
All Saints Twr. E10 78 B7
All Souls Av. NW10 107 H2
**All Souls Pl. W1 17 E2**
Allan Barclay Cl. N15 76 C6
*High Rd.*
Allan Cl., N.Mal. 182 D5
Allan Way W3 106 C5
Allandale Av. N3 72 B3
Allard Cres., Bushey 51 J1
Allard Gdns. SW4 150 D5
Allardyce St. SW4 151 F4
Allbrook Cl., Tedd. 162 B5
Allcroft Rd. NW5 92 A5
Allen Cl., Mitch. 186 B1
Allen Cl., Sun. 178 B1
Allen Ct., Grnf. 86 C5
Allen Edwards Dr. SW8 150 E1
Allen Pl., Twick. 162 D1
*Church St.*
Allen Rd. E3 113 J2
Allen Rd. N16 94 B4
Allen Rd., Beck. 189 G2
Allen Rd., Croy. 187 F7
Allen Rd., Sun. 178 B1
Allen St. W8 128 D3
Allenby Cl., Grnf. 103 G3
Allenby Rd. SE23 171 H3
Allenby Rd., Sthl. 103 G6
Allendale Av., Sthl. 103 G6
Allendale Cl. SE5 152 A1
*Daneville Rd.*
Allendale Cl. SE26 171 G5
Allendale Rd., Grnf. 86 E6
Allens Rd., Enf. 45 F5
Allensbury Pl. NW1 92 D7
Allenswood Rd. SE9 156 B3
Allerford Ct., Har. 67 H5
Allerford Rd. SE6 172 B4
Allerton Ct. NW4 72 A2
*Holders Hill Rd.*
Allerton Rd. N16 93 J2
Allerton Wk. N7 93 F2
*Durham Rd.*
Allestree Rd. SW6 128 B7
Alleyn Cres. SE21 170 A2
Alleyn Pk. SE21 170 A2
Alleyn Pk., Sthl. 123 F4
Alleyn Rd. SE21 170 A3
Alleyndale Rd., Dag. 100 C2
Allfarthing La. SW18 149 E6
Allgood Cl., Mord. 184 A6
**Allgood St. E2 13 G2**
**Allhallows La. EC4 20 B6**
Allhallows Rd. E6 116 B5
Alliance Cl., Wem. 87 G4
Alliance Rd. E13 115 J4
Alliance Rd. SE18 138 A6
Alliance Rd. W3 106 B4

Andover Rd., Orp. 207 G1
Andover Rd., Twick. 162 A1
Andre St. E8 94 D5
**Andrew Borde St. WC2 17 J3**
Andrew Cl., Ilf. 65 G6
Andrew Pl. SW8 150 D1
*Cowthorpe Rd.*
Andrew St. E14 114 C6
Andrewes Gdns. E6 116 B6
Andrews Cl. E6 116 B6
*Linton Gdns.*
Andrews Cl., Buck.H. 63 J2
Andrews Cl., Har. 68 A7
*Bessborough Rd.*
Andrews Cl., Wor.Pk. 198 A2
**Andrews Crosse WC2 18 E4**
Andrews Pl. SE9 156 E6
Andrew's Rd. E8 112 E1
**Andrews Wk. SE17 35 H6**
Andwell Cl. SE2 138 B2
Anerley Gro. SE19 170 C7
Anerley Hill SE19 170 C6
Anerley Pk. SE20 170 D7
Anerley Pk. Rd. SE20 170 E7
Anerley Rd. SE19 170 D7
Anerley Rd. SE20 170 D7
Anerley Sta. Rd. SE20 188 E1
Anerley St. SW11 149 J2
Anerley Vale SE19 170 C7
Anfield Cl. SW12 150 C7
*Belthorn Cres.*
**Angel All. E1 21 G3**
Angel Cl. N18 60 C4
Angel Cor. Par. N18 60 D5
*Fore St.*
**Angel Ct. EC2 20 C3**
Angel Ct. EC2 112 A6
**Angel Ct. SW1 25 G2**
Angel Ct. SW17 167 J4
**Angel Gate EC1 11 H3**
Angel Hill, Sutt. 198/199 E3
*Sutton Common Rd.*
Angel Hill Dr., Sutt. 199 E3
Angel La. E15 96 D6
**Angel Ms. N1 11 F2**
Angel Ms. N1 111 G2
Angel Ms. SW15 147 G7
*Roehampton High St.*
**Angel Pas. EC4 20 B6**
Angel Pl. N18 60 D5
**Angel Pl. SE1 28 B3**
Angel Rd. N18 60 E5
Angel Rd., Har. 68 B6
Angel Rd., T.Ditt. 180 D7
Angel Rd. Wks. N18 61 F5
**Angel Sq. EC1 11 F2**
**Angel St. EC1 19 J3**
Angel St. EC1 111 J6
Angel Wk. W6 127 J4
Angelfield, Houns. 143 H4
Angelica Dr. E6 116 D5
Angelica Gdns., Croy. 203 G1
Angell Pk. Gdns. SW9 151 G3
Angell Rd. SW9 151 G3
Angerstein La. SE3 135 F7
Angle Grn., Dag. 100 C1
Anglers Cl., Rich. 163 F4
*Locksmeade Rd.*
Angler's La. NW5 92 B6
Anglers Reach, Surb. 181 G5
Angles Rd. SW16 169 E4
Anglesea Av. SE18 136 E4
Anglesea Rd. SE18 136 E4
Anglesea Rd., Kings.T. 181 G4
Anglesea Ter. W6 127 H3
*Wellesley Av.*
Anglesey Ct. Rd., Cars. 200 A6
Anglesey Gdns., Cars. 200 A6
Anglesey Rd., Enf. 45 E4
Anglesey Rd., Wat. 50 C5
Anglesmede Cres., Pnr. 67 G3
Anglesmede Way, Pnr. 67 F3
Anglia Cl. N17 60/61 E7
*Park La.*
Anglia Ho. E14 113 H6
Anglia Wk. E6 116 C1
Anglian Rd. E11 96 D3
Anglo Rd. E3 113 J2
Angrave Ct. E8 112 C1
Angrave Pas. E8 112 C1
*Haggerston Rd.*
Angus Cl., Chess. 196 A5
Angus Dr., Ruis. 84 C4
Angus Gdns. NW9 70 D1
Angus Rd. E13 115 J3
Angus St. SE14 133 H7
**Anhalt Rd. SW11 31 H7**
Anhalt Rd. SW11 129 H7
Ankerdine Cres. SE18 136 D7
Anlaby Rd., Tedd. 162 B5
Anley Rd. W14 128 A2
Anmersh Gro., Stan. 69 G1
**Ann La. SW10 30 E7**
Ann La. SW10 129 G7
Ann Moss Way SE16 133 F3
Ann St. SE18 137 G4
Anna Cl. E8 112 C1
Anna Neagle Cl. E7 97 G4
*Dames Rd.*
Annabel Cl. E14 114 B6
Annandale Rd. SE10 135 F6
Annandale Rd. W4 126 E4
Annandale Rd., Croy. 202 D2
Annandale Rd., Sid. 157 H7
Anne Boleyn's Wk., Kings.T. 163 H5
Anne Boleyn's Wk., Sutt. 198 A7
Anne Case Ms., N.Mal. 182 D3
*Sycamore Gro.*
Anne St. E13 115 G4
Anne Way, Ilf. 65 F6
Anne Way, W.Mol. 179 H4
Annesley Av. NW9 70 D3
Annesley Cl. NW10 88 E3
Annesley Dr., Croy. 203 J3
Annesley Rd. SE3 155 H1
Annesley Wk. N19 92 C2
Annett Rd., Walt. 178 A7
Annette Cl., Har. 68 B2
*Spencer Rd.*
Annette Cres. N1 93 J7
*Essex Rd.*
Annette Rd. N7 93 F4
Annie Besant Cl. E3 113 J1
**Anning St. EC2 13 E5**
Annington Rd. N2 73 J3
Annis Rd. E9 95 H6
**Ann's Cl. SW1 24 A4**
**Ann's Pl. E1 21 F2**
Annsworthy Av., Th.Hth. 188 A3
*Grange Pk. Rd.*
Annsworthy Cres. SE25 188 A2
*Grange Rd.*
Ansdell Rd. SE15 153 F2
**Ansdell St. W8 22 B5**
Ansdell St. W8 129 E3
**Ansdell Ter. W8 22 B5**
Ansell Gro., Cars. 200 A1
Ansell Rd. SW17 167 H3
Anselm Cl., Croy. 202 C3
*Park Hill Ri.*
Anselm Rd. SW6 128 D6
Anselm Rd., Pnr. 51 F7
Ansford Rd., Brom. 172 C5
Ansleigh Pl. W11 108 A7
Anson Cl., Rom. 83 H2
Anson Rd. N7 92 D4
Anson Rd. NW2 90 A5
Anson Ter., Nthlt. 85 H6
Anstey Rd. SE15 152 D3
Anstey Wk. N15 75 H4
Anstice Cl. W4 127 E7
Anstridge Path SE9 157 G6
Anstridge Rd. SE9 157 G6
Antelope Rd. SE18 136 C3
Anthony Cl. NW7 55 E4
Anthony Cl., Wat. 50 C1
Anthony Rd. SE25 188 D6
Anthony Rd., Grnf. 104 B2
Anthony Rd., Well. 158 A1
Anthony St. E1 112/113 E6
*Commercial Rd.*
Antigua Cl. SE19 170 A5
*Salters Hill*
Antigua Wk. SE19 170 A5
Antill Rd. E3 113 H3
Antill Rd. N15 76 C4
Antill Ter. E1 113 G6
Antlers Hill E4 46 B5
Anton Cres., Sutt. 198 D3
Anton St. E8 94 D5
Antoneys Cl., Pnr. 66 D2
Antrim Gro. NW3 91 J6
Antrim Mans. NW3 91 H6
Antrim Rd. NW3 91 J6
Antrobus Cl., Sutt. 198 C5
Antrobus Rd. W4 126 C4
Anvil Cl. SW16 168 C7
Anvil Rd., Sun. 178 A3
Anworth Cl., Wdf.Grn. 63 H6
Apex Cl., Beck. 190 B1
Apex Cor. NW7 54 D4
Apex Retail Pk., Felt. 161 F3
Apex Twr., N.Mal. 182 E3
Aplin Way, Islw. 144 B1
Apollo Av., Brom. 191 H1
*Rodway Rd.*
Apollo Av., Nthwd. 50 A5
Apollo Pl. E11 96 E3
**Apollo Pl. SW10 31 E7**
Apollo Pl. SW10 129 G7
Apollo Way SE28 137 G3
*Broadwater Rd.*
Apostle Way, Th.Hth. 187 H2
**Apothecary St. EC4 19 G4**
Appach Rd. SW2 151 G6
Apple Garth, Brent. 125 G4
Apple Gro., Chess. 195 H4
Apple Gro., Enf. 44 B3
Apple Mkt., Kings.T. 181 G2
*Eden St.*
Apple Rd. E11 96 E3
**Apple Tree Yd. SW1 25 G1**
Appleby Cl. E4 62 C6
Appleby Cl. N15 76 A5
Appleby Cl., Twick. 162 A2
Appleby Rd. E8 94 D7
Appleby Rd. E16 115 F6
**Appleby St. E2 13 F1**
Appleby St. E2 112 C2
Appledore Av., Bexh. 159 J1
Appledore Av., Ruis. 84 B3
Appledore Cl. SW17 167 J2
Appledore Cl., Brom. 191 F5
Appledore Cl., Edg. 70 A1
Appledore Cres., Sid. 175 H3
Appleford Rd. W10 108 B4
Applegarth, Croy. 204 B7
Applegarth, Esher 194 C5
Applegarth Dr., Ilf. 81 J4
Applegarth Rd. SE28 138 B1
Applegarth Rd. W14 128 A3
Appleton Gdns., N.Mal. 183 G6
Appleton Rd. SE9 156 B3
Appleton Rd., Loug. 49 E3
Appleton Sq., Mitch. 185 H1
Appletree Cl. SE20 188/189 E1
*Jasmine Gro.*
Appletree Gdns., Barn. 41 H4
Applewood Cl. N20 57 H1
Applewood Cl. NW2 89 H3
**Appold St. EC2 20 D1**
Appold St. EC2 112 B5
Apprentice Way E5 94/95 E4
*Clarence Rd.*
Approach, The NW4 72 A5
Approach, The W3 106 D6
Approach, The, Enf. 44 E2
Approach, The, Orp. 207 J2
Approach Cl. N16 94 B5
*Cowper Rd.*
Approach Rd. E2 113 F2
Approach Rd. SW20 183 J2
Approach Rd., Barn. 41 G4
Approach Rd., W.Mol. 179 G5
Aprey Gdns. NW4 71 J4
April Cl. W7 104 B7
April Cl., Felt. 160 A3
April Cl., Orp. 207 J5
*Briarswood Way*
April Glen SE23 171 G3
April St. E8 94 C4
Apsley Cl., Har. 67 J5
Apsley Rd. SE25 188 E4
Apsley Rd., N.Mal. 182 C3
Apsley Way NW2 89 G2
**Apsley Way W1 24 C3**
Aquarius Business Pk. NW2 89 G1
Aquarius Way, Nthwd. 50 A5
**Aquila St. NW8 7 F1**
Aquila St. NW8 109 G2
**Aquinas St. SE1 27 F2**
Arabella Dr. SW15 147 E4
Arabia Cl. E4 46 D7
Arabin Rd. SE4 153 H4
Aragon Av., T.Ditt. 180 C5
Aragon Cl., Brom. 206 C1
Aragon Cl., Loug. 48 B6
Aragon Dr., Ilf. 65 F7
Aragon Dr., Ruis. 84 D1
**Aragon Ms. E1 29 H1**
Aragon Rd., Kings.T. 163 H5
Aragon Rd., Mord. 184 A6
Aran Dr., Stan. 53 F4
Arandora Cres., Rom. 82 B7
Arbery Rd. E3 113 H3
Arbor Cl., Beck. 190 B2
Arbor Ct. N16 94 A2
*Lordship Rd.*
Arbor Rd. E4 62 D3
Arborfield Cl. SW2 169 F1
Arbour Rd., Enf. 45 G4
Arbour Sq. E1 113 G6
Arbroath Grn., Wat. 50 A3
Arbroath Rd. SE9 156 B3
Arbury Ter. SE26 170/171 E3
*Oaksford Av.*
Arbuthnot La., Bex. 159 E6
Arbuthnot Rd. SE14 153 G2
Arbutus St. E8 112 B1
**Arcade, The EC2 20 D2**
Arcade, The, Croy. 201 J3
*High St.*
Arcadia Av. N3 72 D1
Arcadia Cl., Cars. 200 A4
Arcadia St. E14 114 A6
Arcadian Av., Bex. 158 E6
Arcadian Cl., Bex. 158 E6
Arcadian Gdns. N22 59 F7
Arcadian Rd., Bex. 158 E6
**Arch St. SE1 27 J6**
Arch St. SE1 131 J3
Archangel St. SE16 133 G2
Archbishops Pl. SW2 151 F6
Archdale Pl., N.Mal. 182 B3
Archdale Rd. SE22 152 C5
Archel Rd. W14 128 C6
Archer Cl., Kings.T. 163 H7
Archer Ho. SW11 149 G1
*Vicarage Cres.*
Archer Ms., Hmptn. 161 J6
*Windmill Rd.*
Archer Rd. SE25 188 E4
**Archer St. W1 17 H5**
Archers Dr., Enf. 45 F2
Archers Wk. SE15 152 C1
*Wodehouse Av.*
**Archery Cl. W2 15 H4**
Archery Cl. W2 109 H6
Archery Cl., Har. 68 C3
Archery Rd. SE9 156 C5
Arches, The SW6 148 C2
*Munster Rd.*
**Arches, The WC2 26 B1**
Arches, The, Har. 85 H2
**Archibald Ms. W1 24 C1**
Archibald Ms. W1 130 A1
Archibald Rd. N7 92 D4
Archibald St. E3 114 A3
Archie Cl., West Dr. 120 D2
Archway Cl. N19 92 C2
*St. Johns Way*
Archway Cl. SW19 166 E4
Archway Cl. W10 108 A5
Archway Cl., Wall. 200 D3
Archway Mall N19 92 C2
*Magdala Av.*
Archway Rd. N6 74 A6
Archway Rd. N19 92 C1
Archway St. SW13 147 E3
Arcola St. E8 94 C5
Arctic St. NW5 92 A5
*Gillies St.*
Arcus Rd., Brom. 173 E6
Ardbeg Rd. SE24 152 A6
Arden Cl., Har. 86 A3
Arden Ct. Gdns. N2 73 G6
Arden Cres. E14 134 A4
Arden Cres., Dag. 100 C7
**Arden Est. N1 12 D2**
Arden Est. N1 112 B2
Arden Gro., Orp. 207 E4
Arden Ms. E17 78 B5
Arden Mhor, Pnr. 66 B4
Arden Rd. N3 72 B3
Arden Rd. W13 105 F7
Ardent Cl. SE25 188 B3
Ardfern Av. SW16 187 G3
Ardfillan Rd. SE6 172 D1
Ardgowan Rd. SE6 154 E7
Ardilaun Rd. N5 93 J4
Ardingly Cl., Croy. 203 G3
Ardleigh Gdns., Sutt. 184 D7
Ardleigh Ho., Bark. 117 F1
*St. Ann's*
Ardleigh Ms., Ilf. 98/99 E3
*Bengal Rd.*
Ardleigh Rd. E17 77 J1
Ardleigh Rd. N1 94 A6
Ardleigh Ter. E17 77 J1
Ardley Cl. NW10 88 E3
Ardley Cl. SE6 171 H3
Ardlui Rd. SE27 169 J2
Ardmay Gdns., Surb. 181 H5
Ardmere Rd. SE13 154 D6
Ardmore La., Buck.H. 47 H7
Ardmore Pl., Buck.H. 47 H7
Ardoch Rd. SE6 172 D2
Ardra Rd. N9 61 G3
Ardrossan Gdns., Wor.Pk. 197 G3
Ardshiel Cl. SW15 148 A3
*Bemish Rd.*
Ardwell Av., Ilf. 81 F5

220 Ard–Ash

Ardwell Rd. SW2 169 E2
Ardwick Rd. NW2 90 D4
Arewater Grn., Loug. 48 C1
Argali Ho., Erith 138/139 E3
*Kale Rd.*
Argall Av. E10 77 G7
Argall Way E10 95 G1
**Argent St. SE1 27 H3**
Argenta Way NW10 88 B7
Argon Ms. SW6 128 D7
Argon Rd. N18 61 F5
Argosy La., Stai. 140 A7
Argus Cl., Rom. 83 H1
Argus Way W3 126 B3
Argus Way, Nthlt. 102 E3
Argyle Av., Houns. 143 G6
Argyle Cl. W13 104 D4
Argyle Pas. N17 76 C1
Argyle Pl. W6 127 H4
Argyle Rd. E1 113 G4
Argyle Rd. E15 96 E4
Argyle Rd. E16 115 J6
Argyle Rd. N12 56 D5
Argyle Rd. N17 76 D1
Argyle Rd. N18 60 D4
Argyle Rd. W13 104 D5
Argyle Rd., Barn. 39 J4
Argyle Rd., Grnf. 104 C3
Argyle Rd., Har. 67 H5
Argyle Rd., Houns. 143 H5
Argyle Rd., Ilf. 98 D2
Argyle Rd., Tedd. 162 B5
**Argyle Sq. WC1 10 B3**
Argyle Sq. WC1 111 E3
**Argyle St. WC1 10 A3**
Argyle St. WC1 110 E3
**Argyle Wk. WC1 10 B4**
**Argyle Way SE16 37 J4**
Argyle Way SE16 132 D5
Argyll Av., Sthl. 123 H1
Argyll Cl. SW9 151 F3
*Dalyell Rd.*
Argyll Gdns., Edg. 70 B2
Argyll Rd. W8 128 D2
**Argyll St. W1 17 F4**
Argyll St. W1 110 C6
Arica Rd. SE4 153 H4
Ariel Rd. NW6 90 D6
Ariel Way W12 127 J1
Ariel Way, Houns. 142 B3
Aristotle Rd. SW4 150 D3
Arkell Gro. SE19 169 H7
Arkindale Rd. SE6 172 C3
Arkley Cres. E17 77 J5
Arkley Dr., Barn. 39 G4
Arkley La., Barn. 39 G3
Arkley Pk., Barn. 38 D6
Arkley Rd. E17 77 J5
Arkley Vw., Barn. 39 H4
Arklow Ms., Surb. 195 H2
*Vale Rd. S.*
Arklow Rd. SE14 133 J6
Arkwright Rd. NW3 91 F5
Arlesey Cl. SW15 148 B6
*Lytton Gro.*
Arlesford Rd. SW9 151 E3
Arlingford Rd. SW2 151 G5
Arlington N12 56 D3
Arlington Av. N1 111 J2
Arlington Cl., Sid. 157 H7
Arlington Cl., Sutt. 198 D2
Arlington Cl., Twick. 145 F6
Arlington Ct., Hayes 121 G5
*Shepiston La.*
Arlington Dr., Cars. 199 J2
Arlington Gdns. W4 126 C5
Arlington Gdns., Ilf. 98 D1
Arlington Lo. SW2 151 F4
Arlington Ms., Twick. 144/145 E6
*Arlington Rd.*
Arlington Pl. SE10 134 C7
*Greenwich S. St.*
Arlington Rd. N14 58 B2
Arlington Rd. NW1 110 B1
Arlington Rd. W13 104 E6
Arlington Rd., Rich. 163 G2
Arlington Rd., Surb. 181 G6
Arlington Rd., Tedd. 162 C4
Arlington Rd., Twick. 145 F6
Arlington Rd., Wdf.Grn. 79 G1
Arlington Sq. N1 111 J1
**Arlington St. SW1 25 F1**
Arlington St. SW1 130 C1
**Arlington Way EC1 11 F3**
Arlington Way EC1 111 G3
Arliss Way, Nthlt. 102 C1
Arlow Rd. N21 59 G1
Armada Ct. SE8 134 A6
*Watergate St.*
Armada St. SE8 134 A6
Armada Way E6 117 F7
Armadale Cl. N17 76 E4
Armadale Rd. SW6 128 D7
Armadale Rd., Felt. 142 A5
Armagh Rd. E3 113 J1
Armfield Cl., W.Mol. 179 F5
Armfield Cres., Mitch. 185 J2
Armfield Rd., Enf. 44 A1
Arminger Rd. W12 127 H1
Armistice Gdns. SE25 188 D3
*Penge Rd.*
Armitage Rd. NW11 90 C1
Armitage Rd. SE10 135 F5
Armour Cl. N7 93 F6
*Roman Way*
Armoury Rd. SE8 154 B2
Armoury Way SW18 148 D5
Armstead Wk., Dag. 101 G7
Armstrong Av., Wdf.Grn. 62 E6
Armstrong Cl. E6 116 C6
*Porter Rd.*
Armstrong Cl., Dag. 100 D1
*Palmer Rd.*
Armstrong Cl., Pnr. 66 A6
Armstrong Cl., Walt. 178 A6
*Sunbury La.*
Armstrong Cres., Barn. 41 G3
**Armstrong Rd. SW7 22 E6**
Armstrong Rd. SW7 129 G3
Armstrong Rd. W3 127 F1
Armstrong Rd., Felt. 160 E5
Armstrong Way, Sthl. 123 H2
Armytage Rd., Houns. 122 D7
Arnal Cres. SW18 148 B7
Arncliffe Cl. N11 58 A6
*Kettlewell Cl.*
Arncroft Ct., Bark. 118 B3
*Renwick Rd.*
Arndale Cen. SW18 148 E6
Arndale Wk. SW18 148/149 E5
*Garratt La.*
Arne Gro., Orp. 207 J3
**Arne St. WC2 18 B4**
Arne St. WC2 111 E6
Arne Wk. SE3 155 F4
Arnett Sq. E4 61 J6
*Silver Birch Av.*
**Arneway St. SW1 25 J6**
Arneways Av., Rom. 82 D3
Arnewood Cl. SW15 165 G1
Arney's La., Mitch. 186 A6
Arngask Rd. SE6 154 D7
Arnhem Pl. E14 134 A3
Arnhem Way SE22 152 B5
*East Dulwich Gro.*
Arnhem Wf. E14 134 A3
*Arnhem Pl.*
Arnison Rd., E.Mol. 180 A4
**Arnold Circ. E2 13 F4**
Arnold Circ. E2 112 C3
Arnold Cl., Har. 69 J7
Arnold Cres., Islw. 144 A5
Arnold Dr., Chess. 195 G6
**Arnold Est. SE1 29 G4**
Arnold Est. SE1 132 C2
Arnold Gdns. N13 59 H5
Arnold Rd. E3 114 A3
Arnold Rd. N15 76 C3
Arnold Rd. SW17 167 J7
Arnold Rd., Dag. 101 F7
Arnold Rd., Nthlt. 84 D6
Arnos Gro. N14 58 D4
Arnos Rd. N11 58 C5
Arnott Cl. SE28 118 C7
*Applegarth Rd.*
Arnott Cl. W4 126 D4
*Fishers La.*
Arnould Av. SE5 152 A4
Arnsberg Way, Bexh. 159 G4
Arnside Gdns., Wem. 87 G1
Arnside Rd., Bexh. 159 G1
**Arnside St. SE17 36 A5**
Arnside St. SE17 131 J6
Arnulf St. SE6 172 B4
Arnulls Rd. SW16 169 G6
Arodene Rd. SW2 151 F6
Arosa Rd., Twick. 145 G6
Arragon Gdns. SW16 168 E7
Arragon Gdns., W.Wick. 204 B3
Arragon Rd. E6 116 A1
Arragon Rd. SW18 166 E1
Arragon Rd., Twick. 144 D7
Arran Cl., Wall. 200 B4
Arran Dr. E12 98 A1
Arran Grn., Wat. 50 C1
*Prestwick Rd.*
Arran Ms. W5 125 J1
Arran Rd. SE6 172 B2
Arran Wk. N1 93 J7
Arras Av., Mord. 185 F5
Arrol Rd., Beck. 189 F3
Arrow Rd. E3 114 B3
Arrowscout Wk., Nthlt. 102/103 E3
*Argus Way*
Arrowsmith Cl., Chig. 65 J5
Arrowsmith Path, Chig. 65 J5
Arrowsmith Rd., Chig. 65 H5
Arrowsmith Rd., Loug. 48 B3
Arsenal Rd. SE9 156 C2
Arterberry Rd. SW20 165 J7
Artesian Cl. NW10 88 D7
Artesian Gro., Barn. 41 F4
Artesian Rd. W2 108 D6
Artesian Wk. E11 96 E3
Arthingworth St. E15 114 E1
**Arthur Ct. W2 14 A3**
Arthur Gro. SE18 137 F4
Arthur Henderson Ho. SW6 148 C2
Arthur Horsley Wk. E7 97 F5
*Magpie Cl.*
Arthur Rd. E6 116 C2
Arthur Rd. N7 93 F4
Arthur Rd. N9 60 C2
Arthur Rd. SW19 166 D3
Arthur Rd., Kings.T. 164 A7
Arthur Rd., N.Mal. 183 H5
Arthur Rd., Rom. 82 C7
**Arthur St. EC4 20 C6**
Arthurdon Rd. SE4 154 A5
Artichoke Hill E1 112/113 E7
*Pennington St.*
Artichoke Pl. SE5 152 A1
*Camberwell Ch. St.*
Artillery Cl., Ilf. 81 F6
*Horns Rd.*
**Artillery La. E1 21 E2**
Artillery La. E1 112 B5
Artillery La. W12 107 G6
**Artillery Pas. E1 21 E2**
Artillery Pl. SE18 136 C4
**Artillery Pl. SW1 25 H6**
Artillery Pl., Har. 51 J7
*Chicheley Rd.*
**Artillery Row SW1 25 H6**
Artillery Row SW1 130 D3
Artington Cl., Orp. 207 F4
Artisan Cl. E6 116/117 E6
*Ferndale St.*
**Artizan St. E1 21 E3**
Arundel Av., Mord. 184 C4
Arundel Cl. E15 97 E4
Arundel Cl. SW11 149 H5
*Chivalry Rd.*
Arundel Cl., Bex. 159 F6
Arundel Cl., Croy. 201 H3
Arundel Cl., Hmptn. 161 H5
Arundel Ct. N12 57 H6
Arundel Ct., Har. 85 G4
Arundel Dr., Borwd. 38 C5
Arundel Dr., Har. 85 F4
Arundel Dr., Wdf.Grn. 63 G7
Arundel Gdns. N21 59 G1
Arundel Gdns. W11 108 C7
Arundel Gdns., Edg. 54 D7
Arundel Gdns., Ilf. 100 A2
**Arundel Great Ct. WC2 18 D5**
Arundel Gro. N16 94 B5
Arundel Pl. N1 93 G6
Arundel Rd., Barn. 41 H3
Arundel Rd., Croy. 188 A6
Arundel Rd., Houns. 142 C3
Arundel Rd., Kings.T. 182 B2
Arundel Rd., Sutt. 198 C7
Arundel Sq. N7 93 G6
**Arundel St. WC2 18 D5**
Arundel St. WC2 111 F7
Arundel Ter. SW13 127 H6
Arvon Rd. N5 93 G5
Asbaston Ter., Ilf. 99 F5
*Buttsbury Rd.*
Ascalon St. SW8 130 C7
Ascham Dr. E4 62 B7
*Rushcroft Rd.*
Ascham End E17 77 H1
Ascham St. NW5 92 C5
Aschurch Rd., Croy. 188 C7
Ascot Cl., Borwd. 38 A5
Ascot Cl., Ilf. 65 H6
Ascot Cl., Nthlt. 85 G5
Ascot Gdns., Sthl. 103 F5
Ascot Rd. E6 116 C3
Ascot Rd. N15 76 A5
Ascot Rd. N18 60 D4
Ascot Rd. SW17 168 A6
Ascot Rd., Orp. 193 J4
Ascott Av. W5 125 H2
Ash Cl. SE20 189 F2
Ash Cl., Cars. 199 J2
Ash Cl., Edg. 54 C4
Ash Cl., N.Mal. 182 D2
Ash Cl., Orp. 193 G5
Ash Cl., Sid. 176 B3
Ash Cl., Stan. 52 D6
Ash Ct., Epsom 196 C4
Ash Gro. E8 113 E1
Ash Gro. N13 59 J3
Ash Gro. NW2 90 A4
Ash Gro. SE20 189 F2
Ash Gro. W5 125 H2
Ash Gro., Enf. 44 B7
Ash Gro., Houns. 142 D1
Ash Gro., Sthl. 103 G5
Ash Gro., Wem. 86 D4
Ash Gro., W.Wick. 204 C2
Ash Hill Cl., Bushey 51 H1
Ash Hill Dr., Pnr. 66 C3
Ash Island, E.Mol. 180 A3
Ash Rd. E15 97 E5
Ash Rd., Croy. 204 A2
Ash Rd., Orp. 207 J7
Ash Rd., Sutt. 184 B7
Ash Row, Brom. 192 D7
Ash Tree Cl., Croy. 189 H6
Ash Tree Cl., Surb. 195 H1
Ash Tree Dell NW9 70 C5
Ash Tree Way, Croy. 189 H5
Ash Wk. SW2 169 F1
Ash Wk., Wem. 87 F4
Ashbourne Av. E18 79 H4
Ashbourne Av. N20 57 J2
Ashbourne Av. NW11 72 C5
Ashbourne Av., Bexh. 139 E7
Ashbourne Av., Har. 86 A2
Ashbourne Cl. N12 57 E4
Ashbourne Cl. W5 106 A5
Ashbourne Ct. E5 95 H4
*Daubeney Rd.*
Ashbourne Gro. NW7 54 D5
Ashbourne Gro. SE22 152 C5
Ashbourne Gro. W4 127 E5
Ashbourne Par. W5 105 J4
*Ashbourne Rd.*
Ashbourne Ri., Orp. 207 G4
Ashbourne Rd. W5 105 J5
Ashbourne Rd., Mitch. 168 A6
Ashbourne Ter. SW19 166 D7
Ashbourne Way NW11 72 C5
*Ashbourne Av.*
Ashbridge Rd. E11 79 F7
**Ashbridge St. NW8 7 G6**
Ashbridge St. NW8 109 H4
Ashbrook Rd. N19 92 D1
Ashbrook Rd., Dag. 101 H3
**Ashburn Gdns. SW7 30 C1**
Ashburn Gdns. SW7 129 F4
**Ashburn Pl. SW7 30 C1**
Ashburn Pl. SW7 129 F4
Ashburnham Av., Har. 68 C6
Ashburnham Cl. N2 73 G3
Ashburnham Cl., Wat. 50 A3
*Ashburnham Dr.*
Ashburnham Dr., Wat. 50 A3
Ashburnham Gdns., Har. 68 C6
Ashburnham Gro. SE10 134 B7
Ashburnham Pl. SE10 134 B7
Ashburnham Retreat SE10 134 B7
Ashburnham Rd. NW10 107 J3
Ashburnham Rd. SW10 129 F7
Ashburnham Rd., Belv. 139 J4
Ashburnham Rd., Rich. 163 E3
Ashburton Av., Croy. 202 E1
Ashburton Av., Ilf. 99 H4
Ashburton Cl., Croy. 202 D1
Ashburton Ct., Pnr. 66 D3
Ashburton Gdns., Croy. 202 D2
Ashburton Gro. N7 93 G4
Ashburton Rd. E16 115 G6
Ashburton Rd., Croy. 202 D1
Ashburton Rd., Ruis. 84 A2
Ashburton Ter. E13 115 G2
*Grasmere Rd.*
Ashbury Gdns., Rom. 82 D5
Ashbury Pl. SW19 167 F6
Ashbury Rd. SW11 149 J3
Ashby Av., Chess. 196 A6
Ashby Gro. N1 93 J7
Ashby Ms. SE4 153 J2

Augustus Cl., Brent. 125 F7
Augustus Rd. SW19 166 B1
**Augustus St. NW1 9 E2**
Augustus St. NW1 110 B2
**Aulton Pl. SE11 35 F4**
Aulton Pl. SE11 131 G5
Aultone Way, Cars. 199 J3
Aultone Way, Sutt. 199 E2
Aurelia Gdns., Croy. 187 F5
Aurelia Rd., Croy. 187 E6
Auriga Ms. N16 94 A5
Auriol Cl., Wor.Pk. 196/197 E3
*Auriol Pk. Rd.*
Auriol Dr., Grnf. 86 A7
Auriol Pk. Rd., Wor.Pk. 197 E3
Auriol Rd. W14 128 B4
Austell Gdns. NW7 55 E3
Austen Cl. SE28 138 B1
Austen Cl., Loug. 49 G3
Austen Ho. NW6 108 D3
Austen Rd., Erith 139 H7
Austen Rd., Har. 85 H2
Austin Av., Brom. 192 B5
Austin Cl. SE23 153 J7
Austin Cl., Twick. 145 F5
Austin Ct. E6 115 J1
*Kings Rd.*
**Austin Friars EC2 20 C3**
Austin Friars EC2 112 A6
**Austin Friars Pas. EC2 20 C3**
**Austin Friars Sq. EC2 20 C3**
Austin Rd. SW11 150 A1
Austin Rd., Hayes 121 J2
**Austin St. E2 13 F4**
Austin St. E2 112 C3
Austral Cl., Sid. 175 J3
**Austral St. SE11 35 G1**
Austral St. SE11 131 H4
Australia Rd. W12 107 H7
Austyn Gdns., Surb. 196 B1
Autumn Cl. SW19 167 F6
Autumn Cl., Enf. 44 D1
Autumn St. E3 114 A1
Avalon Cl. SW20 184 B2
Avalon Cl. W13 104 D5
Avalon Cl., Enf. 43 G2
Avalon Rd. SW6 148 E1
Avalon Rd. W13 104 D4
Avard Gdns., Orp. 207 F4
Avarn Rd. SW17 167 J6
**Ave Maria La. EC4 19 H4**
Ave Maria La. EC4 111 H6
Avebury Ct. N1 112 A1
*Poole St.*
Avebury Pk., Surb. 181 G7
Avebury Rd. E11 96 D1
*Southwest Rd.*
Avebury Rd. SW19 184 C1
Avebury Rd., Orp. 207 G3
Avebury St. N1 112 A1
*Poole St.*
**Aveline St. SE11 34 E3**
Aveline St. SE11 131 G5
Aveling Pk. Rd. E17 78 A2
Avenell Rd. N5 93 H3
Avening Rd. SW18 148 D7
*Brathway Rd.*
Avening Ter. SW18 148 D6
Avenons Rd. E13 115 G4
Avenue, The E4 62 D6
Avenue, The (Leytonstone) E11 97 F2
Avenue, The (Wanstead) E11 97 F2
Avenue, The N3 72 D2
Avenue, The N8 75 G3
Avenue, The N10 74 C2
Avenue, The N11 58 B4
Avenue, The N17 76 B2
Avenue, The NW6 108 A1
Avenue, The SE7 135 J7
Avenue, The SE10 134 D7
Avenue, The SW4 150 A5
Avenue, The SW11 149 J7
*Bellevue Rd.*
Avenue, The SW18 149 H7
Avenue, The W4 126 E3
Avenue, The W13 104 E7
Avenue, The, Barn. 40 B3
Avenue, The, Beck. 190 B1
Avenue, The, Bex. 158 D7
Avenue, The, Brom. 192 A3
Avenue, The, Cars. 200 A7
Avenue, The, Croy. 202 B3
Avenue, The, Epsom 197 H7
Avenue, The, Esher 194 B6
Avenue, The, Hmptn. 161 F6
Avenue, The, Har. 68 C1
Avenue, The, Houns. 143 H5
Avenue, The (Cranford), Houns. 142 A1
Avenue, The, Islw. 124 A6
Avenue, The, Kes. 206 A3
Avenue, The, Loug. 48 A6
Avenue, The, Orp. 207 J2
Avenue, The (St. Paul's Cray), Orp. 176 B7
Avenue, The, Pnr. 67 F6
Avenue, The (Hatch End), Pnr. 51 G7
Avenue, The, Rich. 145 J2
Avenue, The, Sun. 178 B1
Avenue, The, Surb. 181 J6
Avenue, The (Cheam), Sutt. 197 J7
Avenue, The, Twick. 145 F5
Avenue, The, Wem. 87 J2
Avenue, The, West Dr. 120 B3
Avenue, The, W.Wick. 190 D7
Avenue, The, Wor.Pk. 197 F2
Avenue Cl. N14 42 C6
Avenue Cl. NW8 109 H1
Avenue Cl., Houns. 142 A1
*The Av.*
Avenue Cl., West Dr. 120 A3
Avenue Cres. W3 126 B2
Avenue Cres., Houns. 122 B7
Avenue Elmers, Surb. 181 H5
Avenue Gdns. SE25 188 D3
Avenue Gdns. SW14 146 E3
Avenue Gdns. W3 126 B2
Avenue Gdns., Houns. 122 A7
*The Av.*
Avenue Gdns., Tedd. 162 C7
Avenue Gate, Loug. 47 J6
Avenue Ind. Est. E4 61 J6
Avenue Ms. N10 74 B3
Avenue Pk. Rd. SE27 169 H2
Avenue Rd. E7 97 H5
Avenue Rd. N6 74 C7
Avenue Rd. N12 57 F4
Avenue Rd. N14 42 C7
Avenue Rd. N15 76 A5
Avenue Rd. NW3 91 G7
Avenue Rd. NW8 109 G1
Avenue Rd. NW10 107 F2
Avenue Rd. SE20 189 F1
Avenue Rd. SE25 188 D2
Avenue Rd. SW16 186 D2
Avenue Rd. SW20 183 H2
Avenue Rd. W3 126 B2
Avenue Rd., Beck. 189 F1
Avenue Rd., Belv. 139 J4
Avenue Rd., Bexh. 158 E3
Avenue Rd., Brent. 125 F5
Avenue Rd., Erith 139 J7
Avenue Rd., Hmptn. 179 H1
Avenue Rd., Islw. 144 C1
Avenue Rd., Kings.T. 181 H3
Avenue Rd., N.Mal. 182 E4
Avenue Rd., Pnr. 66 E3
Avenue Rd. (Chadwell Heath), Rom. 82 B7
Avenue Rd., Sthl. 123 F2
Avenue Rd., Tedd. 162 D7
Avenue Rd., Wall. 200 C7
Avenue Rd., Wdf.Grn. 63 J6
Avenue S., Surb. 181 J7
Avenue Ter., N.Mal. 182 C3
*Kingston Rd.*
Averil Gro. SW16 169 H6
Averill St. W6 128 A6
Avern Gdns., W.Mol. 179 H4
Avern Rd., W.Mol. 179 H5
**Avery Fm. Row SW1 32 C2**
Avery Gdns., Ilf. 80 C5
Avery Hill Rd. SE9 157 G6
**Avery Row W1 16 D5**
Avery Row W1 110 B7
Avey La., Loug. 47 H1
Aviary Cl. E16 115 F5
Aviemore Cl., Beck. 189 J5
Aviemore Way, Beck. 189 H5
Avignon Rd. SE4 153 G3
Avington Ct. SE1 132 B4
*Old Kent Rd.*
Avington Gro. SE20 171 F7
**Avington Way SE15 37 F7**
Avion Cres. NW9 71 G1
Avis Sq. E1 113 G6
Avoca Rd. SW17 168 A4
Avocet Ms. SE28 137 G3
Avon Cl., Hayes 102 C4
Avon Cl., Sutt. 199 F4
Avon Cl., Wor.Pk. 197 G2
Avon Ct., Grnf. 103 H4
*Braund Av.*
Avon Ms., Pnr. 67 F1
Avon Path, S.Croy. 201 J6
**Avon Pl. SE1 28 A4**
Avon Rd. E17 78 D3
Avon Rd. SE4 154 A3
Avon Rd., Grnf. 103 G4
Avon Way E18 79 G3
Avondale Av. N12 56 E5
Avondale Av. NW2 89 E3
Avondale Av., Barn. 57 J1
Avondale Av., Esher 194 D3
Avondale Av., Wor.Pk. 197 F1
Avondale Cl., Loug. 48 C7
Avondale Ct. E11 96 E1
Avondale Ct. E16 114/115 E5
*Avondale Rd.*
Avondale Ct. E18 79 H1
Avondale Cres., Enf. 45 H3
Avondale Cres., Ilf. 80 A5
Avondale Dr., Hayes 122 A1
Avondale Dr., Loug. 48 C7
Avondale Gdns., Houns. 143 F5
Avondale Ms., Brom. 173 G6
*Avondale Rd.*
Avondale Pk. Gdns. W11 108 B7
Avondale Pk. Rd. W11 108 B7
Avondale Pavement SE1 132 D5
*Avondale Sq.*
Avondale Ri. SE15 152 C3
Avondale Rd. E16 115 E5
Avondale Rd. E17 78 A7
Avondale Rd. N3 73 F1
Avondale Rd. N13 59 G2
Avondale Rd. N15 75 H5
Avondale Rd. SE9 174 B2
Avondale Rd. SW14 146 D3
Avondale Rd. SW19 166 E5
Avondale Rd., Brom. 173 E6
Avondale Rd., Har. 68 C3
Avondale Rd., S.Croy. 201 J6
Avondale Rd., Well. 158 C2
**Avondale Sq. SE1 37 H4**
Avondale Sq. SE1 132 D5
Avonley Rd. SE14 133 F7
Avonmore Gdns. W14 128 B4
*Avonmore Rd.*
Avonmore Pl. W14 128 B4
*Avonmore Rd.*
Avonmore Rd. W14 128 C4
**Avonmouth St. SE1 27 J5**
Avonmouth St. SE1 131 J3
Avonwick Rd., Houns. 143 H2
Avril Way E4 62 C5
Avro Way, Wall. 201 E7
Awlfield Av. N17 76 A1
Awliscombe Rd., Well. 157 J2
Axe St., Bark. 117 F1
Axholme Av., Edg. 70 A1
Axminster Cres., Well. 158 C1
Axminster Rd. N7 93 E3
**Aybrook St. W1 16 B2**
Aybrook St. W1 110 A5
Aycliffe Cl., Brom. 192 C4
Aycliffe Rd. W12 127 F1
Aylands Cl., Wem. 87 H2
*Preston Rd.*
Ayles Rd., Hayes 102 B3
Aylesbury Cl. E7 97 F6
*Atherton Rd.*
**Aylesbury Est. SE17 36 C4**
**Aylesbury Rd. SE17 36 C4**
Aylesbury Rd. SE17 132 A5
Aylesbury Rd., Brom. 191 G3
**Aylesbury St. EC1 11 G6**
Aylesbury St. EC1 111 H4
Aylesbury St. NW10 88 D3
Aylesford Av., Beck. 189 H5
**Aylesford St. SW1 33 H3**
Aylesford St. SW1 130 D5
Aylesham Cl. NW7 55 G7
Aylesham Rd., Orp. 193 J7
Aylestone Av. NW6 108 A1
Aylett Rd. SE25 188 E4
Aylett Rd., Islw. 144 B2
Ayley Cft., Enf. 44 D5
Ayliffe Cl., Kings.T. 182 A2
*Cambridge Gdns.*
Aylmer Cl., Stan. 52 D4
Aylmer Dr., Stan. 52 D4
Aylmer Par. N2 73 J5
*Aylmer Rd.*
Aylmer Rd. E11 97 F1
Aylmer Rd. N2 73 H5
Aylmer Rd. W12 127 F2
Aylmer Rd., Dag. 100 E3
Ayloffe Rd., Dag. 101 F6
Aylton Est. SE16 133 F2
*Renforth St.*
Aylward Rd. SE23 171 G2
Aylward Rd. SW20 184 C2
Aylward St. E1 113 F6
Aylwards Ri., Stan. 52 D4
**Aylwyn Est. SE1 29 F5**
Aylwyn Est. SE1 132 B3
Aynhoe Rd. W14 128 A4
Aynscombe La. SW14 146 C3
Aynscombe Path SW14 146 C2
*Thames Bank*
Ayr Ct. W3 106 A5
*Monks Dr.*
Ayres Cl. E13 115 G3
Ayres Cres. NW10 88 D7
**Ayres St. SE1 28 A3**
Ayres St. SE1 131 J2
Ayrsome Rd. N16 94 B3
**Ayrton Rd. SW7 23 E5**
Aysgarth Rd. SE21 152 B6
Aytoun Pl. SW9 151 F2
Aytoun Rd. SW9 151 F2
Azalea Cl. W7 124 C1
Azalea Cl., Ilf. 98 E5
Azalea Ct., Wdf.Grn. 62/63 E7
*The Bridle Path*
Azalea Wk., Pnr. 66 B5
Azalea Wk., Sthl. 123 J2
*Navigator Dr.*
Azenby Rd. SE15 152 C2
Azile Everitt Ho. SE18 137 F5
*Vicarage Pk.*
Azof St. SE10 135 E4


## B


Baalbec Rd. N5 93 H5
Babbacombe Cl., Chess. 195 G5
Babbacombe Gdns., Ilf. 80 B4
Babbacombe Rd., Brom. 191 G1
Baber Dr., Felt. 142 C6
Babington Ri., Wem. 88 A6
Babington Rd. NW4 71 H4
Babington Rd. SW16 168 D5
Babington Rd., Dag. 100 C5
**Babmaes St. SW1 17 G6**
**Bacchus Wk. N1 12 D2**
**Baches St. N1 12 C4**
Baches St. N1 112 A3
**Back Ch. La. E1 21 H5**
Back Ch. La. E1 112 D7
**Back Hill EC1 11 E6**
Back Hill EC1 111 G4
Back La. N8 74 E5
Back La. NW3 91 F4
*Heath St.*
Back La., Bex. 159 G7
Back La., Brent. 125 G6
Back La., Edg. 70 C1
Back La., Rich. 163 F3
Back La., Rom. 82/83 E7
*St. Chad's Rd.*
Back Rd., Sid. 176 A4
**Backhouse Pl. SE17 36 E2**
Backley Gdns. SE25 188 D6
**Bacon Gro. SE1 29 F6**
Bacon Gro. SE1 132 C3
Bacon La. NW9 70 B4
Bacon La., Edg. 70 A1
**Bacon St. E1 13 G5**
Bacon St. E1 112 C4
**Bacon St. E2 13 G5**
Bacon St. E2 112 C4
Bacon Ter., Dag. 100 B5
*Fitzstephen Rd.*
Bacons La. N6 92 A1
Bacton NW5 92 A5
Bacton St. E2 113 F3
*Roman Rd.*
Baddow Cl., Dag. 119 G1
Baddow Cl., Wdf.Grn. 64 A6
Baddow Wk. N1 111 J1
**Baden Pl. SE1 28 B3**
Baden Powell Cl., Dag. 119 E1
Baden Powell Cl., Surb. 195 J2
Baden Rd. N8 74 D4
Baden Rd., Ilf. 98 E5
Badger Cl., Felt. 160 A3
*Sycamore Cl.*
Badger Cl., Houns. 142 C3
Badger Cl., Ilf. 81 F7
Badgers Cl., Enf. 43 H3
Badgers Cl., Har. 68 A6
Badgers Copse, Orp. 207 J2
Badgers Copse, Wor.Pk. 197 F2

Barham Rd., S.Croy. 201 J5
Baring Cl. SE12 173 G2
Baring Rd. SE12 155 G7
Baring Rd., Barn. 41 G3
Baring Rd., Croy. 202 D1
Baring St. N1 112 A1
**Bark Pl. W2 14 A5**
Bark Pl. W2 108 E7
Barkantine Shop. Par., The E14 134 A2
*The Quarterdeck*
Barker Cl., N.Mal. 182 C3
*California Rd.*
Barker Dr. NW1 92 C7
Barker Ms. SW4 150 B4
**Barker St. SW10 30 C5**
Barker St. SW10 129 F6
Barker Wk. SW16 168 D3
Barker Way SE22 170 D1
*Dulwich Common*
Barkham Rd. N17 60 A7
Barking Ind. Pk., Bark. 117 J1
Barking Rd. E6 116 A2
Barking Rd. E13 115 H4
Barking Rd. E16 115 F5
**Barkston Gdns. SW5 30 A3**
Barkston Gdns. SW5 128 E4
Barkway Ct. N4 93 J3
*Queens Dr.*
Barkwood Cl., Rom. 83 J5
Barkworth Rd. SE16 133 E5
Barlborough St. SE14 133 F7
Barlby Gdns. W10 108 A4
Barlby Rd. W10 108 A5
Barley La., Ilf. 82 A7
Barley La., Rom. 82 B6
**Barley Mow Pas. EC1 19 H2**
Barley Mow Pas. W4 126 D5
Barley Shotts Business Pk. W10 108 C5
*St. Ervans Rd.*
Barleycorn Way E14 113 J7
Barleyfields Cl., Rom. 82 B7
Barlow Cl., Wall. 200/201 E6
*Cobham Cl.*
**Barlow Pl. W1 17 E6**
Barlow Rd. NW6 90 C6
Barlow Rd. W3 126 B1
Barlow Rd., Hmptn. 161 G7
**Barlow St. SE17 36 C2**
Barmeston Rd. SE6 172 B2
Barmor Cl., Har. 67 H2
Barmouth Av., Grnf. 104 C2
Barmouth Rd. SW18 149 F6
Barmouth Rd., Croy. 203 G2
Barn Cl., Nthlt. 102 C2
Barn Cres., Stan. 53 F6
Barn Elms Pk. SW15 147 J2
Barn Hill, Wem. 88 B2
Barn Ms., Har. 85 G3
Barn Ri., Wem. 88 A1
Barn St. N16 94 B3
*Stoke Newington Ch. St.*
Barn Way, Wem. 88 A1
Barnabas Ct. N21 43 G5
*Cheyne Wk.*
Barnabas Rd. E9 95 G5
Barnaby Cl., Har. 85 J2
**Barnaby Pl. SW7 31 E2**
Barnaby Pl. SW7 129 G4
Barnaby Way, Chig. 64 E3
Barnard Cl. SE18 136 D4
Barnard Cl., Chis. 193 G1
Barnard Cl., Sun. 160 B7
*Oak Gro.*
Barnard Cl., Wall. 200 D7
Barnard Gdns., Hayes 102 B4
Barnard Gdns., N.Mal. 183 G4
Barnard Gro. E15 97 F7
*Vicarage La.*
Barnard Hill N10 74 A2
Barnard Ms. SW11 149 H4
Barnard Rd. SW11 149 H4
Barnard Rd., Enf. 45 E2
Barnard Rd., Mitch. 186 A3
Barnardo Dr., Ilf. 81 F4
Barnardo St. E1 113 G6
*Devonport St.*
Barnardos Village, Ilf. 81 F3
**Barnard's Inn EC1 19 F3**
Barnby Sq. E15 114/115 E1
*Barnby St.*
Barnby St. E15 114 E1
**Barnby St. NW1 9 G2**
Barnby St. NW1 110 C2
Barncroft Cl., Loug. 48 D5
Barncroft Grn., Loug. 48 D5
Barncroft Rd., Loug. 48 D5
Barnehurst Av., Bexh. 159 J1
Barnehurst Av., Erith 159 J1
Barnehurst Cl., Erith 159 J1
Barnehurst Rd., Bexh. 159 J2
Barnes All., Hmptn. 179 J2
*Hampton Ct. Rd.*
Barnes Av. SW13 127 G7
Barnes Av., Sthl. 123 F4
Barnes Br. SW13 147 E2
Barnes Br. W4 147 E2
Barnes Cl. E12 98 A4
Barnes Ct. E16 115 J5
*Ridgwell Rd.*
Barnes Ct., Wdf.Grn. 64 A5
Barnes End, N.Mal. 183 G5
Barnes High St. SW13 147 F2
Barnes Ho., Bark. 117 G1
*St. Marys*
Barnes Pikle W5 105 F7
Barnes Rd. N18 61 F4
Barnes Rd., Ilf. 99 F5
Barnes St. E14 113 H6
Barnes Ter. SE8 133 J5
Barnesbury Ho. SW4 150 D5
Barnet Bypass, Barn. 38 E3
Barnet Dr., Brom. 206 B2
Barnet Gate La., Barn. 39 F6
**Barnet Gro. E2 13 H3**
Barnet Gro. E2 112 D3
Barnet Hill, Barn. 40 D4
Barnet Ho. N20 57 F2
Barnet La. N20 56 C1
Barnet La., Barn. 40 C6
Barnet Rd. (Arkley), Barn. 39 H5
Barnet Trd. Est., Barn. 40 C3
Barnet Way NW7 38 D7
Barnet Wd. Rd., Brom. 205 J2
Barnett St. E1 112/113 E6
*Cannon St. Rd.*
Barney Cl. SE7 135 J5
Barnfield, N.Mal. 182 E6
Barnfield Av., Croy. 203 F2
Barnfield Av., Kings.T. 163 H5
Barnfield Av., Mitch. 186 B4
Barnfield Cl. N4 74/75 E7
*Crouch Hill*
Barnfield Cl. SW17 167 F3
Barnfield Gdns. SE18 136/137 E6
*Plumstead Common Rd.*
Barnfield Gdns., Kings.T. 163 H4
Barnfield Pl. E14 134 A4
Barnfield Rd. SE18 137 E6
Barnfield Rd. W5 105 F4
Barnfield Rd., Belv. 139 F6
Barnfield Rd., Edg. 70 C1
Barnfield Wd. Cl., Beck. 190 D6
Barnfield Wd. Rd., Beck. 190 D6
Barnham Rd., Grnf. 103 J3
**Barnham St. SE1 28 E3**
Barnham St. SE1 132 B2
Barnhill, Pnr. 66 C5
Barnhill Av., Brom. 191 F5
Barnhill La., Hayes 102 B3
Barnhill Rd., Hayes 102 B3
Barnhill Rd., Wem. 88 C3
Barnhurst Path, Wat. 50 C5
Barningham Way NW9 70 D6
Barnlea Cl., Felt. 161 E2
Barnmead Gdns., Dag. 101 F5
Barnmead Rd., Beck. 189 H1
Barnmead Rd., Dag. 101 F5
Barnsbury Cl., N.Mal. 182 C4
Barnsbury Cres., Surb. 196 C1
Barnsbury Est. N1 111 G1
*Barnsbury Rd.*
Barnsbury Gro. N7 93 F7
Barnsbury La., Surb. 196 B2
Barnsbury Pk. N1 93 G7
**Barnsbury Rd. N1 10 E1**
Barnsbury Rd. N1 111 G2
Barnsbury Sq. N1 93 G7
Barnsbury St. N1 93 G7
Barnsbury Ter. N1 93 F7
Barnscroft SW20 183 H3
Barnsdale Av. E14 134 A4
Barnsdale Rd. W9 108 C4
Barnsley St. E1 113 E4
Barnstaple Rd., Ruis. 84 C3
Barnston Wk. N1 111 J1
*Popham St.*
Barnwell Rd. SW2 151 G5
**Barnwood Cl. W9 6 A6**
Barnwood Cl. W9 108 E4
Baron Cl. N11 58 A5
*Balmoral Av.*
Baron Gdns., Ilf. 81 F3
Baron Gro., Mitch. 185 H4
Baron Rd., Dag. 100 D1
**Baron St. N1 11 E1**
Baron St. N1 111 G2
Baron Wk. E16 115 F5
Baron Wk., Mitch. 185 H4
**Baroness Rd. E2 13 G3**
Baronet Gro. N17 76 D1
*St. Paul's Rd.*
Baronet Rd. N17 76 D1
Barons, The, Twick. 145 E6
Barons Ct., Wall. 200 D3
*Whelan Way*
Barons Ct. Rd. W14 128 B5
Barons Gate, Barn. 41 H6
Barons Keep W14 128 B5
Barons Mead, Har. 68 B4
**Barons Pl. SE1 27 F4**
Barons Pl. SE1 131 G2
Barons Wk., Croy. 189 H6
Baronsfield Rd., Twick. 145 E6
Baronsmead Rd. SW13 147 G1
Baronsmede W5 125 J2
Baronsmere Rd. N2 73 H4
Barque Ms. SE8 134 A6
*Watergate St.*
Barrack Rd., Houns. 142 D4
Barracks La., Barn. 40 B3
*High St.*
Barratt Av. N22 75 F2
Barratt Ind. Pk., Sthl. 123 G2
Barratt Way, Har. 68 A3
*Tudor Rd.*
Barrenger Rd. N10 73 J1
Barrett Rd. E17 78 C4
**Barrett St. W1 16 C4**
Barrett St. W1 110 A6
Barretts Grn. Rd. NW10 106 C2
Barretts Gro. N16 94 B5
Barrhill Rd. SW2 169 E2
**Barrie Est. W2 14 E5**
Barrie Ho. W3 126 B2
Barriedale SE14 153 H2
Barrier App. SE7 136 A3
Barrier Pt. Rd. E16 135 G1
*North Woolwich Rd.*
Barringer Sq. SW17 168 A4
Barrington Cl. NW5 92 A5
Barrington Cl., Ilf. 80 C1
Barrington Cl., Loug. 49 F4
*Barrington Rd.*
Barrington Grn., Loug. 49 F4
Barrington Rd. E12 98 D6
Barrington Rd. N8 74 D5
Barrington Rd. SW9 151 H3
Barrington Rd., Bexh. 158 D2
Barrington Rd., Loug. 49 F3
Barrington Rd., Sutt. 198 D1
Barrington Vil. SE18 156 D1
Barrow Av., Cars. 199 J7
Barrow Cl. N21 59 H3
Barrow Hedges Cl., Cars. 199 H7
Barrow Hedges Way, Cars. 199 H7
Barrow Hill, Wor.Pk. 196 E2
Barrow Hill Cl., Wor.Pk. 196/197 E2
*Barrow Hill*
**Barrow Hill Rd. NW8 7 G2**
Barrow Hill Rd. NW8 109 H2
Barrow Pt. Av., Pnr. 66 E2
Barrow Pt. La., Pnr. 66 E2
Barrow Rd. SW16 168 D6
Barrow Rd., Croy. 201 G5
Barrow Wk., Brent. 125 F5
*Glenhurst Rd.*
Barrowdene Cl., Pnr. 66/67 E2
*Paines La.*
Barrowell Grn. N21 59 H2
Barrowfield Cl. N9 61 E3
Barrowgate Rd. W4 126 C5
Barrs Rd. NW10 88 D7
Barry Av. N15 76 C6
*Craven Pk. Rd.*
Barry Av., Bexh. 138 E7
Barry Cl., Orp. 207 H3
Barry Rd. E6 116 B6
Barry Rd. NW10 88 C7
Barry Rd. SE22 152 D6
Barset Rd. SE15 153 F3
Barson Cl. SE20 171 F7
Barston Rd. SE27 169 J3
Barstow Cres. SW2 169 F1
**Barter St. WC1 18 B2**
Barter St. WC1 111 E5
Barters Wk., Pnr. 66/67 E3
*High St.*
Barth Rd. SE18 137 H4
**Bartholomew Cl. EC1 19 J2**
Bartholomew Cl. EC1 111 J5
Bartholomew Cl. SW18 149 F4
**Bartholomew La. EC2 20 C4**
**Bartholomew Pl. EC1 19 J2**
Bartholomew Rd. NW5 92 C6
Bartholomew Sq. E1 112/113 E4
*Coventry Rd.*
**Bartholomew Sq. EC1 12 A5**
Bartholomew Sq. EC1 111 J4
**Bartholomew St. SE1 28 B6**
Bartholomew St. SE1 132 A3
Bartholomew Vil. NW5 92 C6
Bartle Av. E6 116 B2
Bartle Rd. W11 108 B6
Bartlett Cl. E14 114 A6
**Bartlett Ct. EC4 19 F3**
Bartlett St., S.Croy. 202 A5
**Bartletts Pas. EC4 19 F3**
Barton Av., Rom. 101 H1
Barton Cl. E6 116 C6
Barton Cl. E9 95 F5
*Churchill Wk.*
Barton Cl. NW4 71 G4
Barton Cl. SE15 152/153 E3
*Kirkwood Rd.*
Barton Cl., Bexh. 158 E5
Barton Cl., Chig. 65 F2
Barton Grn., N.Mal. 182 D2
Barton Meadows, Ilf. 81 F4
Barton Rd. W14 128 B5
Barton Rd., Sid. 177 E6
**Barton St. SW1 26 A5**
Barton Way, Borwd. 38 A2
Bartonway NW8 109 G2
*Queen's Ter.*
Bartram Rd. SE4 153 H5
Barville Cl. SE4 153 H4
*St. Norbert Rd.*
Barwick Rd. E7 97 H4
Barwood Av., W.Wick. 204 B1
Basden Gro., Felt. 161 G2
Basedale Rd., Dag. 100 B7
Baseing Cl. E6 116 D7
Bashley Rd. NW10 106 D4
Basil Av. E6 116 B2
Basil Gdns. SE27 169 J5
Basil Gdns., Croy. 203 G1
*Primrose La.*
**Basil St. SW3 23 J5**
Basil St. SW3 129 J3
Basildene Rd., Houns. 142 D2
Basildon Av., Ilf. 80 D1
Basildon Rd. SE2 138 A5
Basilon Rd., Bexh. 158 E2
Basin S. E16 137 E1
Basing Cl., T.Ditt. 180 C7
Basing Ct. SE15 152 C1
Basing Dr., Bex. 159 F6
Basing Hill NW11 90 C1
Basing Hill, Wem. 87 J2
Basing Ho., Bark. 117 G1
*St. Margarets*
**Basing Ho. Yd. E2 13 E3**
**Basing Pl. E2 12 E3**
Basing St. W11 108 C6
Basing Way N3 72 E3
Basing Way, T.Ditt. 180 C7
Basingdon Way SE5 152 A4
Basingfield Rd., T.Ditt. 180 C7
**Basinghall Av. EC2 20 B2**
Basinghall Av. EC2 112 A5
**Basinghall St. EC2 20 B3**
Basinghall St. EC2 111 J5
Basire St. N1 111 J1
Baskerville Rd. SW18 149 H7
Basket Gdns. SE9 156 B5
Baslow Cl., Har. 68 A1
Baslow Wk. E5 95 G4
*Overbury St.*
Basnett Rd. SW11 150 A3
Basque Ct. SE16 133 G2
*Poolmans St.*

| | | |
|---|---|---|
| Bassano St. SE22 | 152 | C5 |
| Bassant Rd. SE18 | 137 | J6 |
| Bassein Pk. Rd. W12 | 127 | F2 |
| Bassett Gdns., Islw. | 123 | J7 |
| Bassett Ho., Dag. | 118 | B1 |
| Bassett Rd. W10 | 108 | A6 |
| Bassett St. NW5 | 92 | A6 |
| Bassett Way, Grnf. | 103 | H6 |
| Bassetts Cl., Orp. | 206 | E4 |
| Bassetts Way, Orp. | 206 | E4 |
| Bassingham Rd. SW18 | 149 | F7 |
| Bassingham Rd., Wem. | 87 | G6 |
| Bassishaw Highwalk EC2 *London Wall* | 111 | J5 |
| Basswood Cl. SE15 *Linden Gro.* | 152/153 | E3 |
| Bastable Av., Bark. | 117 | H2 |
| Bastion Highwalk EC2 *London Wall* | 111 | J5 |
| Bastion Rd. SE2 | 138 | A5 |
| Baston Manor Rd., Brom. | 205 | H3 |
| Baston Rd., Brom. | 205 | H1 |
| **Bastwick St. EC1** | **11** | **J5** |
| Bastwick St. EC1 | 111 | J4 |
| Basuto Rd. SW6 | 148 | D1 |
| Batavia Cl., Sun. | 178 | C1 |
| Batavia Ms. SE14 *Goodwood Rd.* | 133 | H7 |
| Batavia Rd. SE14 | 133 | H7 |
| Batavia Rd., Sun. | 178 | B1 |
| **Batchelor St. N1** | **11** | **E1** |
| Batchelor St. N1 | 111 | G2 |
| Bate St. E14 *Three Colt St.* | 113 | J7 |
| Bateman Cl., Bark. *Glenny Rd.* | 99 | F6 |
| **Bateman Ho. SE17** | **35** | **G6** |
| Bateman Rd. E4 | 62 | A6 |
| **Bateman St. W1** | **17** | **H4** |
| **Bateman's Bldgs. W1** | **17** | **H4** |
| **Bateman's Row EC2** | **12** | **E5** |
| Bateman's Row EC2 | 112 | B4 |
| Bates Cres. SW16 | 168 | C7 |
| Bates Cres., Croy. | 201 | G5 |
| Bateson St. SE18 | 137 | H4 |
| Bath Cl. SE15 *Asylum Rd.* | 132/133 | E7 |
| **Bath Ct. EC1** | **11** | **E6** |
| Bath Ho. Rd., Croy. | 200 | E1 |
| Bath Pas., Kings.T. *St. James Rd.* | 181 | G2 |
| **Bath Pl. EC2** | **12** | **D4** |
| Bath Pl., Barn. | 40 | C3 |
| Bath Rd. E7 | 98 | A6 |
| Bath Rd. N9 | 61 | E2 |
| Bath Rd. W4 | 127 | E4 |
| Bath Rd., Hayes | 141 | F1 |
| Bath Rd., Houns. | 142 | C1 |
| Bath Rd., Mitch. | 185 | G3 |
| Bath Rd., Rom. | 82 | E6 |
| Bath Rd., West Dr. | 140 | A1 |
| **Bath St. EC1** | **12** | **A4** |
| Bath St. EC1 | 112 | A3 |
| **Bath Ter. SE1** | **27** | **J6** |
| Bath Ter. SE1 | 131 | J3 |
| Bathgate Rd. SW19 | 166 | A3 |
| Baths Rd., Brom. | 192 | A4 |
| Bathurst Av. SW19 *Brisbane Av.* | 184/185 | D1 |
| Bathurst Gdns. NW10 | 107 | H2 |
| **Bathurst Ms. W2** | **15** | **E5** |
| Bathurst Rd., Ilf. | 98 | E1 |
| **Bathurst St. W2** | **15** | **E5** |
| Bathurst St. W2 | 109 | G7 |
| Bathway SE18 | 136 | D4 |
| Batley Cl., Mitch. | 185 | J7 |
| Batley Pl. N16 | 94 | C3 |
| Batley Rd. N16 *Stoke Newington High St.* | 94 | C3 |
| Batley Rd., Enf. | 43 | J1 |
| Batman Cl. W12 | 127 | H1 |
| Batoum Gdns. W6 | 127 | J3 |
| Batson St. W12 | 127 | G2 |
| Batsworth Rd., Mitch. | 185 | G3 |
| Batten Cl. E6 *Savage Gdns.* | 116 | C6 |
| Batten St. SW11 | 149 | H3 |
| Battenburg Wk. SE19 *Brabourne Cl.* | 170 | B5 |
| Battersby Rd. SE6 | 172 | D2 |
| **Battersea Br. SW3** | **31** | **F7** |
| **Battersea Br. SW11** | **31** | **F7** |
| Battersea Br. SW11 | 129 | G7 |
| Battersea Br. Rd. SW11 | 129 | H7 |
| Battersea Ch. Rd. SW11 | 149 | G1 |
| Battersea High St. SW11 | 149 | G1 |
| **Battersea Pk. SW11** | **31** | **J7** |
| Battersea Pk. SW11 | 129 | J7 |
| Battersea Pk. Rd. SW8 | 150 | B1 |
| Battersea Pk. Rd. SW11 | 149 | H2 |
| Battersea Ri. SW11 | 149 | H5 |
| Battersea Sq. SW11 *Battersea High St.* | 149 | G1 |
| Battery Rd. SE28 | 137 | H2 |
| Battishall Gdns. N1 *Waterloo Ter.* | 93 | H7 |
| Battishill St. N1 *Waterloo Ter.* | 93 | H7 |
| **Battle Br. La. SE1** | **28** | **D2** |
| Battle Br. La. SE1 | 132 | B1 |
| **Battle Br. Rd. NW1** | **10** | **A2** |
| Battle Br. Rd. NW1 | 110 | E2 |
| Battle Cl. SW19 *North Rd.* | 167 | F6 |
| Battle Rd., Belv. | 139 | J4 |
| Battle Rd., Erith | 139 | J4 |
| Battledean Rd. N5 | 93 | H5 |
| **Batty St. E1** | **21** | **J3** |
| Batty St. E1 | 112 | D6 |
| Baudwin Rd. SE6 | 172 | E2 |
| Baugh Rd., Sid. | 176 | C5 |
| Baulk, The SW18 | 148 | D7 |
| Bavant Rd. SW16 | 187 | E2 |
| Bavaria Rd. N19 | 92 | E2 |
| Bavdene Ms. NW4 *The Burroughs* | 71 | H4 |
| Bavent Rd. SE5 | 151 | J2 |
| Bawdale Rd. SE22 | 152 | C5 |
| Bawdsey Av., Ilf. | 81 | J4 |
| Bawtree Rd. SE14 | 133 | H7 |
| Bawtry Rd. N20 | 57 | J3 |
| Baxendale N20 | 57 | F2 |
| **Baxendale St. E2** | **13** | **H3** |
| Baxendale St. E2 | 112 | D3 |
| Baxter Cl., Sthl. | 123 | H2 |
| Baxter Rd. E16 | 115 | J6 |
| Baxter Rd. N1 | 94 | A6 |
| Baxter Rd. N18 | 60 | E4 |
| Baxter Rd. NW10 | 106 | E4 |
| Baxter Rd., Ilf. | 98 | E5 |
| Bay Ct. W5 *Popes La.* | 125 | H3 |
| Bay Tree Cl., Brom. | 191 | J1 |
| Baycroft Cl., Pnr. | 66 | C3 |
| Baydon Ct., Brom. | 191 | F3 |
| Bayes Cl. SE26 | 171 | F5 |
| Bayfield Rd. SE9 | 156 | A4 |
| Bayford Ms. E8 *Bayford St.* | 94/95 | E7 |
| Bayford Rd. NW10 | 108 | A3 |
| Bayford St. E8 | 95 | E7 |
| **Bayham Pl. NW1** | **9** | **F1** |
| Bayham Pl. NW1 | 110 | C1 |
| Bayham Rd. W4 | 126 | D3 |
| Bayham Rd. W13 | 104 | E7 |
| Bayham Rd., Mord. | 185 | E4 |
| Bayham St. NW1 | 110 | C1 |
| **Bayley St. WC1** | **17** | **H2** |
| Bayley St. WC1 | 110 | D5 |
| Bayley Wk. SE2 *Woolwich Rd.* | 138/139 | E5 |
| Baylin Rd. SW18 *Garratt La.* | 148/149 | E6 |
| **Baylis Rd. SE1** | **27** | **E4** |
| Baylis Rd. SE1 | 131 | G2 |
| Bayliss Av. SE28 | 118 | D7 |
| Bayliss Cl. N21 *Macleod Rd.* | 42/43 | E5 |
| Bayne Cl. E6 *Savage Gdns.* | 116 | C6 |
| Baynes Cl., Enf. | 44 | D2 |
| Baynes Ms. NW3 *Belsize La.* | 91 | G6 |
| Baynes St. NW1 | 92 | C7 |
| Baynham Cl., Bex. | 159 | F6 |
| Bayonne Rd. W6 | 128 | B6 |
| Bayshill Ri., Nthlt. | 85 | H6 |
| Bayston Rd. N16 | 94 | C3 |
| **Bayswater Rd. W2** | **15** | **F5** |
| Bayswater Rd. W2 | 108 | E7 |
| Baythorne St. E3 | 113 | J5 |
| Baytree Cl., Sid. | 175 | J1 |
| Baytree Rd. SW2 | 151 | F4 |
| Bazalgette Cl., N.Mal. | 182 | D5 |
| Bazalgette Gdns., N.Mal. | 182 | D5 |
| Bazely St. E14 | 114 | C7 |
| Bazile Rd. N21 | 43 | G6 |
| Beach Gro., Felt. | 161 | G2 |
| Beacham Cl. SE7 | 136 | A5 |
| Beachborough Rd., Brom. | 172 | C4 |
| Beachcroft Rd. E11 | 97 | E3 |
| Beachcroft Way N19 | 92 | D1 |
| Beachy Rd. E3 | 96 | A7 |
| Beacon Gate SE14 | 153 | G3 |
| Beacon Gro., Cars. | 200 | A4 |
| Beacon Hill N7 | 92 | E5 |
| Beacon Rd. SE13 | 154 | D6 |
| Beacon Rd., Houns. | 140 | D6 |
| Beacon Rd. Roundabout, Houns. | 140 | E6 |
| Beacons Cl. E6 *Oliver Gdns.* | 116 | B5 |
| Beaconsfield Cl. N11 | 58 | A4 |
| Beaconsfield Cl. SE3 | 135 | G6 |
| Beaconsfield Cl. W4 | 126 | C5 |
| Beaconsfield Par. SE9 *Beaconsfield Rd.* | 174 | B4 |
| Beaconsfield Rd. E10 | 96 | C2 |
| Beaconsfield Rd. E16 | 115 | F4 |
| Beaconsfield Rd. E17 | 77 | J6 |
| Beaconsfield Rd. N9 | 60 | D4 |
| Beaconsfield Rd. N11 | 58 | A3 |
| Beaconsfield Rd. N15 | 76 | B4 |
| Beaconsfield Rd. NW10 | 89 | F6 |
| Beaconsfield Rd. SE3 | 135 | F7 |
| Beaconsfield Rd. SE9 | 174 | B2 |
| **Beaconsfield Rd. SE17** | **36** | **C4** |
| Beaconsfield Rd. SE17 | 132 | A5 |
| Beaconsfield Rd. W4 | 126 | D3 |
| Beaconsfield Rd. W5 | 125 | F7 |
| Beaconsfield Rd., Brom. | 192 | A3 |
| Beaconsfield Rd., Croy. | 188 | A6 |
| Beaconsfield Rd., Esher | 194 | B7 |
| Beaconsfield Rd., Hayes | 122 | C1 |
| Beaconsfield Rd. N.Mal. | 182 | D2 |
| Beaconsfield Rd., Sthl. | 122 | D1 |
| Beaconsfield Rd., Surb. | 181 | J7 |
| Beaconsfield Rd., Twick. | 144 | E6 |
| Beaconsfield Ter., Rom. | 82 | D6 |
| Beaconsfield Ter. Rd. W14 | 128 | B3 |
| Beaconsfield Wk. E6 *East Ham Manor Way* | 116 | D6 |
| Beaconsfield Wk. SW6 | 148 | C1 |
| Beacontree Av. E17 | 78 | D1 |
| Beacontree Rd. E11 | 79 | F7 |
| Beadlow Cl., Cars. *Olveston Wk.* | 185 | G6 |
| Beadman Pl. SE27 *Norwood High St.* | 169 | H4 |
| Beadman St. SE27 | 169 | H4 |
| Beadnell Rd. SE23 | 171 | G1 |
| Beadon Rd. W6 | 127 | J4 |
| Beadon Rd., Brom. | 191 | G4 |
| Beaford Gro. SW20 | 184 | B3 |
| Beagle Cl., Felt. | 160 | B4 |
| **Beak St. W1** | **17** | **G5** |
| Beak St. W1 | 110 | C7 |
| Beal Cl., Well. | 158 | A1 |
| Beal Rd., Ilf. | 98 | D2 |
| Beale Cl. N13 | 59 | H5 |
| Beale Pl. E3 | 113 | J2 |
| Beale Rd. E3 | 113 | J1 |
| Beam Av., Dag. | 119 | H1 |
| Beaminster Gdns., Ilf. | 80 | E2 |
| Beamish Dr., Bushey | 51 | J1 |
| Beamish Rd. N9 | 60 | D1 |
| Bean Rd., Bexh. | 158 | D4 |
| Beanacre Cl. E9 | 95 | J6 |
| Beanshaw SE9 | 174 | D4 |
| Beansland Gro., Rom. | 83 | E2 |
| **Bear All. EC4** | **19** | **G3** |
| Bear Cl., Rom. | 83 | H6 |
| **Bear Gdns. SE1** | **27** | **J1** |
| Bear Gdns. SE1 | 131 | J1 |
| **Bear La. SE1** | **27** | **H1** |
| Bear La. SE1 | 131 | H1 |
| Bear Rd., Felt. | 160 | D5 |
| **Bear St. WC2** | **17** | **J5** |
| Beard Rd., Kings.T. | 163 | J5 |
| Beardell St. SE19 | 170 | C6 |
| Beardow Gro. N14 | 42 | C6 |
| Beard's Hill, Hmptn. | 179 | G1 |
| Beard's Hill Cl., Hmptn. *Beard's Hill* | 179 | G1 |
| Beardsfield E13 *Valetta Gro.* | 115 | G1 |
| Beardsley Ter., Dag. *Fitzstephen Rd.* | 100 | B5 |
| Beardsley Way W3 | 126 | D2 |
| Bearfield Rd., Kings.T. | 163 | H7 |
| Bearstead Ri. SE4 | 153 | J5 |
| Bearstead Ter., Beck. *Copers Cope Rd.* | 190 | A1 |
| Beatrice Av. SW16 | 187 | F3 |
| Beatrice Av., Wem. | 87 | H5 |
| Beatrice Cl. E13 *Chargeable La.* | 115 | G4 |
| Beatrice Cl., Pnr. *Reid Cl.* | 66 | A4 |
| Beatrice Ct., Buck.H. | 64 | A2 |
| **Beatrice Pl. W8** | **22** | **A6** |
| Beatrice Pl. W8 | 128 | E3 |
| Beatrice Rd. E17 | 78 | A5 |
| Beatrice Rd. N4 | 75 | G7 |
| Beatrice Rd. N9 | 45 | F7 |
| **Beatrice Rd. SE1** | **37** | **J2** |
| Beatrice Rd. SE1 | 132 | D4 |
| Beatrice Rd., Rich. *Albert Rd.* | 145 | J5 |
| Beatrice Rd., Sthl. | 123 | F1 |
| Beatson Wk. SE16 | 133 | H1 |
| Beattock Ri. N10 | 74 | B4 |
| Beatty Rd. N16 | 94 | B4 |
| Beatty Rd., Stan. | 53 | F6 |
| **Beatty St. NW1** | **9** | **F1** |
| Beatty St. NW1 | 110 | C2 |
| Beattyville Gdns., Ilf. | 80 | D3 |
| Beauchamp Cl. W4 *Church Path* | 126 | C3 |
| **Beauchamp Pl. SW3** | **23** | **H5** |
| Beauchamp Pl. SW3 | 129 | H3 |
| Beauchamp Rd. E7 | 97 | H7 |
| Beauchamp Rd. SE19 | 188 | A1 |
| Beauchamp Rd. SW11 | 149 | H4 |
| Beauchamp Rd., E.Mol. | 179 | H5 |
| Beauchamp Rd., Sutt. | 198 | D5 |
| Beauchamp Rd. Twick. | 144 | D7 |
| Beauchamp Rd., W.Mol. | 179 | H5 |
| **Beauchamp St. EC1** | **19** | **E2** |
| Beauchamp Ter. SW15 *Dryburgh Rd.* | 147 | H3 |
| Beauclerc Rd. W6 | 127 | H3 |
| Beauclerk Cl., Felt. *Florence Rd.* | 160 | B1 |
| Beaudesert Ms., West Dr. | 120 | B2 |
| Beaufort E6 *Newark Knok* | 116 | D5 |
| Beaufort Av., Har. | 68 | D4 |
| Beaufort Cl. E4 *Higham Sta. Av.* | 62 | B6 |
| Beaufort Cl. SW15 | 147 | H7 |
| Beaufort Cl. W5 | 105 | J5 |
| Beaufort Cl., Rom. | 83 | J4 |
| Beaufort Cl., Rich. *Beaufort Rd.* | 163 | F4 |
| Beaufort Dr. NW11 | 72 | D4 |
| Beaufort Gdns. NW4 | 71 | J6 |
| **Beaufort Gdns. SW3** | **23** | **H5** |
| Beaufort Gdns. SW3 | 129 | H3 |
| Beaufort Gdns. SW16 | 169 | F7 |
| Beaufort Gdns., Houns. | 143 | E1 |
| Beaufort Gdns., Ilf. | 98 | D1 |
| Beaufort Ms. SW6 *Lillie Rd.* | 128 | C6 |
| Beaufort Pk. NW11 | 72 | D4 |
| Beaufort Rd. W5 | 105 | J5 |
| Beaufort Rd., Kings.T. | 181 | H4 |
| Beaufort Rd., Twick. | 145 | F7 |
| **Beaufort St. SW3** | **31** | **F6** |
| Beaufort St. SW3 | 129 | G6 |
| Beaufort Way, Epsom | 197 | G7 |
| Beaufoy Rd. N17 | 60 | B7 |
| **Beaufoy Wk. SE11** | **34** | **D2** |
| Beaufoy Wk. SE11 | 131 | F4 |
| Beaulieu Av. E16 | 135 | H1 |
| Beaulieu Av. SE26 | 170 | E4 |
| Beaulieu Cl. NW9 | 71 | E4 |
| Beaulieu Cl. SE5 | 152 | A3 |
| Beaulieu Cl., Houns. | 143 | F5 |
| Beaulieu Cl., Mitch. | 186 | A1 |
| Beaulieu Cl., Twick. | 145 | G7 |
| Beaulieu Cl., Wat. | 50 | C1 |
| Beaulieu Dr., Pnr. | 66 | D6 |
| Beaulieu Gdns. N21 | 43 | J7 |
| Beaulieu Pl. W4 *Rothschild Rd.* | 126 | C3 |
| Beaumanor Gdns. SE9 | 174 | D4 |
| Beaumaris Dr., Wdf.Grn. | 64 | A7 |
| Beaumont Av. W14 | 128 | C5 |

Beaumont Av., Har. 67 H6
Beaumont Av., Rich. 145 J3
Beaumont Av., Wem. 87 F5
Beaumont Cl., Kings.T. 164 A7
Beaumont Cres. W14 128 C5
Beaumont Gdns. NW3 90 D3
Beaumont Gro. E1 113 G4
**Beaumont Ms. W1 16 C1**
**Beaumont Pl. W1 9 G5**
Beaumont Pl. W1 110 C4
Beaumont Pl., Barn. 40 C1
Beaumont Pl., Islw. 144 C5
Beaumont Ri. N19 92 D1
Beaumont Rd. E10 78 B7
Beaumont Rd. E13 115 H3
Beaumont Rd. SE19 169 J6
Beaumont Rd. SW19 148 B7
Beaumont Rd. W4 126 C3
Beaumont Rd., Orp. 193 G6
Beaumont Sq. E1 113 G4
**Beaumont St. W1 16 C1**
Beaumont St. W1 110 A5
Beaumont Wk. NW3 91 J7
Beauvais Ter., Nthlt. 102 D3
Beauval Rd. SE22 152 C6
Beaver Cl. SE20 170 D7
*Lullington Rd.*
Beaver Cl., Hmptn. 179 H1
Beaver Gro., Nthlt. 102/103 E3
*Jetstar Way*
Beaverbank Rd. SE9 175 G1
Beavers Cres., Houns. 142 C4
Beavers La., Houns. 142 C3
Beavers La. Camp, Houns. 142 C3
*Beavers La.*
Beaverwood Rd., Chis. 175 H6
Beavor Gro. W6 127 G4
*Beavor La.*
Beavor La. W6 127 G4
Bebbington Rd. SE18 137 H4
Bebletts Cl., Orp. 207 J5
Bec Cl., Ruis. 84 D3
Beccles Dr., Bark. 99 H6
Beccles St. E14 113 J7
Beck Cl. SE13 154 B1
Beck Ct., Beck. 189 G3
Beck La., Beck. 189 G3
Beck River Pk., Beck. 190 A1
*Rectory Rd.*
Beck Rd. E8 112 E1
Beck Way, Beck. 189 J3
Beckenham Business Cen., Beck. 171 H6
Beckenham Gdns. N9 60 B3
Beckenham Gro., Brom. 190 D2
Beckenham Hill Rd. SE6 172 B5
Beckenham Hill Rd., Beck. 172 B5
Beckenham La., Brom. 191 E2
Beckenham Pl. Pk., Beck. 172 B7
Beckenham Rd., Beck. 189 G1
Beckenham Rd., W.Wick. 190 B7
Beckers, The N16 94 D3
*Rectory Rd.*
Becket Av. E6 116 D3
Becket Cl. SE25 188 D6
Becket Fold, Har. 68 C5
*Courtfield Cres.*
Becket Rd. N18 61 F4
**Becket St. SE1 28 B5**
Beckett Cl. NW10 88 D6
Beckett Cl. SW16 168 D2
Beckett Cl., Belv. 138/139 E3
*Tunstock Way*
Beckett Wk., Beck. 171 H6
Becketts Cl., Felt. 142 B6
Becketts Cl., Orp. 207 J3
Becketts Pl., Kings.T. 181 G1
Beckford Dr., Orp. 193 G7
**Beckford Pl. SE17 36 A4**
Beckford Rd., Croy. 188 C6
Becklow Gdns. W12 127 G2
*Becklow Rd.*
Becklow Ms. W12 127 F2
*Becklow Rd.*
Becklow Rd. W12 127 G2
Becks Rd., Sid. 176 A3
Beckton Pk. Roundabout E16 116 C7
*Royal Albert Way*
Beckton Rd. E16 115 F5
Beckway Rd. SW16 186 D2
**Beckway St. SE17 36 C2**
Beckway St. SE17 132 A4
Beckwith Rd. SE24 152 A6
Beclands Rd. SW17 168 A6
Becmead Av. SW16 168 D4
Becmead Av., Har. 68 E5
Becondale Rd. SE19 170 B5
Becontree Av., Dag. 100 B4
Bective Pl. SW15 148 C4
*Bective Rd.*
Bective Rd. E7 97 G4
Bective Rd. SW15 148 C4
Becton Pl., Erith 139 H7
**Bedale St. SE1 28 B2**
Bedale St. SE1 132 A1
Beddington Cross, Croy. 186/187 E7
*Beddington Fm. Rd.*
Beddington Fm. Rd., Croy. 200 E1
Beddington Gdns., Cars. 200 A6
Beddington Gdns., Wall. 200 B6
Beddington Grn., Orp. 193 J1
Beddington Gro., Wall. 200 D5
Beddington La., Croy. 186 C5
Beddington Path, Orp. 193 J1
Beddington Rd., Ilf. 81 J7
Beddington Rd., Orp. 193 H2
Beddington Trd. Pk. W., Croy. 200 E1
Bede Cl., Pnr. 66 D1
Bede Rd., Rom. 82 C6
**Bedenham Way SE15 37 F7**
Bedens Rd., Sid. 176 E6
Bedfont Cl., Felt. 141 F6
Bedfont Cl., Mitch. 186 A2
Bedfont La., Felt. 141 J7
Bedfont Rd., Stai. 140 B6
**Bedford Av. WC1 17 J2**
Bedford Av. WC1 110 D5
Bedford Av., Barn. 40 C5
Bedford Av., Hayes 102 B6
Bedford Cl. N10 58 A7
Bedford Cl. W4 127 E6
Bedford Cor. W4 126/127 E4
*The Av.*
**Bedford Ct. WC2 18 A6**
Bedford Gdns. W8 128 D1
Bedford Hill SW12 168 B1
Bedford Hill SW16 168 B1
Bedford Ho. SW4 150 D4
Bedford Ms. N2 73 H3
*Bedford Rd.*
Bedford Pk., Croy. 201 J1
Bedford Pk. Cor. W4 126/127 E4
*Bath Rd.*
Bedford Pas. SW6 128 B7
*Dawes Rd.*
**Bedford Pl. W1 17 G1**
**Bedford Pl. WC1 18 A1**
Bedford Pl. WC1 110 E5
Bedford Pl., Croy. 202 A1
Bedford Rd. E6 116 D1
Bedford Rd. E17 78 A2
Bedford Rd. E18 79 G2
Bedford Rd. N2 73 H3
Bedford Rd. N8 74 D6
Bedford Rd. N9 44 E7
Bedford Rd. N15 76 B4
Bedford Rd. N22 74 E1
Bedford Rd. NW7 54 E3
Bedford Rd. SW4 150 E3
Bedford Rd. W4 126 D3
Bedford Rd. W13 104 E7
Bedford Rd., Har. 67 J6
Bedford Rd., Ilf. 99 E3
Bedford Rd., Sid. 175 H3
Bedford Rd., Twick. 162 A3
Bedford Rd., Wor.Pk. 197 J2
**Bedford Row WC1 18 D1**
Bedford Row WC1 111 F5
**Bedford Sq. WC1 17 J2**
Bedford Sq. WC1 110 D5
**Bedford St. WC2 18 A5**
Bedford St. WC2 111 E7
Bedford Ter. SW2 150/151 E5
*Lyham Rd.*
**Bedford Way WC1 9 J6**
Bedford Way WC1 110 D4
**Bedfordbury WC2 18 A5**
Bedgebury Gdns. SW19 166 B2
Bedgebury Rd. SE9 156 A4
Bedivere Rd., Brom. 173 G3
Bedlow Way, Croy. 201 F4
Bedonwell Rd. SE2 138 E6
Bedonwell Rd., Belv. 139 G6
Bedonwell Rd., Bexh. 139 G6
**Bedser Cl. SE11 34 D5**
Bedser Cl., Th.Hth. 187 J3
Bedser Dr., Grnf. 86 A5
Bedster Gdns., W.Mol. 179 H2
Bedwardine Rd. SE19 170 B7
Bedwell Gdns., Hayes 121 H5
Bedwell Rd. N17 76 B1
Bedwell Rd., Belv. 139 G5
Beeby Rd. E16 115 H5
Beech Av. N20 57 H1
Beech Av. W3 126 E1
Beech Av., Brent. 125 E7
Beech Av., Buck.H. 63 H2
Beech Av., Ruis. 84 B1
Beech Av., Sid. 158 A7
Beech Cl. N9 44 D6
Beech Cl. SE8 133 J6
*Clyde St.*
Beech Cl. SW15 147 G7
Beech Cl. SW19 165 J6
Beech Cl., Cars. 199 J2
Beech Cl., Loug. 48/49 E2
*Cedar Dr.*
Beech Cl., Stai. 140 A7
*St. Mary's Cres.*
Beech Cl., Sun. 178 D2
*Harfield Rd.*
Beech Cl., West Dr. 120 D3
Beech Copse, Brom. 192 C2
Beech Copse, S.Croy. 202 B5
Beech Ct. E17 78 D3
Beech Ct. SE9 156 B6
Beech Ct., Ilf. 98 D3
*Riverdene Rd.*
Beech Ct., Surb. 181 H7
Beech Dell, Kes. 206 C4
Beech Dr. N2 73 J3
Beech Gdns. EC2 111 J5
*Aldersgate St.*
Beech Gdns. W5 125 H2
Beech Gdns., Dag. 101 H7
Beech Gro., Ilf. 65 H6
Beech Gro., Mitch. 186 D4
Beech Gro., N.Mal. 182 D3
Beech Hall Cres. E4 62 D7
Beech Hall Rd. E4 62 C7
Beech Hill Av., Barn. 41 F1
Beech Ho., Croy. 204 B6
Beech Ho. Rd., Croy. 202 A3
Beech La., Buck.H. 63 H2
Beech Lawns N12 57 G5
Beech Rd. N11 59 E6
Beech Rd. SW16 187 E2
Beech Rd., Felt. 141 H7
Beech Row, Rich. 163 H4
**Beech St. EC2 19 J1**
Beech St. EC2 111 J5
Beech St., Rom. 83 J4
Beech Tree Cl., Stan. 53 F5
Beech Tree Glade E4 63 F1
*Forest Side*
Beech Tree Pl., Sutt. 198/199 E5
*St. Nicholas Way*
Beech Wk. NW7 54 E6
Beech Way NW10 88 D7
Beech Way, Twick. 161 G3
Beechcroft, Chis. 174 D7
Beechcroft Av. NW11 72 C7
Beechcroft Av., Har. 67 G7
Beechcroft Av., N.Mal. 182 C1
Beechcroft Av., Sthl. 123 F1
Beechcroft Cl., Houns. 122 E7
Beechcroft Cl., Orp. 207 G4
Beechcroft Gdns., Wem. 87 J3
Beechcroft Rd. E18 79 H2
Beechcroft Rd. SW14 146 C3
*Elm Rd.*
Beechcroft Rd. SW17 167 H2
Beechcroft Rd., Chess. 195 J3
Beechcroft Rd., Orp. 207 G4
Beechdale N21 59 F2
Beechdale Rd. SW2 151 F6
Beechen Cliff Way, Islw. 144 C1
*Henley Cl.*
Beechen Gro., Pnr. 67 F3
Beeches, The, Houns. 143 H1
Beeches Av., Cars. 199 H7
Beeches Cl. SE20 189 F1
*Genoa Rd.*
Beeches Ct., Brom. 173 G6
*Avondale Rd.*
Beeches Rd. SW17 167 H3
Beeches Rd., Sutt. 198 B1
Beechfield Cotts., Brom. 191 J2
*Widmore Rd.*
Beechfield Gdns., Rom. 83 J7
Beechfield Rd. N4 75 J6
Beechfield Rd. SE6 171 J1
Beechfield Rd., Brom. 191 J2
Beechhill Rd. SE9 156 D5
Beechmont Cl., Brom. 172 E5
Beechmore Gdns., Sutt. 198 A2
Beechmore Rd. SW11 149 J1
Beechmount Av. W7 104 A5
Beecholme Av., Mitch. 186 B1
Beecholme Est. E5 94/95 E3
*Prout Rd.*
Beechvale Cl. N12 57 H5
Beechway, Bex. 158 D6
Beechwood Av. N3 72 C3
Beechwood Av., Grnf. 103 H3
Beechwood Av., Har. 85 H3
Beechwood Av., Orp. 207 H5
Beechwood Av., Rich. 146 A1
Beechwood Av., Sun. 160 A6
Beechwood Av., Th.Hth. 187 H4
Beechwood Circle, Har. 85 H3
*Beechwood Gdns.*
Beechwood Cl. NW7 54 D5
Beechwood Cl., Surb. 181 F7
Beechwood Ct., Cars. 199 J4
Beechwood Ct., Sun. 160 A6
Beechwood Cres., Bexh. 158 D3
Beechwood Dr., Kes. 206 A4
Beechwood Dr., Wdf.Grn. 63 F5
Beechwood Gdns. NW10 105 J3
*St. Annes Gdns.*
Beechwood Gdns., Har. 85 H3
Beechwood Gdns., Ilf. 80 C5
Beechwood Gro. W3 106/107 E7
*East Acton La.*
Beechwood Gro., Surb. 181 F7
Beechwood Ms. N9 60 D2
Beechwood Pk. E18 79 G3
Beechwood Ri., Chis. 175 E4
Beechwood Rd. E8 94 C6
Beechwood Rd. N8 74 D4
Beechwoods Ct. SE19 170 C5
*Crystal Palace Par.*
Beechworth Cl. NW3 90 D2
Beecroft Rd. SE4 153 H5
Beehive Cl. E8 94 C7
Beehive La., Ilf. 80 C6
**Beehive Pas. EC3 20 D4**
Beehive Pl. SW9 151 G3
Beeken Dene, Orp. 207 F4
*Isabella Dr.*
Beeleigh Rd., Mord. 185 E4
Beeston Cl. E8 94 D5
*Ferncliff Rd.*
Beeston Cl., Wat. 50 D4
**Beeston Pl. SW1 24 E6**
Beeston Pl. SW1 130 B3
Beeston Rd., Barn. 41 G6
Beeston Way, Felt. 142 C6
Beethoven St. W10 108 B3
Beeton Cl., Pnr. 51 G7
Begbie Rd. SE3 155 J1
Beggars Hill, Epsom 197 F7
Beggars Roost La., Sutt. 198 D6
Begonia Cl. E6 116 B5
Begonia Pl., Hmptn. 161 G6
*Gresham Rd.*
Begonia Wk. W12 107 F6
*Du Cane Rd.*
Beira St. SW12 150 B7
Bekesbourne St. E14 113 H6
*Ratcliffe La.*
Belcroft Cl., Brom. 173 F7
*Hope Pk.*
Beldham Gdns., W.Mol. 179 H3
Belfairs Dr., Rom. 82 C7
Belfairs Grn., Wat. 50 D5
*Heysham Dr.*

Bexley Gdns., Rom. 82 B5
Bexley High St., Bex. 159 G7
Bexley La., Sid. 176 C3
Bexley Rd. SE9 156 E5
Bexley Rd., Erith 139 J7
Beynon Rd., Cars. 199 J5
Bianca Ho. N1 112 B2
*Crondall St.*
**Bianca Rd. SE15 37 H6**
Bianca Rd. SE15 132 C6
Bibsworth Rd. N3 72 C2
**Bibury Cl. SE15 37 E6**
Bibury Cl. SE15 132 B6
Bicester Rd., Rich. 146 A3
**Bickenhall St. W1 16 A1**
Bickenhall St. W1 109 J5
Bickersteth Rd. SW17 167 J6
Bickerton Rd. N19 92 C2
Bickley Cres., Brom. 192 B4
Bickley Pk. Rd., Brom. 192 B3
Bickley Rd. E10 78 B7
Bickley Rd., Brom. 192 A2
Bickley St. SW17 167 H5
Bicknell Rd. SE5 151 J3
Bicknoller Rd., Enf. 44 C1
Bicknor Rd., Orp. 193 H7
Bidborough Cl., Brom. 191 F5
**Bidborough St. WC1 10 A4**
Bidborough St. WC1 110 D3
Biddenden Way SE9 174 D4
Bidder St. E16 114 E5
Biddestone Rd. N7 93 F4
**Biddulph Rd. W9 6 A4**
Biddulph Rd. W9 108 E3
Bideford Av., Grnf. 104 E2
Bideford Cl., Edg. 70 A1
Bideford Cl., Felt. 161 F3
Bideford Gdns., Enf. 44 B7
Bideford Rd., Brom. 173 F3
Bideford Rd., Ruis. 84 B3
Bideford Rd., Well. 138 B7
Bidwell Gdns. N11 58 C7
Bidwell St. SE15 153 E1
Big Hill E5 95 E1
Bigbury Cl. N17 60 A7
*Weir Hall Rd.*
Bigbury Rd. N17 60 B7
*Barkham Rd.*
Biggerstaff Rd. E15 114 C1
Biggerstaff St. N4 93 G2
Biggin Av., Mitch. 185 J1
Biggin Hill SE19 169 H7
Biggin Hill Cl., Kings.T. 163 F5
Biggin Way SE19 169 H7
Bigginwood Rd. SW16 169 H7
Biggs Row SW15 148 A3
*Felsham Rd.*
Bigland St. E1 112 E6
Bignell Rd. SE18 136 E5
Bignold Rd. E7 97 G4
Bigwood Rd. NW11 72 E5
Bill Hamling Cl. SE9 174 C2
Bill Nicholson Way N17 76 C3
*High Rd.*
Billet Cl., Rom. 82 D3
Billet Rd. E17 77 G2
Billet Rd., Rom. 82 B3
Billets Hart Cl. W7 124 B2
**Billing Pl. SW10 30 B7**
Billing Pl. SW10 129 E7
**Billing Rd. SW10 30 B7**
Billing Rd. SW10 129 E7
**Billing St. SW10 30 B7**
Billing St. SW10 129 E7
Billingford Cl. SE4 153 G4
Billings Cl., Dag. 100 C7
*Ellerton Rd.*
Billington Rd. SE14 133 G7
**Billiter Sq. EC3 20 E5**
**Billiter St. EC3 20 E4**
Billiter St. EC3 112 B6
Billockby Cl., Chess. 195 J6
Billson St. E14 134 C4
Bilsby Gro. SE9 174 A4
Bilton Rd., Grnf. 105 F1
Bilton Way, Enf. 45 H1
Bilton Way, Hayes 122 B2
**Bina Gdns. SW5 30 C2**
Bina Gdns. SW5 129 F4
Bincote Rd., Enf. 43 F3
Binden Rd. W12 127 F3
Bindon Grn., Mord. 185 E4
Binfield Rd. SW4 151 E1
Binfield Rd., S.Croy. 202 C5
Bingfield St. N1 111 E1
Bingham Ct. N1 93 H7
*Halton Rd.*
**Bingham Pl. W1 16 B1**
Bingham Rd., Croy. 202 D1
Bingham St. N1 94 A6
Bingley Rd. E16 115 J6
Bingley Rd., Grnf. 103 J5
Bingley Rd., Sun. 160 A7
**Binney St. W1 16 C5**
Binney St. W1 110 A6
Binns Rd. W4 126 E5
Binns Ter. W4 126/127 E5
*Binns Rd.*
Binsey Wk. SE2 138 C1
Binyon Cres., Stan. 52 C5
Birbetts Rd. SE9 174 C2
Birch Av. N13 59 J3
Birch Cl. E16 115 E5
Birch Cl. N19 92 C2
*Hargrave Pk.*
Birch Cl. SE15 152 D2
*Bournemouth Rd.*
Birch Cl., Brent. 124 E7
Birch Cl., Buck.H. 64 A3
Birch Cl., Houns. 144 A3
Birch Cl., Rom. 83 H3
Birch Cl., Tedd. 162 D5
Birch Gdns., Dag. 101 J3
Birch Grn. NW9 54/55 E7
*Clayton Fld.*
Birch Gro. E11 96 E3
Birch Gro. SE12 155 F7
Birch Gro. W3 126 A1
Birch Gro., Well. 158 A4
Birch Hill, Croy. 203 G5
Birch Mead, Orp. 206 D2
Birch Pk., Har. 51 J7
Birch Rd., Felt. 160 D5
Birch Rd., Rom. 83 H3
Birch Row, Brom. 192 D7
Birch Tree Av., W.Wick. 205 F5
Birch Tree Way, Croy. 202 E2
Birch Wk., Borwd. 38 A1
Birch Wk., Erith 139 J6
Birch Wk., Mitch. 186 B1
Bircham Path SE4 153 G4
*St. Norbert Rd.*
Birchanger Rd. SE25 188 D5
Birchdale Gdns., Rom. 82 D7
Birchdale Rd. E7 97 J5
Birchdene Dr. SE28 138 A2
Birchen Cl. NW9 88 D2
Birchen Gro. NW9 88 D2
Birchend Cl., S.Croy. 202 A6
Birches, The N21 43 F6
Birches, The SE7 135 H6
Birches, The, Orp. 206 D4
Birches Cl., Mitch. 185 J3
Birches Cl., Pnr. 66 E5
Birchfield St. E14 114 A7
**Birchin La. EC3 20 C4**
Birchin La. EC3 112 A6
Birchington Cl., Bexh. 159 H1
Birchington Rd. N8 74 D6
Birchington Rd. NW6 108 D1
Birchington Rd., Surb. 181 J7
Birchlands Av. SW12 149 J7
Birchmead Av., Pnr. 66 C4
Birchmere Row SE3 155 F2
Birchmore Wk. N5 93 J3
Birchville Ct., Bushey 52 B1
*Heathbourne Rd.*
Birchway, Hayes 122 A1
Birchwood Av. N10 74 A3
Birchwood Av., Beck. 189 J4
Birchwood Av., Sid. 176 B2
Birchwood Av., Wall. 200 A3
Birchwood Cl., Mord. 184 E4
Birchwood Ct. N13 59 H5
Birchwood Ct., Edg. 70 C2
Birchwood Dr. NW3 91 E3
Birchwood Gro., Hmptn. 161 G6
Birchwood Rd. SW17 168 B5
Birchwood Rd., Orp. 193 G4
Bird in Bush Rd. SE15 132 D7
**Bird St. W1 16 C4**
Bird Wk., Twick. 161 F1
Bird-in-Hand La., Brom. 192 A2
Bird-in-Hand Pas. SE23 171 F2
*Dartmouth Rd.*
Birdbrook Cl., Dag. 101 J7
Birdbrook Rd. SE3 155 J3
**Birdcage Wk. SW1 25 G4**
Birdcage Wk. SW1 130 C2
Birdham Cl., Brom. 192 B5
Birdhurst Av., S.Croy. 202 A4
Birdhurst Gdns., S.Croy. 202 A4
Birdhurst Ri., S.Croy. 202 B5
Birdhurst Rd. SW18 149 F4
Birdhurst Rd. SW19 167 H6
Birdhurst Rd., S.Croy 202 B5
**Birdlip Cl. SE15 36 D6**
Birdlip Cl. SE15 132 B6
Birds Fm. Av., Rom. 83 H1
Birdsfield La. E3 113 J1
Birdwood Cl., Tedd. 162 B4
Birkbeck Av. W3 106 C7
Birkbeck Av., Grnf. 103 J1
Birkbeck Gdns., Wdf.Grn. 63 F2
Birkbeck Gro. W3 126 D2
Birkbeck Hill SE21 169 H2
Birkbeck Ms. E8 94 C5
*Sandringham Rd.*
Birkbeck Pl. SE21 169 J1
Birkbeck Rd. E8 94 C5
Birkbeck Rd. N8 75 E4
Birkbeck Rd. N12 57 F5
Birkbeck Rd. N17 76 C1
Birkbeck Rd. NW7 55 F5
Birkbeck Rd. SW19 167 E5
Birkbeck Rd. W3 126 D1
Birkbeck Rd. W5 125 F4
Birkbeck Rd., Beck. 189 F2
Birkbeck Rd., Enf. 44 A1
Birkbeck Rd., Ilf. 81 G5
Birkbeck Rd., Sid. 176 A3
Birkbeck St. E2 113 E3
Birkbeck Way, Grnf. 103 J1
Birkdale Av., Pnr. 67 G3
Birkdale Cl. SE16 132/133 E5
*Masters Dr.*
Birkdale Cl., Orp. 193 G7
Birkdale Gdns., Croy. 203 G4
Birkdale Gdns., Wat. 50 D3
Birkdale Rd. SE2 138 A4
Birkdale Rd. W5 105 H5
Birkenhead Av., Kings.T. 181 J2
**Birkenhead St. WC1 10 B3**
Birkenhead St. WC1 111 E3
Birkhall Rd. SE6 172 D1
Birkwood Cl. SW12 150 D7
Birley Rd. N20 57 F2
Birley St. SW11 150 A2
Birnam Rd. N4 93 F2
Birse Cres. NW10 89 E4
Birstall Grn., Wat. 50 D4
Birstall Rd. N15 76 B5
Biscay Rd. W6 128 A5
Biscoe Cl., Houns. 123 G6
Biscoe Way SE13 154 D3
Bisenden Rd., Croy. 202 B2
Bisham Cl., Cars. 199 J1
Bisham Gdns. N6 92 A1
Bishop Butt Cl., Orp. 207 J3
*Stapleton Rd.*
Bishop Cl. W4 126 C5
Bishop Fox Way, W.Mol. 179 F4
Bishop Ken Rd., Har. 68 C2
Bishop Kings Rd. W14 128 B4
Bishop Rd. N14 42 B7
Bishop St. N1 111 J1
Bishop Way NW10 88 E7
Bishop Wilfred Wd. Cl. SE15 152 D2
*Moncrieff St.*
Bishop's Av. E13 115 H1
Bishop's Av. SW6 148 A2
Bishops Av., Brom. 191 J2
Bishops Av., Rom. 82 C6
Bishops Av., The N2 73 G7
**Bishops Br. W2 14 D2**
Bishops Br. W2 109 F5
**Bishops Br. Rd. W2 14 B4**
Bishops Br. Rd. W2 109 F6
Bishops Cl. E17 78 B4
Bishops Cl. N19 92 C3
*Wyndham Cres.*
Bishops Cl. SE9 175 F2
Bishops Cl., Barn. 40 A6
Bishops Cl., Enf. 44/45 E2
*Central Av.*
Bishops Cl., Rich. 163 G3
Bishop's Cl., Sutt. 198 D3
**Bishop's Ct. EC4 19 G3**
**Bishop's Ct. WC2 18 E3**
Bishops Dr., Felt. 141 G6
Bishops Dr., Nthlt. 103 E1
Bishops Gro. N2 73 G6
Bishops Gro., Hmptn. 161 F4
Bishop's Hall, Kings.T. 181 G2
Bishops Hill, Walt. 178 A7
Bishop's Pk. SW6 148 A2
Bishop's Pk. Rd. SW6 148 A2
Bishops Pk. Rd. SW16 187 E1
Bishops Pl., Sutt. 199 F5
*Lind Rd.*
Bishops Rd. N6 74 A6
Bishops Rd. SW6 148 C1
Bishops Rd. W7 124 B2
Bishops Rd., Croy. 187 H7
**Bishops Ter. SE11 35 F1**
Bishops Ter. SE11 131 G4
Bishops Wk., Chis. 193 F1
Bishops Wk., Croy. 203 G5
Bishop's Wk., Pnr. 66/67 E3
*High St.*
Bishops Way E2 113 E2
Bishopsford Rd., Mord. 185 F7
**Bishopsgate EC2 20 E2**
Bishopsgate EC2 112 B6
**Bishopsgate Arc. EC2 20 E2**
**Bishopsgate Chyd. EC2 20 D3**
Bishopsthorpe Rd. SE26 171 G4
Bishopswood Rd. N6 73 J7
Bisley Cl., Wor.Pk. 197 J1
Bispham Rd. NW10 105 J3
Bisson Rd. E15 114 C2
Bisterne Av. E17 78 D3
Bittacy Cl. NW7 56 A6
Bittacy Hill NW7 56 A6
Bittacy Pk. Av. NW7 56 A6
Bittacy Ri. NW7 55 J6
Bittacy Rd. NW7 56 A6
Bittern Cl., Hayes 102 D5
**Bittern St. SE1 27 J4**
Bittoms, The, Kings.T. 181 G3
Bixley Cl., Sthl. 123 F4
Black Boy La. N15 75 J5
Black Fan Cl., Enf. 43 J1
**Black Friars Ct. EC4 19 G5**
**Black Friars La. EC4 19 G5**
Black Friars La. EC4 111 H7
Black Gates, Pnr. 67 F3
*Church La.*
**Black Horse Ct. SE1 28 C5**
Black Lion La. W6 127 G4
Black Lion Ms. W6 127 G4
*Black Lion La.*
Black Path E10 77 G7
**Black Prince Rd. SE1 34 C2**
Black Prince Rd. SE1 131 F4
**Black Prince Rd. SE11 34 D2**
Black Prince Rd. SE11 131 F4
Black Rod Cl., Hayes 121 J3
**Black Swan Yd. SE1 28 E3**
**Blackall St. EC2 12 D5**
Blackberry Fm. Cl., Houns. 122 E7
Blackbird Hill NW9 88 C2
**Blackbird Yd. E2 13 G3**
Blackborne Rd., Dag. 101 G6
Blackbrook La., Brom. 192 D3
Blackburn Rd. NW6 90 E6
Blackburn Trd. Est., Stai. 140 C6
**Blackburne's Ms. W1 16 B5**
Blackburne's Ms. W1 110 A7
Blackbush Av., Rom. 82 D5
Blackbush Cl., Sutt. 199 E7
Blackdown Cl. N2 73 F2
Blackdown Ter. SE18 136 D7
*Prince Imperial Rd.*
Blackett St. SW15 148 A3
Blackfen Rd., Sid. 157 H5
Blackford Rd., Wat. 50 D5
Blackford's Path SW15 147 G7
*Roehampton High St.*
**Blackfriars Br. EC4 19 G5**
Blackfriars Br. EC4 111 H7
**Blackfriars Br. SE1 19 G5**
Blackfriars Br. SE1 111 H7
**Blackfriars Pas. EC4 19 G5**
**Blackfriars Rd. SE1 27 G4**
Blackfriars Rd. SE1 131 H1
Blackheath Av. SE10 134 D7
Blackheath Gro. SE3 155 F2
Blackheath Hill SE10 154 C1
Blackheath Pk. SE3 155 F3
Blackheath Ri. SE13 154 C2
Blackheath Rd. SE10 154 B1
Blackheath Vale SE3 155 E2
Blackheath Village SE3 155 F2
Blackhorse La. E17 77 G4
Blackhorse La., Croy. 188 D7
Blackhorse Ms. E17 77 G3
*Blackhorse La.*
Blackhorse Rd. E17 77 G4
Blackhorse Rd. SE8 133 H5

Blackhorse Rd., Sid. 176 A4
Blacklands Rd. SE6 172 C4
**Blacklands Ter. SW3 31 J2**
Blacklands Ter. SW3 129 J4
Blackmore Av., Sthl. 124 A1
Blackmore Rd., Buck.H. 48 B7
Blackmores Gro., Tedd. 162 D6
Blackpool Rd. SE15 152 E2
Blacks Rd. W6 127 J4
*Queen Caroline St.*
Blackshaw Pl. N1 94 B7
*Hertford Rd.*
Blackshaw Rd. SW17 167 F4
Blacksmiths Cl., Rom. 82 C6
Blackstock Ms. N4 93 H2
*Blackstock Rd.*
Blackstock Rd. N4 93 H2
Blackstock Rd. N5 93 H2
Blackstone Est. E8 94 E7
Blackstone Rd. NW2 89 J5
Blackthorn Av., West Dr. 120 D4
Blackthorn Ct., Houns. 122 E7
Blackthorn Gro., Bexh. 158 E3
Blackthorn St. E3 114 A4
Blackthorne Av., Croy. 189 F7
Blackthorne Dr. E4 62 D4
Blacktree Ms. SW9 151 G3
Blackwall La. SE10 135 E5
Blackwall Pier E14 114 E7
Blackwall Tunnel E14 134 D1
Blackwall Tunnel App. SE10 134 E2
Blackwall Tunnel Northern App. E3 114 A2
Blackwall Tunnel Northern App. E14 114 A2
Blackwall Way E14 114 C7
Blackwater Cl. E7 97 F4
Blackwater Rd., Sutt. 198/199 E4
*High St.*
Blackwater St. SE22 152 C5
Blackwell Cl. E5 95 G4
Blackwell Cl., Har. 52 A7
Blackwell Gdns., Edg. 54 A3
**Blackwood St. SE17 36 B3**
Blackwood St. SE17 132 A5
Blade Ms. SW15 148 C4
*Deodar Rd.*
Blades Ct. SW15 148 C4
*Deodar Rd.*
Bladindon Dr., Bex. 158 C7
Bladon Gdns., Har. 67 H6
Blagdens Cl. N14 58 C2
Blagdens La. N14 58 D2
Blagdon Rd. SE13 154 B6
Blagdon Rd., N.Mal. 183 F4
Blagdon Wk., Tedd. 163 F6
Blagrove Rd. W10 108 B5
Blair Av. NW9 70 E7
Blair Cl. N1 93 J6
Blair Cl., Hayes 122 A4
Blair Cl., Sid. 157 H5
Blair St. E14 114 C6
Blairderry Rd. SW2 169 E2
Blairhead Dr., Wat. 50 B3
Blake Av., Bark. 117 H1
Blake Cl. W10 107 J5
Blake Cl., Cars. 185 H7
Blake Cl., Well. 157 H1
Blake Gdns. SW6 148 E1
Blake Hall Cres. E11 97 G1
Blake Hall Rd. E11 79 G7
Blake Ho., Beck. 172 A6
Blake Rd. E16 115 F4
Blake Rd. N11 58 C7
Blake Rd., Croy. 202 B2
Blake Rd., Mitch. 185 H3
Blake St. SE8 134 A6
*Watergate St.*
Blakeden Dr., Esher 194 C6
Blakehall Rd., Cars. 199 J6
Blakeley Cotts. SE10 134 D2
*Tunnel Av.*
Blakemore Rd. SW16 168 E3
Blakemore Rd., Th.Hth. 187 F5
Blakemore Way, Belv. 139 E3
Blakeney Av., Beck. 189 J1
Blakeney Cl. E8 94 D5
*Ferncliff Rd.*
Blakeney Cl. N20 57 F1
Blakeney Cl. NW1 92 D7
*Rossendale Way*
Blakeney Rd., Beck. 171 J7
Blakenham Rd. SW17 167 J4
Blaker Ct. SE7 135 J7
*Fairlawn*
Blaker Rd. E15 114 C1
Blakes Av., N.Mal. 183 F5
Blake's Grn., W.Wick. 204 C1
Blakes La., N.Mal. 183 F5
**Blakes Rd. SE15 36 E7**
Blakes Rd. SE15 132 B7
Blakes Ter., N.Mal. 183 G5
Blakesley Av. W5 105 F6
Blakesley Wk. SW20 184 C2
*Kingston Rd.*
Blakesware Gdns. N9 44 A7
Blakewood Cl., Felt. 160 C4
Blanch Cl. SE15 133 F7
*Culmore Rd.*
Blanchard Cl. SE9 174 B3
Blanchard Way E8 94 D6
Blanche St. E16 115 F4
Blanchedowne SE5 152 A4
Blanchland Rd., Mord. 184 E5
Bland St. SE9 156 A4
Blandfield Rd. SW12 150 A6
Blandford Av., Beck. 189 H2
Blandford Av., Twick. 161 H1
Blandford Cl. N2 73 F4
Blandford Cl., Croy. 201 E3
Blandford Cl., Rom. 83 H4
Blandford Cres. E4 46 C7
Blandford Rd. W4 126 E3
Blandford Rd. W5 125 G2
Blandford Rd., Beck. 189 F2
Blandford Rd., Sthl. 123 G4
Blandford Rd., Tedd. 162 A5
**Blandford Sq. NW1 7 H6**
Blandford Sq. NW1 109 H4
**Blandford St. W1 16 A3**
Blandford St. W1 110 A5
Blandford Waye, Hayes 102 C6
Blaney Cres. E6 116 E3
Blanmerle Rd. SE9 174 E1
Blann Cl. SE9 156 A6
**Blantyre St. SW10 30 E7**
Blantyre St. SW10 129 G7
**Blantyre Wk. SW10 30 E7**
Blashford NW3 91 J7
Blashford St. SE13 154 D7
Blasker Wk. E14 134 A5
Blawith Rd., Har. 68 B4
Blaydon Cl. N17 60 E7
Blaydon Wk. N17 60 E7
Bleak Hill La. SE18 137 J6
Blean Gro. SE20 171 F7
Bleasdale Av., Grnf. 104 D2
Blechynden St. W10 108 A7
*Bramley Rd.*
Bleddyn Cl., Sid. 158 C6
Bledlow Cl. SE28 118 C7
Bledlow Ri., Grnf. 103 J2
**Bleeding Heart Yd. EC1 19 F2**
Blegborough Rd. SW16 168 C6
Blendon Dr., Bex. 158 D6
Blendon Path, Brom. 173 F7
Blendon Rd., Bex. 158 D6
Blendon Ter. SE18 137 F5
**Blendworth Way SE15 37 E7**
Blenheim Av., Ilf. 80 D6
Blenheim Cl. N21 59 J1
*Elm Pk. Rd.*
Blenheim Cl. SW20 183 J3
Blenheim Cl., Grnf. 104 A2
*Leaver Gdns.*
Blenheim Cl., Rom. 83 J4
Blenheim Cl., Wall. 200 C7
Blenheim Ct. N19 92/93 E2
*Marlborough Rd.*
Blenheim Ct., Sid. 175 G3
Blenheim Cres. W11 108 B6
Blenheim Cres., S.Croy. 201 J7
Blenheim Dr., Well. 157 J1
Blenheim Gdns. NW2 89 J5
Blenheim Gdns. SW2 151 F6
Blenheim Gdns., Kings.T. 164 B7
Blenheim Gdns., Wall. 200 C6
Blenheim Gdns., Wem. 87 H3
Blenheim Gro. SE15 152 D2
**Blenheim Pas. NW8 6 C1**
Blenheim Ri. N15 76 C4
*Talbot Rd.*
Blenheim Rd. E6 116 A3
Blenheim Rd. E15 97 E4
Blenheim Rd. E17 77 G3
**Blenheim Rd. NW8 6 C1**
Blenheim Rd. NW8 109 F2
Blenheim Rd. SE20 171 F7
*Maple Rd.*
Blenheim Rd. SW20 183 J3
Blenheim Rd. W4 126 E3
Blenheim Rd., Barn. 40 A3
Blenheim Rd., Brom. 192 B4
Blenheim Rd., Har. 67 H6
Blenheim Rd., Nthlt. 85 H6
Blenheim Rd., Sid. 176 C1
Blenheim Rd., Sutt. 198 D3
**Blenheim St. W1 16 D4**
**Blenheim Ter. NW8 6 C1**
Blenheim Ter. NW8 109 F2
Blenheim Way, Islw. 144 D1
Blenkarne Rd. SW11 149 J6
Bleriot Rd., Houns. 122 C7
Blessbury Rd., Edg. 70 C1
Blessing Way, Bark. 118 C3
Blessington Cl. SE13 154 D3
Blessington Rd. SE13 154 D3
Bletchingley Cl., Th.Hth. 187 H4
**Bletchley Ct. N1 12 B2**
Bletchley Ct. N1 112 A2
**Bletchley St. N1 12 A2**
Bletchley St. N1 111 J2
Bletchmore Cl., Hayes 121 G5
**Bletsoe Wk. N1 12 A1**
Blewbury Ho. SE2 138 D2
*Yarnton Way*
Blincoe Cl. SW19 166 A2
Blind La., Loug. 47 E2
Bliss Cres. SE13 154 B2
*Coldbath St.*
Blissett St. SE10 154 C1
Blisworth Cl., Hayes 102/103 E4
*Braunston Dr.*
Blithbury Rd., Dag. 100 B6
Blithdale Rd. SE2 138 A4
**Blithfield St. W8 22 A6**
Blithfield St. W8 128 E3
Blockley Rd., Wem. 86 E2
Bloemfontein Av. W12 127 H1
Bloemfontein Rd. W12 107 H7
**Blomfield Rd. W9 14 D1**
Blomfield Rd. W9 109 F5
**Blomfield St. EC2 20 C2**
Blomfield St. EC2 112 A5
**Blomfield Vil. W2 14 B2**
Blomfield Vil. W2 109 E5
Blomville Rd., Dag. 101 E3
Blondel St. SW11 150 A2
Blondell Cl., West Dr. 120 A6
Blondin Av. W5 125 F4
Blondin St. E3 114 A2
Bloom Gro. SE27 169 H3
Bloom Pk. Rd. SW6 128 C7
**Bloomburg St. SW1 33 G2**
Bloomfield Cres., Ilf. 81 E6
**Bloomfield Pl. W1 16 E5**
Bloomfield Pl. W1 110 B7
Bloomfield Rd. N6 74 A6
Bloomfield Rd. SE18 137 E5
Bloomfield Rd., Brom. 192 A5
Bloomfield Rd., Kings.T. 181 H4
**Bloomfield Ter. SW1 32 C3**
Bloomfield Ter. SW1 130 A5
Bloomhall Rd. SE19 170 A5
Bloomsbury Cl. W5 105 J7
**Bloomsbury Ct. WC1 18 B2**
Bloomsbury Ct., Pnr. 67 F3
Bloomsbury Ho. SW4 150 D6
Bloomsbury Pl. SW18 149 F5
*Fullerton Rd.*
**Bloomsbury Pl. WC1 18 B1**
Bloomsbury Pl. WC1 111 E5
**Bloomsbury Sq. WC1 18 B2**
Bloomsbury Sq. WC1 111 E5
**Bloomsbury St. WC1 17 J2**
Bloomsbury St. WC1 110 D5
**Bloomsbury Way WC1 18 A3**
Bloomsbury Way WC1 110 E6
Blore Cl. SW8 150 D1
*Thessaly Rd.*
**Blore Ct. W1 17 H4**
Blossom Cl. W5 125 H2
*Almond Av.*
Blossom Cl., Dag. 119 F1
Blossom Cl., S.Croy. 202 C5
Blossom La., Enf. 43 J1
**Blossom Pl. E1 13 E6**
**Blossom St. E1 21 E1**
Blossom St. E1 112 B4
Blossom Way, West Dr. 120 D4
Blossom Waye, Houns. 122 E7
Blount St. E14 113 H5
Bloxam Gdns. SE9 156 B5
Bloxhall Rd. E10 95 J1
Bloxham Cres., Hmptn. 179 F1
Bloxworth Cl., Wall. 200 C3
Blucher Rd. SE5 131 J7
Blue Anchor All., Rich. 145 H4
*Kew Rd.*
**Blue Anchor La. SE16 37 J1**
Blue Anchor La. SE16 132 D4
**Blue Anchor Yd. E1 21 H5**
Blue Anchor Yd. E1 112 D7
**Blue Ball Yd. SW1 25 F2**
Bluebell Av. E12 98 B5
Bluebell Cl. E9 113 F1
*Moulins Rd.*
Bluebell Cl. SE26 170 C4
Bluebell Cl., Orp. 207 F2
Bluebell Cl., Wall. 200 B1
Bluebell Way, Ilf. 98 E6
Blueberry Cl., Wdf.Grn. 63 G6
Bluefield Cl., Hmptn. 161 G5
Bluegates, Epsom 197 G7
Bluehouse Rd. E4 63 E3
Blundell Rd., Edg. 70 D1
Blundell St. N7 93 E7
Blunden Cl., Dag. 100 C1
Blunt Rd., S.Croy. 202 A5
Blunts Av., West Dr. 120 D7
Blunts Rd. SE9 156 D5
Blurton Rd. E5 95 F4
Blyth Cl. E14 134 D4
*Manchester Rd.*
Blyth Cl., Twick. 144 C6
*Grimwood Rd.*
Blyth Rd. E17 77 J7
Blyth Rd. SE28 118 C7
Blyth Rd., Brom. 191 F1
Blyth Rd., Hayes 121 H2
Blythe Cl. SE6 153 J7
Blythe Hill SE6 153 J7
Blythe Hill, Orp. 193 J1
Blythe Hill La. SE6 153 J7
Blythe Rd. W14 128 A3
Blythe St. E2 112 E3
Blythe Vale SE6 171 J1
Blythswood Rd., Ilf. 100 A1
Blythwood Rd. N4 75 E7
Blythwood Rd., Pnr. 66 D1
Boades Ms. NW3 91 G4
*New End*
Boadicea St. N1 111 F1
*Copenhagen St.*
Boakes Cl. NW9 70 C4
Boardman Av. E4 46 B5
Boardman Cl., Barn. 40 B5
Boardwalk Pl. E14 134 C1
Boar's Head Yd., Brent. 125 G7
*Brent Way*
Boat Lifter Way SE16 133 H4
*Sweden Gate*
**Boathouse Wk. SE15 37 G7**
Boathouse Wk. SE15 132 C7
Boathouse Wk., Rich. 145 H1
Bob Anker Cl. E13 115 G3
*Chesterton Rd.*
Bob Marley Way SE24 151 G4
*Mayall Rd.*
Bobbin Cl. SW4 150 C3
Bobby Moore Way N10 57 J7
Bockhampton Rd., Kings.T. 163 J7
Bocking St. E8 112 E1
Boddicott Cl. SW19 166 B2
Bodiam Cl., Enf. 44 A2
Bodiam Rd. SW16 168 D7
Bodley Cl., N.Mal. 182 E5
Bodley Manor Way SW2 151 G7
*Papworth Way*
Bodley Rd., N.Mal. 182 D6
Bodmin Cl., Har. 85 F3
Bodmin Gro., Mord. 185 E5
Bodmin St. SW18 166 D1
Bodnant Gdns. SW20 183 G3

Bodney Rd. E8 94 E5
Boeing Way, Sthl. 122 B3
Boevey Path, Belv. 139 F6
Bogey La., Orp. 206 D7
Bognor Gdns., Wat. 50 C5
*Bowring Grn.*
Bognor Rd., Well. 158 D1
Bohemia Pl. E8 95 E6
Bohun Gro., Barn. 41 H6
Boileau Par. W5 105 J6
*Boileau Rd.*
Boileau Rd. SW13 127 G7
Boileau Rd. W5 105 J6
Bolden St. SE8 154 B2
Bolderwood Way, W.Wick. 204 B2
Boldmere Rd., Pnr. 66 C7
Boleyn Av., Enf. 44 E1
Boleyn Cl. E17 78 A4
Boleyn Cl., Loug. 48 B6
*Roding Gdns.*
Boleyn Ct., Buck.H. 63 G1
Boleyn Dr., Ruis. 84 D2
Boleyn Dr., W.Mol. 179 F3
Boleyn Gdns., Dag. 101 J7
Boleyn Gdns., W.Wick. 204 B2
Boleyn Gro., W.Wick. 204 C2
Boleyn Rd. E6 116 A2
Boleyn Rd. E7 97 G7
Boleyn Rd. N16 94 B5
Boleyn Way, Barn. 41 F3
Boleyn Way, Ilf. 65 F6
Bolina Rd. SE16 133 F5
Bolingbroke Gro. SW11 149 H4
Bolingbroke Rd. W14 128 A3
Bolingbroke Wk. SW11 129 G7
Bolingbroke Way, Hayes 121 G1
Bolliger Ct. NW10 106 C4
*Park Royal Rd.*
Bollo Br. Rd. W3 126 B3
Bollo La. W3 126 B2
Bollo La. W4 126 C4
**Bolney Gate SW7 23 G4**
Bolney St. SW8 131 F7
Bolney Way, Felt. 161 E3
**Bolsover St. W1 9 E6**
Bolsover St. W1 110 B4
Bolstead Rd., Mitch. 186 B1
**Bolt Ct. EC4 19 F4**
Boltmore Cl. NW4 72 A3
Bolton Cl. SE20 188 D2
*Selby Rd.*
Bolton Cl., Chess. 195 G6
**Bolton Cres. SE5 35 F6**
Bolton Cres. SE5 131 H6
Bolton Gdns. NW10 108 A2
**Bolton Gdns. SW5 30 B3**
Bolton Gdns. SW5 129 E5
Bolton Gdns., Brom. 173 F6
Bolton Gdns., Tedd. 162 D6
**Bolton Gdns. Ms. SW10 30 C3**
Bolton Gdns. Ms. SW10 129 E5
Bolton Rd. E15 97 F6
Bolton Rd. N18 60 C5
Bolton Rd. NW8 109 E1
Bolton Rd. NW10 107 E1
Bolton Rd. W4 126 C7
Bolton Rd., Chess. 195 G6
Bolton Rd., Har. 67 J4
**Bolton St. W1 24 E1**
Bolton St. W1 130 B1
Bolton Wk. N7 93 F2
*Durham Rd.*
**Boltons, The SW10 30 C3**
Boltons, The SW10 129 F5
Boltons, The, Wem. 86 C4
Boltons, The, Wdf.Grn. 63 G4
Boltons La., Hayes 121 F7
**Boltons Pl. SW5 30 C3**
Boltons Pl. SW5 129 F5
Bombay St. SE16 132 E4
Bomer Cl., West Dr. 120 D7
Bomore Rd. W11 108 A7
Bon Marche Ter. Ms. SE27 170 B4
*Gipsy Rd.*
Bonar Pl., Chis. 174 B7
Bonar Rd. SE15 132 D7
Bonchester Cl., Chis. 174 D7
Bonchurch Cl., Sutt. 199 E7
Bonchurch Rd. W10 108 B5
Bonchurch Rd. W13 124 E1
**Bond Ct. EC4 20 B4**
Bond Ct. EC4 112 A6
Bond Gdns., Wall. 200 C4
Bond Rd., Mitch. 185 H2
Bond Rd., Surb. 195 J2
Bond St. E15 96 E5
Bond St. W4 126 E4
Bond St. W5 105 G7
Bondfield Av., Hayes 102 A3
Bondfield Rd. E6 116 B5
*Lovage App.*
Bonding Yd. Wk. SE16 133 H3
*Finland St.*
**Bondway SW8 34 B5**
Bondway SW8 131 E6
Boneta Rd. SE18 136 C3
Bonfield Rd. SE13 154 C4
Bonham Gdns., Dag. 100 D2
Bonham Rd. SW2 151 F5
Bonham Rd., Dag. 100 D2
Bonheur Rd. W4 126 D2
**Bonhill St. EC2 12 C6**
Bonhill St. EC2 112 A4
Boniface Gdns., Har. 51 H7
Boniface Wk., Har. 51 H7
Bonner Hill Rd., Kings.T. 181 J3
Bonner Rd. E2 113 F2
Bonner St. E2 113 F2
Bonnersfield Cl., Har. 68 C6
Bonnersfield La., Har. 68 D6
Bonneville Gdns. SW4 150 C6
**Bonnington Sq. SW8 34 C5**
Bonnington Sq. SW8 131 F6
Bonnington Twr., Brom. 192 B6
Bonny St. NW1 92 C7
Bonser Rd., Twick. 162 C2
Bonsor St. SE5 132 B7
Bonville Gdns. NW4 71 G4
*Handowe Cl.*
Bonville Rd., Brom. 173 F5
**Book Ms. WC2 17 J4**
Bookbinders' Cotts. N20 57 J3
*Manor Dr.*
Booker Cl. E14 113 J5
*Wallwood St.*
Booker Rd. N18 60 D5
Boone Ct. N9 61 F3
Boone St. SE13 155 E4
Boones Rd. SE13 155 E4
Boord St. SE10 135 E3
**Boot St. N1 12 D4**
Boot St. N1 112 B3
Booth Cl. E9 112/113 E1
*Victoria Pk. Rd.*
Booth Cl. SE28 118 B7
Booth Rd. NW9 70 E2
Booth Rd., Croy. 201 H2
*Waddon New Rd.*
Boothby Rd. N19 92 D2
**Booth's Pl. W1 17 G2**
Bordars Rd. W7 104 B5
Bordars Wk. W7 104 B5
Borden Av., Enf. 44 A6
Border Cres. SE26 170 E5
Border Gdns., Croy. 204 B4
Border Rd. SE26 171 E5
Bordergate, Mitch. 185 H1
Borders La., Loug. 48 D4
Bordesley Rd., Mord. 185 E4
Bordon Wk. SW15 147 G7
**Boreas Wk. N1 11 H2**
Boreham Av. E16 115 G6
Boreham Cl. E11 96 C1
*Hainault Rd.*
Boreham Rd. N22 75 J2
Borehamwood Ind. Pk., Borwd. 38 D2
Borgard Rd. SE18 136 C4
Borkwood Pk., Orp. 207 J4
Borkwood Way, Orp. 207 H4
Borland Rd. SE15 153 F4
Borland Rd., Tedd. 163 E6
Borneo St. SW15 147 J3
**Borough High St. SE1 27 J4**
Borough High St. SE1 131 J2
Borough Hill, Croy. 201 H3
**Borough Rd. SE1 27 G5**
Borough Rd. SE1 131 H3
Borough Rd., Islw. 144 B1
Borough Rd., Kings.T. 182 A1
Borough Rd., Mitch. 185 H2
**Borough Sq. SE1 27 J4**
**Borrett Cl. SE17 35 J4**
Borrodaile Rd. SW18 149 E6
Borrowdale Av., Har. 68 D2
Borrowdale Cl., Ilf. 80 B4
Borrowdale Ct., Enf. 43 J1
Borthwick Ms. E15 96/97 E4
*Borthwick Rd.*
Borthwick Rd. E15 96 E4
Borthwick Rd. NW9 71 F6
*West Hendon Bdy.*
Borthwick St. SE8 134 A5
Borwick Av. E17 77 J3
Bosbury Rd. SE6 172 C3
Boscastle Rd. NW5 92 B3
Bosco Cl., Orp. 207 J4
*Strickland Way*
**Boscobel Pl. SW1 32 C1**
Boscobel Pl. SW1 130 A4
**Boscobel St. NW8 7 F6**
Boscobel St. NW8 109 G4
Boscombe Av. E10 78 D7
Boscombe Cl. E5 95 H5
Boscombe Gdns. SW16 169 E6
Boscombe Rd. SW17 168 A6
Boscombe Rd. SW19 184 E1
Boscombe Rd. W12 127 G1
Boscombe Rd., Wor.Pk. 197 J1
Bosgrove E4 62 C1
**Boss St. SE1 29 F3**
Bostal Row, Bexh. 159 F3
*Harlington Rd.*
Bostall Heath SE2 138 C5
Bostall Hill SE2 138 A5
Bostall La. SE2 138 B5
Bostall Manorway SE2 138 B4
Bostall Pk. Av., Bexh. 138 E7
Bostall Rd., Orp. 176 B7
Boston Gdns. W4 127 E6
Boston Gdns. W7 124 D4
Boston Gdns., Brent. 124 D4
Boston Manor Rd., Brent. 124 E4
Boston Pk. Rd., Brent. 125 F5
**Boston Pl. NW1 7 J6**
Boston Pl. NW1 109 J4
Boston Rd. E6 116 B3
Boston Rd. E17 78 A6
Boston Rd. W7 124 B1
Boston Rd., Croy. 187 F6
Boston Rd., Edg. 54 C7
**Boston St. E2 13 H1**
Boston Vale W7 124 D4
Bostonthorpe Rd. W7 124 B2
Bosun Cl. E14 134 A2
*Byng St.*
**Boswell Ct. WC1 18 B1**
Boswell Path, Hayes 121 J4
*Croyde Av.*
Boswell Rd., Th.Hth. 187 J4
**Boswell St. WC1 18 B1**
Boswell St. WC1 111 E5
Bosworth Cl. E17 77 J1
Bosworth Rd. N11 58 D6
Bosworth Rd. W10 108 B4
Bosworth Rd., Barn. 40 D3
Bosworth Rd., Dag. 101 G4
Botany Bay La., Chis. 193 F2
Botany Cl., Barn. 41 H4
Boteley Cl. E4 62 D2
Botha Rd. E13 115 H5
Botham Cl., Edg. 54 C7
*Pavilion Way*
Bothwell Cl. E16 115 F5
Bothwell St. W6 128 A6
*Delorme St.*
**Botolph All. EC3 20 D5**
**Botolph La. EC3 20 D5**
Botsford Rd. SW20 184 B2
Botts Ms. W2 108 D6
*Chepstow Rd.*
Botts Pas. W2 108 D6
*Chepstow Rd.*
Botwell La., Hayes 121 H1
Boucher Cl., Tedd. 162 C5
Boughton Av., Brom. 191 F7
Boughton Rd. SE28 137 H3
Boulcott St. E1 113 G6
Boulevard, The SW17 168 A2
*Balham High Rd.*
Boulevard, The, Pnr. 67 G4
*Pinner Rd.*
Boulevard 25 Retail Pk., Borwd. 38 A3
Boulogne Rd., Croy. 187 J6
Boulton Ho., Brent. 125 H5
*Green Dragon La.*
Boulton Rd., Dag. 101 E3
Boultwood Rd. E6 116 B6
Bounces La. N9 60 E2
Bounces Rd. N9 60 E1
Boundaries Rd. SW12 167 J2
Boundaries Rd., Felt. 160 C1
Boundary Av. E17 77 J7
Boundary Cl. SE20 188 D2
*Haysleigh Gdns.*
Boundary Cl., Barn. 40 C1
Boundary Cl., Ilf. 99 H4
*Loxford La.*
Boundary Cl., Kings.T. 182 B3
Boundary Cl., Sthl. 123 G5
Boundary La. E13 116 A3
**Boundary La. SE17 36 A6**
Boundary La. SE17 131 J6
**Boundary Pas. E2 13 F5**
Boundary Rd. E13 115 J3
Boundary Rd. E17 77 J7
Boundary Rd. N9 45 F6
Boundary Rd. N22 75 H3
Boundary Rd. NW8 109 E1
Boundary Rd. SW19 167 G6
Boundary Rd., Bark. 117 F2
Boundary Rd., Cars. 200 B6
Boundary Rd., Pnr. 66 D6
Boundary Rd., Sid. 157 H5
Boundary Rd., Wall. 200 B6
Boundary Rd., Wem. 87 H3
**Boundary Row SE1 27 G3**
**Boundary St. E2 13 F4**
Boundary St. E2 112 C4
Boundary Way, Croy. 204 A5
Boundfield Rd. SE6 172 E3
Bounds Grn. Rd. N11 58 C6
Bounds Grn. Rd. N22 58 C6
**Bourchier St. W1 17 H5**
**Bourdon Pl. W1 16 E5**
Bourdon Rd. SE20 189 F2
**Bourdon St. W1 16 D6**
Bourdon St. W1 110 B7
Bourke Cl. NW10 88/89 E6
*Mayo Rd.*
Bourke Cl. SW4 150 E6
**Bourlet Cl. W1 17 F2**
Bourn Av. N15 76 A4
Bourn Av., Barn. 41 G5
Bournbrook Rd. SE3 156 A3
Bourne, The N14 58 D1
Bourne Av. N14 58 E2
Bourne Av., Hayes 121 F3
Bourne Av., Ruis. 84 C5
Bourne Ct., Ruis. 84 B5
Bourne Dr., Mitch. 185 G2
**Bourne Est. EC1 18 E1**
Bourne Est. EC1 111 G5
Bourne Gdns. E4 62 B4
Bourne Hill N13 58 E1
Bourne Pl. W4 126 D5
*Dukes Av.*
Bourne Rd. E7 97 F3
Bourne Rd. N8 75 E6
Bourne Rd., Bex. 159 H6
Bourne Rd., Brom. 192 A4
Bourne Rd., Dart. 159 J6
**Bourne St. SW1 32 B2**
Bourne St. SW1 130 A4
Bourne St., Croy. 201 H2
*Waddon New Rd.*
**Bourne Ter. W2 14 A1**
Bourne Ter. W2 108 E5
Bourne Vale, Brom. 191 G7
Bourne Vw., Grnf. 86 C6
Bourne Way, Brom. 205 F2
Bourne Way, Epsom 196 C4
Bourne Way, Sutt. 198 C5
Bournemead Av., Nthlt. 102 A2
Bournemead Cl., Nthlt. 102 A2
Bournemead Way, Nthlt. 102 B2
Bournemouth Cl. SE15 152 D2
Bournemouth Rd. SE15 152 D2
Bournemouth Rd. SW19 184 D1
Bourneside Cres. N14 58 D1
Bourneside Gdns. SE6 172 C5
Bournevale Rd. SW16 168 E4
Bournewood Rd. SE18 138 A7
Bournville Rd. SE6 154 A7
Bournwell Cl., Barn. 41 J3
Bourton Cl., Hayes 122 A1
*Avondale Dr.*
Bousfield Rd. SE14 153 G2
Boutflower Rd. SW11 149 H4
Bouverie Gdns., Har. 69 G6
Bouverie Ms. N16 94 B2
*Bouverie Rd.*
**Bouverie Pl. W2 15 F3**

| Name | Page | Grid |
|---|---|---|
| Bouverie Pl. W2 | 109 | G6 |
| Bouverie Rd. N16 | 94 | B2 |
| Bouverie Rd., Har. | 67 | J6 |
| **Bouverie St. EC4** | **19** | **F4** |
| Bouverie St. EC4 | 111 | G6 |
| Boveney Rd. SE23 | 153 | G7 |
| Bovill Rd. SE23 | 153 | G7 |
| Bovingdon Av., Wem. | 88 | A6 |
| Bovingdon Cl. N19 | 92 | C2 |
| *Junction Rd.* | | |
| Bovingdon La. NW9 | 71 | E1 |
| Bovingdon Rd. SW6 | 148 | E1 |
| Bovingdon Sq., Mitch. | 186/187 | E4 |
| *Leicester Av.* | | |
| Bow Br. Est. E3 | 114 | B3 |
| **Bow Chyd. EC4** | **20** | **A4** |
| Bow Common La. E3 | 113 | H4 |
| Bow Ind. Pk. E15 | 96 | A7 |
| **Bow La. EC4** | **20** | **A4** |
| Bow La. EC4 | 111 | A6 |
| Bow La. N12 | 73 | F1 |
| Bow La., Mord. | 184 | B6 |
| Bow Rd. E3 | 113 | J3 |
| Bow St. E15 | 96 | E5 |
| **Bow St. WC2** | **18** | **B4** |
| Bow St. WC2 | 111 | E6 |
| Bowater Cl. NW9 | 70 | D5 |
| Bowater Cl. SW2 | 150 | E6 |
| Bowater Pl. SE3 | 135 | H7 |
| Bowater Rd. SE18 | 136 | A3 |
| **Bowden St. SE11** | **35** | **F4** |
| Bowden St. SE11 | 131 | G5 |
| Bowditch SE8 | 133 | J5 |
| Bowdon Rd. E17 | 78 | A7 |
| Bowen Dr. SE21 | 170 | B3 |
| Bowen Rd., Har. | 67 | J7 |
| Bowen St. E14 | 114 | B6 |
| Bower Av. SE10 | 154 | E1 |
| Bower Cl., Nthlt. | 102 | C2 |
| Bower St. E1 | 113 | G6 |
| Bowerdean St. SW6 | 148 | E1 |
| Bowerman Av. SE14 | 133 | H6 |
| Bowers Wk. E6 | 116 | C6 |
| Bowes Cl., Sid. | 158 | B6 |
| Bowes Rd. N11 | 58 | B5 |
| Bowes Rd. N13 | 58 | E5 |
| Bowes Rd. W3 | 106 | E7 |
| Bowes Rd., Dag. | 100 | C4 |
| Bowfell Rd. W6 | 127 | J6 |
| Bowford Av., Bexh. | 158 | E1 |
| Bowhill Cl. SW9 | 131 | G7 |
| Bowie Cl. SW4 | 150 | D7 |
| **Bowl Ct. EC2** | **13** | **E6** |
| Bowl Ct. EC2 | 112 | B4 |
| Bowland Rd. SW4 | 150 | D4 |
| Bowland Rd., Wdf.Grn. | 63 | J6 |
| **Bowland Yd. SW1** | **24** | **A4** |
| **Bowles Rd. SE1** | **37** | **H5** |
| Bowley Cl. SE19 | 170 | C6 |
| Bowley La. SE19 | 170 | C5 |
| Bowling Grn. Cl. SW15 | 147 | H7 |
| **Bowling Grn. La. EC1** | **11** | **F5** |
| Bowling Grn. La. EC1 | 111 | G4 |
| **Bowling Grn. Pl. SE1** | **28** | **B3** |
| Bowling Grn. Pl. SE1 | 132 | A2 |
| Bowling Grn. Row SE18 | 136 | C3 |
| *Samuel St.* | | |
| **Bowling Grn. St. SE11** | **35** | **E5** |
| Bowling Grn. St. SE11 | 131 | G6 |
| **Bowling Grn. Wk. N1** | **12** | **D3** |
| Bowls, The, Chig. | 65 | H4 |
| Bowls Cl., Stan. | 52 | E5 |
| Bowman Av. E16 | 115 | F7 |
| Bowman Ms. SW18 | 166 | C5 |
| Bowman's Cl. W13 | 124 | E1 |
| Bowmans Lea SE23 | 153 | F7 |
| Bowmans Meadow, Wall. | 200 | B3 |
| **Bowmans Ms. E1** | **21** | **H5** |
| Bowmans Ms. N7 | 92/93 | E3 |
| *Seven Sisters Rd.* | | |
| Bowmans Pl. N7 | 92/93 | E3 |
| *Holloway Rd.* | | |
| Bowman's Trd. Est. NW9 | 69 | J3 |
| *Westmoreland Rd.* | | |
| Bowmead SE9 | 174 | C2 |
| Bowmore Wk. NW1 | 92 | D7 |
| *St. Paul's Cres.* | | |
| Bowness Cl. E8 | 94 | C6 |
| *Beechwood Rd.* | | |
| Bowness Cres. SW15 | 164 | E5 |
| Bowness Dr., Houns. | 143 | E4 |
| Bowness Rd. SE6 | 154 | B7 |
| Bowness Rd., Bexh. | 159 | H2 |
| Bowood Rd. SW11 | 150 | A4 |
| Bowood Rd., Enf. | 45 | G2 |
| Bowring Grn., Wat. | 50 | C5 |
| Bowrons Av., Wem. | 87 | G7 |
| Bowsley Ct., Felt. | 160 | A1 |
| *Highfield Rd.* | | |
| Bowyer Cl. E6 | 116 | C5 |
| **Bowyer Pl. SE5** | **36** | **A7** |
| Bowyer Pl. SE5 | 132 | A7 |
| **Bowyer St. SE5** | **35** | **J7** |
| Bowyer St. SE5 | 131 | J7 |
| Box La., Bark. | 118 | B2 |
| Boxall Rd. SE21 | 152 | B6 |
| Boxgrove Rd. SE2 | 138 | C3 |
| Boxley Rd., Mord. | 185 | F4 |
| Boxley St. E16 | 135 | H1 |
| Boxmoor Rd., Har. | 68 | C4 |
| Boxoll Rd., Dag. | 101 | F4 |
| Boxted Cl., Buck.H. | 64 | B1 |
| Boxtree La., Har. | 67 | J1 |
| Boxtree Rd., Har. | 52 | A7 |
| Boxwood Cl., West Dr. | 120 | C2 |
| *Hawthorne Cres.* | | |
| Boxworth Cl. N12 | 57 | G5 |
| Boxworth Gro. N1 | 111 | F1 |
| *Richmond La.* | | |
| Boyard Rd. SE18 | 136 | E5 |
| **Boyce St. SE1** | **26** | **D2** |
| Boyce Way E13 | 115 | G4 |
| Boycroft Av. NW9 | 70 | C6 |
| Boyd Av., Sthl. | 123 | F1 |
| Boyd Cl., Kings.T. | 164 | A7 |
| *Crescent Rd.* | | |
| Boyd Rd. SW19 | 167 | G6 |
| **Boyd St. E1** | **21** | **H4** |
| Boyd St. E1 | 112 | D6 |
| Boydell Ct. NW8 | 91 | G7 |
| *St. John's Wd. Pk.* | | |
| **Boyfield St. SE1** | **27** | **H4** |
| Boyfield St. SE1 | 131 | H2 |
| Boyland Rd., Brom. | 173 | F5 |
| Boyle Av., Stan. | 52 | D6 |
| Boyle Frm. Island, T.Ditt. | 180 | D6 |
| Boyle Frm. Rd., T.Ditt. | 180 | D6 |
| **Boyle St. W1** | **17** | **F5** |
| Boyne Av. NW4 | 72 | A4 |
| Boyne Rd. SE13 | 154 | C3 |
| Boyne Rd., Dag. | 101 | G3 |
| Boyne Ter. Ms. W11 | 128 | C1 |
| Boyseland Ct., Edg. | 54 | C2 |
| **Boyson Rd. SE17** | **36** | **B5** |
| Boyson Rd. SE17 | 132 | A6 |
| Boyton Cl. E1 | 113 | G4 |
| *Stayner's Rd.* | | |
| Boyton Cl. N8 | 75 | E3 |
| Boyton Rd. N8 | 75 | E3 |
| **Brabant Ct. EC3** | **20** | **D5** |
| Brabant Rd. N22 | 75 | F2 |
| Brabazon Av., Wall. | 200 | E7 |
| Brabazon Rd., Houns. | 122 | C7 |
| Brabazon Rd., Nthlt. | 103 | G2 |
| Brabazon St. E14 | 114 | B6 |
| Brabourn Gro. SE15 | 153 | F2 |
| Brabourne Cl. SE19 | 170 | B5 |
| Brabourne Cres., Bexh. | 139 | F6 |
| Brabourne Hts. NW7 | 55 | E3 |
| Brabourne Ri., Beck. | 190 | C5 |
| Bracewell Av., Grnf. | 86 | C5 |
| Bracewell Rd. W10 | 107 | J5 |
| Bracewood Gdns., Croy. | 202 | C3 |
| Bracey Ms. N4 | 92/93 | E2 |
| *Bracey St.* | | |
| Bracey St. N4 | 93 | E2 |
| Bracken, The E4 | 62 | C2 |
| *Hortus Rd.* | | |
| Bracken Av. SW12 | 150 | A6 |
| Bracken Cl. E6 | 116 | C5 |
| Bracken Cl., Borwd. | 38 | B1 |
| Bracken Cl., Twick. | 143 | G7 |
| *Hedley Rd.* | | |
| Bracken Dr., Chig. | 65 | E6 |
| Bracken End, Islw. | 144 | A5 |
| Bracken Gdns. SW13 | 147 | G2 |
| Bracken Hill Cl., Brom. | 191 | F1 |
| *Bracken Hill La.* | | |
| Bracken Hill La., Brom. | 191 | F1 |
| Bracken Ind. Est., Ilf. | 65 | J7 |
| Bracken Ms. E4 | 62 | C2 |
| *Hortus Rd.* | | |
| Bracken Ms., Rom. | 83 | G6 |
| Brackenbridge Dr., Ruis. | 84 | D3 |
| Brackenbury Gdns. W6 | 127 | H3 |
| Brackenbury Rd. N2 | 73 | F3 |
| Brackenbury Rd. W6 | 127 | H3 |
| Brackendale N21 | 59 | F2 |
| Brackendale Cl., Houns. | 143 | H1 |
| Brackenfield Cl. E5 | 94/95 | E4 |
| *Tiger Way* | | |
| Brackens, The, Enf. | 44 | B7 |
| Brackenwood, Sun. | 178 | A1 |
| Brackley Cl., Wall. | 201 | E7 |
| Brackley Rd. W4 | 127 | E6 |
| Brackley Rd., Beck. | 171 | J7 |
| Brackley Sq., Wdf.Grn. | 64 | A7 |
| **Brackley St. EC1** | **19** | **J1** |
| Brackley Ter. W4 | 127 | E6 |
| **Bracklyn Cl. N1** | **12** | **B1** |
| **Bracklyn Ct. N1** | **12** | **B1** |
| **Bracklyn St. N1** | **12** | **B1** |
| Bracklyn St. N1 | 112 | A2 |
| Bracknell Cl. N22 | 75 | G1 |
| Bracknell Gdns. NW3 | 90 | E4 |
| Bracknell Gate NW3 | 90 | E5 |
| Bracknell Way NW3 | 90 | E4 |
| Braconable Rd. SE2 | 138 | A4 |
| **Brad St. SE1** | **27** | **F2** |
| Bradbourne Rd., Bex. | 159 | G7 |
| Bradbourne St. SW6 | 148 | D2 |
| Bradbury Cl., Borwd. | 38 | B1 |
| Bradbury Cl., Sthl. | 123 | F4 |
| Bradbury Ms. N16 | 94 | B5 |
| *Bradbury St.* | | |
| Bradbury St. N16 | 94 | B5 |
| Braddock Cl., Islw. | 144 | C3 |
| Braddon Rd., Rich. | 145 | J3 |
| Braddyll St. SE10 | 134 | E5 |
| **Braden St. W9** | **6** | **A6** |
| Bradenham Av., Well. | 158 | A4 |
| **Bradenham Cl. SE17** | **36** | **B5** |
| Bradenham Cl. SE17 | 132 | A6 |
| Bradenham Rd., Har. | 68 | C4 |
| Bradfield Dr., Bark. | 100 | A5 |
| Bradfield Rd. E16 | 135 | G2 |
| Bradfield Rd., Ruis. | 85 | E5 |
| Bradford Cl. N17 | 60 | B6 |
| *Commercial Rd.* | | |
| Bradford Cl. SE26 | 170/171 | E4 |
| *Coombe Rd.* | | |
| Bradford Cl., Brom. | 206 | C1 |
| Bradford Dr., Epsom | 197 | F6 |
| Bradford Rd. W3 | 126/127 | E2 |
| *Warple Way* | | |
| Bradford Rd., Ilf. | 99 | G1 |
| Bradgate Rd. SE6 | 154 | A6 |
| Brading Cres. E11 | 97 | H2 |
| Brading Rd. SW2 | 151 | F7 |
| Brading Rd., Croy. | 187 | F6 |
| Bradiston Rd. W9 | 108 | C3 |
| Bradley Cl. N7 | 93 | F6 |
| *Sutterton St.* | | |
| Bradley Gdns. W13 | 104 | E6 |
| Bradley Ms. SW17 | 167 | J1 |
| *Bellevue Rd.* | | |
| Bradley Rd. N22 | 75 | F2 |
| Bradley Rd. SE19 | 169 | J6 |
| Bradley Stone Rd. E6 | 116 | C5 |
| **Bradley's Cl. N1** | **11** | **F1** |
| Bradman Row, Edg. | 54 | C7 |
| *Pavilion Way* | | |
| Bradmead SW8 | 130 | B7 |
| Bradmore Ho. E1 | 113 | F5 |
| Bradmore Pk. Rd. W6 | 127 | H3 |
| Bradshaw Cl. SW19 | 166 | D6 |
| Bradshaws Cl. SE25 | 188 | D3 |
| Bradstock Rd. E9 | 95 | G6 |
| Bradstock Rd., Epsom | 197 | G5 |
| Bradwell Av., Dag. | 101 | G2 |
| Bradwell Cl. E18 | 79 | F4 |
| Bradwell Ms. N18 | 60 | D4 |
| *Lyndhurst Rd.* | | |
| Bradwell Rd., Buck.H. | 64 | B1 |
| Bradwell St. E1 | 113 | G3 |
| Brady Av., Loug. | 49 | F2 |
| Brady St. E1 | 112 | E4 |
| Bradymead E6 | 116/117 | E6 |
| *Warwall* | | |
| Braemar Av. N22 | 75 | E1 |
| Braemar Av. NW10 | 88 | D3 |
| Braemar Av. SW19 | 166 | D2 |
| Braemar Av., Bexh. | 159 | J4 |
| Braemar Av., Th.Hth. | 187 | G3 |
| Braemar Av., Wem. | 87 | G7 |
| Braemar Gdns. NW9 | 70 | D1 |
| Braemar Gdns., Sid. | 175 | G3 |
| Braemar Gdns., W.Wick. | 204 | C1 |
| Braemar Rd. E13 | 115 | F4 |
| Braemar Rd. N15 | 76 | B5 |
| Braemar Rd., Brent. | 125 | H6 |
| Braemar Rd., Wor.Pk. | 197 | H3 |
| Braes St. N1 | 93 | H7 |
| Braeside, Beck. | 172 | A5 |
| Braeside Av. SW19 | 184 | B1 |
| Braeside Cl., Pnr. | 51 | G7 |
| *The Av.* | | |
| Braeside Cres., Bexh. | 159 | J4 |
| Braeside Rd. SW16 | 168 | C7 |
| Braesyde Cl., Belv. | 139 | F4 |
| Brafferton Rd., Croy. | 201 | J4 |
| **Braganza St. SE17** | **35** | **G3** |
| Braganza St. SE17 | 131 | H5 |
| Bragg Cl., Dag. | 100 | B6 |
| *Porters Av.* | | |
| **Braham St. E1** | **21** | **G3** |
| Braham St. E1 | 112 | C6 |
| Braid Av. W3 | 106 | E6 |
| Braid Cl., Felt. | 161 | F2 |
| Braidwood Rd. SE6 | 172 | D1 |
| **Braidwood St. SE1** | **28** | **D2** |
| Brailsford Cl., Mitch. | 167 | H7 |
| Brailsford Rd. SW2 | 151 | G5 |
| Brainton Av., Felt. | 142 | B7 |
| Braintree Av., Ilf. | 80 | B4 |
| Braintree Rd., Dag. | 101 | G3 |
| Braintree Rd., Ruis. | 84 | B4 |
| Braintree St. E2 | 113 | F3 |
| Braithwaite Av., Rom. | 83 | G7 |
| Braithwaite Gdns., Stan. | 69 | F1 |
| Braithwaite Rd., Enf. | 45 | J3 |
| Bramah Grn. SW9 | 151 | G1 |
| Bramalea Cl. N6 | 74 | A6 |
| Bramall Cl. E15 | 97 | F5 |
| *Idmiston Rd.* | | |
| Bramber Ct., Brent. | 125 | H4 |
| *Sterling Pl.* | | |
| Bramber Rd. N12 | 57 | H5 |
| Bramber Rd. W14 | 128 | C6 |
| Bramble Cl., Croy. | 204 | A4 |
| Bramble Cl., Stan. | 53 | G7 |
| Bramble Cft., Erith | 139 | J4 |
| Bramble Gdns. W12 | 107 | F7 |
| *Wallflower St.* | | |
| Bramble La., Hmptn. | 161 | F6 |
| Brambleacres Cl., Sutt. | 198 | D7 |
| Bramblebury Rd. SE18 | 137 | F5 |
| Brambledown Cl., W.Wick. | 191 | E5 |
| Brambledown Rd., Cars. | 200 | A7 |
| Brambledown Rd., S.Croy. | 202 | B7 |
| Brambledown Rd., Wall. | 200 | B7 |
| Brambles, The, Chig. | 65 | F5 |
| *Clayside* | | |
| Brambles, The, West Dr. | 120 | B4 |
| Brambles Cl., Islw. | 124 | E7 |
| Bramblewood Cl., Cars. | 199 | H1 |
| Brambles, The, E4 | 62 | D4 |
| Bramcote Av., Mitch. | 185 | J4 |
| Bramcote Ct., Mitch. | 185 | J4 |
| Bramcote Gro. SE16 | 133 | F5 |
| Bramcote Rd. SW15 | 147 | H4 |
| Bramdean Cres. SE12 | 173 | G1 |
| Bramdean Gdns. SE12 | 173 | G1 |
| Bramerton Rd., Beck. | 189 | J3 |
| **Bramerton St. SW3** | **31** | **G5** |
| Bramfield Ct. N4 | 93 | J2 |
| *Queens Dr.* | | |
| Bramfield Rd. SW11 | 149 | H6 |
| Bramford Ct. N14 | 58 | D2 |
| Bramford Rd. SW18 | 149 | F4 |
| **Bramham Gdns. SW5** | **30** | **A3** |
| Bramham Gdns. SW5 | 129 | E5 |
| Bramham Gdns., Chess. | 195 | G4 |
| Bramhope La. SE7 | 135 | H6 |
| Bramlands Cl. SW11 | 149 | H3 |
| Bramley Cl. E17 | 77 | H2 |
| Bramley Cl. N14 | 42 | B5 |
| Bramley Cl., Hayes | 102 | A7 |
| *Orchard Rd.* | | |
| Bramley Cl., Orp. | 207 | E1 |
| Bramley Cl., S.Croy. | 201 | H5 |
| Bramley Cl., Twick. | 143 | J6 |

**Bride La. EC4 19 G4**
Bride St. N7 93 F6
Brideale Cl. SE15 132 C7
*Colegrove Rd.*
**Bridewain St. SE1 29 G5**
Bridewain St. SE1 132 C3
Bridewell Pl. E1 132/133 E1
*Brewhouse La.*
**Bridewell Pl. EC4 19 G4**
**Bridford Ms. W1 16 E1**
Bridge, The, Har. 68 B3
Bridge App. NW1 92 A7
Bridge Av. W6 127 J5
Bridge Av. W7 104 A5
Bridge Cl. W10 108 A6
*Kingsdown Cl.*
Bridge Cl., Enf. 45 E2
Bridge Cl., Tedd. 162 C4
*Shacklegate La.*
Bridge Dr. N13 59 F4
Bridge End E17 78 C1
Bridge Gdns., E.Mol. 180 A4
Bridge Gate N21 43 J7
*Ridge Av.*
Bridge Ho. Quay E14 134 C1
*Prestons Rd.*
Bridge La. NW11 72 B5
Bridge La. SW11 149 H1
Bridge Meadows SE14 133 G6
Bridge Pk. SW18 148 D5
**Bridge Pl. SW1 33 E1**
Bridge Pl. SW1 130 B4
Bridge Pl., Croy. 188 A7
Bridge Rd. E6 98 C7
Bridge Rd. E15 96 D7
Bridge Rd. E17 77 J7
Bridge Rd. N9 60 D3
*The Bdy.*
Bridge Rd. N22 75 E1
Bridge Rd. NW10 88 E6
Bridge Rd., Beck. 171 J7
Bridge Rd., Bexh. 159 E2
Bridge Rd., Chess. 195 H5
Bridge Rd., Croy. 201 J3
*Duppas Hill Rd.*
Bridge Rd., E.Mol. 180 B4
Bridge Rd., Houns. 144 A3
Bridge Rd., Islw. 144 A3
Bridge Rd., Sthl. 123 F2
Bridge Rd., Sutt. 199 E6
Bridge Rd., Twick. 144 E6
Bridge Rd., Wall. 200 C5
Bridge Rd., Wem. 88 A3
Bridge Row, Croy. 202 A1
*Cross Rd.*
**Bridge St. SW1 26 A4**
Bridge St. SW1 130 E2
Bridge St. W4 126 D4
Bridge St., Pnr. 66 D3
Bridge St., Rich. 145 G5
Bridge Ter. E15 96 D7
Bridge Vw. W6 127 J5
Bridge Way N11 58 C3
*Pymmes Grn. Rd.*
Bridge Way NW11 72 C5
Bridge Way, Twick. 143 J7
Bridge Wf. Rd., Islw. 144/145 E3
*Church St.*
**Bridge Yd. SE1 28 C1**
Bridgefield Rd., Sutt. 198 D6
**Bridgefoot SE1 34 A4**
Bridgefoot SE1 131 E5
Bridgeland Rd. E16 115 G7
Bridgeman Rd. N1 93 F7
Bridgeman Rd., Tedd. 162 D6
**Bridgeman St. NW8 7 G2**
Bridgeman St. NW8 109 H2
Bridgen Rd., Bex. 158 E6
Bridgend Rd. SW18 149 F4
Bridgenhall Rd., Enf. 44 C1
**Bridgeport Pl. E1 29 J1**
Bridges Ct. SW11 149 G3
Bridges La., Croy. 200 E4
Bridges Ms. SW19 166/167 E6
*Bridges Rd.*
Bridges Pl. SW6 148 C1
Bridges Rd. SW19 166 E6
Bridges Rd., Stan. 52 C5
Bridges Rd. Ms. SW19 166/167 E6
*Bridges Rd.*
Bridgetown Cl. SE19 170 B5
*St. Kitts Ter.*
Bridgeview Ct., Ilf. 65 G6
Bridgewater Cl., Chis. 193 H3
Bridgewater Gdns., Edg. 69 J2
Bridgewater Rd., Ruis. 84 A4
Bridgewater Rd., Wem. 87 F7
**Bridgewater Sq. EC2 19 J1**
**Bridgewater St. EC2 19 J1**
Bridgeway, Bark. 99 J7
Bridgeway, Wem. 87 H7
**Bridgeway St. NW1 9 H2**
Bridgeway St. NW1 110 C2
Bridgewood Cl. SE20 170 E7
Bridgewood Rd. SW16 168 D7
Bridgewood Rd., Wor.Pk. 197 G4
Bridgford St. SW18 167 F3
Bridgman Rd. W4 126 C3
Bridgwater Rd. E15 114 C1
Bridle Cl., Epsom 196 D5
Bridle Cl., Kings.T. 181 G4
Bridle Cl., Sun. 178 A3
*Forge La.*
**Bridle La. W1 17 G5**
Bridle La., Twick. 144/145 E6
*Crown Rd.*
Bridle Path, Croy. 201 F3
Bridle Path, The, Wdf.Grn. 62 E7
Bridle Rd., Croy. 204 A3
Bridle Rd., Esher 194 E6
Bridle Rd., Pnr. 66 C6
Bridle Way, Croy. 204 A5
Bridle Way, Orp. 207 F4
Bridleway, The, Wall. 200 C4
Bridlington Rd. N9 44 E7
Bridlington Rd., Wat. 50 D3
Bridport Av., Rom. 83 H6
**Bridport Pl. N1 12 C1**
Bridport Pl. N1 112 A2
Bridport Rd. N18 60 B5
Bridport Rd., Grnf. 103 H1
Bridport Rd., Th.Hth. 187 G3
Bridport Ter. SW8 150 D1
*Wandsworth Rd.*
Bridstow Pl. W2 108 D6
*Talbot Rd.*
Brief St. SE5 151 H1
Brierley, Croy. 204 B6
Brierley Av. N9 61 F1
Brierley Cl. SE25 188 D4
Brierley Rd. E11 96 D4
Brierley Rd. SW12 168 C2
Brierly Gdns. E2 113 F2
*Royston St.*
Brig Ms. SE8 134 A6
*Watergate St.*
Brigade Cl., Har. 86 A2
Brigade St. SE3 155 F2
*Royal Par.*
Brigadier Av., Enf. 43 J1
Briggeford Cl. E5 94 D2
*Geldeston Rd.*
Briggs Cl., Mitch. 186 B1
Bright Cl., Belv. 138 D4
Bright St. E14 114 B6
Brightfield Rd. SE12 155 F5
Brightling Rd. SE4 153 J6
Brightlingsea Pl. E14 113 J7
Brightman Rd. SW18 167 G1
Brighton Av. E17 77 J5
Brighton Dr., Nthlt. 85 G6
Brighton Gro. SE14 153 H1
*New Cross Rd.*
Brighton Rd. E6 116 D3
Brighton Rd. N2 73 F2
Brighton Rd. N16 94 B4
Brighton Rd., S.Croy. 201 J5
Brighton Rd., Surb. 181 F6
Brighton Ter. SW9 151 F4
Brightside, The, Enf. 45 G1
Brightside Rd. SE13 154 D6
Brightwell Cl., Croy. 201 G1
*Sumner Rd.*
Brightwell Cres. SW17 167 J5
Brigstock Rd., Belv. 139 H4
Brigstock Rd., Th.Hth. 187 G5
**Brill Pl. NW1 9 J2**
Brill Pl. NW1 110 D2
Brim Hill N2 73 F4
Brimpsfield Cl. SE2 138 B3
Brimsdown Av., Enf. 45 H2
Brimsdown Ind. Est., Enf. 45 J2
Brindle Gate, Sid. 175 H1
Brindley Cl., Bexh. 159 H3
Brindley Cl., Wem. 105 G1
Brindley St. SE14 153 J1
Brindley Way, Brom. 173 G5
Brindley Way, Sthl. 103 H7
Brindwood Rd. E4 61 J3
Brinkburn Cl. SE2 138 A4
Brinkburn Cl., Edg. 70 B2
Brinkburn Gdns., Edg. 70 A3
Brinkley Rd., Wor.Pk. 197 H2
Brinklow Cres. SE18 137 E7
**Brinklow Ho. W2 14 A1**
Brinklow Ho. W2 108 E5
Brinkworth Rd., Ilf. 80 B3
Brinkworth Way E9 95 J6
Brinsdale Rd. NW4 72 A4
Brinsley Rd., Har. 68 A2
Brinsley St. E1 112/113 E6
*Watney St.*
Brinsworth Cl., Twick. 162 A2
**Brinton Wk. SE1 27 G2**
Brion Pl. E14 114 C5
Brisbane Av. SW19 184 E1
Brisbane Ct. N10 58 B7
*Sydney Rd.*
Brisbane Rd. E10 96 B2
Brisbane Rd. W13 124 D2
Brisbane Rd., Ilf. 81 E7
Brisbane St. SE5 132 A7
Briscoe Cl. E11 97 F2
Briscoe Rd. SW19 167 G6
Briset Rd. SE9 156 A3
**Briset St. EC1 19 G1**
Briset Way N7 93 F2
Bristol Cl., Stai. 140 B6
Bristol Gdns. SW15 147 J7
*Portsmouth Rd.*
**Bristol Gdns. W9 6 B6**
Bristol Gdns. W9 109 E4
**Bristol Ms. W9 6 B6**
Bristol Pk. Rd. E17 77 H4
Bristol Rd. E7 97 J6
Bristol Rd., Grnf. 103 H1
Bristol Rd., Mord. 185 F5
Briston Gro. N8 75 E6
Briston Ms. NW7 55 G7
Bristow Rd. SE19 170 B5
Bristow Rd., Bexh. 159 E1
Bristow Rd., Croy. 200 E4
Bristow Rd., Houns. 143 J3
Britannia Cl. SW4 150 D4
*Bowland Rd.*
Britannia Cl., Nthlt. 102 D3
Britannia Gate E16 135 G1
Britannia La., Twick. 143 J7
Britannia Rd. E14 134 A4
Britannia Rd. N12 57 F3
Britannia Rd. SW6 128 E7
Britannia Rd., Ilf. 98 E3
Britannia Rd., Surb. 181 J7
Britannia Row N1 111 H1
**Britannia St. WC1 10 C3**
Britannia St. WC1 111 F3
**Britannia Wk. N1 12 B3**
Britannia Wk. N1 112 A2
Britannia Way NW10 106 B4
Britannia Way SW6 148/149 E1
*Britannia Rd.*
Britannia Way, Stai. 140 A7
British Gro. W4 127 F5
British Gro. Pas. W4 127 F5
British Gro. S. W4 127 F5
*British Gro. Pas.*
British Legion Rd. E4 63 F2
British St. E3 113 J3
Brittain Rd., Dag. 101 E3
Britten Cl. NW11 90 E1
Britten Dr., Sthl. 103 G6
**Britten St. SW3 31 G4**
Britten St. SW3 129 H5
Brittenden Cl., Orp. 207 H6
Britten's Ct. E1 112 E7
Britton Cl. SE6 154 D7
*Brownhill Rd.*
**Britton St. EC1 11 G6**
Britton St. EC1 111 H4
Brixham Cres., Ruis. 84 A1
Brixham Gdns., Ilf. 99 H5
Brixham Rd., Well. 158 D1
Brixham St. E16 136 D1
Brixton Est., Edg. 70 B2
Brixton Hill SW2 151 E7
Brixton Hill Pl. SW2 150/151 E7
*Brixton Hill*
Brixton Oval SW2 151 G4
Brixton Rd. SW9 151 G2
Brixton Sta. Rd. SW9 151 G4
Brixton Water La. SW2 151 F5
**Broad Ct. WC2 18 B4**
Broad Grn. Av., Croy. 187 H7
**Broad La. EC2 20 D1**
Broad La. EC2 112 B5
Broad La. N8 75 F5
*Tottenham La.*
Broad La. N15 76 C4
Broad La., Hmptn. 161 G6
Broad Lawn SE9 174 D2
Broad Oak, Wdf.Grn. 63 H5
Broad Oak Cl. E4 62 A5
*Royston Av.*
**Broad Sanctuary SW1 25 J4**
Broad Sanctuary SW1 130 D2
Broad St., Dag. 101 G7
Broad St., Tedd. 162 C6
**Broad St. Av. EC2 20 D2**
**Broad St. Pl. EC2 20 C2**
Broad Vw. NW9 70 A6
Broad Wk. N21 59 F2
**Broad Wk. NW1 8 D4**
Broad Wk. NW1 110 B3
Broad Wk. SE3 155 J2
**Broad Wk. W1 24 B1**
Broad Wk. W1 130 A1
Broad Wk., Houns. 142 D1
Broad Wk., Rich. 125 J7
**Broad Wk., The W8 22 B1**
Broad Wk., The W8 129 E1
Broad Wk., The, E.Mol. 180 C3
Broad Wk. La. NW11 72 C7
**Broad Yd. EC1 11 G6**
Broadbent Cl. N6 92 B1
**Broadbent St. W1 16 D5**
Broadberry Ct. N18 60 E5
Broadbridge Cl. SE3 135 G7
Broadcoombe, S.Croy. 203 F7
Broadcroft Av., Stan. 69 G2
Broadcroft Rd., Orp. 193 G7
Broadfield Cl. NW2 89 J3
Broadfield Cl., Croy. 201 F2
*Progress Way*
Broadfield Ct., Bushey 52 B2
Broadfield La. NW1 92 E7
Broadfield Rd. SE6 154 E7
Broadfield Sq., Enf. 45 E2
Broadfield Way, Buck.H. 63 J3
Broadfields, E.Mol. 180 A6
Broadfields, Har. 67 H2
Broadfields Av. N21 43 G7
Broadfields Av., Edg. 54 B4
Broadfields Hts., Edg. 54 B4
Broadfields La., Wat. 50 B1
Broadfields Way NW10 89 F5
Broadgate E13 115 J2
Broadgate EC2 112 B5
*Liverpool St.*
**Broadgate Circle EC2 20 D1**
Broadgate Rd. E16 116 A6
*Fulmer Rd.*
Broadgates Av., Barn. 41 E1
Broadgates Rd. SW18 167 G1
*Ellerton Rd.*
Broadhead Strand NW9 71 F1
Broadheath Dr., Chis. 174 C5
Broadhinton Rd. SW4 150 B3
Broadhurst Av., Edg. 54 B4
Broadhurst Av., Ilf. 99 J4
Broadhurst Cl. NW6 91 F6
*Broadhurst Gdns.*
Broadhurst Cl., Rich. 145 J5
*Lower Gro. Rd.*
Broadhurst Gdns. NW6 90 E6
Broadhurst Gdns., Chig. 65 F4
Broadhurst Gdns., Ruis. 84 C2
Broadlands, Felt. 161 F3
Broadlands Av. SW16 168 E2
Broadlands Av., Enf. 45 E3
Broadlands Cl. N6 74 A7
Broadlands Cl. SW16 168 E2
Broadlands Cl., Enf. 45 E3
Broadlands Rd. N6 73 J7
Broadlands Rd., Brom. 173 H4
Broadlands Way, N.Mal. 183 F6
Broadlawns Ct., Har. 68 C1
**Broadley St. NW8 15 F1**
Broadley St. NW8 109 H5
**Broadley Ter. NW1 7 H6**
Broadley Ter. NW1 109 H4
**Broadmayne SE17 36 B3**
Broadmead SE6 172 A3
Broadmead Av., Wor.Pk. 183 G7

Brook's Ms. W1 110 B7
Brooks Rd. E13 115 G1
Brooks Rd. W4 126 A5
Brooksbank St. E9 95 G6
Brooksby Ms. N1 93 G7
*Brooksby St.*
Brooksby St. N1 93 G7
Brooksby's Wk. E9 95 G5
Brookscroft Rd. E17 78 B1
Brookshill, Har. 52 A5
Brookshill Av., Har. 52 A5
Brookshill Dr., Har. 52 A5
Brookside N21 43 F6
Brookside, Barn. 41 H6
Brookside, Cars. 200 A5
Brookside, Ilf. 65 F6
Brookside, Orp. 193 J7
Brookside Cl., Barn. 40 B6
Brookside Cl., Felt. 160 A3
*Sycamore Cl.*
Brookside Cl., Har. 69 G5
Brookside Cl. 85 E4
(Kenton), Har.
Brookside Cres., 197 G1
Wor.Pk.
*Green La.*
Brookside Rd. N9 60 E4
Brookside Rd. N19 92 C2
*Junction Rd.*
Brookside Rd. NW11 72 B6
Brookside Rd., 102 C7
Hayes
Brookside S., Barn. 42 A7
Brookside Wk. N3 72 B2
Brookside Wk. N12 56 D6
Brookside Wk. NW4 72 A5
Brookside Wk. NW11 72 B4
Brookside Way, Croy. 189 G6
Brooksville Av. NW6 108 B1
Brookview Rd. 168 C5
SW16
Brookville Rd. SW6 128 C7
Brookway SE3 155 G3
Brookwood Av. 147 F2
SW13
Brookwood Cl., Brom. 191 F4
Brookwood Rd. 166 C1
SW18
Brookwood Rd., 143 H1
Houns.
Broom Cl., Brom. 192 B6
Broom Cl., Tedd. 163 G7
Broom Gdns., Croy. 204 A3
Broom Lock, Tedd. 163 F6
Broom Mead, Bexh. 159 G5
Broom Pk., Tedd. 163 G7
Broom Rd., Croy. 204 A3
Broom Rd., Tedd. 163 F6
Broom Water, Tedd. 163 F6
Broom Water W., 163 F5
Tedd.
Broomcroft Av., 102 C3
Nthlt.
Broome Rd., Hmptn. 161 F7
Broome Way SE5 131 J7
Broomfield E17 77 J7
Broomfield, Sun. 178 A1
Broomfield Av. N13 59 F5
Broomfield Av., Loug. 48 C6
Broomfield La. N13 59 F5
Broomfield Pl. 124/125 E1
W13
*Broomfield Rd.*
Broomfield Rd. N13 59 F5
Broomfield Rd. W13 125 E1
Broomfield Rd., 189 H3
Beck.
Broomfield Rd., Bexh. 159 G5
Broomfield Rd., Rich. 145 J1
Broomfield Rd., Rom. 82 D7
Broomfield Rd., 195 J1
Surb.
Broomfield Rd., Tedd. 163 F6
*Melbourne Rd.*
Broomfield St. E14 114 A5
Broomgrove Gdns., 70 A1
Edg.
Broomgrove Rd. SW9 151 F2
Broomhill Ri., Bexh. 159 G5
Broomhill Rd. SW18 148 D5
Broomhill Rd., Ilf. 100 A2
Broomhill Rd., 63 G6
Wdf.Grn.
Broomhill Wk., 63 F7
Wdf.Grn.
Broomhouse La. 148 D2
SW6
Broomhouse Rd. 148 D2
SW6
Broomloan La., Sutt. 198 D2
Broomsleigh St. 90 C5
NW6
Broomwood Cl., 189 G5
Croy.

Broomwood Rd. 149 J6
SW11
Broseley Gro. SE26 171 H5
Broster Gdns. SE25 188 C3
Brough Cl. SW8 130/131 E7
*Kenchester Cl.*
Brough Cl., Kings.T. 163 G5
Brougham Rd. E8 112 D1
Brougham Rd. W3 106 C6
Brougham St. SW11 149 J2
Broughinge Rd., 38 B2
Borwd.
Broughton Av. N3 72 B3
Broughton Av., Rich. 163 E3
Broughton Dr. SW9 151 G4
Broughton Gdns. N6 74 C6
Broughton Rd. SW6 148 E2
Broughton Rd. W13 105 E7
Broughton Rd., Orp. 207 G2
Broughton Rd., 187 G6
Th.Hth.
Broughton Rd. 148/149 E2
App. SW6
*Wandsworth Br. Rd.*
Broughton St. SW8 150 A2
Brouncker Rd. W3 126 C2
Browells La., Felt. 160 B2
Brown Cl., Wall. 200 E7
**Brown Hart Gdns.** 16 C5
W1
Brown Hart Gdns. 110 A7
W1
**Brown St. W1** 15 J3
Brown St. W1 109 J6
Brownfield St. E14 114 B6
Browngraves Rd., 121 F7
Hayes
Brownhill Rd. SE6 154 B7
Browning Av. W7 104 C6
Browning Av., Sutt. 199 H4
Browning Av., 197 H1
Wor.Pk.
Browning Cl. E17 78 C4
**Browning Cl. W9** 6 D6
Browning Cl., 161 F4
Hmptn.
Browning Cl., Well. 157 H1
**Browning Est. SE17** 36 A3
Browning Est. SE17 131 J5
Browning Ho. W12 107 J6
*Wood La.*
**Browning Ms. W1** 16 D2
Browning Rd. E11 79 F7
Browning Rd. E12 98 C6
**Browning St. SE17** 36 A3
Browning St. SE17 131 J5
Browning Way, 142 D1
Houns.
**Brownlow Ms. WC1** 10 D6
Brownlow Ms. WC1 111 F4
Brownlow Rd. E7 97 H4
*Woodford Rd.*
Brownlow Rd. E8 112 C1
Brownlow Rd. N3 56 E7
Brownlow Rd. N11 58 E6
Brownlow Rd. NW10 89 E7
Brownlow Rd. W13 124 D1
Brownlow Rd., 38 A4
Borwd.
Brownlow Rd., 202 B4
Croy.
**Brownlow St. WC1** 18 D2
**Brown's Bldgs. EC3** 20 E4
Brown's Bldgs. EC3 112 B6
Browns La. NW5 92 B5
Browns Rd. E17 78 A3
Browns Rd., Surb. 181 J7
Brownspring Dr. SE9 175 E4
Brownswood Rd. N4 93 H3
Broxash Rd. SW11 150 A6
Broxbourne Av. E18 79 H4
Broxbourne Rd. E7 97 G3
Broxbourne Rd., 193 J7
Orp.
Broxholm Rd. SE27 169 G3
Broxted Rd. SE6 171 J2
Broxwood Way NW8 109 H1
Bruce Castle Rd. 76 C1
N17
Bruce Cl. W10 108 B5
*Ladbroke Gro.*
Bruce Cl., Well. 158 B1
Bruce Gdns. N20 57 J3
*Balfour Gro.*
Bruce Gro. N17 76 B1
Bruce Hall Ms. SW17 168 A4
*Brudenell Rd.*
Bruce Rd. E3 114 B3
Bruce Rd. NW10 88 D7
Bruce Rd. SE25 188 A4
Bruce Rd., Barn. 40 B4
*St. Albans Rd.*

Bruce Rd., Har. 68 B2
Bruce Rd., Mitch. 168 A7
Bruckner St. W10 108 C3
Brudenell Rd. SW17 167 J3
Bruffs Meadow, 85 E6
Nthlt.
Bruges Pl. NW1 92 C7
*Randolph St.*
Brumfield Rd., Epsom 196 C5
Brummel Cl., Bexh. 159 J3
**Brune St. E1** 21 F2
Brune St. E1 112 C5
Brunel Cl. SE19 170 C6
Brunel Cl., Houns. 122 B7
Brunel Cl., Nthlt. 103 F3
Brunel Est. W2 108 D5
Brunel Pl., Sthl. 103 H6
Brunel Rd. E17 77 H6
Brunel Rd. SE16 133 F2
Brunel Rd. W3 106 E5
Brunel Rd., Wdf.Grn. 64 C5
Brunel St. E16 115 F6
*Victoria Dock Rd.*
Brunel Wk. N15 76 B4
Brunel Wk., Twick. 143 G7
*Stephenson Rd.*
Brunner Cl. NW11 73 F5
Brunner Rd. E17 77 J5
Brunner Rd. W5 105 G4
Bruno Pl. NW9 88 C2
Brunswick Av. N11 58 A3
**Brunswick Cen. WC1** 10 A5
Brunswick Cl., Bexh. 158 D4
Brunswick Cl., Pnr. 67 E6
Brunswick Cl., 194 C1
T.Ditt.
Brunswick Cl., 162 A3
Twick.
Brunswick Ct. EC1 111 H3
*Northampton Sq.*
**Brunswick Ct. SE1** 29 E4
Brunswick Ct. SE1 132 B2
Brunswick Ct., Barn. 41 G5
Brunswick Cres. N11 58 A3
Brunswick Gdns. W5 105 H3
Brunswick Gdns. W8 128 D1
Brunswick Gdns., Ilf. 65 F7
Brunswick Gro. N11 58 A3
Brunswick Ind. Pk. 58 B4
N11
Brunswick Ms. SW16 168 D6
*Potters La.*
**Brunswick Ms. W1** 16 A3
Brunswick Pk. SE5 152 A1
Brunswick Pk. Gdns. 58 A2
N11
**Brunswick Pk. Rd. N11** 58 A2
**Brunswick Pl. N1** 12 C4
Brunswick Pl. N1 112 A3
Brunswick Pl. SE19 170 D7
Brunswick Quay 133 G3
SE16
Brunswick Rd. E10 96 C1
Brunswick Rd. E14 114 C6
*Blackwall Tunnel*
*Northern App.*
Brunswick Rd. N15 76 B5
Brunswick Rd. W5 105 G4
Brunswick Rd., Bexh. 158 D4
Brunswick Rd., 174 C7
Kings.T.
Brunswick Rd., Sutt. 199 E4
Brunswick Sq. N17 60 C6
**Brunswick Sq. WC1** 10 B6
Brunswick Sq. WC1 111 E4
Brunswick Vil. SE5 152 B1
Brunswick Way N11 58 B4
Brunton Pl. E14 113 H6
**Brushfield St. E1** 21 E2
Brushfield St. E1 112 B5
Brussels Rd. SW11 149 G4
Bruton Cl., Chis. 174 C7
**Bruton La. W1** 17 E6
Bruton La. W1 110 B7
**Bruton Pl. W1** 17 E6
Bruton Pl. W1 110 B7
Bruton Rd., Mord. 185 F5
**Bruton St. W1** 16 E6
Bruton St. W1 110 B7
Bruton Way W13 104 D5
Bryan Av. NW10 89 H7
Bryan Cl., Sun. 160 A7
Bryan Rd. SE16 133 J2
Bryan's All. SW6 128/129 E2
*Wandsworth Br. Rd.*
Bryanston Av., 161 H1
Twick.
Bryanston Cl., Sthl. 123 F4
**Bryanston Ms. E. W1** 15 J2
**Bryanston Ms. W. W1** 15 J2
**Bryanston Pl. W1** 15 J2
Bryanston Pl. W1 109 J5
**Bryanston Sq. W1** 15 J2

Bryanston Sq. W1 109 J5
**Bryanston St. W1** 15 J4
Bryanston St. W1 109 J6
Bryanstone Rd. N8 74 D5
Bryant Cl., Barn. 40 C5
**Bryant Ct. E2** 13 F1
Bryant Ct. E2 112 C2
Bryant Rd., Nthlt. 102 C3
Bryant St. E15 96 D7
Bryantwood Rd. N7 93 G5
Bryce Rd., Dag. 100 C4
Brycedale Cres. N14 58 D4
Bryden Cl. SE26 171 H6
**Brydges Pl. WC2** 18 A6
Brydges Rd. E15 96 D5
Brydon Wk. N1 110/111 E1
*Outram Pl.*
Bryer Ct. EC2 111 J5
*Aldersgate St.*
Bryett Rd. N7 93 E3
Brymay Cl. E3 114 A3
Bryn-y-Mawr Rd., 44 C4
Enf.
Brynmaer Rd. SW11 149 J1
Bryony Cl., Loug. 48 E4
Bryony Rd. W12 107 G7
Buchan Rd. SE15 153 F3
Buchanan Cl. N21 43 F5
Buchanan Ct., Borwd. 38 C2
Buchanan Gdns. 107 H2
NW10
Bucharest Rd. SW18 149 F7
Buck Hill Wk. W2 15 F6
Buck La. NW9 70 D5
Buck St. NW1 92 B7
Buck Wk. E17 78 D4
*Foresters Dr.*
Buckden Cl. N2 73 J4
*Southern Rd.*
Buckden Cl. SE12 155 F6
*Upwood Rd.*
Buckfast Rd., Mord. 185 E4
**Buckfast St. E2** 13 J4
Buckfast St. E2 112 D3
Buckhold Rd. SW18 148 D6
Buckhurst Av., Cars. 199 H1
Buckhurst St. E1 113 E4
Buckhurst Way, 64 A4
Buck.H.
Buckingham Arc. 18 B6
WC2
Buckingham Av. N20 41 F7
Buckingham Av., 142 B6
Felt.
Buckingham Av., 104 D1
Grnf.
Buckingham Av., 187 G1
Th.Hth.
Buckingham Av., 157 H4
Well.
Buckingham Av., 179 H3
W.Mol.
Buckingham Cl. W5 105 F5
Buckingham Cl., Enf. 44 B2
Buckingham Cl., 161 F5
Hmptn.
Buckingham Cl., 193 H7
Orp.
Buckingham Cl. NW4 71 G3
Buckingham Dr., 175 E5
Chis.
Buckingham Gdns. 53 J7
Edg.
Buckingham Gdns., 187 G2
Th.Hth.
Buckingham Gdns., 179 H2
W.Mol.
*Buckingham Av.*
**Buckingham Gate** 25 F4
SW1
Buckingham Gate 130 C3
SW1
Buckingham La. 153 H7
SE23
Buckingham Ms. N1 94 B6
Buckingham Ms. 107 F2
NW10
*Buckingham Rd.*
**Buckingham Ms.** 25 F5
SW1
**Buckingham Palace** 32 D2
Rd. SW1
Buckingham Palace 130 B4
Rd. SW1
**Buckingham Pl. SW1** 25 F5
Buckingham Rd. E10 96 B3
Buckingham Rd. E11 79 J5
Buckingham Rd. E15 97 F5
Buckingham Rd. E18 79 F1
Buckingham Rd. N1 94 B6
Buckingham Rd. N22 74 E1
Buckingham Rd. 107 F2
NW10

Buckingham Rd., Borwd. 38 D4
Buckingham Rd., Edg. 53 J7
Buckingham Rd., Hmptn. 161 F5
Buckingham Rd., Har. 68 A5
Buckingham Rd., Ilf. 99 G2
Buckingham Rd., Kings.T. 181 J4
Buckingham Rd., Mitch. 186 E5
Buckingham Rd., Rich. 163 G2
**Buckingham St. WC2 18 B6**
Buckland Cres. NW3 91 G7
Buckland Ri., Pnr. 66 C1
Buckland Rd. E10 96 C2
Buckland Rd., Chess. 195 J5
Buckland Rd., Orp. 207 H4
**Buckland St. N1 12 C2**
Buckland St. N1 112 A2
Buckland Wk. W3 126 C2
*Church Rd.*
Buckland Wk., Mord. 185 F4
Buckland Way, Wor.Pk. 197 J1
Bucklands Rd., Tedd. 163 F6
**Buckle St. E1 21 G3**
Buckleigh Av. SW20 184 B3
Buckleigh Rd. SW16 168 D6
Buckleigh Way SE19 188 C1
Buckler Gdns. SE9 174 C3
*Southold Ri.*
Bucklers All. SW6 128 C6
Bucklers Way, Cars. 199 J3
**Bucklersbury EC4 20 B4**
Bucklersbury EC4 112 A6
**Bucklersbury Pas. EC4 20 B4**
Buckles Ct., Belv. 138 D3
*Fendyke Rd.*
Buckley Rd. NW6 90 C7
**Buckley St. SE1 26 E2**
Buckmaster Cl. SW9 151 F3
*Stockwell Pk. Rd.*
Buckmaster Rd. SW11 149 H4
**Bucknall St. WC2 17 J3**
Bucknall St. WC2 110 D6
Bucknell Cl. SW2 151 F4
Buckner Rd. SW2 151 F4
Buckrell Rd. E4 62 D2
Buckstone Cl. SE23 153 F6
Buckstone Rd. N18 60 D5
Buckters Rents SE16 133 H1
Buckthorne Rd. SE4 153 H6
Budd Cl. N12 57 E4
Buddings Circle, Wem. 88 C3
Budd's All., Twick. 145 F5
*Arlington Cl.*
Budge La., Mitch. 185 J7
**Budge Row EC4 20 B5**
**Budge's Wk. W2 22 C1**
Budge's Wk. W2 109 F7
Budleigh Cres., Well. 158 C1
Budoch Ct., Ilf. 100 A2
Budoch Dr., Ilf. 100 A2
Buer Rd. SW6 148 B2
Bugsby's Way SE7 135 H4
Bugsby's Way SE10 135 F4
Bulganak Rd., Th.Hth. 187 J4
**Bulinga St. SW1 34 A2**
Bulinga St. SW1 130 D4
Bull All., Well. 158 B3
*Welling High St.*
**Bull Inn Ct. WC2 18 B6**
Bull La. N18 60 B5
Bull La., Chis. 175 G7
Bull La., Dag. 101 H3
Bull Rd. E15 115 F2
**Bull Wf. La. EC4 20 A5**
Bullace Row SE5 151 J1
*Camberwell Rd.*
Bullards Pl. E2 113 G3
Bullbanks Rd., Belv. 139 J4
Bullen St. SW11 149 H2
Buller Cl. SE15 132 D7
Buller Rd. N17 76 D2
Buller Rd. N22 75 G2
Buller Rd. NW10 108 A3
*Chamberlayne Rd.*
Buller Rd., Bark. 99 H7
Buller Rd., Th.Hth. 188 A2
Bullers Cl., Sid. 176 E5
Bullers Wd. Dr., Chis. 174 B7
Bullescroft Rd., Edg. 54 A3
Bullhead Rd., Borwd. 38 C3
**Bullied Way SW1 32 E2**
Bullivant St. E14 114 C7
Bullrush Cl., Croy. 188 B6
Bull's All. SW14 146 D2
Bulls Br. Ind. Est., Sthl. 122 B3
*Hayes Rd.*
Bulls Br. Rd., Sthl. 122 B3
**Bulls Gdns. SW3 31 H1**
**Bull's Head Pas. EC3 20 D4**
Bullsbrook Rd., Hayes 122 C1
Bulmer Gdns., Har. 69 G7
Bulmer Ms. W11 108 D7
*Ladbroke Rd.*
Bulmer Pl. W11 128 D1
Bulow Est. SW6 148/149 E2
*Broughton Rd.*
Bulstrode Av., Houns. 143 F2
Bulstrode Gdns., Houns. 143 F3
**Bulstrode Pl. W1 16 C2**
Bulstrode Rd., Houns. 143 G3
**Bulstrode St. W1 16 C3**
Bulstrode St. W1 110 A6
Bulwer Ct. Rd. E11 96 D1
Bulwer Gdns., Barn. 41 F4
*Bulwer Rd.*
Bulwer Rd. E11 78 D7
Bulwer Rd. N18 60 B4
Bulwer Rd., Barn. 41 E4
Bulwer St. W12 127 J1
Bunces La., Wdf.Grn. 63 F7
Bungalow Rd. SE25 188 B4
Bungalows, The SW16 168 B7
Bungalows, The, Wall. 200 B5
**Bunhill Row EC1 12 B5**
Bunhill Row EC1 112 A4
**Bunhouse Pl. SW1 32 B3**
Bunhouse Pl. SW1 130 A5
Bunkers Hill NW11 73 F7
Bunkers Hill, Belv. 139 G4
Bunkers Hill, Sid. 177 F3
Bunning Way N7 93 E7
Bunns La. NW7 55 F6
Bunsen St. E3 113 H2
*Kenilworth Rd.*
Bunting Cl. N9 61 G1
*Dunnock Cl.*
Bunting Cl., Mitch. 185 J5
Buntingbridge Rd., Ilf. 81 G5
Bunton St. SE18 136 D3
Bunyan Rd. E17 77 H3
**Buonaparte Ms. SW1 33 H3**
**Burbage Cl. SE1 28 B6**
Burbage Cl. SE1 132 A3
Burbage Rd. SE21 152 A6
Burbage Rd. SE24 151 J6
Burberry Cl., N.Mal. 182 E2
Burbridge Way N17 76 C2
Burcham St. E14 114 B6
Burcharbro Rd. SE2 138 D6
Burchell Rd. E10 96 B1
Burchell Rd. SE15 153 E1
Burchett Way, Rom. 83 F6
Burcote Rd. SW18 167 G1
Burden Cl., Brent. 125 F5
Burden Way E11 97 H2
*Brading Cres.*
Burdenshott Av., Rich. 146 B4
Burder Cl. N1 94 B6
Burder Rd. N1 94 B6
*Balls Pond Rd.*
Burdett Av. SW20 183 G1
Burdett Cl. W7 124 C2
*Cherington Rd.*
Burdett Cl., Sid. 176 E5
Burdett Ms. NW3 91 G6
*Belsize Cres.*
**Burdett Ms. W2 14 A3**
Burdett Rd. E3 113 J4
Burdett Rd. E14 113 J4
Burdett Rd., Croy. 188 A6
Burdett Rd., Rich. 145 J3
**Burdett St. SE1 27 E5**
Burdetts Rd., Dag. 119 F1
Burdock Cl., Croy. 203 G1
Burdock Rd. N17 76 D3
Burdon La., Sutt. 198 B7
Burfield Cl. SW17 167 G4
Burford Cl., Dag. 100 C3
Burford Cl., Ilf. 81 F4
Burford Gdns. N13 59 F3
Burford Rd. E6 116 B3
Burford Rd. E15 96 D7
Burford Rd. SE6 171 J2
Burford Rd., Brent. 125 H5
Burford Rd., Brom. 192 B4
Burford Rd., Sutt. 198 D2
Burford Rd., Wor.Pk. 183 F7
Burford Wk. SW6 128/129 E7
*Cambria St.*
Burford Way, Croy. 204 C6
**Burge St. SE1 28 C6**
Burge St. SE1 132 A3
Burges Ct. E6 98 D7
Burges Gro. SW13 127 H7
Burges Rd. E6 98 B7
Burgess Av. NW9 70 D6
Burgess Cl., Felt. 160 E4
Burgess Hill NW2 90 D4
Burgess Rd. E15 96 E4
Burgess Rd., Sutt. 198 E4
Burgess St. E14 114 A5
**Burgh St. N1 11 H1**
Burgh St. N1 111 H2
Burghill Rd. SE26 171 H4
Burghley Av., Borwd. 38 C5
Burghley Av., N.Mal. 182 D1
Burghley Hall Cl. SW19 166 B1
*Princes Way*
Burghley Pl., Mitch. 186 A5
Burghley Rd. E11 97 E1
Burghley Rd. N8 75 G3
Burghley Rd. NW5 92 B5
Burghley Rd. SW19 166 A4
Burghley Twr. W3 107 F7
**Burgon St. EC4 19 H4**
Burgos Cl., Croy. 201 G6
Burgos Gro. SE10 154 B1
Burgoyne Rd. N4 75 H6
Burgoyne Rd. SE25 188 C4
Burgoyne Rd. SW9 151 F3
Burham Cl. SE20 171 F7
*Maple Rd.*
Burhill Gro., Pnr. 66 E2
Burke Cl. SW15 147 E4
Burke St. E16 115 F6
Burket Cl., Sthl. 123 F4
*Kingsbridge Rd.*
Burland Rd. SW11 149 J5
Burleigh Av., Sid. 157 J5
Burleigh Av., Wall. 200 A3
Burleigh Gdns. N14 58 C1
Burleigh Ho. W10 108 A5
*St. Charles Sq.*
Burleigh Pl. SW15 148 A5
Burleigh Rd., Enf. 44 B4
Burleigh Rd., Sutt. 198 B1
**Burleigh St. WC2 18 C5**
Burleigh Wk. SE6 172 C1
*Muirkirk Rd.*
Burleigh Way, Enf. 44 A3
*Church St.*
Burley Cl. E4 62 A5
Burley Cl. SW16 186 D2
Burley Rd. E16 115 J6
**Burlington Arc. W1 17 F6**
Burlington Arc. W1 110 C7
Burlington Av., Rich. 146 A1
Burlington Av., Rom. 83 H6
Burlington Cl. E6 116 B6
*Northumberland Rd.*
Burlington Cl. W9 108 C4
Burlington Cl., Felt. 141 G7
Burlington Cl., Orp. 206 E2
Burlington Cl., Pnr. 66 B3
**Burlington Gdns. W1 17 F6**
Burlington Gdns. W1 110 C7
Burlington Gdns. W3 126 C1
Burlington Gdns. W4 126 C5
Burlington Gdns., Rom. 83 E7
Burlington La. W4 126 E7
Burlington Ms. SW15 148 C5
*Upper Richmond Rd.*
Burlington Ms. W3 126 C1
Burlington Pl. SW6 148 B2
*Burlington Rd.*
Burlington Pl., Wdf.Grn. 63 G3
Burlington Ri., Barn. 57 H1
Burlington Rd. N10 74 A2
*Tetherdown*
Burlington Rd. N17 76 D1
Burlington Rd. SW6 148 B2
Burlington Rd. W4 126 C5
Burlington Rd., Enf. 44 A1
Burlington Rd., Islw. 144 A1
Burlington Rd., N.Mal. 183 G4
Burlington Rd., Th.Hth. 187 J2
Burma Rd. N16 94 A4
Burmester Rd. SW17 167 F3
Burn Side N9 61 F3
Burnaby Cres. W4 126 B6
Burnaby Gdns. W4 126 C6
Burnaby St. SW10 129 F7
Burnbrae Cl. N12 57 E6
Burnbury Rd. SW12 168 C1
Burncroft Av., Enf. 45 F2
Burne Jones Ho. W14 128 C4
**Burne St. NW1 15 G1**
Burne St. NW1 109 H5
Burnell Av., Rich. 163 F5
Burnell Av., Well. 158 A2
Burnell Gdns., Stan. 69 G1
Burnell Rd., Sutt. 199 E4
**Burnell Wk. SE1 37 G3**
Burnels Av. E6 116 D3
Burness Cl. N7 93 F6
*Roman Way*
Burnett Cl. E9 95 F5
Burney Av., Surb. 181 J5
Burney Dr., Loug. 49 E2
Burney St. SE10 134 C7
Burnfoot Av. SW6 148 B1
Burnfoot Ct. SE22 170 E1
Burnham NW3 91 H7
Burnham Cl. NW7 55 G7
**Burnham Cl. SE1 37 G2**
Burnham Cl., Har. 68 D4
Burnham Ct. NW4 71 J4
Burnham Cres. E11 79 J4
Burnham Dr., Wor.Pk. 198 A2
Burnham Gdns., Croy. 188 C7
Burnham Gdns., Hayes 121 G3
Burnham Gdns., Houns. 142 B1
Burnham Rd. E4 61 J5
Burnham Rd., Dag. 100 B7
Burnham Rd., Mord. 185 E5
Burnham Rd., Sid. 176 E2
Burnham St. E2 113 F3
Burnham St., Kings.T. 182 A1
Burnham Way SE26 171 J5
Burnham Way W13 124 E4
Burnhill Rd., Beck. 190 A2
Burnley Cl., Wat. 50 C5
Burnley Rd. NW10 89 G5
Burnley Rd. SW9 151 F2
Burns Av., Felt. 142 A6
Burns Av., Rom. 82 C7
Burns Av., Sid. 158 B6
Burns Av., Sthl. 103 G7
Burns Cl. E17 78 C4
Burns Cl. SW19 167 G6
*North Rd.*
Burns Cl., Well. 157 J1
Burns Rd. NW10 107 F1
Burns Rd. SW11 149 J2
Burns Rd. W13 124 E2
Burns Rd., Wem. 105 G2
Burns Way, Houns. 142 D2
**Burnsall St. SW3 31 H3**
Burnsall St. SW3 129 H5
Burnside Av. E4 61 J6
Burnside Cl. SE16 133 G1
Burnside Cl., Barn. 40 D3
Burnside Cl., Twick. 144 D6
Burnside Cres., Wem. 105 G1
Burnside Rd., Dag. 100 C2
Burnt Ash Hill SE12 155 F6
Burnt Ash La., Brom. 173 G6
Burnt Ash Rd. SE12 155 F5
Burnt Oak Bdy., Edg. 54 B7
Burnt Oak Flds., Edg. 70 C1
Burnt Oak La., Sid. 158 A6
Burnthwaite Rd. SW6 128 D7
Burntwood Cl. SW18 167 G1
Burntwood Gra. Rd. SW18 167 G1
Burntwood La. SW17 167 H2
Burntwood Vw. SE19 170 C5
*Bowley La.*
Buross St. E1 112/113 E6
*Commercial Rd.*
**Burr Cl. E1 29 H1**
Burr Cl. E1 132 D1
Burr Cl., Bexh. 159 F3
Burr Rd. SW18 148 D7
Burrage Gro. SE18 137 F4
Burrage Pl. SE18 137 E5
Burrage Rd. SE18 137 F5
Burrard Rd. E16 115 H6
Burrard Rd. NW6 90 D4
Burrell Cl., Croy. 189 H6
Burrell Cl., Edg. 54 B2
Burrell Row, Beck. 190 A2
*High St.*
**Burrell St. SE1 27 G1**
Burrell St. SE1 131 H1
Burrell Twr. E10 78 A7
Burrells Wf. Sq. E14 134 B5
Burritt Rd., Kings.T. 182 A2
Burroughs, The NW4 71 H5
Burroughs Gdns. NW4 71 H4

| Name | No. | Grid |
|---|---|---|
| Caistor Ms. SW12 | 150 | B7 |
| *Caistor Rd.* | | |
| Caistor Pk. Rd. E15 | 115 | F1 |
| Caistor Rd. SW12 | 150 | B7 |
| Caithness Gdns., Sid. | 157 | H8 |
| Caithness Rd. W14 | 128 | A4 |
| Caithness Rd., Mitch. | 168 | B7 |
| Calabria Rd. N5 | 93 | H6 |
| Calais Gate SE5 | 151 | H1 |
| *Calais St.* | | |
| Calais St. SE5 | 151 | H1 |
| Calbourne Rd. SW12 | 149 | J7 |
| Calcott Wk. SE9 | 174 | A4 |
| Caldbeck Av., Wor.Pk. | 197 | G2 |
| Caldecot Rd. SE5 | 151 | J2 |
| Caldecott Way E5 | 95 | G3 |
| Calder Av., Grnf. | 104 | C2 |
| Calder Cl., Enf. | 44 | B3 |
| Calder Gdns., Edg. | 70 | A3 |
| Calder Rd., Mord. | 185 | F5 |
| Calderon Pl. W10 | 107 | J5 |
| *St. Quintin Gdns.* | | |
| Calderon Rd. E11 | 96 | C4 |
| Caldervale Rd. SW4 | 150 | D5 |
| Calderwood St. SE18 | 136 | D4 |
| Caldicot Grn. NW9 | 70/71 | E6 |
| *Snowdon Dr.* | | |
| Caldwell Rd., Wat. | 50 | D4 |
| Caldwell St. SW9 | 131 | F7 |
| Caldwell Yd. EC4 | 111 | J7 |
| *Upper Thames St.* | | |
| Caldy Rd., Belv. | 139 | H3 |
| Caldy Rd. N1 | 93 | J6 |
| *Clephane Rd.* | | |
| Cale St. SW3 | 31 | G3 |
| Cale St. SW3 | 129 | H5 |
| Caleb St. SE1 | 27 | J3 |
| Caledon Rd. E6 | 116 | C1 |
| Caledon Rd., Wall. | 200 | A4 |
| Caledonia St. N1 | 10 | B2 |
| Caledonia St. N1 | 111 | E2 |
| Caledonian Cl., Ilf. | 100 | B1 |
| Caledonian Rd. N1 | 10 | B2 |
| Caledonian Rd. N1 | 111 | F2 |
| Caledonian Rd. N7 | 93 | F5 |
| Caledonian Wf. E14 | 134 | D4 |
| Caletock Way SE10 | 135 | F5 |
| Calico Row SW11 | 149 | F3 |
| *York Pl.* | | |
| Calidore Cl. SW2 | 151 | F6 |
| *Endymion Rd.* | | |
| California La., Bushey | 52 | A1 |
| California Rd., N.Mal. | 182 | C4 |
| Callaby Ter. N1 | 94 | A6 |
| *Wakeham St.* | | |
| Callaghan Cl. SE13 | 154/155 | E4 |
| *Glenton Rd.* | | |
| Callander Rd. SE6 | 172 | B2 |
| Callard Av. N13 | 59 | H5 |
| Callcott Rd. NW6 | 90 | C7 |
| Callcott St. W8 | 128 | D1 |
| *Hillgate Pl.* | | |
| Callendar Rd. SW7 | 22 | E5 |
| Callendar Rd. SW7 | 129 | G3 |
| Callingham Cl. E14 | 113 | J5 |
| *Wallwood St.* | | |
| Callis Fm. Cl., Stai. | 140 | B6 |
| *Bedfont Rd.* | | |
| Callis Rd. E17 | 77 | J6 |
| Callow St. SW3 | 30 | D5 |
| Callow St. SW3 | 129 | G6 |
| Calmont Rd., Brom. | 172 | D6 |
| Calne Av., Ilf. | 80 | E1 |
| Colonne Rd. SW19 | 166 | A4 |
| Calshot Rd., Houns. | 140 | D2 |
| Calshot St. N1 | 10 | C1 |
| Calshot St. N1 | 111 | F2 |
| Calshot Way, Enf. | 43 | H3 |
| Calshot Way, Houns. | 140/141 | E2 |
| *Calshot Rd.* | | |
| Calthorpe Gdns., Edg. | 53 | H5 |
| *Jesmond Way* | | |
| Calthorpe Gdns., Sutt. | 199 | F3 |
| Calthorpe St. WC1 | 10 | D5 |
| Calthorpe St. WC1 | 111 | F4 |
| Calton Av. SE21 | 152 | B5 |
| Calton Rd., Barn. | 41 | F6 |
| Calverley Cl., Beck. | 172 | B6 |
| Calverley Cres., Dag. | 101 | G2 |
| Calverley Gdns., Har. | 69 | G7 |
| Calverley Gro. N19 | 92 | D1 |
| Calverley Rd., Epsom | 197 | G6 |
| Calvert Av. E2 | 13 | E4 |
| Calvert Av. E2 | 112 | B3 |
| Calvert Cl., Belv. | 139 | G4 |
| Calvert Cl., Sid. | 176 | E6 |
| Calvert Rd. SE10 | 135 | F5 |
| Calvert Rd., Barn. | 40 | A2 |
| Calvert St. NW1 | 110 | A1 |
| *Chalcot Rd.* | | |
| Calverton SE5 | 38 | D5 |
| Calverton Rd. E6 | 116 | D1 |
| Calvert's Bldgs. SE1 | 28 | B2 |
| Calvin St. E1 | 13 | F6 |
| Calvin St. E1 | 112 | C4 |
| Calydon Rd. SE7 | 135 | H5 |
| Calypso Way SE16 | 133 | J3 |
| Cam Rd. E15 | 114 | D1 |
| Camac Rd., Twick. | 162 | A1 |
| Cambalt Rd. SW15 | 148 | A5 |
| Camberley Av. SW20 | 183 | H2 |
| Camberley Av., Enf. | 44 | B4 |
| Camberley Cl., Sutt. | 198 | A3 |
| Camberley Rd., Houns. | 140 | D3 |
| Cambert Way SE3 | 155 | H4 |
| Camberwell Ch. St. SE5 | 152 | A1 |
| Camberwell Glebe SE5 | 152 | A1 |
| Camberwell Grn. SE5 | 152 | A1 |
| Camberwell New Rd. SE5 | 35 | E6 |
| Camberwell New Rd. SE5 | 131 | G7 |
| Camberwell Pas. SE5 | 151 | J1 |
| *Camberwell Grn.* | | |
| Camberwell Rd. SE5 | 36 | A6 |
| Camberwell Rd. SE5 | 131 | J6 |
| Camberwell Sta. Rd. SE5 | 151 | J1 |
| Cambeys Rd., Dag. | 101 | H5 |
| Camborne Av. W13 | 125 | E2 |
| Camborne Ms. W11 | 108 | B6 |
| *St. Marks Rd.* | | |
| Camborne Rd. SW18 | 148 | D7 |
| Camborne Rd., Croy. | 188 | D7 |
| Camborne Rd., Houns. | 140 | D3 |
| Camborne Rd., Mord. | 184 | A5 |
| Camborne Ms., Sid. | 176 | C3 |
| Camborne Rd., Sutt. | 198 | D7 |
| Camborne Rd., Well. | 157 | J2 |
| Camborne Way, Houns. | 143 | G1 |
| Cambourne Av. N9 | 45 | G7 |
| Cambray Rd. SW12 | 168 | C1 |
| Cambray Rd., Orp. | 193 | J7 |
| Cambria Cl., Houns. | 143 | G4 |
| Cambria Cl., Sid. | 175 | G1 |
| Cambria Ct., Felt. | 142 | B7 |
| *Hounslow Rd.* | | |
| Cambria Gdns., Stai. | 140 | B7 |
| Cambria Rd. SE5 | 151 | J3 |
| Cambria St. SW6 | 129 | E7 |
| Cambrian Av., Ilf. | 81 | H5 |
| Cambrian Cl. SE27 | 169 | H3 |
| Cambrian Rd. E10 | 78 | A7 |
| Cambrian Rd., Rich. | 145 | J6 |
| Cambridge Av. NW6 | 108 | D2 |
| Cambridge Av., Grnf. | 86 | C5 |
| Cambridge Av., N.Mal. | 183 | F2 |
| Cambridge Av., Well. | 157 | J4 |
| Cambridge Barracks Rd. SE18 | 136 | C4 |
| Cambridge Circ. WC2 | 17 | J4 |
| Cambridge Circ. WC2 | 110 | D6 |
| Cambridge Cl. E17 | 77 | J6 |
| Cambridge Cl. N22 | 75 | G1 |
| *Pellatt Gro.* | | |
| Cambridge Cl. NW10 | 88 | C3 |
| Cambridge Cl. SW20 | 183 | H1 |
| Cambridge Cl., Houns. | 143 | E4 |
| Cambridge Cl., West Dr. | 120 | A6 |
| Cambridge Cotts., Rich. | 126 | A6 |
| Cambridge Cres. E2 | 112 | E2 |
| Cambridge Cres., Tedd. | 162 | D5 |
| Cambridge Dr. SE12 | 155 | G5 |
| Cambridge Dr., Ruis. | 84 | C2 |
| Cambridge Gdns. N10 | 74 | B1 |
| Cambridge Gdns. N13 | 59 | G5 |
| Cambridge Gdns. N17 | 60 | A7 |
| *Great Cambridge Rd.* | | |
| Cambridge Gdns. N21 | 44 | A7 |
| Cambridge Gdns. NW6 | 108 | D2 |
| Cambridge Gdns. W10 | 108 | B6 |
| Cambridge Gdns., Enf. | 44 | D2 |
| Cambridge Gdns., Kings.T. | 182 | A2 |
| **Cambridge Gate NW1** | 8 | E4 |
| **Cambridge Gate Ms. NW1** | 8 | E4 |
| Cambridge Grn. SE9 | 174 | E1 |
| Cambridge Gro. W6 | 127 | H4 |
| Cambridge Gro. Rd., Kings.T. | 182 | A2 |
| Cambridge Heath Rd. E1 | 113 | E2 |
| Cambridge Heath Rd. E2 | 113 | E2 |
| Cambridge Mans. SW11 | 149 | J1 |
| *Cambridge Rd.* | | |
| Cambridge Par., Enf. | 44 | D1 |
| *Great Cambridge Rd.* | | |
| Cambridge Pk. E11 | 79 | G7 |
| Cambridge Pk., Twick. | 145 | G7 |
| Cambridge Pk. Rd. E11 | 79 | F7 |
| *Cambridge Pk.* | | |
| **Cambridge Pl. W8** | 22 | B4 |
| Cambridge Pl. W8 | 129 | E2 |
| Cambridge Rd. E4 | 62 | D1 |
| Cambridge Rd. E11 | 79 | F6 |
| Cambridge Rd. NW6 | 108 | D3 |
| Cambridge Rd. SE20 | 188 | E3 |
| Cambridge Rd. SW11 | 149 | J1 |
| Cambridge Rd. SW13 | 147 | F2 |
| Cambridge Rd. SW20 | 183 | G1 |
| Cambridge Rd. W7 | 124 | C2 |
| Cambridge Rd., Bark. | 99 | F7 |
| Cambridge Rd., Brom. | 173 | G7 |
| Cambridge Rd., Cars. | 199 | H6 |
| Cambridge Rd., Hmptn. | 161 | F7 |
| Cambridge Rd., Har. | 67 | G5 |
| Cambridge Rd., Houns. | 143 | E4 |
| Cambridge Rd., Ilf. | 99 | H1 |
| Cambridge Rd., Kings.T. | 181 | J2 |
| Cambridge Rd., Mitch. | 186 | C3 |
| Cambridge Rd., N.Mal. | 182 | E4 |
| Cambridge Rd., Rich. | 126 | A7 |
| Cambridge Rd., Sid. | 175 | H4 |
| Cambridge Rd., Sthl. | 123 | F1 |
| Cambridge Rd., Tedd. | 162 | C4 |
| Cambridge Rd., Twick. | 145 | G6 |
| Cambridge Rd., Walt. | 178 | B6 |
| Cambridge Rd., W.Mol. | 179 | F4 |
| Cambridge Rd. N. W4 | 126 | B5 |
| Cambridge Rd. S. W4 | 126 | B5 |
| *Oxford Rd. S.* | | |
| Cambridge Row SE18 | 137 | E5 |
| **Cambridge Sq. W2** | 15 | G3 |
| Cambridge Sq. W2 | 109 | H6 |
| **Cambridge St. SW1** | 32 | E2 |
| Cambridge St. SW1 | 130 | B5 |
| Cambridge Ter. N13 | 59 | G5 |
| **Cambridge Ter. NW1** | 8 | E4 |
| **Cambridge Ter. Ms. NW1** | 8 | E4 |
| Cambstone Cl. N11 | 58 | A2 |
| Cambus Cl., Hayes | 103 | E5 |
| Cambus Rd. E16 | 115 | G5 |
| Camdale Rd. SE18 | 137 | J7 |
| Camden Av., Felt. | 160 | C2 |
| Camden Av., Hayes | 102 | C7 |
| Camden Cl., Chis. | 175 | F7 |
| Camden Est. SE15 | 152 | C1 |
| Camden Gdns. NW1 | 92 | B7 |
| *Kentish Town Rd.* | | |
| Camden Gdns., Sutt. | 198 | E5 |
| Camden Gdns., Th.Hth. | 187 | H3 |
| Camden Gro., Chis. | 175 | E6 |
| Camden High St. NW1 | 110 | B1 |
| Camden Hill Rd. SE19 | 170 | B6 |
| Camden Lock Pl. NW1 | 92 | B7 |
| *Chalk Fm. Rd.* | | |
| Camden Ms. NW1 | 92 | D6 |
| Camden Pk. Rd. NW1 | 92 | D6 |
| Camden Pk. Rd., Chis. | 174 | C7 |
| Camden Pas. N1 | 111 | H1 |
| Camden Rd. E11 | 79 | H6 |
| Camden Rd. E17 | 77 | J6 |
| Camden Rd. N7 | 92 | D5 |
| Camden Rd. NW1 | 92 | C7 |
| Camden Rd., Bex. | 177 | F1 |
| Camden Rd., Cars. | 199 | J4 |
| Camden Rd., Sutt. | 198 | D5 |
| Camden Row SE3 | 155 | E2 |
| Camden Sq. NW1 | 92 | D6 |
| Camden Sq. SE15 | 152 | C1 |
| *Watts St.* | | |
| Camden St. NW1 | 92 | C7 |
| Camden Ter. NW1 | 92 | D6 |
| *North Vil.* | | |
| Camden Wk. N1 | 111 | H1 |
| Camden Way, Chis. | 174 | C7 |
| Camden Way, Th.Hth. | 187 | H3 |
| Camdenhurst St. E14 | 113 | H6 |
| Camel Gro., Kings.T. | 163 | G5 |
| Camel Rd. E16 | 136 | A1 |
| Camelford Wk. W11 | 108 | B6 |
| Camellia Ct., Wdf.Grn. | 62/63 | E7 |
| *The Bridle Path* | | |
| Camellia Pl., Twick. | 143 | H7 |
| Camellia St. SW8 | 130 | E7 |
| Camelot Cl. SE28 | 137 | G2 |
| Camelot Cl. SW19 | 166 | D4 |
| Camelot St. SE15 | 132/133 | E7 |
| *Bird in Bush Rd.* | | |
| **Camera Pl. SW10** | 30 | E5 |
| Camera Pl. SW10 | 129 | G6 |
| Cameron Cl. N18 | 61 | E4 |
| Cameron Cl. N20 | 57 | H2 |
| *Myddelton Pk.* | | |
| Cameron Pl. E1 | 112/113 | E6 |
| *Varden St.* | | |
| Cameron Rd. SE6 | 171 | J2 |
| Cameron Rd., Brom. | 191 | G4 |
| Cameron Rd., Croy. | 187 | H6 |
| Cameron Rd., Ilf. | 99 | H1 |
| Cameron Sq., Mitch. | 185 | H1 |
| Camerton Cl. E8 | 94 | C6 |
| *Buttermere Wk.* | | |
| Camgate Cen., Stai. | 140 | C6 |
| Camilla Rd. SE16 | 132 | E4 |
| Camille Cl. SE25 | 188 | D3 |
| Camlan Rd., Brom. | 173 | F4 |
| **Camlet St. E2** | 13 | F5 |
| Camlet St. E2 | 112 | C4 |
| Camlet Way, Barn. | 40 | D2 |
| **Camley St. NW1** | 9 | J1 |
| Camley St. NW1 | 92 | D7 |
| Camm Gdns., Kings.T. | 181 | J2 |
| *Church Rd.* | | |
| Camm Gdns., T.Ditt. | 180 | B7 |
| Camms Ter., Dag. | 101 | J5 |
| Camomile Av., Mitch. | 185 | J1 |
| **Camomile St. EC3** | 20 | D3 |
| Camomile St. EC3 | 112 | B6 |
| Camp Rd. SW19 | 165 | J5 |
| Camp Vw. SW19 | 165 | H5 |
| Campana Rd. SW6 | 148 | D1 |
| Campbell Av., Ilf. | 81 | F4 |
| Campbell Cl. SE18 | 156 | D1 |
| *Moordown* | | |
| Campbell Cl. SW16 | 168 | D4 |
| Campbell Cl., Ruis. | 66 | A6 |
| Campbell Cl., Twick. | 162 | A2 |
| Campbell Ct. N17 | 76 | C1 |
| Campbell Cft., Edg. | 54 | A5 |
| Campbell Gordon Way NW2 | 89 | H4 |
| Campbell Rd. E3 | 114 | A3 |
| Campbell Rd. E6 | 116 | B1 |
| Campbell Rd. E15 | 97 | F4 |
| *Trevelyan Rd.* | | |
| Campbell Rd. E17 | 77 | J4 |
| Campbell Rd. N17 | 76 | D1 |
| Campbell Rd. W7 | 104 | B7 |
| Campbell Rd., Croy. | 187 | H7 |
| Campbell Rd., E.Mol. | 180 | C3 |
| *Hampton Ct. Rd.* | | |
| Campbell Rd., Twick. | 162 | A2 |
| Campbell Wk. N1 | 110/111 | E1 |
| *Outram Pl.* | | |
| Campdale Rd. N7 | 92 | D3 |
| Campden Cres., Dag. | 100 | B4 |
| Campden Cres., Wem. | 87 | E2 |
| Campden Gro. W8 | 128 | D2 |
| Campden Hill W8 | 128 | D2 |
| Campden Hill Gdns. W8 | 128 | D1 |
| Campden Hill Gate W8 | 128 | D2 |
| *Duchess of Bedford's Wk.* | | |
| Campden Hill Pl. W11 | 128 | C1 |
| *Holland Pk. Av.* | | |
| Campden Hill Rd. W8 | 128 | D1 |
| Campden Hill Sq. W8 | 128 | C1 |
| Campden Ho. Cl. W8 | 128 | D2 |
| *Hornton St.* | | |

**Carlos Pl. W1 16 C6**
Carlos Pl. W1 110 A7
**Carlow St. NW1 9 F1**
Carlton Av. N14 42 D5
Carlton Av., Felt. 142 C6
Carlton Av., Har. 68 E5
Carlton Av., Hayes 121 H4
Carlton Av., S.Croy. 202 B7
Carlton Av. E., Wem. 87 H1
Carlton Av. W., Wem. 86 E2
Carlton Cl. NW3 90 D2
Carlton Cl., Borwd. 38 D4
Carlton Cl., Chess. 195 G6
Carlton Cl., Edg. 54 A5
Carlton Cl., Nthlt. 85 J5
*Whitton Av. W.*
Carlton Ct. SW9 151 H1
Carlton Ct., Ilf. 81 G3
Carlton Cres., Sutt. 198 B4
Carlton Dr. SW15 148 B5
Carlton Dr., Ilf. 81 G3
**Carlton Gdns. SW1 25 H2**
Carlton Gdns. SW1 130 D1
Carlton Gdns. W5 105 F6
Carlton Gro. SE15 152 E1
**Carlton Hill NW8 6 B2**
Carlton Hill NW8 109 E2
Carlton Ho., Felt. 141 J7
**Carlton Ho. Ter. SW1 25 H2**
Carlton Ho. Ter. SW1 130 D1
Carlton Pk. Av. SW20 183 J2
Carlton Rd. E11 97 F1
Carlton Rd. E12 98 A4
Carlton Rd. E17 77 H1
Carlton Rd. N4 75 G7
Carlton Rd. N11 58 A5
Carlton Rd. SW14 146 C3
Carlton Rd. W4 126 D2
Carlton Rd. W5 105 F7
Carlton Rd., Erith 139 H6
Carlton Rd., N.Mal. 182 E2
Carlton Rd., Sid. 175 J5
Carlton Rd., S.Croy. 202 A6
Carlton Rd., Walt. 178 B7
Carlton Rd., Well. 158 B3
Carlton Sq. E1 113 G4
*Argyle Rd.*
**Carlton St. SW1 17 H6**
Carlton Ter. E11 79 H5
Carlton Ter. N18 60 A3
Carlton Ter. SE26 171 F3
**Carlton Twr. Pl. SW1 24 A5**
Carlton Twr. Pl. SW1 129 J3
Carlton Vale NW6 108 E2
Carlton Vil. SW15 147 J5
*St. John's Av.*
Carlwell St. SW17 167 H5
Carlyle Av., Brom. 192 A3
Carlyle Av., Sthl. 103 F7
Carlyle Cl. N2 73 F6
Carlyle Cl. NW10 106 D1
Carlyle Cl., W.Mol. 179 H2
Carlyle Gdns., Sthl. 103 F7
Carlyle Ms. E1 113 G4
*Alderney Rd.*
Carlyle Pl. SW15 148 A4
Carlyle Rd. E12 98 B4
Carlyle Rd. SE28 118 B7
Carlyle Rd. W5 125 F5
Carlyle Rd., Croy. 202 D2
**Carlyle Sq. SW3 31 F4**
Carlyle Sq. SW3 129 G5
Carlyon Av., Har. 85 F4
Carlyon Cl., Wem. 105 H1
Carlyon Rd., Hayes 102 C6
Carlyon Rd., Wem. 105 H2
Carmalt Gdns. SW15 147 J4
Carmarthen Gdn. NW9 70/71 E6
*Snowdon Dr.*
**Carmel Ct. W8 22 A3**
Carmel Ct., Wem. 88 B2
Carmelite Cl., Har. 67 J1
Carmelite Rd., Har. 67 J1
**Carmelite St. EC4 19 F5**
Carmelite St. EC4 111 G7
Carmelite Wk., Har. 67 J1
Carmelite Way, Har. 67 J2
Carmen St. E14 114 B6
Carmichael Cl. SW11 149 G3
*Darien Rd.*
Carmichael Cl., Ruis. 84 A4
Carmichael Ms. SW18 149 G7
Carmichael Rd. SE25 188 D5
Carminia Rd. SW17 168 B2
**Carnaby St. W1 17 F4**
Carnaby St. W1 110 C6
Carnac St. SE27 170 A4
Carnanton Rd. E17 78 D1
Carnarvon Av., Enf. 44 C3
Carnarvon Dr., Hayes 121 F3
Carnarvon Rd. E10 78 C6
Carnarvon Rd. E15 97 F6
Carnarvon Rd. E18 79 F1
Carnarvon Rd., Barn. 40 B3
Carnation St. SE2 138 B5
Carnbrook Rd. SE3 156 A3
Carnecke Gdns. SE9 156 B5
Carnegie Cl., Surb. 195 J2
*Fullers Av.*
Carnegie Pl. SW19 166 A3
Carnegie St. N1 111 F1
Carnforth Cl., Epsom 196 B6
Carnforth Rd. SW16 168 D7
Carnie Lo. SW17 168 B3
*Manville Rd.*
Carnoustie Dr. N1 93 F7
Carnwath Rd. SW6 148 D3
Carol St. NW1 110 C1
Carolina Cl. E15 96 E5
Carolina Rd., Th.Hth. 187 H2
Caroline Cl. N10 74 B2
*Alexandra Pk. Rd.*
Caroline Cl. SW16 169 F4
**Caroline Cl. W2 14 B6**
Caroline Cl., Croy. 202 B4
*Brownlow Rd.*
Caroline Cl., Islw. 124 A7
Caroline Cl., West Dr. 120 A2
Caroline Ct., Stan. 52 D6
*The Chase*
Caroline Gdns. SE15 132 E7
Caroline Pl. SW11 150 A2
**Caroline Pl. W2 14 B5**
Caroline Pl. W2 109 E7
Caroline Pl., Hayes 121 H7
**Caroline Pl. Ms. W2 14 B6**
Caroline Rd. SW19 166 C7
Caroline St. E1 113 G6
**Caroline Ter. SW1 32 B2**
Caroline Ter. SW1 130 A4
Caroline Wk. W6 128 B6
Carpenders Av., Wat. 50 E3
Carpenders Pk., Wat. 51 E2
Carpenter Gdns. N21 59 H2
**Carpenter St. W1 16 D6**
Carpenters Ct., Twick. 162 B2
Carpenters Pl. SW4 150 D4
Carpenters Rd. E15 96 B6
Carr Gro. SE18 136 B4
Carr Rd. E17 77 J2
Carr Rd., Nthlt. 85 H6
Carr St. E14 113 H5
Carrara Wk. SW9 151 G4
*Somerleyton Rd.*
**Carriage Dr. E. SW11 32 B7**
Carriage Dr. E. SW11 130 A7
**Carriage Dr. N. SW11 32 C6**
Carriage Dr. N. SW11 130 A6
Carriage Dr. S. SW11 149 J1
Carriage Dr. W. SW11 129 J7
Carriage Ms., Ilf. 99 F2
Carriage Pl. N16 94 A3
Carrick Cl., Islw. 144 D3
Carrick Dr., Ilf. 81 F1
Carrick Gdns. N17 60 B7
*Flexmere Rd.*
Carrick Ms. SE8 134 A6
*Watergate St.*
Carrill Way, Belv. 138 D4
Carrington Av., Borwd. 38 B5
Carrington Av., Houns. 143 H5
Carrington Cl., Barn. 39 G5
Carrington Cl., Borwd. 38 C5
Carrington Cl., Croy. 189 H7
Carrington Cl., Kings.T. 164 C5
Carrington Gdns. E7 97 H4
*Woodford Rd.*
Carrington Rd., Rich. 146 A4
Carrington Sq., Har. 51 J7
**Carrington St. W1 24 D2**
Carrol Cl. NW5 92 B4
Carroll Cl. E15 97 F5
Carroll Hill, Loug. 48 C3
Carron Cl. E14 114 B6
Carronade Pl. SE28 137 F3
**Carroun Rd. SW8 34 C7**
Carroun Rd. SW8 131 F7
Carrow Rd., Dag. 100 B7
Carroway La., Grnf. 104 A3
*Cowgate Rd.*
Carrs La. N21 43 J5
Carshalton Gro., Sutt. 199 G4
Carshalton Pk. Rd., Cars. 199 J5
Carshalton Pl., Cars. 200 A4
Carshalton Rd., Cars. 199 F5
Carshalton Rd., Mitch. 186 A4
Carshalton Rd., Sutt. 199 F5
Carslake Rd. SW15 147 J6
Carson Rd. E16 115 G4
Carson Rd. SE21 170 A2
Carson Rd., Barn. 41 J4
Carstairs Rd. SE6 172 C3
Carston Cl. SE12 155 G5
Carswell Cl., Ilf. 80 A4
*Roding La. S.*
Carswell Rd. SE6 154 C7
Cart La. E4 46 D7
Carter Cl., Wall. 200 D7
Carter Ct. EC4 111 H6
*Carter La.*
**Carter La. EC4 19 H4**
Carter La. EC4 111 H6
**Carter Pl. SE17 36 A4**
Carter Pl. SE17 131 J5
Carter Rd. E13 115 H1
Carter Rd. SW19 167 G6
**Carter St. SE17 35 J5**
Carter St. SE17 131 J6
**Carteret St. SW1 25 H4**
Carteret St. SW1 130 D2
Carteret Way SE8 133 H4
Carterhatch La., Enf. 44 D2
Carterhatch Rd., Enf. 45 F2
Carters Cl., Wor.Pk. 198 A2
Carters Hill Cl. SE9 173 J1
Carters La. SE23 171 H2
Carters Yd. SW18 148 D5
*Wandsworth High St.*
Carthew Rd. W6 127 H3
Carthew Vil. W6 127 H3
**Carthusian St. EC1 19 J1**
Carthusian St. EC1 111 J5
Cartier Circle E14 134 B1
**Carting La. WC2 18 B6**
Carting La. WC2 111 E7
Cartmel Cl. N17 60/61 E7
*Heybourne Rd.*
Cartmel Gdns., Mord. 185 F5
Cartmel Rd., Bexh. 159 G1
**Carton St. W1 16 A3**
**Cartwright Gdns. WC1 10 A4**
Cartwright Gdns. WC1 110 E3
Cartwright Rd., Dag. 101 F7
**Cartwright St. E1 21 G5**
Cartwright St. E1 112 C7
Cartwright Way SW13 127 H7
Carver Cl. W4 126 C3
Carver Rd. SE24 151 J6
Carville Cres., Brent. 125 H5
Cary Rd. E11 97 E4
Carysfort Rd. N8 74 D5
Carysfort Rd. N16 94 A3
Cascade Av. N10 74 C4
Cascade Cl., Buck.H. 64 A2
*Cascade Rd.*
Cascade Rd., Buck.H. 64 A2
Casella Rd. SE14 133 G7
Casewick Rd. SE27 169 H4
Casimir Rd. E5 95 E3
Casino Av. SE24 151 J5
**Caspian St. SE5 36 B7**
Caspian St. SE5 132 A7
Caspian Wk. E16 116 A6
Caspian Wf. E3 114 B5
*Violet Rd.*
Cassandra Cl., Nthlt. 86 A4
Casselden Rd. NW10 88 D7
Cassidy Rd. SW6 128 D7
Cassilda Rd. SE2 138 A4
Cassilis Rd., Twick. 145 E5
Cassiobury Av., Felt. 141 J6
Cassiobury Rd. E17 77 G5
Cassis Ct., Loug. 49 F4
Cassland Rd. E9 95 F7
Cassland Rd., Th.Hth. 188 A4
Casslee Rd. SE6 153 J7
**Casson St. E1 21 H2**
Casson St. E1 112 D5
Castalia Sq. E14 134 C2
*Roserton St.*
Castalia St. E14 134 C2
*Plevna St.*
Castell Rd., Loug. 49 F1
**Castellain Rd. W9 6 C6**
Castellain Rd. W9 108 E4
Castellane Cl., Stan. 52 C7
*Daventer Dr.*
Castello Av. SW15 147 J5
Castelnau SW13 127 H6
Castelnau Gdns. SW13 127 H6
*Arundel Ter.*
Castelnau Pl. SW13 127 H6
*Castelnau*
Castelnau Row SW13 127 H6
*Lonsdale Rd.*
Casterbridge NW6 109 E1
Casterbridge Rd. SE3 155 G3
Casterton St. E8 94/95 E6
*Wilton Way*
Castile Rd. SE18 136 D4
Castillon Rd. SE6 172 E2
Castlands Rd. SE6 171 J2
Castle Av. E4 62 D5
**Castle Baynard St. EC4 19 H5**
Castle Cl. E9 95 H5
*Swinnerton St.*
Castle Cl. SW19 166 A3
Castle Cl. W3 126 B2
*Park Rd. E.*
Castle Cl., Brom. 190 E3
**Castle Ct. EC3 20 C4**
Castle Ct. SE26 171 H4
*Champion Rd.*
Castle Dr., Ilf. 80 B6
**Castle La. SW1 25 G5**
Castle La. SW1 130 C3
Castle Ms. N12 57 F5
*Castle Rd.*
Castle Ms. NW1 92 B6
*Castle Rd.*
Castle Par., Epsom 197 G7
*Ewell Bypass*
Castle Pl. NW1 92 B6
Castle Pl. W4 126/127 E4
*Windmill Rd.*
Castle Pt. E13 115 J2
Castle Rd. N12 57 F5
Castle Rd. NW1 92 B6
Castle Rd., Dag. 118 B1
Castle Rd., Enf. 45 H1
Castle Rd., Islw. 144 C2
Castle Rd., Nthlt. 85 H6
Castle Rd., Sthl. 123 F3
Castle St. E6 115 J2
Castle St., Kings.T. 181 H2
Castle Wk., Sun. 178 C3
*Elizabeth Gdns.*
Castle Way SW19 166 A3
Castle Way, Felt. 160 C4
Castle Yd. N6 74 A7
*North Rd.*
**Castle Yd. SE1 27 H1**
Castle Yd., Rich. 145 G5
*Hill St.*
Castlebar Hill W5 105 E5
Castlebar Ms. W5 105 F5
Castlebar Pk. W5 105 E5
Castlebar Rd. W5 105 F5
**Castlebrook Cl. SE11 35 G1**
Castlebrook Cl. SE11 131 H4
Castlecombe Dr. SW19 148 A7
Castlecombe Rd. SE9 174 B4
Castledine Rd. SE20 170 E7
Castleford Av. SE9 174 E1
Castleford Cl. N17 60 C6
Castlegate, Rich. 145 J3
Castlehaven Rd. NW1 92 B7
Castleleigh Ct., Enf. 44 A5
Castlemaine Av., S.Croy. 202 C5
Castlemaine Twr. SW11 149 J1
**Castlereagh St. W1 15 J3**
Castleton Av., Wem. 87 H4
Castleton Cl., Croy. 189 H6
Castleton Gdns., Wem. 87 H3
Castleton Rd. E17 78 D2
Castleton Rd. SE9 174 A4
Castleton Rd., Ilf. 100 A1
Castleton Rd., Mitch. 186 D4
Castleton Rd., Ruis. 84 D1
Castletown Rd. W14 128 B5
Castleview Cl. N4 93 J1
Castleview Gdns., Ilf. 80 B6
Castlewood Dr. SE9 156 C2
Castlewood Rd. N15 76 D6
Castlewood Rd. N16 76 D7
Castlewood Rd., Barn. 41 G3
Castor La. E14 114 B7
Cat Hill, Barn. 41 H6
Caterham Av., Ilf. 80 C2
Caterham Rd. SE13 154 C3
**Catesby St. SE17 36 C2**
Catesby St. SE17 132 A4
Catford Bdy. SE6 154 B7
Catford Hill SE6 171 J2
Catford Ms. SE6 154 B7
*Holbeach Rd.*
Catford Rd. SE6 154 A7
Cathall Rd. E11 96 D3
Cathay St. SE16 133 E2
Cathay Wk., Nthlt. 103 G2
*Brabazon Rd.*

Cathcart Dr., Orp. 207 H2
Cathcart Hill N19 92 C3
**Cathcart Rd. SW10** 30 B5
Cathcart Rd. SW10 129 F6
Cathcart St. NW5 92 B6
**Cathedral Piazza SW1** 25 F6
**Cathedral Pl. EC4** 19 J3
**Cathedral St. SE1** 28 B1
Cathedral St. SE1 132 A1
Catherall Rd. N5 93 J3
Catherine Cl., Loug. 48 C6
  *Roding Gdns.*
Catherine St. N14 42 C5
  *Conisbee Ct.*
Catherine Dr., Rich. 145 H4
Catherine Gdns., 144 A4
  Houns.
**Catherine Griffiths Ct. EC1** 11 F5
**Catherine Gro. SE10** 154 B1
**Catherine Pl. SW1** 25 F5
Catherine Rd., Surb. 181 G5
**Catherine St. WC2** 18 C5
Catherine St. WC2 111 F7
**Catherine Wheel All. E1** 20 E2
Catherine Wheel Rd., 125 G7
  Brent.
**Catherine Wheel Yd. SW1** 25 F2
Catherine's Cl., 120 A3
  West Dr.
  *Money La.*
Cathles Rd. SW12 150 B6
Cathnor Rd. W12 127 H2
Catlin St. SE16 37 J3
Catlin St. SE16 132 D5
Catling Cl. SE23 171 F3
Catlins La., Pnr. 66 B3
Cato Rd. SW4 150 D3
**Cato St. W1** 15 H2
Cato St. W1 109 H5
Cator La., Beck. 189 J2
Cator Rd. SE26 171 G6
Cator St., Cars. 199 J3
**Cator St. SE15** 37 F6
Cator St. SE15 132 C6
Catterick Cl. N11 58 A6
Cattistock Rd. SE9 174 B5
Cattley Cl., Barn. 40 B4
  *Wood St.*
**Catton St. WC1** 18 C2
Catton St. WC1 111 F5
Caulfield Rd. E6 98 C7
Caulfield Rd. SE15 153 E2
Causeway, The N2 73 H4
Causeway, The SW18 148 E4
Causeway, The SW19 166 A5
Causeway, The, Cars. 200 A3
Causeway, The, 195 H4
  Chess.
Causeway, The, Esher 194 C7
Causeway, The, Felt. 142 A4
Causeway, The, 162 C6
  Tedd.
  *Broad St.*
Causewayare Rd. N9 45 E7
Causton Rd. N6 74 B7
**Causton St. SW1** 33 J2
Causton St. SW1 130 D4
Cautley Av. SW4 150 C5
Cavalier Cl., Rom. 82 D4
Cavalry Barracks, 142 D3
  Houns.
Cavalry Cres., Houns. 142 D4
Cavalry Gdns. SW15 148 C5
  *Upper Richmond Rd.*
**Cavaye Pl. SW10** 30 D4
Cave Rd. E13 115 H2
Cave Rd., Rich. 163 F4
**Cave St. N1** 10 D1
Cavell Dr., Enf. 43 G2
Cavell Rd. N17 60 A7
Cavell St. E1 113 E5
**Cavendish Av. N3** 72 D2
**Cavendish Av. NW8** 7 F2
Cavendish Av. NW8 109 G2
Cavendish Av. W13 104 D5
Cavendish Av., Erith 139 J6
Cavendish Av., Har. 86 A4
Cavendish Av., 183 H5
  N.Mal.
Cavendish Av., Ruis. 84 B5
Cavendish Av., Sid. 158 A7
Cavendish Av., Well. 157 J3
Cavendish Av., 79 H1
  Wdf.Grn.
Cavendish Cl. N18 60/61 E5
  *Cavendish Rd.*
Cavendish Cl. NW6 90 C7
  *Cavendish Rd.*
**Cavendish Cl. NW8** 7 F3

Cavendish Cl. NW8 109 G3
**Cavendish Ct. EC3** 20 E3
Cavendish Cres., 38 A4
  Borwd.
Cavendish Dr. E11 96 D1
Cavendish Dr., Edg. 53 J6
Cavendish Dr., Esher 194 B5
Cavendish Gdns., 99 H5
  Bark.
Cavendish Gdns., Ilf. 98 D1
Cavendish Gdns., 83 E5
  Rom.
**Cavendish Ms. N. W1** 16 E1
**Cavendish Ms. S. W1** 16 E2
Cavendish Par., 142/143 E2
  Houns.
  *Bath Rd.*
**Cavendish Pl. W1** 16 E3
Cavendish Pl. W1 110 B6
Cavendish Rd. E4 62 C6
Cavendish Rd. N4 75 G6
Cavendish Rd. N18 60 E5
Cavendish Rd. NW6 90 B7
Cavendish Rd. SW12 150 B6
Cavendish Rd. SW19 167 G7
Cavendish Rd. W4 146 C1
Cavendish Rd., Barn. 39 J3
Cavendish Rd., Croy. 201 H1
Cavendish Rd., 183 F5
  N.Mal.
Cavendish Rd., Sutt. 199 F7
Cavendish Sq. W1 16 E3
Cavendish Sq. W1 110 B6
Cavendish St. N1 112 A2
**Cavendish St. N1** 12 B2
  *High St.*
Cavendish Way, 204 B1
  W.Wick.
Cavenham Gdns., Ilf. 99 G3
Caverleigh Way, 197 G1
  Wor.Pk.
Caversham Av. N13 59 G3
Caversham Av., 198 B2
  Sutt.
**Caversham Flats SW3** 31 J5
Caversham Rd. N15 75 J4
Caversham Rd. NW5 92 C6
Caversham Rd., 181 J2
  Kings.T.
**Caversham St. SW3** 31 J5
Caversham St. SW3 129 J6
Caverswall St. W12 107 J6
Caveside Cl., Chis. 192 D1
Cawdor Cres. W7 124 D4
Cawnpore St. SE19 170 B5
Caxton Gro. E3 114 A3
Caxton Ms., Brent. 125 G6
  *The Butts*
Caxton Rd. N22 75 F2
Caxton Rd. SW19 167 F5
Caxton Rd. W12 128 A2
Caxton Rd., Sthl. 122 D3
**Caxton St. SW1** 25 G5
Caxton St. SW1 130 C3
Caxton St. N. E16 115 F7
  *Victoria Dock Rd.*
Caygill Cl., Brom. 191 F4
Cayley Cl., Wall. 200 E7
Cayley Rd., Sthl. 123 H3
  *McNair Rd.*
**Cayton Pl. EC1** 12 B4
Cayton Rd., Grnf. 104 B2
**Cayton St. EC1** 12 B4
Cazenove Pl. SW1 25 J6
Cazenove Rd. E17 78 A1
Cazenove Rd. N16 94 C2
Cearns Ho. E6 116 A1
Cecil Av., Bark. 99 G7
Cecil Av., Enf. 44 C4
Cecil Av., Wem. 87 J5
Cecil Cl. W5 105 G5
  *Helena Rd.*
Cecil Cl., Chess. 195 G4
**Cecil Ct. WC2** 17 J6
Cecil Ct., Barn. 40 A3
Cecil Pk., Pnr. 67 E4
Cecil Pl., Mitch. 185 J5
Cecil Rd. E11 97 E3
Cecil Rd. E13 115 G1
Cecil Rd. E17 78 A1
Cecil Rd. N10 74 B2
Cecil Rd. N14 58 C1
Cecil Rd. NW9 70 E3
Cecil Rd. NW10 106 E1
Cecil Rd. SW19 166 E7
Cecil Rd. W3 106 C5
Cecil Rd., Croy. 187 F6
Cecil Rd., Enf. 44 A4
Cecil Rd., Har. 68 B3
Cecil Rd., Houns. 143 J2
Cecil Rd., Ilf. 98 E4
Cecil Rd., Rom. 82 D7
Cecil Rd., Sutt. 198 C6

Cecil Way, Brom. 205 G1
Cecile Pk. N8 75 E6
Cecilia Cl. N2 73 F3
Cecilia Rd. E8 94 D5
Cedar Av., Barn. 41 H7
Cedar Av., Enf. 45 F2
Cedar Av., Hayes 102 A6
Cedar Av., Rom. 82 E5
Cedar Av., Ruis. 84 C6
Cedar Av., Sid. 158 A7
Cedar Av., Twick. 143 H6
Cedar Av., West Dr. 120 C1
Cedar Cl. SE21 169 J1
Cedar Cl. SW15 164 D4
Cedar Cl., Borwd. 38 B4
Cedar Cl., Brom. 206 B3
Cedar Cl., Buck.H. 64 A2
Cedar Cl., Cars. 199 J6
Cedar Cl., E.Mol. 180 B4
  *Cedar Rd.*
Cedar Cl., Rom. 83 J4
Cedar Copse, Brom. 192 C2
Cedar Ct. E8 94 C7
Cedar Ct. N1 93 J7
  *Essex Rd.*
Cedar Ct. SE9 156 B6
Cedar Ct. SW19 166 A3
Cedar Cres., Brom. 206 B3
Cedar Dr. N2 73 H4
Cedar Dr., Loug. 49 E2
Cedar Dr., Pnr. 51 G6
Cedar Gdns., Sutt. 199 F6
Cedar Gro. W5 125 H3
Cedar Gro., Bex. 158 C6
Cedar Gro., Sthl. 103 G5
Cedar Hts., Rich. 163 H1
Cedar Ho., Croy. 204 B6
Cedar Lawn Av., 40 B5
  Barn.
Cedar Mt. SE9 174 A1
Cedar Pk., Chig. 64/65 E4
  *High Rd.*
Cedar Pk. Gdns., 82 D7
  Rom.
Cedar Pl. SE7 135 J5
  *Floyd Rd.*
Cedar Ri. N14 42 A7
Cedar Rd. N17 76 C1
Cedar Rd. NW2 89 J4
Cedar Rd., Brom. 191 J2
Cedar Rd., Croy. 202 B2
Cedar Rd., E.Mol. 180 B4
Cedar Rd., Houns. 142 C2
Cedar Rd., Rom. 83 J4
Cedar Rd., Sutt. 199 F6
Cedar Rd., Tedd. 162 D5
Cedar Ter., Rich. 145 J4
Cedar Tree Gro. SE27 169 H5
Cedar Vista, Rich. 145 H1
  *Kew Rd.*
Cedar Wk., Esher 194 C6
Cedar Way NW1 92 D7
Cedarcroft Rd., 195 J4
  Chess.
Cedarhurst, 172/173 E7
  Brom.
  *Elstree Hill*
Cedarhurst Dr. SE9 155 J5
Cedarne Rd. SW6 128 E7
Cedars, The E15 115 F1
  *Portway*
Cedars, The W13 105 F6
  *Heronsforde*
Cedars, The, Buck.H. 63 G1
Cedars, The, Tedd. 162 C6
  *Adelaide Rd.*
Cedars Av. E17 78 A5
Cedars Av., Mitch. 186 A4
Cedars Cl. NW4 72 A3
  *Church St.*
Cedars Ct. N9 60 B2
Cedars Ms. SW4 150 B4
  *Cedars Rd.*
Cedars Rd. E15 97 E6
Cedars Rd. N9 60 D2
  *Church St.*
Cedars Rd. N21 59 H2
Cedars Rd. SW4 150 B3
Cedars Rd. SW13 147 F2
Cedars Rd. W4 126 C5
Cedars Rd., Beck. 189 H2
Cedars Rd., Croy. 201 E3
Cedars Rd., Kings.T. 181 F1
Cedars Rd., Mord. 184 D4
Cedarville Gdns. 169 F6
  SW16
Cedra Ct. N16 94 D1
Cedric Rd. SE9 175 F3
Celandine Cl. E14 114 A5
Celandine Dr. E8 94 C7
  *Richmond Rd.*
Celandine Dr. SE28 138 B1
Celandine Way E15 115 E3

**Celbridge Ms. W2** 14 B3
Celestial Gdns. SE13 154 D4
Celia Rd. N19 92 C4
Celtic Av., Brom. 190 E3
Celtic St. E14 114 B5
Cemetery La. SE7 136 B6
Cemetery Rd. E7 97 F4
Cemetery Rd. N17 60 B7
Cemetery Rd. SE2 138 B7
Cenacle Cl. NW3 90 D3
**Centaur St. SE1** 26 D5
Centaur St. SE1 131 F3
Centaurs Business 124 D6
  Cen., Islw.
Centenary Est., Enf. 45 J4
Centenary Rd., Enf. 45 J4
Centenary Wk., Loug. 47 H3
Central Av. E11 96 D2
Central Av. N2 73 G2
Central Av. N9 60 B3
Central Av. SW11 129 J7
Central Av., Enf. 44 E2
Central Av., Hayes 102 A7
Central Av., Houns. 143 H4
Central Av., Pnr. 67 F6
Central Av., Wall. 201 E5
Central Av., Well. 157 J2
Central Av., W.Mol. 179 F4
Central Circ. NW4 71 H5
  *Hendon Way*
Central Gdns., 184/185 E5
  Mord.
  *Central Rd.*
Central Hill SE19 170 A5
Central Mkts. EC1 19 H2
Central Mkts. EC1 111 H5
Central Par., Felt. 142 C7
Central Par., Grnf. 104 D3
Central Par., Houns. 123 G7
  *Heston Rd.*
Central Par., Surb. 181 H6
  *St. Mark's Hill*
Central Pk. Av., Dag. 101 H3
Central Pk. Est., 142 D5
  Houns.
Central Pk. Rd. E6 116 A2
Central Pl. SE25 188/189 E4
  *Portland Rd.*
Central Rd., Mord. 184 D5
Central Rd., Wem. 86 E5
Central Rd., Wor.Pk. 197 G2
Central Sch. 146 C3
  Footpath NW10
Central Sq. NW11 72 E6
Central Sq., Wem. 87 H5
  *Station Gro.*
Central Sq., W.Mol. 179 F4
**Central St. EC1** 11 J4
Central St. EC1 111 J3
Central Way NW10 106 C2
Central Way SE28 118 A7
Central Way, Cars. 199 H7
Central Way, Felt. 142 B5
Centre, The, Felt. 160 A2
Centre Av. W3 126 D1
Centre Av. W10 107 J3
  *Harrow Rd.*
Centre Common Rd., 175 F6
  Chis.
Centre Rd. E7 97 G2
Centre Rd. E11 97 G2
Centre Rd., Dag. 119 H2
Centre St. E2 113 E2
Centre Way E17 62 C7
Centre Way N9 61 F2
Centreway, Ilf. 99 F2
Centric Cl. NW1 110 B1
  *Oval Rd.*
Centurion Cl. N7 93 F7
Centurion Ct., Wall. 200 B2
  *Wandle Rd.*
Centurion La. E3 113 J2
  *Libra Rd.*
Centurion Way, Erith 139 G3
Century Cl. NW4 72 A5
Century Ms. E5 95 F4
  *Lower Clapton Rd.*
Century Rd. E17 77 H3
Cephas Av. E1 113 F4
Cephas St. E1 113 F4
Ceres Rd. SE18 137 J4
Cerise Rd. SE15 152 D1
Cerne Cl., Hayes 102 D7
Cerne Rd., Mord. 185 F6
**Cerney Ms. W2** 15 E5
**Cervantes Ct. W2** 14 B4
  *Inverness Ter.*
Cester St. E2 112 D1
  *Whiston Rd.*
Ceylon Rd. W14 128 A3
Chadacre Av., Ilf. 80 C3
Chadacre Rd., Epsom 197 H6
Chadbourn St. E14 114 B5
Chadd Dr., Brom. 192 B3
Chadd Grn. E13 115 G1
Chadview Ct., Rom. 82 D7

Chadville Gdns., Rom. 82 D5
Chadway, Dag. 100 C1
Chadwell Av., Rom. 82 B7
Chadwell Heath La., Rom. 82 B5
**Chadwell St. EC1 11 F3**
Chadwell St. EC1 111 G3
Chadwick Av. E4 62 D4
Chadwick Av. N21 43 F5
Chadwick Av. SW19 166 D6
Chadwick Cl. SW15 147 F7
Chadwick Cl. W7 104 C5
*Westcott Cres.*
Chadwick Cl., Tedd. 162 D6
Chadwick Pl., Surb. 181 F7
Chadwick Rd. E11 79 E7
Chadwick Rd. NW10 107 F1
Chadwick Rd. SE15 152 C2
Chadwick Rd., Ilf. 99 E3
**Chadwick St. SW1 25 J6**
Chadwick St. SW1 130 D3
Chadwick Way SE28 118 D7
Chadwin Rd. E13 115 H5
Chadworth Way, Esher 194 A5
Chaffinch Av., Croy. 189 G6
Chaffinch Cl. N9 61 G1
Chaffinch Cl., Croy. 189 G6
Chaffinch Cl., Surb. 196 A3
Chaffinch Rd., Beck. 189 H1
Chafford Way, Rom. 82 C4
**Chagford St. NW1 7 J6**
Chagford St. NW1 109 J4
Chailey Av., Enf. 44 C2
Chailey Cl., Houns. 142 D1
*Springwell Rd.*
Chailey St. E5 95 F3
Chalbury Wk. N1 111 F2
Chalcombe Rd. SE2 138 B3
Chalcot Cl., Sutt. 198 D7
Chalcot Cres. NW1 109 J1
Chalcot Gdns. NW3 91 J6
Chalcot Ms. SW16 168 E3
Chalcot Rd. NW1 92 A7
Chalcot Sq. NW1 92 A7
Chalcott Gdns., Surb. 195 F1
Chalcroft Rd. SE13 154 E5
Chaldon Path, Th.Hth. 187 H4
Chaldon Rd. SW6 128 B7
Chale Rd. SW2 150 E6
Chalet Est. NW7 55 G4
Chalfont Av., Wem. 88 B6
Chalfont Ct. NW9 71 F3
Chalfont Grn. N9 60 B3
Chalfont Rd. N9 60 C3
Chalfont Rd. SE25 188 C3
Chalfont Rd., Hayes 122 A2
Chalfont Wk., Pnr. 66 C2
*Willows Cl.*
Chalfont Way W13 124 E3
Chalford Cl., W.Mol. 179 G4
Chalford Rd. SE21 170 A4
Chalford Wk., Wdf.Grn. 80 A1
Chalgrove Av., Mord. 184 D5
Chalgrove Cres., Ilf. 80 D2
Chalgrove Gdns. N3 72 B3
Chalgrove Rd. N17 76 E1
Chalgrove Rd., Sutt. 199 G7
Chalice Cl., Wall. 200 D6
*Lavender Vale*
Chalk Fm. Rd. NW1 92 A7
Chalk Hill Rd. W6 128 A4
*Shortlands*
Chalk La., Barn. 41 J4
Chalk Pit Way, Sutt. 199 F5
Chalk Rd. E13 115 J5
Chalkenden Cl. SE20 170 E7
Chalkhill Rd., Wem. 88 B3
Chalklands, Wem. 88 C3
Chalkley Cl., Mitch. 185 J2
Chalkmill Rd., Enf. 44 E3
Chalkstone Cl., Well. 158 A1
Chalkwell Pk. Av., Enf. 44 B4
Challice Way SW2 169 F1
Challin St. SE20 189 F1
Challis Rd., Brent. 125 G5
Challoner Cl. N2 73 G2
Challoner Cres. W14 128 C5
*Challoner St.*
Challoner St. W14 128 C5
Challoners Cl., E.Mol. 180 A4
**Chalmers Wk. SE17 35 H6**
Chalmers Way, Felt. 142 A5
**Chaloner Ct. SE1 28 B3**
Chalsey Rd. SE4 153 J4
Chalton Dr. N2 73 F6
**Chalton St. NW1 9 J3**
Chalton St. NW1 110 D2
**Chamber St. E1 21 G5**
Chamber St. E1 112 C7
Chamberlain Cl. SE28 137 G3
*Broadwater Rd.*
Chamberlain Cotts. SE5 152 A1
*Camberwell Gro.*
Chamberlain Cres., W.Wick. 204 B1
Chamberlain Gdns., Houns. 143 J1
*Gresham Rd.*
Chamberlain La., Pnr. 66 A4
Chamberlain Pl. E17 77 H3
Chamberlain Rd. N2 73 F2
Chamberlain Rd. N9 60 D3
Chamberlain Rd. W13 124 D2
*Midhurst Rd.*
Chamberlain St. NW1 91 J7
*Regents Pk. Rd.*
Chamberlain Wk., Felt. 160/161 E4
*Burgess Cl.*
Chamberlain Way, Pnr. 66 B3
Chamberlain Way, Surb. 181 H7
Chamberlayne Rd. NW10 108 A3
Chambers Gdns. N2 73 G1
Chambers La. NW10 89 H7
Chambers Pl., S.Croy. 202 A7
*Rolleston Rd.*
Chambers Rd. N7 92 E4
**Chambers St. SE16 29 H3**
Chambers St. SE16 132 D2
**Chambord St. E2 13 G4**
Chambord St. E2 112 C3
Champion Cres. SE26 171 H4
Champion Gro. SE5 152 A3
Champion Hill SE5 152 A3
Champion Hill Est. SE5 152 B3
Champion Pk. SE5 152 A2
Champion Pk. Est. SE5 152 A3
*Denmark Hill*
Champion Rd. SE26 171 H4
Champness Cl. SE27 170 A4
*Rommany Rd.*
Champneys Cl., Sutt. 198 C7
**Chance St. E1 13 F5**
Chance St. E1 112 C4
**Chance St. E2 13 F5**
Chance St. E2 112 C4
**Chancel St. SE1 27 G1**
Chancel St. SE1 131 H1
Chancellor Gro. SE21 169 J2
Chancellor Pas. E14 134 A1
*South Colonnade*
Chancellor Pl. NW9 71 F2
Chancellors Rd. W6 127 J5
Chancellors St. W6 127 J5
Chancelot Rd. SE2 138 B4
**Chancery La. WC2 18 E3**
Chancery La. WC2 111 G5
Chancery La., Beck. 190 B2
Chancery Ms. SW17 167 H2
*Beechcroft Rd.*
Chanctonbury Cl. SE9 175 E3
Chanctonbury Gdns., Sutt. 198 E7
Chanctonbury Way N12 56 C4
Chandler Av. E16 115 G5
Chandler Cl., Hmptn. 179 G1
Chandler Rd., Loug. 49 E1
Chandler St. E1 132/133 E1
*Wapping La.*
Chandler Way SE15 132 C7
Chandlers Cl., Felt. 141 J7
Chandlers Ms. E14 134 A2
Chandlers Way SW2 151 G7
Chandos Av. E17 78 A2
Chandos Av. N14 58 C3
Chandos Av. N20 57 F1
Chandos Av. W5 125 F4
Chandos Cl., Buck.H. 63 H2
Chandos Cres., Edg. 53 J7
Chandos Par., Edg. 53 J7
*Chandos Cres.*
**Chandos Pl. WC2 18 A6**
Chandos Pl. WC2 110 E7
Chandos Rd. E15 96 D5
Chandos Rd. N2 73 G2
Chandos Rd. N17 76 B2
Chandos Rd. NW2 89 J5
Chandos Rd. NW10 106 E4
Chandos Rd., Har. 67 J5
Chandos Rd., Pnr. 66 C7
**Chandos St. W1 16 E2**
Chandos St. W1 110 B5
Chandos Way NW11 90 E1
**Change All. EC3 20 C4**
Channel Cl., Houns. 143 G1
Channel Gate Rd. NW10 107 F3
*Old Oak La.*
Channelsea Rd. E15 114 D1
Chant Sq. E15 96 D7
Chant St. E15 96 D7
Chantress Cl., Dag. 119 J1
Chantrey Rd. SW9 151 F3
Chantry Cl. NW7 39 F6
*Hendon Wd. La.*
Chantry Cl., Har. 69 J5
Chantry Cl., Sid. 176/177 E5
*Ellenborough Rd.*
Chantry La., Brom. 192 A5
*Bromley Common*
Chantry Pl., Har. 67 H1
Chantry Pt. W9 108 C4
Chantry Rd., Chess. 195 J5
Chantry Rd., Har. 67 H1
Chantry St. N1 111 H1
Chantry Way, Mitch. 185 G3
Chapel Ct. N2 73 H3
**Chapel Ct. SE1 28 B3**
Chapel Fm. Rd. SE9 174 C3
Chapel Ho. St. E14 134 B5
Chapel La., Chig. 65 J3
Chapel La., Pnr. 66 D3
Chapel La., Rom. 82 D7
**Chapel Mkt. N1 10 E1**
Chapel Mkt. N1 111 G2
Chapel Path E11 79 G6
**Chapel Pl. EC2 12 D4**
**Chapel Pl. N1 11 F1**
Chapel Pl. N17 60 C7
*White Hart La.*
**Chapel Pl. W1 16 D4**
Chapel Pl. W1 110 B6
Chapel Rd. SE27 169 H4
Chapel Rd. W13 125 E1
Chapel Rd., Bexh. 159 G4
Chapel Rd., Houns. 143 H3
Chapel Rd., Ilf. 98 D3
Chapel Rd., Twick. 145 E7
**Chapel Side W2 14 A5**
Chapel Side W2 108 E7
Chapel Stones N17 76 C1
**Chapel St. NW1 15 G2**
Chapel St. NW1 109 H5
**Chapel St. SW1 24 C5**
Chapel St. SW1 130 A3
Chapel St., Enf. 43 J3
Chapel Ter., Loug. 48 B4
*Forest Rd.*
Chapel Vw., S.Croy. 203 E6
Chapel Wk. NW4 71 H4
Chapel Wk., Croy. 201 J2
*Wellesley Rd.*
Chapel Way N7 93 F3
*Sussex Way*
Chapel Yd. SW18 148 D5
*Wandsworth High St.*
Chapelmount Rd., Wdf.Grn. 64 C6
**Chaplin Cl. SE1 27 F3**
Chaplin Cl. SE1 131 G2
Chaplin Rd. E15 115 E2
Chaplin Rd. N17 76 C3
Chaplin Rd. NW2 89 G6
Chaplin Rd., Dag. 101 E7
Chaplin Rd., Wem. 87 F6
Chaplin Sq. N12 57 G7
Chapman Cl., West Dr. 120 C3
Chapman Cres., Har. 69 H5
Chapman Pk. Ind. Est. NW10 89 F6
Chapman Rd. E9 95 J6
Chapman Rd., Belv. 139 G5
Chapman Rd., Croy. 201 G1
Chapman Sq. SW19 166 A2
Chapman St. E1 112 E7
Chapman's La. SE2 138 C4
Chapman's La., Belv. 138 D4
**Chapone Pl. W1 17 H4**
Chapter Cl. W4 126 C3
*Beaumont Rd.*
**Chapter Ho. Ct. EC4 19 J4**
Chapter Rd. NW2 89 G5
**Chapter Rd. SE17 35 H4**
Chapter Rd. SE17 131 H5
**Chapter St. SW1 33 H2**
Chapter St. SW1 130 D4
Chapter Way, Hmptn. 161 G4
Chara Pl. W4 126 D6
Charcroft Gdns., Enf. 45 G4
Chardin Rd. W4 126/127 E4
*Elliott Rd.*
Chardmore Rd. N16 94 D1
Chardwell Cl. E6 116 B6
*Northumberland Rd.*
Charecroft Way W12 128 A2
**Charfield Ct. W9 6 A6**
Charford Rd. E16 115 G5
Chargeable La. E13 115 F4
Chargeable St. E16 115 F4
Chargrove Cl. SE16 133 G2
*Marlow Way*
Charing Cl., Orp. 207 J4
**Charing Cross SW1 26 A1**
**Charing Cross Rd. WC2 17 J3**
Charing Cross Rd. WC2 110 D6
**Charlbert St. NW8 7 G1**
Charlbert St. NW8 109 H2
Charlbury Av., Stan. 53 G5
Charlbury Gdns., Ilf. 99 J2
Charlbury Gro. W5 105 F6
Charldane Rd. SE9 174 E3
Charlecote Gro. SE26 171 E3
Charlecote Rd., Dag. 100 E3
Charlemont Rd. E6 116 C3
Charles Babbage Cl., Chess. 195 G6
*Ashlyns Way*
Charles Barry Cl. SW4 150 C3
Charles Burton Ct. E5 95 H5
*Ashenden Rd.*
Charles Cl., Sid. 176 B4
Charles Cobb Gdns., Croy. 201 G5
Charles Coveney Rd. SE15 152 C1
Charles Cres., Har. 68 A7
Charles Dickens Ho. E2 112 E3
Charles Flemwell Ms. E16 135 G1
*Hanameel St.*
Charles Grinling Wk. SE18 136 D4
Charles Ho. N17 60 C7
*Love La.*
**Charles La. NW8 7 F2**
**Charles Pl. NW1 9 G4**
Charles Rd. E7 97 J7
*Lens Rd.*
Charles Rd. SW19 184 D1
Charles Rd. W13 104 D5
Charles Rd., Rom. 82 D7
**Charles II St. SW1 25 H1**
Charles II St. SW1 130 D1
Charles Sevright Dr. NW7 56 A5
**Charles Sq. N1 12 C4**
Charles Sq. N1 112 A3
Charles Sq. Est. N1 112 A3
*Pitfield St.*
Charles St. E16 136 A1
Charles St. SW13 147 E2
**Charles St. W1 24 D1**
Charles St. W1 130 B1
Charles St., Croy. 201 J3
Charles St., Enf. 44 C5
Charles St., Houns. 143 F2
Charles Whincup Rd. E16 135 H1
Charlesfield SE9 173 J3
Charleston Cl., Felt. 160 A3
*Vineyard Rd.*
**Charleston St. SE17 36 A2**
Charleston St. SE17 131 J4
Charleville Circ. SE26 170 D5
Charleville Rd. W14 128 B5
Charlieville Rd., Erith 139 J7
*Northumberland Pk.*
Charlmont Rd. SW17 167 J6
Charlotte Cl., Bexh. 158 E5
Charlotte Cl., Ilf. 80 C1
*Fullwell Av.*
Charlotte Despard Av. SW11 150 A1
**Charlotte Ms. W1 17 G1**
Charlotte Ms. W10 108 A6
Charlotte Ms. W14 128 B4
*Munden St.*
Charlotte Pl. NW9 70 C5
*Uphill Dr.*
**Charlotte Pl. SW1 33 F2**
**Charlotte Pl. W1 17 G2**
**Charlotte Rd. EC2 12 D5**
Charlotte Rd. EC2 112 B4
Charlotte Rd. SW13 147 F1
Charlotte Rd., Dag. 101 H6
Charlotte Rd., Wall. 200 C6
Charlotte Row SW4 150 C3
*North St.*
Charlotte Sq., Rich. 145 J6
*Greville Rd.*
**Charlotte St. W1 17 G2**

| Name | Page | Grid |
|---|---|---|
| Child's Pl. SW5 | 128 | D4 |
| Child's St. SW5 | 128 | D4 |
| Child's Wk. SW5 | 128 | D4 |
| *Child's Pl.* | | |
| Childs Way NW11 | 72 | C5 |
| Chilham Cl., Bex. | 159 | F7 |
| Chilham Cl., Grnf. | 104 | D2 |
| Chilham Rd. SE9 | 174 | B4 |
| Chilham Way, Brom. | 191 | G7 |
| Chillerton Rd. SW17 | 168 | A5 |
| Chillingworth Gdns., Twick. | 162 | C3 |
| *Tower Rd.* | | |
| Chillingworth Rd. N7 | 93 | G5 |
| *Liverpool Rd.* | | |
| Chilmark Gdns., N.Mal. | 183 | F7 |
| Chilmark Rd. SW16 | 186 | D2 |
| Chiltern Av., Twick. | 161 | G1 |
| Chiltern Cl., Croy. | 202 | B3 |
| Chiltern Cl., Wor.Pk. | 197 | J2 |
| *Cotswold Way* | | |
| Chiltern Dene, Enf. | 43 | F4 |
| Chiltern Dr., Surb. | 182 | B5 |
| Chiltern Gdns. NW2 | 90 | A3 |
| Chiltern Gdns., Brom. | 191 | F4 |
| Chiltern Rd. E3 | 114 | A4 |
| Chiltern Rd., Ilf. | 81 | H4 |
| Chiltern Rd., Pnr. | 66 | C5 |
| **Chiltern St. W1** | **16** | **B1** |
| Chiltern St. W1 | 110 | A5 |
| Chiltern Way, Wdf.Grn. | 63 | G3 |
| Chilthorne Cl. SE6 | 153 | J7 |
| *Ravensbourne Pk. Cres.* | | |
| Chilton Av. W5 | 125 | G4 |
| Chilton Gro. SE8 | 133 | G4 |
| Chilton Rd., Edg. | 54 | A6 |
| *Manor Pk. Cres.* | | |
| Chilton Rd., Rich. | 146 | A3 |
| **Chilton St. E2** | **13** | **G5** |
| Chilton St. E2 | 112 | C4 |
| Chiltonian Ind. Est. SE12 | 155 | F6 |
| Chiltons, The E18 | 79 | G2 |
| *Grove Hill* | | |
| Chilver St. SE10 | 135 | F5 |
| Chilwell Gdns., Wat. | 50 | C4 |
| Chilworth Ct. SW19 | 166 | A1 |
| *Windlesham Gro.* | | |
| Chilworth Gdns., Sutt. | 199 | F3 |
| **Chilworth Ms. W2** | **14** | **D4** |
| Chilworth Ms. W2 | 109 | F6 |
| **Chilworth St. W2** | **14** | **D4** |
| Chilworth St. W2 | 109 | F6 |
| Chimes Av. N13 | 59 | G5 |
| Chinbrook Cres. SE12 | 173 | H3 |
| Chinbrook Est. SE9 | 174 | A3 |
| Chinbrook Rd. SE12 | 173 | H3 |
| Chinchilla Dr., Houns. | 142 | C2 |
| Chine, The N10 | 74 | C4 |
| Chine, The N21 | 43 | H6 |
| Chine, The, Wem. | 87 | E5 |
| **Ching Ct. WC2** | **18** | **A4** |
| Ching Way E4 | 61 | J6 |
| Chingdale Rd. E4 | 62 | E3 |
| Chingford Av. E4 | 62 | B3 |
| Chingford Hall Est. E4 | 61 | J6 |
| Chingford Ind. Cen. E4 | 61 | H5 |
| Chingford La., Wdf.Grn. | 63 | E4 |
| Chingford Mt. Rd. E4 | 62 | A4 |
| Chingford Rd. E4 | 62 | A6 |
| Chingford Rd. E17 | 78 | B1 |
| Chingley Cl., Brom. | 173 | E6 |
| Chinnor Cres., Grnf. | 103 | H2 |
| Chip St. SW4 | 150 | D4 |
| Chipka St. E14 | 134 | C2 |
| Chipley St. SE14 | 133 | H6 |
| Chipmunk Gro., Nthlt. | 102/103 | E3 |
| *Argus Way* | | |
| Chippendale St. E5 | 95 | G3 |
| Chippenham Av., Wem. | 88 | B5 |
| Chippenham Gdns. NW6 | 108 | D3 |
| Chippenham Ms. W9 | 108 | D4 |
| Chippenham Rd. W9 | 108 | D4 |
| Chipping Cl., Barn. | 40 | B3 |
| *St. Albans Rd.* | | |
| Chipstead Av., Th.Hth. | 187 | H4 |
| Chipstead Cl. SE19 | 170 | C7 |
| Chipstead Gdns. NW2 | 89 | H2 |
| Chipstead St. SW6 | 148 | D1 |
| Chirk Cl., Hayes | 102/103 | E4 |
| *Braunston Dr.* | | |
| Chisenhale Rd. E3 | 113 | H2 |
| Chisholm Rd., Croy. | 202 | B2 |
| Chisholm Rd., Rich. | 145 | J6 |
| Chisledon Wk. E9 | 95 | J6 |
| *Osborne Rd.* | | |
| Chislehurst Av. N12 | 57 | F7 |
| Chislehurst Rd., Brom. | 192 | A2 |
| Chislehurst Rd., Chis. | 192 | A2 |
| Chislehurst Rd., Orp. | 193 | H4 |
| Chislehurst Rd., Rich. | 145 | H6 |
| Chislehurst Rd., Sid. | 176 | A5 |
| Chislet Cl., Beck. | 172 | A7 |
| *Abbey La.* | | |
| Chisley Rd. N15 | 76 | B6 |
| Chiswell Sq. SE3 | 155 | H2 |
| *Brook La.* | | |
| **Chiswell St. EC1** | **20** | **A1** |
| Chiswell St. EC1 | 111 | J5 |
| Chiswick Br. SW14 | 146 | C2 |
| Chiswick Br. W4 | 146 | C2 |
| Chiswick Cl., Croy. | 201 | F3 |
| Chiswick Common Rd. W4 | 126 | D4 |
| Chiswick Ct., Pnr. | 67 | F3 |
| Chiswick High Rd. W4 | 126 | D4 |
| Chiswick High Rd., Brent. | 125 | J5 |
| Chiswick Ho. Grds. W4 | 126 | D6 |
| Chiswick La. W4 | 127 | E5 |
| Chiswick La. S. W4 | 127 | F5 |
| Chiswick Mall W4 | 127 | F6 |
| Chiswick Mall W6 | 127 | F6 |
| Chiswick Quay W4 | 146 | C1 |
| Chiswick Rd. N9 | 60 | D2 |
| Chiswick Rd. W4 | 126 | C4 |
| Chiswick Roundabout W4 | 126 | A5 |
| *Chiswick High Rd.* | | |
| Chiswick Sq. W4 | 126/127 | E6 |
| *Hogarth Roundabout* | | |
| Chiswick Staithe W4 | 146 | C1 |
| Chiswick Ter. W4 | 126 | C4 |
| *Acton La.* | | |
| Chiswick Village W4 | 126 | B5 |
| Chiswick Wf. W4 | 127 | F6 |
| Chitterfield Gate, West Dr. | 120 | D7 |
| **Chitty St. W1** | **17** | **G1** |
| Chitty St. W1 | 110 | C5 |
| Chitty's La., Dag. | 100 | D2 |
| Chivalry Rd. SW11 | 149 | H5 |
| Chivenor Gro., Kings.T. | 163 | G5 |
| Chivers Rd. E4 | 62 | B3 |
| Choats Manor Way, Bark. | 118 | C4 |
| Choats Rd., Bark. | 118 | C2 |
| Choats Rd., Dag. | 118 | E3 |
| Chobham Gdns. SW19 | 166 | A2 |
| Chobham Rd. E15 | 96 | D5 |
| Cholmeley Cres. N6 | 74 | B7 |
| Cholmeley Pk. N6 | 92 | B1 |
| Cholmley Gdns. NW6 | 90 | D5 |
| *Fortune Grn. Rd.* | | |
| Cholmley Rd., T.Ditt. | 180 | E6 |
| Cholmondeley Av. NW10 | 107 | G2 |
| Cholmondeley Wk., Rich. | 145 | F5 |
| Choppins Ct. E1 | 132/133 | E1 |
| *Wapping La.* | | |
| Chopwell Cl. E15 | 96 | D7 |
| *Bryant La.* | | |
| Chorleywood Cres., Orp. | 193 | J2 |
| Choumert Gro. SE15 | 152 | D2 |
| Choumert Rd. SE15 | 152 | C3 |
| Choumert Sq. SE15 | 152 | D2 |
| Chow Sq. E8 | 94 | C5 |
| *Arcola St.* | | |
| Chrisalene Cl. (Stanwell), Stai. | 140 | A6 |
| *High St.* | | |
| Chrisp St. E14 | 114 | B5 |
| **Christ Ch. Pas. EC1** | **19** | **H3** |
| Christ Ch. Path, Hayes | 121 | F3 |
| Christ Ch. Rd., Beck. | 190 | A2 |
| *Fairfield Rd.* | | |
| Christ Ch. Rd., Surb. | 181 | J6 |
| Christchurch Av. N12 | 57 | H4 |
| Christchurch Av. NW6 | 90 | B7 |
| Christchurch Av., Har. | 69 | E4 |
| Christchurch Av., Tedd. | 162 | D5 |
| Christchurch Av., Wem. | 87 | H6 |
| Christchurch Cl. SW19 | 167 | G7 |
| Christchurch Gdns., Enf. | 43 | J1 |
| Christchurch Gdns., Har. | 68 | D4 |
| Christchurch Grn., Wem. | 87 | H6 |
| Christchurch Hill NW3 | 91 | G3 |
| Christchurch La., Barn. | 40 | B2 |
| Christchurch Pk., Sutt. | 199 | F7 |
| Christchurch Pas. NW3 | 91 | F3 |
| Christchurch Pas., Barn. | 40 | B3 |
| Christchurch Rd. N8 | 74 | E6 |
| Christchurch Rd. SW2 | 169 | F1 |
| Christchurch Rd. SW14 | 146 | B5 |
| Christchurch Rd. SW19 | 167 | G7 |
| Christchurch Rd. Houns. | 140 | D3 |
| *Courtney Rd.* | | |
| Christchurch Rd., Ilf. | 99 | E1 |
| Christchurch Rd., Sid. | 175 | J4 |
| Christchurch Sq. E9 | 113 | F1 |
| *Victoria Pk. Rd.* | | |
| **Christchurch St. SW3** | **31** | **J5** |
| Christchurch St. SW3 | 129 | J6 |
| **Christchurch Ter. SW3** | **31** | **J5** |
| Christchurch Way SE10 | 135 | E4 |
| Christian Ct. SE16 | 133 | J1 |
| Christian Flds. SW16 | 169 | G7 |
| **Christian St. E1** | **21** | **J3** |
| Christian St. E1 | 112 | D6 |
| Christie Dr., Croy. | 188 | D5 |
| Christie Gdns., Rom. | 82 | B6 |
| Christie Rd. E9 | 95 | H6 |
| Christina Sq. N4 | 93 | H1 |
| *Adolphus Rd.* | | |
| **Christina St. EC2** | **12** | **D5** |
| Christine Worsley Cl. N21 | 59 | H2 |
| *Highfield Rd.* | | |
| Christopher Av. W7 | 124 | D3 |
| Christopher Cl. SE16 | 133 | G2 |
| Christopher Cl., Sid. | 157 | J7 |
| Christopher Gdns., Dag. | 100 | D5 |
| *Wren Rd.* | | |
| **Christopher Pl. NW1** | **9** | **J4** |
| Christopher Rd., Sthl. | 122 | B4 |
| **Christopher St. EC2** | **12** | **C6** |
| Christopher St. EC2 | 112 | A4 |
| Christopher's Ms. W11 | 128 | B1 |
| *Penzance St.* | | |
| Chryssell Rd. SW9 | 131 | G7 |
| Chubworthy St. SE14 | 133 | H6 |
| Chudleigh Cres., Ilf. | 99 | H4 |
| Chudleigh Gdns., Sutt. | 199 | F3 |
| Chudleigh Rd. NW6 | 90 | A7 |
| Chudleigh Rd. SE4 | 153 | J5 |
| Chudleigh Rd., Twick. | 144 | C7 |
| Chudleigh St. E1 | 113 | G6 |
| Chudleigh Way, Ruis. | 84 | A1 |
| Chulsa Rd. SE26 | 170 | E5 |
| **Chumleigh St. SE5** | **36** | **D5** |
| Chumleigh St. SE5 | 132 | B6 |
| Chumleigh Wk., Surb. | 181 | J4 |
| Church All., Croy. | 201 | G1 |
| Church App. SE21 | 170 | A3 |
| Church App., Stai. | 140 | A6 |
| Church Av. E4 | 62 | D6 |
| Church Av. NW1 | 92 | B6 |
| *Kentish Town Rd.* | | |
| Church Av. SW14 | 146 | D3 |
| Church Av., Beck. | 190 | A1 |
| Church Av., Nthlt. | 85 | F7 |
| Church Av., Pnr. | 67 | E6 |
| Church Av., Sid. | 176 | A5 |
| Church Av., Sthl. | 123 | E3 |
| Church Cl. N20 | 57 | H3 |
| **Church Cl. W8** | **22** | **A3** |
| Church Cl., Edg. | 54 | C5 |
| Church Cl., Loug. | 48 | C2 |
| Church Cl., West Dr. | 120 | B3 |
| Church Cl., Rich. | 145 | G5 |
| *George St.* | | |
| Church Cres. E9 | 95 | G7 |
| Church Cres. N3 | 72 | C1 |
| Church Cres. N10 | 74 | B4 |
| Church Cres. N20 | 57 | H3 |
| Church Dr. NW9 | 88 | D1 |
| Church Dr., Har. | 67 | F6 |
| Church Dr., W.Wick. | 205 | E3 |
| Church Elm La., Dag. | 101 | G6 |
| Church End E17 | 78 | B4 |
| Church End NW4 | 71 | H3 |
| **Church Entry EC4** | **19** | **H4** |
| Church Fm. La., Sutt. | 198 | B6 |
| Church Gdns. W5 | 125 | G2 |
| Church Gdns., Wem. | 86 | D4 |
| Church Gate SW6 | 148 | B3 |
| Church Gro. SE13 | 154 | B4 |
| Church Gro., Kings.T. | 181 | F1 |
| Church Hill E17 | 78 | A4 |
| Church Hill N21 | 43 | F7 |
| Church Hill SE18 | 136 | C3 |
| Church Hill SW19 | 166 | C5 |
| Church Hill, Cars. | 199 | J5 |
| Church Hill, Har. | 86 | B1 |
| Church Hill, Loug. | 48 | B3 |
| Church Hill Rd. E17 | 78 | B4 |
| Church Hill Rd., Barn. | 41 | J7 |
| Church Hill Rd., Surb. | 181 | H5 |
| Church Hill Rd., Sutt. | 198 | A4 |
| Church Hill Wd., Orp. | 193 | J5 |
| Church Hyde SE18 | 137 | H6 |
| *Old Mill Rd.* | | |
| Church La. E11 | 97 | E1 |
| Church La. E17 | 78 | B4 |
| Church La. N2 | 73 | G3 |
| Church La. N8 | 75 | F4 |
| Church La. N9 | 60 | D2 |
| Church La. N17 | 76 | B1 |
| Church La. NW9 | 88 | C2 |
| Church La. SW17 | 168 | B4 |
| Church La. SW19 | 184 | C1 |
| Church La. W5 | 125 | F2 |
| Church La., Brom. | 206 | B1 |
| Church La., Chess. | 195 | J6 |
| Church La., Chis. | 193 | F1 |
| Church La., Dag. | 101 | H6 |
| Church La., Enf. | 44 | A3 |
| Church La., Har. | 68 | C1 |
| Church La., Loug. | 48 | C3 |
| Church La., Pnr. | 67 | E3 |
| Church La., Rich. | 163 | H1 |
| Church La., Tedd. | 162 | C5 |
| Church La., T.Ditt. | 180 | C6 |
| Church La., Twick. | 162 | D1 |
| Church La., Wall. | 200 | D3 |
| Church Manor Est. SW9 | 131 | G7 |
| *Vassall Rd.* | | |
| Church Manorway SE2 | 137 | J4 |
| Church Meadow, Surb. | 195 | F2 |
| Church Mt. N2 | 73 | G5 |
| Church Paddock Ct., Wall. | 200 | D3 |
| Church Pas. EC2 | 111 | J6 |
| *Gresham St.* | | |
| Church Pas., Barn. | 40 | C4 |
| *Wood St.* | | |
| Church Pas., Surb. | 181 | H5 |
| Church Path E11 | 79 | G5 |
| Church Path E17 | 78 | B4 |
| *St. Mary Rd.* | | |
| Church Path N12 | 57 | F5 |
| Church Path N17 | 60 | B7 |
| *White Hart La.* | | |
| Church Path N20 | 57 | F4 |
| Church Path NW10 | 89 | E7 |
| Church Path SW14 | 146 | D3 |
| Church Path SW19 | 184 | D2 |
| Church Path W4 | 126 | C3 |
| Church Path W7 | 123 | G1 |
| Church Path, Croy. | 201 | J2 |
| Church Path, Mitch. | 185 | H3 |
| Church Path, Sthl. | 123 | F3 |
| **Church Pl. SW1** | **17** | **G6** |
| Church Pl. W5 | 125 | G2 |
| *Church Gdns.* | | |
| Church Pl., Mitch. | 185 | H3 |
| Church Pl., Twick. | 162/163 | E1 |
| *Church St.* | | |
| Church Ri. SE23 | 171 | G1 |
| Church Ri., Chess. | 195 | J6 |
| Church Rd. E10 | 96 | B2 |
| Church Rd. E12 | 98 | B5 |
| Church Rd. E17 | 77 | H2 |
| Church Rd. N6 | 74 | A6 |
| Church Rd. N17 | 76 | B1 |
| Church Rd. NW4 | 71 | H4 |
| Church Rd. NW10 | 89 | E6 |
| Church Rd. SE19 | 188 | B1 |
| Church Rd. SW13 | 147 | F2 |
| Church Rd. (Wimbledon) SW19 | 166 | B4 |
| Church Rd. W3 | 126 | C1 |
| Church Rd. W7 | 124 | C1 |
| Church Rd., Bark. | 99 | F6 |
| Church Rd., Bexh. | 159 | F2 |
| Church Rd., Brom. | 191 | G2 |
| Church Rd. (Shortlands), Brom. | 190 | E3 |
| Church Rd., Buck.H. | 63 | H1 |
| Church Rd., Croy. | 201 | H3 |
| Church Rd., E.Mol. | 180 | A4 |
| Church Rd., Enf. | 45 | F6 |
| Church Rd. (West Ewell), Epsom | 196 | D7 |
| Church Rd., Esher | 194 | C6 |

Clivedon Ct. W13 104 E5
Clivedon Rd. E4 62 E5
Clivesdale Dr., Hayes 122 B1
**Cloak La. EC4 20 A5**
Cloak La. EC4 111 J7
Clock Ho. Rd., Beck. 189 H3
Clock Twr. Ms. N1 111 J1 *Arlington Av.*
Clock Twr. Ms. SE28 118 B7
Clock Twr. Pl. N7 92 E6
Clock Twr. Rd., Islw. 144 C3
Clockhouse Av., Bark. 117 F1
Clockhouse Cl. SW19 165 J3
Clockhouse Pl. SW15 148 B5
Cloister Cl., Tedd. 162 E5
Cloister Gdns. SE25 188 E6
Cloister Gdns., Edg. 54 C5
Cloister Rd. NW2 90 C3
Cloister Rd. W3 106 C5
Cloisters Av., Brom. 192 C5
Cloisters Mall, Kings.T. 181 G2 *Union St.*
Clonard Way, Pnr. 51 G6
Clonbrock Rd. N16 94 B4
Cloncurry St. SW6 148 A2
Clonmel Cl., Har. 86 A1
Clonmel Rd. SW6 128 C7
Clonmel Rd., Tedd. 162 A4
Clonmell Rd. N17 76 A3
Clonmore St. SW18 166 C1
Cloonmore Av., Orp. 207 J4
Clorane Gdns. NW3 90 D3
Close, The E4 62 C7 *Beech Hall Rd.*
Close, The N14 58 D2
Close, The N20 56 C2
Close, The SE3 154 D2 *Heath La.*
Close, The, Barn. 41 J6
Close, The, Beck. 189 H4
Close, The, Bex. 159 G6
Close, The, Har. 67 J2
Close, The, Islw. 144 A2
Close, The, Mitch. 185 J4
Close, The, N.Mal. 182 C2
Close, The, Orp. 193 H6
Close, The (Eastcote), Pnr. 66 C7
Close, The (Rayners La.), Pnr. 67 F7
Close, The, Rich. 146 B3
Close, The, Rom. 82 E6
Close, The, Sid. 176 B5
Close, The, Sutt. 184 C7
Close, The (Barnhill Rd.), Wem. 88 C3
Close, The (Lyon Pk. Av.), Wem. 87 H6
**Cloth Ct. EC1 19 H2**
**Cloth Fair EC1 19 H2**
Cloth Fair EC1 111 H5
**Cloth St. EC1 19 J1**
**Clothier St. E1 21 E3**
Clothworkers Rd. SE18 137 G7
Cloudesdale Rd. SW17 168 B2
Cloudesley Pl. N1 111 G1
Cloudesley Rd. N1 111 G1
Cloudesley Rd., Bexh. 159 F1
Cloudesley Sq. N1 111 G1
Cloudesley St. N1 111 G1
Clouston Cl., Wall. 200 E5
Clova Rd. E7 97 F6
Clove Cres. E14 114 D7
Clove Hitch Quay SW11 149 F3
Clove St. E13 115 G4 *Barking Rd.*
Clovelly Av. NW9 71 F4
Clovelly Cl., Pnr. 66 B3
Clovelly Gdns. SE19 188 C1
Clovelly Gdns., Enf. 44 B7
Clovelly Gdns., Rom. 83 H1
Clovelly Rd. N8 74 D4
Clovelly Rd. W4 126 C2
Clovelly Rd. W5 125 F2
Clovelly Rd., Bexh. 138 E6
Clovelly Rd., Houns. 143 G2
Clovelly Way E1 113 F6 *Jamaica St.*
Clovelly Way, Har. 85 F2
Clovelly Way, Orp. 193 J6
Clover Cl. E11 96 D2 *Norman Rd.*
**Clover Ms. SW3 31 J5**
Clover Way, Wall. 200 A1
Cloverdale Gdns., Sid. 157 J6
Cloverleys, Loug. 48 A5
Clowders Rd. SE6 171 J3
Clowser Cl., Sutt. 199 F5 *Turnpike La.*
Cloyster Wd., Edg. 53 G7
**Cloysters Grn. E1 29 H1**
Cloysters Grn. E1 132 D1
Club Gdns. Rd., Brom. 191 G7
**Club Row E1 13 F5**
Club Row E1 112 C4
**Club Row E2 13 F5**
Club Row E2 112 C4
Clunbury Av., Sthl. 123 F5
**Clunbury St. N1 12 C2**
**Cluny Est. SE1 28 D5**
Cluny Ms. SW5 128 D4
**Cluny Pl. SE1 28 D5**
**Cluse Ct. N1 11 J1**
Clutton St. E14 114 B5
Clydach Rd., Enf. 44 C4
Clyde Circ. N15 76 B4
Clyde Pl. E10 78 B7
Clyde Rd. N15 76 B4
Clyde Rd. N22 74 D1
Clyde Rd., Croy. 202 C1
Clyde Rd., Sutt. 198 D5
Clyde Rd., Wall. 200 C5
Clyde St. SE8 133 J6
Clyde Ter. SE23 171 F2
Clyde Vale SE23 171 F2
Clydesdale, Enf. 45 G4
Clydesdale Av., Stan. 69 G3
Clydesdale Cl., Borwd. 38 D5
Clydesdale Cl., Islw. 144 C3
Clydesdale Gdns., Rich. 146 B4
Clydesdale Ho., Erith 138/139 E2 *Kale Rd.*
Clydesdale Rd. W11 108 C6
Clymping Dene, Felt. 142 B7
Clyston St. SW8 150 C2
**Coach & Horses Yd. W1 17 E5**
Coach Ho. La. N5 93 H4 *Highbury Hill*
Coach Ho. La. SW19 166 A4
Coach Ho. Ms. SE23 153 G6
Coach Ho. Yd. SW18 148/149 E4 *Ebner St.*
Coach Yd. Ms. N19 92/93 E1 *Trinder Rd.*
Coachhouse Ms. SE20 170 E7
Coal Wf. Rd. W12 128 A2 *Shepherds Bush Pl.*
Coaldale Wk. SE21 151 J7 *Lairdale Cl.*
Coalecroft Rd. SW15 147 J4
**Coate St. E2 13 J2**
Coate St. E2 112 D2
Coates Av. SW18 149 G6
Coates Hill Rd., Brom. 192 D2
Coates Wk., Brent. 125 H5
Cobb Cl., Borwd. 38 C5
**Cobb St. E1 21 F2**
Cobb St. E1 112 C5
Cobbett Rd. SE9 156 B3
Cobbett Rd., Twick. 161 G1
Cobbett St. SW8 131 F7
Cobbetts Av., Ilf. 80 A5
Cobblers Wk., E.Mol. 180 D1
Cobblers Wk., Hmptn. 161 J7
Cobblers Wk., Kings.T. 180 D1
Cobblers Wk., Tedd. 162 A7
Cobblestone Pl., Croy. 201 J1 *Oakfield Rd.*
Cobbold Est. NW10 89 F6
Cobbold Ms. W12 127 F2 *Cobbold Rd.*
Cobbold Rd. E11 97 F3
Cobbold Rd. NW10 89 F6
Cobbold Rd. W12 127 F2
Cobb's Ct. EC4 111 H6 *Carter La.*
Cobb's Rd., Houns. 143 F4
Cobden Rd. E11 97 E3
Cobden Rd. SE25 188 D5
Cobden Rd., Orp. 207 G4
Cobham Av., N.Mal. 183 G5
Cobham Cl. SW11 149 H6
Cobham Cl., Brom. 192 B7
Cobham Cl., Edg. 70 B2
Cobham Cl., Sid. 158 B6 *Park Mead*
Cobham Cl., Wall. 200 E6
Cobham Ho., Bark. 117 F1 *St. Margarets*
Cobham Ms. NW1 92 D7 *Agar Gro.*
Cobham Pl., Bexh. 158 D5
Cobham Rd. E17 78 C1
Cobham Rd. N22 75 H3
Cobham Rd., Houns. 122 C7
Cobham Rd., Ilf. 99 H2
Cobham Rd., Kings.T. 182 A1
Cobland Rd. SE12 173 J4
Coborn Rd. E3 113 J3
Coborn St. E3 113 J3
**Cobourg Rd. SE5 37 F5**
Cobourg Rd. SE5 132 C6
**Cobourg St. NW1 9 G4**
Cobourg St. NW1 110 C3
**Coburg Cl. SW1 33 G1**
Coburg Cres. SW2 169 F1
Coburg Gdns., Ilf. 80 A2
Coburg Rd. N22 75 F3
**Cochrane Ms. NW8 7 F2**
Cochrane Rd. SW19 166 C7
**Cochrane St. NW8 7 F2**
Cochrane St. NW8 109 G2
**Cock Hill E1 21 E2**
**Cock La. EC1 19 G2**
Cock La. EC1 111 H5
Cockayne Way SE8 133 H5
Cockerell Rd. E17 77 H6
Cockfosters Rd., Barn. 41 J2
**Cockpit Steps SW1 25 J4**
**Cockpit Yd. WC1 18 D1**
Cocks Cres., N.Mal. 183 F4
Cocksett Av., Orp. 207 H6
**Cockspur Ct. SW1 25 J1**
**Cockspur St. SW1 25 J1**
Cockspur St. SW1 130 D1
Cocksure La., Sid. 177 G3
**Code St. E1 13 G6**
Code St. E1 112 C4
Codicote Ter. N4 93 J2 *Green Las.*
**Codling Cl. E1 29 J2**
Codling Way, Wem. 87 G4
Codrington Hill SE23 153 H7
Codrington Ms. W11 108 B6 *Blenheim Cres.*
Cody Cl., Har. 69 G3
Cody Cl., Wall. 200 D7 *Alcock Cl.*
Cody Rd. E16 114 D4
Cody Rd. Business Cen. E16 114 D4
Coe Av. SE25 188 D6
Coe's All., Barn. 40 B4 *Wood St.*
Coffers Circle, Wem. 88 B3
Cogan Av. E17 77 H1
**Coin St. SE1 27 E1**
Coin St. SE1 131 G1
Coity Rd. NW5 92 A6
**Coke St. E1 21 H3**
Coke St. E1 112 D6
Cokers La. SE21 170 A1 *Perifield*
Colas Ms. NW6 108 D1 *Birchington Rd.*
**Colbeck Ms. SW7 30 B2**
Colbeck Ms. SW7 129 E4
Colbeck Rd., Har. 67 J7
Colberg Pl. N16 76 B7
Colborne Way, Wor.Pk. 197 J3
Colbrook Av., Hayes 121 G3
Colbrook Cl., Hayes 121 G3
Colburn Av., Pnr. 51 E6
Colburn Way, Sutt. 199 G3
Colby Ms. SE19 170 B5 *Gipsy Hill*
Colby Rd. SE19 170 B5
Colchester Av. E12 98 C3
Colchester Dr., Pnr. 66 D5
Colchester Rd. E10 78 C7
Colchester Rd. E17 78 A6
Colchester Rd., Edg. 54 C7
Colchester Rd., Nthwd. 66 A2
**Colchester St. E1 21 G3**
Cold Blow La. SE14 133 G7
Cold Blows, Mitch. 186 A3
Cold Harbour E14 134 C2
**Coldbath Sq. EC1 11 E5**
Coldbath St. SE13 154 B1
Coldershaw Rd. W13 124 D1
Coldfall Av. N10 73 J2
Coldharbour La. SE5 151 G4
Coldharbour La. SW9 151 G4
Coldharbour La., Hayes 102 A7
Coldharbour Pl. SE5 151 J2 *Denmark Hill*
Coldharbour Rd., Croy. 201 G5
Coldharbour Way, Croy. 201 G5
Coldstream Gdns. SW18 148 C6
Cole Cl. SE28 138 B1
Cole Gdns., Houns. 122 A7
Cole Pk. Gdns., Twick. 144 D6
Cole Pk. Rd., Twick. 144 D6
Cole Pk. Vw., Twick. 144 D6 *Hill Vw. Rd.*
Cole Rd., Twick. 144 D6
**Cole St. SE1 28 A4**
Cole St. SE1 131 J2
Colebeck Ms. N1 93 H6
Colebert Av. E1 113 F4
Colebrook Cl. SW15 148 A7 *West Hill*
Colebrook Gdns., Loug. 49 E2
Colebrook Ho. E14 114 B6 *Brabazon St.*
Colebrook La., Loug. 49 E2
Colebrook Path, Loug. 49 E2
Colebrook Rd. SW16 187 E1
Colebrook Way N11 58 B5
Colebrooke Av. W13 104 E6
Colebrooke Dr. E11 79 H7
Colebrooke Pl. N1 111 H1 *St. Peters St.*
Colebrooke Ri., Brom. 191 E2
**Colebrooke Row N1 11 G2**
Colebrooke Row N1 111 H2
Coleby Path SE5 132 A7 *Harris St.*
Coledale Dr., Stan. 69 F1
Coleford Rd. SW18 149 F5
Colegrave Rd. E15 96 D5
**Colegrove Rd. SE15 37 G6**
Colegrove Rd. SE15 132 C7
**Coleherne Ct. SW5 30 B4**
Coleherne Ct. SW5 129 E5
**Coleherne Ms. SW10 30 A4**
Coleherne Ms. SW10 128 E5
**Coleherne Rd. SW10 30 A4**
Coleherne Rd. SW10 128 E5
Colehill Gdns. SW6 148 B2 *Fulham Palace Rd.*
Colehill La. SW6 148 B1
Coleman Cl. SE25 188 D2 *Warminster Rd.*
Coleman Flds. N1 111 J1
**Coleman Rd. SE5 36 D7**
Coleman Rd. SE5 132 B7
Coleman Rd., Belv. 139 G4
Coleman Rd., Dag. 101 E6
**Coleman St. EC2 20 B3**
Coleman St. EC2 112 A6
Colemans Heath SE9 174 E3
Colenso Dr. NW7 55 G7 *Bunns La.*
Colenso Rd. E5 95 F4
Colenso Rd., Ilf. 99 H1
Colepits Wd. Rd. SE9 157 F5
Coleraine Rd. N8 75 G3
Coleraine Rd. SE3 135 F6
Coleridge Av. E12 98 B6
Coleridge Av., Sutt. 199 H4
Coleridge Cl. SW8 150 B2
Coleridge Gdns. NW6 91 F7 *Fairhazel Gdns.*
Coleridge La. N8 74/75 E6 *Coleridge Rd.*
Coleridge Rd. E17 77 J4
Coleridge Rd. N4 93 G2
Coleridge Rd. N8 74 D6
Coleridge Rd. N12 57 F5
Coleridge Rd., Croy. 189 F7
Coleridge Sq. W13 104 D6 *Berners Dr.*
Coleridge Wk. NW11 72 D4
Coleridge Way, Hayes 102 A6
Coleridge Way, West Dr. 120 C4
Coles Cres., Har. 85 H2
Coles Grn., Bushey 51 J1
Coles Grn., Loug. 48 D1
Coles Grn. Ct. NW2 89 G2
Coles Grn. Rd. NW2 89 G1
Colesburg Rd., Beck. 189 J3
Coleshill Rd., Tedd. 162 B6
Colestown St. SW11 149 H2
Colet Cl. N13 59 H6
Colet Gdns. W14 128 A4
**Coley St. WC1 10 D6**
Coley St. WC1 111 F4
Colfe Rd. SE23 171 H1
Colham Av., West Dr. 120 B1
Colham Mill Rd., West Dr. 120 A2
Colin Cl. NW9 71 E4

| Street | Page | Grid |
|---|---|---|
| Colin Cl., Croy. | 203 | J3 |
| Colin Cl., W.Wick. | 205 | F3 |
| Colin Cres. NW9 | 71 | F4 |
| Colin Dr. NW9 | 71 | F5 |
| Colin Gdns. NW9 | 71 | F5 |
| Colin Par. NW9 | 70/71 | E4 |
| *Edgware Rd.* | | |
| Colin Pk. Rd. NW9 | 70 | E4 |
| Colin Rd. NW10 | 89 | G6 |
| Colina Ms. N15 | 75 | H5 |
| *Harringay Rd.* | | |
| Colina Rd. N15 | 75 | H5 |
| Colindale Av. NW9 | 70 | D3 |
| Colindale Business Pk. NW9 | 70 | C3 |
| Colindeep Gdns. NW4 | 71 | G5 |
| Colindeep La. NW4 | 70 | E3 |
| Colindeep La. NW9 | 70 | E3 |
| Colinette Rd. SW15 | 147 | J4 |
| Colinton Rd., Ilf. | 100 | B2 |
| Coliston Pas. SW18 | 148 | D7 |
| *Coliston Rd.* | | |
| Coliston Rd. SW18 | 148 | D7 |
| Collamore Av. SW18 | 167 | H1 |
| Collapit Cl., Har. | 67 | H5 |
| Collard Av., Loug. | 49 | F2 |
| Collard Grn., Loug. | 49 | F2 |
| *Collard Av.* | | |
| College App. SE10 | 134 | C6 |
| College Av., Har. | 68 | B1 |
| College Cl. E9 | 95 | F5 |
| *Median Rd.* | | |
| College Cl. N18 | 60 | C5 |
| College Cl., Har. | 52 | B7 |
| College Cl., Twick. | 162 | A1 |
| *Meadway* | | |
| College Cres. NW3 | 91 | G6 |
| College Cross N1 | 93 | G7 |
| College Dr., Ruis. | 66 | A7 |
| College Gdns. E4 | 46 | B7 |
| College Gdns. N18 | 60 | C5 |
| College Gdns. SE21 | 170 | B1 |
| College Gdns. SW17 | 167 | H2 |
| College Gdns., Enf. | 44 | A1 |
| College Gdns., Ilf. | 80 | B5 |
| College Gdns., N.Mal. | 183 | F5 |
| College Grn. SE19 | 170 | B7 |
| College Gro. NW1 | 110 | D1 |
| *St. Pancras Way* | | |
| **College Hill EC4** | **20** | **A5** |
| College Hill Rd., Har. | 68 | C1 |
| College La. NW5 | 92 | B4 |
| **College Ms. SW1** | **26** | **A5** |
| College Ms. SW18 | 148/149 | E5 |
| *St. Ann's Hill* | | |
| College Pk. Cl. SE13 | 154 | D4 |
| College Pk. Rd. N17 | 60 | C6 |
| *College Rd.* | | |
| College Pl. E17 | 78 | E4 |
| College Pl. NW1 | 110 | C1 |
| **College Pl. SW10** | **30** | **C7** |
| College Pt. E15 | 97 | F6 |
| College Rd. E17 | 78 | C5 |
| College Rd. N17 | 60 | C6 |
| College Rd. N21 | 59 | G2 |
| College Rd. NW10 | 107 | J2 |
| College Rd. SE19 | 170 | C5 |
| College Rd. SE21 | 152 | B7 |
| College Rd. SW19 | 167 | G6 |
| College Rd. W13 | 104 | E6 |
| College Rd., Brom. | 173 | G7 |
| College Rd., Croy. | 202 | A2 |
| College Rd., Enf. | 44 | A2 |
| College Rd. (Harrow on the Hill), Har. | 68 | B6 |
| College Rd. (Harrow Weald), Har. | 68 | B1 |
| College Rd., Islw. | 144 | C1 |
| College Rd., Wem. | 87 | G1 |
| College Row E9 | 95 | G5 |
| College Slip, Brom. | 191 | G1 |
| **College St. EC4** | **20** | **B5** |
| College Ter. E3 | 113 | J3 |
| College Ter. N3 | 72 | C2 |
| *Hendon La.* | | |
| College Vw. SE9 | 174 | A1 |
| College Wk., Kings.T. | 181 | H2 |
| *Grange Rd.* | | |
| College Yd. NW5 | 92 | B4 |
| *College La.* | | |
| Collent St. E9 | 95 | F6 |
| Colless Rd. N15 | 76 | C5 |
| **Collett Rd. SE16** | **29** | **J6** |
| Collett Rd. SE16 | 132 | D3 |
| Collett Way, Sthl. | 123 | H1 |
| Collier Cl. E6 | 116/117 | E6 |
| *Trader Rd.* | | |
| Collier Cl., Epsom | 196 | A6 |
| Collier Dr., Edg. | 70 | A2 |
| Collier Row Rd., Rom. | 83 | F1 |
| **Collier St. N1** | **10** | **C2** |
| Collier St. N1 | 111 | F2 |
| Colliers Shaw, Kes. | 206 | A4 |
| Colliers Water La., Th.Hth. | 187 | G5 |
| Collindale Av., Erith | 139 | H6 |
| Collindale Av., Sid. | 176 | A1 |
| Collingbourne Rd. W12 | 127 | H1 |
| **Collingham Gdns. SW5** | **30** | **B2** |
| Collingham Gdns. SW5 | 129 | E4 |
| **Collingham Pl. SW5** | **30** | **A2** |
| Collingham Pl. SW5 | 128 | E4 |
| **Collingham Rd. SW5** | **30** | **B1** |
| Collingham Rd. SW5 | 129 | E4 |
| Collings Cl. N22 | 59 | F6 |
| *Whittington Rd.* | | |
| Collingtree Rd. SE26 | 171 | F4 |
| Collingwood Av. N10 | 74 | A3 |
| Collingwood Av., Surb. | 196 | C1 |
| Collingwood Cl. SE20 | 189 | E1 |
| Collingwood Cl., Twick. | 143 | G6 |
| Collingwood Rd. E17 | 78 | A6 |
| Collingwood Rd. N15 | 76 | B4 |
| Collingwood Rd., Mitch. | 185 | H2 |
| Collingwood Rd., Sutt. | 198 | D3 |
| Collingwood St. E1 | 113 | E4 |
| Collins Av., Stan. | 69 | H2 |
| Collins Dr., Ruis. | 84 | C2 |
| Collins Rd. N5 | 93 | J4 |
| Collins Sq. SE3 | 155 | F2 |
| *Tranquil Vale* | | |
| Collins St. SE3 | 155 | E2 |
| Collin's Yd. N1 | 111 | H1 |
| *Islington Grn.* | | |
| **Collinson St. SE1** | **27** | **J4** |
| **Collinson Wk. SE1** | **27** | **J4** |
| Collinwood Av., Enf. | 45 | F3 |
| Collinwood Gdns., Ilf. | 80 | C5 |
| Collis All., Twick. | 162 | B1 |
| *The Grn.* | | |
| Colls Rd. SE15 | 153 | F1 |
| Collyer Av., Croy. | 200 | E4 |
| Collyer Pl. SE15 | 152 | D1 |
| *Peckham High St.* | | |
| Collyer Rd., Croy. | 201 | E4 |
| Colman Rd. E16 | 115 | J5 |
| Colmar Cl. E1 | 113 | G4 |
| *Alderney Rd.* | | |
| Colmer Pl., Har. | 52 | A7 |
| Colmer Rd. SW16 | 187 | E1 |
| Colmore Ms. SE15 | 153 | E1 |
| Colmore Rd., Enf. | 45 | F4 |
| **Colnbrook St. SE1** | **27** | **G6** |
| Colnbrook St. SE1 | 131 | H3 |
| Colne Ct., Epsom | 196 | C4 |
| Colne Ho., Bark. | 99 | E6 |
| Colne Rd. E5 | 95 | H4 |
| Colne Rd. N21 | 44 | A7 |
| Colne Rd., Twick. | 162 | B1 |
| Colne St. E13 | 115 | G3 |
| *Grange Rd.* | | |
| Colney Hatch La. N10 | 74 | B2 |
| Colney Hatch La. N11 | 57 | J6 |
| Cologne Rd. SW11 | 149 | G4 |
| Colomb St. SE10 | 135 | E5 |
| Colombo Rd., Ilf. | 99 | F1 |
| **Colombo St. SE1** | **27** | **G2** |
| Colombo St. SE1 | 131 | H1 |
| Colonels Wk., Enf. | 43 | H3 |
| Colonial Av., Twick. | 143 | J5 |
| Colonial Rd., Felt. | 141 | H7 |
| **Colonnade WC1** | **10** | **A6** |
| Colonnade WC1 | 110 | E4 |
| **Colonnade Wk. SW1** | **32** | **D2** |
| **Colonnades, The W2** | **14** | **B3** |
| Colonnades, The W2 | 109 | E6 |
| Colson Gdns., Loug. | 48/49 | E4 |
| *Colson Rd.* | | |
| Colson Grn., Loug. | 48/49 | E4 |
| *Colson Rd.* | | |
| Colson Path, Loug. | 48 | D4 |
| Colson Rd., Croy. | 202 | B2 |
| Colson Rd., Loug. | 48 | E4 |
| Colson Way SW16 | 168 | C4 |
| Colsterworth Rd. N15 | 76 | C4 |
| Colston Av., Cars. | 199 | H4 |
| Colston Cl., Cars. | 199 | J4 |
| *West St.* | | |
| Colston Rd. E7 | 98 | A6 |
| Colston Rd. SW14 | 146 | C4 |
| Colthurst Cres. N4 | 93 | J2 |
| Coltness Cres. SE2 | 138 | B5 |
| Colton Gdns. N17 | 75 | J3 |
| Colton Rd., Har. | 68 | B5 |
| Columbia Av., Edg. | 70 | B1 |
| Columbia Av., Ruis. | 84 | B1 |
| Columbia Av., Wor.Pk. | 183 | F7 |
| Columbia Ctyd. E14 | 134 | A1 |
| *West India Av.* | | |
| **Columbia Rd. E2** | **13** | **F3** |
| Columbia Rd. E2 | 112 | C3 |
| Columbia Rd. E13 | 115 | F4 |
| Columbia Sq. SW14 | 146 | C4 |
| *Upper Richmond Rd. W.* | | |
| Columbine Av. E6 | 116 | B5 |
| Columbine Av., S.Croy. | 201 | H7 |
| Columbine Way SE13 | 154 | C2 |
| Columbus Ct. SE16 | 133 | F1 |
| *Rotherhithe St.* | | |
| Columbus Ctyd. E14 | 134 | A1 |
| *West India Av.* | | |
| Columbus Gdns., Nthwd. | 66 | A1 |
| Colva Wk. N19 | 92 | B2 |
| *Chester Rd.* | | |
| Colvestone Cres. E8 | 94 | C5 |
| Colview Ct. SE9 | 174 | A1 |
| *Mottingham La.* | | |
| Colville Est. N1 | 112 | B1 |
| Colville Gdns. W11 | 108 | C6 |
| Colville Hos. W11 | 108 | C6 |
| Colville Ms. W11 | 108 | C6 |
| *Lonsdale Rd.* | | |
| **Colville Pl. W1** | **17** | **G2** |
| Colville Rd. E11 | 96 | C3 |
| Colville Rd. E17 | 77 | H2 |
| Colville Rd. N9 | 60 | E1 |
| Colville Rd. W3 | 126 | B3 |
| Colville Rd. W11 | 108 | C6 |
| Colville Sq. W11 | 108 | C6 |
| Colville Sq. Ms. W11 | 108 | C6 |
| *Portobello Rd.* | | |
| Colville Ter. W11 | 108 | C6 |
| Colvin Cl. SE26 | 171 | F5 |
| Colvin Gdns. E4 | 62 | C3 |
| Colvin Gdns. E11 | 79 | H4 |
| Colvin Gdns., Ilf. | 81 | F1 |
| Colvin Rd. E6 | 98 | B7 |
| Colvin Rd., Th.Hth. | 187 | G5 |
| Colwall Gdns., Wdf.Grn. | 63 | G5 |
| Colwell Rd. SE22 | 152 | C5 |
| Colwick Cl. N6 | 74 | D7 |
| Colwith Rd. W6 | 127 | J6 |
| Colwood Gdns. SW19 | 167 | G7 |
| **Colworth Gro. SE17** | **36** | **A2** |
| Colworth Rd. E11 | 78 | E6 |
| Colworth Rd., Croy. | 202 | D1 |
| Colwyn Av., Grnf. | 104 | C2 |
| Colwyn Cl. SW16 | 168 | C5 |
| Colwyn Cres., Houns. | 143 | J1 |
| Colwyn Grn. NW9 | 70/71 | E6 |
| *Snowdon Dr.* | | |
| Colwyn Rd. NW2 | 89 | H3 |
| **Colyer Cl. N1** | **10** | **D1** |
| Colyer Cl. N1 | 111 | F2 |
| Colyer Cl. SE9 | 175 | E2 |
| Colyers La., Erith | 159 | J1 |
| Colyton Cl., Well. | 158 | D1 |
| Colyton Cl., Wem. | 87 | F6 |
| *Bridgewater Rd.* | | |
| Colyton Rd. SE22 | 153 | E5 |
| Colyton Way N18 | 60 | D5 |
| Combe Av. SE3 | 135 | F7 |
| Combe Lo. SE7 | 135 | J6 |
| *Elliscombe Rd.* | | |
| Combe Martin, Kings.T. | 164 | C5 |
| Combe Ms. SE3 | 135 | F7 |
| Combedale Rd. SE10 | 135 | G5 |
| Combemartin Rd. SW18 | 148 | B7 |
| Comber Cl. NW2 | 89 | H3 |
| Comber Gro. SE5 | 151 | J1 |
| Combermere Rd. SW9 | 151 | F3 |
| Combermere Rd., Mord. | 185 | E6 |
| Comberton Rd. E5 | 95 | E2 |
| Combeside SE18 | 137 | J7 |
| Combwell Cres. SE2 | 138 | A3 |
| Comely Bank Rd. E17 | 78 | C5 |
| Comer Cres., Sthl. | 123 | J2 |
| *Windmill Av.* | | |
| Comeragh Ms. W14 | 128 | B5 |
| Comeragh Rd. W14 | 128 | B5 |
| Comerford Rd. SE4 | 153 | H4 |
| Comet Cl. E12 | 98 | A4 |
| Comet Pl. SE8 | 134 | A7 |
| Comet Rd., Stai. | 140 | A7 |
| Comet St. SE8 | 134 | A7 |
| Commerce Rd. N22 | 75 | F1 |
| Commerce Rd., Brent. | 125 | F7 |
| Commerce Way, Croy. | 201 | F2 |
| **Commercial Rd. E1** | **21** | **H3** |
| Commercial Rd. E1 | 112 | D6 |
| Commercial Rd. E14 | 113 | F6 |
| Commercial Rd. N17 | 60 | B6 |
| Commercial Rd. N18 | 60 | B5 |
| **Commercial St. E1** | **13** | **F6** |
| Commercial St. E1 | 112 | C4 |
| Commercial Way NW10 | 106 | B2 |
| Commercial Way SE15 | 132 | C7 |
| Commerell St. SE10 | 135 | E5 |
| **Commodity Quay E1** | **21** | **G6** |
| Commodore Sq. SW10 | 149 | G1 |
| Commodore St. E1 | 113 | H4 |
| Common, The W5 | 105 | H7 |
| Common, The, Rich. | 163 | G3 |
| Common, The, Sthl. | 122 | C4 |
| Common, The, Stan. | 52 | B2 |
| Common La., Esher | 194 | D7 |
| Common Rd. SW13 | 147 | G3 |
| Common Rd., Esher | 194 | D6 |
| Common Rd., Stan. | 52 | A4 |
| Commondale SW15 | 147 | J3 |
| Commonfield La. SW17 | 167 | H5 |
| *Tooting Gro.* | | |
| Commonside, Kes. | 205 | J4 |
| Commonside E., Mitch. | 185 | J3 |
| Commonside W., Mitch. | 185 | J3 |
| Commonwealth Av. W12 | 107 | H7 |
| Commonwealth Rd. N17 | 60 | D7 |
| Commonwealth Way SE2 | 138 | B5 |
| Community Cl., Houns. | 142 | B1 |
| Community La. N7 | 92 | D5 |
| Community Rd. E15 | 96 | D5 |
| Community Rd., Grnf. | 103 | J1 |
| Como Rd. SE23 | 171 | H2 |
| Compass Hill, Rich. | 145 | G6 |
| Compayne Gdns. NW6 | 90 | E7 |
| Compton Av. E6 | 116 | A2 |
| Compton Av. N1 | 93 | H6 |
| Compton Av. N6 | 73 | H7 |
| Compton Cl. E3 | 114 | A5 |
| **Compton Cl. NW1** | **9** | **E4** |
| Compton Cl. NW11 | 90 | A3 |
| *The Vale* | | |
| Compton Cl. W13 | 104 | D6 |
| Compton Cl., Edg. | 54 | C7 |
| *Pavilion Way* | | |
| Compton Ct. SE19 | 170 | B5 |
| *Victoria Cres.* | | |
| Compton Cres. N17 | 59 | J7 |
| Compton Cres. W4 | 126 | C6 |
| Compton Cres., Chess. | 195 | H6 |
| Compton Cres., Nthlt. | 102 | D1 |
| **Compton Pas. EC1** | **11** | **H5** |
| **Compton Pl. WC1** | **10** | **A5** |
| Compton Pl., Wat. | 50 | E3 |
| Compton Ri., Pnr. | 67 | E5 |
| Compton Rd. N1 | 93 | H6 |
| Compton Rd. N21 | 59 | G1 |
| Compton Rd. NW10 | 108 | A3 |
| Compton Rd. SW19 | 166 | C6 |
| Compton Rd., Croy. | 202 | E1 |
| **Compton St. EC1** | **11** | **G5** |
| Compton St. EC1 | 111 | H4 |
| Compton Ter. N1 | 93 | H6 |
| Comreddy Cl., Enf. | 43 | H1 |
| **Comus Pl. SE17** | **36** | **D2** |
| Comus Pl. SE17 | 132 | B4 |
| Comyn Rd. SW11 | 149 | H4 |
| Comyns, The, Bushey | 51 | J1 |
| Comyns Cl. E16 | 115 | F5 |
| Comyns Rd., Dag. | 101 | G7 |
| **Conant Ms. E1** | **21** | **H5** |
| Concanon Rd. SW2 | 151 | F4 |
| **Concert Hall App. SE1** | **26** | **D2** |
| Concert Hall App. SE1 | 131 | F1 |
| Concord Cl., Nthlt. | 102 | D3 |
| *Britannia Cl.* | | |
| Concord Rd. W3 | 106 | B4 |
| Concord Rd., Enf. | 45 | F5 |
| Concorde Cl., Houns. | 143 | H2 |
| *Lampton Rd.* | | |
| Concorde Dr. E6 | 116 | C5 |
| Concourse, The N9 | 60 | D2 |
| *New Rd.* | | |
| Concourse, The NW9 | 71 | F1 |
| Condell Rd. SW8 | 150 | C1 |
| Conder St. E14 | 113 | H6 |
| *Salmon La.* | | |

| Name | No. | Grid |
|---|---|---|
| Conderton Rd. SE5 | 151 | J3 |
| Condor Path, Nthlt. | 103 | G2 |
| *Brabazon Rd.* | | |
| Condover Cres. SE18 | 136 | E7 |
| Condray Pl. SW11 | 129 | H7 |
| Conduit Av. SE10 | 154 | D1 |
| *Crooms Hill* | | |
| **Conduit Ct. WC2** | **18** | **A5** |
| Conduit La. N18 | 61 | F5 |
| Conduit La., Croy. | 202 | D5 |
| Conduit La., Enf. | 45 | H6 |
| *Morson Rd.* | | |
| Conduit La., S.Croy. | 202 | D5 |
| **Conduit Ms. W2** | **14** | **E4** |
| Conduit Ms. W2 | 109 | G4 |
| **Conduit Pas. W2** | **15** | **E4** |
| **Conduit Pl. W2** | **15** | **E4** |
| Conduit Rd. NW10 | 109 | G6 |
| Conduit Rd. SE18 | 137 | E5 |
| **Conduit St. W1** | **17** | **E5** |
| Conduit St. W1 | 110 | B7 |
| Conduit Way NW10 | 88 | C7 |
| Conewood St. N5 | 93 | H3 |
| Coney Acre SE21 | 169 | J1 |
| Coney Burrows E4 | 62/63 | E2 |
| *Wyemead Cres.* | | |
| Coney Hill Rd., W.Wick. | 205 | E2 |
| **Coney Way SW8** | **34** | **D6** |
| Coney Way SW8 | 131 | F6 |
| Coneygrove Path, Nthlt. | 84/85 | E6 |
| *Arnold Rd.* | | |
| Conference Cl. E4 | 62 | C2 |
| *Greenbank Cl.* | | |
| Conference Rd. SE2 | 138 | C4 |
| Congleton Gro. SE18 | 137 | F5 |
| Congo Rd. SE18 | 137 | G5 |
| Congress Rd. SE2 | 138 | C4 |
| Congreve Rd. SE9 | 156 | C3 |
| **Congreve St. SE17** | **36** | **D1** |
| Congreve St. SE17 | 132 | B4 |
| Congreve Wk. E16 | 116 | A5 |
| Conical Cor., Enf. | 43 | J2 |
| Conifer Cl., Orp. | 207 | G4 |
| Conifer Gdns. SW16 | 169 | E3 |
| Conifer Gdns., Enf. | 44 | B6 |
| Conifer Gdns., Sutt. | 198 | E2 |
| Conifer Way, Hayes | 102 | A7 |
| *Longmead Rd.* | | |
| Conifer Way, Wem. | 87 | F3 |
| Conifers Cl., Tedd. | 163 | E7 |
| Coniger Rd. SW6 | 148 | D2 |
| Coningham Ms. W12 | 127 | G1 |
| *Percy Rd.* | | |
| Coningham Rd. W12 | 127 | H1 |
| Coningsby Cotts. W5 | 125 | G2 |
| *Coningsby Rd.* | | |
| Coningsby Gdns. E4 | 62 | B6 |
| Coningsby Rd. N4 | 75 | H7 |
| Coningsby Rd. W5 | 125 | G2 |
| Conington Rd. SE13 | 154 | B2 |
| Conisbee Ct. N14 | 42 | C5 |
| Conisborough Cres. SE6 | 172 | C3 |
| Coniscliffe Cl., Chis. | 192 | D1 |
| Coniscliffe Rd. N13 | 59 | J3 |
| Coniston Av., Bark. | 99 | H7 |
| Coniston Av., Grnf. | 105 | E3 |
| Coniston Av., Well. | 157 | H3 |
| Coniston Cl. N20 | 57 | F3 |
| Coniston Cl. SW13 | 172 | C3 |
| *Lonsdale Rd.* | | |
| Coniston Cl. SW20 | 184 | A6 |
| Coniston Cl. W4 | 146 | C1 |
| Coniston Cl., Bark. | 99 | H7 |
| *Coniston Av.* | | |
| Coniston Cl., Bexh. | 159 | J1 |
| Coniston Gdns. N9 | 61 | J1 |
| Coniston Gdns. NW9 | 70 | D5 |
| Coniston Gdns., Ilf. | 80 | B4 |
| Coniston Gdns., Pnr. | 66 | A4 |
| Coniston Gdns., Sutt. | 199 | G6 |
| Coniston Gdns., Wem. | 87 | F1 |
| **Coniston Ho. SE5** | **35** | **J7** |
| Coniston Ho. SE5 | 131 | J7 |
| Coniston Rd. N10 | 74 | B2 |
| Coniston Rd. N17 | 60 | D6 |
| Coniston Rd., Bexh. | 159 | J1 |
| Coniston Rd., Brom. | 172 | E6 |
| Coniston Rd., Croy. | 188 | D7 |
| Coniston Rd., Twick. | 143 | H6 |
| Coniston Wk. E9 | 95 | F5 |
| *Clifden Rd.* | | |
| Coniston Way, Chess. | 195 | H3 |
| Conistone Way N7 | 93 | E7 |
| Conlan St. W10 | 108 | B4 |
| Conley Rd. NW10 | 89 | E6 |
| Conley St. SE10 | 134/135 | E5 |
| *Pelton Rd.* | | |
| Connaught Av. E4 | 46 | D7 |
| Connaught Av. SW14 | 146 | C3 |
| Connaught Av., Barn. | 57 | J1 |
| Connaught Av., Enf. | 44 | B2 |
| Connaught Av., Houns. | 143 | E5 |
| Connaught Av., Loug. | 48 | A4 |
| Connaught Br. E16 | 116 | A7 |
| Connaught Cl. E10 | 95 | H2 |
| **Connaught Cl. W2** | **15** | **G4** |
| Connaught Cl., Enf. | 44 | B2 |
| Connaught Cl., Sutt. | 199 | G2 |
| Connaught Dr. NW11 | 72 | D4 |
| Connaught Gdns. N10 | 74 | B5 |
| Connaught Gdns. N13 | 59 | H4 |
| Connaught Gdns., Mord. | 185 | F4 |
| Connaught Hill, Loug. | 48 | A4 |
| Connaught La., Ilf. | 99 | G2 |
| *Connaught Rd.* | | |
| **Connaught Ms. SE18** | 136 | D5 |
| **Connaught Ms. W2** | **15** | **J4** |
| Connaught Ms., Ilf. | 99 | G2 |
| *Connaught Rd.* | | |
| **Connaught Pl. W2** | **15** | **J5** |
| Connaught Pl. W2 | 109 | J7 |
| Connaught Rd. E4 | 46 | E7 |
| Connaught Rd. E11 | 96 | D1 |
| Connaught Rd. E16 | 136 | A1 |
| Connaught Rd. E17 | 78 | A5 |
| Connaught Rd. N4 | 75 | G7 |
| Connaught Rd. NW10 | 107 | E1 |
| Connaught Rd. SE18 | 136 | D5 |
| Connaught Rd. W13 | 104 | E7 |
| Connaught Rd., Barn. | 40 | A6 |
| Connaught Rd., Har. | 68 | C1 |
| Connaught Rd., Ilf. | 99 | G2 |
| Connaught Rd., N.Mal. | 183 | E4 |
| Connaught Rd., Rich. | 145 | J5 |
| *Albert Rd.* | | |
| Connaught Rd., Sutt. | 199 | G2 |
| Connaught Rd., Tedd. | 162 | A5 |
| Connaught Roundabout E16 | 116 | A7 |
| *Connaught Br.* | | |
| **Connaught Sq. W2** | **15** | **J4** |
| Connaught Sq. W2 | 109 | J6 |
| **Connaught St. W2** | **15** | **G4** |
| Connaught St. W2 | 109 | H6 |
| Connaught Way N13 | 59 | H4 |
| Connell Cres. W5 | 105 | J4 |
| Connemara Cl., Borwd. | 38 | D6 |
| *Percheron Rd.* | | |
| Connington Cres. E4 | 62 | D3 |
| Connor Cl., Ilf. | 80 | C1 |
| *Fullwell Av.* | | |
| Connor Rd., Dag. | 101 | F4 |
| Connor St. E9 | 113 | G1 |
| *Lauriston Rd.* | | |
| Conolly Rd. W7 | 124 | B1 |
| Conrad Dr., Wor.Pk. | 197 | J1 |
| Conrad Ho. N16 | 94 | B5 |
| **Cons St. SE1** | **27** | **F3** |
| Consfield Av., N.Mal. | 183 | G4 |
| Consort Ms., Islw. | 144 | A5 |
| Consort Rd. SE15 | 152 | E1 |
| Constable Av. E16 | 135 | H1 |
| *Wesley Av.* | | |
| Constable Cl. NW11 | 73 | E6 |
| Constable Cres. N15 | 76 | D5 |
| Constable Gdns., Edg. | 70 | A1 |
| Constable Gdns., Islw. | 144 | A5 |
| Constable Ms., Dag. | 100 | B4 |
| *Stonard Rd.* | | |
| Constable Wk. SE21 | 170 | C3 |
| Constance Cres., Brom. | 191 | F7 |
| Constance Rd., Croy. | 187 | H7 |
| Constance Rd., Enf. | 44 | B6 |
| Constance Rd., Sutt. | 199 | F4 |
| Constance Rd., Twick. | 143 | H7 |
| Constance St. E16 | 136 | B1 |
| *Albert Rd.* | | |
| Constantine Rd. NW3 | 91 | H4 |
| **Constitution Hill SW1** | **24** | **D3** |
| Constitution Hill SW1 | 130 | B2 |
| Constitution Ri. SE18 | 156 | D1 |
| Consul Av., Dag. | 119 | J3 |
| **Content St. SE17** | **36** | **A2** |
| Content St. SE17 | 132 | A4 |
| Contessa Cl., Orp. | 207 | H5 |
| Control Twr. Rd., Houns. | 140 | D3 |
| Convair Wk., Nthlt. | 102 | D3 |
| *Kittiwake Rd.* | | |
| Convent Cl., Beck. | 172 | C7 |
| Convent Gdns. W5 | 125 | F4 |
| Convent Gdns. W11 | 108 | C6 |
| *Kensington Pk. Rd.* | | |
| Convent Hill SE19 | 169 | J6 |
| Convent Way, Sthl. | 122 | C4 |
| Conway Cl., Stan. | 52 | D6 |
| Conway Cres., Grnf. | 104 | B2 |
| Conway Cres., Rom. | 82 | C7 |
| Conway Dr., Hayes | 121 | F3 |
| Conway Dr., Sutt. | 198 | E6 |
| Conway Gdns., Mitch. | 186 | D4 |
| Conway Gdns., Wem. | 69 | F7 |
| **Conway Ms. W1** | **9** | **F6** |
| Conway Rd. N14 | 59 | E3 |
| Conway Rd. N15 | 75 | H5 |
| Conway Rd. NW2 | 89 | J2 |
| Conway Rd. SE18 | 137 | G4 |
| Conway Rd. SW20 | 183 | J1 |
| Conway Rd., Felt. | 160 | D5 |
| Conway Rd., Houns. | 143 | F7 |
| Conway Rd. (Heathrow Airport), Houns. | 140/141 | E3 |
| *Inner Ring E.* | | |
| Conway St. E13 | 115 | G4 |
| **Conway St. W1** | **9** | **F6** |
| Conway St. W1 | 110 | C5 |
| Conway Wk., Hmptn. | 161 | F6 |
| *Fearnley Cres.* | | |
| Conybeare NW3 | 91 | H7 |
| *King Henry's Rd.* | | |
| Conyer St. E3 | 113 | H2 |
| Conyers Cl., Wdf.Grn. | 62 | E6 |
| Conyers Rd. SW16 | 168 | D5 |
| Conyers Way, Loug. | 49 | E3 |
| Cooden Cl., Brom. | 173 | H7 |
| *Plaistow La.* | | |
| Cooderidge Cl. N17 | 60 | C6 |
| *Brantwood Rd.* | | |
| Cook Cl. SE16 | 133 | F1 |
| *Rotherhithe St.* | | |
| Cook Rd., Dag. | 118 | E1 |
| Cooke Cl. E14 | 134 | A1 |
| *Cabot Sq.* | | |
| Cookes Cl. E11 | 97 | F2 |
| Cookes La., Sutt. | 198 | B6 |
| Cookham Cl., Sthl. | 123 | H2 |
| Cookham Cres. SE16 | 133 | G2 |
| *Marlow Way* | | |
| Cookham Dene Cl., Chis. | 193 | G1 |
| Cookham Rd., Sid. | 177 | G7 |
| Cookhill Rd. SE2 | 138 | B2 |
| Cooks Cl., Rom. | 83 | J1 |
| Cooks Rd. E15 | 114 | B2 |
| **Cooks Rd. SE17** | **35** | **G5** |
| Cooks Rd. SE17 | 131 | H6 |
| Cookson Gro., Erith | 139 | H7 |
| Cool Oak La. NW9 | 71 | E7 |
| Coolfin Rd. E16 | 115 | G6 |
| Coolgardie Av. E4 | 62 | C5 |
| Coolgardie Av., Chig. | 64 | D3 |
| Coolhurst Rd. N8 | 74 | D6 |
| Coomassie Rd. W9 | 108 | C4 |
| *Bravington Rd.* | | |
| Coombe Av., Croy. | 202 | B4 |
| Coombe Bank, Kings.T. | 182 | E1 |
| Coombe Cl., Edg. | 69 | J2 |
| Coombe Cl., Houns. | 143 | G4 |
| Coombe Cor. N21 | 59 | H1 |
| Coombe Cres. Hmptn. | 161 | E7 |
| Coombe Dr., Kings.T. | 164 | D7 |
| Coombe Dr., Ruis. | 84 | B1 |
| Coombe End, Kings.T. | 164 | D7 |
| Coombe Gdns. SW20 | 183 | G2 |
| Coombe Gdns., N.Mal. | 183 | F4 |
| Coombe Hts., Kings.T. | 165 | E7 |
| Coombe Hill Glade, Kings.T. | 165 | E7 |
| Coombe Hill Rd., Kings.T. | 164 | E7 |
| Coombe Ho. Chase, N.Mal. | 182 | D1 |
| Coombe La. SW20 | 183 | H2 |
| Coombe La., Croy. | 202 | C6 |
| Coombe La. W., Kings.T. | 183 | G1 |
| Coombe Lea, Brom. | 192 | B3 |
| Coombe Neville, Kings.T. | 164 | D7 |
| Coombe Pk., Kings.T. | 164 | D5 |
| Coombe Ridings, Kings.T. | 164 | C5 |
| Coombe Ri., Kings.T. | 182 | C1 |
| Coombe Rd. N22 | 75 | G1 |
| Coombe Rd. NW10 | 88 | D3 |
| Coombe Rd. SE26 | 170 | E4 |
| Coombe Rd. W4 | 127 | E5 |
| Coombe Rd. W13 | 124/125 | E3 |
| *Northcroft Rd.* | | |
| Coombe Rd., Croy. | 202 | A4 |
| Coombe Rd., Hmptn. | 161 | F6 |
| Coombe Rd., Kings.T. | 182 | A1 |
| Coombe Rd., N.Mal. | 182 | E3 |
| Coombe Wk., Sutt. | 198 | E3 |
| Coombe Wd. Rd., Kings.T. | 164 | C5 |
| Coombefield Cl., N.Mal. | 183 | E5 |
| Coombehurst Cl., Barn. | 41 | J2 |
| Coomber Way, Croy. | 186 | D7 |
| Coombes Rd., Dag. | 119 | F1 |
| Coombewood Dr., Rom. | 83 | F6 |
| **Coombs St. N1** | **11** | **H2** |
| Coombs St. N1 | 111 | H2 |
| Coomer Ms. SW6 | 128 | C6 |
| *Coomer Pl.* | | |
| Coomer Pl. SW6 | 128 | C6 |
| Coomer Rd. SW6 | 128 | C6 |
| *Coomer Pl.* | | |
| Cooms Wk., Edg. | 70 | C1 |
| *East Rd.* | | |
| Cooper Av. E17 | 77 | G1 |
| **Cooper Cl. SE1** | **27** | **F4** |
| Cooper Ct. E15 | 96 | B5 |
| *Clays La.* | | |
| Cooper Cres., Cars. | 199 | J3 |
| Cooper Rd. NW4 | 72 | A6 |
| Cooper Rd. NW10 | 89 | G5 |
| Cooper Rd., Croy. | 201 | G4 |
| Cooper St. E16 | 115 | F5 |
| *Lawrence St.* | | |
| Cooperage Cl. N17 | 60 | C6 |
| *Brantwood Rd.* | | |
| Coopers Cl. E1 | 113 | F4 |
| Coopers Cl., Dag. | 101 | H6 |
| Coopers Cres., Borwd. | 38 | C1 |
| Coopers La. E10 | 96 | B1 |
| **Coopers La. NW1** | **9** | **J1** |
| Coopers La. NW1 | 110 | D2 |
| Cooper's La. SE12 | 173 | H2 |
| **Coopers Rd. SE1** | **37** | **G4** |
| Coopers Rd. SE1 | 132 | C5 |
| **Cooper's Row EC3** | **21** | **F5** |
| Coopers Wk. E15 | 96 | D5 |
| *Maryland St.* | | |
| Cooper's Yd. SE19 | 170 | B6 |
| *Westow Hill* | | |
| Coopersale Cl., Wdf.Grn. | 63 | J7 |
| *Navestock Cres.* | | |
| Coopersale Rd. E9 | 95 | G5 |
| Coote Gdns., Dag. | 101 | F3 |
| Coote Rd., Bexh. | 159 | F1 |
| Coote Rd., Dag. | 101 | F3 |
| Cope Pl. W8 | 128 | D3 |
| Cope St. SE16 | 133 | G4 |
| Copeland Dr. E14 | 134 | A4 |
| Copeland Rd. E17 | 78 | B5 |
| Copeland Rd. SE15 | 152 | D2 |
| Copeman Cl. SE26 | 171 | F5 |
| Copenhagen Gdns. W4 | 126 | D2 |
| Copenhagen Pl. E14 | 113 | J6 |
| Copenhagen St. N1 | 111 | E1 |
| Copers Cope Rd., Beck. | 171 | J6 |
| Copford Cl., Wdf.Grn. | 64 | B6 |
| Copford Wk. N1 | 111 | J1 |
| *Popham St.* | | |
| Copgate Path SW16 | 169 | F6 |
| Copinger Wk., Edg. | 70 | B1 |
| *North Rd.* | | |
| Copland Av., Wem. | 87 | G5 |
| Copland Cl., Wem. | 87 | F5 |
| Copland Ms., Wem. | 87 | H6 |
| *Copland Rd.* | | |
| Copland Rd., Wem. | 87 | H6 |
| Copleston Ms. SE15 | 152 | C2 |
| *Copleston Rd.* | | |
| Copleston Pas. SE15 | 152 | C3 |
| Copleston Rd. SE15 | 152 | C3 |
| **Copley Cl. SE17** | **35** | **H6** |
| Copley Cl. W7 | 104 | C5 |
| Copley Dene, Brom. | 192 | A1 |
| Copley Pk. SW16 | 169 | F6 |
| Copley Rd., Stan. | 53 | F5 |
| Copley St. E1 | 113 | G5 |
| *Stepney Grn.* | | |
| **Copnor Way SE15** | **37** | **E7** |
| Coppard Gdns., Chess. | 195 | F6 |
| Copped Hall SE21 | 170 | A2 |
| *Glazebrook Cl.* | | |

Coppelia Rd. SE3 155 F4
Coppen Rd., Dag. 83 F7
Copper Beech Cl. NW3 91 G6
*Daleham Ms.*
Copper Beech Cl., Ilf. 80 D1
Copper Beech Ct., Loug. 48 D1
Copper Beeches, Islw. 144 A1
*Eversley Cres.*
Copper Cl. SE19 170 C7
*Auckland Rd.*
Copper Mead Cl. NW2 89 J3
Copper Mill Dr., Islw. 144 C2
Copper Mill La. SW17 167 F4
**Copper Row SE1 29 F2**
Copper Row SE1 132 C1
Copperas St. SE8 134 B6
Copperbeech Cl. NW3 91 G5
*Akenside Rd.*
Copperdale Rd., Hayes 122 A2
Copperfield, Chig. 65 G6
Copperfield App., Chig. 65 G6
Copperfield Ct., Pnr. 67 F4
*Copperfield Way*
Copperfield Dr. N15 76 C4
Copperfield Ms. N18 60 B5
Copperfield Rd. E3 113 H4
Copperfield Rd. SE28 118 C6
**Copperfield St. SE1 27 H3**
Copperfield St. SE1 131 H2
Copperfield Way, Chis. 175 F6
Copperfield Way, Pnr. 67 F4
Coppergate Cl., Brom. 191 H1
Coppermill La. E17 77 F6
Coppetts Cl. N12 57 H7
Coppetts Rd. N10 74 A2
Coppice, The, Enf. 43 H4
Coppice Cl. SW20 183 J3
Coppice Cl., Stan. 52 C6
Coppice Dr. SW15 147 H6
Coppice Wk. N20 56 D3
Coppice Way E18 79 F4
Coppies Gro. N11 58 A4
Copping Cl., Croy. 202 B4
*Tipton Dr.*
Coppins, The, Croy. 204 B6
Coppins, The, Har. 52 B6
Coppock Cl. SW11 149 H2
Coppsfield, W.Mol. 179 G3
*Hurst Rd.*
Copse, The E4 63 F1
Copse Av., W.Wick. 204 B3
Copse Cl. SE7 135 H6
Copse Cl., West Dr. 120 A3
Copse Glade, Surb. 195 G1
Copse Hill SW20 165 H7
Copse Hill, Sutt. 199 E7
Copsewood Cl., Sid. 157 H6
Coptefield Dr., Belv. 138 D3
**Copthall Av. EC2 20 C3**
Copthall Av. EC2 112 A6
**Copthall Bldgs. EC2 20 B3**
**Copthall Cl. EC2 20 B3**
Copthall Ct. EC2 112 A6
Copthall Dr. NW7 55 G7
Copthall Gdns. NW7 55 G7
Copthall Gdns., Twick. 162 C1
Copthorne Av. SW12 150 D7
Copthorne Av., Brom. 206 C2
Copthorne Av., Ilf. 65 E6
Copthorne Ms., Hayes 121 H4
**Coptic St. WC1 18 A2**
Coptic St. WC1 110 E5
Copwood Cl. N12 57 G4
Coral Cl., Rom. 82 C3
Coral Row SW11 149 F3
*Gartons Way*
**Coral St. SE1 27 F4**
Coral St. SE1 131 G2
Coraline Cl., Sthl. 103 F3
Coralline Wk. SE2 138 C2
**Coram St. WC1 10 A6**
Coram St. WC1 110 E4
Coran Cl. N9 45 G7
Corban Rd., Houns. 143 G3
Corbet Cl., Wall. 200 A1
**Corbet Ct. EC3 20 C4**
**Corbet Pl. E1 21 F1**
Corbett Gro. N22 58 E7
Corbett Ho., Wat. 50 C3
Corbett Rd. E11 79 J6
Corbett Rd. E17 78 C3
Corbetts La. SE16 133 F4
*Rotherhithe New Rd.*
Corbetts Pas. SE16 133 F4
*Rotherhithe New Rd.*
Corbicum E11 79 E7
Corbiere Ct. SW19 166 A6
*Thornton Rd.*
Corbiere Ho. N1 112 B1
Corbins La., Har. 85 H3
Corbridge Cres. E2 112 E2
Corby Cres., Enf. 43 E4
Corby Rd. NW10 106 D2
Corby Way E3 114 A4
*Knapp Rd.*
Corbylands Rd., Sid. 157 H7
Corbyn St. N4 93 E1
Cord Way E14 134 A3
*Mellish St.*
Cordelia Cl. SE24 151 H4
Cordelia Gdns., Stai. 140 B7
Cordelia Rd., Stai. 140 B7
Cordelia St. E14 114 B6
Cording St. E14 114 B5
*Chrisp St.*
Cordova Rd. E3 113 H3
Cordwainers Wk. E13 115 G2
*Clegg St.*
Cordwell Rd. SE13 154 E5
Corelli Rd. SE3 156 B2
Corfe Av., Har. 85 G4
Corfe Cl., Hayes 102 C6
Corfe Twr. W3 126 B2
Corfield Rd. N21 43 F5
Corfield St. E2 113 E3
Corfton Rd. W5 105 H6
Coriander Av. E14 114 D6
Cories Cl., Dag. 100 D2
Corinium Cl., Wem. 87 J4
Corinne Rd. N19 92 C4
Corinthian Way, Stai. 140 A7
*Clare Rd.*
Cork Sq. E1 132/133 E1
*Smeaton St.*
**Cork St. W1 17 F6**
Cork St. W1 110 C7
**Cork St. Ms. W1 17 F6**
Cork Tree Way E4 61 H5
Corker Wk. N7 93 F2
Corkran Rd., Surb. 181 G7
Corkscrew Hill, W.Wick. 204 D2
**Corlett St. NW1 15 G1**
Corlett St. NW1 109 H5
Cormont Rd. SE5 151 H1
Cormorant Cl. E17 77 G7
*Banbury Rd.*
Cormorant Pl., Sutt. 198 B2
*Gander Grn. La.*
Cormorant Rd. E7 97 F5
Corn Mill Dr., Orp. 193 J7
Corn Way E11 96 D3
Cornbury Rd., Edg. 53 G7
Cornelia St. N7 93 F6
Cornell Cl., Sid. 177 E6
Corner Grn. SE3 155 G2
**Corner Ho. St. WC2 26 A1**
Corner Mead NW9 55 F7
Corney Reach Way W4 127 E7
Corney Rd. W4 127 E6
Cornflower La., Croy. 203 G1
Cornflower Ter. SE22 152 E6
Cornford Cl., Brom. 191 G5
Cornford Gro. SW12 168 B2
**Cornhill EC3 20 C4**
Cornhill EC3 112 A6
Cornish Ct. N9 44 E7
Cornish Gro. SE20 171 E7
**Cornish Ho. SE17 35 G6**
Cornish Ho., Brent. 125 J5
*Green Dragon La.*
Cornmill La. SE13 154 B3
Cornmow Dr. NW10 89 F5
Cornshaw Rd., Dag. 100 D1
Cornthwaite Rd. E5 95 F3
Cornwall Av. E2 113 F3
Cornwall Av. N3 56 D7
Cornwall Av. N22 75 E1
Cornwall Av., Esher 194 C7
*The Causeway*
Cornwall Av., Sthl. 103 F5
Cornwall Av., Well. 157 H3
Cornwall Cl., Bark. 99 J6
Cornwall Cres. W11 108 B7
Cornwall Dr., Orp. 176 C7
Cornwall Gdns. NW10 • 89 H6
**Cornwall Gdns. SW7 22 B6**
Cornwall Gdns. SW7 129 F3
**Cornwall Gdns. Wk. SW7 22 B6**
Cornwall Gro. W4 127 E5
**Cornwall Ms. S. SW7 22 C6**
Cornwall Ms. S. SW7 129 F3
**Cornwall Ms. W. SW7 22 B6**
Cornwall Rd. N4 75 G7
Cornwall Rd. N15 76 A5
Cornwall Rd. N18 60 D5
*Fairfield Rd.*
**Cornwall Rd. SE1 26 E1**
Cornwall Rd. SE1 131 G1
Cornwall Rd., Croy. 201 H2
Cornwall Rd., Esher 194 D7
Cornwall Rd., Har. 67 J6
Cornwall Rd., Pnr. 51 F7
Cornwall Rd., Sutt. 198 C7
Cornwall Rd., Twick. 162 D1
Cornwall St. E1 112/113 E7
*Watney St.*
**Cornwall Ter. NW1 8 A6**
**Cornwall Ter. Ms. NW1 8 A6**
Cornwallis Av. N9 61 E2
Cornwallis Av. SE9 175 G2
Cornwallis Gro. N9 61 E2
Cornwallis Rd. E17 77 G4
Cornwallis Rd. N9 61 E2
Cornwallis Rd. N19 92 E2
Cornwallis Rd., Dag. 100 D4
Cornwallis Sq. N19 92 E2
Cornwallis Wk. SE9 156 C3
Cornwood Cl. N2 73 G5
Cornwood Dr. E1 113 F6
Cornworthy Rd., Dag. 100 C5
Corona Rd. SE12 155 G7
Coronation Av. N16 94 C3
*Victorian Rd.*
Coronation Cl., Bex. 158 D6
Coronation Cl., Ilf. 81 F4
Coronation Rd. E13 115 J3
Coronation Rd. NW10 105 J3
Coronation Rd., Hayes 121 J4
Coronation Wk., Twick. 161 F1
**Coronet St. N1 12 D4**
Coronet St. N1 112 B3
Corporation Av., Houns. 142 E4
**Corporation Row EC1 11 F5**
Corporation Row EC1 111 G4
Corporation St. E15 115 E2
Corporation St. N7 92 E5
Corrance Rd. SW2 151 E4
Corri Av. N14 58 D4
Corrib Dr., Sutt. 199 H5
Corringham Ct. NW11 72/73 E7
*Corringham Rd.*
Corringham Rd. NW11 72 D7
Corringham Rd., Wem. 88 A2
Corringway NW11 72 E7
Corringway W5 106 A4
Corsair Cl., Stai. 140 A7
Corsair Rd., Stai. 140 B7
Corscombe Cl., Kings.T. 164 C5
Corsehill St. SW16 168 C6
**Corsham St. N1 12 C4**
Corsham St. N1 112 A3
Corsica St. N5 93 H6
Corsley Way E9 95 J6
*Osborne Rd.*
Cortayne Rd. SW6 148 C2
Cortis Rd. SW15 147 H6
Cortis Ter. SW15 147 H6
Corunna Rd. SW8 150 C1
Corunna Ter. SW8 150 C1
Corvette Sq. SE10 134 D6
*Feathers Pl.*
Coryton Path W9 108 C4
*Ashmore Rd.*
Cosbycote Av. SE24 151 J5
Cosdach Av., Wall. 200 D7
Cosedge Cres., Croy. 201 G5
Cosgrove Cl. N21 59 J2
Cosgrove Cl., Hayes 102/103 E4
*Kingsash Dr.*
**Cosmo Pl. WC1 18 B1**
Cosmur Cl. W12 127 F3
Cossall Wk. SE15 153 E1
**Cosser St. SE1 26 E5**
Cosser St. SE1 131 G3
Costa St. SE15 152 D2
Coston Wk. SE4 153 G4
*Frendsbury Rd.*
Costons Av., Grnf. 104 A3
Costons La., Grnf. 104 A3
**Cosway St. NW1 15 H1**
Cosway St. NW1 109 H5
Cotall St. E14 114 A6
Coteford Cl., Loug. 48 E2
Coteford Cl., Pnr. 66 A5
Coteford St. SW17 167 J4
Cotelands, Croy. 202 B3
Cotesbach Rd. E5 95 F3
Cotesmore Gdns., Dag. 100 C4
Cotford Rd., Th.Hth. 187 J4
**Cotham St. SE17 36 A2**
Cotherstone Rd. SW2 169 F1
Cotleigh Av., Bex. 176 D2
Cotleigh Rd. NW6 90 D7
Cotman Cl. NW11 73 F6
Cotman Cl. SW15 148 A6
*Westleigh Av.*
Cotman Gdns., Edg. 70 A2
Cotman Ms., Dag. 100 C5
*Highgrove Rd.*
Cotmans Cl., Hayes 122 A1
Coton Rd., Well. 158 A3
Cotsford Av., N.Mal. 182 C5
Cotswold Cl., Esher 194 C3
Cotswold Cl., Kings.T. 164 B6
Cotswold Ct. N11 58 A4
Cotswold Gdns. E6 116 A3
Cotswold Gdns. NW2 90 A2
Cotswold Gdns., Ilf. 81 G7
Cotswold Gate NW2 90 B1
*Cotswold Gdns.*
Cotswold Grn., Enf. 43 F4
*Cotswold Way*
Cotswold Ms. SW11 149 G1
*Battersea High St.*
Cotswold Ri., Orp. 193 J6
Cotswold Rd., Hmptn. 161 G6
Cotswold St. SE27 169 H4
*Norwood High St.*
Cotswold Way, Enf. 43 F4
Cotswold Way, Wor.Pk. 197 J2
Cottage Av., Brom. 206 B1
Cottage Fld. Cl., Sid. 176 C1
**Cottage Grn. SE5 36 C7**
Cottage Grn. SE5 132 A7
Cottage Gro. SW9 150 E3
Cottage Gro., Surb. 181 G6
Cottage Homes NW7 55 G4
**Cottage Pl. SW3 23 G5**
Cottage Pl. SW3 129 H3
Cottage Rd., Epsom 196 D7
Cottage St. E14 114 B7
Cottage Wk. N16 94 C3
*Smalley Cl.*
Cottage Wk. SE15 132 C7
*Sumner Est.*
Cottenham Dr. NW9 71 F3
Cottenham Dr. SW20 165 H7
Cottenham Par. SW20 183 H2
*Durham Rd.*
Cottenham Pk. Rd. SW20 165 H7
Cottenham Pl. SW20 165 H7
Cottenham Rd. E17 77 J4
Cotterill Rd., Surb. 195 H2
Cottesbrook St. SE14 133 H7
*Nynehead St.*
**Cottesloe Ms. SE1 27 F5**
Cottesmore Av., Ilf. 80 D2
**Cottesmore Gdns. W8 22 B5**
Cottesmore Gdns. W8 129 E3
Cottimore Cres., Walt. 178 B7
Cottimore Ter., Walt. 178 B7
Cottingham Chase, Ruis. 84 A3
Cottingham Rd. SE20 171 G7
**Cottingham Rd. SW8 34 D6**
Cottingham Rd. SW8 131 F7
Cottington Rd., Felt. 160 D4
**Cottington St. SE11 35 F3**
Cottle St. SE16 133 F2
*St. Marychurch St.*
Cotton Av. W3 106 D6
Cotton Cl., Dag. 100 C7
*Ellerton Rd.*
Cotton Hill, Brom. 172 D4
Cotton Row SW11 149 F3
Cotton St. E14 114 C7
Cottongrass Cl., Croy. 203 G1
*Cornflower La.*
**Cottons Gdns. E2 13 E3**
**Cottons La. SE1 28 C1**
Cotts Cl. W7 104 C5
*Westcott Cres.*
Couchmore Av., Esher 194 B2
Couchmore Av., Ilf. 80 C2
Coulgate St. SE4 153 H3
Coulson Cl., Dag. 82 C7
**Coulson St. SW3 31 J3**
Coulson St. SW3 129 J4
Coulter Cl., Hayes 102 E4

**Cranleigh St. NW1 9 G2**
Cranleigh St. NW1 110 C2
Cranley Dene Ct. N10 74 B4
Cranley Dr., Ilf. 81 F7
Cranley Gdns. N10 74 C4
Cranley Gdns. N13 59 F3
**Cranley Gdns. SW7 30 D3**
Cranley Gdns. SW7 129 F5
Cranley Gdns., Wall. 200 C7
**Cranley Ms. SW7 30 D3**
Cranley Ms. SW7 129 F5
Cranley Par. SE9 174 B4
*Beaconsfield Rd.*
**Cranley Pl. SW7 31 E2**
Cranley Pl. SW7 129 G4
Cranley Rd. E13 115 H5
Cranley Rd., Ilf. 81 F6
Cranmer Av. W13 125 E3
Cranmer Cl., Mord. 184 A6
Cranmer Cl., Ruis. 84 D1
Cranmer Cl., Stan. 53 F7
**Cranmer Ct. SW3 31 H2**
Cranmer Ct. SW4 150 D3
Cranmer Ct., Hmptn. 161 H5
*Cranmer Rd.*
Cranmer Fm. Cl., Mitch. 185 J4
Cranmer Gdns., Dag. 101 J4
Cranmer Rd. E7 97 H4
**Cranmer Rd. SW9 35 F7**
Cranmer Rd. SW9 131 G7
Cranmer Rd., Croy. 201 H3
Cranmer Rd., Edg. 54 B3
Cranmer Rd., Hmptn. 161 H5
Cranmer Rd., Kings.T. 163 H5
Cranmer Rd., Mitch. 185 J4
Cranmer Ter. SW17 167 G5
Cranmore Av., Islw. 123 J7
Cranmore Rd., Brom. 173 E3
Cranmore Rd., Chis. 174 C5
Cranmore Way N10 74 C4
Cranston Cl., Houns. 143 E2
**Cranston Est. N1 12 C2**
Cranston Est. N1 112 A2
Cranston Gdns. E4 62 B5
Cranston Rd. SE23 171 H1
Cranswick Rd. SE16 133 E5
Crantock Rd. SE6 172 B2
Cranwell Cl. E3 114 B4
Cranwell Rd., Houns. 140 E2
Cranwich Av. N21 44 A7
Cranwich Rd. N16 76 A7
**Cranwood St. EC1 12 B4**
Cranwood St. EC1 112 A3
Cranworth Cres. E4 62 D1
Cranworth Gdns. SW9 151 G1
Craster Rd. SW2 151 F7
Crathie Rd. SE12 155 H6
Cravan Av., Felt. 160 A2
Craven Av. W5 105 F7
Craven Av., Sthl. 103 F5
Craven Cl., Hayes 102 A6
Craven Gdns. SW19 166 D5
Craven Gdns., Bark. 117 H2
Craven Gdns., Ilf. 81 G2
**Craven Hill W2 14 D5**
Craven Hill W2 109 F7
**Craven Hill Gdns. W2 14 C5**
Craven Hill Gdns. W2 109 F7
**Craven Hill Ms. W2 14 D5**
Craven Hill Ms. W2 109 F7
Craven Ms. SW11 150 A3
*Taybridge Rd.*
Craven Pk. NW10 106 E1
Craven Pk. Ms. NW10 106 E1
Craven Pk. Rd. N15 76 C6
Craven Pk. Rd. NW10 107 E1
**Craven Pas. WC2 26 A1**
Craven Pas. WC2 130 E1
Craven Rd. NW10 106 D1
**Craven Rd. W2 14 D5**
Craven Rd. W2 109 F7
Craven Rd. W5 105 F7
Craven Rd., Croy. 202 E1
Craven Rd., Kings.T. 181 J1
**Craven St. WC2 26 A1**
Craven St. WC2 130 E1
**Craven Ter. W2 14 D5**
Craven Ter. W2 109 F7
Craven Wk. N16 76 D7
Crawford Av., Wem. 87 G5
Crawford Cl., Islw. 144 B2
Crawford Est. SE5 151 J2
Crawford Gdns. N13 59 H3
Crawford Gdns., Nthlt. 103 F3
**Crawford Ms. W1 15 J2**
**Crawford Pas. EC1 11 E6**
**Crawford Pl. W1 15 H3**
Crawford Pl. W1 109 H6
Crawford Rd. SE5 151 J1
**Crawford St. W1 15 J2**
Crawford St. W1 109 J5
Crawley Rd. E10 96 B1
Crawley Rd. N22 75 J2
Crawley Rd., Enf. 44 B7
Crawshay Ct. SW9 151 G1
*Eythorne Rd.*
Crawthew Gro. SE22 152 C4
Cray Rd., Belv. 139 G6
Cray Rd., Sid. 176 C7
Craybrooke Rd., Sid. 176 B4
Craybury End SE9 175 F2
Crayford Cl. E6 116 B5
*Neatscourt Rd.*
Crayford Rd. N7 92 D4
Crayke Hill, Chess. 195 H7
Crealock Gro., Wdf.Grn. 63 F5
Crealock St. SW18 149 E6
**Creasy Est. SE1 28 D6**
Creasy Est. SE1 132 B3
Crebor St. SE22 152 D6
Credenhall Dr., Brom. 206 C1
Credenhill St. SW16 168 C6
Crediton Hill NW6 90 E5
Crediton Rd. E16 115 G6
*Pacific Rd.*
Crediton Rd. NW10 108 A1
Crediton Way, Esher 194 D5
Credon Rd. E13 115 J2
Credon Rd. SE16 133 E5
**Creechurch La. EC3 21 E4**
Creechurch La. EC3 112 B6
**Creechurch Pl. EC3 21 E4**
Creed Ct. EC4 111 H6
*Ludgate Hill*
**Creed La. EC4 19 H4**
Creek, The, Sun. 178 A5
Creek Rd. SE8 134 A6
Creek Rd. SE10 134 A6
Creek Rd., Bark. 117 J3
Creek Rd., E.Mol. 180 B4
Creekside SE8 134 B7
Creeland Gro. SE6 171 J1
*Catford Hill*
Crefeld Cl. W6 128 A6
Creffield Rd. W3 105 J7
Creffield Rd. W5 105 J7
Creighton Av. E6 116 A2
Creighton Av. N2 73 H3
Creighton Av. N10 73 H3
Creighton Cl. W12 107 H7
*Bloemfontein Rd.*
Creighton Rd. N17 60 B7
Creighton Rd. NW6 108 A2
Creighton Rd. W5 125 G3
**Cremer St. E2 13 F2**
Cremer St. E2 112 C2
**Cremorne Est. SW10 31 E7**
Cremorne Rd. SW10 129 F7
**Crescent EC3 21 F5**
Crescent, The E17 77 H5
Crescent, The N11 57 J4
Crescent, The NW2 89 H3
Crescent, The SW13 147 F2
Crescent, The SW19 166 D3
Crescent, The W3 106 E6
Crescent, The, Barn. 40 E3
Crescent, The, Beck. 190 A1
Crescent, The, Bex. 158 C7
Crescent, The, Croy. 188 A5
Crescent, The, Har. 86 A1
Crescent, The, Hayes 121 F7
Crescent, The, Ilf. 80 D6
Crescent, The, Loug. 48 A5
Crescent, The, N.Mal. 182 C2
Crescent, The, Sid. 175 J4
Crescent, The, Sthl. 123 F2
Crescent, The, Surb. 181 H5
Crescent, The, Sutt. 199 G4
Crescent, The, Wem. 86 E2
Crescent, The, W.Mol. 179 G4
Crescent, The, W.Wick. 190 E6
Crescent Ct., Surb. 181 G5
Crescent Dr., Orp. 193 E6
Crescent Gdns. SW19 166 D3
Crescent Gdns., Ruis. 66 B6
Crescent Gro. SW4 150 C4
Crescent Gro., Mitch. 185 H4
Crescent La. SW4 150 D5
Crescent Ms. N22 74/75 E1
*Palace Gates Rd.*
**Crescent Pl. SW3 31 G1**
Crescent Pl. SW3 129 H4
Crescent Ri. N22 74 D1
Crescent Ri., Barn. 41 H5
Crescent Rd. E4 47 E7
Crescent Rd. E6 115 J1
Crescent Rd. E10 96 B2
Crescent Rd. E13 115 G1
Crescent Rd. E18 79 J2
Crescent Rd. N3 72 C1
Crescent Rd. N8 74 D7
Crescent Rd. N9 60 D1
Crescent Rd. N11 57 J4
Crescent Rd. N15 75 H3
*Carlingford Rd.*
Crescent Rd. N22 74 D1
Crescent Rd. SE18 136 E5
Crescent Rd. SW20 184 A1
Crescent Rd., Barn. 41 H5
Crescent Rd., Beck. 190 B2
Crescent Rd., Brom. 173 G7
Crescent Rd., Dag. 101 H4
Crescent Rd., Enf. 43 H3
Crescent Rd., Kings.T. 164 A7
Crescent Rd., Sid. 175 J3
**Crescent Row EC1 11 J6**
Crescent Stables SW15 148 B4
*Upper Richmond Rd.*
Crescent St. N1 93 F7
Crescent Vw., Loug. 48 A6
Crescent Way N12 57 H6
Crescent Way SE4 154 A3
Crescent Way SW16 169 F7
Crescent Way, Orp. 207 H5
Crescent Wd. Rd. SE26 170 D3
Cresford Rd. SW6 148 E1
Crespigny Rd. NW4 71 H6
Cressage Cl., Sthl. 103 G4
Cresset Rd. E9 95 F6
Cresset St. SW4 150 D3
Cressfield Cl. NW5 92 A5
Cressida Rd. N19 92 C1
Cressingham Gro., Sutt. 199 F4
Cressingham Rd. SE13 154 C3
Cressingham Rd., Edg. 54 D6
Cressington Cl. N16 94 B5
*Wordsworth Rd.*
**Cresswell Gdns. SW5 30 C3**
Cresswell Gdns. SW5 129 F5
Cresswell Pk. SE3 155 F3
**Cresswell Pl. SW10 30 C3**
Cresswell Pl. SW10 129 F5
Cresswell Rd. SE25 188 D4
Cresswell Rd., Felt. 160 E4
Cresswell Rd., Twick. 145 G6
Cresswell Way N21 43 G7
Cressy Ct. E1 113 F5
*Cressy Pl.*
Cressy Ct. W6 127 H3
Cressy Pl. E1 113 F5
Cressy Rd. NW3 91 J4
Crest, The N13 59 G4
Crest, The NW4 71 J5
Crest, The, Surb. 182 A5
Crest Gdns., Ruis. 84 C3
Crest Rd. NW2 89 F3
Crest Rd., Brom. 191 F7
Crest Rd., S.Croy. 202 E7
Crest Vw., Pnr. 66 D4
Crest Vw. Dr., Orp. 193 E5
Crestbrook Av. N13 59 H3
Crestbrook Pl. N13 59 H3
**Crestfield St. WC1 10 B3**
Crestfield St. WC1 111 E3
Creston Way, Wor.Pk. 198 A1
Crestway SW15 147 H6
Crestwood Way, Houns. 143 F5
Creswick Rd. W3 106 B7
Creswick Wk. E3 114 A3
*Malmesbury Rd.*
Creswick Wk. NW11 72 C4
Creton St. SE18 136 D3
Crewdson Rd. SW9 131 G7
Crewe Pl. NW10 107 F3
Crews St. E14 134 A4
Crewys Rd. NW2 90 C2
Crewys Rd. SE15 153 E2
Crichton Av., Wall. 200 D5
Crichton Rd., Cars. 199 J6
Cricket Grn., Mitch. 185 J3
Cricket Grd. Rd., Chis. 192 E1
Cricket La., Beck. 171 H6
Cricketers Arms Rd., Enf. 43 J2
Cricketers Cl. N14 42 C7
Cricketers Cl., Chess. 195 G4
**Cricketers Ct. SE11 35 G2**
Cricketers Ct. SE11 131 H4
Cricketers Ms. SW18 148/149 E5
*East Hill*
Cricketers Ter., Cars. 199 H3
*Wrythe La.*
Cricketfield Rd. E5 95 E4
Cricklade Av. SW2 169 E2
Cricklewood Bdy. NW2 90 A3
Cricklewood La. NW2 90 A4
Cricklewood Trd. Est. NW2 90 B3
Cridland St. E15 115 F1
*Church St.*
Crieff Ct., Tedd. 163 F7
Crieff Rd. SW18 149 F6
Criffel Av. SW2 168 D2
**Crimscott St. SE1 29 E6**
Crimscott St. SE1 132 B3
Crimsworth Rd. SW8 150 D1
**Crinan St. N1 10 B1**
Crinan St. N1 111 E2
**Cringle St. SW8 33 F7**
Cringle St. SW8 130 C7
**Cripplegate St. EC2 19 J1**
Cripps Grn., Hayes 102 B4
*Stratford Rd.*
Crisp Rd. W6 127 J5
Crispe Ho., Bark. 117 G2
*Dovehouse Mead*
Crispen Rd., Felt. 160 E4
Crispian Cl. NW10 89 E4
Crispin Cl., Croy. 200/201 E2
*Harrington Cl.*
Crispin Cres., Croy. 200 D3
Crispin Rd., Edg. 54 C6
**Crispin St. E1 21 F2**
Crispin St. E1 112 C5
Cristowe Rd. SW6 148 C2
Criterion Ms. N19 92 D2
Crockerton Rd. SW17 167 J2
Crockham Way SE9 174 D4
Crocus Cl., Croy. 203 G1
*Cornflower La.*
Crocus Fld., Barn. 40 C6
Croft, The E4 62 E2
Croft, The NW10 107 F2
Croft, The W5 105 H5
Croft, The, Barn. 40 A4
Croft, The, Houns. 123 E6
Croft, The, Loug. 48 D2
Croft, The, Pnr. 67 F7
*Rayners La.*
Croft, The, Ruis. 84 C4
Croft, The, Wem. 87 F5
Croft Av., W.Wick. 204 C1
Croft Cl. NW7 54 E3
Croft Cl., Belv. 139 F5
Croft Cl., Chis. 174 C4
Croft Cl., Hayes 121 F7
Croft End Cl., Chess. 195 J3
*Ashcroft Rd.*
Croft Gdns. W7 124 D2
Croft Lo. Cl., Wdf.Grn. 63 H6
Croft Ms. N12 57 F3
Croft Rd. SW16 187 G1
Croft Rd. SW19 167 F7
Croft Rd., Brom. 173 G6
Croft Rd., Enf. 45 H1
Croft Rd., Sutt. 199 H5
Croft St. SE8 133 H4
Croft Way NW3 90 D4
*Ferncroft Av.*
Croft Way, Sid. 175 H3
Croftdown Rd. NW5 92 A3
Crofters Cl., Islw. 144 A5
*Ploughmans End*
Crofters Ct. SE8 133 H4
*Croft St.*
Crofters Way NW1 110 D1
Crofton Av. W4 126 D7
Crofton Av., Bex. 158 D7
Crofton Av., Orp. 207 F2
Crofton Gro. E4 62 D4
Crofton La., Orp. 193 H7
Crofton Pk. Rd. SE4 153 J6
Crofton Rd. E13 115 H4
Crofton Rd. SE5 152 B1
Crofton Rd., Orp. 206 D3
Crofton Ter. E5 95 H5
*Studley Cl.*
Crofton Ter., Rich. 145 J4
Crofton Way, Barn. 40/41 E6
*Wycherley Cres.*
Crofton Way, Enf. 43 G2
Croftongate Way SE4 153 H5
Crofts La. N22 59 G7
*Glendale Av.*
Crofts Rd., Har. 68 D6
**Crofts St. E1 21 H6**
Crofts St. E1 112 D7
Croftside SE25 188 D3
*Sunny Bank*
Croftway NW3 90 D4
Croftway, Rich. 163 E3
Crogsland Rd. NW1 92 A7
Croham Cl., S.Croy. 202 B6
Croham Manor Rd., S.Croy. 202 B7

Dale Wd. Rd., Orp. 193 H7
Dalebury Rd. SW17 167 H2
Daleham Gdns. NW3 91 G5
Daleham Ms. NW3 91 G6
**Dalehead NW1 9 F2**
Dalehead NW1 110 C2
Dalemain Ms. E16 135 G1
*Hanover Av.*
Dales Path, Borwd. 38 D5
*Farriers Way*
Dales Rd., Borwd. 38 D5
Daleside Gdns., Chig. 65 F3
Daleside Rd. SW16 168 B5
Daleside Rd., Epsom 196 D6
Daleview Rd. N15 76 B6
Dalewood Gdns., Wor.Pk. 197 H2
Daley St. E9 95 G6
Daley Thompson Way SW8 150 B2
Dalgarno Gdns. W10 107 J5
Dalgarno Way W10 107 J4
Dalgleish St. E14 113 H6
Daling Way E3 113 H1
Dalkeith Gro., Stan. 53 G5
Dalkeith Rd. SE21 169 J1
Dalkeith Rd., Ilf. 99 F3
Dallas Rd. NW4 71 G7
Dallas Rd. SE26 170 E4
Dallas Rd. W5 105 J5
Dallas Rd., Sutt. 198 B6
Dallas Ter., Hayes 121 J3
Dallin Rd. SE18 137 E7
Dallin Rd., Bexh. 158 D4
Dalling Rd. W6 127 H3
Dallinger Rd. SE12 155 F6
**Dallington St. EC1 11 H5**
Dallington St. EC1 111 H4
Dalmain Rd. SE23 171 G1
Dalmally Rd., Croy. 188 C7
Dalmeny Av. N7 92 D4
Dalmeny Av. SW16 187 G2
Dalmeny Cl., Wem. 87 F6
Dalmeny Cres., Houns. 144 A4
Dalmeny Rd. N7 92 D3
Dalmeny Rd., Barn. 41 F6
Dalmeny Rd., Cars. 200 A7
Dalmeny Rd., Erith 159 H1
Dalmeny Rd., Wor.Pk. 197 H3
Dalmeyer Rd. NW10 89 F6
Dalmore Av., Esher 194 C6
Dalmore Rd. SE21 169 J2
Dalrymple Cl. N14 42 D7
Dalrymple Rd. SE4 153 H4
Dalston Cross Shop. Cen. E8 94 C6
Dalston Gdns., Stan. 69 H1
Dalston La. E8 94 C6
Dalton Av., Mitch. 185 H2
Dalton Cl., Orp. 207 H3
Dalton Rd., Har. 68 A2
Dalton St. SE27 169 H2
Dalwood St. SE5 152 B1
Daly Ct. E15 96 C5
*Clays La.*
Dalyell Rd. SW9 151 F3
Damascene Wk. SE21 169 J1
*Lovelace Rd.*
Damask Cres. E16 114/115 E4
*Cranberry La.*
**Dame St. N1 11 J1**
Dame St. N1 111 J2
Damer Ter. SW10 129 F7
*Tadema Rd.*
Dames Rd. E7 97 G3
Damien St. E1 113 E6
Damon Cl., Sid. 176 B3
Damsonwood Rd., Sthl. 123 G3
Dan Leno Wk. SW6 128/129 E7
*Britannia Rd.*
Danbrook Rd. SW16 187 E1
Danbury Cl., Rom. 82 D3
Danbury Ms., Wall. 200 B4
Danbury Rd., Loug. 48 B7
**Danbury St. N1 11 H1**
Danbury St. N1 111 H2
Danbury Way, Wdf.Grn. 63 J6
Danby St. SE15 152 C3
Dancer Rd. SW6 148 C1
Dancer Rd., Rich. 146 A3
Dando Cres. SE3 155 H3
Dandridge Cl. SE10 135 F5
Dane Cl., Bex. 159 G7
Dane Cl., Orp. 207 G5
Dane Pl. E3 113 H2
*Roman Rd.*
Dane Rd. N18 61 F3
Dane Rd. SW19 185 F1
Dane Rd. W13 125 F1
Dane Rd., Ilf. 99 F5
Dane Rd., Sthl. 103 E7
**Dane St. WC1 18 C2**
Danebury, Croy. 204 B6
Danebury Av. SW15 147 E6
Daneby Rd. SE6 172 B3
Danecourt Gdns., Croy. 202 C3
Danecroft Rd. SE24 151 J5
Danehill Wk., Sid. 176 A3
*Hatherley Rd.*
Danehurst Gdns., Ilf. 80 B5
Danehurst St. SW6 148 B1
Daneland, Barn. 41 J6
Danemead Gro., Nthlt. 85 H5
Danemere St. SW15 147 J3
Danes Ct., Wem. 88 B3
Danes Gate, Har. 68 B3
Danes Rd., Rom. 83 J7
Danesbury Rd., Felt. 160 B1
Danescombe SE12 173 G1
*Winn Rd.*
Danescourt Cres., Sutt. 199 F2
Danescroft NW4 72 A5
Danescroft Av. NW4 72 A5
Danescroft Gdns. NW4 72 A5
Danesdale Rd. E9 95 H6
**Danesfield SE5 36 D5**
Daneswood Av. SE6 172 C3
Danethorpe Rd., Wem. 87 G6
Danetree Cl., Epsom 196 C7
Danetree Rd., Epsom 196 C7
Danette Gdns., Dag. 101 F2
Daneville Rd. SE5 152 A1
Dangan Rd. E11 79 G6
Daniel Bolt Cl. E14 114 B5
*Uamvar St.*
Daniel Cl. N18 61 F4
Daniel Cl. SW17 167 H6
**Daniel Gdns. SE15 37 F7**
Daniel Gdns. SE15 132 C7
Daniel Pl. NW4 71 H7
Daniel Rd. W5 105 J7
Daniell Way, Croy. 201 E1
Daniels Ms. SE4 153 J4
Daniels Rd. SE15 153 F3
**Dansey Pl. W1 17 H5**
Dansington Rd., Well. 158 A4
Danson Cres., Well. 158 B3
Danson La., Well. 158 B4
Danson Mead, Well. 158 C3
Danson Pk., Bexh. 158 C4
Danson Rd., Bex. 158 D5
Danson Rd., Bexh. 158 D5
Danson Underpass, Sid. 158 C6
*Danson Rd.*
**Dante Pl. SE11 35 H1**
**Dante Rd. SE11 35 G1**
Dante Rd. SE11 131 H4
**Danube St. SW3 31 H3**
Danvers Rd. N8 74 D4
**Danvers St. SW3 31 F6**
Danvers St. SW3 129 G6
Danziger Way, Borwd. 38 C1
Daphne Gdns. E4 62 C3
*Gunners Gro.*
Daphne St. SW18 149 F6
**Daplyn St. E1 21 H1**
**D'Arblay St. W1 17 G4**
D'Arblay St. W1 110 C6
Darby Cres., Sun. 178 C2
Darby Gdns., Sun. 178 C2
Darcy Av., Wall. 200 C4
Darcy Cl. N20 57 G2
D'Arcy Dr., Har. 69 G4
Darcy Gdns., Dag. 119 F1
D'Arcy Gdns., Har. 69 H4
Darcy Rd. SW16 186 E2
Darcy Rd., Islw. 144 D1
*London Rd.*
D'Arcy Rd., Sutt. 198 A4
Dare Gdns., Dag. 100/101 E3
*Grafton Rd.*
Darell Rd., Rich. 146 A3
Darenth Rd. N16 76 C7
Darenth Rd., Well. 158 A1
Darfield Rd. SE4 153 J5
Darfield Way W10 108 A6
Darfur St. SW15 148 A3
Dargate Cl. SE19 170 C7
*Chipstead Cl.*
Darien Rd. SW11 149 G3
Darlan Rd. SW6 128 C7
Darlaston Rd. SW19 166 A7
Darley Cl., Croy. 189 H6
Darley Dr., N.Mal. 182 D2
Darley Gdns., Mord. 185 E6
Darley Rd. N9 60 C1
Darley Rd. SW11 149 J6
Darling Rd. SE4 154 A3
Darling Row E1 113 E4
Darlington Rd. SE27 169 H5
Darmaine Cl., S.Croy. 201 J7
*Churchill Rd.*
Darndale Cl. E17 77 J2
Darnley Ho. E14 113 H6
Darnley Rd. E9 95 E6
Darnley Rd., Wdf.Grn. 79 G1
Darnley Ter. W11 128 B1
*St. James's Gdns.*
Darrell Rd. SE22 152 D5
Darren Cl. N4 75 F7
Darrick Wd. Rd., Orp. 207 G2
Darris Cl., Hayes 103 E4
Darsley Dr. SW8 150 E1
Dart St. W10 108 B3
Dartford Av. N9 45 F6
Dartford Gdns., Rom. 82 B6
*Heathfield Pk. Dr.*
Dartford Rd., Bex. 177 J1
**Dartford St. SE17 36 A5**
Dartford St. SE17 131 J6
Dartmoor Wk. E14 134 A4
*Charnwood Gdns.*
Dartmouth Cl. W11 108 C6
Dartmouth Gro. SE10 154 C1
Dartmouth Hill SE10 154 C1
Dartmouth Pk. Av. NW5 92 B3
Dartmouth Pk. Hill N19 92 B1
Dartmouth Pk. Hill NW5 92 B4
Dartmouth Pk. Rd. NW5 92 B4
Dartmouth Pl. SE23 171 F2
*Dartmouth Rd.*
Dartmouth Pl. W4 127 E6
Dartmouth Rd. E16 115 G6
*Fords Pk. Rd.*
Dartmouth Rd. NW2 90 A6
Dartmouth Rd. NW4 71 G6
Dartmouth Rd. SE23 171 F3
Dartmouth Rd. SE26 171 F3
Dartmouth Rd., Brom. 191 G7
Dartmouth Rd., Ruis. 84 A3
Dartmouth Row SE10 154 C1
**Dartmouth St. SW1 25 H4**
Dartmouth St. SW1 130 D2
Dartmouth Ter. SE10 154 D1
Dartnell Rd., Croy. 188 C7
**Dartrey Wk. SW10 30 D7**
Darville Rd. N16 94 C3
Darwell Cl. E6 116 D2
Darwin Cl. N11 58 B3
Darwin Cl., Orp. 207 G5
Darwin Dr., Sthl. 103 H6
Darwin Gdns., Wat. 50 C5
*Barnhurst Path*
Darwin Rd. N22 75 H1
Darwin Rd. W5 125 F5
Darwin Rd., Well. 157 J3
**Darwin St. SE17 36 C1**
Darwin St. SE17 132 A4
Daryngton Dr., Grnf. 104 A2
Dashwood Cl., Bexh. 159 G5
Dashwood Rd. N8 75 F6
Dassett Rd. SE27 169 H5
Datchelor Pl. SE5 152 A1
Datchet Rd. SE6 171 J3
Datchworth Ct. N4 93 J3
*Queens Dr.*
**Date St. SE17 36 B4**
Date St. SE17 131 J5
Daubeney Gdns. N17 59 J7
Daubeney Rd. E5 95 H4
Daubeney Rd. N17 59 J7
Daubeney Twr. SE8 133 J4
Dault Rd. SW18 149 F6
Davema Cl., Chis. 192 D1
*Brenchley Cl.*
Davenant Rd. N19 92 D2
Davenant Rd., Croy. 201 H4
*Duppas Hill Rd.*
**Davenant St. E1 21 J2**
Davenant St. E1 112 D5
Davenport Cl., Tedd. 162 D6
Davenport Rd. SE6 154 B6
Davenport Rd., Sid. 176 D2
Daventer Dr., Stan. 52 C7
Daventry Av. E17 78 A5
**Daventry St. NW1 15 G1**
Daventry St. NW1 109 H5
Davern Cl. SE10 135 F4
Davey Cl. N7 93 F6
Davey Rd. E9 96 A7
**Davey St. SE15 37 G6**
Davey St. SE15 132 C6
David Av., Grnf. 104 B3
David Cl., Hayes 121 G7
**David Ms. W1 16 A1**
David Rd., Dag. 100 E2
David St. E15 96 D6
**Davidge St. SE1 27 G4**
Davidge St. SE1 131 H2
Davids Rd. SE23 171 F1
David's Way, Ilf. 65 H7
Davidson Gdns. SW8 130 E7
Davidson La., Har. 68 C7
*Grove Hill*
Davidson Rd., Croy. 188 C6
Davies Cl., Croy. 188 D6
Davies La. E11 97 E2
**Davies Ms. W1 16 D5**
**Davies St. W1 16 D5**
Davies St. W1 110 B7
Davington Gdns., Dag. 100 B5
Davington Rd., Dag. 100 B6
Davinia Cl., Wdf.Grn. 64 C6
*Deacon Way*
Davis Rd. W3 127 F1
Davis Rd., Chess. 196 A4
Davis St. E13 115 H2
Davisville Rd. W12 127 G2
Dawes Av., Islw. 144 D5
**Dawes Ho. SE17 36 C2**
Dawes Rd. SW6 128 B7
**Dawes St. SE17 36 C3**
Dawes St. SE17 132 A5
Dawley Rd., Hayes 121 H3
Dawlish Av. N13 58 E4
Dawlish Av. SW18 166 E2
Dawlish Av., Grnf. 104 D2
Dawlish Dr., Ilf. 99 H4
Dawlish Dr., Pnr. 67 E5
Dawlish Dr., Ruis. 84 A2
Dawlish Rd. E10 96 C2
Dawlish Rd. N17 76 D3
Dawlish Rd. NW2 90 A6
Dawn Cl., Houns. 143 E3
Dawn Cres. E15 114 D1
*Bridge Rd.*
Dawnay Gdns. SW18 167 G2
Dawnay Rd. SW18 167 F2
Dawpool Rd. NW2 89 F2
Daws Hill E4 46 C3
Daws La. NW7 55 F5
Dawson Av., Bark. 99 J7
Dawson Cl. SE18 137 F4
Dawson Gdns., Bark. 99 J7
*Dawson Av.*
Dawson Hts. Est. SE22 152 D7
Dawson Pl. W2 108 D7
Dawson Rd. NW2 89 J5
Dawson Rd., Kings.T. 181 J3
**Dawson St. E2 13 G2**
Dawson St. E2 112 C2
Dax Ct., Sun. 178 C3
*Thames St.*
Daybrook Rd. SW19 184 E2
Daylesford Av. SW15 147 G4
Daymer Gdns., Pnr. 66 B4
Days La., Sid. 157 H7
Daysbrook Rd. SW2 169 F1
Dayton Gro. SE15 153 F1
De Barowe Ms. N5 93 H4
*Leigh Rd.*
De Beauvoir Cres. N1 112 B1
De Beauvoir Est. N1 112 A1
De Beauvoir Rd. N1 112 B1
De Beauvoir Sq. N1 94 B7
De Bohun Av. N14 42 B6
De Brome Rd., Felt. 160 C1
De Crespigny Pk. SE5 152 A2
De Frene Rd. SE26 171 G4
De Havilland Rd., Edg. 70 B2
De Havilland Rd., Houns. 122 C7
De Havilland Rd., Wall. 201 E7
De Havilland Way, Stai. 140 A6
**De Laune St. SE17 35 G4**
De Laune St. SE17 131 H5
De Luci Rd., Erith 139 J5
De Lucy St. SE2 138 B4
De Mandeville Gate, Enf. 44 D4
*Southbury Rd.*
De Montfort Par. SW16 168/169 E3
*Streatham High Rd.*
De Montfort Rd. SW16 168 E3
De Morgan Rd. SW6 149 E3
De Quincey Ms. E16 135 G1
*Wesley Av.*
De Quincey Rd. N17 76 A1
**De Vere Gdns. W8 22 C4**

De Vere Gdns. W8 129 F2
De Vere Gdns., Ilf. 98 C2
**De Vere Ms. W8 22 C5**
**De Walden St. W1 16 C2**
Deacon Ms. N1 94 A7
Deacon Rd. NW2 89 G5
Deacon Rd., Kings.T. 181 J1
**Deacon Way SE17 35 J1**
Deacon Way SE17 131 J4
Deacon Way, Wdf.Grn. 64 C7
Deacons Cl., Borwd. 38 A4
Deacons Cl., Pnr. 66 B2
Deacons Leas, Orp. 207 G4
Deacons Ri. N2 73 G5
Deacons Wk., Hmptn. 161 F4
*Bishops Gro.*
Deal Ms. W5 125 G4
*Darwin Rd.*
Deal Porters Way SE16 133 F3
Deal Rd. SW17 168 A6
**Deal St. E1 21 H1**
Deal St. E1 112 D5
Deal Wk. SW9 131 G7
*Mandela St.*
Deal's Gateway SE10 154 B1
*Blackheath Rd.*
Dealtry Rd. SW15 147 J4
**Dean Bradley St. SW1 26 A6**
Dean Bradley St. SW1 130 E3
Dean Cl. E9 95 F5
*Churchill Wk.*
Dean Cl. SE16 133 G1
*Surrey Water Rd.*
Dean Ct., Wem. 87 E3
Dean Dr., Stan. 69 H2
**Dean Farrar St. SW1 25 H5**
Dean Farrar St. SW1 130 D3
Dean Gdns. E17 78 D4
Dean Gdns. W13 124/125 E1
*Northfield Av.*
Dean Rd. NW2 89 J6
Dean Rd. SE28 118 A7
Dean Rd., Croy. 202 A4
Dean Rd., Hmptn. 161 G5
Dean Rd., Houns. 143 H5
**Dean Ryle St. SW1 34 A1**
Dean Ryle St. SW1 130 E4
**Dean Stanley St. SW1 26 A6**
Dean Stanley St. SW1 130 E3
Dean St. E7 97 G5
**Dean St. W1 17 H3**
Dean St. W1 110 D6
**Dean Trench St. SW1 26 A6**
Dean Trench St. SW1 130 E3
Dean Wk., Edg. 54 C6
*Deansbrook Rd.*
Dean Way, Sthl. 123 H2
Deancross St. E1 113 F6
Deane Av., Ruis. 84 C5
Deane Cft. Rd., Pnr. 66 C6
Deane Way, Ruis. 66 B6
Deanery Cl. N2 73 H4
**Deanery Ms. W1 24 C1**
Deanery Rd. E15 97 E6
**Deanery St. W1 24 C1**
Deanery St. W1 130 A1
Deanhill Rd. SW14 146 B4
**Deans Bldgs. SE17 36 B2**
Deans Bldgs. SE17 132 A4
Deans Cl. W4 126 B6
Dean's Cl., Croy. 202 C3
Deans Cl., Edg. 54 C6
**Deans Ct. EC4 19 H4**
Deans Dr. N13 59 H6
Deans Dr., Edg. 54 D5
Dean's Gate Cl. SE23 171 G3
Deans La. W4 126 B6
Deans La., Edg. 54 C6
**Deans Ms. W1 16 E3**
**Dean's Pl. SW1 33 H3**
Dean's Pl. SW1 130 D5
Deans Rd. W7 124 C1
Deans Rd., Sutt. 198 E3
Deans Way, Edg. 54 C5
**Dean's Yd. SW1 25 J5**
Deansbrook Cl., Edg. 54 C7
Deansbrook Rd., Edg. 54 C6
Deanscroft Av. NW9 88 C2
Deansway N2 73 G4
Deansway N9 60 B3
De'Arn Gdns., Mitch. 185 H3
Dearne Cl., Stan. 52 D5
Dearsley Rd., Enf. 44 D3
Deason St. E15 114 C1
*High St.*
Debden Cl., Kings.T. 163 G5
Debden Cl., Wdf.Grn. 63 J7
Debnams Rd. SE16 133 F4
*Rotherhithe New Rd.*
Deborah Cl., Islw. 144 B1
Deburgh Rd. SW19 167 F7
**Decima St. SE1 28 D5**
Decima St. SE1 132 B3
Deck Cl. SE16 133 G2
*Thame Rd.*
Decoy Av. NW11 72 B5
Dee Rd., Rich. 145 J4
Dee St. E14 114 C6
Deeley Rd. SW8 150 D1
Deena Cl. W3 105 J6
Deepdale SW19 166 A4
Deepdale Av., Brom. 191 F4
Deepdale Cl. N11 58 A6
*Ribblesdale Av.*
Deepdene W5 105 J4
Deepdene Av., Croy. 202 C3
Deepdene Cl. E11 79 G4
Deepdene Ct. N21 43 H6
Deepdene Gdns. SW2 151 F7
Deepdene Path, Loug. 48 D4
Deepdene Rd. SE5 152 A4
Deepdene Rd., Loug. 48 D4
Deepdene Rd., Well. 158 A3
Deepwell Cl., Islw. 144 D1
Deepwood La., Grnf. 104 A3
*Cowgate Rd.*
Deer Pk. Cl., Kings.T. 164 B7
Deer Pk. Gdns., Mitch. 185 G3
Deer Pk. Rd. SW19 185 E2
Deer Pk. Way, W.Wick. 205 F2
Deerbrook Rd. SE24 169 H1
Deerdale Rd. SE24 151 J4
Deerhurst Cl., Felt. 160 A4
Deerhurst Cres., Hmptn. 161 J5
Deerhurst Rd. NW2 90 A6
Deerhurst Rd. SW16 169 F5
Deerings Dr., Pnr. 66 A5
Deerleap Gro. E4 46 B5
Deeside Rd. SW17 167 G3
Defiance Wk. SE18 136 C3
Defiant Way, Wall. 200 E7
Defoe Av., Rich. 126 A7
Defoe Cl. SE16 133 J2
*Vaughan St.*
Defoe Cl. SW17 167 H6
Defoe Rd. N16 94 B2
Degema Rd., Chis. 174 E5
Dehar Cres. NW9 71 F7
Dehavilland Cl., Nthlt. 102 D3
Dekker Rd. SE21 152 B6
Delacourt Rd. SE3 135 H7
*Old Dover Rd.*
Delafield Rd. SE7 135 H5
Delaford Rd. SE16 133 E5
Delaford St. SW6 128 B7
Delamare Cres., Croy. 189 F6
Delamere Gdns. NW7 54 D6
Delamere Rd. SW20 184 A1
Delamere Rd. W5 125 H1
Delamere Rd., Borwd. 38 B1
Delamere Rd., Hayes 102 D7
**Delamere Ter. W2 14 B1**
Delamere Ter. W2 109 E5
Delancey Pas. NW1 110 B1
*Delancey St.*
Delancey St. NW1 110 B1
**Delaware Rd. W9 6 A5**
Delaware Rd. W9 108 E4
Delawyk Cres. SE24 151 J6
Delcombe Av., Wor.Pk. 197 J1
Delft Way SE22 152 B5
*East Dulwich Gro.*
Delhi Rd., Enf. 44 C7
Delhi St. N1 111 E1
Delia St. SW18 149 E7
Delisle Rd. SE28 137 H1
*Merbury Rd.*
Delius Gro. E15 114 D2
Dell, The SE2 138 A5
Dell, The SE19 188 C1
Dell, The, Brent. 125 F6
Dell, The, Felt. 142 B7
*Harlington Rd. W.*
Dell, The, Pnr. 66 D2
Dell, The, Wem. 87 E5
Dell, The, Wdf.Grn. 63 H3
Dell Cl. E15 114 D1
Dell Cl., Wall. 200 D4
Dell Cl., Wdf.Grn. 63 H3
Dell La., Epsom 197 G5
Dell Rd., Epsom 197 G6
Dell Rd., West Dr. 120 C3
Dell Wk., N.Mal. 183 E2
Dell Way W13 105 F6
Della Path E5 94/95 E3
*Napoleon Rd.*
Dellbow Rd., Felt. 142 B5
*Central Way*
Dellfield Cl., Beck. 172 C7
*Foxgrove Rd.*
Dellors Cl., Barn. 40 A5
Dellow Cl., Ilf. 81 G7
Dellow St. E1 113 E7
Dells Cl. E4 46 B7
**Dell's Ms. SW1 33 G2**
Dellwood Gdns., Ilf. 80 D3
Delmare Cl. SW9 151 F4
*Brighton Ter.*
Delme Cres. SE3 155 H2
Delmey Cl., Croy. 202 C3
*Radcliffe Rd.*
Deloraine St. SE8 154 A1
Delorme St. W6 128 A6
Delta Cl., Wor.Pk. 197 F3
Delta Ct. NW2 89 G2
Delta Gain, Wat. 50 D2
Delta Gro., Nthlt. 102 D3
Delta Rd., Wor.Pk. 197 E3
**Delta St. E2 13 H3**
Delvan Cl. SE18 136 D7
*Ordnance Rd.*
Delvers Mead, Dag. 101 J4
**Delverton Rd. SE17 35 H4**
Delverton Rd. SE17 131 H5
Delvino Rd. SW6 148 D1
Demesne Rd., Wall. 200 D5
Demeta Cl., Wem. 88 C3
Dempster Cl., Surb. 195 F1
Dempster Rd. SW18 149 F5
Den Cl., Beck. 190 D3
Den Rd., Brom. 190 D3
Denbar Par., Rom. 83 J4
*Mawney Rd.*
Denberry Dr., Sid. 176 B3
Denbigh Cl. NW10 88 E7
Denbigh Cl. W11 108 C7
Denbigh Cl., Chis. 174 C6
Denbigh Cl., Sthl. 103 F6
Denbigh Cl., Sutt. 198 C5
Denbigh Dr., Hayes 121 F2
Denbigh Gdns., Rich. 145 J5
**Denbigh Ms. SW1 33 F2**
**Denbigh Pl. SW1 33 F3**
Denbigh Pl. SW1 130 C5
Denbigh Rd. E6 116 A3
Denbigh Rd. W11 108 C7
Denbigh Rd. W13 105 E7
Denbigh Rd., Houns. 143 H2
Denbigh Rd., Sthl. 103 F6
**Denbigh St. SW1 33 F2**
Denbigh St. SW1 130 C4
Denbigh Ter. W11 108 C7
Denbridge Rd., Brom. 192 C2
Dene, The W13 104 E5
Dene, The, Croy. 203 G4
Dene, The, Wem. 87 H4
Dene, The, W.Mol. 179 F5
Dene Av., Houns. 143 F3
Dene Av., Sid. 158 B7
Dene Cl. SE4 153 H3
Dene Cl., Brom. 205 F1
Dene Cl., Wor.Pk. 197 F2
Dene Ct., Stan. 53 F5
*Marsh La.*
Dene Gdns., Stan. 53 F5
Dene Gdns., T.Ditt. 194 D2
Dene Rd. N11 57 J1
Dene Rd., Buck.H. 64 A1
Denehurst Gdns. NW4 71 J6
Denehurst Gdns. W3 126 B1
Denehurst Gdns., Rich. 146 A4
Denehurst Gdns., Twick. 144 A7
Denehurst Gdns., Wdf.Grn. 63 H4
Denewood, Barn. 41 F5
Denewood Rd. N6 73 J6
Dengie Wk. N1 111 J1
*Basire St.*
Denham Cl., Well. 158 C3
*Park Vw. Rd.*
Denham Cres., Mitch. 185 J4
Denham Dr., Ilf. 81 F6
Denham Rd. N20 57 J3
Denham Rd., Felt. 142 C6
Denham St. SE10 135 G5
Denham Way, Bark. 117 H1
Denham Way, Borwd. 38 D1
Denholme Rd. W9 108 C3
Denison Cl. N2 73 F3
Denison Rd. SW19 167 G6
Denison Rd. W5 105 F4
Deniston Av., Bex. 176 E1
Denleigh Gdns. N21 59 G1
Denleigh Gdns., T.Ditt. 180 B6
Denman Dr. NW11 72 D5
Denman Dr., Esher 194 D5
Denman Dr. N. NW11 72 D5
Denman Dr. S. NW11 72 D5
Denman Rd. SE15 152 C1
**Denman St. W1 17 H6**
Denmark Av. SW19 166 B7
Denmark Ct., Mord. 184 D5
Denmark Gdns., Cars. 200 A3
**Denmark Gro. N1 11 E1**
Denmark Gro. N1 111 G2
Denmark Hill SE5 152 A1
Denmark Hill Dr. NW9 71 F4
Denmark Hill Est. SE5 152 A4
**Denmark Pl. WC2 17 J3**
Denmark Rd. N8 75 F4
Denmark Rd. NW6 108 C2
Denmark Rd. SE5 151 J1
Denmark Rd. SE25 188 D5
Denmark Rd. SW19 166 A6
Denmark Rd. W13 105 E7
Denmark Rd., Brom. 191 H1
Denmark Rd., Cars. 199 J3
Denmark Rd., Kings.T. 181 H3
Denmark Rd., Twick. 162 A3
Denmark St. E11 96/97 E3
*High Rd. Leytonstone*
Denmark St. E13 115 H5
Denmark St. N17 76 E1
**Denmark St. WC2 17 J4**
Denmark St. WC2 110 D6
Denmark Wk. SE27 169 J4
Denmead Ho. SW15 147 F6
*Highcliffe Dr.*
Denmead Rd., Croy. 201 H1
**Denmead Way SE15 37 F7**
Dennan Rd., Surb. 195 J1
Denne Ter. E8 112 C1
Denner Rd. E4 62 A2
Dennett Rd., Croy. 187 G7
Dennetts Gro. SE14 153 G2
*Dennetts Rd.*
Dennetts Rd. SE14 153 F1
Denning Av., Croy. 201 G4
**Denning Cl. NW8 6 D3**
Denning Cl. NW8 109 F3
Denning Cl., Hmptn. 161 F6
Denning Rd. NW3 91 G4
Dennington Cl. E5 94/95 E2
*Detmold Rd.*
Dennington Pk. Rd. NW6 90 D6
Denningtons, The, Wor.Pk. 197 E2
Dennis Av., Wem. 87 J5
Dennis Gdns., Stan. 53 F5
Dennis La., Stan. 52 E3
Dennis Pk. Cres. SW20 184 B1
Dennis Reeve Cl., Mitch. 185 J1
Dennis Rd., E.Mol. 179 J4
Dennis Way SW4 150 D3
*Gauden Rd.*
Dennison Pt. E15 96 C7
Denny Cl. E6 116 B5
*Linton Gdns.*
**Denny Cres. SE11 35 F2**
Denny Gdns., Dag. 100 B7
*Canonsleigh Rd.*
Denny Rd. N9 60 E1
**Denny St. SE11 35 F3**
Denny St. SE11 131 G5
Densham Rd. E15 115 E1
Densole Cl., Beck. 189 H1
*Kings Hall Rd.*
Densworth Gro. N9 61 F2
Denton Cl., Barn. 39 J5
Denton Rd. N8 75 F5
Denton Rd. N18 60 B4
Denton Rd., Twick. 145 G6
Denton Rd., Well. 138 C7
Denton St. SW18 149 E6
Denton Way E5 95 G3
Dents Rd. SW11 149 J6
Denver Cl., Orp. 193 H6
Denver Rd. N16 76 B7
**Denyer St. SW3 31 H2**
Denyer St. SW3 129 H4
Denzil Rd. NW10 89 F5
Deodar Rd. SW15 148 B4
Deodara Cl. N20 57 H3
Depot Rd., Houns. 144 A3
Deptford Br. SE8 154 A1
Deptford Bdy. SE8 154 A1
Deptford Ch. St. SE8 134 A6

Dobree Av. NW10 89 H7
Dobson Cl. NW6 91 G7
Dock Hill Av. SE16 133 G2
Dock Rd. E16 115 F7
Dock Rd., Brent. 125 G7
**Dock St. E1 21 H5**
Dock St. E1 112 D7
Dockers Tanner Rd. E14 134 A3
**Dockhead SE1 29 G4**
Dockhead SE1 132 C2
Dockland St. E16 136 D1
**Dockley Rd. SE16 29 H6**
Dockley Rd. SE16 132 D3
Dockwell Cl., Felt. 142 A4
Dockyard Ind. Est. SE18 136 B3
*Woolwich Ch. St.*
Doctor Johnson Av. SW17 168 B3
Doctors Cl. SE26 171 F5
Docwra's Bldgs. N1 94 B6
Dod St. E14 114 A6
Dodbrooke Rd. SE27 169 G3
**Doddington Gro. SE17 35 G5**
Doddington Gro. SE17 131 H6
**Doddington Pl. SE17 35 G5**
Doddington Pl. SE17 131 H6
Dodsley Pl. N9 61 E3
**Dodson St. SE1 27 F4**
Dodson St. SE1 131 G2
Doebury Wk. SE18 138 A6
*Prestwood Cl.*
Doel Cl. SW19 167 F7
Dog Kennel Hill SE22 152 B3
Dog Kennel Hill Est. SE22 152 B3
Dog La. NW10 89 E4
Doggets Ct., Barn. 41 H5
Doggett Rd. SE6 154 A7
Doghurst Av., Hayes 121 E7
Doghurst Dr., West Dr. 121 E7
Doherty Rd. E13 115 G4
Dokal Ind. Est., Sthl. 122 E2
**Dolben St. SE1 27 G2**
Dolben St. SE1 131 H1
**Dolby Ct. EC4 20 A5**
Dolby Rd. SW6 148 C2
**Dolland St. SE11 34 D4**
Dolland St. SE11 131 F5
Dollis Av. N3 72 C1
Dollis Brook Wk., Barn. 40 B6
Dollis Cres., Ruis. 84 C1
Dollis Hill Av. NW2 89 H3
Dollis Hill Est. NW2 89 G3
Dollis Hill La. NW2 89 H3
Dollis Ms. N3 72 C1
*Dollis Pk.*
Dollis Pk. N3 72 C1
Dollis Rd. N3 56 B7
Dollis Rd. NW7 56 B7
Dollis Valley Grn. Wk. N20 57 F2
*Totteridge La.*
Dollis Valley Grn. Wk., Barn. 40 B6
Dollis Valley Way, Barn. 40 C6
Dolman Cl. N3 73 F2
*Avondale Rd.*
Dolman Rd. W4 126 D4
Dolman St. SW4 151 F4
Dolphin Cl. SE16 133 G2
*Kinburn St.*
Dolphin Cl. SE28 118 D6
Dolphin Cl., Surb. 181 G6
Dolphin Ct. NW11 72 B6
Dolphin La. E14 114 B7
Dolphin Rd., Nthlt. 103 F2
**Dolphin Sq. SW1 33 G4**
Dolphin Sq. SW1 130 C5
Dolphin Sq. W4 126 E7
Dolphin St., Kings.T. 181 H1
**Dombey St. WC1 18 C1**
Dombey St. WC1 111 F5
Dome Hill Pk. SE26 170 C4
Domett Cl. SE5 152 A4
Domfe Pl. E5 95 F4
*Rushmore Rd.*
**Domingo St. EC1 11 J5**
Dominica Cl. E13 115 J2
Dominion Rd., Croy. 188 C7
Dominion Rd., Sthl. 123 E3
**Dominion St. EC2 20 C1**
Domonic Dr. SE9 174 E4
Domville Cl. N20 57 G2
Don Phelan Cl. SE5 152 A1
Donald Dr., Rom. 82 C5
Donald Rd. E13 115 H1
Donald Rd., Croy. 187 F6
Donald Wds. Gdns., Surb. 196 B2
Donaldson Rd. NW6 108 C1
Donaldson Rd. SE18 156 D1
Doncaster Dr., Nthlt. 85 F5
Doncaster Gdns. N4 75 J6
*Stanhope Gdns.*
Doncaster Gdns., Nthlt. 85 F5
Doncaster Grn., Wat. 50 C5
Doncaster Rd. N9 44 E7
Doncel Ct. E4 46 D7
**Donegal St. N1 10 D2**
Donegal St. N1 111 F2
Doneraile St. SW6 148 A2
Dongola Rd. E13 115 H3
Dongola Rd. N17 76 B3
Dongola Rd. W. E13 115 H3
*Balaam St.*
Donington Av., Ilf. 81 F5
Donkey All. SE22 152 D7
Donkey La., Enf. 44 D2
Donne Ct. SE24 151 J6
**Donne Pl. SW3 31 H1**
Donne Pl. SW3 129 H4
Donne Pl., Mitch. 186 B4
Donne Rd., Dag. 100 C2
Donnefield Av., Edg. 53 H7
Donnington Rd. NW10 89 H7
Donnington Rd., Har. 69 G5
Donnington Rd., Wor.Pk. 197 G2
Donnybrook Rd. SW16 168 C7
Donovan Av. N10 74 B2
**Doon St. SE1 26 E2**
Doone Cl., Tedd. 162 D6
Dora Rd. SW19 166 D5
Dora St. E14 113 J6
Doral Way, Cars. 199 J5
Doran Gro. SE18 137 H7
Doran Mans. N2 73 J5
*Great N. Rd.*
Doran Wk. E15 96 C7
Dorchester Av. N13 59 J4
Dorchester Av., Bex. 176 D1
Dorchester Av., Har. 67 J6
Dorchester Cl., Nthlt. 85 H5
Dorchester Cl., Orp. 176 A7
*Grovelands Rd.*
Dorchester Ct. N14 42 B7
Dorchester Ct. SE24 151 J5
Dorchester Dr. SE24 151 J5
Dorchester Dr., Felt. 141 H6
Dorchester Gdns. E4 62 A4
Dorchester Gdns. NW11 72 D4
Dorchester Gro. W4 127 E5
Dorchester Ms., N.Mal. 182 D4
*Elm Rd.*
Dorchester Ms., Twick. 145 F7
Dorchester Rd., Mord. 185 E7
Dorchester Rd., Nthlt. 85 H5
Dorchester Rd., Wor.Pk. 197 J1
Dorchester Way, Har. 69 J6
Dorchester Waye, Hayes 102 C6
Dorcis Av., Bexh. 158 E2
Dordrecht Rd. W3 127 E1
Dore Av. E12 98 D5
Dore Gdns., Mord. 185 E7
Doreen Av. NW9 88 D1
Dorell Cl., Sthl. 103 F5
Doria Rd. SW6 148 C2
**Doric Way NW1 9 H3**
Doric Way NW1 110 D3
Dorien Rd. SW20 184 A2
Doris Av., Erith 159 J1
Doris Rd. E7 97 G7
Dorking Cl. SE8 133 J6
Dorking Cl., Wor.Pk. 198 A2
Dorlcote Rd. SW18 149 H7
Dorma Trd. Pk. E10 95 G1
Dorman Pl. N9 60 D2
*Balham Rd.*
Dorman Wk. NW10 88 D5
*Garden Way*
Dorman Way NW8 109 G1
Dormay St. SW18 148 E5
Dormer Cl. E15 97 F6
Dormer Cl., Barn. 40 A5
Dormers Av., Sthl. 103 G6
Dormers Ri., Sthl. 103 H6
Dormers Wells La., Sthl. 103 G6
Dornberg Cl. SE3 135 G7
Dornberg Rd. SE3 135 H7
*Banchory Rd.*
Dorncliffe Rd. SW6 148 B2
Dorney NW3 91 H7
Dorney Ri., Orp. 193 J4
Dorney Way, Houns. 143 E5
Dornfell St. NW6 90 C5
Dornton Rd. SW12 168 B2
Dornton Rd., S.Croy. 202 A5
Dorothy Av., Wem. 87 H7
Dorothy Evans Cl., Bexh. 159 H4
Dorothy Gdns., Dag. 100 B4
Dorothy Rd. SW11 149 J3
Dorrell Pl. SW9 151 G4
*Brixton Rd.*
Dorrien Wk. SW16 168 D2
Dorrington Ct. SE25 188 B2
Dorrington Pt. E3 114 B3
*Bromley High St.*
**Dorrington St. EC1 19 E1**
Dorrington St. EC1 111 G5
Dorrit Ms. N18 60 B4
Dorrit Way, Chis. 175 F6
Dors Cl. NW9 88 D1
Dorset Av., Sthl. 123 G4
Dorset Av., Well. 157 J4
**Dorset Bldgs. EC4 19 G4**
**Dorset Cl. NW1 15 J1**
Dorset Dr., Edg. 53 J6
**Dorset Est. E2 13 G3**
Dorset Est. E2 112 C3
Dorset Gdns., Mitch. 187 F4
Dorset Ms. N3 72 D1
**Dorset Ms. SW1 24 D5**
Dorset Pl. E15 96 D6
**Dorset Pl. SW1 33 H3**
**Dorset Ri. EC4 19 G4**
Dorset Ri. EC4 111 H6
Dorset Rd. E7 97 J7
Dorset Rd. N15 76 A4
Dorset Rd. N22 75 E1
Dorset Rd. SE9 174 B2
**Dorset Rd. SW8 34 B7**
Dorset Rd. SW8 131 F7
Dorset Rd. SW19 184 D1
Dorset Rd. W5 125 F3
Dorset Rd., Beck. 189 G3
Dorset Rd., Har. 67 J6
Dorset Rd., Mitch. 185 H2
**Dorset Sq. NW1 7 J6**
Dorset Sq. NW1 109 J4
**Dorset St. W1 16 A2**
Dorset St. W1 110 A5
Dorset Way, Twick. 162 A1
Dorset Waye, Houns. 123 F7
Dorville Cres. W6 127 H3
Dorville Rd. SE12 155 F5
Dothill Rd. SE18 137 G7
Douai Gro., Hmptn. 179 J1
Doubleday Rd., Loug. 49 F3
**Doughty Ms. WC1 10 C6**
Doughty Ms. WC1 111 F4
**Doughty St. WC1 10 C5**
Doughty St. WC1 111 F4
Douglas Av. E17 78 A1
Douglas Av., N.Mal. 183 H4
Douglas Av., Wem. 87 H7
Douglas Cl., Stan. 52 D5
Douglas Cl., Wall. 201 E7
Douglas Cres., Hayes 102 C4
Douglas Dr., Croy. 204 A3
Douglas Est. N1 93 J6
Douglas Ms. NW2 90 B3
Douglas Rd. E4 47 E7
Douglas Rd. E16 115 G5
Douglas Rd. N1 93 J7
Douglas Rd. N22 75 G1
Douglas Rd. NW6 108 C1
Douglas Rd., Houns. 143 H3
Douglas Rd., Ilf. 82 A6
Douglas Rd., Kings.T. 182 B2
Douglas Rd., Stai. 140 A6
Douglas Rd., Surb. 195 J2
Douglas Rd., Well. 158 B1
Douglas Sq., Mord. 184 D6
**Douglas St. SW1 33 H2**
Douglas St. SW1 130 D4
Douglas Ter. E17 78 A1
*Douglas Av.*
Douglas Way SE8 133 J7
Doulton Ms. NW6 90/91 E6
*Lymington Rd.*
Dounesforth Gdns. SW18 166 E1
**Douro Pl. W8 22 B5**
Douro Pl. W8 129 E3
Douro St. E3 114 A2
**Douthwaite Sq. E1 29 J1**
Dove App. E6 116 B5
Dove Cl. NW7 55 F7
*Bunns La.*
Dove Cl., Nthlt. 102 D4
*Wayfarer Rd.*
**Dove Ct. EC2 20 B4**
Dove Ho. Gdns. E4 62 A2
**Dove Ms. SW5 30 C2**
Dove Ms. SW5 129 F4
Dove Pk., Pnr. 51 G7
Dove Rd. N1 94 A6
Dove Row E2 112 D1
**Dove Wk. SW1 32 B3**
Dovecot Cl., Pnr. 66 B5
Dovecote Av. N22 75 G3
Dovecote Gdns. SW14 146 D3
*Avondale Rd.*
Dovecott Gdns. SW14 146 D3
*North Worple Way*
Dovedale Av., Har. 69 F6
Dovedale Av., Ilf. 80 D2
Dovedale Cl., Well. 158 A2
Dovedale Ri., Mitch. 167 J7
Dovedale Rd. SE22 153 E5
Dovedon Cl. N14 58 E2
Dovehouse Mead, Bark. 117 G2
**Dovehouse St. SW3 31 G3**
Dovehouse St. SW3 129 G5
Dover Cl. NW2 90 A2
*Brent Ter.*
Dover Cl., Rom. 83 J2
Dover Flats SE1 132 B4
*Old Kent Rd.*
Dover Gdns., Cars. 199 J3
Dover Ho. Rd. SW15 147 G4
Dover Pk. Dr. SW15 147 H6
Dover Patrol SE3 155 H2
*Kidbrooke Way*
Dover Rd. E12 97 J2
Dover Rd. N9 61 F2
Dover Rd. SE19 170 A6
Dover Rd., Rom. 82 E6
**Dover St. W1 17 E6**
Dover St. W1 110 B7
**Dover Yd. W1 25 F1**
Dovercourt Av., Th.Hth. 187 G4
Dovercourt Est. N1 94 A6
Dovercourt Gdns., Stan. 53 H5
Dovercourt La., Sutt. 199 F3
Dovercourt Rd. SE22 152 B6
Doverfield Rd. SW2 151 E6
Doveridge Gdns. N13 59 H4
Doves Cl., Brom. 206 B2
Dove's Yd. N1 111 G1
Doveton Rd., S.Croy. 202 A5
Doveton St. E1 113 F4
*Malcolm Rd.*
Dowanhill Rd. SE6 172 D1
Dowdeswell Cl. SW15 147 E4
Dowding Pl., Stan. 52 D6
**Dowgate Hill EC4 20 B5**
Dowgate Hill EC4 112 A7
Dowland St. W10 108 B2
**Dowlas Est. SE5 36 D7**
**Dowlas St. SE5 36 D7**
Dowlas St. SE5 132 B7
Dowlerville Rd., Orp. 207 J6
Dowman Cl. SW19 184/185 E1
*Nelson Gro. Rd.*
Down Cl., Nthlt. 102 B2
Down Hall Rd., Kings.T. 181 G1
Down Pl. W6 127 H4
Down Rd., Tedd. 163 E6
**Down St. W1 24 D2**
Down St. W1 130 B1
Down St., W.Mol. 179 G5
**Down St. Ms. W1 24 D2**
Down Way, Nthlt. 102 B3
Downage NW4 71 J3
Downalong, Bushey 52 A1
Downbarns Rd., Ruis. 84 D3
Downbury Ms. SW18 148 D6
*Merton Rd.*
Downderry Rd., Brom. 172 D3
Downe Cl., Well. 138 C7
Downe Rd., Mitch. 185 J2
Downend SE18 136/137 E7
*Moordown*
Downers Cotts. SW4 150 C4
*The Pavement*
Downes Cl., Twick. 144/145 E6
*St. Margarets Rd.*
Downes Ct. N21 59 G1
Downfield, Wor.Pk. 197 F1
**Downfield Cl. W9 6 A6**
Downfield Cl. W9 108 E4
Downham La., Brom. 172 D5
*Downham Way*
Downham Rd. N1 94 A7
Downham Way, Brom. 172 D5
Downhills Av. N17 76 A3
Downhills Pk. Rd. N17 75 J3

| | | |
|---|---|---|
| Downhills Way N17 | 75 | J3 |
| Downhurst Av. NW7 | 54 | D6 |
| Downing Cl., Har. | 67 | J3 |
| Downing Dr., Grnf. | 104 | A1 |
| Downing Rd., Dag. | 119 | F1 |
| **Downing St. SW1** | **26** | **A3** |
| Downing St. SW1 | 130 | E2 |
| Downings E6 | 116 | D6 |
| Downland Cl. N20 | 57 | F1 |
| Downleys Cl. SE9 | 174 | B2 |
| Downman Rd. SE9 | 156 | B3 |
| Downs, The SW20 | 166 | A7 |
| Downs Av., Chis. | 174 | C5 |
| Downs Av., Pnr. | 67 | F6 |
| Downs Br. Rd., Beck. | 190 | D1 |
| Downs Hill, Beck. | 190 | D1 |
| Downs La. E5 | 94/95 | E4 |
| *Downs Rd.* | | |
| Downs Pk. Rd. E5 | 94 | D5 |
| Downs Pk. Rd. E8 | 94 | C5 |
| Downs Rd. E5 | 94 | D4 |
| Downs Rd., Beck. | 190 | B2 |
| Downs Rd., Enf. | 44 | B4 |
| Downs Rd., Th.Hth. | 187 | J1 |
| Downs Vw., Islw. | 124 | C7 |
| Downsbury Ms. SW18 | 148 | D5 |
| *Merton Rd.* | | |
| Downsell Rd. E15 | 96 | C4 |
| Downsfield Rd. E17 | 77 | H6 |
| Downshall Av., Ilf. | 81 | H6 |
| Downshire Hill NW3 | 91 | G4 |
| Downside, Sun. | 178 | A1 |
| Downside, Twick. | 162 | C3 |
| Downside Cl. SW19 | 167 | F6 |
| Downside Cres. NW3 | 91 | H5 |
| Downside Cres. W13 | 104 | D4 |
| Downside Rd., Sutt. | 199 | G6 |
| Downside Wk., Nthlt. | 103 | F3 |
| Downsview Gdns. SE19 | 169 | H7 |
| Downsview Rd. SE19 | 169 | J7 |
| Downsway, Orp. | 207 | H5 |
| Downton Av. SW2 | 169 | E2 |
| Downtown Rd. SE16 | 133 | H2 |
| Downway N12 | 57 | H7 |
| Dowrey St. N1 | 111 | G1 |
| *Richmond Av.* | | |
| Dowsett Rd. N17 | 76 | C2 |
| Dowson Cl. SE5 | 152 | A4 |
| **Doyce St. SE1** | **27** | **J3** |
| Doyle Gdns. NW10 | 107 | G1 |
| Doyle Rd. SE25 | 188 | D4 |
| **D'Oyley St. SW1** | **32** | **B1** |
| D'Oyley St. SW1 | 130 | A4 |
| Doynton St. N19 | 92 | B2 |
| **Draco St. SE17** | **35** | **J5** |
| Draco St. SE17 | 131 | J6 |
| Dragmire La., Mitch. | 185 | G4 |
| **Dragon Rd. SE15** | **36** | **D6** |
| Dragon Rd. SE15 | 132 | B6 |
| Dragonfly Cl. E13 | 115 | H3 |
| *Hollybush St.* | | |
| Dragoon Rd. SE8 | 133 | J5 |
| Dragor Rd. NW10 | 106 | C4 |
| Drake Cl. SE16 | 133 | G2 |
| *Middleton Dr.* | | |
| Drake Ct. SE19 | 170 | C5 |
| Drake Ct., Har. | 85 | F1 |
| Drake Cres. SE28 | 118 | C6 |
| Drake Rd. SE4 | 154 | A3 |
| Drake Rd., Chess. | 196 | A5 |
| Drake Rd., Croy. | 187 | F7 |
| Drake Rd., Har. | 85 | F2 |
| Drake Rd., Mitch. | 186 | A6 |
| **Drake St. WC1** | **18** | **C2** |
| Drake St., Enf. | 44 | A1 |
| Drakefell Rd. SE4 | 153 | G2 |
| Drakefell Rd. SE14 | 153 | G2 |
| Drakefield Rd. SW17 | 168 | A3 |
| Drakeley Ct. N5 | 93 | H4 |
| *Highbury Hill* | | |
| Drakes Ctyd. NW6 | 90 | C7 |
| Drakes Wk. E6 | 116 | C1 |
| Drakewood Rd. SW16 | 168 | D7 |
| Draper Cl., Belv. | 139 | F4 |
| Draper Cl., Islw. | 124 | A7 |
| *Thornbury Rd.* | | |
| Draper Pl. N1 | 111 | H1 |
| *Essex Rd.* | | |
| Drapers Gdns. EC2 | 112 | A6 |
| *Copthall Av.* | | |
| Drapers Rd. E15 | 96 | D4 |
| Drapers Rd. N17 | 76 | C3 |
| Drapers Rd., Enf. | 43 | H2 |
| **Drappers Way SE16** | **37** | **J1** |
| Draven Cl., Brom. | 191 | F7 |
| Drawdock Rd. SE10 | 134 | D1 |
| Drawell Cl. SE18 | 137 | H5 |
| Drax Av. SW20 | 165 | G7 |
| Draxmont SW19 | 166 | B6 |
| Dray Gdns. SW2 | 151 | F5 |
| Draycot Rd. E11 | 79 | H6 |
| Draycot Rd., Surb. | 196 | A1 |
| **Draycott Av. SW3** | **31** | **H1** |
| Draycott Av. SW3 | 129 | H4 |
| Draycott Av., Har. | 69 | E6 |
| Draycott Cl., Har. | 69 | E6 |
| Draycott Ms. SW6 | 148 | C2 |
| *New Kings Rd.* | | |
| **Draycott Pl. SW3** | **31** | **J2** |
| Draycott Pl. SW3 | 129 | J4 |
| **Draycott Ter. SW3** | **32** | **A1** |
| Draycott Ter. SW3 | 129 | J4 |
| Drayford Cl. W9 | 108 | C4 |
| Draymans Way, Islw. | 144 | C3 |
| Drayside Ms., Sthl. | 123 | F2 |
| *Kingston Rd.* | | |
| Drayson Ms. W8 | 128 | D2 |
| Drayton Av. W13 | 104 | D7 |
| Drayton Av., Loug. | 48 | C6 |
| Drayton Av., Orp. | 207 | E1 |
| Drayton Br. Rd. W7 | 104 | C7 |
| Drayton Br. Rd. W13 | 104 | C7 |
| Drayton Cl., Houns. | 143 | F5 |
| *Bramley Way* | | |
| Drayton Cl., Ilf. | 99 | G1 |
| Drayton Gdns. N21 | 43 | H7 |
| **Drayton Gdns. SW10** | **30** | **D3** |
| Drayton Gdns. SW10 | 129 | F5 |
| Drayton Gdns. W13 | 104 | D7 |
| Drayton Gdns., West Dr. | 120 | B2 |
| Drayton Grn. W13 | 104 | D7 |
| Drayton Grn. Rd. W13 | 104 | E7 |
| Drayton Gro. W13 | 104 | D7 |
| Drayton Pk. N5 | 93 | G5 |
| Drayton Pk. Ms. N5 | 93 | G5 |
| *Drayton Pk.* | | |
| Drayton Rd. E11 | 96 | D1 |
| Drayton Rd. N17 | 76 | B2 |
| Drayton Rd. NW10 | 107 | F1 |
| Drayton Rd. W13 | 104 | D7 |
| Drayton Rd., Borwd. | 38 | A4 |
| Drayton Rd., Croy. | 201 | H2 |
| Drayton Waye, Har. | 69 | E6 |
| Dreadnought St. SE10 | 135 | E3 |
| Dresden Cl. NW6 | 91 | E6 |
| Dresden Rd. N19 | 92 | D1 |
| Dressington Av. SE4 | 154 | A6 |
| Drew Av. NW7 | 56 | B6 |
| Drew Gdns., Grnf. | 86 | C6 |
| Drew Rd. E16 | 136 | B1 |
| Drewstead Rd. SW16 | 168 | D2 |
| Driffield Rd. E3 | 113 | H2 |
| Drift, The, Brom. | 206 | A3 |
| Drift Way, Rich. | 163 | J1 |
| Driftway, The, Mitch. | 186 | A1 |
| Drinkwater Rd., Har. | 85 | H2 |
| Drive, The E4 | 46 | D7 |
| Drive, The E17 | 78 | B4 |
| Drive, The E18 | 79 | G4 |
| Drive, The N3 | 56 | D7 |
| Drive, The N6 | 73 | J5 |
| *Fordington Rd.* | | |
| Drive, The N11 | 58 | C6 |
| Drive, The NW10 | 107 | F1 |
| *Longstone Av.* | | |
| Drive, The NW11 | 72 | B7 |
| Drive, The SW6 | 148 | B2 |
| *Fulham Rd.* | | |
| Drive, The SW16 | 187 | F3 |
| Drive, The SW20 | 165 | J7 |
| Drive, The W3 | 106 | C6 |
| Drive, The, Bark. | 99 | J7 |
| Drive, The, Barn. | 40 | B3 |
| Drive, The (New Barnet), Barn. | 41 | F6 |
| Drive, The, Beck. | 190 | A2 |
| Drive, The, Bex. | 158 | C6 |
| Drive, The, Buck.H. | 47 | J7 |
| Drive, The, Chis. | 193 | J3 |
| Drive, The (Scadbury Pk.), Chis. | 193 | H1 |
| Drive, The, Edg. | 54 | A5 |
| Drive, The, Enf. | 44 | A1 |
| Drive, The, Epsom | 197 | F6 |
| Drive, The, Erith | 139 | H7 |
| Drive, The, Felt. | 142 | C7 |
| Drive, The, Har. | 67 | G7 |
| Drive, The, Houns. | 144 | A2 |
| Drive, The, Ilf. | 98 | C1 |
| Drive, The, Islw. | 144 | A2 |
| Drive, The, Kings.T. | 164 | C7 |
| Drive, The, Loug. | 48 | B3 |
| Drive, The, Mord. | 185 | G5 |
| Drive, The, Orp. | 207 | J2 |
| Drive, The, Rom. | 83 | J1 |
| Drive, The, Sid. | 176 | B3 |
| Drive, The, Surb. | 181 | H7 |
| Drive, The, Th.Hth. | 188 | A4 |
| Drive, The, Wem. | 88 | C2 |
| Drive, The, W.Wick. | 190 | D7 |
| Driveway, The E17 | 78 | B6 |
| *Hoe St.* | | |
| Droitwich Cl. SE26 | 170 | D3 |
| Dromey Gdns., Har. | 52 | C7 |
| Dromore Rd. SW15 | 148 | B6 |
| Dronfield Gdns., Dag. | 100 | C5 |
| Droop St. W10 | 108 | B4 |
| Drover La. SE15 | 133 | E7 |
| Drovers Pl. SE15 | 133 | E7 |
| Drovers Rd., S.Croy. | 202 | A5 |
| Droveway, Loug. | 49 | E2 |
| Druce Rd. SE21 | 152 | B6 |
| **Druid St. SE1** | **28** | **E3** |
| Druid St. SE1 | 132 | B2 |
| Druids Way, Brom. | 190 | D4 |
| **Drum St. E1** | **21** | **G3** |
| Drumaline Ridge, Wor.Pk. | 197 | E2 |
| **Drummond Cres. NW1** | **9** | **H3** |
| Drummond Cres. NW1 | 110 | D3 |
| Drummond Dr., Stan. | 52 | C7 |
| **Drummond Gate SW1** | **33** | **J3** |
| Drummond Gate SW1 | 130 | D5 |
| Drummond Pl., Rich. | 145 | H4 |
| Drummond Pl., Twick. | 144 | E6 |
| Drummond Rd. E11 | 79 | J6 |
| Drummond Rd. SE16 | 132 | E3 |
| Drummond Rd., Croy. | 201 | J2 |
| **Drummond St. NW1** | **9** | **F5** |
| Drummond St. NW1 | 110 | C4 |
| Drummonds, The, Buck.H. | 63 | H2 |
| Drury Cres., Croy. | 201 | G2 |
| **Drury La. WC2** | **18** | **B4** |
| Drury La. WC2 | 111 | E6 |
| Drury Rd., Har. | 67 | J7 |
| Drury Way NW10 | 88 | D5 |
| Drury Way Ind. Est. NW10 | 88 | C5 |
| Dryad St. SW15 | 148 | A3 |
| Dryburgh Gdns. NW9 | 70 | A3 |
| Dryburgh Rd. SW15 | 147 | H3 |
| Dryden Av. W7 | 104 | C6 |
| Dryden Cl., Ilf. | 65 | J6 |
| **Dryden Ct. SE11** | **35** | **F2** |
| Dryden Ct. SE11 | 131 | G4 |
| Dryden Rd. SW19 | 167 | F6 |
| Dryden Rd., Enf. | 44 | B6 |
| Dryden Rd., Har. | 68 | C1 |
| Dryden Rd., Well. | 157 | H1 |
| **Dryden St. WC2** | **18** | **B4** |
| Dryfield Cl. NW10 | 88 | C6 |
| Dryfield Rd., Edg. | 54 | C6 |
| Dryfield Wk. SE8 | 134 | A6 |
| *New King St.* | | |
| Dryhill Rd., Belv. | 139 | F6 |
| Dryland Av., Orp. | 207 | J4 |
| Drylands Rd. N8 | 75 | E6 |
| Drysdale Av. E4 | 46 | B7 |
| **Drysdale Pl. N1** | **12** | **E3** |
| **Drysdale St. N1** | **12** | **E3** |
| Drysdale St. N1 | 112 | B3 |
| Du Burstow Ter. W7 | 124 | B2 |
| Du Cane Cl. W12 | 107 | J6 |
| Du Cane Ct. SW17 | 168 | A1 |
| Du Cane Rd. W12 | 107 | F6 |
| Du Cros Dr., Stan. | 53 | F6 |
| Du Cros Rd. W3 | 126/127 | E1 |
| *The Vale* | | |
| Dublin Av. E8 | 112 | D1 |
| **Ducal St. E2** | **13** | **G4** |
| Duchess Cl. N11 | 58 | B5 |
| Duchess Cl., Sutt. | 199 | F4 |
| Duchess Gro., Buck.H. | 63 | H2 |
| **Duchess Ms. W1** | **16** | **E2** |
| Duchess of Bedford's Wk. W8 | 128 | D2 |
| **Duchess St. W1** | **16** | **E2** |
| Duchess St. W1 | 110 | B5 |
| **Duchy St. SE1** | **27** | **F1** |
| Duchy St. SE1 | 131 | G1 |
| Ducie St. SW4 | 151 | F4 |
| **Duck La. W1** | **17** | **H4** |
| Duck Lees La., Enf. | 45 | H4 |
| Duckett Ms. N4 | 75 | H6 |
| *Duckett Rd.* | | |
| Duckett Rd. N4 | 75 | H6 |
| Duckett St. E1 | 113 | G5 |
| Ducks Wk., Twick. | 145 | F5 |
| Dudden Hill La. NW10 | 89 | F4 |
| Duddington Cl. SE9 | 174 | A4 |
| Dudley Av., Har. | 69 | F3 |
| Dudley Ct. NW11 | 72 | C4 |
| Dudley Dr., Mord. | 184 | B7 |
| Dudley Dr., Ruis. | 84 | B5 |
| Dudley Gdns. W13 | 125 | E2 |
| Dudley Gdns., Har. | 86 | A1 |
| Dudley Rd. E17 | 78 | A2 |
| Dudley Rd. N3 | 72 | E2 |
| Dudley Rd. NW6 | 108 | B2 |
| Dudley Rd. SW19 | 166 | D6 |
| Dudley Rd., Har. | 85 | J2 |
| Dudley Rd., Ilf. | 99 | E4 |
| Dudley Rd., Kings.T. | 181 | J3 |
| Dudley Rd., Rich. | 145 | J2 |
| Dudley Rd., Sthl. | 122 | D2 |
| Dudley Rd., Walt. | 178 | A6 |
| **Dudley St. W2** | **14** | **E2** |
| Dudley St. W2 | 109 | G5 |
| Dudlington Rd. E5 | 95 | F2 |
| **Dudmaston Ms. SW3** | **31** | **F3** |
| Dudsbury Rd., Sid. | 176 | B6 |
| Dudset La., Houns. | 142 | A1 |
| Duff St. E14 | 114 | B6 |
| **Dufferin Av. EC1** | **12** | **B6** |
| **Dufferin St. EC1** | **12** | **A6** |
| Dufferin St. EC1 | 111 | J4 |
| Duffield Cl., Har. | 68 | C5 |
| Duffield Dr. N15 | 76 | C4 |
| *Copperfield Dr.* | | |
| **Dufour's Pl. W1** | **17** | **G4** |
| **Dugard Way SE11** | **35** | **G1** |
| Dugard Way SE11 | 131 | H4 |
| Duke Gdns., Ilf. | 81 | G4 |
| *Duke Rd.* | | |
| Duke Humphrey Rd. SE3 | 155 | E1 |
| Duke of Cambridge Cl., Twick. | 144 | A6 |
| Duke of Edinburgh Rd., Sutt. | 199 | G2 |
| **Duke of Wellington Pl. SW1** | **24** | **C3** |
| Duke of Wellington Pl. SW1 | 130 | A2 |
| **Duke of York St. SW1** | **25** | **G1** |
| Duke of York St. SW1 | 130 | C1 |
| Duke Rd. W4 | 126 | D5 |
| Duke Rd., Ilf. | 81 | G4 |
| Duke Shore Pl. E14 | 113 | J7 |
| *Narrow St.* | | |
| Duke Shore Wf. E14 | 113 | J7 |
| *Narrow St.* | | |
| **Duke St. SW1** | **25** | **G1** |
| Duke St. SW1 | 130 | C1 |
| **Duke St. W1** | **16** | **C3** |
| Duke St. W1 | 110 | A6 |
| Duke St., Rich. | 145 | G4 |
| Duke St., Sutt. | 199 | G4 |
| **Duke St. Hill SE1** | **28** | **C1** |
| Dukes Av. N3 | 72 | E1 |
| Dukes Av. N10 | 74 | C3 |
| Dukes Av. W4 | 126 | D5 |
| Dukes Av., Edg. | 53 | J6 |
| Dukes Av., Har. | 67 | F6 |
| Dukes Av. (Wealdstone), Har. | 68 | B4 |
| Dukes Av., Houns. | 142 | E4 |
| Dukes Av., Kings.T. | 163 | F4 |
| Dukes Av., N.Mal. | 183 | F3 |
| Dukes Av., Nthlt. | 85 | E7 |
| Dukes Av., Rich. | 163 | F4 |
| Dukes Cl., Hmptn. | 161 | F5 |
| Dukes Ct. E6 | 116 | D1 |
| Dukes Grn. Av., Felt. | 142 | A5 |
| Dukes Head Yd. N6 | 92 | B1 |
| *Highgate High St.* | | |
| Dukes La. W8 | 128 | D2 |
| Duke's Meadows W4 | 146 | C2 |
| *Great Chertsey Rd.* | | |
| Dukes Ms. N10 | 74 | B3 |
| *Dukes Av.* | | |
| **Duke's Ms. W1** | **16** | **C3** |
| Dukes Orchard, Bex. | 177 | J1 |
| Duke's Pas. E17 | 78 | C4 |
| **Dukes Pl. EC3** | **21** | **E4** |
| Dukes Pl. EC3 | 112 | B6 |
| Dukes Rd. E6 | 116 | D1 |
| Dukes Rd. W3 | 106 | A5 |
| **Duke's Rd. WC1** | **9** | **J4** |
| Duke's Rd. WC1 | 110 | D3 |
| Dukes Way, W.Wick. | 205 | E3 |
| **Duke's Yd. W1** | **16** | **C5** |
| Dukesthorpe Rd. SE26 | 171 | G4 |
| Dulas St. N4 | 93 | F1 |
| *Everleigh St.* | | |
| Dulford St. W11 | 108 | B7 |
| Dulka Rd. SW11 | 149 | J5 |
| Dulverton Rd. SE9 | 175 | F2 |
| Dulverton Rd., Ruis. | 84 | A1 |
| Dulwich Common SE21 | 170 | B1 |
| Dulwich Common SE22 | 170 | B1 |
| Dulwich Lawn Cl. SE22 | 152 | C5 |
| *Colwell Rd.* | | |
| Dulwich Oaks, The SE21 | 170 | B3 |
| Dulwich Rd. SE24 | 151 | G5 |
| Dulwich Village SE21 | 152 | B6 |
| Dulwich Wd. Av. SE19 | 170 | B4 |
| Dulwich Wd. Pk. SE19 | 170 | B4 |

Dumbarton Rd. SW2 151 E6
Dumbleton Cl., Kings.T. 182 B1
*Gloucester Rd.*
Dumbreck Rd. SE9 156 D4
Dumont Rd. N16 94 B3
Dumpton Pl. NW1 92 A7
*Gloucester Av.*
Dunbar Av. SW16 187 G2
Dunbar Av., Beck. 189 H4
Dunbar Av., Dag. 101 G3
Dunbar Cl., Hayes 102 A5
Dunbar Ct., Sutt. 199 G5
Dunbar Gdns., Dag. 101 G5
Dunbar Rd. E7 97 G6
Dunbar Rd. N22 75 G1
Dunbar Rd., N.Mal. 182 C4
Dunbar St. SE27 169 J3
Dunblane Cl., Edg. 54 B2
*Tayside Dr.*
Dunblane Rd. SE9 156 B3
Dunboyne Rd. NW3 91 J5
**Dunbridge St. E2 13 J5**
Dunbridge St. E2 112 D4
Duncan Cl., Barn. 41 F4
Duncan Gro. W3 106 E6
Duncan Rd. E8 112 E1
Duncan Rd., Rich. 145 H4
**Duncan St. N1 11 G1**
Duncan St. N1 111 H2
**Duncan Ter. N1 11 G2**
Duncan Ter. N1 111 H2
**Duncannon St. WC2 18 A6**
Duncannon St. WC2 110 E7
Dunch St. E1 112/113 E6
*Watney St.*
Duncombe Hill SE23 153 H7
Duncombe Rd. N19 92 D1
Duncrievie Rd. SE13 154 D6
Duncroft SE18 137 H7
Dundalk Rd. SE4 153 H3
Dundas Gdns., W.Mol. 179 H3
Dundas Rd. SE15 153 F2
Dundee Rd. E13 115 H2
Dundee Rd. SE25 188 E5
Dundee St. E1 132 E1
Dundee Way, Enf. 45 H3
Dundela Gdns., Wor.Pk. 197 H4
Dundonald Cl. E6 116 B6
*Northumberland Rd.*
Dundonald Rd. NW10 108 A1
Dundonald Rd. SW19 166 B7
Dunedin Rd. E10 96 B3
Dunedin Rd., Ilf. 99 F1
Dunedin Way, Hayes 102 C4
Dunelm Gro. SE27 169 J4
Dunelm St. E1 113 G6
Dunfield Gdns. SE6 172 B4
Dunfield Rd. SE6 172 B5
Dunford Rd. N7 93 F4
Dungarvan Av. SW15 147 G4
Dunheved Cl., Th.Hth. 187 G6
Dunheved Rd. N., Th.Hth. 187 G6
Dunheved Rd. S., Th.Hth. 187 G6
Dunheved Rd. W., Th.Hth. 187 G6
Dunholme Grn. N9 60 C3
Dunholme La. N9 60 C3
*Dunholme Rd.*
Dunholme Rd. N9 60 C3
Dunkeld Rd. SE25 188 A4
Dunkeld Rd., Dag. 100 B2
Dunkery Rd. SE9 174 A4
Dunkirk St. SE27 169 J4
*Waring St.*
Dunlace Rd. E5 95 F4
Dunleary Cl., Houns. 143 F7
Dunley Dr., Croy. 204 B7
Dunlin Ho. W13 104 C4
Dunloe Av. N17 76 A3
**Dunloe St. E2 13 F2**
Dunloe St. E2 112 C2
**Dunlop Pl. SE16 29 G6**
**Dunmore Pt. E2 13 F4**
Dunmore Rd. NW6 108 B1
Dunmore Rd. SW20 183 J1
Dunmow Cl., Felt. 160 E4
Dunmow Cl., Loug. 48 B6
Dunmow Cl., Rom. 82 C5
Dunmow Ho., Dag. 118 B1
Dunmow Rd. E15 96 D4
Dunmow Wk. N1 111 J1
*Popham St.*
Dunn Mead NW9 55 F7
*Field Mead*
Dunn St. E8 94 C5
Dunnage Cres. SE16 133 H4
*Plough Way*
Dunnock Cl. N9 61 G1
Dunnock Cl., Borwd. 38 A4
Dunnock Rd. E6 116 B6
**Dunns Pas. WC1 18 B3**
Dunollie Pl. NW5 92 C5
*Dunollie Rd.*
Dunollie Rd. NW5 92 C5
Dunoon Rd. SE23 153 F7
Dunraven Dr., Enf. 43 G2
Dunraven Rd. W12 127 G1
**Dunraven St. W1 16 A5**
Dunsany Rd. W14 128 A3
Dunsfold Way, Croy. 204 B7
Dunsford Way SW15 147 H6
*Dover Pk. Dr.*
Dunsmore Cl., Hayes 102/103 E4
*Kingsash Dr.*
Dunsmore Rd., Walt. 178 B6
Dunsmure Rd. N16 94 B1
Dunspring La., Ilf. 80 E2
**Dunstable Ms. W1 16 C1**
Dunstable Rd., Rich. 145 H4
Dunstable Rd., W.Mol. 179 F4
Dunstall Rd. SW20 165 H6
Dunstall Way, W.Mol. 179 H3
Dunstan Cl. N2 73 F3
*Thomas More Way*
Dunstan Rd. NW11 90 C1
Dunstans Gro. SE22 152 E6
Dunstans Rd. SE22 152 D7
Dunster Av., Mord. 198 A1
Dunster Cl., Barn. 40 A4
Dunster Cl., Rom. 83 J2
**Dunster Ct. EC3 20 E5**
Dunster Dr. NW9 88 C1
Dunster Gdns. NW6 90 C7
Dunster Way, Har. 85 E3
**Dunsterville Way SE1 28 C4**
Dunston Rd. E8 112 C1
Dunston Rd. SW11 150 A2
Dunston St. E8 112 C1
Dunton Cl., Surb. 195 H1
Dunton Rd. E10 78 B7
**Dunton Rd. SE1 37 F3**
Dunton Rd. SE1 132 C5
Duntshill Rd. SW18 167 E1
Dunvegan Cl., W.Mol. 179 H4
Dunvegan Rd. SE9 156 C4
Dunwich Rd., Bexh. 159 F1
Dunworth Ms. W11 108 C6
*Portobello Rd.*
**Duplex Ride SW1 24 A4**
Dupont Rd. SW20 184 A2
Dupont St. E14 113 H5
*Maroon St.*
Duppas Av., Croy. 201 H4
*Violet La.*
Duppas Hill La., Croy. 201 H4
*Duppas Hill Rd.*
Duppas Hill Rd., Croy. 201 H4
Duppas Hill Ter., Croy. 201 H3
Duppas Rd., Croy. 201 G3
Dupree Rd. SE7 135 H5
Dura Den Cl., Beck. 172 B7
Durand Cl., Cars. 199 J1
Durand Gdns. SW9 151 F1
Durand Way NW10 88 C7
Durands Wk. SE16 133 J2
**Durant St. E2 13 H3**
Durant St. E2 112 D3
Durants Pk. Av., Enf. 45 G4
Durants Rd., Enf. 45 F4
Durban Gdns., Dag. 101 J7
Durban Rd. E15 114 E3
Durban Rd. E17 77 J1
Durban Rd. N17 60 B6
Durban Rd. SE27 169 J4
Durban Rd., Beck. 189 J2
Durban Rd., Ilf. 99 H1
Durbin Rd., Chess. 195 H4
Durdans Rd., Sthl. 103 F6
Durell Gdns., Dag. 100 D5
Durell Rd., Dag. 100 D5
Durford Cres. SW15 165 H1
Durham Av., Brom. 191 F4
Durham Av., Houns. 123 F5
Durham Av., Wdf.Grn. 64 A5
Durham Cl. SW20 183 H2
*Durham Rd.*
Durham Hill, Brom. 173 F4
**Durham Ho. St. WC2 18 B6**
**Durham Pl. SW3 31 J4**
Durham Pl., Ilf. 99 F4
*Eton Rd.*
Durham Ri. SE18 137 F5
Durham Rd. E12 98 A4
Durham Rd. E16 115 E4
Durham Rd. N2 73 H3
Durham Rd. N7 93 F2
Durham Rd. N9 60 D2
Durham Rd. SW20 183 H1
Durham Rd. W5 125 G3
Durham Rd., Borwd. 38 C3
Durham Rd., Brom. 191 F3
Durham Rd., Dag. 101 J5
Durham Rd., Felt. 142 C7
Durham Rd., Har. 67 H5
Durham Rd., Sid. 176 B5
Durham Row E1 113 H5
**Durham St. SE11 34 C4**
Durham St. SE11 131 F5
**Durham Ter. W2 14 A3**
Durham Ter. W2 108 E6
Durham Wf., Brent. 125 F7
*London Rd.*
Durham Yd. E2 112/113 E3
*Teesdale St.*
Durley Av., Pnr. 67 E7
Durley Rd. N16 76 B7
Durlston Rd. E5 94 D2
Durlston Rd., Kings.T. 163 H6
Durnell Way, Loug. 48 D3
Durnford St. N15 76 B5
Durnford St. SE10 134 C6
*Greenwich Ch. St.*
Durning Rd. SE19 170 A5
Durnsford Av. SW19 166 D2
Durnsford Rd. N11 74 D1
Durnsford Rd. SW19 166 D2
Durrant Way, Orp. 207 G5
Durrell Rd. SW6 148 C1
Durrington Av. SW20 183 J1
Durrington Pk. Rd. SW20 165 J7
Durrington Rd. E5 95 H4
Dursley Cl. SE3 155 J2
Dursley Gdns. SE3 156 A1
Dursley Rd. SE3 155 J2
Durward St. E1 112 E5
**Durweston Ms. W1 16 A1**
**Durweston St. W1 16 A1**
Durweston St. W1 109 J5
Dury Rd., Barn. 40 C1
Dutch Barn Cl., Stai. 140 A6
Dutch Gdns., Kings.T. 164 B6
*Windmill Ri.*
Dutch Yd. SW18 148 D5
*Wandsworth High St.*
Duthie St. E14 114 C7
*Prestons Rd.*
Dutton St. SE10 154 C1
Duxberry Cl., Brom. 192 B5
*Southborough La.*
Duxford Ho. SE2 138 D2
*Wolvercote Rd.*
Dwight Ct. SW6 148 B2
*Burlington Rd.*
Dye Ho. La. E3 114 A1
**Dyer's Bldgs. EC1 19 E2**
Dyers Hall Rd. E11 96 E1
Dyers La. SW15 147 H4
Dykes Way, Brom. 191 F3
Dylan Rd. SE24 151 H4
Dylan Rd., Belv. 139 G3
Dylan Thomas Ho. N8 75 F4
Dylways SE5 152 A4
Dymchurch Cl., Ilf. 80 D2
Dymchurch Cl., Orp. 207 H4
Dymes Path SW19 166 A2
*Queensmere Rd.*
Dymock St. SW6 148 E3
Dymond Est. SW17 167 H3
*Glenburnie Rd.*
Dyne Rd. NW6 90 C7
Dyneley Rd. SE12 173 J4
Dynevor Rd. N16 94 B3
Dynevor Rd., Rich. 145 H5
Dynham Rd. NW6 90 D7
**Dyott St. WC1 18 A3**
Dyott St. WC1 110 D6
Dysart Av., Kings.T. 163 F5
**Dysart St. EC2 12 D6**
Dyson Rd. E11 79 E6
Dyson Rd. E15 97 F6
Dysons Rd. N18 61 E5

## E

Eade Rd. N4 75 J7
Eagans Cl. N2 73 H3
*Market Pl.*
Eagle Av., Rom. 82 E6
Eagle Cl. SE16 133 F5
*Varcoe Rd.*
Eagle Cl., Enf. 45 F4
Eagle Cl., Wall. 201 E6
**Eagle Ct. EC1 19 G1**
Eagle Ct. EC1 111 H5
Eagle Dr. NW9 71 E2
Eagle Hill SE19 170 A6
Eagle La. E11 79 G4
Eagle Ms. N1 94 B6
*Tottenham Rd.*
**Eagle Pl. SW1 17 G6**
**Eagle Pl. SW7 30 D3**
Eagle Rd., Wem. 87 G7
**Eagle St. WC1 18 C2**
Eagle St. WC1 111 F5
Eagle Ter., Wdf.Grn. 63 H7
Eagle Wf. E14 114 B5
*Broomfield St.*
**Eagle Wf. Rd. N1 12 A1**
Eagle Wf. Rd. N1 111 J2
Eaglesfield Rd. SE18 137 E7
Ealdham Sq. SE9 155 J4
Ealing Cl., Borwd. 38 D1
Ealing Downs Ct., Grnf. 104 D3
*Perivale La.*
Ealing Grn. W5 125 G1
Ealing Pk. Gdns. W5 125 F4
Ealing Rd., Brent. 125 G5
Ealing Rd., Nthlt. 85 G7
Ealing Rd., Wem. 105 H1
Ealing Village W5 105 H6
**Eamont St. NW8 7 G1**
Eamont St. NW8 109 H2
Eardley Cres. SW5 128 D5
Eardley Pt. SE18 136/137 E4
*Wilmount St.*
Eardley Rd. SW16 168 C5
Eardley Rd., Belv. 139 G5
Earl Cl. N11 58 B5
Earl Ri. SE18 137 G4
Earl Rd. SW14 146 C4
*Elm Rd.*
**Earl St. EC2 20 D1**
Earl St. EC2 112 A5
Earldom Rd. SW15 147 J4
Earle Gdns., Kings.T. 163 H6
Earlham Gro. E7 97 F5
Earlham Gro. N22 59 F7
**Earlham St. WC2 17 J4**
Earlham St. WC2 110 D6
**Earls Ct. Gdns. SW5 30 A2**
Earls Ct. Gdns. SW5 128 E4
Earls Ct. Rd. SW5 128 D4
Earls Ct. Rd. W8 128 D3
**Earls Ct. Sq. SW5 30 A3**
Earls Ct. Sq. SW5 128 E5
Earls Cres., Har. 68 B4
Earl's Path, Loug. 47 J2
Earls Ter. W8 128 C3
Earls Wk. W8 128 D3
Earls Wk., Dag. 100 B4
Earls Way, Orp. 207 J2
*Station Rd.*
Earlsdown Ho., Bark. 117 G2
*Wheelers Cross*
Earlsferry Way N1 111 F1
Earlsfield Rd. SW18 167 F1
Earlshall Rd. SE9 156 C4
Earlsmead, Har. 85 F4
Earlsmead Rd. N15 76 C5
Earlsmead Rd. NW10 107 J2
Earlsthorpe Ms. SW12 150 A6
Earlsthorpe Rd. SE26 171 G4
**Earlstoke St. EC1 11 G3**
Earlston Gro. E9 113 E1
Earlswood Av., Th.Hth. 187 G5
Earlswood Cl. SE10 134/135 E5
*Earlswood St.*
Earlswood Gdns., Ilf. 80 D3
Earlswood St. SE10 135 E5
Early Ms. NW1 110 B1
*Arlington Rd.*
**Earnshaw St. WC2 17 J3**
Earnshaw St. WC2 110 D6
Earsby St. W14 128 B4
Easby Cres., Mord. 185 E6
Easebourne Rd., Dag. 100 C5
Easedale Ho., Islw. 144 C5
*Summerwood Rd.*
**Easley's Ms. W1 16 C3**
East Acton La. W3 126 E1
East Arbour St. E1 113 G6
East Av. E12 98 B7
East Av. E17 78 B4
East Av., Hayes 121 J2
East Av., Sthl. 103 F7
East Av., Wall. 201 F5
East Bank N16 76 B7
East Barnet Rd., Barn. 41 H6
East Churchfield Rd. W3 126 D1
East Cl. W5 106 A4
East Cl., Barn. 42 A4
East Cl., Grnf. 103 J2
East Ct., Wem. 87 F2
East Cres. N11 57 J4
East Cres., Enf. 44 C5

| | | |
|---|---|---|
| East Cross Route E3 | 114 | A1 |
| East Duck Lees La., Enf. | 45 | H4 |
| East Dulwich Gro. SE22 | 152 | B6 |
| East Dulwich Rd. SE15 | 152 | C4 |
| East Dulwich Rd. SE22 | 152 | C4 |
| East End Rd. N2 | 73 | F3 |
| East End Rd. N3 | 72 | D2 |
| East End Way, Pnr. | 67 | E3 |
| East Entrance, Dag. | 119 | H2 |
| East Ferry Rd. E14 | 134 | B3 |
| East Gdns. SW17 | 167 | H6 |
| East Ham Ind. Est. E6 | 116 | B4 |
| East Ham Manor Way E6 | 116 | D6 |
| **East Harding St. EC4** | **19** | **F3** |
| East Heath Rd. NW3 | 91 | G3 |
| East Hill SW18 | 149 | E5 |
| East Hill, Wem. | 88 | A2 |
| East India Dock Rd. E14 | 114 | D6 |
| **East La. SE16** | **29** | **H4** |
| East La. SE16 | 132 | D2 |
| East La., Kings.T. *High St.* | 181 | G3 |
| East La., Wem. | 87 | G3 |
| East Mascalls SE7 *Mascalls Rd.* | 135 | J6 |
| East Mead, Ruis. | 84 | D3 |
| East Mt. St. E1 | 113 | E5 |
| East Pk. Cl., Rom. | 82 | D5 |
| East Parkside SE10 | 135 | E2 |
| **East Pas. EC1** | **19** | **H1** |
| East Pier E1 *Wapping High St.* | 132/133 | E1 |
| East Pl. SE27 *Pilgrim Hill* | 169 | J4 |
| **East Poultry Av. EC1** | **19** | **G2** |
| East Ramp, Houns. | 140 | E1 |
| East Rd. E15 | 115 | G1 |
| **East Rd. N1** | **12** | **B4** |
| East Rd. N1 | 112 | A3 |
| East Rd. SW19 | 167 | F6 |
| East Rd., Barn. | 58 | A1 |
| East Rd., Edg. | 70 | B1 |
| East Rd., Felt. | 141 | G7 |
| East Rd., Kings.T. | 181 | H1 |
| East Rd. (Chadwell Heath), Rom. | 82 | E5 |
| East Rd., Well. | 158 | B2 |
| East Rd., West Dr. | 120 | C4 |
| East Rochester Way SE9 | 157 | H4 |
| East Rochester Way, Bex. | 159 | J7 |
| East Rochester Way, Sid. | 157 | H4 |
| East Row E11 | 79 | G6 |
| East Row W10 | 108 | B4 |
| East Sheen Av. SW14 | 146 | D4 |
| **East Smithfield E1** | **21** | **G6** |
| East Smithfield E1 | 112 | C7 |
| **East St. SE17** | **36** | **A3** |
| East St. SE17 | 131 | J5 |
| East St., Bark. | 99 | F7 |
| East St., Bexh. | 159 | G4 |
| East St., Brent. | 125 | F7 |
| East St., Brom. | 191 | G2 |
| East Surrey Gro. SE15 | 132 | C7 |
| **East Tenter St. E1** | **21** | **G4** |
| East Tenter St. E1 | 112 | C6 |
| East Twrs., Pnr. | 66 | D5 |
| East Vw. E4 | 62 | C5 |
| East Vw., Barn. | 40 | C3 |
| East Wk., Barn. | 42 | A7 |
| East Wk., Hayes | 122 | A1 |
| East Way E11 | 79 | H5 |
| East Way, Brom. | 191 | G7 |
| East Way, Croy. | 203 | H2 |
| East Way, Hayes | 122 | A1 |
| East Way, Ruis. | 84 | A1 |
| East Woodside, Bex. | 177 | E1 |
| Eastbank Rd., Hmptn. | 161 | J5 |
| Eastbourne Av. W3 | 106 | D6 |
| Eastbourne Gdns. SW14 | 146 | C3 |
| **Eastbourne Ms. W2** | **14** | **D3** |
| Eastbourne Ms. W2 | 109 | F6 |
| Eastbourne Rd. E6 | 116 | D3 |
| Eastbourne Rd. E15 | 115 | E1 |
| Eastbourne Rd. N15 | 76 | B6 |
| Eastbourne Rd. SW17 | 168 | A6 |
| Eastbourne Rd. W4 | 126 | C6 |
| Eastbourne Rd., Brent. | 125 | F5 |
| Eastbourne Rd., Felt. | 160 | D2 |
| **Eastbourne Ter. W2** | **14** | **D3** |
| Eastbourne Ter. W2 | 109 | F6 |
| Eastbournia Av. N9 | 61 | E3 |
| Eastbrook Av. N9 | 45 | F7 |
| Eastbrook Av., Dag. | 101 | J4 |
| Eastbrook Rd. SE3 | 135 | H7 |
| Eastbury Av., Bark. | 117 | H1 |
| Eastbury Av., Enf. | 44 | B1 |
| Eastbury Ct., Bark. | 117 | H1 |
| Eastbury Gro. W4 | 127 | E5 |
| Eastbury Ho., Bark. | 117 | J1 |
| Eastbury Rd. E6 | 116 | D4 |
| Eastbury Rd., Kings.T. | 163 | H7 |
| Eastbury Rd., Orp. | 193 | G6 |
| Eastbury Sq., Bark. | 117 | J1 |
| Eastbury Ter. E1 | 113 | G4 |
| **Eastcastle St. W1** | **17** | **F3** |
| Eastcastle St. W1 | 110 | C6 |
| **Eastcheap EC3** | **20** | **C5** |
| Eastcheap EC3 | 112 | A7 |
| Eastchurch Rd., Houns. | 141 | H2 |
| Eastcombe Av. SE7 | 135 | H6 |
| Eastcote, Orp. | 207 | J1 |
| Eastcote Av., Grnf. | 86 | D5 |
| Eastcote Av., Har. | 85 | H2 |
| Eastcote Av., W.Mol. | 179 | F5 |
| Eastcote La., Har. | 85 | G3 |
| Eastcote La., Nthlt. | 85 | G7 |
| Eastcote La. N., Nthlt. | 85 | F6 |
| Eastcote Pl., Pnr. | 66 | B6 |
| Eastcote Rd., Har. | 85 | J3 |
| Eastcote Rd., Pnr. | 66 | D5 |
| Eastcote Rd. (Eastcote Village), Pnr. | 66 | A6 |
| Eastcote Rd., Well. | 157 | G2 |
| Eastcote St. SW9 | 151 | F2 |
| Eastcote Vw., Pnr. | 66 | C4 |
| Eastcroft Rd., Epsom | 197 | E7 |
| Eastdown Pk. SE13 | 154 | D4 |
| Eastern Av. E11 | 79 | J6 |
| Eastern Av., Ilf. | 80 | B6 |
| Eastern Av., Pnr. | 66 | D7 |
| Eastern Av., Rom. | 82 | C4 |
| Eastern Av. W., Rom. | 82 | E4 |
| Eastern Ind. Est., Erith | 139 | G2 |
| Eastern Perimeter Rd., Houns. | 141 | J3 |
| Eastern Rd. E13 | 115 | H2 |
| Eastern Rd. E17 | 78 | C5 |
| Eastern Rd. N2 | 73 | J3 |
| Eastern Rd. N22 | 75 | E1 |
| Eastern Rd. SE4 | 154 | A4 |
| Eastern Way SE2 | 138 | D1 |
| Eastern Way SE28 | 138 | A2 |
| Eastern Way, Belv. | 139 | H2 |
| Eastern Way, Erith | 138 | D1 |
| Easternville Gdns., Ilf. | 81 | F6 |
| Eastfield Cotts., Hayes | 121 | H5 |
| Eastfield Gdns., Dag. | 101 | G4 |
| Eastfield Rd. E17 | 78 | A4 |
| Eastfield Rd. N8 | 74 | E3 |
| Eastfield Rd., Dag. | 101 | G4 |
| Eastfields, Pnr. | 66 | C5 |
| Eastfields Rd. W3 | 106 | C5 |
| Eastfields Rd., Mitch. | 186 | A2 |
| Eastgate Cl. SE28 | 118 | D6 |
| Eastglade, Pnr. | 67 | E3 |
| Eastham Cl., Barn. | 40 | B5 |
| Eastholm NW11 | 73 | E4 |
| Eastholme, Hayes | 122 | A1 |
| Eastlake Rd. SE5 | 151 | H2 |
| Eastlands Cres. SE21 | 152 | C6 |
| Eastlea Ms. E16 *Desford Rd.* | 114/115 | E4 |
| Eastleigh Av., Har. | 85 | H2 |
| Eastleigh Cl. NW2 | 89 | E3 |
| Eastleigh Cl., Sutt. | 199 | E7 |
| Eastleigh Rd. E17 | 77 | J2 |
| Eastleigh Rd., Bexh. | 159 | J2 |
| Eastleigh Rd., Houns. *Cranford La.* | 141 | J3 |
| Eastleigh Wk. SW15 | 147 | G7 |
| Eastleigh Way, Felt. | 160 | A1 |
| Eastman Rd. W3 | 126 | D1 |
| Eastmead Av., Grnf. | 103 | H3 |
| Eastmead Cl., Brom. | 192 | B2 |
| Eastmearn Rd. SE21 | 169 | J2 |
| Eastmont Rd., Esher | 194 | B2 |
| Eastmoor Pl. SE7 *Eastmoor St.* | 136 | A3 |
| Eastmoor St. SE7 | 136 | A3 |
| Eastney Rd., Croy. | 201 | H1 |
| Eastney St. SE10 | 134 | D5 |
| Eastnor Rd. SE9 | 175 | F1 |
| Easton Gdns., Borwd. | 38 | D4 |
| **Easton St. WC1** | **10** | **E4** |
| Eastry Av., Brom. | 191 | F6 |
| Eastry Rd., Erith | 139 | G7 |
| Eastside Rd. NW11 | 72 | C4 |
| Eastview Av. SE18 | 137 | H7 |
| Eastville Av. NW11 | 72 | C6 |
| Eastway E9 | 95 | J6 |
| Eastway E10 | 96 | C4 |
| Eastway E15 | 96 | A5 |
| Eastway, Mord. | 184 | A5 |
| Eastway, Wall. | 200 | C4 |
| Eastway Commercial Cen. E9 | 96 | A5 |
| Eastwell Cl., Beck. | 189 | H1 |
| Eastwood Cl. E18 *George La.* | 79 | G2 |
| Eastwood Cl. N17 *Northumberland Gro.* | 60/61 | E7 |
| Eastwood Rd. E18 | 79 | G2 |
| Eastwood Rd. N10 | 74 | A2 |
| Eastwood Rd., Ilf. | 82 | A7 |
| Eastwood Rd., West Dr. | 120 | D2 |
| Eastwood St. SW16 | 168 | C6 |
| Eatington Rd. E10 | 78 | D5 |
| **Eaton Cl. SW1** | **32** | **B2** |
| Eaton Cl. SW1 | 130 | A4 |
| Eaton Cl., Stan. | 53 | E4 |
| Eaton Dr. SW9 | 151 | H4 |
| Eaton Dr., Kings.T. | 164 | A7 |
| Eaton Gdns., Dag. | 100 | E7 |
| **Eaton Gate SW1** | **32** | **B1** |
| Eaton Gate SW1 | 130 | A4 |
| **Eaton La. SW1** | **24** | **E6** |
| Eaton La. SW1 | 130 | B3 |
| **Eaton Ms. N. SW1** | **32** | **B1** |
| Eaton Ms. N. SW1 | 130 | A3 |
| **Eaton Ms. S. SW1** | **32** | **C1** |
| Eaton Ms. S. SW1 | 130 | B3 |
| **Eaton Ms. W. SW1** | **32** | **C1** |
| Eaton Ms. W. SW1 | 130 | A4 |
| Eaton Pk. Rd. N13 | 59 | G2 |
| **Eaton Pl. SW1** | **24** | **B6** |
| Eaton Pl. SW1 | 130 | A3 |
| Eaton Ri. E11 | 79 | J5 |
| Eaton Ri. W5 | 105 | G6 |
| Eaton Rd. NW4 | 71 | J5 |
| Eaton Rd., Enf. | 44 | B3 |
| Eaton Rd., Houns. | 144 | A4 |
| Eaton Rd., Sid. | 176 | D2 |
| Eaton Rd., Sutt. | 199 | G6 |
| **Eaton Row SW1** | **24** | **D6** |
| Eaton Row SW1 | 130 | B3 |
| **Eaton Sq. SW1** | **24** | **D5** |
| Eaton Sq. SW1 | 130 | A4 |
| **Eaton Ter. SW1** | **32** | **B1** |
| Eaton Ter. SW1 | 130 | A4 |
| **Eaton Ter. Ms. SW1** | **32** | **B1** |
| Eaton Wk. SE15 *Sumner Est.* | 132 | C7 |
| Eatons Mead E4 | 62 | A2 |
| Eatonville Rd. SW17 | 167 | J2 |
| Eatonville Vil. SW17 *Eatonville Rd.* | 167 | J2 |
| **Ebbisham Dr. SW8** | **34** | **C5** |
| Ebbisham Dr. SW8 | 131 | F6 |
| Ebbisham Rd., Wor.Pk. | 197 | J2 |
| Ebbsfleet Rd. NW2 | 90 | B4 |
| Ebdon Way SE3 | 155 | H3 |
| **Ebenezer St. N1** | **12** | **B3** |
| Ebenezer St. N1 | 112 | A3 |
| Ebenezer Wk. SW16 | 186 | C1 |
| **Ebley Cl. SE15** | **37** | **F6** |
| Ebley Cl. SE15 | 132 | C6 |
| Ebner St. SW18 | 149 | E5 |
| **Ebor St. E1** | **13** | **F5** |
| Ebor St. E1 | 112 | C4 |
| Ebrington Rd., Har. | 69 | G6 |
| Ebsworth St. SE23 | 153 | G7 |
| Eburne Rd. N7 | 93 | E3 |
| **Ebury Br. SW1** | **32** | **D3** |
| Ebury Br. SW1 | 130 | B5 |
| **Ebury Br. Est. SW1** | **32** | **D3** |
| Ebury Br. Est. SW1 | 130 | B5 |
| **Ebury Br. Rd. SW1** | **32** | **C4** |
| Ebury Br. Rd. SW1 | 130 | A5 |
| Ebury Cl., Kes. | 206 | B3 |
| Ebury Ms. SE27 | 169 | H3 |
| **Ebury Ms. SW1** | **32** | **D1** |
| Ebury Ms. SW1 | 130 | B4 |
| **Ebury Ms. E. SW1** | **32** | **D1** |
| **Ebury Sq. SW1** | **32** | **C2** |
| Ebury Sq. SW1 | 130 | A4 |
| **Ebury St. SW1** | **32** | **D1** |
| Ebury St. SW1 | 130 | A4 |
| Eccles Rd. SW11 | 149 | J4 |
| Ecclesbourne Cl. N13 | 59 | G5 |
| Ecclesbourne Gdns. N13 | 59 | G5 |
| Ecclesbourne Rd. N1 | 93 | J7 |
| Ecclesbourne Rd., Th.Hth. | 187 | J5 |
| **Eccleston Br. SW1** | **32** | **E1** |
| Eccleston Br. SW1 | 130 | B4 |
| Eccleston Cl., Barn. | 41 | J4 |
| Eccleston Cl., Orp. | 207 | G1 |
| Eccleston Cres., Rom. | 82 | A7 |
| **Eccleston Ms. SW1** | **24** | **C6** |
| Eccleston Ms. SW1 | 130 | A3 |
| **Eccleston Pl. SW1** | **32** | **D1** |
| Eccleston Pl. SW1 | 130 | B4 |
| Eccleston Rd. W13 | 104 | D7 |
| **Eccleston Sq. SW1** | **33** | **E2** |
| Eccleston Sq. SW1 | 130 | B4 |
| **Eccleston Sq. Ms. SW1** | **33** | **F2** |
| **Eccleston St. SW1** | **24** | **D6** |
| Eccleston St. SW1 | 130 | A3 |
| Ecclestone Ct., Wem. *St. John's Rd.* | 87 | H5 |
| Ecclestone Pl., Wem. | 87 | J5 |
| Echo Hts. E4 *Mount Echo Dr.* | 62 | B1 |
| Eckersley St. E1 *Buxton St.* | 112 | D4 |
| **Eckford St. N1** | **10** | **E1** |
| Eckford St. N1 | 111 | G2 |
| Eckstein Rd. SW11 | 149 | H4 |
| Eclipse Rd. E13 | 115 | H5 |
| Ector Rd. SE6 | 172 | E2 |
| Edbrooke Rd. W9 | 108 | D4 |
| Eddiscombe Rd. SW6 | 148 | C2 |
| Eddy Cl., Rom. | 83 | H6 |
| Eddystone Rd. SE4 | 153 | H5 |
| Eddystone Wk., Stai. | 140 | B7 |
| Ede Cl., Houns. | 143 | F3 |
| Eden Cl. NW3 | 90 | D2 |
| Eden Cl. W8 *Adam & Eve Ms.* | 128 | D3 |
| Eden Cl., Wem. | 105 | G1 |
| Eden Gro. E17 | 78 | B5 |
| Eden Gro. N7 | 93 | F5 |
| Eden Ms. SW17 *Huntspill St.* | 167 | F3 |
| Eden Pk. Av., Beck. | 189 | H4 |
| Eden Rd. E17 | 78 | B5 |
| Eden Rd. SE27 | 169 | H5 |
| Eden Rd., Beck. | 189 | H4 |
| Eden Rd., Bex. | 177 | J4 |
| Eden Rd., Croy. | 202 | A4 |
| Eden St., Kings.T. | 181 | G2 |
| Eden Wk., Kings.T. *Eden St.* | 181 | H2 |
| Eden Way, Beck. | 189 | J5 |
| Edenbridge Cl. SE16 *Masters Dr.* | 132/133 | E5 |
| Edenbridge Rd. E9 | 95 | G7 |
| Edenbridge Rd., Enf. | 44 | B6 |
| Edencourt Rd. SW16 | 168 | B6 |
| Edenfield Gdns., Wor.Pk. | 197 | F3 |
| Edenham Way W10 *Elkstone Rd.* | 108 | C5 |
| Edenhurst Av. SW6 | 148 | C3 |
| Edensor Gdns. W4 | 127 | E7 |
| Edensor Rd. W4 | 126 | E7 |
| Edenvale Cl., Mitch. *Edenvale Rd.* | 168 | A7 |
| Edenvale Rd., Mitch. | 168 | A7 |
| Edenvale St. SW6 | 149 | E2 |
| Ederline Av. SW16 | 187 | F3 |
| Edgar Kail Way SE22 | 152 | B4 |
| Edgar Rd. E3 | 114 | B3 |
| Edgar Rd., Houns. | 143 | F7 |
| Edgar Rd., Rom. | 82 | D7 |
| Edgarley Ter. SW6 | 148 | B1 |
| Edgbaston Rd., Wat. | 50 | B3 |
| Edge Hill SE18 | 136 | E6 |
| Edge Hill SW19 | 166 | A7 |
| Edge Hill Av. N3 | 72 | D3 |
| Edge Hill Ct. SW19 | 166 | A7 |
| Edge St. W8 *Kensington Ch. St.* | 128 | D1 |
| Edgeborough Way, Brom. | 174 | A7 |
| Edgebury, Chis. | 175 | E4 |
| Edgebury Wk., Chis. | 175 | F4 |
| Edgecombe Ho. SW19 | 166 | B1 |
| Edgecoombe, S.Croy. | 203 | F7 |
| Edgecoombe Cl., Kings.T. | 164 | D7 |
| Edgecot Gro. N15 *Oulton Rd.* | 76 | A5 |
| Edgecote Cl. W3 *Cheltenham Pl.* | 126 | C1 |
| Edgefield Av., Bark. | 99 | J7 |
| Edgehill Gdns., Dag. | 101 | G4 |
| Edgehill Rd. W13 | 105 | F5 |
| Edgehill Rd., Chis. | 175 | F3 |
| Edgehill Rd., Mitch. | 186 | B1 |
| Edgel St. SW18 *Ferrier St.* | 148/149 | E4 |
| Edgeley La. SW4 *Edgeley Rd.* | 150 | D3 |
| Edgeley Rd. SW4 | 150 | D3 |
| Edgepoint Cl. SE27 *Knights Hill* | 169 | H5 |
| Edgewood Dr., Orp. | 207 | J5 |
| Edgewood Grn., Croy. | 203 | G1 |
| Edgeworth Av. NW4 | 71 | G5 |
| Edgeworth Cl. NW4 | 71 | G5 |
| Edgeworth Cres. NW4 | 71 | G5 |

Elkington Rd. E13 115 H4
Elkstone Rd. W10 108 C5
Ella Rd. N8 75 E7
Ellaline Rd. W6 128 A6
Ellanby Cres. N18 60 E5
Elland Rd. SE15 153 F4
Ellement Cl., Pnr. 66 D5
Ellen Cl., Brom. 192 A3
Ellen Ct. N9 61 F2
*Densworth Gro.*
**Ellen St. E1 21 J4**
Ellen St. E1 112 D6
Ellen Webb Dr., Har. 68 B3
Ellenborough Pl. SW15 147 G4
Ellenborough Rd. N22 75 J1
Ellenborough Rd., Sid. 176 D5
Elleray Rd., Tedd. 162 C6
Ellerby St. SW6 148 A1
Ellerdale Cl. NW3 91 F4
*Ellerdale Rd.*
Ellerdale Rd. NW3 91 F5
Ellerdale St. SE13 154 B4
Ellerdine Rd., Houns. 143 J4
Ellerker Gdns., Rich. 145 H6
Ellerman Av., Twick. 161 F1
Ellerslie Gdns. NW10 107 G1
Ellerslie Rd. W12 127 H1
Ellerslie Sq. Ind. Est. SW2 150 E5
Ellerton Gdns., Dag. 100 C7
Ellerton Rd. SW13 147 G1
Ellerton Rd. SW18 167 G1
Ellerton Rd. SW20 165 G7
Ellerton Rd., Dag. 100 C7
Ellerton Rd., Surb. 195 J2
Ellery Rd. SE19 170 A7
Ellery St. SE15 153 E2
Ellesborough Cl., Wat. 50 C5
Ellesmere Av. NW7 54 D3
Ellesmere Av., Beck. 190 B2
Ellesmere Cl. E11 79 F5
Ellesmere Gdns., Ilf. 80 B5
Ellesmere Gro., Barn. 40 C5
Ellesmere Rd. E3 113 H2
Ellesmere Rd. NW10 89 G5
Ellesmere Rd. W4 126 D6
Ellesmere Rd., Grnf. 103 J4
Ellesmere Rd., Twick. 145 F6
Ellesmere St. E14 114 B6
Ellingfort Rd. E8 95 E7
Ellingham Rd. E15 96 D4
Ellingham Rd. W12 127 G2
Ellingham Rd., Chess. 195 G6
Ellington Rd. N10 74 B4
Ellington Rd., Houns. 143 H2
Ellington St. N7 93 G6
Elliot Cl. E15 96 E7
Elliot Rd. NW4 71 H6
Elliot Rd., Stan. 52 D6
Elliott Av., Ruis. 84 B2
Elliott Cl., Wem. 87 J3
Elliott Rd. SW9 131 H7
Elliott Rd. W4 126 E4
Elliott Rd., Brom. 192 A4
Elliott Rd., Th.Hth. 187 H4
Elliott Sq. NW3 91 H7
Elliott's Pl. N1 111 H1
*St. Peters St.*
**Elliotts Row SE11 35 G1**
Elliotts Row SE11 131 H4
Ellis Cl. NW10 89 H6
*High Rd.*
Ellis Cl. SE9 175 F2
Ellis Ct. W7 104 C5
Ellis Ms. SE7 135 J6
Ellis Rd., Mitch. 185 J6
Ellis Rd., Sthl. 123 J1
**Ellis St. SW1 32 A1**
Ellis St. SW1 129 J4
Elliscombe Rd. SE7 135 J5
Ellisfield Dr. SW15 147 F7
Ellison Gdns., Sthl. 123 F4
Ellison Rd. SW13 147 F2
Ellison Rd. SW16 168 D7
Ellison Rd., Sid. 175 G1
Elliston Ho. SE18 136 D4
Ellora Rd. SW16 168 D5
Ellsworth St. E2 113 E3
**Ellwood Ct. W9 6 A6**
Elm Av. W5 125 H1
Elm Av., Ruis. 84 A1
Elm Bank, Brom. 192 A2
Elm Bank Gdns. SW13 147 E2
Elm Cl. E11 79 H6
Elm Cl. N19 92 C2
*Hargrave Pk.*
Elm Cl. NW4 72 A5
Elm Cl. SW20 183 J4
*Grand Dr.*
Elm Cl., Buck.H. 64 A2
Elm Cl., Cars. 199 J1
Elm Cl., Har. 67 H6
Elm Cl., Hayes 102 A6
Elm Cl., Rom. 83 H2
Elm Cl., S.Croy. 202 B6
Elm Cl., Surb. 182 C7
Elm Cl., Twick. 161 H2
**Elm Ct. EC4 19 E5**
Elm Ct., Mitch. 185 J2
*Armfield Cres.*
Elm Cres. W5 125 H1
Elm Cres., Kings.T. 181 H1
Elm Dr., Har. 67 H6
Elm Dr., Sun. 178 C2
Elm Friars Wk. NW1 92 D7
Elm Gdns. N2 73 F3
Elm Gdns., Esher 194 C6
Elm Gdns., Mitch. 186 D4
Elm Grn. W3 106 E6
Elm Gro. N8 75 E6
Elm Gro. NW2 90 A4
Elm Gro. SE15 152 C2
Elm Gro. SW19 166 B7
Elm Gro., Har. 67 G7
Elm Gro., Kings.T. 181 H1
Elm Gro., Orp. 207 J1
Elm Gro., Sutt. 199 E4
Elm Gro., Wdf.Grn. 63 F5
Elm Gro. Par., Wall. 200 A3
*Butter Hill*
Elm Gro. Rd. SW13 147 G2
Elm Gro. Rd. W5 125 H2
Elm Hall Gdns. E11 79 H5
Elm La. SE6 171 J2
Elm Ms., Rich. 145 J6
*Grove Rd.*
Elm Pk. SW2 151 F6
Elm Pk., Stan. 53 E5
Elm Pk. Av. N15 76 C5
Elm Pk. Ct., Pnr. 66 C3
Elm Pk. Gdns. NW4 72 A5
**Elm Pk. Gdns. SW10 31 E4**
Elm Pk. Gdns. SW10 129 G5
**Elm Pk. La. SW3 30 E4**
Elm Pk. La. SW3 129 G5
**Elm Pk. Mans. SW10 30 D5**
Elm Pk. Rd. E10 95 H1
Elm Pk. Rd. N3 56 C7
Elm Pk. Rd. N21 43 J7
Elm Pk. Rd. SE25 188 C3
**Elm Pk. Rd. SW3 30 E5**
Elm Pk. Rd. SW3 129 G6
Elm Pk. Rd., Pnr. 66 C2
**Elm Pl. SW7 31 E3**
Elm Pl. SW7 129 G5
**Elm Quay Ct. SW8 33 H5**
Elm Quay Ct. SW8 130 D6
Elm Rd. E7 97 F6
Elm Rd. E11 96 D2
Elm Rd. E17 78 C5
Elm Rd. N22 75 H1
*Granville Rd.*
Elm Rd. SW14 146 C3
Elm Rd., Barn. 40 C4
Elm Rd., Beck. 189 J2
Elm Rd., Chess. 195 H4
Elm Rd., Epsom 197 F6
Elm Rd., Esher 194 C6
Elm Rd., Kings.T. 181 J1
Elm Rd., N.Mal. 182 D4
Elm Rd., Rom. 83 H2
Elm Rd., Sid. 176 A4
Elm Rd., Th.Hth. 188 A4
Elm Rd., Wall. 200 A1
Elm Rd., Wem. 87 H5
Elm Rd. W., Sutt. 184 C7
Elm Row NW3 91 F3
**Elm St. WC1 10 D6**
Elm St. WC1 111 F4
Elm Ter. NW2 90 D3
Elm Ter. NW3 91 H4
*Constantine Rd.*
Elm Ter. SE9 156 D6
Elm Ter., Har. 52 A7
Elm Tree Av., Esher 180 A7
**Elm Tree Cl. NW8 7 E3**
Elm Tree Cl. NW8 109 G3
Elm Tree Cl., Nthlt. 103 F2
**Elm Tree Rd. NW8 6 E3**
Elm Tree Rd. NW8 109 G3
Elm Wk. NW3 90 D2
Elm Wk. SW20 183 J4
Elm Wk., Orp. 206 C3
Elm Way N11 58 A6
Elm Way NW10 88 E4
Elm Way, Epsom 196 D5
Elm Way, Wor.Pk. 197 J3
Elmar Rd. N15 76 A4
Elmbank N14 43 E7
Elmbank Av., Barn. 39 J4
Elmbank Way W7 104 A5
Elmbourne Dr., Belv. 139 H4
Elmbourne Rd. SW17 168 A3
Elmbridge Av., Surb. 182 B5
Elmbridge Cl., Ruis. 66 A6
Elmbridge Wk. E8 94 D7
*Wilman Gro.*
Elmbrook Cl., Sun. 178 B1
Elmbrook Gdns. SE9 156 B4
Elmbrook Rd., Sutt. 198 C4
Elmcourt Rd. SE27 169 H2
Elmcroft N8 75 F5
Elmcroft Av. E11 79 H5
Elmcroft Av. N9 44 E6
Elmcroft Av. NW11 72 C7
Elmcroft Av., Sid. 157 J6
Elmcroft Cl. E11 79 H4
Elmcroft Cl. W5 105 G6
Elmcroft Cl., Chess. 195 H3
Elmcroft Cl., Felt. 141 J6
Elmcroft Cres. NW11 72 B7
Elmcroft Cres., Har. 67 G3
Elmcroft Dr., Chess. 195 H3
Elmcroft Gdns. NW9 70 A5
Elmcroft St. E5 95 F4
Elmdale Rd. N13 59 F5
Elmdene, Surb. 196 C1
Elmdene Cl., Beck. 189 J5
Elmdene Rd. SE18 136 E5
Elmdon Rd., Houns. 142 D2
Elmdon Rd. 141 J3
(Hatton Cross), Houns.
Elmer Cl., Enf. 43 F3
Elmer Gdns., Edg. 54 B7
Elmer Gdns., Islw. 144 A3
Elmer Rd. SE6 154 C7
Elmers Dr., Tedd. 162/163 E6
*Kingston Rd.*
Elmers End Rd. SE20 189 F2
Elmers End Rd., Beck. 189 F2
Elmers Rd. SE25 188 D7
Elmerside Rd., Beck. 189 H4
Elmfield Av. N8 74 E5
Elmfield Av., Mitch. 186 A1
Elmfield Av., Tedd. 162 C5
Elmfield Cl., Har. 86 B2
Elmfield Pk., Brom. 191 G3
Elmfield Rd. E4 62 C2
Elmfield Rd. E17 77 G6
Elmfield Rd. N2 73 G3
Elmfield Rd. SW17 168 A2
Elmfield Rd., Brom. 191 G3
Elmfield Rd., Sthl. 123 E3
Elmfield Way W9 108 D5
Elmgate Av., Felt. 160 B3
Elmgate Gdns., Edg. 54 D5
Elmgreen Cl. E15 114/115 E1
*Church St. N.*
Elmgrove Cres., Har. 68 C5
Elmgrove Gdns., Har. 68 D5
Elmgrove Rd., Croy. 188 E7
Elmgrove Rd., Har. 68 C5
Elmhurst, Belv. 139 E6
Elmhurst Av. N2 73 G3
Elmhurst Av., Mitch. 168 B7
Elmhurst Dr. E18 79 G2
Elmhurst Gdns. E18 79 H1
*Elmhurst Dr.*
Elmhurst Rd. E7 97 H7
Elmhurst Rd. N17 76 C2
Elmhurst Rd. SE9 174 B2
Elmhurst St. SW4 150 D3
Elmhurst Vil. SE15 153 F4
*Cheltenham Rd.*
Elmhurst Way, Loug. 48 C7
Elmington Cl., Bex. 159 H6
**Elmington Est. SE5 36 C7**
Elmington Est. SE5 132 A7
Elmington Rd. SE5 152 A1
Elmira St. SE13 154 B3
Elmlee Cl., Chis. 174 C6
Elmley Cl. E6 116 B5
*Northumberland Rd.*
Elmley St. SE18 137 G4
Elmore Cl., Wem. 105 H2
Elmore Rd. E11 96 C3
Elmore Rd., Enf. 45 G1
Elmore St. N1 93 J7
Elmores, Loug. 48 D3
Elms, The SW13 147 F3
Elms Av. N10 74 B3
Elms Av. NW4 72 A5
Elms Ct., Wem. 86 C4
Elms Cres. SW4 150 C6
Elms Gdns., Dag. 101 F4
Elms Gdns., Wem. 86 D4
Elms La., Wem. 86 D4
**Elms Ms. W2 14 E5**
Elms Ms. W2 109 G7
Elms Pk. Av., Wem. 86 D4
Elms Rd. SW4 150 C5
Elms Rd., Har. 52 B7
Elmscott Gdns. N21 43 J6
Elmscott Rd., Brom. 173 F5
Elmsdale Rd. E17 77 J4
Elmshaw Rd. SW15 147 G5
Elmshurst Cres. N2 73 G4
Elmside, Croy. 204 B6
Elmside Rd., Wem. 88 A3
Elmsleigh Av., Har. 69 E4
Elmsleigh Ct., Sutt. 198 E3
Elmsleigh Rd., Twick. 162 A2
Elmslie Cl., Wdf.Grn. 64 C6
Elmslie Pt. E3 113 J5
Elmstead Av., Chis. 174 C5
Elmstead Av., Wem. 87 H1
Elmstead Cl. N20 56 D2
Elmstead Cl., Epsom 197 E5
Elmstead Cres., Well. 138 C6
Elmstead Gdns., Wor.Pk. 197 G3
Elmstead Glade, Chis. 174 C6
Elmstead La., Chis. 174 C5
Elmstead Rd., Ilf. 99 H2
Elmstone Rd. SW6 148 D1
Elmsworth Av., Houns. 143 H2
Elmton Way E5 94 D3
*Rendlesham Rd.*
Elmtree Rd., Tedd. 162 B4
Elmwood Av. N13 59 E5
Elmwood Av., Borwd. 38 B4
Elmwood Av., Felt. 160 A2
Elmwood Av., Har. 68 D5
Elmwood Cl., Epsom 197 G7
Elmwood Cl., Wall. 200 A2
Elmwood Ct., Wem. 86 D3
Elmwood Cres. NW9 70 C4
Elmwood Dr., Bex. 158 E7
Elmwood Dr., Epsom 197 G6
Elmwood Gdns. W7 104 B6
Elmwood Rd. SE24 152 A5
Elmwood Rd. W4 126 C6
Elmwood Rd., Croy. 187 H7
Elmwood Rd., Mitch. 185 J3
Elmworth Gro. SE21 170 A2
**Elnathan Ms. W9 6 B6**
Elphinstone Rd. E17 77 J2
Elphinstone St. N5 93 H4
*Avenell Rd.*
Elrington Rd. E8 94 D6
Elrington Rd., Wdf.Grn. 63 G5
Elruge Cl., West Dr. 120 A3
Elsa Rd., Well. 158 B2
Elsa St. E1 113 H5
Elsdale St. E9 95 F6
Elsden Ms. E2 113 F2
*Old Ford Rd.*
Elsden Rd. N17 76 C1
Elsenham Rd. E12 98 D5
Elsenham St. SW18 166 C1
Elsham Rd. E11 96 E3
Elsham Rd. W14 128 B2
Elsham Ter. W14 128 B2
Elsie Rd. SE22 152 C4
Elsiedene Rd. N21 43 J7
Elsiemaud Rd. SE4 153 J5
Elsinore Av., Stai. 140 B7
Elsinore Gdns. NW2 90 B3
Elsinore Rd. SE23 171 H1
Elsinore Way, Rich. 146 B3
*Lower Richmond Rd.*
Elsley Rd. SW11 149 J3
Elspeth Rd. SW11 149 J4
Elspeth Rd., Wem. 87 H5
Elsrick Av., Mord. 184 D5
*Chalgrove Av.*
Elstan Way, Croy. 189 H7
**Elsted St. SE17 36 C2**
Elsted St. SE17 132 A4
Elstow Cl. SE9 156 D5
Elstow Cl., Ruis. 66 D7
Elstow Gdns., Dag. 118 E1
Elstow Rd., Dag. 100 E7
Elstree Gdns. N9 61 E1
Elstree Gdns., Belv. 139 E4
Elstree Gdns., Ilf. 99 F5
Elstree Hill, Brom. 173 E7
Elstree Pk., Borwd. 38 D6
Elstree Way, Borwd. 38 B3
Elswick Rd. SE13 154 B2
Elswick St. SW6 149 F2
Elsworthy, T.Ditt. 180 B6
Elsworthy Ri. NW3 91 H7
Elsworthy Rd. NW3 109 H1
Elsworthy Ter. NW3 91 H7
Elsynge Rd. SW18 149 G5
Eltham Grn. SE9 155 J5
Eltham Grn. Rd. SE9 155 J4
Eltham High St. SE9 156 C6
Eltham Hill SE9 156 A5
Eltham Palace Rd. SE9 155 J6
Eltham Pk. Gdns. SE9 156 D4
Eltham Rd. SE9 155 J5
Eltham Rd. SE12 155 F5

| | | |
|---|---|---|
| Elthiron Rd. SW6 | 148 | D1 |
| Elthorne Av. W7 | 124 | C2 |
| Elthorne Ct., Felt. | 160 | C1 |
| Elthorne Pk. Rd. W7 | 124 | C2 |
| Elthorne Rd. N19 | 92 | D2 |
| Elthorne Rd. NW9 | 70 | D7 |
| Elthorne Way NW9 | 70 | D6 |
| Elthruda Rd. SE13 | 154 | D6 |
| Eltisley Rd., Ilf. | 98 | E4 |
| Elton Av., Barn. | 40 | C5 |
| Elton Av., Grnf. | 86 | C6 |
| Elton Av., Wem. | 87 | E5 |
| Elton Cl., Kings.T. | 163 | F7 |
| Elton Ho. E3 | 113 | J1 |
| Elton Pl. N16 | 94 | B5 |
| Elton Rd., Kings.T. | 181 | J1 |
| Eltringham St. SW18 | 149 | F4 |
| **Elvaston Ms. SW7** | **22** | **D5** |
| Elvaston Ms. SW7 | 129 | F3 |
| **Elvaston Pl. SW7** | **22** | **C6** |
| Elvaston Pl. SW7 | 129 | F3 |
| Elveden Pl. NW10 | 106 | A2 |
| Elveden Rd. NW10 | 106 | A2 |
| Elvendon Rd. N13 | 58 | E6 |
| **Elver Gdns. E2** | **13** | **J3** |
| Elverson Rd. SE8 | 154 | B2 |
| **Elverton St. SW1** | **33** | **H1** |
| Elverton St. SW1 | 130 | D4 |
| Elvington Grn., Brom. | 191 | F5 |
| Elvington La. NW9 | 70 | E1 |
| Elvino Rd. SE26 | 171 | H5 |
| Elvis Rd. NW2 | 89 | J6 |
| Elwill Way, Beck. | 190 | C4 |
| **Elwin St. E2** | **13** | **H3** |
| Elwin St. E2 | 112 | D3 |
| Elwood St. N5 | 93 | H3 |
| Elwyn Gdns. SE12 | 155 | G7 |
| Ely Cl., N.Mal. | 183 | F2 |
| **Ely Ct. EC1** | **19** | **F2** |
| Ely Gdns., Borwd. | 38 | D5 |
| Ely Gdns., Dag. | 101 | J3 |
| Ely Gdns., Ilf. | 80 | B7 |
| *Canterbury Av.* | | |
| **Ely Pl. EC1** | **19** | **F2** |
| Ely Pl., Wdf.Grn. | 64 | D6 |
| Ely Rd. E10 | 78 | C6 |
| Ely Rd., Croy. | 188 | A5 |
| Ely Rd. (Heathrow Airport), Houns. | 141 | J2 |
| *Eastern Perimeter Rd.* | | |
| Ely Rd. (Hounslow W.), Houns. | 142 | C3 |
| Elyne Rd. N4 | 75 | G6 |
| Elysian Av., Orp. | 193 | J6 |
| Elysium Pl. SW6 | 148 | C2 |
| *Fulham Pk. Gdns.* | | |
| Elysium St. SW6 | 148 | C2 |
| *Fulham Pk. Gdns.* | | |
| Elystan Business Cen., Hayes | 102 | C7 |
| **Elystan Pl. SW3** | **31** | **H3** |
| Elystan Pl. SW3 | 129 | H5 |
| **Elystan St. SW3** | **31** | **G2** |
| Elystan St. SW3 | 129 | H4 |
| Elystan Wk. N1 | 111 | G1 |
| *Cloudesley Rd.* | | |
| Emanuel Av. W3 | 106 | C6 |
| Emanuel Dr., Hmptn. | 161 | F5 |
| **Emba St. SE16** | **29** | **J4** |
| Emba St. SE16 | 132 | D2 |
| Embankment SW15 | 148 | A2 |
| Embankment, The, Twick. | 162 | D1 |
| **Embankment Gdns. SW3** | **32** | **A5** |
| Embankment Gdns. SW3 | 129 | J6 |
| **Embankment Pl. WC2** | **26** | **B1** |
| Embankment Pl. WC2 | 131 | E1 |
| Embassy Ct., Sid. | 176 | B3 |
| Embassy Ct., Well. | 158 | B3 |
| *Welling High St.* | | |
| Embassy Gdns., Beck. | 189 | J1 |
| *Blakeney Rd.* | | |
| Ember Cl., Orp. | 193 | F7 |
| Ember Fm. Av., E.Mol. | 180 | A6 |
| Ember Fm. Way, E.Mol. | 180 | A6 |
| Ember Gdns., T.Ditt. | 180 | B7 |
| Ember La., E.Mol. | 194 | A1 |
| Ember La., Esher | 180 | A7 |
| Embercourt Rd., T.Ditt. | 180 | B6 |
| **Emberton SE5** | **36** | **C5** |
| Embleton Rd. SE13 | 154 | B3 |
| Embleton Rd., Wat. | 50 | A3 |
| Embleton Wk., Hmptn. | 161 | F6 |
| *Fearnley Cres.* | | |
| Embley Pt. E5 | 94/95 | E4 |
| *Tiger Way* | | |
| Embry Cl., Stan. | 52 | D4 |
| Embry Dr., Stan. | 52 | D6 |
| Embry Way, Stan. | 52 | D5 |
| Emden Cl., West Dr. | 120 | D2 |
| Emden St. SW6 | 149 | E1 |
| Emerald Cl. E16 | 116 | B6 |
| Emerald Gdns., Dag. | 101 | G1 |
| Emerald Sq., Sthl. | 122 | D3 |
| **Emerald St. WC1** | **18** | **C1** |
| Emerald St. WC1 | 111 | F5 |
| Emerson Gdns., Har. | 69 | J6 |
| Emerson Rd., Ilf. | 80 | D7 |
| **Emerson St. SE1** | **27** | **J1** |
| Emerson St. SE1 | 131 | J1 |
| Emerton Cl., Bexh. | 159 | E4 |
| **Emery Hill St. SW1** | **25** | **G6** |
| Emery Hill St. SW1 | 130 | C3 |
| **Emery St. SE1** | **27** | **F5** |
| Emes Rd., Erith | 139 | J7 |
| Emilia Cl., Enf. | 45 | E5 |
| Emily Pl. N7 | 93 | G4 |
| Emlyn Gdns. W12 | 127 | E2 |
| Emlyn Rd. W12 | 127 | E3 |
| Emma Rd. E13 | 115 | F2 |
| Emma St. E2 | 112 | E2 |
| Emmanuel Rd. SW12 | 168 | C1 |
| Emmaus Way, Chig. | 64 | D5 |
| Emmott Av., Ilf. | 81 | F5 |
| Emmott Cl. E1 | 113 | H4 |
| Emmott Cl. NW11 | 73 | F6 |
| Emms Pas., Kings.T. | 181 | G2 |
| *High St.* | | |
| **Emperor's Gate SW7** | **22** | **B6** |
| Emperor's Gate SW7 | 129 | E3 |
| Empire Av. N18 | 59 | J5 |
| Empire Ct., Wem. | 88 | B3 |
| Empire Rd., Grnf. | 105 | F1 |
| Empire Sq. N7 | 92/93 | E3 |
| *Holloway Rd.* | | |
| Empire Way, Wem. | 87 | J4 |
| Empire Wf. Rd. E14 | 134 | D4 |
| Empire Yd. N7 | 92/93 | E3 |
| *Holloway Rd.* | | |
| Empress Av. E4 | 62 | A7 |
| Empress Av. E12 | 97 | J2 |
| Empress Av., Ilf. | 98 | C2 |
| Empress Av., Wdf.Grn. | 63 | F7 |
| Empress Dr., Chis. | 174 | E6 |
| Empress Pl. SW6 | 128 | D5 |
| **Empress St. SE17** | **36** | **A5** |
| Empress St. SE17 | 131 | J6 |
| Empson St. E3 | 114 | B4 |
| Emsworth Cl. N9 | 61 | F1 |
| Emsworth Rd., Ilf. | 81 | E2 |
| Emsworth St. SW2 | 169 | F2 |
| Emu Rd. SW8 | 150 | B2 |
| Ena Rd. SW16 | 186 | E3 |
| Enbrook St. W10 | 108 | B3 |
| Endale Cl., Cars. | 199 | J2 |
| Endeavour Way SW19 | 166 | E4 |
| Endeavour Way, Bark. | 118 | A2 |
| Endeavour Way, Croy. | 186 | D7 |
| **Endell St. WC2** | **18** | **A3** |
| Endell St. WC2 | 110 | E6 |
| Enderby St. SE10 | 134 | E5 |
| Enderley Cl., Har. | 68 | B1 |
| *Enderley Rd.* | | |
| Enderley Rd., Har. | 68 | B1 |
| Endersby Rd., Barn. | 39 | J5 |
| Endersleigh Gdns. NW4 | 71 | G4 |
| Endlebury Rd. E4 | 62 | C2 |
| Endlesham Rd. SW12 | 150 | A7 |
| **Endsleigh Gdns. WC1** | **9** | **H5** |
| Endsleigh Gdns. WC1 | 110 | D4 |
| Endsleigh Gdns., Ilf. | 98 | C2 |
| Endsleigh Gdns., Surb. | 181 | F6 |
| **Endsleigh Pl. WC1** | **9** | **J5** |
| Endsleigh Pl. WC1 | 110 | D4 |
| Endsleigh Rd. W13 | 104 | D7 |
| Endsleigh Rd., Sthl. | 123 | E4 |
| **Endsleigh St. WC1** | **9** | **H5** |
| Endsleigh St. WC1 | 110 | D4 |
| Endway, Surb. | 182 | A7 |
| Endwell Rd. SE4 | 153 | H2 |
| Endymion Rd. N4 | 75 | G7 |
| Endymion Rd. SW2 | 151 | F6 |
| Energen Cl. NW10 | 88 | E6 |
| Enfield Retail Pk., Enf. | 44 | E3 |
| Enfield Rd. N1 | 94 | B7 |
| Enfield Rd. W3 | 126 | B2 |
| Enfield Rd., Brent. | 125 | G5 |
| Enfield Rd., Enf. | 42 | D4 |
| Enfield Rd., Houns. | 141 | H2 |
| *Eastern Perimeter Rd.* | | |
| Enfield Wk., Brent. | 125 | G5 |
| **Enford St. W1** | **15** | **J1** |
| Enford St. W1 | 109 | J5 |
| Engadine Cl., Croy. | 202 | C3 |
| Engadine St. SW18 | 166 | C1 |
| Engate St. SE13 | 154 | C4 |
| Engel Pk. NW7 | 55 | J6 |
| Engineer Cl. SE18 | 136 | D6 |
| Engineers Way, Wem. | 88 | A4 |
| England Way, N.Mal. | 182 | C3 |
| *California Rd.* | | |
| Englands La. NW3 | 91 | J6 |
| Englands La., Loug. | 48 | D2 |
| Englefield Cl., Croy. | 187 | J6 |
| *Queen's Rd.* | | |
| Englefield Cl., Enf. | 43 | G2 |
| Englefield Cl., Orp. | 193 | J4 |
| Englefield Cres., Orp. | 193 | J4 |
| Englefield Path, Orp. | 193 | J4 |
| Englefield Rd. N1 | 94 | A6 |
| Engleheart Dr., Felt. | 141 | J6 |
| Engleheart Rd. SE6 | 154 | B7 |
| Englewood Rd. SW12 | 150 | B6 |
| **English Grds. SE1** | **28** | **D2** |
| English St. E3 | 113 | J4 |
| **Enid St. SE16** | **29** | **G5** |
| Enid St. SE16 | 132 | C3 |
| Enmore Av. SE25 | 188 | D5 |
| Enmore Gdns. SW14 | 146 | D5 |
| Enmore Rd. SE25 | 188 | D5 |
| Enmore Rd. SW15 | 147 | J4 |
| Enmore Rd., Sthl. | 103 | G4 |
| Ennerdale Av., Stan. | 69 | F3 |
| Ennerdale Cl. (Cheam), Sutt. | 198 | C4 |
| Ennerdale Dr. NW9 | 70 | E5 |
| Ennerdale Gdns., Wem. | 87 | G1 |
| Ennerdale Ho. E3 | 113 | J4 |
| Ennerdale Rd., Bexh. | 159 | G1 |
| Ennerdale Rd., Rich. | 145 | J2 |
| Ennersdale Rd. SE13 | 154 | D5 |
| Ennis Rd. N4 | 93 | G1 |
| Ennis Rd. SE18 | 137 | F6 |
| Ennismore Av. W4 | 127 | F4 |
| Ennismore Av., Grnf. | 86 | B6 |
| **Ennismore Gdns. SW7** | **23** | **G4** |
| Ennismore Gdns. SW7 | 129 | H2 |
| Ennismore Gdns., T.Ditt. | 180 | B6 |
| **Ennismore Gdns. Ms. SW7** | **23** | **G5** |
| Ennismore Gdns. Ms. SW7 | 129 | H3 |
| **Ennismore Ms. SW7** | **23** | **G4** |
| Ennismore Ms. SW7 | 129 | H2 |
| **Ennismore St. SW7** | **23** | **G5** |
| Ennismore St. SW7 | 129 | H3 |
| Ensign Dr. N13 | 59 | J3 |
| **Ensign St. E1** | **21** | **H5** |
| Ensign St. E1 | 112 | D7 |
| Enslin Rd. SE9 | 156 | D6 |
| **Ensor Ms. SW7** | **30** | **E3** |
| Enstone Rd., Enf. | 45 | H3 |
| Enterprise Cl., Croy. | 201 | G1 |
| Enterprise Way NW10 | 107 | G3 |
| Enterprise Way SW18 | 148 | D4 |
| Enterprise Way, Tedd. | 162 | C5 |
| Enterprize Way SE8 | 133 | J4 |
| Epirus Ms. SW6 | 128 | D7 |
| Epirus Rd. SW6 | 128 | C7 |
| Epping Cl. E14 | 134 | A4 |
| Epping Cl., Rom. | 83 | H3 |
| Epping Glade E4 | 46 | C6 |
| Epping New Rd., Buck.H. | 63 | H2 |
| Epping New Rd., Loug. | 47 | H5 |
| Epping Pl. N1 | 93 | G6 |
| *Liverpool Rd.* | | |
| Epping Way E4 | 46 | B6 |
| Epple Rd. SW6 | 148 | C1 |
| Epsom Cl., Bexh. | 159 | H3 |
| Epsom Cl., Nthlt. | 85 | F5 |
| Epsom Rd. E10 | 78 | C6 |
| Epsom Rd., Croy. | 201 | G4 |
| Epsom Rd., Ilf. | 81 | J6 |
| Epsom Rd., Mord. | 184 | C6 |
| Epsom Rd., Sutt. | 184 | C7 |
| Epsom Sq., Houns. | 141 | J2 |
| *Eastern Perimeter Rd.* | | |
| Epstein Rd. SE28 | 138 | A1 |
| Epworth Rd., Islw. | 124 | E7 |
| **Epworth St. EC2** | **12** | **C6** |
| Epworth St. EC2 | 112 | A4 |
| Equity Sq. E2 | 112 | C3 |
| *Shacklewell St.* | | |
| **Erasmus St. SW1** | **33** | **J2** |
| Erasmus St. SW1 | 130 | D4 |
| Erconwald St. W12 | 107 | F6 |
| Eresby Dr., Beck. | 204 | A1 |
| Eresby Pl. NW6 | 90 | D7 |
| Eric Clarke La., Bark. | 117 | E4 |
| Eric Cl. E7 | 97 | G4 |
| Eric Rd. E7 | 97 | G4 |
| Eric Rd. NW10 | 89 | F6 |
| *Church Rd.* | | |
| Eric Rd., Rom. | 82 | D7 |
| Eric St. E3 | 113 | J4 |
| Erica Gdns., Croy. | 204 | B4 |
| Erica St. W12 | 107 | G7 |
| Ericcson Cl. SW18 | 148 | D5 |
| Eridge Rd. W4 | 126 | D3 |
| Erin Cl., Brom. | 172 | E7 |
| Erin Cl., Ilf. | 82 | A6 |
| Erindale SE18 | 137 | G6 |
| Erindale Ter. SE18 | 137 | G6 |
| Erith Cres., Rom. | 83 | J1 |
| Erith Rd., Belv. | 139 | G5 |
| Erith Rd., Bexh. | 159 | H4 |
| Erith Rd., Erith | 159 | H4 |
| Erlanger Rd. SE14 | 153 | G1 |
| Erlesmere Gdns. W13 | 124 | D3 |
| Ermine Cl., Houns. | 142 | C2 |
| Ermine Ho. N17 | 60 | C7 |
| *Moselle St.* | | |
| Ermine Rd. N15 | 76 | C6 |
| Ermine Rd. SE13 | 154 | B3 |
| Ermine Side, Enf. | 44 | D5 |
| Ermington Rd. SE9 | 175 | F2 |
| Ernald Av. E6 | 116 | B2 |
| Erncroft Way, Twick. | 144 | C6 |
| Ernest Av. SE27 | 169 | H4 |
| Ernest Cl., Beck. | 190 | A5 |
| Ernest Gdns. W4 | 126 | B6 |
| Ernest Gro., Beck. | 189 | J5 |
| Ernest Rd., Kings.T. | 182 | B2 |
| Ernest Sq., Kings.T. | 182 | B2 |
| Ernest St. E1 | 113 | G4 |
| Ernle Rd. SW20 | 165 | H7 |
| Ernshaw Pl. SW15 | 148 | B5 |
| *Carlton Dr.* | | |
| Erpingham Rd. SW15 | 147 | J3 |
| Erridge Rd. SW19 | 184 | D2 |
| Errington Rd. W9 | 108 | C4 |
| Errol Gdns., Hayes | 102 | B4 |
| Errol Gdns., N.Mal. | 183 | G4 |
| **Errol St. EC1** | **12** | **A6** |
| Errol St. EC1 | 111 | J4 |
| Erskine Cl., Sutt. | 199 | H3 |
| Erskine Cres. N17 | 76 | E4 |
| Erskine Hill NW11 | 72 | D5 |
| Erskine Ms. NW3 | 91 | J7 |
| *Erskine Rd.* | | |
| Erskine Rd. E17 | 77 | J4 |
| Erskine Rd. NW3 | 91 | J7 |
| Erskine Rd., Sutt. | 199 | G4 |
| Erskine Rd., Wat. | 50 | C3 |
| Erwood Rd. SE7 | 136 | B5 |
| Esam Way SW16 | 169 | G5 |
| Escot Way, Barn. | 39 | J5 |
| Escott Gdns. SE9 | 174 | B4 |
| Escreet Gro. SE18 | 136 | D4 |
| Esher Av., Rom. | 83 | J6 |
| Esher Av., Sutt. | 198 | A3 |
| Esher Av., Walt. | 178 | A7 |
| Esher Bypass, Chess. | 195 | F4 |
| Esher Bypass, Cob. | 195 | E7 |
| Esher Cl., Bex. | 176 | E1 |
| Esher Cres., Houns. | 141 | H2 |
| *Eastern Perimeter Rd.* | | |
| Esher Gdns. SW19 | 166 | A2 |
| Esher Ms., Mitch. | 185 | J3 |
| Esher Rd., E.Mol. | 180 | A6 |
| Esher Rd., Ilf. | 99 | H3 |
| Esk Rd. E13 | 115 | G4 |
| Eskdale Av., Nthlt. | 103 | F1 |
| Eskdale Cl., Wem. | 87 | G2 |
| Eskdale Rd., Bexh. | 159 | G2 |
| Eskmont Ridge SE19 | 170 | B7 |
| Esmar Cres. NW9 | 71 | G7 |
| Esme Ho. SW15 | 147 | F4 |
| **Esmeralda Rd. SE1** | **37** | **J2** |
| Esmeralda Rd. SE1 | 132 | D4 |
| Esmond Rd. NW6 | 108 | C1 |
| Esmond Rd. W4 | 126 | D4 |
| Esmond St. SW15 | 148 | B4 |
| Esparto St. SW18 | 149 | E7 |
| Essenden Rd., Belv. | 139 | G5 |
| Essenden Rd., S.Croy. | 202 | B7 |
| Essendine Rd. W9 | 108 | D4 |
| Essex Av., Islw. | 144 | B3 |
| Essex Cl. E17 | 77 | H4 |
| Essex Cl., Mord. | 184 | A7 |
| Essex Cl., Rom. | 83 | H4 |
| Essex Cl., Ruis. | 84 | D1 |
| **Essex Ct. EC4** | **18** | **E4** |
| Essex Ct. SW13 | 147 | F2 |
| Essex Gdns. N4 | 75 | H6 |
| Essex Gro. SE19 | 170 | A6 |
| Essex Ho. E14 | 114 | B6 |
| *Giraud St.* | | |
| Essex Pk. N3 | 56 | E6 |
| Essex Pk. Ms. W3 | 126 | E1 |
| Essex Pl. W4 | 126 | C4 |
| Essex Pl. Sq. W4 | 126 | D4 |
| *Essex Pl.* | | |

Essex Rd. E4 62 E1
Essex Rd. E10 78 C6
Essex Rd. E12 98 B5
Essex Rd. E17 77 H6
Essex Rd. E18 79 H2
Essex Rd. N1 111 H1
Essex Rd. NW10 89 E7
Essex Rd. W3 106 C7
Essex Rd. W4 126 D4
*Belmont Rd.*
Essex Rd., Bark. 99 G7
Essex Rd., Borwd. 38 A3
Essex Rd., Dag. 101 J5
Essex Rd., Enf. 44 A4
Essex Rd., Rom. 83 H4
Essex Rd. (Chadwell Heath), Rom. 82 C7
Essex Rd. S. E11 78 D7
Essex St. E7 97 G5
**Essex St. WC2 18 E5**
Essex Twr. SE20 189 E1
Essex Vil. W8 128 D2
Essex Wf. E5 95 G2
Essian St. E1 113 H5
Essoldo Way, Edg. 69 J3
Estate Way E10 95 J1
Estcourt Rd. SE25 189 E6
Estcourt Rd. SW6 128 C7
Este Rd. SW11 149 H3
Estella Av., N.Mal. 183 H4
Estelle Rd. NW3 91 J4
**Esterbrooke St. SW1 33 H2**
Esterbrooke St. SW1 130 D4
Esther Cl. N21 43 G7
Esther Rd. E11 78 E7
Estoria Cl. SW2 151 G7
Estreham Rd. SW16 168 D6
Estridge Cl., Houns. 143 G4
Estuary Cl., Bark. 118 B3
Eswyn Rd. SW17 167 J4
Etchingham Pk. Rd. N3 57 E7
Etchingham Rd. E15 96 C4
Eternit Wk. SW6 147 J1
Etfield Gro., Sid. 176 B5
Ethel Rd. E16 115 H6
**Ethel St. SE17 35 J2**
Ethelbert Cl., Brom. 191 G3
Ethelbert Gdns., Ilf. 80 C5
Ethelbert Rd. SW20 184 A1
Ethelbert Rd., Brom. 191 G3
Ethelbert Rd., Erith 139 J7
Ethelbert St. SW12 168 B1
*Fernlea Rd.*
Ethelburga St. SW11 149 H1
Ethelden Rd. W12 127 H1
Etheldene Av. N10 74 C4
Etheridge Grn., Loug. 49 F3
*Etheridge Rd.*
Etheridge Rd. NW2 71 J7
Etheridge Rd., Loug. 49 E2
Etherley Rd. N15 75 J5
Etherow St. SE22 152 D6
Etherstone Grn. SW16 169 G4
*Etherstone Rd.*
Etherstone Rd. SW16 169 G4
Ethnard Rd. SE15 132 E6
Ethronvi Rd., Bexh. 159 E3
Etloe Rd. E10 96 A2
Eton Av. N12 57 F7
Eton Av. NW3 91 G7
Eton Av., Barn. 41 H6
Eton Av., Houns. 123 F6
Eton Av., N.Mal. 182 D5
Eton Av., Wem. 87 E4
Eton Cl. SW18 149 E7
Eton College Rd. NW3 91 J6
Eton Ct. NW3 91 G7
*Eton Av.*
Eton Ct., Wem. 87 F4
*Eton Av.*
Eton Garages NW3 91 H6
*Lambolle Pl.*
Eton Gro. NW9 70 A3
Eton Gro. SE13 154 E3
Eton Hall NW3 91 J6
*Eton College Rd.*
Eton Pl. NW3 92 A7
*Haverstock Hill*
Eton Ri. NW3 91 J6
*Eton College Rd.*
Eton Rd. NW3 91 J7
Eton Rd., Hayes 121 J7
Eton Rd., Ilf. 99 F5
Eton St., Rich. 145 H5
Eton Vil. NW3 91 J6
Etta St. SE8 133 H6
Ettrick St. E14 114 C6
Etwell Pl., Surb. 181 J6
Eugenia Rd. SE16 133 F4
Eureka Rd., Kings.T. 182 A2
*Washington Rd.*
**Europa Pl. EC1 11 J4**
Europe Rd. SE18 136 C3
Eustace Rd. E6 116 B3
Eustace Rd. SW6 128 D7
Eustace Rd., Rom. 82 D7
Euston Cen. NW1 110 C4
*Triton Sq.*
**Euston Gro. NW1 9 H4**
Euston Gro. NW1 110 D3
**Euston Rd. N1 10 A3**
Euston Rd. N1 110 D4
**Euston Rd. NW1 9 E6**
Euston Rd. NW1 110 B4
Euston Rd., Croy. 201 G1
**Euston Sq. NW1 9 H4**
Euston Sq. NW1 110 D3
**Euston Sta. Colonnade NW1 9 H4**
**Euston St. NW1 9 G5**
Euston St. NW1 110 C3
Eva Rd., Rom. 82 C7
Evandale Rd. SW9 151 G2
Evangelist Rd. NW5 92 B4
Evans Cl. E8 94 C6
*Buttermere Wk.*
Evans Gro., Felt. 161 G2
Evans Rd. SE6 173 E2
Evanston Av. E4 62 C7
Evanston Gdns., Ilf. 80 B6
Eve Rd. E11 96 E4
Eve Rd. E15 115 E2
Eve Rd. N17 76 B3
Eve Rd., Islw. 144 D4
Evelina Rd. SE15 153 F3
Evelina Rd. SE20 171 G7
**Eveline Lowe Est. SE16 29 H6**
Eveline Lowe Est. SE16 132 D3
Eveline Rd., Mitch. 185 J1
Evelyn Av. NW9 70 D4
Evelyn Cl., Twick. 143 H7
**Evelyn Ct. N1 12 B2**
Evelyn Denington Rd. E6 116 B4
Evelyn Dr., Pnr. 50 D7
Evelyn Fox Ct. W10 107 J5
**Evelyn Gdns. SW7 30 E4**
Evelyn Gdns. SW7 129 G5
Evelyn Gdns., Rich. 145 H4
*Kew Rd.*
Evelyn Gro. W5 125 J1
Evelyn Gro., Sthl. 103 F6
Evelyn Rd. E16 135 H1
Evelyn Rd. E17 78 C4
Evelyn Rd. SW19 166 E5
Evelyn Rd. W4 126 D3
Evelyn Rd., Barn. 41 J4
Evelyn Rd., Rich. 145 H3
Evelyn Rd. (Ham), Rich. 163 F3
Evelyn St. SE8 133 H5
Evelyn Ter., Rich. 145 H3
**Evelyn Wk. N1 12 B2**
Evelyn Wk. N1 112 A2
Evelyn Way, Wall. 200 D4
**Evelyn Yd. W1 17 H3**
Evening Hill, Beck. 172 C7
Evenwood Cl. SW15 148 B5
Everard Av., Brom. 205 G1
Everard Way, Wem. 87 H3
Everatt Cl. SW18 148 C6
*Amerland Rd.*
Everdon Rd. SW13 127 G6
Everest Pl. E14 114 C5
Everest Rd. SE9 156 C5
Everest Rd., Stai. 140 A7
Everett Cl., Bushey 52 B1
Everett Wk., Belv. 139 F5
*Osborne Rd.*
Everglade Strand NW9 71 F1
Evergreen Ct., Stai. 140 A7
*Evergreen Way*
Evergreen Way, Stai. 140 A7
Everilda St. N1 111 F1
Evering Rd. E5 94 C3
Evering Rd. N16 94 C3
Everington Rd. N10 73 J2
Everington St. W6 128 A6
Everitt Rd. NW10 106 D3
Everleigh St. N4 93 F1
Eversfield Gdns. NW7 54 E7
Eversfield Rd., Rich. 145 J2
Evershed Wk. W4 126 D4
**Eversholt St. NW1 9 G1**
Eversholt St. NW1 110 C2
Evershot Rd. N4 93 F1
Eversleigh Rd. E6 116 A1
Eversleigh Rd. N3 56 C7
Eversleigh Rd. SW11 150 A2
Eversleigh Rd., Barn. 41 F5
Eversley Av., Wem. 88 A2
Eversley Cl. N21 43 F6
Eversley Cres. N21 43 F6
Eversley Cres., Islw. 144 A1
Eversley Mt. N21 43 F6
Eversley Pk. SW19 165 H5
Eversley Pk. Rd. N21 43 F6
Eversley Rd. SE7 135 H6
Eversley Rd. SE19 170 A7
Eversley Rd., Surb. 181 J4
Eversley Way, Croy. 204 A4
Everthorpe Rd. SE15 152 C3
**Everton Bldgs. NW1 9 F4**
Everton Dr., Stan. 69 J3
Everton Rd., Croy. 202 D1
Evesham Av. E17 78 A2
Evesham Cl., Grnf. 103 H2
Evesham Cl., Sutt. 198 D7
Evesham Grn., Mord. 184 E6
Evesham Rd. E15 115 F1
Evesham Rd. N11 58 C5
Evesham Rd., Felt. 142 C7
*Sparrow Fm. Dr.*
Evesham Rd., Mord. 185 E6
Evesham St. W11 108 A7
Evesham Wk. SE5 152 A2
*Love Wk.*
Evesham Wk. SW9 151 G2
Evesham Way SW11 150 A3
Evesham Way, Ilf. 80 D3
Evry Rd., Sid. 176 C6
Ewald Rd. SW6 148 C2
Ewanrigg Ter., Wdf.Grn. 63 J5
Ewart Gro. N22 75 G1
Ewart Pl. E3 113 J2
Ewart Rd. SE23 153 G7
Ewe Cl. N7 93 E6
Ewell Bypass, Epsom 197 G7
Ewell Ct. Av., Epsom 197 E5
Ewell Pk. Gdns., Epsom 197 G7
Ewell Pk. Way, Epsom 197 G6
Ewell Rd., Surb. 181 H6
Ewell Rd. (Long Ditton), Surb. 180 E7
Ewell Rd., Sutt. 198 B6
Ewellhurst Rd., Ilf. 80 B2
Ewelme Rd. SE23 171 F1
Ewen Cres. SW2 169 G1
**Ewer St. SE1 27 J2**
Ewer St. SE1 131 J1
Ewhurst Ho. E1 113 F5
Ewhurst Rd. SE4 153 J6
Exbury Rd. SE6 172 A2
**Excel Ct. WC2 17 J6**
Excelsior Cl., Kings.T. 182 A2
*Washington Rd.*
Excelsior Gdns. SE13 154 C2
**Exchange Arc. EC2 20 E1**
Exchange Bldgs. E1 112 B6
*Cutler St.*
**Exchange Ct. WC2 18 B6**
**Exchange Pl. EC2 20 D1**
**Exchange Sq. EC2 20 D1**
Exchange Sq. EC2 112 B5
Exeter Cl. E6 116 C6
*Harper Rd.*
Exeter Gdns., Ilf. 98 B1
Exeter Ho. SW15 147 J6
*Putney Heath*
Exeter Ms. NW6 90/91 E6
*West Hampstead Ms.*
Exeter Rd. E16 115 G5
Exeter Rd. E17 78 A5
Exeter Rd. N9 61 F2
Exeter Rd. N14 58 B1
Exeter Rd. NW2 90 B5
Exeter Rd., Croy. 188 B7
Exeter Rd., Dag. 101 H6
Exeter Rd., Enf. 45 G3
Exeter Rd., Felt. 161 F3
Exeter Rd., Har. 85 E2
Exeter Rd., Houns. 141 H2
Exeter Rd., Well. 157 J2
**Exeter St. WC2 18 B5**
Exeter St. WC2 111 E7
Exeter Way SE14 133 J7
Exeter Way, Houns. 141 H3
Exford Gdns. SE12 173 H1
Exford Rd. SE12 173 H2
Exhibition Cl. W12 107 J7
**Exhibition Rd. SW7 23 F4**
Exhibition Rd. SW7 129 G2
Exmoor Cl., Ilf. 81 F1
Exmoor St. W10 108 A4
**Exmouth Mkt. EC1 11 E5**
Exmouth Mkt. EC1 111 G4
**Exmouth Ms. NW1 9 G4**
Exmouth Pl. E8 94 E7
Exmouth Rd. E17 77 J5
Exmouth Rd., Brom. 191 H3
Exmouth Rd., Ruis. 84 C3
Exmouth Rd., Well. 158 C1
Exmouth St. E1 113 F6
*Commercial Rd.*
Exning Rd. E16 115 F4
**Exon St. SE17 36 D3**
Exon St. SE17 132 B5
Express Dr., Ilf. 100 B1
Exton Cres. NW10 88 C7
Exton Gdns., Dag. 100 C5
**Exton St. SE1 27 E2**
Exton St. SE1 131 G1
Eyebright Cl., Croy. 203 G1
*Primrose La.*
Eyhurst Cl. NW2 89 G2
Eylewood Rd. SE27 169 J5
Eynella Rd. SE22 152 C7
Eynham Rd. W12 107 J6
Eynsford Cl., Orp. 193 F7
Eynsford Cres., Bex. 176 C1
Eynsford Rd., Ilf. 99 H2
Eynsham Dr. SE2 138 A4
Eynswood Dr., Sid. 176 B5
Eyot Gdns. W6 127 F5
Eyot Grn. W4 127 F6
*Chiswick Mall*
**Eyre Ct. NW8 7 E1**
**Eyre St. Hill EC1 11 E6**
Eythorne Rd. SW9 151 G1
**Ezra St. E2 13 G3**
Ezra St. E2 112 C3

**F**

Faber Gdns. NW4 71 G5
Fabian Rd. SW6 128 C7
Fabian St. E6 116 C4
Factory La. N17 76 C2
Factory La., Croy. 201 G1
Factory Rd. E16 136 B1
Factory Sq. SW16 168 E6
Factory Yd. W7 124 B1
*Uxbridge Rd.*
Faggs Rd., Felt. 142 A5
Fair Acres, Brom. 191 G5
**Fair St. SE1 29 E3**
Fair St., Houns. 143 J3
*High St.*
Fairacre, N.Mal. 182 E3
Fairacres SW15 147 G4
Fairbairn Grn. SW9 151 G1
Fairbank Av., Orp. 206 E2
Fairbanks Rd. N17 76 C3
Fairbourne Rd. N17 76 B3
Fairbridge Rd. N19 92 D2
Fairbrook Cl. N13 59 G5
Fairbrook Rd. N13 59 G6
Fairburn Cl., Borwd. 38 A1
Fairburn Ct. SW15 148 B5
*Mercier Rd.*
Fairby Rd. SE12 155 H5
Faircharm Trd. Est. SE8 134 B7
Fairchild Cl. SW11 149 G2
*Wye St.*
**Fairchild Pl. EC2 12 E6**
**Fairchild St. EC2 13 E6**
**Fairclough St. E1 21 J4**
Fairclough St. E1 112 D6
Faircross Av., Bark. 99 F6
Fairdale Gdns. SW15 147 H4
Fairdale Gdns., Hayes 122 A1
Fairey Av., Hayes 121 J4
Fairfax Gdns. SE3 156 A1
Fairfax Ms. E16 135 H1
*Wesley Av.*
Fairfax Ms. SW15 147 J4
*Upper Richmond Rd.*
Fairfax Pl. NW6 91 F7
Fairfax Rd. N8 75 G4
Fairfax Rd. NW6 91 F7
Fairfax Rd. W4 127 E3
Fairfax Rd., Tedd. 162 D6
Fairfax Way N10 58 A7
*Cromwell Rd.*
Fairfield Av. NW4 71 H6
Fairfield Av., Edg. 54 B6
Fairfield Av., Twick. 161 H1
Fairfield Av., Wat. 50 C3
Fairfield Cl. N12 57 F4
Fairfield Cl., Enf. 45 H4
*Scotland Grn. Rd. N.*
Fairfield Cl., Epsom 196 E5
Fairfield Cl., Mitch. 167 H7
Fairfield Cl., Sid. 157 J6
Fairfield Ct. NW10 107 G1
Fairfield Cres., Edg. 54 B6
Fairfield Dr. SW18 149 E5
Fairfield Dr., Grnf. 105 F1
Fairfield Dr., Har. 67 J3
Fairfield E., Kings.T. 181 H2
Fairfield Gdns. N8 74/75 E5
*Elder Av.*
Fairfield Gro. SE7 136 A5

Farrins Rents SE16 133 H1
Farrow La. SE14 133 F7
Farrow Pl. SE16 133 H3
*Ropemaker Rd.*
**Farthing All. SE1 29 H4**
Farthing Flds. E1 132/133 E1
*Raine St.*
Farthing St., Orp. 206 C7
Farthingale Wk. E15 96 D7
Farthings, The, Kings.T. 182 A1
*Brunswick Rd.*
Farthings Cl. E4 63 E3
Farthings Cl., Pnr. 66 B6
Farwell Rd., Sid. 176 B3
Farwig La., Brom. 191 F1
**Fashion St. E1 21 F2**
Fashion St. E1 112 C5
Fashoda Rd., Brom. 192 A4
Fassett Rd. E8 94 D6
Fassett Rd., Kings.T. 181 H4
Fassett Sq. E8 94 D6
Fauconberg Rd. W4 126 C6
Faulkner Cl., Dag. 82 D7
Faulkner St. SE14 153 F1
**Faulkner's All. EC1 19 G1**
Fauna Cl., Rom. 82 C7
**Faunce St. SE17 35 G5**
Favart Rd. SW6 148 D1
Faversham Av. E4 63 E1
Faversham Av., Enf. 44 A6
Faversham Rd. SE6 153 J7
Faversham Rd., Beck. 189 J2
Faversham Rd., Mord. 185 E6
Fawcett Cl. SW11 149 G2
Fawcett Cl. SW16 169 G4
Fawcett Est. E5 94 D1
Fawcett Rd. NW10 107 F1
Fawcett Rd., Croy. 201 H3
**Fawcett St. SW10 30 C5**
Fawcett St. SW10 129 F6
Fawcus Cl., Esher 194 C6
*Dalmore Av.*
Fawe Pk. Rd. SW15 148 C4
Fawe St. E14 114 B5
Fawley Rd. NW6 90 E5
Fawn Rd. E13 115 J2
Fawn Rd., Chig. 65 J5
Fawnbrake Av. SE24 151 H5
Fawood Av. NW10 88 D7
Faygate Cres., Bexh. 159 G5
Faygate Rd. SW2 169 F2
Fayland Av. SW16 168 C5
Fearnley Cres., Hmptn. 161 F5
Fearon St. SE10 135 G5
Featherbed La., Croy. 203 J7
Feathers Pl. SE10 134 D6
Featherstone Av. SE23 171 E2
Featherstone Gdns., Borwd. 38 C4
Featherstone Ind. Est., Sthl. 123 E2
Featherstone Rd. NW7 55 H6
Featherstone Rd., Sthl. 122 E3
**Featherstone St. EC1 12 B5**
Featherstone St. EC1 112 A4
Featherstone Ter., Sthl. 123 E3
Featley Rd. SW9 151 H3
Federal Rd., Grnf. 105 F2
Federation Rd. SE2 138 B4
Fee Fm. Rd., Esher 194 C7
Felbridge Av., Stan. 68 D1
Felbridge Cl. SW16 169 G4
Felbrigge Rd., Ilf. 99 J2
Felday Rd. SE13 154 B6
Felden Cl., Pnr. 51 E7
Felden St. SW6 148 C1
Feldman Cl. N16 94 D1
Felgate Ms. W6 127 H4
Felhampton Rd. SE9 174 E2
Felhurst Cres., Dag. 101 H4
Felix Av. N8 74 E6
Felix Rd. W13 104 D7
Felix Rd., Walt. 178 A6
Felix St. E2 112/113 E2
*Hackney Rd.*
Felixstowe Ct. E16 136/137 E2
*Barge Ho. Rd.*
Felixstowe Rd. N9 60 D4
Felixstowe Rd. N17 76 C3
Felixstowe Rd. NW10 107 H3
Felixstowe Rd. SE2 138 B3
Fell Rd., Croy. 201 J3
Fell Wk., Edg. 70 B1
*East Rd.*
Fellbrigg Rd. SE22 152 C5
Fellbrigg St. E1 112/113 E4
*Headlam St.*
Fellbrook, Rich. 163 E3
Fellmongers Yd., Croy. 201 J2
*Surrey St.*
Fellowes Cl., Hayes 102 D4
*Paddington Cl.*
Fellowes Rd., Cars. 199 H3
**Fellows Ct. E2 13 F2**
Fellows Ct. E2 112 C2
Fellows Rd. NW3 91 G7
Felltram Way SE7 135 G5
*Woolwich Rd.*
Felmersham Cl. SW4 150 D4
*Haselrigge Rd.*
Felmingham Rd. SE20 189 F2
Felnex Trd. Est., Wall. 200 A2
Fels Cl., Dag. 101 H3
Fels Fm. Av., Dag. 101 J3
Felsberg Rd. SW2 151 E6
Felsham Rd. SW15 148 A3
Felspar Cl. SE18 137 J5
Felstead Av., Ilf. 80 D1
Felstead Gdns. E14 134 C5
*Ferry St.*
Felstead Rd. E11 79 G7
Felstead Rd., Loug. 48 B7
Felstead St. E9 95 J6
Felsted Rd. E16 116 A6
Feltham Av., E.Mol. 180 B4
Feltham Business Complex, Felt. 160 B2
Feltham Hill Rd., Felt. 160 A4
Feltham Rd., Mitch. 185 J2
Felthambrook Way, Felt. 160 B3
Felton Cl., Orp. 192 E6
Felton Gdns., Bark. 117 H1
*Sutton Rd.*
Felton Lea, Sid. 175 J5
Felton Rd. W13 125 F2
*Camborne Av.*
Felton Rd., Bark. 117 H2
*Sutton Rd.*
Felton St. N1 112 A1
**Fen Ct. EC3 20 D5**
Fen Gro., Sid. 157 J6
Fen St. E16 115 F7
*Victoria Dock Rd.*
Fencepiece Rd., Chig. 65 F5
Fencepiece Rd., Ilf. 65 F5
**Fenchurch Av. EC3 20 D4**
Fenchurch Av. EC3 112 B6
**Fenchurch Bldgs. EC3 20 E4**
**Fenchurch Pl. EC3 20 E5**
**Fenchurch St. EC3 20 D5**
Fenchurch St. EC3 112 B7
Fendall Rd., Epsom 196 C5
**Fendall St. SE1 29 E6**
Fendall St. SE1 132 B3
Fendt Cl. E16 115 F7
*Bowman Av.*
Fendyke Rd., Belv. 138 D3
Fenelon Pl. W14 128 C4
Fenham Rd. SE15 132 D7
Fenman Ct. N17 76/77 E1
*Shelbourne Rd.*
Fenman Gdns., Ilf. 100 B1
Fenn Cl., Brom. 173 G6
Fenn St. E9 95 F5
Fennel Cl. E16 114/115 E4
*Cranberry La.*
Fennel Cl., Croy. 203 G1
*Primrose La.*
Fennel St. SE18 136 D6
Fenner Cl. SE16 132/133 E4
*Layard Rd.*
Fenner Sq. SW11 149 G3
*Thomas Baines Rd.*
**Fenning St. SE1 28 D3**
Fenstanton Av. N12 57 G5
Fenswood Cl., Bex. 159 G5
**Fentiman Rd. SW8 34 B6**
Fentiman Rd. SW8 131 E6
Fenton Cl. E8 94 C6
*Laurel St.*
Fenton Cl. SW9 151 F2
Fenton Cl., Chis. 174 C5
Fenton Rd. N17 59 J7
Fentons Av. E13 115 H2
Fenwick Cl. SE18 136 D6
*Ritter St.*
Fenwick Gro. SE15 152 D3
Fenwick Pl. SW9 150 E3
Fenwick Rd. SE15 152 D3
Ferdinand Pl. NW1 92 A7
*Ferdinand St.*
Ferdinand St. NW1 92 A6
Fergus Rd. N5 93 H5
*Calabria Rd.*
Ferguson Av., Surb. 181 J5
Ferguson Cl. E14 134 A4
Ferguson Cl., Brom. 190 C3
Ferguson Dr. W3 106 D6
Ferme Pk. Rd. N4 75 E5
Ferme Pk. Rd. N8 75 E5
Fermor Rd. SE23 171 H1
Fermoy Rd. W9 108 C4
Fermoy Rd., Grnf. 103 H4
Fern Av., Mitch. 186 D4
Fern Dene W13 104/105 E5
*Templewood*
Fern Gro., Felt. 142 B7
Fern La., Houns. 123 F5
Fern St. E3 114 A4
**Fern Wk. SE16 37 J4**
Fernbank, Buck.H. 63 H1
Fernbank Av., Walt. 179 E7
Fernbank Av., Wem. 86 C4
Fernbank Ms. SW12 150 C6
Fernbrook Av., Sid. 157 H5
*Blackfen Rd.*
Fernbrook Cres. SE13 154 E6
Fernbrook Dr., Har. 67 H7
Fernbrook Rd. SE13 154 E6
Ferncliff Rd. E8 94 D5
Ferncroft Av. N12 57 H6
Ferncroft Av. NW3 90 D3
Ferncroft Av., Ruis. 84 C2
Ferndale, Brom. 191 J2
Ferndale Av. E17 78 D5
Ferndale Av., Houns. 143 E3
Ferndale Cl., Bexh. 158 E1
Ferndale Ct. SE3 135 F7
Ferndale Rd. E7 97 H7
Ferndale Rd. E11 97 E2
Ferndale Rd. N15 76 C6
Ferndale Rd. SE25 188 E5
Ferndale Rd. SW4 150 E4
Ferndale Rd. SW9 151 F3
Ferndale Rd., Rom. 83 J2
Ferndale St. E6 116 E7
Ferndale Ter., Har. 68 C4
Ferndale Way, Orp. 207 G5
Fernden Way, Rom. 83 H6
Ferndene Rd. SE24 151 J4
Ferndown, Nthwd. 66 A2
Ferndown Av., Orp. 207 G1
Ferndown Cl., Pnr. 50 E7
Ferndown Cl., Sutt. 199 G6
Ferndown Rd. SE9 156 A7
Ferndown Rd., Wat. 50 C3
Ferney Meade Way, Islw. 144 D2
Ferney Rd., Barn. 42 A7
Fernhall Dr., Ilf. 80 A5
Fernham Rd., Th.Hth. 187 J3
Fernhead Rd. W9 108 C4
Fernhill Ct. E17 78 D2
Fernhill Gdns., Kings.T. 163 G5
Fernhill St. E16 136 C1
Fernholme Rd. SE15 153 G5
Fernhurst Gdns., Edg. 54 A6
Fernhurst Rd. SW6 148 B1
Fernhurst Rd., Croy. 188 D7
Fernlea Rd. SW12 168 B1
Fernlea Rd., Mitch. 186 A2
Fernleigh Cl., Croy. 201 G4
*Stafford Rd.*
Fernleigh Ct., Har. 67 H2
Fernleigh Ct., Wem. 87 H2
Fernleigh Rd. N21 59 G2
Ferns Rd. E15 97 F6
**Fernsbury St. WC1 10 E4**
**Fernshaw Rd. SW10 30 C6**
Fernshaw Rd. SW10 129 F6
Fernside NW11 90 D2
*Finchley Rd.*
Fernside, Buck.H. 63 H1
Fernside Av. NW7 54 D3
Fernside Av., Felt. 160 B4
Fernside Rd. SW12 167 J1
Fernthorpe Rd. SW16 168 C6
Ferntower Rd. N5 94 A5
Fernways, Ilf. 98/99 E4
*Cecil Rd.*
Fernwood Av. SW16 168 D4
Fernwood Av., Wem. 87 F5
*Bridgewater Rd.*
Fernwood Cl., Brom. 191 J2
Fernwood Cres. N20 57 J3
Ferranti Cl. SE18 136 A3
Ferraro Cl., Houns. 123 G6
Ferrers Av., Wall. 200 D4
Ferrers Av., West Dr. 120 A2
Ferrers Rd. SW16 168 D5
Ferrestone Rd. N8 75 F4
Ferriby Cl. N1 93 G7
*Bewdley St.*
Ferrier Pt. E16 115 H5
*Forty Acre La.*
Ferrier St. SW18 149 E4
Ferring Cl., Har. 85 J1
Ferrings SE21 170 B2
Ferris Av., Croy. 203 J3
Ferris Rd. SE22 152 D4
Ferron Rd. E5 94 E3
Ferrour Ct. N2 73 G3
Ferry La. N17 76 E4
Ferry La. SW13 127 F6
Ferry La., Brent. 125 H6
Ferry La., Rich. 125 J6
Ferry Pl. SE18 136 D3
*Woolwich High St.*
Ferry Rd. SW13 127 G7
Ferry Rd., Tedd. 162 E5
Ferry Rd., T.Ditt. 180 E6
Ferry Rd., Twick. 162 E1
Ferry Rd., W.Mol. 179 G3
Ferry Sq., Brent. 125 G6
Ferry St. E14 134 C5
Ferryhills Cl., Wat. 50 C3
Ferrymead Av., Grnf. 103 G3
Ferrymead Dr., Grnf. 103 G2
Ferrymead Gdns., Grnf. 103 J2
Ferrymoor, Rich. 163 E3
Festing Rd. SW15 148 A3
Festival Cl., Bex. 176 D1
Festival Wk., Cars. 199 J5
**Fetter La. EC4 19 F4**
Fetter La. EC4 111 G6
Ffinch St. SE8 134 A7
Field Cl. E4 62 B6
Field Cl., Brom. 191 J2
Field Cl., Buck.H. 63 J3
Field Cl., Chess. 195 F5
Field Cl., Hayes 121 F7
Field Cl., Houns. 142 B1
Field Cl., W.Mol. 179 H5
**Field Ct. WC1 18 D2**
Field End, Barn. 39 H4
Field End, Nthlt. 84 D6
Field End, Ruis. 84 C6
Field End, Twick. 162 C4
Field End Rd., Pnr. 66 B6
Field End Rd., Ruis. 85 E4
Field La., Brent. 125 F7
Field La., Tedd. 162 D5
Field Mead NW7 55 E7
Field Mead NW9 55 E7
Field Pl., N.Mal. 183 F6
Field Rd. E7 97 G4
Field Rd. N17 76 A3
Field Rd. W6 128 B5
Field Rd., Felt. 142 B6
**Field St. WC1 10 C3**
Field St. WC1 111 F3
Field Way NW10 88 C7
*Twybridge Way*
Field Way, Croy. 204 B6
Field Way, Grnf. 103 H1
Fieldcommon La., Walt. 179 F7
Fieldend Rd. SW16 186 C1
Fielders Cl., Enf. 44 B4
*Woodfield Cl.*
Fielders Cl., Har. 85 J1
Fieldfare Rd. SE28 118 C7
Fieldgate La., Mitch. 185 H3
**Fieldgate St. E1 21 J2**
Fieldgate St. E1 112 D5
Fieldhouse Cl. E18 79 G1
Fieldhouse Rd. SW12 168 C1
Fielding Av., Twick. 161 J3
Fielding Ho. NW6 108 D3
Fielding Ms. SW13 127 H6
*Castelnau*
Fielding Rd. W4 126 D3
Fielding Rd. W14 128 A3
**Fielding St. SE17 35 J5**
Fielding St. SE17 131 J6
Fielding Wk. W13 124 E3
Fieldings, The SE23 171 F1
Fields Est. E8 94 D7
Fields Pk. Cres., Rom. 82 D5
Fieldsend Rd., Sutt. 198 B5
Fieldside Cl., Orp. 207 F4
*State Fm. Av.*
Fieldside Rd., Brom. 172 D5
Fieldview SW18 167 G1
Fieldway, Dag. 100 B4
Fieldway, Orp. 193 G6
Fieldway Cres. N5 93 G5
Fiennes Cl., Dag. 100 C1
Fiesta Dr., Dag. 119 J4
Fife Rd. E16 115 G5
Fife Rd. N22 59 H7
Fife Rd. SW14 146 C5
Fife Rd., Kings.T. 181 H2
**Fife Ter. N1 10 D1**
Fife Ter. N1 111 F2
Fifield Path SE23 171 G3
*Bampton Rd.*
Fifth Av. E12 98 C4
Fifth Av. W10 108 B3
Fifth Av., Hayes 121 J1
Fifth Cross Rd., Twick. 162 A2

Florence Rd., Beck. 189 G2
Florence Rd., Brom. 191 G1
Florence Rd., Felt. 160 B1
Florence Rd., Kings.T. 163 J7
Florence Rd., Sthl. 122 D4
Florence Rd., Walt. 178 B7
Florence St. E16 115 F4
Florence St. N1 93 H7
Florence St. NW4 71 J4
Florence Ter. SE14 153 J1
Florence Way SW12 167 J1
Florfield Pas. E8 94/95 E6
*Reading La.*
Florfield Rd. E8 94/95 E6
*Reading La.*
Florian Av., Sutt. 199 G4
Florian Rd. SW15 148 B4
Florida Cl., Bushey 52 A2
Florida Rd., Th.Hth. 187 H1
**Florida St. E2 13 H4**
Florida St. E2 112 D3
Floriston Cl., Stan. 69 E1
Floriston Gdns., Stan. 69 E1
Floss St. SW15 147 J2
**Flower & Dean Wk. E1 21 G2**
Flower La. NW7 55 F5
Flower Pot Cl. N15 76 C6
*St. Ann's Rd.*
**Flower Wk., The SW7 22 C4**
Flower Wk., The SW7 129 F2
Flowers Ms. N19 92 C2
*Tollhouse Way*
Flowersmead SW17 168 A2
Floyd Rd. SE7 135 J5
Fludyer St. SE13 154 E4
Foley Ms., Esher 194 B7
Foley Rd., Esher 194 B7
**Foley St. W1 17 F2**
Foley St. W1 110 C5
**Folgate St. E1 21 E1**
Folgate St. E1 112 B5
Foliot St. W12 107 F6
Folkestone Rd. E6 116 D2
Folkestone Rd. E17 78 B4
Folkestone Rd. N18 60 D4
Folkingham La. NW9 70 D1
Folkington Cor. N12 56 C5
Follett St. E14 114 C6
Folly La. E4 61 J7
Folly La. E17 77 H1
Folly Ms. W11 108 C6
*Portobello Rd.*
Folly Wall E14 134 C2
Font Hills N2 73 F2
Fontaine Rd. SW16 169 F7
Fontarabia Rd. SW11 150 A4
Fontayne Av., Chig. 65 F4
Fontenoy Rd. SW12 168 B2
Fonteyne Gdns., Wdf.Grn. 80 A2
*Lechmere Av.*
Fonthill Cl. SE20 188 D2
*Selby Rd.*
Fonthill Ms. N4 93 G2
*Lennox Rd.*
Fonthill Rd. N4 93 F1
Fontley Way SW15 147 G7
Fontwell Cl., Har. 52 B7
Fontwell Cl., Nthlt. 85 G6
Fontwell Dr., Brom. 192 D5
Football La., Har. 86 B1
Footpath, The SW15 147 G5
Foots Cray High St., Sid. 176 C6
Foots Cray La., Sid. 176 C1
Footscray Rd. SE9 156 D6
Footway, The SE9 157 F7
Forbes Cl. NW2 89 G3
Forbes Ct. SE19 170 B5
**Forbes St. E1 21 J4**
Forbes Way, Ruis. 84 B2
Forburg Rd. N16 94 D1
Ford Cl. E3 113 H2
*Roman Rd.*
Ford Cl., Har. 68 A7
Ford Cl., Th.Hth. 187 H6
Ford End, Wdf.Grn. 63 H6
Ford Rd. E3 113 H1
Ford Rd., Dag. 101 F7
Ford Sq. E1 113 E5
Ford St. E3 113 H1
Ford St. E16 115 F6
Forde Av., Brom. 191 J3
Fordel Rd. SE6 172 D1
Fordham Cl., Barn. 41 H3
Fordham Rd., Barn. 41 G3
**Fordham St. E1 21 J3**
Fordham St. E1 112 D6
Fordhook Av. W5 105 J7
Fordingley Rd. W9 108 C3
Fordington Rd. N6 73 J5
Fordmill Rd. SE6 172 A2
Fords Gro. N21 59 J1
Fords Pk. Rd. E16 115 G6
Fordwich Cl., Orp. 193 J7
Fordwych Rd. NW2 90 B5
Fordyce Rd. SE13 154 C6
Fordyke Rd., Dag. 101 F2
**Fore St. EC2 20 A2**
Fore St. EC2 111 J5
Fore St. N9 60 D5
Fore St. N18 60 C6
Fore St., Pnr. 66 A5
**Fore St. Av. EC2 20 B2**
Foreland Ct. NW4 72 B1
Foreland St. SE18 137 G4
*Plumstead Rd.*
Foreman Ct. W6 127 J4
*Hammersmith Bdy.*
Foremark Cl., Ilf. 65 J5
Foreshore SE8 133 J4
Forest, The E11 79 E4
Forest App. E4 47 E7
Forest App., Wdf.Grn. 63 F7
Forest Av. E4 47 E7
Forest Av., Chig. 64 D5
Forest Business Pk. E17 77 G7
Forest Cl. E11 79 F5
Forest Cl., Chis. 192 D1
Forest Cl., Wdf.Grn. 63 H3
Forest Ct. E4 63 F1
Forest Ct. E11 79 E4
Forest Cft. SE23 171 E2
Forest Dr. E12 98 A3
Forest Dr., Kes. 206 B4
Forest Dr., Wdf.Grn. 62 D7
Forest Dr. E. E11 78 D7
Forest Dr. W. E11 78 C7
Forest Edge, Buck.H. 63 J4
Forest Gdns. N17 76 C2
Forest Gate NW9 70 E5
Forest Glade E4 62 E4
Forest Glade E11 79 E6
Forest Gro. E8 94 C7
Forest Hts., Buck.H. 63 G2
Forest Hill Business Cen. SE23 171 F2
Forest Hill Ind. Est. SE23 171 F2
*Perry Vale*
Forest Hill Rd. SE22 153 E5
Forest Hill Rd. SE23 153 E5
Forest Ind. Pk., Ilf. 81 H1
Forest La. E7 97 E5
Forest La. E15 97 E5
Forest La., Chig. 64 D5
Forest Mt. Rd., Wdf.Grn. 62 D7
Forest Ridge, Beck. 190 A3
Forest Ridge, Kes. 206 B4
Forest Ri. E17 78 D5
Forest Rd. E7 97 G4
Forest Rd. E8 94 C6
Forest Rd. E11 78 D7
Forest Rd. E17 77 F4
Forest Rd. N9 61 E1
Forest Rd. N17 77 F4
Forest Rd., Felt. 160 C2
Forest Rd., Ilf. 81 H1
Forest Rd., Loug. 48 A3
Forest Rd., Rich. 126 A7
Forest Rd., Rom. 83 H3
Forest Rd., Sutt. 198 D1
Forest Rd., Wdf.Grn. 78 B3
Forest Side E4 47 F7
Forest Side E7 97 H4
*Capel Rd.*
Forest Side, Buck.H. 63 J1
Forest Side, Wor.Pk. 197 F1
Forest St. E7 97 G5
Forest Vw. E4 46 D7
Forest Vw. E11 79 F7
*High Rd. Leytonstone*
Forest Vw. Av. E10 78 D5
Forest Vw. Rd. E12 98 B4
Forest Vw. Rd. E17 78 C1
Forest Vw. Rd., Loug. 48 A4
Forest Way N19 92 C2
*Hargrave Pk.*
Forest Way, Orp. 193 J5
Forest Way, Sid. 157 G7
Forest Way, Wdf.Grn. 63 H4
Forestdale N14 58 D4
Forester Rd. SE15 153 E4
Foresters Cl., Wall. 200 D7
Foresters Cres., Bexh. 159 H4
Foresters Dr. E17 78 D4
Foresters Dr., Wall. 200 D7
Forestholme Cl. SE23 171 F2
Forfar Rd. N22 75 H1
Forfar Rd. SW11 150 A1
Forge Cl., Brom. 205 G1
Forge Cl., Hayes 121 G6
*High St.*
Forge Cotts. W5 125 G1
*Ealing Grn.*
Forge Dr., Esher 194 D7
Forge La., Felt. 160 E5
Forge La., Sun. 178 A3
Forge La., Sutt. 198 B7
Forge Ms., Sun. 178 A3
*Forge La.*
Forge Pl. NW1 92 A6
*Malden Cres.*
Forlong Path, Nthlt. 84/85 E6
*Arnold Rd.*
Forman Pl. N16 94 C4
*Farleigh Rd.*
Formby Av., Stan. 69 F3
**Formosa St. W9 6 C6**
Formosa St. W9 109 E4
Formunt Cl. E16 115 F5
*Vincent St.*
Forres Gdns. NW11 72 D6
Forrest Gdns. SW16 187 F3
Forrester Path SE26 171 G4
Forris Av., Hayes 121 J1
**Forset St. W1 15 H3**
Forset St. W1 109 H6
Forstal Cl., Brom. 191 G3
*Ridley Rd.*
Forster Rd. E17 77 H6
Forster Rd. N17 76 C3
Forster Rd. SW2 150 E7
Forster Rd., Beck. 189 H3
Forster Rd., Croy. 187 J7
*Windmill Rd.*
Forsters Cl., Rom. 83 F6
Forster's Way SW18 166 E1
Forsters Way, Hayes 102 B6
**Forston St. N1 12 B1**
Forsyte Cres. SE19 188 B1
**Forsyth Gdns. SE17 35 H5**
Forsyth Gdns. SE17 131 H6
Forsyth Pl., Enf. 44 B5
Forsythia Cl., Ilf. 98 E5
**Fort Rd. SE1 37 G2**
Fort Rd. SE1 132 C4
Fort Rd., Nthlt. 85 G7
**Fort St. E1 21 E2**
Fort St. E16 135 H1
Forterie Gdns., Ilf. 100 A3
Fortescue Av. E8 94/95 E7
*Mentmore Ter.*
Fortescue Av., Twick. 161 J3
Fortescue Rd. SW19 167 G7
Fortescue Rd., Edg. 70 D1
Fortess Gro. NW5 92 B5
*Fortess Rd.*
Fortess Rd. NW5 92 B5
Fortess Wk. NW5 92 B5
*Fortess Rd.*
Forthbridge Rd. SW11 150 A4
Fortis Cl. E16 115 J6
Fortis Grn. N2 73 H4
Fortis Grn. N10 73 H4
Fortis Grn. Av. N2 73 J3
Fortis Grn. Rd. N10 74 A3
Fortismere Av. N10 74 A3
Fortnam Rd. N19 92 D2
Fortnums Acre, Stan. 52 C6
Fortrose Gdns. SW2 168 D1
*New Pk. Rd.*
Fortuna Cl. N7 93 F6
*Vulcan Way*
Fortune Gate Rd. NW10 107 E1
Fortune Grn. Rd. NW6 90 D4
**Fortune St. EC1 12 A6**
Fortune St. EC1 111 J4
Fortune Wk. SE28 137 G3
*Broadwater Rd.*
Fortune Way NW10 107 G3
Fortunes Mead, Nthlt. 85 E6
Forty Acre La. E16 115 G5
Forty Av., Wem. 87 J3
Forty Cl., Wem. 87 J2
Forty Footpath SW14 146 C3
Forty La., Wem. 88 B2
Forum, The, W.Mol. 179 H4
Forum Way, Edg. 54 A6
*High St.*
Forumside, Edg. 54 A6
*High St.*
Forval Cl., Mitch. 185 J5
Forward Dr., Har. 68 C4
**Fosbury Ms. W2 14 B6**
Foscote Ms. W9 108 D5
*Amberley Rd.*
Foscote Rd. NW4 71 H6
Foskett Rd. SW6 148 C2
Foss Av., Croy. 201 G5
Foss Rd. SW17 167 G4
Fossdene Rd. SE7 135 H5
Fossdyke Cl., Hayes 103 E5
Fosse Way W13 104 D5
Fossil Rd. SE13 154 A3
Fossington Rd., Belv. 138 D4
Fossway, Dag. 100 C2
**Foster La. EC2 19 J3**
Foster La. EC2 111 J6
Foster Rd. E13 115 G4
Foster Rd. W3 106 E7
Foster Rd. W4 126 D5
Foster St. NW4 71 J4
Foster Wk. NW4 71 J4
*New Brent St.*
Fosters Cl. E18 79 H1
Fosters Cl., Chis. 174 C5
Fothergill Cl. E13 115 G2
Fothergill Dr. N21 43 F5
Fotheringham Rd., Enf. 44 C4
**Foubert's Pl. W1 17 F4**
Foubert's Pl. W1 110 C6
Foulden Rd. N16 94 C4
Foulden Ter. N16 94 C4
*Foulden Rd.*
**Foulis Ter. SW7 31 F3**
Foulis Ter. SW7 129 G5
Foulser Rd. SW17 167 J3
Foulsham Rd., Th.Hth. 187 J3
Founder Cl. E6 116/117 E6
*Trader Rd.*
**Founders Ct. EC2 20 B3**
Founders Gdns. SE19 169 J7
Foundry Cl. SE16 133 H1
**Foundry Ms. NW1 9 G5**
Fount St. SW8 130 D7
**Fountain Ct. EC4 19 E5**
Fountain Dr. SE19 170 C4
Fountain Dr., Cars. 199 J1
Fountain Grn. Sq. SE16 132 D2
*Bermondsey Wall E.*
Fountain Ms. N5 93 J4
*Kelross Rd.*
Fountain Pl. SW9 151 G1
Fountain Rd. SW17 167 G5
Fountain Rd., Th.Hth. 187 J2
**Fountain Sq. SW1 32 D1**
Fountain Sq. SW1 130 B4
Fountain St. E2 112 C3
*Columbia Rd.*
Fountains, The, Loug. 47 J7
*Fallow Flds.*
Fountains Av., Felt. 161 F3
Fountains Cl., Felt. 161 F2
Fountains Cres. N14 42 E7
Fountayne Rd. N15 76 D4
Fountayne Rd. N16 94 D2
Four Seasons Cl. E3 114 A2
Four Seasons Cres., Sutt. 198 C2
*Kimpton Rd.*
Four Wents, The E4 62 D2
*Kings Rd.*
Fouracres SW12 168 B2
*Little Dimocks*
Fouracres, Enf. 45 H1
Fourland Wk., Edg. 54 C6
**Fournier St. E1 21 F1**
Fournier St. E1 112 C5
Fourth Av. E12 98 C4
Fourth Av. W10 108 B4
Fourth Av., Hayes 121 J1
Fourth Cross Rd., Twick. 162 A2
Fourth Way, Wem. 88 C4
Fowey Av., Ilf. 80 A5
Fowey Cl. E1 132/133 E1
*Kennet St.*
Fowler Cl. SW11 149 G3
Fowler Rd. E7 97 G4
Fowler Rd. N1 93 H7
*Halton Rd.*
Fowler Rd., Mitch. 186 A2
Fowlers Cl., Sid. 176/177 E5
*Thursland Rd.*
Fowlers Wk. W5 105 G4
Fownes St. SW11 149 H3
**Fox & Knot St. EC1 19 H1**
Fox Cl. E1 113 F4
Fox Cl. E16 115 G5
Fox Gro., Walt. 178 B7
Fox Hill SE19 170 C7
Fox Hill, Kes. 205 J5
Fox Hill Gdns. SE19 170 C7
Fox Hollow Cl. SE18 137 H5
Fox Hollow Dr., Bexh. 158 D3
Fox Ho. Rd., Belv. 139 H4
Fox La. N13 59 F3
Fox La. W5 105 H4
Fox La., Kes. 205 H5
Fox Rd. E16 115 F5
Foxberry Rd. SE4 153 H3
Foxborough Gdns. SE4 154 A5
Foxbourne Rd. SW17 168 A2

Fulbourne Rd. E17 78 C1
Fulbourne St. E1 112/113 E5 *Durward St.*
Fulbrook Ms. N19 92 C4 *Junction Rd.*
Fulbrook Rd. N19 92 C4 *Junction Rd.*
Fulford Gro., Wat. 50 B2
Fulford Rd., Epsom 196 D7
Fulford St. SE16 133 E2
Fulham Bdy. SW6 128 D7
Fulham Ct. SW6 128 D7 *Fulham Rd.*
Fulham High St. SW6 148 B2
Fulham Palace Rd. SW6 128 A7
Fulham Palace Rd. W6 127 J5
Fulham Pk. Gdns. SW6 148 C2
Fulham Pk. Rd. SW6 148 C2
**Fulham Rd. SW3 30 E4**
Fulham Rd. SW3 129 F6
**Fulham Rd. SW6 30 B7**
Fulham Rd. SW6 148 B2
**Fulham Rd. SW10 30 E4**
Fulham Rd. SW10 129 E7
Fullbrooks Av., Wor.Pk. 197 F1
**Fuller Cl. E2 13 H5**
Fuller Cl., Orp. 207 J5
Fuller Rd., Dag. 100 B3
Fuller St. NW4 71 J4
Fuller Ter., Ilf. 99 F5 *Oaktree Gro.*
Fuller Way, Hayes 121 J5
Fullers Av., Surb. 195 J2
Fullers Av., Wdf.Grn. 63 F7
Fullers Rd. E18 79 F1
Fullers Way N., Surb. 195 J3
Fullers Way S., Chess. 195 H4
Fullers Wd., Croy. 204 A5
Fullerton Rd. SW18 149 F5
Fullerton Rd., Croy. 188 C7
Fullwell Av., Ilf. 80 C1
Fullwell Cross Roundabout, Ilf. 81 G2 *Fencepiece Rd.*
**Fullwoods Ms. N1 12 C3**
Fulmar Ct., Surb. 181 J6
Fulmead St. SW6 149 E1
Fulmer Cl., Hmptn. 161 E5
Fulmer Rd. E16 116 A5
Fulmer Way W13 124 E3
Fulready Rd. E10 78 D5
Fulstone Cl., Houns. 143 F4
Fulthorp Rd. SE3 155 F2
**Fulton Ms. W2 14 C5**
Fulton Rd., Wem. 88 A3
Fulwell Pk. Av., Twick. 161 H2
Fulwell Rd., Tedd. 162 A4
Fulwood Av., Wem. 105 J1
Fulwood Gdns., Twick. 144 C6
**Fulwood Pl. WC1 18 D2**
Fulwood Pl. WC1 111 F5
Fulwood Wk. SW19 166 B1
Furber St. W6 127 H3
Furham Feild, Pnr. 51 G7
Furley Rd. SE15 132 D7
Furlong Cl., Wall. 200 A1
Furlong Rd. N7 93 G6
Furmage St. SW18 149 E7
Furneaux Av. SE27 169 H5
Furness Rd. NW10 107 G2
Furness Rd. SW6 149 E2
Furness Rd., Har. 67 H7
Furness Rd., Mord. 185 E7
**Furnival St. EC4 19 E3**
Furnival St. EC4 111 G6
Furrow La. E9 95 F5
Fursby Av. N3 56 D6
Further Acre NW9 71 F2
Further Grn. Rd. SE6 155 E7
Furtherfield Cl., Croy. 187 G6
Furze Cl., Wat. 50 C5
Furze Fm. Cl., Rom. 83 E2
Furze Rd., Th.Hth. 187 J3
Furze St. E3 114 A5
Furzedown Dr. SW17 168 B5
Furzedown Rd. SW17 168 B5
Furzefield Cl., Chis. 174 E6
Furzefield Rd. SE3 135 H6
Furzeground Way, Uxb. 121 F1
Furzeham Rd., West Dr. 120 B2
Furzehill Rd., Borwd. 38 A4
Furzewood, Sun. 178 A1
Fuschia Ct., Wdf.Grn. 62/63 E7 *The Bridle Path*
Fyfe Way, Brom. 191 G2 *Widmore Rd.*
Fyfield Cl., Brom. 190 D4
Fyfield Ct. E7 97 G6
Fyfield Rd. E17 78 D3
Fyfield Rd. SW9 151 G3
Fyfield Rd., Enf. 44 B3
Fyfield Rd., Wdf.Grn. 63 J7
**Fynes St. SW1 33 H1**
Fynes St. SW1 130 D4

## G

G.E.C. Est., Wem. 87 G3
Gable Cl., Pnr. 51 G7
Gable Ct. SE26 170/171 E5 *Lawrie Pk. Av.*
Gables, The, Wem. 87 J4
Gables Cl. SE5 152 B1
Gables Cl. SE12 173 G1
Gabriel Cl., Felt. 160 D4
Gabriel St. SE23 153 G7
Gabrielle Cl., Wem. 87 J3
Gabrielle Ct. NW3 91 G6
Gad Cl. E13 115 H3
Gaddesden Av., Wem. 87 J6
Gade Cl., Hayes 122 B1
Gadesden Rd., Epsom 196 C6
Gadsbury Cl. NW9 71 F6
Gadwall Cl. E16 115 H6 *Freemasons Rd.*
Gadwall Way SE28 137 G2
Gage Rd. E16 114/115 E5 *Malmesbury Rd.*
**Gage St. WC1 18 B1**
Gainford St. N1 111 G1 *Richmond Av.*
Gainsboro Gdns., Grnf. 86 B5
Gainsborough Av. E12 98 D5
Gainsborough Cl., Beck. 172 A7
Gainsborough Cl., Esher 194 B1 *Lime Tree Av.*
Gainsborough Ct. N12 57 E5
Gainsborough Ct. W12 127 J2 *Lime Gro.*
Gainsborough Gdns. NW3 91 G3
Gainsborough Gdns. NW11 72 C7
Gainsborough Gdns., Edg. 69 J2
Gainsborough Gdns., Islw. 144 A5
Gainsborough Ms. SE26 170/171 E3 *Panmure Rd.*
Gainsborough Pl., Chig. 65 J3
Gainsborough Rd. E11 79 E7
Gainsborough Rd. E15 114 E3
Gainsborough Rd. N12 57 E5
Gainsborough Rd. W4 127 F4
Gainsborough Rd., Dag. 100 B4
Gainsborough Rd., N.Mal. 182 D7
Gainsborough Rd., Rich. 145 J3
Gainsborough Rd., Wdf.Grn. 64 B6
Gainsborough Sq., Bexh. 158 D3 *Regency Way*
Gainsford Rd. E17 77 J4
**Gainsford St. SE1 29 F3**
Gainsford St. SE1 132 C2
Gairloch Rd. SE5 152 B2
Gaisford St. NW5 92 C6
Gaitskell Rd. SE9 175 F1
Galahad Rd., Brom. 173 G3
Galata Rd. SW13 127 G7
Galatea Sq. SE15 152/153 E3 *Scylla Rd.*
Galbraith St. E14 134 C3
Galdana Av., Barn. 41 F3
Gale Cl., Hmptn. 160/161 E6 *Stewart Cl.*
Gale Cl., Mitch. 185 G3
Gale St. E3 114 A5
Gale St., Dag. 118 D1
Galeborough Av., Wdf.Grn. 62 D7
**Galen Pl. WC1 18 B2**
Galena Ho. SE18 137 J5 *Grosmont Rd.*
Galena Rd. W6 127 H4
Gales Gdns. E2 113 E3
Gales Way, Wdf.Grn. 64 B7
Galesbury Rd. SW18 149 F6
Galgate Cl. SW19 166 B1
Gallants Fm. Rd., Barn. 41 H7
Galleon Cl. SE16 133 G2 *Kinburn St.*
Galleons Dr., Bark. 117 H3 *Thames Rd.*
Gallery Gdns., Nthlt. 102 D2
Gallery Rd. SE21 170 A1
Galley La., Barn. 39 H3
Galleywall Rd. SE16 132 E4
Gallia Rd. N5 93 H5
Galliard Cl. N9 45 F6
Galliard Rd. N9 60 D1
Gallions Cl., Bark. 118 A3
Gallions Rd. E16 117 E7
Gallions Rd. SE7 135 H4
Gallions Roundabout E16 116 E7
Gallions Vw. Rd. SE28 137 G2 *Goldfinch Rd.*
Gallon Cl. SE7 135 J4
Gallop, The, S.Croy. 203 E7
Gallop, The, Sutt. 199 F7
Gallosson Rd. SE18 137 H4
Galloway Path, Croy. 202 A4
Galloway Rd. W12 127 G1
Gallus Cl. N21 43 F6
Gallus Sq. SE3 155 H3
Galpins Rd., Th.Hth. 187 F4
Galsworthy Av., Rom. 82 B7
Galsworthy Cl. SE28 138 B1
Galsworthy Cres. SE3 155 J1 *Merriman Rd.*
Galsworthy Rd. NW2 90 B4
Galsworthy Rd., Kings.T. 164 B7
Galsworthy Ter. N16 94 B3 *Hawksley Rd.*
Galton St. W10 108 B4
Galva Cl., Barn. 42 A4
Galvani Way, Croy. 201 F1 *Ampere Way*
Galveston Rd. SW15 148 C5
Galway Cl. SE16 132/133 E5 *Masters Dr.*
**Galway St. EC1 12 A4**
Galway St. EC1 111 J3
Gambetta St. SW8 150 B2
**Gambia St. SE1 27 H2**
Gambole Rd. SW17 167 H4
Games Rd., Barn. 41 J3
Gamlen Rd. SW15 148 A4
Gamuel Cl. E17 78 A6
Gander Grn. Cres., Hmptn. 179 G1
Gander Grn. La., Sutt. 198 B2
Gandhi Cl. E17 78 A6
**Gandolfi St. SE15 36 E6**
Gane Cl., Wall. 200/201 E7 *Kingsford Av.*
**Ganton St. W1 17 F5**
Ganton Wk., Wat. 50/51 E4 *Woodhall La.*
Gantshill Cres., Ilf. 80 D5
Gantshill Cross, Ilf. 80 D6 *Eastern Av.*
Gap Rd. SW19 166 D5
Garage Rd. W3 106 A6
**Garbutt Pl. W1 16 C1**
**Gard St. EC1 11 H3**
Garden Av., Bexh. 159 G3
Garden Av., Mitch. 168 B7
Garden City, Edg. 54 A6
Garden Cl. E4 62 A5
Garden Cl. SE12 173 H3
Garden Cl. SW15 147 H7
Garden Cl., Barn. 39 J4
Garden Cl., Hmptn. 161 F5
Garden Cl., Nthlt. 103 E1
Garden Cl., Wall. 200 E5
**Garden Ct. EC4 18 E5**
Garden Ct. SE15 152 C1 *Sumner Est.*
Garden Ct., Rich. 145 J1 *Lichfield Rd.*
Garden Ct., Stan. 53 F5 *Marsh La.*
Garden Ct., W.Mol. 179 H4 *Avern Rd.*
Garden La. SW2 169 F1 *Christchurch Rd.*
Garden La., Brom. 173 H6
Garden Ms. W2 108 D7 *Linden Gdns.*
**Garden Rd. NW8 6 D3**
Garden Rd. NW8 109 F3
Garden Rd. SE20 189 F1
Garden Rd., Brom. 173 H7
Garden Rd., Rich. 146 A3
Garden Rd., Walt. 178 B6
**Garden Row SE1 27 G6**
Garden Row SE1 131 H3
Garden St. E1 113 G5
**Garden Ter. SW1 33 H3**
**Garden Wk. EC2 12 D4**
Garden Wk., Beck. 189 J1 *Hayne Rd.*
Garden Way NW10 88 C6
Gardeners Cl. N11 58 A2
Gardeners Rd., Croy. 201 H1
Gardenia Rd., Enf. 44 B6
Gardenia Way, Wdf.Grn. 63 G5
Gardens, The SE22 152 D4
Gardens, The, Beck. 190 C2
Gardens, The, Felt. 141 G5
Gardens, The, Har. 67 J6
Gardens, The, Pnr. 67 F6
Gardiner Av. NW2 89 J5
Gardiner Cl., Dag. 100 D4
Gardiner Cl., Enf. 45 G6
Gardner Cl. E11 79 H6
Gardner Gro., Felt. 161 F2
Gardner Rd. E13 115 H4
**Gardners La. EC4 19 J5**
Gardnor Rd. NW3 91 G4 *Flask Wk.*
Garendon Gdns., Mord. 184 E7
Garendon Rd., Mord. 184 E7
Gareth Cl., Wor.Pk. 198 A2 *Burnham Dr.*
Gareth Gro., Brom. 173 G4
Garfield Ms. SW11 150 A3 *Garfield Rd.*
Garfield Rd. E4 62 D1
Garfield Rd. E13 115 F4
Garfield Rd. SW11 150 A3
Garfield Rd. SW19 167 F5
Garfield Rd., Enf. 45 F4
Garfield Rd., Twick. 162 D1
Garford St. E14 114 A7
Garganey Wk. SE28 118 D7
Garibaldi St. SE18 137 H4
Garland Rd. SE18 137 G7
Garland Rd., Stan. 69 H1
Garlands Ct., Croy. 202 A4 *Chatsworth Rd.*
**Garlick Hill EC4 20 A5**
Garlick Hill EC4 111 J7
Garlies Rd. SE23 171 H3
Garlinge Rd. NW2 90 C6
Garman Cl. N18 60 A5
Garman Rd. N17 61 F7
**Garnault Ms. EC1 11 F4**
**Garnault Pl. EC1 11 F4**
Garner Rd. E17 78 C1
**Garner St. E2 13 J2**
Garnet Rd. NW10 89 E6
Garnet Rd., Th.Hth. 188 A4
Garnet St. E1 113 F7
Garnet Wk. E6 116 B5 *Kingfisher St.*
Garnett Cl. SE9 156 C3
Garnett Rd. NW3 91 J5
Garnett Way E17 77 H1 *McEntee Av.*
Garnham Cl. N16 94 C2 *Garnham St.*
Garnham St. N16 94 C2
**Garnies Cl. SE15 37 F7**
Garnies Cl. SE15 132 C7
Garrad's Rd. SW16 168 D3
Garrard Cl., Bexh. 159 G3
Garrard Cl., Chis. 175 E5
Garrard Wk. NW10 88/89 E6 *Garnet Rd.*
Garratt Cl., Croy. 200 E4
Garratt La. SW17 167 G4
Garratt La. SW18 148 E5
Garratt Rd., Edg. 54 A7
Garratt Ter. SW17 167 H4
Garrett Cl. W3 106 D5 *Jenner Av.*
**Garrett St. EC1 12 A5**
Garrick Av. NW11 72 B6
Garrick Cl. SW18 149 F4
Garrick Cl. W5 105 H4
Garrick Cl., Rich. 145 G5 *The Grn.*
Garrick Cres., Croy. 202 B2
Garrick Dr. NW4 71 J2
Garrick Dr. SE28 137 G3 *Broadwater Rd.*
Garrick Gdns., W.Mol. 179 G3
Garrick Pk. NW4 72 A2
Garrick Rd. NW9 71 F6
Garrick Rd., Grnf. 103 H4

| | | |
|---|---|---|
| Garrick Rd., Rich. | 146 | A2 |
| **Garrick St. WC2** | **18** | **A5** |
| Garrick St. WC2 | 110 | E7 |
| Garrick Way NW4 | 72 | A4 |
| Garrison Cl. SE18 | 136 | D7 |
| *Red Lion La.* | | |
| Garrison Cl., Houns. | 143 | F5 |
| Garrison La., Chess. | 195 | G7 |
| Garsdale Cl. N11 | 58 | A6 |
| Garside Cl. SE28 | 137 | G3 |
| *Goosander Way* | | |
| Garside Cl., Hmptn. | 161 | H6 |
| Garsington Ms. SE4 | 153 | J3 |
| Garter Way SE16 | 133 | G2 |
| *Poolmans St.* | | |
| Garth, The, Hmptn. | 161 | H6 |
| *Uxbridge Rd.* | | |
| Garth, The, Har. | 69 | J6 |
| Garth Cl. W4 | 126 | D5 |
| Garth Cl., Kings.T. | 163 | J5 |
| Garth Cl., Mord. | 184 | A7 |
| Garth Cl., Ruis. | 84 | D1 |
| Garth Ct. W4 | 126 | D5 |
| *Garth Rd.* | | |
| Garth Ms. W5 | 105 | H4 |
| *Greystoke Gdns.* | | |
| Garth Rd. NW2 | 90 | C2 |
| Garth Rd. W4 | 126 | D6 |
| Garth Rd., Kings.T. | 163 | J5 |
| Garth Rd., Mord. | 183 | J6 |
| Garth Rd. Ind. Cen., Mord. | 184 | A7 |
| Garthland Dr., Barn. | 39 | H5 |
| Garthorne Rd. SE23 | 153 | G7 |
| Garthside, Rich. | 163 | H5 |
| Garthway N12 | 57 | H6 |
| Gartmoor Gdns. SW19 | 166 | C1 |
| Gartmore Rd., Ilf. | 99 | J1 |
| Garton Pl. SW18 | 149 | F6 |
| Gartons Cl., Enf. | 45 | F5 |
| Gartons Way SW11 | 149 | F3 |
| Garvary Rd. E16 | 115 | H6 |
| **Garway Rd. W2** | **14** | **A4** |
| Garway Rd. W2 | 108 | E6 |
| Gascoigne Gdns., Wdf.Grn. | 63 | E7 |
| **Gascoigne Pl. E2** | **13** | **F4** |
| Gascoigne Pl. E2 | 112 | C3 |
| Gascoigne Rd., Bark. | 117 | F1 |
| Gascony Av. NW6 | 90 | D7 |
| Gascoyne Rd. E9 | 95 | G7 |
| Gaselee St. E14 | 114 | C7 |
| **Gasholder Pl. SE11** | **34** | **D4** |
| Gaskarth Rd. SW12 | 150 | B6 |
| Gaskarth Rd., Edg. | 70 | C1 |
| Gaskell Rd. N6 | 73 | J6 |
| Gaskell St. SW4 | 150 | E2 |
| Gaskin St. N1 | 111 | H1 |
| **Gaspar Cl. SW5** | **30** | **B1** |
| **Gaspar Ms. SW5** | **30** | **B1** |
| Gassiot Rd. SW17 | 167 | J4 |
| Gassiot Way, Sutt. | 199 | G3 |
| Gastein Rd. W6 | 128 | A6 |
| Gaston Bell Cl., Rich. | 145 | J3 |
| Gaston Rd., Mitch. | 186 | A3 |
| Gataker St. SE16 | 133 | E3 |
| Gatcombe Rd. E16 | 135 | G1 |
| Gatcombe Rd. N19 | 92 | D3 |
| Gatcombe Way, Barn. | 41 | J3 |
| Gate Cl., Borwd. | 38 | C1 |
| Gate End, Nthwd. | 50 | A7 |
| **Gate Ms. SW7** | **23** | **H4** |
| Gate Ms. SW7 | 129 | H2 |
| **Gate St. WC2** | **18** | **C3** |
| **Gateforth St. NW8** | **7** | **G6** |
| Gateforth St. NW8 | 109 | H4 |
| Gatehouse Cl., Kings.T. | 164 | C7 |
| Gatehouse Sq. SE1 | 131 | J1 |
| *Southwark Br. Rd.* | | |
| Gateley Rd. SW9 | 151 | F3 |
| Gater Dr., Enf. | 44 | A1 |
| Gates Grn. Rd., Kes. | 205 | G4 |
| Gates Grn. Rd., W.Wick. | 205 | F3 |
| **Gatesborough St. EC2** | **12** | **D5** |
| Gateside Rd. SW17 | 167 | J3 |
| Gatestone Rd. SE19 | 170 | B6 |
| **Gateway SE17** | **36** | **A5** |
| Gateway SE17 | 131 | J6 |
| Gateway Arc. N1 | 111 | H2 |
| *SET* | | |
| Gateway Ind. Est. NW10 | 107 | F3 |
| Gateway Ms. E8 | 94 | C5 |
| *Shacklewell La.* | | |
| Gateway Rd. E10 | 96 | B3 |
| **Gateways, The SW3** | **31** | **H2** |
| Gateways, The SW3 | 129 | J4 |
| Gatfield Gro., Felt. | 161 | G2 |
| Gathorne Rd. N22 | 75 | G2 |
| Gathorne St. E2 | 113 | G2 |
| *Mace St.* | | |
| Gatley Av., Epsom | 196 | B5 |
| **Gatliff Rd. SW1** | **32** | **D4** |
| Gatliff Rd. SW1 | 130 | B5 |
| Gatling Rd. SE2 | 138 | A5 |
| Gatting Cl., Edg. | 54 | C7 |
| *Pavilion Way* | | |
| Gatton Rd. SW17 | 167 | H4 |
| Gattons Way, Sid. | 177 | F4 |
| Gatward Cl. N21 | 43 | H6 |
| Gatward Grn. N9 | 60 | B2 |
| Gatwick Rd. SW18 | 148 | C7 |
| Gauden Cl. SW4 | 150 | D3 |
| Gauden Rd. SW4 | 150 | D2 |
| Gaumont Ter. W12 | 127 | J2 |
| *Lime Gro.* | | |
| **Gaunt St. SE1** | **27** | **J5** |
| Gauntlet Cl., Nthlt. | 84 | E7 |
| Gauntlett Ct., Wem. | 86 | E5 |
| Gauntlett Rd., Sutt. | 199 | G5 |
| Gautrey Rd. SE15 | 153 | F2 |
| Gautrey Sq. E6 | 116 | C6 |
| **Gavel St. SE17** | **36** | **C1** |
| Gaverick St. E14 | 134 | A4 |
| Gavestone Cres. SE12 | 155 | H7 |
| Gavestone Rd. SE12 | 155 | H7 |
| Gaviller Pl. E5 | 94/95 | E4 |
| *Clarence Rd.* | | |
| Gavin St. SE18 | 137 | H4 |
| Gavina Cl., Mord. | 185 | H5 |
| Gawber St. E2 | 113 | F3 |
| Gawsworth Cl. E15 | 96/97 | E5 |
| *Ash Rd.* | | |
| Gawthorne Av. NW7 | 56 | B5 |
| *Lane App.* | | |
| Gawthorne Ct. E3 | 114 | A2 |
| *Mostyn Gro.* | | |
| Gay Cl. NW2 | 89 | H5 |
| Gay Gdns., Dag. | 101 | J4 |
| Gay Rd. E15 | 114 | D2 |
| Gay St. SW15 | 148 | A3 |
| **Gaydon Ho. W2** | **14** | **B1** |
| Gaydon Ho. W2 | 109 | E5 |
| Gaydon La. NW9 | 70 | E1 |
| Gayfere Rd., Epsom | 197 | G5 |
| Gayfere Rd., Ilf. | 80 | C3 |
| **Gayfere St. SW1** | **26** | **A6** |
| Gayfere St. SW1 | 130 | E3 |
| Gayford Rd. W12 | 127 | F2 |
| **Gayhurst SE17** | **36** | **C5** |
| Gayhurst Rd. E8 | 94 | D7 |
| Gaylor Rd., Nthlt. | 85 | F5 |
| Gaynes Hill Rd., Wdf.Grn. | 64 | B6 |
| Gaynesford Rd. SE23 | 171 | G2 |
| Gaynesford Rd., Cars. | 199 | J7 |
| Gaysham Av., Ilf. | 80 | D5 |
| Gaysham Hall, Ilf. | 80 | E3 |
| Gayton Ct., Har. | 68 | C6 |
| Gayton Cres. NW3 | 91 | G4 |
| Gayton Rd. NW3 | 91 | G4 |
| Gayton Rd. SE2 | 138 | C3 |
| *Florence Rd.* | | |
| Gayton Rd., Har. | 68 | C6 |
| Gayville Rd. SW11 | 149 | J6 |
| Gaywood Cl. SW2 | 169 | F1 |
| **Gaywood Est. SE1** | **27** | **H6** |
| Gaywood Est. SE1 | 131 | H3 |
| Gaywood Rd. E17 | 78 | A3 |
| **Gaywood St. SE1** | **27** | **H6** |
| **Gaza St. SE17** | **35** | **G4** |
| Geariesville Gdns., Ilf. | 81 | E4 |
| Geary Rd. NW10 | 89 | G5 |
| Geary St. N7 | 93 | F5 |
| Geddes Pl., Bexh. | 159 | G4 |
| *Market Pl.* | | |
| Gedeney Rd. N17 | 75 | J1 |
| **Gedling Pl. SE1** | **29** | **G5** |
| Gedling Pl. SE1 | 132 | C2 |
| **Gee St. EC1** | **11** | **J5** |
| Gee St. EC1 | 111 | J4 |
| Geere Rd. E15 | 115 | F1 |
| **Gees Ct. W1** | **16** | **C4** |
| **Geffrye Ct. N1** | **12** | **E2** |
| Geffrye Est. N1 | 112 | B2 |
| *Stanway St.* | | |
| **Geffrye St. E2** | **13** | **F1** |
| Geffrye St. E2 | 112 | C2 |
| Geldart Rd. SE15 | 132 | E7 |
| Geldeston Rd. E5 | 94 | D2 |
| Gellatly Rd. SE14 | 153 | F2 |
| Gemini Gro., Nthlt. | 102/103 | E3 |
| *Javelin Way* | | |
| General Gordon Pl. SE18 | 136 | E4 |
| General Wolfe Rd. SE10 | 154 | D1 |
| Genesta Rd. SE18 | 137 | E6 |
| Geneva Dr. SW9 | 151 | G4 |
| Geneva Gdns., Rom. | 82 | E5 |
| Geneva Rd., Kings.T. | 181 | H4 |
| Geneva Rd., Th.Hth. | 187 | J5 |
| Genever Cl. E4 | 62 | A5 |
| Genista Rd. N18 | 61 | E5 |
| Genoa Av. SW15 | 147 | J5 |
| Genoa Rd. SE20 | 189 | F1 |
| Genotin Rd., Enf. | 44 | A3 |
| Genotin Ter., Enf. | 44 | A3 |
| *Genotin Rd.* | | |
| Gentian Row SE13 | 154 | C1 |
| *Sparta St.* | | |
| Gentlemans Row, Enf. | 43 | J3 |
| Gentry Gdns. E13 | 115 | G4 |
| *Whitwell Rd.* | | |
| Geoffrey Cl. SE5 | 151 | J2 |
| Geoffrey Gdns. E6 | 116 | B2 |
| Geoffrey Rd. SE4 | 153 | J3 |
| George Beard Rd. SE8 | 133 | J4 |
| George Comberton Wk. E12 | 98 | D5 |
| *Gainsborough Av.* | | |
| **George Ct. WC2** | **18** | **B6** |
| George Cres. N10 | 58 | A7 |
| George Downing Est. N16 | 94 | C2 |
| *Cazenove Rd.* | | |
| George V Av., Pnr. | 67 | G3 |
| George V Cl., Pnr. | 67 | G3 |
| *George V Av.* | | |
| George V Way, Grnf. | 105 | E1 |
| George Gange Way, Har. | 68 | B3 |
| George Gro. Rd. SE20 | 188 | D1 |
| **George Inn Yd. SE1** | **28** | **B2** |
| George La. E18 | 79 | G2 |
| George La. SE13 | 154 | C6 |
| George La., Brom. | 205 | H1 |
| George Lansbury Ho. N22 | 75 | G1 |
| *Progress Way* | | |
| **George Loveless Ho. E2** | **13** | **G3** |
| **George Lowe Ct. W2** | **14** | **A1** |
| **George Mathers Rd. SE11** | **35** | **G1** |
| George Mathers Rd. SE11 | 131 | H4 |
| **George Ms. NW1** | **9** | **F4** |
| George Ms., Enf. | 44 | A3 |
| *Sydney Rd.* | | |
| George Pl. N17 | 76 | B3 |
| *Dongola Rd.* | | |
| George Rd. E4 | 62 | A6 |
| George Rd., Kings.T. | 164 | B7 |
| George Rd., N.Mal. | 183 | F4 |
| **George Row SE16** | **29** | **H4** |
| George Row SE16 | 132 | D2 |
| George Sq. SW19 | 184 | C3 |
| *Mostyn Rd.* | | |
| George St. E16 | 115 | F6 |
| **George St. W1** | **16** | **A3** |
| George St. W1 | 110 | A6 |
| George St. W7 | 124 | B1 |
| *The Bdy.* | | |
| George St., Bark. | 99 | F7 |
| George St., Croy. | 202 | A2 |
| George St., Houns. | 143 | F2 |
| George St., Rich. | 145 | G5 |
| George St., Sthl. | 122 | E4 |
| George St., Sutt. | 198 | E5 |
| George Wyver Cl. SW19 | 148 | B7 |
| *Beaumont Rd.* | | |
| **George Yd. EC3** | **20** | **C4** |
| **George Yd. W1** | **16** | **C5** |
| George Yd. W1 | 110 | A7 |
| George's Rd. N7 | 93 | F5 |
| Georges Sq. SW6 | 128 | C6 |
| *North End Rd.* | | |
| Georgetown Cl. SE19 | 170 | A5 |
| *St. Kitts Ter.* | | |
| Georgette Pl. SE10 | 134 | C7 |
| *King George St.* | | |
| Georgeville Gdns., Ilf. | 81 | E4 |
| Georgia Rd., N.Mal. | 182 | C4 |
| Georgia Rd., Th.Hth. | 187 | H1 |
| Georgian Cl., Brom. | 191 | H7 |
| Georgian Cl., Stan. | 52 | D7 |
| Georgian Ct. SW16 | 168/169 | E4 |
| *Gleneldon Rd.* | | |
| Georgian Ct., Wem. | 88 | A6 |
| Georgian Way, Har. | 86 | A2 |
| Georgiana St. NW1 | 110 | C1 |
| **Georgina Gdns. E2** | **13** | **G3** |
| Geraint Rd., Brom. | 173 | G4 |
| **Gerald Ms. SW1** | **32** | **C1** |
| Gerald Rd. E16 | 115 | F4 |
| **Gerald Rd. SW1** | **32** | **C1** |
| Gerald Rd. SW1 | 130 | A4 |
| Gerald Rd., Dag. | 101 | F2 |
| Geraldine Rd. SW18 | 149 | F5 |
| Geraldine Rd. W4 | 126 | A6 |
| **Geraldine St. SE11** | **27** | **G6** |
| Geraldine St. SE11 | 131 | H3 |
| Gerard Av., Houns. | 143 | G7 |
| *Redfern Av.* | | |
| Gerard Rd. SW13 | 147 | F1 |
| Gerard Rd., Har. | 68 | D6 |
| Gerards Cl. SE16 | 133 | F5 |
| Gerda Rd. SE9 | 175 | F2 |
| Germander Way E15 | 115 | E3 |
| Gernon Rd. E3 | 113 | H2 |
| Geron Way NW2 | 89 | H1 |
| Gerrard Gdns., Pnr. | 66 | A5 |
| **Gerrard Pl. W1** | **17** | **J5** |
| **Gerrard Rd. N1** | **11** | **H1** |
| Gerrard Rd. N1 | 111 | H2 |
| **Gerrard St. W1** | **17** | **H5** |
| Gerrard St. W1 | 110 | D7 |
| Gerrards Cl. N14 | 42 | C5 |
| **Gerridge St. SE1** | **27** | **F4** |
| Gerridge St. SE1 | 131 | G3 |
| Gerry Raffles Sq. E15 | 96 | D6 |
| *Salway Rd.* | | |
| Gertrude Rd., Belv. | 139 | G4 |
| **Gertrude St. SW10** | **30** | **D6** |
| Gertrude St. SW10 | 129 | F6 |
| Gervase Cl., Wem. | 88 | C3 |
| Gervase Rd., Edg. | 70 | C1 |
| Gervase St. SE15 | 133 | E7 |
| Ghent St. SE6 | 172 | A2 |
| Ghent Way E8 | 94 | C6 |
| *Tyssen St.* | | |
| Giant Arches Rd. SE24 | 151 | J7 |
| Giant Tree Hill, Bushey | 52 | A1 |
| Gibbard Ms. SW19 | 166 | A5 |
| Gibbfield Cl., Rom. | 82 | E3 |
| Gibbins Rd. E15 | 96 | C7 |
| Gibbon Rd. SE15 | 153 | F2 |
| Gibbon Rd. W3 | 106 | E7 |
| Gibbon Rd., Kings.T. | 181 | H1 |
| Gibbon Wk. SW15 | 147 | G4 |
| *Swinburne Rd.* | | |
| Gibbons Rd. NW10 | 88 | D6 |
| Gibbs Av. SE19 | 170 | A5 |
| Gibbs Cl. SE19 | 170 | A5 |
| Gibbs Couch, Wat. | 50 | D3 |
| Gibbs Grn. W14 | 128 | C5 |
| Gibbs Grn., Edg. | 54 | C5 |
| Gibbs Rd. N18 | 61 | F4 |
| Gibbs Sq. SE19 | 170 | A5 |
| **Gibraltar Wk. E2** | **13** | **G4** |
| Gibraltar Wk. E2 | 112 | C3 |
| Gibson Cl. E1 | 113 | F4 |
| *Colebert Av.* | | |
| Gibson Cl. N21 | 43 | G6 |
| Gibson Cl., Chess. | 195 | F6 |
| Gibson Cl., Islw. | 144 | A3 |
| Gibson Gdns. N16 | 94 | C2 |
| *Northwold Rd.* | | |
| **Gibson Rd. SE11** | **34** | **D2** |
| Gibson Rd. SE11 | 131 | F4 |
| Gibson Rd., Dag. | 100 | C1 |
| Gibson Rd., Sutt. | 198 | E5 |
| Gibson Sq. N1 | 111 | G1 |
| Gibson St. SE10 | 134 | E5 |
| Gibson's Hill SW16 | 169 | G6 |
| Gideon Cl., Belv. | 139 | H4 |
| Gideon Ms. W5 | 125 | G2 |
| Gideon Rd. SW11 | 150 | A3 |
| Giesbach Rd. N19 | 92 | C2 |
| Giffard Rd. N18 | 60 | B5 |
| Giffin St. SE8 | 134 | A7 |
| Gifford Gdns. W7 | 104 | A5 |
| Gifford St. N1 | 93 | E7 |
| Gift La. E15 | 115 | E1 |
| Giggs Hill Gdns., T.Ditt. | 194 | D1 |
| Giggs Hill Rd., T.Ditt. | 180 | D7 |
| Gilbert Cl. SE18 | 156 | C1 |
| Gilbert Gro., Edg. | 70 | D1 |
| Gilbert Ho. SE8 | 134 | A6 |
| *McMillan St.* | | |
| **Gilbert Pl. WC1** | **18** | **A2** |
| **Gilbert Rd. SE11** | **35** | **F2** |
| Gilbert Rd. SE11 | 131 | G4 |
| Gilbert Rd. SW19 | 167 | F7 |
| Gilbert Rd., Belv. | 139 | G3 |
| Gilbert Rd., Brom. | 173 | G7 |
| Gilbert Rd., Pnr. | 66 | D4 |
| Gilbert St. E15 | 96 | E4 |
| **Gilbert St. W1** | **16** | **C5** |
| Gilbert St. W1 | 110 | A6 |
| Gilbert St., Houns. | 143 | J3 |
| *High St.* | | |
| Gilbert Way, Croy. | 200/201 | E1 |
| *Beddington Fm. Rd.* | | |
| Gilbey Rd. SW17 | 167 | H4 |
| Gilbeys Yd. NW1 | 110 | B1 |
| *Oval Rd.* | | |
| Gilbourne Rd. SE18 | 137 | J6 |

Gilda Av., Enf. 45 H5
Gilda Cres. N16 94 D1
Gildea Cl., Pnr. 51 G7
**Gildea St. W1** 17 E2
Gilden Cres. NW5 92 A5
Gilders Rd., Chess. 195 J6
Gildersome St. SE18 136 D6
*Nightingale Vale*
Giles Coppice SE19 170 C4
Gilkes Cres. SE21 152 B6
Gilkes Pl. SE21 152 B6
Gill Av. E16 115 G6
Gill St. E14 113 J6
Gillan Grn., Bushey 51 J2
Gillards Ms. E17 78 A4
*Gillards Way*
Gillards Way E17 78 A4
Gillender St. E3 114 C4
Gillender St. E14 114 C4
Gillespie Rd. N5 93 G3
Gillett Av. E6 116 B2
Gillett Pl. N16 94 B5
*Gillett St.*
Gillett Rd., Th.Hth. 188 A4
Gillett St. N16 94 B5
Gillette Cor., Islw. 124 D7
**Gillfoot NW1** 9 G2
Gillfoot NW1 110 C2
Gillham Ter. N17 60 D6
Gillian Pk. Rd., Sutt. 198 C1
Gillian St. SE13 154 B5
Gillies St. NW5 92 A5
Gilling Ct. NW3 91 H6
**Gillingham Ms. SW1** 33 F1
Gillingham Rd. NW2 90 B3
**Gillingham Row SW1** 33 F1
**Gillingham St. SW1** 33 F1
Gillingham St. SW1 130 B4
**Gillison Wk. SE16** 29 J5
Gillman Dr. E15 115 F1
Gillum Cl., Barn. 57 J1
Gilmore Rd. SE13 154 D4
Gilpin Av. SW14 146 D4
Gilpin Cl., Mitch. 185 H2
Gilpin Cres. N18 60 C5
Gilpin Cres., Twick. 143 H7
Gilpin Rd. E5 95 H4
Gilpin Way, Hayes 121 G7
Gilsland Rd., Th.Hth. 188 A4
Gilstead Ho., Bark. 118 B2
Gilstead Rd. SW6 149 E2
**Gilston Rd. SW10** 30 D4
Gilston Rd. SW10 129 F5
Gilton Rd. SE6 173 E3
**Giltspur St. EC1** 19 H3
Giltspur St. EC1 111 H6
Gilwell Cl. E4 46 B4
*Antlers Hill*
Gilwell La. E4 46 C4
Gilwell Pk. E4 46 C3
Gippeswyck Cl., Pnr. 66 D1
*Uxbridge Rd.*
Gipsy Hill SE19 170 B5
Gipsy La. SW15 147 G3
Gipsy Rd. SE27 169 J4
Gipsy Rd., Well. 158 D1
Gipsy Rd. Gdns. 169 J4
SE27
Giralda Cl. E16 116 A5
*Fulmer Rd.*
Giraud St. E14 114 B6
Girdlers Rd. W14 128 A4
Girdlestone Wk. N19 92 C2
Girdwood Rd. SW18 148 B7
Girling Way, Felt. 142 A3
Gironde Rd. SW6 128 C7
Girton Av. NW9 70 A3
Girton Cl., Nthlt. 85 J6
Girton Gdns., Croy. 204 A3
Girton Rd. SE26 171 G5
Girton Rd., Nthlt. 85 J6
Girton Vil. W10 108 A6
Gisbourne Cl., Wall. 200 D3
Gisburn Rd. N8 75 F4
Gissing Wk. N1 93 G7
*Lofting Rd.*
Gittens Cl., Brom. 173 F4
Given Wilson Wk. E13 115 F2
Glacier Way, Wem. 105 G2
Gladbeck Way, Enf. 43 H4
Gladding Rd. E12 98 A4
Glade, The N21 43 F6
Glade, The SE7 135 J7
Glade, The, Brom. 192 A2
Glade, The, Croy. 189 G5
Glade, The, Enf. 43 G3
Glade, The, Epsom 197 G5
Glade, The, Ilf. 80 C1
Glade, The, W.Wick. 204 B3
Glade, The, Wdf.Grn. 63 H3
Glade Cl., Surb. 195 G2
Glade Ct., Ilf. 80 C1
*The Glade*

Glade Gdns., Croy. 189 H7
Glade La., Sthl. 123 H2
Glades Pl., Brom. 191 G2
*Widmore Rd.*
Glades Shop. Cen., 191 G2
The, Brom.
Gladeside N21 43 F6
Gladeside, Croy. 189 G6
Gladeside Cl., Chess. 195 G7
*Leatherhead Rd.*
Gladesmore Rd. N15 76 C6
Gladeswood Rd., 139 H4
Belv.
Gladiator St. SE23 153 H6
Glading Ter. N16 94 C3
Gladioli Cl., Hmptn. 161 G6
*Gresham Rd.*
Gladsdale Dr., Pnr. 66 A4
Gladsmuir Rd. N19 92 C1
Gladsmuir Rd., Barn. 40 B2
Gladstone Av. E12 98 B7
Gladstone Av. N22 75 G2
Gladstone Av., Felt. 142 A6
Gladstone Av., 144 A7
Twick.
Gladstone Gdns., 143 J1
Houns.
*Gresham Rd.*
Gladstone Ms. NW6 90 C7
*Cavendish Rd.*
Gladstone Ms. SE20 171 F7
Gladstone Par. NW2 89 H1
*Edgware Rd.*
Gladstone Pk. Gdns. 89 H3
NW2
Gladstone Pl. E3 113 J2
*Roman Rd.*
Gladstone Pl., Barn. 40 A4
Gladstone Rd. SW19 166 D7
Gladstone Rd. W4 126 D3
*Acton La.*
Gladstone Rd., 63 H1
Buck.H.
Gladstone Rd., Croy. 188 A7
Gladstone Rd., 182 A3
Kings.T.
Gladstone Rd., Orp. 207 F5
Gladstone Rd., Sthl. 122 E3
Gladstone Rd., Surb. 195 G2
**Gladstone St. SE1** 27 G5
Gladstone St. SE1 131 H3
Gladstone Ter. SE27 169 J4
Gladstone Ter. SW8 150 B1
Gladstone Way, Har. 68 B3
Gladwell Rd. N8 75 F6
Gladwell Rd., Brom. 173 G6
Gladwyn Rd. SW15 148 A3
Gladys Rd. NW6 90 D7
Glamis Cres., Hayes 121 F3
Glamis Pl. E1 113 F7
Glamis Rd. E1 113 F7
Glamis Way, Nthlt. 85 J6
Glamorgan Cl., 187 E3
Mitch.
Glamorgan Rd., 163 F7
Kings.T.
Glanfield Rd., Beck. 189 J4
Glanleam Rd., Stan. 53 G4
Glanville Rd. SW2 151 E5
Glanville Rd., Brom. 191 H3
Glasbrook Av., 161 F1
Twick.
Glasbrook Rd. SE9 156 A7
Glaserton Rd. N16 76 B7
Glasford St. SW17 167 J6
Glasgow Ho. W9 6 B3
Glasgow Ho. W9 109 E2
Glasgow Rd. E13 115 H2
Glasgow Rd. N18 60/61 E5
*Aberdeen Rd.*
**Glasgow Ter. SW1** 33 F4
Glasgow Ter. SW1 130 C5
Glass St. E2 112/113 E4
*Coventry Rd.*
Glass Yd. SE18 136 D3
*Woolwich High St.*
Glasse Cl. W13 104 D7
**Glasshill St. SE1** 27 H3
Glasshill St. SE1 131 H2
**Glasshouse All. EC4** 19 F4
*Glasshouse Flds. E1* 113 G7
**Glasshouse St. W1** 17 G6
Glasshouse St. W1 110 C7
**Glasshouse Wk. SE11** 34 B3
Glasshouse Wk. SE11 131 E5
**Glasshouse Yd. EC1** 19 J1
Glasslyn Rd. N8 74 D5
Glassmill La., Brom. 191 F2
Glastonbury Av., 64 A7
Wdf.Grn.
Glastonbury Rd. N9 60 C1
Glastonbury Rd., 184 D7
Mord.
Glastonbury St. NW6 90 C5

Glaucus St. E3 114 B5
Glazbury Rd. W14 128 B4
Glazebrook Cl. SE21 170 A2
Glazebrook Rd., Tedd. 162 C7
Glebe, The SE3 154 E3
Glebe, The SW16 168 D4
Glebe, The, Chis. 193 F1
Glebe, The, West Dr. 120 C4
Glebe, The, Wor.Pk. 197 F1
Glebe Av., Enf. 43 H3
Glebe Av., Har. 69 H3
Glebe Av., Mitch. 185 H2
Glebe Av., Ruis. 84 B6
Glebe Av., Wdf.Grn. 63 G6
Glebe Cl. W4 126/127 E5
*Glebe St.*
Glebe Cotts., 198/199 E4
Sutt.
*Vale Rd.*
Glebe Ct. W7 104 A7
Glebe Ct., Mitch. 185 J3
Glebe Ct., Stan. 53 F5
*Glebe Rd.*
Glebe Cres. NW4 71 J4
Glebe Cres., Har. 69 H3
Glebe Gdns., N.Mal. 183 E7
Glebe Ho. Dr., Brom. 205 H1
Glebe Hyrst SE19 170 C4
*Giles Coppice*
Glebe La., Barn. 39 G5
Glebe La., Har. 69 H4
Glebe Path, Mitch. 185 H3
**Glebe Pl. SW3** 31 G5
Glebe Pl. SW3 129 H6
Glebe Rd. E8 94 C7
*Middleton Rd.*
Glebe Rd. N3 73 F1
Glebe Rd. N8 75 F4
Glebe Rd. NW10 89 F6
Glebe Rd. SW13 147 G2
Glebe Rd., Brom. 191 G1
Glebe Rd., Cars. 199 J6
Glebe Rd., Dag. 101 H6
Glebe Rd., Hayes 121 J1
Glebe Rd., Stan. 53 F5
Glebe Side, Twick. 144 C6
Glebe St. W4 126 E5
Glebe Ter. E3 114 A3
*Bow Rd.*
Glebe Way, Felt. 161 G3
Glebe Way, W.Wick. 204 C2
Glebelands, W.Mol. 179 H5
Glebelands Av. E18 79 G2
Glebelands Av., Ilf. 81 G7
Glebelands Cl. SE5 152 B3
*Grove Hill Rd.*
Glebelands Rd., Felt. 142 A7
Glebeway, Wdf.Grn. 63 J5
**Gledhow Gdns.** 30 C2
SW5
Gledhow Gdns. SW5 129 F4
Gledstanes Rd. W14 128 B5
Gleed Av., Bushey 52 A2
Gleeson Dr., Orp. 207 J5
Glegg Pl. SW15 148 A4
Glen, The, Brom. 190 E2
Glen, The, Croy. 203 G2
Glen, The, Enf. 43 H4
Glen, The, Orp. 206 C3
Glen, The, Pnr. 67 E7
Glen, The, (Eastcote), 66 B5
Pnr.
Glen, The, Sthl. 123 F5
Glen, The, Wem. 87 G4
Glen Albyn Rd. SW19 166 A2
Glen Cres., Wdf.Grn. 63 H6
Glen Gdns., Croy. 201 G3
Glen Ri., Wdf.Grn. 63 H6
Glen Rd. E13 115 J4
Glen Rd. E17 77 J5
Glen Rd., Chess. 195 H3
Glen Ter. E14 134 C2
*Manchester Rd.*
Glen Wk., Islw. 144 A5
Glena Mt., Sutt. 199 F4
Glenaffric Av. E14 134 D4
Glenalmond Rd., Har. 69 H4
Glenalvon Way SE18 136 B4
Glenarm Rd. E5 95 F5
Glenavon Cl., Esher 194 D7
Glenavon Rd. E15 97 E7
Glenbarr Cl. SE9 156/157 E3
*Dumbreck Rd.*
Glenbow Rd., Brom. 172 E6
Glenbrook N., Enf. 43 F4
Glenbrook Rd. NW6 90 D5
Glenbrook S., Enf. 43 F4
Glenbuck Ct., Surb. 181 H6
*Glenbuck Rd.*
Glenbuck Rd., Surb. 181 G6
Glenburnie Rd. 167 J3
SW17
Glencairn Dr. W5 105 F4
Glencairn Rd. SW16 168 E7

Glencairne Cl. E16 116 A5
Glencoe Av., Ilf. 81 G7
Glencoe Dr., Dag. 101 G4
Glencoe Rd., Hayes 102 D5
Glencorse Grn., Wat. 50 D4
*Caldwell Rd.*
Glendale Av. N22 59 G7
Glendale Av., Edg. 53 J4
Glendale Av., Rom. 82 C7
Glendale Cl. SE9 156 D3
*Dumbreck Rd.*
Glendale Dr. SW19 166 C5
Glendale Gdns., Wem. 87 G1
Glendale Ms., Beck. 190 B1
Glendale Rd., Erith 139 J4
Glendale Way SE28 118 C7
Glendall St. SW9 151 F4
Glendarvon St. SW15 148 A3
Glendevon Cl., Edg. 54 B3
*Tayside Dr.*
Glendish Rd. N17 76 E1
Glendor Gdns. NW7 54 D4
Glendower Gdns. 146 D3
SW14
*Glendower Rd.*
Glendower Pl. SW7 31 E1
Glendower Pl. SW7 129 G4
Glendower Rd. E4 62 D1
Glendower Rd. SW14 146 D3
Glendown Rd. SE2 138 A5
Glendun Rd. W3 107 E7
Gleneagle Ms. SW16 168 D5
*Ambleside Av.*
Gleneagle Rd. SW16 168 D5
Gleneagles, Stan. 52 E6
Gleneagles Cl. 132/133 E5
SE16
*Ryder Dr.*
Gleneagles Cl., Orp. 207 G1
Gleneagles Cl., Stai. 140 A6
Gleneagles Cl., Wat. 50 D4
Gleneagles Grn., Orp. 207 G1
*Tandridge Dr.*
Gleneagles Twr., 103 J6
Sthl.
Gl02 Gleneldon Ms. SW16 168 E4
Gleneldon Rd. SW16 168 E4
Glenelg Rd. SW2 151 E5
Glenesk Rd. SE9 156 D3
Glenfarg Rd. SE6 172 D1
Glenfield Rd. SW12 168 C1
Glenfield Rd. W13 125 E2
Glenfield Ter. W13 124 E2
**Glenfinlas Way SE5** 35 H7
Glenfinlas Way SE5 131 H7
Glenforth St. SE10 135 F5
Glengall Causeway 134 A3
E14
Glengall Gro. E14 134 C3
Glengall Rd. NW6 108 C1
**Glengall Rd. SE15** 37 G5
Glengall Rd. SE15 132 C6
Glengall Rd., Bexh. 159 E3
Glengall Rd., Edg. 54 B3
Glengall Rd., 63 G6
Wdf.Grn.
**Glengall Ter. SE15** 37 G5
Glengall Ter. SE15 132 C6
Glengarnock Av. E14 134 C4
Glengarry Rd. SE22 152 B5
Glenham Dr., Ilf. 80 E5
Glenhaven Av., 38 A3
Borwd.
Glenhead Cl. SE9 156/157 E3
*Dumbreck Rd.*
Glenhill Cl. N3 72 D2
Glenhouse Rd. SE9 156 D5
Glenhurst Av. NW5 92 A4
Glenhurst Av., Bex. 177 F1
Glenhurst Ct. SE19 170 C5
Glenhurst Ri. SE19 169 J7
Glenhurst Rd. N12 57 G5
Glenhurst Rd., Brent. 125 F6
Glenilla Rd. NW3 91 H6
Glenister Ho., Hayes 122 B1
Glenister Pk. Rd. 168 D7
SW16
Glenister Rd. SE10 135 F5
Glenister St. E16 136 D1
Glenlea Rd. SE9 156 C5
Glenloch Rd. NW3 91 H6
Glenloch Rd., Enf. 45 F2
Glenluce Rd. SE3 135 G6
Glenlyon Rd. SE9 156 D5
Glenmere Av. NW7 55 G7
Glenmill, Hmptn. 161 F5
Glenmore Rd. NW3 91 H6
Glenmore Rd., Well. 157 J1
Glenmore Way, Bark. 118 A2
Glenmount Path SE18 137 F5
*Raglan Rd.*
Glennie Rd. SE27 169 G3
Glenny Rd., Bark. 99 F6
Glenorchy Cl., Hayes 103 E5

| Name | Page | Grid |
|---|---|---|
| Gordon Av. SW14 | 146 | E4 |
| Gordon Av., Stan. | 52 | E6 |
| Gordon Av., Twick. | 144 | D5 |
| Gordon Cl. E17 | 78 | A6 |
| Gordon Cl. N19 | 92 | C1 |
| *Highgate Hill* | | |
| Gordon Ct. W12 | 107 | J6 |
| Gordon Cres., Croy. | 202 | B1 |
| Gordon Cres., Hayes | 122 | A3 |
| Gordon Gdns., Edg. | 70 | B2 |
| Gordon Gro. SE5 | 151 | H2 |
| Gordon Hill, Enf. | 43 | J1 |
| Gordon Ho. Rd. NW5 | 92 | A4 |
| Gordon Pl. W8 | 128 | D2 |
| Gordon Rd. E4 | 47 | E7 |
| Gordon Rd. E11 | 79 | G6 |
| Gordon Rd. E15 | 96 | C4 |
| Gordon Rd. E18 | 79 | H1 |
| Gordon Rd. N3 | 56 | C7 |
| Gordon Rd. N9 | 61 | E2 |
| Gordon Rd. N11 | 58 | D7 |
| Gordon Rd. SE15 | 152 | E2 |
| Gordon Rd. W4 | 126 | B6 |
| Gordon Rd. W5 | 105 | F7 |
| Gordon Rd. W13 | 105 | E7 |
| Gordon Rd., Bark. | 117 | H1 |
| Gordon Rd., Beck. | 189 | J3 |
| Gordon Rd., Belv. | 139 | J4 |
| Gordon Rd., Cars. | 199 | J6 |
| Gordon Rd., Enf. | 43 | J1 |
| Gordon Rd., Esher | 194 | B6 |
| Gordon Rd., Har. | 68 | B3 |
| Gordon Rd., Houns. | 143 | J4 |
| Gordon Rd., Ilf. | 99 | G3 |
| Gordon Rd., Kings.T. | 181 | J1 |
| Gordon Rd., Rich. | 145 | J2 |
| Gordon Rd., Rom. | 83 | F6 |
| Gordon Rd., Sid. | 157 | H5 |
| Gordon Rd., Sthl. | 123 | E4 |
| Gordon Rd., Surb. | 181 | J7 |
| Gordon Sq. WC1 | 9 | J6 |
| Gordon Sq. WC1 | 110 | D4 |
| Gordon St. E13 | 115 | G3 |
| *Grange Rd.* | | |
| Gordon St. WC1 | 9 | H5 |
| Gordon St. WC1 | 110 | D4 |
| Gordon Way, Barn. | 40 | C4 |
| Gordon Way, Brom. | 191 | G1 |
| Gordonbrock Rd. SE4 | 154 | A5 |
| Gordondale Rd. SW19 | 166 | D2 |
| Gossington Cl., Chis. | 174/175 | E4 |
| *Beechwood Ri.* | | |
| Gosterwood St. SE8 | 133 | H6 |
| Gostling Rd., Twick. | 161 | G1 |
| Goston Gdns., Th.Hth. | 187 | G3 |
| Goswell Rd. EC1 | 11 | J6 |
| Goswell Rd. EC1 | 111 | H3 |
| Gothic Ct., Hayes | 121 | G6 |
| *Sipson La.* | | |
| Gothic Rd., Twick. | 162 | A2 |
| Gottfried Ms. NW5 | 92 | C4 |
| *Fortess Rd.* | | |
| Goudhurst Rd., Brom. | 173 | E5 |
| Gough Rd. E15 | 97 | F4 |
| Gough Rd., Enf. | 44 | E2 |
| Gough Sq. EC4 | 19 | F3 |
| Gough Sq. EC4 | 111 | G6 |
| Gough St. WC1 | 10 | D5 |
| Gough St. WC1 | 111 | F4 |
| Gough Wk. E14 | 114 | A6 |
| *Saracen St.* | | |
| Gould Ct. SE19 | 170 | C5 |
| Gould Rd., Felt. | 141 | H7 |
| Gould Rd., Twick. | 162 | B1 |
| Gould Ter. E8 | 94/95 | E5 |
| *Kenmure Rd.* | | |
| Goulding Gdns., Th.Hth. | 187 | H2 |
| Goulston St. E1 | 21 | F3 |
| Goulston St. E1 | 112 | C6 |
| Goulton Rd. E5 | 95 | E4 |
| Gourley Pl. N15 | 76 | B5 |
| Gourley St. N15 | 76 | B5 |
| Gourock Rd. SE9 | 156 | D5 |
| Govan St. E2 | 112 | D1 |
| *Whiston Rd.* | | |
| Govier Cl. E15 | 97 | E7 |
| Gowan Av. SW6 | 148 | B1 |
| Gowan Rd. NW10 | 89 | H6 |
| Gower Cl. SW4 | 150 | C6 |
| Gower Ct. WC1 | 9 | H5 |
| Gower Ms. WC1 | 17 | H2 |
| Gower Ms. WC1 | 110 | D5 |
| Gower Pl. WC1 | 9 | G5 |
| Gower Pl. WC1 | 110 | C4 |
| Gower Rd. E7 | 97 | G6 |
| Gower Rd., Islw. | 124 | C6 |
| Gower St. WC1 | 9 | H4 |
| Gower St. WC1 | 110 | C4 |
| Gower's Wk. E1 | 21 | H3 |
| Gower's Wk. E1 | 112 | D6 |
| Gowland Pl., Beck. | 189 | J2 |
| Gowlett Rd. SE15 | 152 | D3 |
| Gowrie Rd. SW11 | 150 | A3 |
| Graburn Way, E.Mol. | 180 | A3 |
| Grace Av., Bexh. | 159 | F2 |
| Grace Cl. SE9 | 174 | A3 |
| Grace Cl., Borwd. | 38 | D1 |
| Grace Cl., Edg. | 54 | C7 |
| *Pavilion Way* | | |
| Grace Cl., Ilf. | 65 | J6 |
| Grace Jones Cl. E8 | 94 | D6 |
| *Parkholme Rd.* | | |
| Grace Path SE26 | 171 | F4 |
| *Silverdale* | | |
| Grace Pl. E3 | 114 | B3 |
| *St. Leonards St.* | | |
| Grace Rd., Croy. | 187 | J6 |
| Grace St. E3 | 114 | B3 |
| Gracechurch St. EC3 | 20 | C5 |
| Gracechurch St. EC3 | 112 | A7 |
| Gracedale Rd. SW16 | 168 | B5 |
| Gracefield Gdns. SW16 | 169 | E3 |
| Grace's All. E1 | 21 | H5 |
| Grace's All. E1 | 112 | D7 |
| Graces Ms. SE5 | 152 | B2 |
| Graces Rd. SE5 | 152 | B2 |
| Gradient, The SE26 | 170 | D4 |
| Graeme Rd., Enf. | 44 | A2 |
| Graemesdyke Av. SW14 | 146 | B4 |
| Grafton Cl. W13 | 104 | D6 |
| Grafton Cl., Houns. | 161 | E1 |
| Grafton Cl., Wor.Pk. | 197 | E3 |
| Grafton Cres. NW1 | 92 | B6 |
| Grafton Gdns. N4 | 75 | J6 |
| Grafton Gdns., Dag. | 101 | E2 |
| Grafton Ho. E3 | 114 | A3 |
| Grafton Ms. W1 | 9 | F6 |
| Grafton Pk. Rd., Wor.Pk. | 196 | E2 |
| Grafton Pl. NW1 | 9 | H4 |
| Grafton Pl. NW1 | 110 | D3 |
| Grafton Rd. NW5 | 92 | A5 |
| Grafton Rd. W3 | 106 | C7 |
| Grafton Rd., Croy. | 201 | G1 |
| Grafton Rd., Dag. | 101 | E2 |
| Grafton Rd., Enf. | 43 | F3 |
| Grafton Rd., Har. | 67 | J5 |
| Grafton Rd., N.Mal. | 182 | E3 |
| Grafton Rd., Wor.Pk. | 196 | D3 |
| Grafton Sq. SW4 | 150 | C3 |
| **Grafton St. W1** | **17** | **E6** |
| Grafton St. W1 | 110 | B7 |
| Grafton Ter. NW5 | 91 | J5 |
| **Grafton Way W1** | **9** | **F6** |
| Grafton Way W1 | 110 | C4 |
| **Grafton Way WC1** | **9** | **F6** |
| Grafton Way WC1 | 110 | C4 |
| Grafton Way, W.Mol. | 179 | F4 |
| Grafton Yd. NW5 | 92 | B6 |
| Graftons, The NW2 | 90 | D3 |
| *Hermitage La.* | | |
| Graham Av. W13 | 124 | E2 |
| Graham Av., Mitch. | 186 | A1 |
| Graham Cl., Croy. | 204 | A2 |
| Graham Gdns., Surb. | 195 | H1 |
| Graham Rd. E8 | 94 | D6 |
| Graham Rd. E13 | 115 | G4 |
| Graham Rd. N15 | 75 | H3 |
| Graham Rd. NW4 | 71 | H6 |
| Graham Rd. SW19 | 166 | C7 |
| Graham Rd. W4 | 126 | D3 |
| Graham Rd., Bexh. | 159 | G4 |
| Graham Rd., Hmptn. | 161 | G4 |
| Graham Rd., Har. | 68 | B3 |
| Graham Rd., Mitch. | 186 | A1 |
| **Graham St. N1** | **11** | **H2** |
| Graham St. N1 | 111 | H2 |
| **Graham Ter. SW1** | **32** | **B2** |
| Graham Ter. SW1 | 130 | A4 |
| Grahame Pk. Est. NW9 | 71 | F1 |
| Grahame Pk. Way NW7 | 55 | F7 |
| Grahame Pk. Way NW9 | 71 | F2 |
| Grainger Cl., Nthlt. | 85 | J5 |
| *Lancaster Rd.* | | |
| Grainger Rd. N22 | 75 | J1 |
| Grainger Rd., Islw. | 144 | C2 |
| Gramer Cl. E11 | 96 | D2 |
| *Norman Rd.* | | |
| Grampian Cl., Hayes | 121 | G7 |
| Grampian Cl., Orp. | 193 | J6 |
| *Cotswold Ri.* | | |
| Grampian Gdns. NW2 | 90 | B1 |
| Granard Av. SW15 | 147 | H5 |
| Granard Rd. SW12 | 149 | J7 |
| Granary Cl. N9 | 45 | F7 |
| *Turin Rd.* | | |
| Granary Rd. E1 | 112 | E4 |
| Granary St. NW1 | 110 | D1 |
| **Granby Bldgs. SE11** | **34** | **C2** |
| Granby Rd. SE9 | 156 | C2 |
| **Granby St. E2** | **13** | **G5** |
| Granby St. E2 | 112 | C4 |
| **Granby Ter. NW1** | **9** | **F2** |
| Granby Ter. NW1 | 110 | C2 |
| **Grand Av. EC1** | **19** | **H1** |
| Grand Av. N10 | 74 | A4 |
| Grand Av., Surb. | 182 | B5 |
| Grand Av., Wem. | 88 | A5 |
| Grand Av., E., Wem. | 88 | B5 |
| Grand Depot Rd. SE18 | 136 | D5 |
| Grand Dr. SW20 | 183 | J2 |
| Grand Dr., Sthl. | 123 | J2 |
| **Grand Junct. Wf. N1** | **11** | **J2** |
| Grand Junct. Wf. N1 | 111 | J2 |
| Grand Par. Ms. SW15 | 148 | B5 |
| *Upper Richmond Rd.* | | |
| Grand Union Canal Wk. W7 | 108 | C5 |
| *Woodfield Rd.* | | |
| Grand Union Cres. E8 | 94 | D7 |
| Grand Union Ind. Est. NW10 | 106 | B2 |
| Grand Union Wk. NW1 | 92 | B7 |
| Grand Wk. E1 | 113 | H4 |
| *Solebay St.* | | |
| Granden Rd. SW16 | 187 | E2 |
| Grandison Rd. SW11 | 149 | J5 |
| Grandison Rd., Wor.Pk. | 197 | J2 |
| Granfield St. SW11 | 149 | G1 |
| Grange, The N2 | 73 | G2 |
| *Central Av.* | | |
| Grange, The N20 | 57 | F1 |
| **Grange, The SE1** | **29** | **F5** |
| Grange, The SE1 | 132 | C3 |
| Grange, The SW19 | 166 | A6 |
| Grange, The, Croy. | 203 | J2 |
| Grange, The, Wem. | 88 | A7 |
| Grange, The, Wor.Pk. | 196 | D3 |
| Grange Av. N12 | 57 | F5 |
| Grange Av. N20 | 40 | B7 |
| Grange Av. SE25 | 188 | B2 |
| Grange Av., Barn. | 57 | J1 |
| Grange Av., Stan. | 69 | E2 |
| Grange Av., Twick. | 162 | B2 |
| Grange Av., Wdf.Grn. | 63 | G6 |
| Grange Cl., Edg. | 54 | C5 |
| Grange Cl., Houns. | 123 | F6 |
| Grange Cl., Sid. | 176 | A3 |
| Grange Cl., W.Mol. | 179 | H4 |
| Grange Cl., Wdf.Grn. | 63 | G7 |
| Grange Ct. E8 | 94 | C7 |
| **Grange Ct. WC2** | **18** | **D4** |
| Grange Ct., Chig. | 65 | F2 |
| Grange Ct., Loug. | 48 | A5 |
| Grange Ct., Nthlt. | 102 | C2 |
| Grange Cres. SE28 | 118 | C6 |
| Grange Cres., Chig. | 65 | G5 |
| Grange Dr., Chis. | 174 | B6 |
| Grange Fm. Cl., Har. | 85 | J2 |
| Grange Gdns. N14 | 58 | D1 |
| Grange Gdns. NW3 | 91 | E3 |
| Grange Gdns. SE25 | 188 | B2 |
| Grange Gdns., Pnr. | 67 | F4 |
| Grange Gro. N1 | 93 | J6 |
| Grange Hill SE25 | 188 | B2 |
| Grange Hill, Edg. | 54 | C5 |
| Grange Ho., Bark. | 117 | G1 |
| *St. Margarets* | | |
| Grange La. SE21 | 170 | C2 |
| Grange Mans., Epsom | 197 | F3 |
| Grange Ms. SE10 | 134 | D7 |
| *Crooms Hill* | | |
| Grange Pk. W5 | 125 | H1 |
| Grange Pk. Av. N21 | 43 | H6 |
| Grange Pk. Pl. SW20 | 165 | H7 |
| Grange Pk. Rd. E10 | 96 | B1 |
| Grange Pk. Rd., Th.Hth. | 188 | A4 |
| Grange Rd. E10 | 96 | A1 |
| Grange Rd. E13 | 115 | F3 |
| Grange Rd. E17 | 77 | H5 |
| Grange Rd. N6 | 74 | A6 |
| Grange Rd. N17 | 60 | D6 |
| Grange Rd. N18 | 60 | D6 |
| Grange Rd. NW10 | 89 | H6 |
| **Grange Rd. SE1** | **28** | **E6** |
| Grange Rd. SE1 | 132 | B3 |
| Grange Rd. SE19 | 188 | A4 |
| Grange Rd. SE25 | 188 | A4 |
| Grange Rd. SW13 | 147 | G1 |
| Grange Rd. W4 | 126 | B5 |
| Grange Rd. W5 | 125 | G1 |
| Grange Rd., Chess. | 195 | H4 |
| Grange Rd., Edg. | 54 | D6 |
| Grange Rd., Har. | 68 | D6 |
| Grange Rd. (South Harrow), Har. | 86 | A2 |
| Grange Rd., Ilf. | 99 | E4 |
| Grange Rd., Kings.T. | 181 | H3 |
| Grange Rd., Orp. | 207 | F2 |
| Grange Rd., Sthl. | 122 | E2 |
| Grange Rd., Sutt. | 198 | A4 |
| Grange Rd., Th.Hth. | 188 | A4 |
| Grange Rd., W.Mol. | 179 | H4 |
| Grange St. N1 | 112 | A1 |
| Grange Vale, Sutt. | 199 | E7 |
| Grange Vw. Rd. N20 | 57 | F1 |
| **Grange Wk. SE1** | **28** | **E5** |
| Grange Wk. SE1 | 132 | B3 |
| **Grange Yd. SE1** | **29** | **F6** |
| Grange Yd. SE1 | 132 | C3 |
| Grangecliffe Gdns. SE25 | 188 | B2 |
| Grangecourt Rd. N16 | 94 | B1 |
| Grangehill Pl. SE9 | 156 | C3 |
| *Westmount Rd.* | | |
| Grangehill Rd. SE9 | 156 | C3 |
| Grangemill Rd. SE6 | 172 | A3 |
| Grangemill Way SE6 | 172 | A2 |
| Grangeway N12 | 57 | E4 |
| Grangeway NW6 | 90 | D7 |
| *Messina Av.* | | |
| Grangeway, Wdf.Grn. | 63 | J4 |
| Grangeway, The N21 | 43 | H6 |
| Grangeway Gdns., Ilf. | 80 | B5 |
| Grangeway, Bexh. | 177 | F1 |
| *Hurst Rd.* | | |
| Grangewood Cl., Pnr. | 66 | A5 |
| Grangewood La., Beck. | 171 | J6 |
| Grangewood St. E6 | 115 | J1 |
| Grangewood Ter. SE25 | 188 | A3 |
| *Grange Rd.* | | |
| Granham Gdns. N9 | 60 | C2 |
| Granite St. SE18 | 137 | J5 |
| Granleigh Rd. E11 | 96 | E2 |
| Gransden Av. E8 | 95 | E7 |
| Gransden Rd. W12 | 127 | F2 |
| *Wendell Rd.* | | |
| Grant Cl. N14 | 42 | C7 |
| Grant Pl., Croy. | 202 | C1 |
| Grant Rd. SW11 | 149 | G4 |
| Grant Rd., Croy. | 202 | C1 |
| Grant Rd., Har. | 68 | C3 |

Grant St. E13 115 G3
**Grant St. N1 11 E1**
Grant Way, Islw. 124 D6
**Grantbridge St. N1 11 H1**
Grantbridge St. N1 111 H2
Grantchester Cl., Har. 86 C3
Grantham Cl., Edg. 53 H3
Grantham Gdns., Rom. 83 F6
Grantham Grn., Borwd. 38 C5
**Grantham Pl. W1 24 D2**
Grantham Rd. E12 98 D4
Grantham Rd. SW9 151 E2
Grantham Rd. W4 126 E7
Grantley Rd., Houns. 142 C2
Grantley St. E1 113 G3
Grantock Rd. E17 78 D1
Granton Rd. SW16 186 C1
Granton Rd., Ilf. 100 A1
Granton Rd., Sid. 176 C6
Grants Cl. NW7 55 J7
**Grantully Rd. W9 6 A4**
Grantully Rd. W9 108 E3
Granville Av. N9 61 F3
Granville Av., Felt. 160 A2
Granville Av., Houns. 143 G5
Granville Cl., Croy. 202 B2
Granville Ct. N1 112 A1
Granville Gdns. SW16 187 F1
Granville Gdns. W5 125 J1
Granville Gro. SE13 154 C3
Granville Ms., Sid. 176 A4
Granville Pk. SE13 154 C3
Granville Pl. (North Finchley) N12 57 F7
*High Rd.*
**Granville Pl. W1 16 B4**
Granville Pl. W1 110 A6
Granville Pl., Pnr. 66 D2
*Elm Pk. Rd.*
Granville Rd. E17 78 B6
Granville Rd. E18 79 H2
Granville Rd. N4 75 F6
Granville Rd. N12 57 E7
Granville Rd. N13 59 F6
*Russell Rd.*
Granville Rd. N22 75 H1
Granville Rd. NW2 90 C2
Granville Rd. NW6 108 D2
Granville Rd. SW18 148 D7
Granville Rd. SW19 166 D7
*Russell Rd.*
Granville Rd., Barn. 39 J4
Granville Rd., Hayes 121 J4
Granville Rd., Ilf. 98 E1
Granville Rd., Sid. 176 A4
Granville Rd., Well. 158 C3
Granville Sq. SE15 132 B7
**Granville Sq. WC1 10 D4**
Granville Sq. WC1 111 F3
**Granville St. WC1 10 D4**
**Grape St. WC2 18 A3**
**Graphite Sq. SE11 34 C3**
Grapsome Cl., Chess. 195 G6
*Ashlyns Way*
Grasdene Rd. SE18 138 A7
Grasmere Av. SW15 164 D4
Grasmere Av. SW19 184 D3
Grasmere Av. W3 106 C7
Grasmere Av., Houns. 143 H6
Grasmere Av., Orp. 206 E3
Grasmere Av., Wem. 69 G7
Grasmere Cl., Loug. 48 C2
Grasmere Ct. N22 59 F6
*Palmerston Rd.*
Grasmere Gdns., Har. 68 D2
Grasmere Gdns., Ilf. 80 C5
Grasmere Gdns., Orp. 206 E3
Grasmere Rd. E13 115 G2
Grasmere Rd. N10 74 B1
Grasmere Rd. N17 60 D6
Grasmere Rd. SE25 189 E6
Grasmere Rd. SW16 169 F5
Grasmere Rd., Bexh. 159 J1
Grasmere Rd., Brom. 191 F1
Grasmere Rd., Orp. 206 E3
Grass Pk. N3 72 C1
Grassington Cl. N11 58 A6
*Ribblesdale Av.*
Grassington Rd., Sid. 176 A4
Grassmount SE23 171 E2
Grassway, Wall. 200 C4
Grasvenor Av., Barn. 40 D6
**Grately Way SE15 37 F7**
Gratton Rd. W14 128 B3
Gratton Ter. NW2 90 A3
Gravel Hill N3 72 C2
Gravel Hill, Bexh. 159 H5
Gravel Hill, Croy. 203 G6
Gravel Hill Cl., Bexh. 159 H5
**Gravel La. E1 21 F3**
Gravel Pit La. SE9 157 F5
Gravel Rd., Brom. 206 B2
Gravel Rd., Twick. 162 B1
Graveley Av., Borwd. 38 C4
Gravelly Ride SW19 165 H4
Gravelwood Cl., Chis. 175 F3
Graveney Gro. SE20 171 F7
Graveney Rd. SW17 167 H4
Gravesend Rd. W12 107 G7
Gray Av., Dag. 101 F1
**Gray St. SE1 27 F4**
Grayham Cres., N.Mal. 182 D4
Grayham Rd., N.Mal. 182 D4
Grayland Cl., Brom. 192 A1
Grayling Cl. E16 114/115 E4
*Cranberry La.*
Grayling Rd. N16 94 A2
**Grayling Sq. E2 13 J3**
Grayling Sq. E2 112 D3
**Gray's Inn WC1 18 D1**
Gray's Inn WC1 111 G5
**Gray's Inn Pl. WC1 18 D2**
**Gray's Inn Rd. WC1 10 C4**
Gray's Inn Rd. WC1 111 F4
**Gray's Inn Sq. WC1 18 D1**
**Gray's Yd. W1 16 C4**
Grayscroft Rd. SW16 168 D7
Grayshott Rd. SW11 150 A2
Grayswood Gdns. SW20 183 H2
*Farnham Gdns.*
Graywood Ct. N12 57 F7
Grazebrook Rd. N16 94 A2
Grazeley Cl., Bexh. 159 J5
Grazeley Ct. SE19 170 B4
*Gipsy Hill*
Great Acre Ct. SW4 150 D4
*St. Alphonsus Rd.*
**Great Bell All. EC2 20 B3**
Great Benty, West Dr. 120 B4
Great Brownings SE21 170 C4
Great Bushey Dr. N20 57 E1
Great Cambridge Rd. N9 60 C1
Great Cambridge Rd. N17 60 A5
Great Cambridge Rd. N18 60 A5
Great Cambridge Rd., Enf. 44 D4
**Great Castle St. W1 17 E3**
Great Castle St. W1 110 C6
Great Cen. Av., Ruis. 84 C5
**Great Cen. St. NW1 15 J1**
Great Cen. St. NW1 109 J5
Great Cen. Way NW10 88 E5
Great Cen. Way, Wem. 88 C4
**Great Chapel St. W1 17 H3**
Great Chapel St. W1 110 D6
Great Chertsey Rd. W4 146 C2
Great Chertsey Rd., Felt. 161 G3
Great Ch. La. W6 128 A5
**Great College St. SW1 26 A5**
Great College St. SW1 130 E3
Great Cross Av. SE10 134 E7
**Great Cumberland Ms. W1 15 J4**
**Great Cumberland Pl. W1 15 J3**
Great Cumberland Pl. W1 109 J6
**Great Dover St. SE1 28 A4**
Great Dover St. SE1 132 A2
Great Eastern Rd. E15 96 D7
**Great Eastern St. EC2 12 D4**
Great Eastern St. EC2 112 B3
**Great Eastern Wk. EC2 20 E2**
Great Elms Rd., Brom. 191 J4
Great Fld. NW9 71 E1
Great Fleete Way, Bark. 118 C2
Great Galley Cl., Bark. 118 B3
**Great George St. SW1 25 J4**
Great George St. SW1 130 D2
**Great Guildford St. SE1 27 J1**
Great Guildford St. SE1 131 J1
Great Harry Dr. SE9 174 D3
**Great James St. WC1 10 C6**
Great James St. WC1 111 F5
**Great Marlborough St. W1 17 F4**
Great Marlborough St. W1 110 C6
**Great Maze Pond SE1 28 C3**
Great Maze Pond SE1 132 A2
**Great New St. EC4 19 F3**
Great Newport St. WC2 110 D7
*Cranbourn St.*
Great N. Rd. N2 73 H4
Great N. Rd. N6 73 H4
Great N. Rd. (New Barnet), Barn. 40 D5
Great N. Way NW4 71 J2
Great Oaks, Chig. 65 F4
**Great Ormond St. WC1 18 B1**
Great Ormond St. WC1 111 E5
Great Owl Rd., Chig. 64 D3
**Great Percy St. WC1 10 D3**
Great Percy St. WC1 111 F3
**Great Peter St. SW1 25 H6**
Great Peter St. SW1 130 D3
**Great Portland St. W1 17 E1**
Great Portland St. W1 110 B5
**Great Pulteney St. W1 17 G5**
Great Pulteney St. W1 110 C7
**Great Queen St. WC2 18 B4**
Great Queen St. WC2 111 E6
**Great Russell St. WC1 17 J3**
Great Russell St. WC1 110 E5
**Great St. Helens EC3 20 D3**
Great St. Helens EC3 112 B6
**Great St. Thomas Apostle EC4 20 A5**
**Great Scotland Yd. SW1 26 A2**
Great Scotland Yd. SW1 130 E1
**Great Smith St. SW1 25 J5**
Great Smith St. SW1 130 D3
Great South-West Rd., Felt. 141 F7
Great South-West Rd., Houns. 141 J4
Great Spilmans SE22 152 B5
Great Strand NW9 71 F1
**Great Suffolk St. SE1 27 H2**
Great Suffolk St. SE1 131 H2
**Great Sutton St. EC1 11 H6**
Great Sutton St. EC1 111 H4
**Great Swan All. EC2 20 B3**
Great Thrift, Orp. 193 F4
**Great Titchfield St. W1 17 F3**
Great Titchfield St. W1 110 C6
**Great Twr. St. EC3 20 D5**
Great Twr. St. EC3 112 B7
**Great Trinity La. EC4 20 A5**
**Great Turnstile WC1 18 D2**
Great W. Rd. W4 126 B5
Great W. Rd. W6 127 F5
Great W. Rd., Brent. 126 B5
Great W. Rd., Houns. 142 D2
Great W. Rd., Islw. 124 C7
Great Western Rd. W2 108 C5
Great Western Rd. W9 108 C5
Great Western Rd. W11 108 C5
Great Wf. Rd. E14 134 B1
*Churchill Pl.*
**Great Winchester St. EC2 20 C3**
Great Winchester St. EC2 112 A6
**Great Windmill St. W1 17 H5**
Great Windmill St. W1 110 D7
**Great Yd. SE1 28 E3**
Greatdown Rd. W7 104 C4
Greatfield Av. E6 116 C4
Greatfield Cl. N19 92 C4
*Warrender Rd.*
Greatfield Cl. SE4 154 A4
Greatfields Rd., Bark. 117 G1
Greatham Wk. SW15 165 G1
**Greatorex St. E1 21 H1**
Greatorex St. E1 112 D5
Greatwood, Chis. 174 D7
Greaves Cl., Bark. 99 H7
*Norfolk Rd.*
Greaves Pl. SW17 167 H4
Grebe Av., Hayes 102 D6
*Cygnet Way*
Grebe Cl. E7 97 F5
*Cormorant Rd.*
Grebe Cl. E17 61 H7
Grebe Cl., Bark. 117 H3
*Thames Rd.*
Grebe Ct., Sutt. 198 B2
*Gander Grn. La.*
Grecian Cres. SE19 169 H6
Gredo Ho., Bark. 118 B3
**Greek Ct. W1 17 J4**
**Greek St. W1 17 J4**
Greek St. W1 110 D6
**Greek Yd. WC2 18 A5**
Green, The E4 62 C1
Green, The E11 79 H6
Green, The E15 97 E6
Green, The N9 60 D2
Green, The N14 58 D3
Green, The N21 43 G7
Green, The SW14 146 C3
Green, The SW19 166 A5
Green, The W3 107 E6
Green, The W5 125 G1
*High St.*
Green, The, Bexh. 159 G1
Green, The, Brom. 191 G7
Green, The, Cars. 200 A4
Green, The, Esher 194 C6
Green, The, Felt. 160 B2
Green, The, Houns. 123 G6
*Heston Rd.*
Green, The, Mord. 184 B4
Green, The, N.Mal. 182 C3
Green, The (St. Paul's Cray), Orp. 176 B7
*The Av.*
Green, The, Rich. 145 G5
Green, The, Sid. 176 A4
Green, The, Sthl. 123 E3
Green, The, Sutt. 198 E3
Green, The, Twick. 162 B1
Green, The, Well. 157 H4
Green, The, Wem. 86 D2
Green, The, West Dr. 120 A3
Green, The, Wdf.Grn. 63 G5
Green Acres, Croy. 202 C3
**Green Arbour Ct. EC1 19 G3**
Green Av. NW7 54 D4
Green Av. W13 125 E3
Green Bank E1 132 E1
Green Bank N12 57 E4
Green Cl. NW9 70 C6
Green Cl. NW11 73 F7
Green Cl., Brom. 190 E3
Green Cl., Cars. 199 J2
Green Cl., Felt. 160 E5
Green Cft., Edg. 54 C5
*Deans La.*
Green Dale SE5 152 A4
Green Dale SE22 152 B5
Green Dale Cl. SE22 152 B5
*Green Dale*
**Green Dragon Ct. SE1 28 B1**
Green Dragon La. N21 43 H6
Green Dragon La., Brent. 125 H5
**Green Dragon Yd. E1 21 H2**
Green Dr., Sthl. 123 G1
Green End N21 59 H2
Green End, Chess. 195 H4
Green Gdns., Orp. 207 F5
Green Hill, Buck.H. 63 J1
Green Hundred Rd. SE15 132 D6
Green La. E4 46 E3
Green La. NW4 72 A5
Green La. SE9 174 D2
Green La. SE20 171 G7
Green La. SW16 169 F7
Green La. W7 124 B2
Green La., Chig. 65 G2
Green La., Chis. 174 E4
Green La., Dag. 100 D2
Green La., Edg. 54 A5
Green La., Felt. 160 E5
Green La., Har. 86 B3
Green La., Houns. 142 B3
Green La., Ilf. 99 F2
Green La., Mord. 184 E6
Green La., N.Mal. 182 C5
Green La., Stan. 52 E4
Green La., Th.Hth. 187 G1
Green La., Wat. 50 C1
Green La., W.Mol. 179 H5
Green La., Wor.Pk. 197 G1
Green La. Gdns., Th.Hth. 187 J2
Green Las. N4 93 J1
Green Las. N8 75 H3
Green Las. N13 59 F6
Green Las. N15 75 H3
Green Las. N16 93 J3
Green Las. N21 59 H1
Green Lawns, Ruis. 84 C1
Green Leaf Av., Wall. 200 D4
Green Man Gdns. W13 104 D7
Green Man La. W13 124 D1
Green Man La., Felt. 142 A4
Green Man Pas. W13 104 D7
Green Man Roundabout E11 79 F7

Green Moor Link N21 43 H7
Green Pk. Way, Grnf. 104 B1
Green Pt. E15 97 E6
Green Pond Cl. E17 77 J3
Green Pond Rd. E17 77 H3
Green Ride, Loug. 47 G5
Green Rd. N14 42 B6
Green Rd. N20 57 F3
Green Shield Ind. Est. E16 135 G1 *Bradfield Rd.*
Green St. E7 97 H6
Green St. E13 115 J1
**Green St. W1 16 B5**
Green St. W1 110 A7
Green St., Enf. 45 F2
Green St., Sun. 178 A1
Green Vale W5 105 J6
Green Vale, Bexh. 158 D5
Green Verges, Stan. 53 G7
Green Vw., Chess. 195 J7
Green Wk. NW4 72 A5
**Green Wk. SE1 28 D6**
Green Wk., Buck.H. 48 B7
Green Wk., Hmptn. 161 F6 *Orpwood Cl.*
Green Wk., Sthl. 123 G5
Green Wk., Wdf.Grn. 64 B6
Green Wk., The E4 62 C1
Green Way SE9 156 A5
Green Way, Brom. 192 B6
Green Way, Sun. 178 A4
Green Wrythe Cres., Cars. 199 H1
Green Wrythe La., Cars. 185 G6
Greenacre Cl., Nthlt. 85 F5 *Eastcote La.*
Greenacre Gdns. E17 78 C4
Greenacre Pl., Wall. 200 B2 *Park Rd.*
Greenacre Sq. SE16 133 G2 *Fishermans Dr.*
Greenacre Wk. N14 58 E3
Greenacres SE9 156 D6
Greenacres, Bushey 52 A2
Greenacres Cl., Orp. 207 F4
Greenacres Dr., Stan. 52 E7
Greenaway Gdns. NW3 90 E4
Greenbank Av., Wem. 86 D5
Greenbank Cl. E4 62 C2
Greenbank Cres. NW4 72 B4
Greenbay Rd. SE7 136 A7
**Greenberry St. NW8 7 G2**
Greenberry St. NW8 109 H2
Greenbrook Av., Barn. 41 F1
**Greencoat Pl. SW1 33 G1**
Greencoat Pl. SW1 130 C4
**Greencoat Row SW1 25 G6**
Greencourt Av., Croy. 203 E2
Greencourt Av., Edg. 70 B1
Greencourt Gdns., Croy. 203 E1
Greencourt Rd., Orp. 193 G5
Greencrest Pl. NW2 89 H3 *Dollis Hill La.*
Greencroft Av., Ruis. 84 C2
Greencroft Cl. E6 116 B5 *Neatscourt Rd.*
Greencroft Gdns. NW6 91 E7
Greencroft Gdns., Enf. 44 B3
Greencroft Rd., Houns. 143 F1
Greenend Rd. W4 126 E2
Greenfarm Cl., Orp. 207 J5
Greenfield Av., Surb. 182 B7
Greenfield Av., Wat. 50 D2
Greenfield Gdns. NW2 90 B2
Greenfield Gdns., Dag. 118 D1
Greenfield Gdns., Orp. 193 G7
**Greenfield Rd. E1 21 J2**
Greenfield Rd. E1 112 D5
Greenfield Rd. N15 76 B5
Greenfield Rd., Dag. 118 C1
Greenfield Way, Har. 67 H3
Greenfields, Loug. 48 D4
Greenfields Cl., Loug. 48 D4
Greenford Av. W7 104 B4
Greenford Av., Sthl. 103 F7
Greenford Gdns., Grnf. 103 H3
Greenford Rd., Grnf. 103 J5
Greenford Rd., Har. 104 A2
Greenford Rd., Sthl. 123 J1
Greenford Rd., Sutt. 198 E4
Greengate, Grnf. 86 E6
Greengate St. E13 115 H2
Greenhalgh Wk. N2 73 F4
**Greenham Cl. SE1 27 E4**
Greenham Cl. SE1 131 G2
Greenham Cres. E4 61 J6
Greenham Rd. N10 74 A2
Greenheys Dr. E18 79 F3
Greenhill NW3 91 G4 *Hampstead High St.*
Greenhill SE18 136 C5
Greenhill, Sutt. 199 F2
Greenhill, Wem. 88 B2
Greenhill Gdns., Nthlt. 103 F2
Greenhill Gro. E12 98 B4
Greenhill Pk. NW10 106 E1
Greenhill Pk., Barn. 40 E5
Greenhill Rd. NW10 106 E1
Greenhill Rd., Har. 68 B6
Greenhill Ter. SE18 136 C5
Greenhill Ter., Nthlt. 103 F2
Greenhill Way, Har. 68 B6
Greenhill Way, Wem. 88 B2
**Greenhill's Rents EC1 19 H1**
Greenhills Ter. N1 94 A6 *Baxter Rd.*
Greenhithe Cl., Sid. 157 H7
Greenholm Rd. SE9 156 E5
Greenhurst Rd. SE27 169 G5
Greening St. SE2 138 C4
Greenland Cres., Sthl. 122 C3
Greenland Ms. SE8 133 G5 *Trundleys Rd.*
Greenland Pl. NW1 110 B1 *Greenland Rd.*
Greenland Quay SE16 133 G4
Greenland Rd. NW1 110 C1
Greenland Rd., Barn. 39 J6
Greenland St. NW1 110 B1 *Camden High St.*
Greenlaw Gdns., N.Mal. 183 F7
Greenlaw St. SE18 136 D3
Greenlea Pk. SW19 185 G1
Greenleaf Cl. SW2 151 G7 *Tulse Hill*
Greenleaf Rd. E6 115 J1 *Redclyffe Rd.*
Greenleaf Rd. E17 77 J3
Greenleafe Dr., Ilf. 81 E4
Greenman St. N1 93 J7
Greenmead Cl. SE25 188 D5
Greenmoor Rd., Enf. 45 F2
Greenoak Pl., Barn. 41 J3 *Cockfosters Rd.*
Greenoak Way SW19 166 A4
Greenock Rd. SW16 186 D1
Greenock Rd. W3 126 B3
Greenpark Ct., Wem. 87 F7
Greens Cl., The, Loug. 48 D2
**Green's Ct. W1 17 H5**
Green's End SE18 136 E4
Greenshank Cl. E17 61 H7 *Banbury Rd.*
Greenside, Bex. 177 E1
Greenside, Dag. 100 C1
Greenside Cl. N20 57 G2
Greenside Cl. SE6 172 D2
Greenside Rd. W12 127 G3
Greenside Rd., Croy. 187 G7
Greenslade Rd., Bark. 99 G7
Greenstead Av., Wdf.Grn. 63 J7
Greenstead Cl., Wdf.Grn. 63 J6 *Greenstead Gdns.*
Greenstead Gdns. SW15 147 G5
Greenstead Gdns., Wdf.Grn. 63 J6
Greensted Rd., Loug. 48 B7
Greenstone Ms. E11 79 G6
Greenvale Rd. SE9 156 C4
Greenview Av., Beck. 189 H6
Greenview Av., Croy. 189 H6
Greenway N14 58 E2
Greenway N20 56 D2
Greenway SW20 183 J4
Greenway, Chis. 174 D5
Greenway, Dag. 100 C2
Greenway, Har. 69 H5
Greenway, Hayes 102 B4
Greenway, Pnr. 66 B2
Greenway, Wall. 200 C4
Greenway, Wdf.Grn. 63 J5
Greenway, The NW9 70 D2
Greenway, The, Har. 68 B1
Greenway, The, Houns. 143 F4
Greenway, The, Pnr. 67 F6
Greenway Av. E17 78 D4
Greenway Cl. N4 93 J2
Greenway Cl. N11 58 A6
Greenway Cl. N15 76 C4 *Copperfield Dr.*
Greenway Cl. N20 56 D2
Greenway Cl. NW9 70 D2
Greenway Gdns. NW9 70 D2
Greenway Gdns., Croy. 203 J3
Greenway Gdns., Grnf. 103 G3
Greenway Gdns., Har. 68 B1
Greenways, Beck. 190 A2
Greenways, Esher 194 B4
Greenways, The, Twick. 144 D6 *South Western Rd.*
**Greenwell St. W1 9 E6**
Greenwell St. W1 110 B4
Greenwich Ch. St. SE10 134 C6
Greenwich Cres. E6 116 B5 *Swan App.*
Greenwich Foot Tunnel E14 134 C5
Greenwich Foot Tunnel SE10 134 C5
Greenwich High Rd. SE10 154 B1
Greenwich Ind. Est. SE7 135 H4
Greenwich Mkt. SE10 134 C6
Greenwich Pk. SE10 134 D7
Greenwich Pk. St. SE10 134 D5
Greenwich S. St. SE10 154 B1
Greenwich Vw. Pl. E14 134 B3
Greenwood Av., Dag. 101 H4
Greenwood Av., Enf. 45 H2
Greenwood Cl., Mord. 184 B4
Greenwood Cl., Orp. 193 H6
Greenwood Cl., Sid. 176 A2 *Hurst Rd.*
Greenwood Cl., T.Ditt. 194 D1
**Greenwood Ct. SW1 33 F3**
Greenwood Ct. SW1 130 C5
Greenwood Dr. E4 62 C5 *Avril Way*
Greenwood Gdns. N13 59 H3
Greenwood Gdns., Ilf. 65 F7
Greenwood La., Hmptn. 161 H5
Greenwood Pk., Kings.T. 165 E7
Greenwood Pl. NW5 92 B5 *Highgate Rd.*
Greenwood Rd. E8 94 D6
Greenwood Rd. E13 115 F2 *Maud Rd.*
Greenwood Rd., Croy. 187 H7
Greenwood Rd., Islw. 144 B3
Greenwood Rd., Mitch. 186 D3
Greenwood Rd., T.Ditt. 194 D1
Greenwood Ter. NW10 106 D1
Greenwoods, The, Har. 85 J2 *Sherwood Rd.*
Greer Rd., Har. 67 J1
**Greet St. SE1 27 F2**
Greet St. SE1 131 G1
Greg Cl. E10 78 C6
Gregor Ms. SE3 135 G7
Gregory Cres. SE9 156 A7
**Gregory Pl. W8 22 A3**
Gregory Pl. W8 128 E2
Gregory Rd., Rom. 82 D4
Gregory Rd., Sthl. 123 G3
Gregson Cl., Borwd. 38 C1
Greig Cl. N8 74 E5
**Greig Ter. SE17 35 H5**
Grena Gdns., Rich. 145 J4
Grena Rd., Rich. 145 J4
Grenaby Av., Croy. 188 A7
Grenaby Rd., Croy. 188 A7
Grenada Rd. SE7 135 J7
Grenade St. E14 113 J7
Grenadier St. E16 136 D1
Grendon Gdns., Wem. 88 A2
**Grendon St. NW8 7 G5**
Grendon St. NW8 109 H4
Grenfell Cl., Borwd. 38 C1
Grenfell Gdns., Har. 69 H7
Grenfell Rd. W11 108 A7
Grenfell Rd., Mitch. 167 J6
Grenfell Twr. W11 108 A7
Grenfell Wk. W11 108 A7
Grennell Cl., Sutt. 199 G2
Grennell Rd., Sutt. 199 F2
Grenoble Gdns. N13 59 G6
Grenville Cl. N3 72 C1
Grenville Cl., Surb. 196 C1
Grenville Gdns., Wdf.Grn. 79 J1
**Grenville Ms. SW7 30 D1**
Grenville Ms. SW7 129 F4
Grenville Ms., Hmptn. 161 H5
Grenville Pl. NW7 54 D5
**Grenville Pl. SW7 22 C6**
Grenville Pl. SW7 129 F3
Grenville Rd. N19 92 E1
**Grenville St. WC1 10 B6**
Grenville St. WC1 111 E4
Gresham Av. N20 57 J4
Gresham Cl., Bex. 159 E6
Gresham Cl., Enf. 43 J3
Gresham Dr., Rom. 82 B5
Gresham Gdns. NW11 90 B1
Gresham Rd. E6 116 C2
Gresham Rd. E16 115 H6
Gresham Rd. NW10 88 D5
Gresham Rd. SE25 188 D4
Gresham Rd. SW9 151 G3
Gresham Rd., Beck. 189 H2
Gresham Rd., Edg. 53 J6
Gresham Rd., Hmptn. 161 G6
Gresham Rd., Houns. 143 J1
**Gresham St. EC2 19 J3**
Gresham St. EC2 111 J6
Gresham Way SW19 166 D3
Gresley Cl. E17 77 H6
Gresley Cl. N15 76 A4 *Clinton Rd.*
Gresley Rd. N19 92 C1
**Gresse St. W1 17 H2**
Gresse St. W1 110 D5
Gressenhall Rd. SW18 148 C6
Gresswell Cl., Sid. 176 A3
Greswell St. SW6 148 A1
Gretton Rd. N17 60 B7
Greville Cl., Twick. 144 E7
**Greville Hall NW6 6 A1**
Greville Hall NW6 109 E2
**Greville Pl. NW6 6 B1**
Greville Pl. NW6 109 E2
Greville Rd. E17 78 C4
Greville Rd. NW6 108 E1
Greville Rd., Rich. 145 J6
**Greville St. EC1 19 F2**
Greville St. EC1 111 G5
Grey Cl. NW11 73 F6
**Grey Eagle St. E1 21 F1**
Grey Eagle St. E1 112 C5
**Greycoat Pl. SW1 25 H6**
Greycoat Pl. SW1 130 D3
**Greycoat St. SW1 25 H6**
Greycoat St. SW1 130 D3
Greycot Rd., Beck. 172 A5
Greyfell Cl., Stan. 52/53 E5 *Coverdale Cl.*
**Greyfriars Pas. EC1 19 H3**
Greyhound Hill NW4 71 G3
Greyhound La. SW16 168 D6
Greyhound Rd. N17 76 B3
Greyhound Rd. NW10 107 H3
Greyhound Rd. W6 128 A6
Greyhound Rd. W14 128 A6
Greyhound Rd., Sutt. 199 F5
Greyhound Ter. SW16 186 C1
Greys Pk. Cl., Kes. 205 J5
Greystead Rd. SE23 153 F7
Greystoke Av., Pnr. 67 G3
Greystoke Gdns. W5 105 H4
Greystoke Gdns., Enf. 42 D4
Greystoke Pk. Ter. W5 105 G3
**Greystoke Pl. EC4 19 E3**
Greystone Gdns., Har. 69 F6
Greystone Gdns., Ilf. 81 F2
Greystone Path E11 79 F7 *Grove Rd.*
Greyswood St. SW16 168 B6
Grierson Rd. SE23 153 G7
Griffin Cen., The, Felt. 142 B5
Griffin Cl. NW10 89 H5
Griffin Manor Way SE28 137 G3
Griffin Rd. N17 76 B2
Griffin Rd. SE18 137 G5
Griffin Way, Sun. 178 A2
Griffith Cl., Dag. 100 C1 *Gibson Rd.*
Griffiths Cl., Wor.Pk. 197 H2
Griffiths Rd. SW19 166 D7
Griggs App., Ilf. 99 F2
**Griggs Pl. SE1 28 E6**
Griggs Rd. E10 78 C6

Grilse Cl. N9 61 E4
Grimsby Gro. E16 136/137 E2
*Barge Ho. Rd.*
**Grimsby St. E2 13 G6**
Grimsdyke Cres., Barn. 39 J3
Grimsdyke Rd., Pnr. 51 E7
**Grimsel Path SE5 35 H7**
Grimshaw Cl. N6 74 A7
Grimston Rd. SW6 148 C2
Grimwade Av., Croy. 202 D3
Grimwade Cl. SE15 153 F3
Grimwade Cres. SE15 153 F3
*Evelina Rd.*
Grimwood Rd., Twick. 144 C7
**Grindal St. SE1 26 E4**
Grindall Cl., Croy. 201 H4
*Hillside Rd.*
Grindleford Av. N11 58 A2
Grindley Gdns., Croy. 188 C6
Grinling Pl. SE8 134 A6
Grinstead Rd. SE8 133 H5
Grittleton Av., Wem. 88 B6
Grittleton Rd. W9 108 D4
Grizedale Ter. SE23 171 E2
**Grocer's Hall Ct. EC2 20 B4**
Grogan Cl., Hmptn. 161 F6
Groom Cres. SW18 149 G7
**Groom Pl. SW1 24 C5**
Groom Pl. SW1 130 A3
Groombridge Cl., Well. 158 A5
Groombridge Rd. E9 95 G7
Groomfield Cl. SW17 168 A4
Grooms Dr., Pnr. 66 A5
Grosmont Rd. SE18 137 J5
Grosse Way SW15 147 H6
Grosvenor Av. N5 93 J5
Grosvenor Av. SW14 146 E3
Grosvenor Av., Cars. 199 J6
Grosvenor Av., Har. 67 H6
Grosvenor Av., Rich. 145 H5
*Grosvenor Rd.*
Grosvenor Cl., Loug. 48 E1
**Grosvenor Cotts. SW1 32 B1**
Grosvenor Ct. N14 42 C7
Grosvenor Ct. NW6 108 A1
*Christchurch Av.*
Grosvenor Cres. NW9 70 A4
**Grosvenor Cres. SW1 24 C4**
Grosvenor Cres. SW1 130 A2
**Grosvenor Cres. Ms. SW1 24 B4**
Grosvenor Cres. Ms. SW1 130 A2
Grosvenor Dr., Loug. 49 E1
**Grosvenor Est. SW1 33 J1**
Grosvenor Est. SW1 130 D4
Grosvenor Gdns. E6 116 A3
Grosvenor Gdns. N10 74 C3
Grosvenor Gdns. N14 42 D5
Grosvenor Gdns. NW2 89 J5
Grosvenor Gdns. NW11 72 C6
**Grosvenor Gdns. SW1 24 D5**
Grosvenor Gdns. SW1 130 B3
Grosvenor Gdns. SW14 146 E3
Grosvenor Gdns., Kings.T. 163 G6
Grosvenor Gdns., Wall. 200 C7
Grosvenor Gdns., Wdf.Grn. 63 G6
**Grosvenor Gdns. Ms. E. SW1 24 E5**
**Grosvenor Gdns. Ms. N. SW1 24 D6**
**Grosvenor Gdns. Ms. S. SW1 24 E6**
**Grosvenor Gate W1 16 A6**
Grosvenor Gate W1 109 J7
Grosvenor Hill SW19 166 B6
**Grosvenor Hill W1 16 D5**
Grosvenor Hill W1 110 B7
**Grosvenor Pk. SE5 35 J6**
Grosvenor Pk. SE5 131 J6
Grosvenor Pk. Rd. E17 78 A5
Grosvenor Path, Loug. 49 E1
**Grosvenor Pl. SW1 24 C4**
Grosvenor Pl. SW1 130 A2
Grosvenor Ri. E. E17 78 B5
Grosvenor Rd. E6 116 A1
Grosvenor Rd. E7 97 H6
Grosvenor Rd. E10 96 C1
Grosvenor Rd. E11 79 G5
Grosvenor Rd. N3 56 C7
Grosvenor Rd. N9 60 E1
Grosvenor Rd. N10 74 B1
Grosvenor Rd. SE25 188 D4
**Grosvenor Rd. SW1 33 J4**
Grosvenor Rd. SW1 130 B6
Grosvenor Rd. W4 126 B5
Grosvenor Rd. W7 124 D1
Grosvenor Rd., Belv. 139 G6
Grosvenor Rd., Bexh. 158 D5
Grosvenor Rd., Borwd. 38 A3
Grosvenor Rd., Brent. 125 G6
Grosvenor Rd., Dag. 101 F1
Grosvenor Rd., Houns. 143 F3
Grosvenor Rd., Ilf. 99 F3
Grosvenor Rd., Orp. 193 H6
Grosvenor Rd., Rich. 145 H5
Grosvenor Rd., Sthl. 123 F3
Grosvenor Rd., Twick. 144 D7
Grosvenor Rd., Wall. 200 B6
Grosvenor Rd., W.Wick. 204 B1
**Grosvenor Sq. W1 16 C5**
Grosvenor Sq. W1 110 A7
**Grosvenor St. W1 16 D5**
Grosvenor St. W1 110 B7
**Grosvenor Ter. SE5 35 J7**
Grosvenor Ter. SE5 131 H7
Grosvenor Way E5 95 F2
Grosvenor Wf. Rd. E14 134 D4
Grote's Bldgs. SE3 155 E2
Grote's Pl. SE3 154 E2
Groton Rd. SW18 167 E2
**Grotto Pas. W1 16 C1**
Grotto Rd., Twick. 162 C2
Grove, The E15 96 E6
Grove, The N3 72 D1
Grove, The N4 75 F7
Grove, The N6 92 A1
Grove, The N8 74 D5
Grove, The N13 59 G4
Grove, The N14 42 C5
Grove, The NW9 70 D5
Grove, The NW11 72 B7
Grove, The W5 125 G1
Grove, The, Bexh. 158 D4
Grove, The, Edg. 54 B4
Grove, The, Enf. 43 G2
Grove, The, Grnf. 103 J6
Grove, The, Islw. 144 B1
Grove, The, Sid. 177 E4
Grove, The, Stan. 52 D2
Grove, The, Tedd. 162 D4
Grove, The, Twick. 144/145 E6
*Bridge Rd.*
Grove, The, Walt. 178 B7
Grove, The, W.Wick. 204 B3
Grove Av. N3 56 D7
Grove Av. N10 74 C2
Grove Av. W7 104 B6
Grove Av., Pnr. 67 E4
Grove Av., Sutt. 198 D6
Grove Av., Twick. 162 C1
Grove Bank, Wat. 50 D1
Grove Cl. N14 42 B7
*Avenue Rd.*
Grove Cl. SE23 171 G1
Grove Cl., Brom. 205 G2
Grove Cl., Felt. 160 E4
Grove Cl., Kings.T. 181 J4
**Grove Cotts. SW3 31 H5**
Grove Cotts. SW3 129 H6
Grove Ct. SE3 155 G1
Grove Ct., E.Mol. 180 A5
*Walton Rd.*
Grove Cres. E18 79 F2
Grove Cres. NW9 70 C4
Grove Cres. SE5 152 B2
Grove Cres., Felt. 160 E4
Grove Cres., Kings.T. 181 H3
Grove Cres., Walt. 178 B7
Grove Cres. Rd. E15 96 D6
Grove End E18 79 F2
*Grove Hill*
Grove End NW5 92 B4
*Chetwynd Rd.*
Grove End La., Esher 194 A1
**Grove End Rd. NW8 6 E3**
Grove End Rd. NW8 109 G3
Grove Fm. Ct., Mitch. 185 J4
*Brookfields Av.*
Grove Footpath, Surb. 181 H4
Grove Gdns. E15 96 E6
Grove Gdns. NW4 71 G4
**Grove Gdns. NW8 7 H4**
Grove Gdns., Dag. 101 J3
Grove Gdns., Enf. 45 G1
Grove Gdns., Tedd. 162 D4
Grove Grn. Rd. E11 96 C3
**Grove Hall Ct. NW8 6 D3**
Grove Hill E18 79 F2
Grove Hill, Har. 68 B7
Grove Hill Rd. SE5 152 B3
Grove Hill Rd., Har. 68 B7
Grove Ho. Rd. N8 74 E4
Grove La. SE5 152 A1
Grove La., Chig. 65 J3
Grove La., Kings.T. 181 H4
Grove La. Ter. SE5 152 B3
*Grove La.*
Grove Mkt. Pl. SE9 156 C6
Grove Ms. W6 127 J3
Grove Ms. W11 108 C6
*Portobello Rd.*
Grove Mill Pl., Cars. 200 A3
Grove Pk. E11 79 H6
Grove Pk. NW9 70 C4
Grove Pk. SE5 152 B2
Grove Pk. Av. E4 62 B7
Grove Pk. Br. W4 126 C7
Grove Pk. Gdns. W4 126 B6
Grove Pk. Ms. W4 126 C7
Grove Pk. Rd. N15 76 B4
Grove Pk. Rd. SE9 173 J3
Grove Pk. Rd. W4 126 B7
Grove Pk. Ter. W4 126 B6
Grove Pas. E2 113 E2
Grove Pas., Tedd. 162 D5
Grove Pl. NW3 91 G4
*Christchurch Hill*
Grove Pl. SW12 150 B6
*Cathles Rd.*
Grove Pl. W3 126 C1
Grove Pl. W5 125 G1
*The Gro.*
Grove Pl., Bark. 117 F1
*Clockhouse Av.*
Grove Rd. E3 113 G1
Grove Rd. E4 62 B4
Grove Rd. E11 79 F7
Grove Rd. E17 78 B5
Grove Rd. E18 79 F2
Grove Rd. N11 58 B5
Grove Rd. N12 57 G5
Grove Rd. N15 76 B5
Grove Rd. NW2 89 J6
Grove Rd. SW13 147 F2
Grove Rd. SW19 167 F7
Grove Rd. W3 126 C1
Grove Rd. W5 105 G7
Grove Rd., Barn. 41 H3
Grove Rd., Belv. 139 F6
Grove Rd., Bexh. 159 J4
Grove Rd., Borwd. 38 A1
Grove Rd., Brent. 125 F5
Grove Rd., E.Mol. 180 A4
Grove Rd., Edg. 54 A6
Grove Rd., Houns. 143 G4
Grove Rd., Islw. 144 B1
Grove Rd., Mitch. 186 B2
Grove Rd., Pnr. 67 F5
Grove Rd., Rich. 145 J6
Grove Rd., Rom. 82 B7
Grove Rd., Surb. 181 G5
Grove Rd., Sutt. 199 E6
Grove Rd., Th.Hth. 187 G4
Grove Rd., Twick. 162 A3
Grove St. N18 60 C6
Grove St. SE8 133 J4
Grove Ter. NW5 92 B3
Grove Ter., Tedd. 162 D4
Grove Ter. Ms. NW5 92 B3
*Grove Ter.*
Grove Vale SE22 152 C4
Grove Vale, Chis. 174 D6
Grove Vil. E14 114 B7
Grove Way, Esher 179 J7
Grove Way, Wem. 88 B5
Grovebury Rd. SE2 138 B2
Grovedale Rd. N19 92 D2
Groveland Av. SW16 169 F7
**Groveland Ct. EC4 20 A4**
Groveland Rd., Beck. 189 J3
Groveland Way, N.Mal. 182 C5
Grovelands, W.Mol. 179 G4
Grovelands Cl. SE5 152 B2
Grovelands Cl., Har. 85 H3
Grovelands Ct. N14 42 D7
Grovelands Rd. N13 59 F4
Grovelands Rd. N15 76 D6
Grovelands Rd., Orp. 176 A7
Groveside Cl. W3 106 A6
Groveside Cl., Cars. 199 H2
Groveside Rd. E4 63 E2
Grovestile Waye, Felt. 141 G7
Groveway SW9 151 F1
Groveway, Dag. 100 D4
Grovewood, Rich. 146 A1
*Sandycombe Rd.*
Grovewood Pl., Wdf.Grn. 64 C6
Grummant Rd. SE15 152 C1
Grundy St. E14 114 B6
Gruneisen Rd. N3 56 E7
Gubyon Av. SE24 151 H5
Guerin Sq. E3 113 J3
*Malmesbury Rd.*
Guernsey Cl., Houns. 143 G1
Guernsey Gro. SE24 151 J7
Guernsey Rd. E11 96 D1
Guibal Rd. SE12 155 H7
Guild Rd. SE7 136 A5
Guildersfield Rd. SW16 168 E7
Guildford Gro. SE10 154 B1
Guildford Rd. E6 116 B6
Guildford Rd. E17 78 C1
Guildford Rd. SW8 151 E1
Guildford Rd., Croy. 188 A6
Guildford Rd., Ilf. 99 H2
Guildford Way, Wall. 201 E5
Guildhall Bldgs. EC2 112 A6
*Basinghall St.*
**Guildhall Yd. EC2 20 B3**
**Guildhouse St. SW1 33 F1**
Guildhouse St. SW1 130 C4
Guildown Av. N12 56 E4
Guildsway E17 77 J1
Guilford Av., Surb. 181 J5
**Guilford Pl. WC1 10 C6**
Guilford Pl. WC1 111 F4
**Guilford St. WC1 10 A6**
Guilford St. WC1 111 E4
Guilford Vil., Surb. 181 J6
*Alpha Rd.*
Guilsborough Cl. NW10 88 E7
**Guinness Bldgs. SE1 28 D6**
Guinness Bldgs. SE1 132 B4
Guinness Cl. E9 95 H7
Guinness Cl., Hayes 121 G3
**Guinness Sq. SE1 36 D1**
**Guinness Trust Bldgs. SE11 35 H3**
Guinness Trust Bldgs. SE11 131 H5
**Guinness Trust Bldgs. SW3 31 J2**
Guinness Trust Bldgs. SW9 151 H4
Guinness Trust Est. N16 94 B1
*Holmleigh Rd.*
Guion Rd. SW6 148 C2
Gull Cl., Wall. 200 E7
Gulland Wk. N1 93 J6
*Clephane Rd.*
Gulliver Cl., Nthlt. 103 F1
Gulliver Rd., Sid. 175 H2
Gulliver St. SE16 133 J3
**Gulston Wk. SW3 32 A2**
Gulston Wk. W11 108 C6
*Basing St.*
Gumleigh Rd. W5 125 F4
Gumley Gdns., Islw. 144 D3
Gumping Rd., Orp. 207 F2
**Gun St. E1 21 F2**
Gun St. E1 112 C5
Gundulph Rd., Brom. 191 J3
Gunmakers La. E3 113 H1
Gunnell Cl. SE26 170 D5
Gunnell Cl., Croy. 188 D6
Gunner La. SE18 136 D5
Gunners Gro. E4 62 C3
Gunners Rd. SW18 167 G2
Gunnersbury Av. W3 126 A3
Gunnersbury Av. W4 126 A3
Gunnersbury Av. W5 125 J1
Gunnersbury Cl. W4 126 B5
*Grange Rd.*
Gunnersbury Ct. W3 126 B2
*Bollo La.*
Gunnersbury Cres. W3 126 A2
Gunnersbury Dr. W5 125 J2
Gunnersbury Gdns. W3 126 A2
Gunnersbury La. W3 126 A3
Gunnersbury Ms. W4 126 B5
*Chiswick High Rd.*
Gunnersbury Pk. W3 125 J4
Gunnersbury Pk. W5 125 J4
Gunning St. SE18 137 H4
**Gunpowder Sq. EC4 19 F3**
Gunstor Rd. N16 94 B4
**Gunter Gro. SW10 30 C6**
Gunter Gro. SW10 129 F6
Gunter Gro., Edg. 70 D1
Gunterstone Rd. W14 128 B4
**Gunthorpe St. E1 21 G2**
Gunthorpe St. E1 112 C6
Gunton Rd. E5 95 E3
Gunton Rd. SW17 168 A6
Gunwhale Cl. SE16 133 G1
Gurdon Rd. SE7 135 G5
Gurnell Gro. W13 104 C4

Gurney Cl. E15 96/97 E5
*Gurney Rd.*
Gurney Cl. E17 77 G1
Gurney Cl., Bark. 98 E6
Gurney Cres., Croy. 201 F1
Gurney Dr. N2 73 F5
Gurney Rd. E15 96 E5
Gurney Rd., Cars. 200 A4
Gurney Rd., Nthlt. 102 B3
**Guthrie St. SW3 31 G3**
Gutter La. EC2 20 A3
Gutter La. EC2 111 J6
Guy Barnett Gro. SE3 155 G3
*Casterbridge Rd.*
Guy Rd., Wall. 200 D3
**Guy St. SE1 28 C3**
Guy St. SE1 132 A2
Guyatt Gdns., Mitch. 186 A2
*Ormerod Gdns.*
Guyscliff Rd. SE13 154 C5
Gwalior Rd. SW15 148 A3
*Felsham Rd.*
Gwendolen Av. SW15 148 A5
Gwendolen Cl. SW15 148 A5
Gwendoline Av. E13 115 H1
Gwendwr Rd. W14 128 B5
Gwillim Cl., Sid. 158 A5
Gwydor Rd., Beck. 189 G4
Gwydyr Rd., Brom. 191 F3
Gwyn Cl. SW6 129 F7
Gwynne Av., Croy. 189 G7
Gwynne Cl. W4 127 F6
Gwynne Pk. Av., 64 C6
Wdf.Grn.
**Gwynne Pl. WC1 10 D4**
Gwynne Rd. SW11 149 G2
Gylcote Cl. SE5 152 A4
Gyles Pk., Stan. 69 F1
Gyllyngdune Gdns., 99 J2
Ilf.

## H

Ha-Ha Rd. SE18 136 C6
Haarlem Rd. W14 128 A3
**Haberdasher Pl. N1 12 C3**
**Haberdasher St. N1 12 C3**
Haberdasher St. N1 112 A3
Habgood Rd., Loug. 48 B3
Haccombe Rd. SW19 167 F6
*Haydons Rd.*
Hackbridge Grn., 200 A2
Wall.
Hackbridge Pk. 200 A2
Gdns., Cars.
Hackbridge Rd., Wall. 200 A2
Hackford Rd. SW9 151 F1
Hackforth Cl., Barn. 39 H5
Hackington Cres., 172 A6
Beck.
Hackney Cl., Borwd. 38 D5
Hackney Gro. E8 94/95 E6
*Reading La.*
**Hackney Rd. E2 13 F4**
Hackney Rd. E2 112 C3
Hadden Rd. SE28 137 H3
Hadden Way, Grnf. 86 A6
Haddington Rd., 172 D3
Brom.
Haddo St. SE10 134 B6
Haddon Cl., Borwd. 38 A3
Haddon Cl., Enf. 44 D6
Haddon Cl., N.Mal. 183 F5
Haddon Gro., Sid. 158 A7
Haddon Rd., Sutt. 198 E4
Haddonfield SE8 133 G4
Hadfield Cl., Sthl. 103 F3
*Adrienne Av.*
Hadfield Rd., Stai. 140 A6
Hadleigh Cl. E1 113 F4
*Mantus Rd.*
Hadleigh Cl. SW20 184 C2
Hadleigh Rd. N9 44 E7
Hadleigh St. E2 113 F4
Hadleigh Wk. E6 116 B6
Hadley Cl. N21 43 G6
Hadley Common, 40 D2
Barn.
Hadley Gdns. W4 126 D5
Hadley Gdns., Sthl. 123 F5
Hadley Grn., Barn. 40 C2
Hadley Grn. Rd., 40 C2
Barn.
Hadley Grn. W., Barn. 40 C2
Hadley Gro., Barn. 40 B2
Hadley Highstone, 40 C1
Barn.
Hadley Ridge, Barn. 40 C3
Hadley Rd. (New 41 E4
Barnet), Barn.
Hadley Rd., Belv. 139 F4
Hadley Rd., Mitch. 186 D4
Hadley St. NW1 92 B6
Hadley Way N21 43 G6

Hadlow Pl. SE19 170 D7
Hadlow Rd., Sid. 176 A4
Hadlow Rd., Well. 138 C7
Hadrian Cl., Wall. 201 E7
**Hadrian Est. E2 13 J2**
Hadrian Est. E2 112 D2
Hadrian St. SE10 134 E5
Hadrian Way, Stai. 140 B7
Hadyn Pk. Rd. W12 127 G2
Hafer Rd. SW11 149 J4
Hafton Rd. SE6 173 E1
Haggard Rd., Twick. 144 E7
Haggerston Rd. E8 94 C7
**Hague St. E2 13 J4**
Haig Pl., Mord. 184 D6
*Green La.*
Haig Rd., Stan. 53 F5
Haig Rd. E. E13 115 J3
Haig Rd. W. E13 115 J3
Haigville Gdns., Ilf. 81 E4
Hailes Cl. SW19 167 F6
*North Rd.*
Hailey Rd., Erith 139 G2
Haileybury Av., Enf. 44 C6
Hailsham Av. SW2 169 F2
Hailsham Cl., Surb. 181 G7
Hailsham Dr., Har. 68 A3
Hailsham Rd. SW17 168 A6
Hailsham Ter. N18 59 J5
Haimo Rd. SE9 156 A5
Hainault Ct. E17 78 D4
Hainault Gore, Rom. 83 E5
Hainault Gro., Chig. 65 F4
Hainault Rd. E11 96 C1
Hainault Rd., Chig. 65 E3
Hainault Rd., Rom. 83 J2
Hainault Rd. 83 F6
(Chadwell Heath), Rom.
Hainault Rd. 82 B3
(Hainault), Rom.
Hainault St. SE9 175 E1
Hainault St., Ilf. 99 E2
Haines Wk., Mord. 184/185 E7
*Dorchester Rd.*
Hainford Cl. SE4 153 G4
Haining Cl. W4 126 A5
*Wellesley Rd.*
Hainthorpe Rd. SE27 169 H3
Hainton Cl. E1 113 E6
Halberd Ms. E5 94/95 E2
*Knightland Rd.*
Halbutt Gdns., Dag. 101 F3
Halbutt St., Dag. 101 F4
Halcomb St. N1 112 B1
Halcot Av., Bexh. 159 H5
Halcrow St. E1 112/113 E5
*Newark St.*
Halcyon Cl., Wem. 88 B3
*Coffers Circle*
Haldan Rd. E4 62 C6
Haldane Cl. N10 58 B7
Haldane Pl. SW18 166 E1
Haldane Rd. E6 116 A3
Haldane Rd. SE28 118 D7
Haldane Rd. SW6 128 C7
Haldane Rd., Sthl. 103 J6
Haldon Cl., Chig. 65 H5
*Arrowsmith Rd.*
Haldon Rd. SW18 148 C5
Hale, The E4 62 D7
Hale, The N17 76 D4
Hale Cl. E4 62 C3
Hale Cl., Edg. 54 C5
Hale Cl., Orp. 207 F4
Hale Dr. NW7 54 C6
Hale End Cl., Ruis. 66 A6
Hale End Rd. E4 62 D6
Hale End Rd. E17 78 D1
Hale End Rd., 62 D7
Wdf.Grn.
Hale Gdns. N17 76 D3
Hale Gdns. W3 126 A1
Hale Gro. Gdns. NW7 54 D5
Hale La. NW7 54 D5
Hale La., Edg. 54 B5
Hale Path SE27 169 H4
Hale Rd. E6 116 B4
Hale Rd. N17 76 D3
Hale St. E14 114 B7
Hale Wk. W7 104 B5
Halefield Rd. N17 76 D1
Hales St. SE8 134 A7
*Deptford High St.*
Halesowen Rd., 184 E7
Mord.
Halesworth Cl. E5 95 F2
*Theydon Rd.*
Halesworth Rd. SE13 154 B3
Haley Rd. NW4 71 J6
Half Acre, Brent. 125 G6
Half Acre Rd. W7 124 B1
**Half Moon Ct. EC1 19 J2**
**Half Moon Cres. N1 10 D1**

Half Moon Cres. N1 111 F2
Half Moon La. SE24 151 J6
**Half Moon Pas. E1 21 G4**
**Half Moon St. W1 24 E1**
Half Moon St. W1 130 B1
Halford Cl., Edg. 70 B2
Halford Rd. E10 78 D5
Halford Rd. SW6 128 D6
Halford Rd., Rich. 145 H5
Halfway St., Sid. 157 G7
Haliburton Rd., Twick. 144 D5
Haliday Wk. N1 94 A6
*Balls Pond Rd.*
Halidon Cl. E9 95 F5
*Urswick Rd.*
Halifax Rd., Enf. 43 J2
Halifax Rd., Grnf. 103 H1
Halifax St. SE26 171 E4
Halifield Dr., Belv. 138 E3
Haling Gro., S.Croy. 201 J7
Haling Pk., S.Croy. 201 J6
Haling Pk. Gdns., 201 H6
S.Croy.
Haling Pk. Rd., 201 H5
S.Croy.
Haling Rd., S.Croy. 202 A6
**Halkin Arc. SW1 24 B5**
Halkin Arc. SW1 130 A3
**Halkin Ms. SW1 24 B5**
**Halkin Pl. SW1 24 B5**
Halkin Pl. SW1 130 A3
**Halkin St. SW1 24 C4**
Halkin St. SW1 130 A2
Hall, The SE3 155 G3
Hall Av. N18 60 A6
*Weir Hall Av.*
Hall Cl. W5 105 H5
Hall Ct., Tedd. 162 C5
*Teddington Pk.*
Hall Dr. SE26 171 F5
Hall Dr. W7 104 B6
Hall Fm. Cl., Stan. 52 E4
Hall Fm. Dr., Twick. 144 A7
Hall Gdns. E4 61 J4
**Hall Gate NW8 6 D3**
Hall La. E4 61 H5
Hall La. NW4 71 G1
Hall La., Hayes 121 G7
*Maygrove Rd.*
**Hall Pl. W2 7 E6**
Hall Pl. W2 109 G4
Hall Pl. Cres., Bex. 159 J5
Hall Rd. E6 116 C1
Hall Rd. E15 96 D4
**Hall Rd. NW8 6 D4**
Hall Rd. NW8 109 F3
Hall Rd., Islw. 144 A5
Hall Rd., Rom. 82 C6
**Hall St. EC1 11 H3**
Hall St. EC1 111 H3
Hall St. N12 57 F5
Hall Vw. SE9 174 A2
Hallam Cl., Chis. 174 C5
Hallam Gdns., Pnr. 51 E7
**Hallam Ms. W1 16 E1**
Hallam Rd. N15 75 H4
Hallam Rd. SW13 147 H3
**Hallam St. W1 8 E6**
Hallam St. W1 110 B5
Halley Gdns. SE13 154 D4
Halley Rd. E7 97 J6
Halley Rd. E12 98 A6
Halley St. E14 113 H5
**Hallfield Est. W2 14 C4**
Hallfield Est. W2 109 F6
Halliards, The, Walt. 178 A6
*Felix Rd.*
Halliday Sq., Sthl. 124 A1
Halliford St. N1 93 J7
Hallingbury Ct. E17 78 B3
Halliwell Rd. SW2 151 F6
Halliwick Rd. N10 74 A1
Hallmark Trd. Est. 88 C4
NW10
*Great Cen. Way*
Hallmead Rd., Sutt. 198 E3
Hallowell Av., Croy. 200 E4
Hallowell Cl., Mitch. 186 A3
Hallowes Cres., Wat. 50 A3
*Hayling Rd.*
Hallowfield Way, 185 H3
Mitch.
Hallsville Rd. E16 115 F6
Hallswelle Rd. NW11 72 C5
Hallywell Cres. E6 116 C5
Halons Rd. SE9 156 D7
**Halpin Pl. SE17 36 C2**
Halsbrook Rd. SE3 156 A3
Halsbury Cl., Stan. 52 E4
Halsbury Rd. W12 127 H1
Halsbury Rd. E., Nthlt. 85 J4
Halsbury Rd. W., 85 H5
Nthlt.

Halsend, Hayes 122 B1
**Halsey Ms. SW3 31 J1**
**Halsey St. SW3 31 J1**
Halsey St. SW3 129 J4
Halsham Cres., Bark. 99 J6
Halsmere Rd. SE5 151 H1
Halstead Cl., Croy. 201 J3
*Charles St.*
**Halstead Ct. N1 12 C2**
Halstead Gdns. N21 60 A1
Halstead Rd. E11 79 G5
Halstead Rd. N21 59 J1
Halstead Rd., Enf. 44 B4
Halston Cl. SW11 149 J6
Halstow Rd. NW10 108 A3
Halstow Rd. SE10 135 G5
Halsway, Hayes 122 A1
Halt Robin La., Belv. 139 H4
*Halt Robin Rd.*
Halt Robin Rd., Belv. 139 G4
Halter Cl., Borwd. 38 D5
*Clydesdale Cl.*
Halton Cross St. N1 111 H1
Halton Pl. N1 111 J1
*Dibden St.*
Halton Rd. N1 93 H7
Ham, The, Brent. 125 F7
Ham Cl., Rich. 163 F3
Ham Common, Rich. 163 J4
Ham Fm. Rd., Rich. 163 G4
Ham Gate Av., Rich. 163 G3
Ham Pk. Rd. E7 97 F7
Ham Pk. Rd. E15 97 F7
Ham Ridings, Rich. 163 J5
Ham St., Rich. 163 F2
Ham Vw., Croy. 189 H6
**Ham Yd. W1 17 H5**
Hambalt Rd. SW4 150 C5
Hamble Cl., Kings.T. 163 G7
Hamble St. SW6 149 E3
Hamble Wk., Nthlt. 103 G2
*Brabazon Rd.*
Hambledon Gdns. 188 C3
SE25
Hambledon Pl. SE21 170 B1
Hambledon Rd. SW18 148 C7
Hambledown Rd., 157 G7
Sid.
Hambleton Cl., 197 J2
Wor.Pk.
*Cotswold Way*
Hambridge Way SW2 151 G7
Hambro Av., Brom. 205 G1
Hambro Rd. SW16 168 D6
Hambrook Rd. SE25 188 E3
Hambrough Rd., Sthl. 122 E1
Hamden Cres., Dag. 101 H3
Hamel Cl., Har. 69 G3
Hamelin St. E14 114 C6
*St. Leonards Rd.*
Hameway E6 116 D4
Hamfrith Rd. E15 97 F6
Hamilton Av. N9 44 D7
Hamilton Av., Ilf. 81 E4
Hamilton Av., Surb. 196 B1
Hamilton Av., Sutt. 198 B2
Hamilton Cl. N17 76 C3
**Hamilton Cl. NW8 6 E4**
Hamilton Cl. NW8 109 G3
Hamilton Cl. SE16 133 H2
*Somerford Way*
Hamilton Cl., Barn. 41 H4
Hamilton Cl., Stan. 52 C2
Hamilton Cl. W5 105 J7
**Hamilton Ct. W9 6 C3**
Hamilton Cres. N13 59 G4
Hamilton Cres., Har. 85 F3
Hamilton Cres., 143 H5
Houns.
**Hamilton Gdns. NW8 6 D3**
Hamilton Gdns. NW8 109 F3
Hamilton La. N5 93 H4
*Hamilton Pk.*
**Hamilton Ms. W1 24 D3**
Hamilton Pk. N5 93 H4
Hamilton Pk. W. N5 93 H4
*Wedmore St.*
**Hamilton Pl. W1 24 C2**
Hamilton Pl. W1 130 A1
Hamilton Pl., Sun. 160 B7
Hamilton Rd. E15 115 E3
Hamilton Rd. E17 77 H2
Hamilton Rd. N2 73 F3
Hamilton Rd. N9 44 D7
Hamilton Rd. NW10 89 G5
Hamilton Rd. NW11 72 A7
Hamilton Rd. SE27 170 H4
Hamilton Rd. SW19 167 E7
Hamilton Rd. W4 126 E2
Hamilton Rd. W5 105 H7
Hamilton Rd., Barn. 41 H4
Hamilton Rd., Bexh. 159 E2
Hamilton Rd., Brent. 125 G6

Harecastle Cl., Hayes 102/103 E4
*Braunston Dr.*
Harecourt Rd. N1 93 J6
Haredale Rd. SE24 151 J4
Haredon Cl. SE23 153 F7
Harefield, Esher 194 B4
Harefield Cl., Enf. 43 G1
Harefield Ms. SE4 153 J3
Harefield Rd. N8 74 D5
Harefield Rd. SE4 153 J3
Harefield Rd. SW16 169 F7
Harefield Rd., Sid. 176 D2
Haresfield Rd., Dag. 101 G6
**Harewood Av. NW1 7 H6**
Harewood Av. NW1 109 H4
Harewood Av., Nthlt. 85 E7
Harewood Cl., Nthlt. 85 F7
Harewood Dr., Ilf. 80 C2
**Harewood Pl. W1 16 E4**
Harewood Rd. SW19 167 H6
Harewood Rd., Islw. 124 C7
Harewood Rd., S.Croy. 202 B6
Harewood Rd., Wat. 50 B3
**Harewood Row NW1 15 H1**
Harewood Ter., Sthl. 123 F4
Harfield Gdns. SE5 152 B3
Harfield Rd., Sun. 178 D2
Harford Cl. E4 46 B7
Harford Rd. E4 46 B7
Harford St. E1 113 H4
Harford Wk. N2 73 G5
Hargood Cl., Har. 69 H6
Hargood Rd. SE3 155 J1
Hargrave Pk. N19 92 C2
Hargrave Pl. N7 92 D5
*Brecknock Rd.*
Hargrave Rd. N19 92 C2
Hargwyne St. SW9 151 F3
Haringey Pk. N8 75 E6
Haringey Pas. N4 75 H6
Haringey Pas. N8 75 G4
Haringey Rd. N8 74 E4
Harington Ter. N9 60 A3
Harington Ter. N18 60 A3
Harkett Cl., Har. 68 C2
*Byron Rd.*
Harkett Ct., Har. 68 C2
Harland Av., Croy. 202 C3
Harland Av., Sid. 175 G3
Harland Cl. SW19 184 E3
Harland Rd. SE12 173 G1
Harlands Gro., Orp. 206/207 E4
*Pinecrest Gdns.*
Harlech Gdns., Houns. 122 C6
Harlech Gdns., Pnr. 66 D7
Harlech Rd. N14 59 E3
Harlech Twr. W3 126 B2
Harlequin Av., Brent. 124 D6
Harlequin Cl., Hayes 102 D5
*Cygnet Way*
Harlequin Cl., Islw. 144 B5
Harlequin Ho., Erith 138/139 E3
*Kale Rd.*
Harlequin Rd., Tedd. 162 E7
Harlescott Rd. SE15 153 G4
Harlesden Gdns. NW10 107 F1
Harlesden La. NW10 107 G1
Harlesden Rd. NW10 107 G1
Harleston Cl. E5 95 F2
*Theydon Rd.*
Harley Cl., Wem. 87 G6
Harley Ct. E11 79 G7
*Blake Hall Rd.*
Harley Cres., Har. 68 A4
**Harley Gdns. SW10 30 D4**
Harley Gdns. SW10 129 F5
Harley Gdns., Orp. 207 H4
Harley Gro. E3 113 J3
**Harley Pl. W1 16 D2**
Harley Pl. W1 110 B5
Harley Rd. NW3 91 G7
Harley Rd. NW10 106 E2
Harley Rd., Har. 68 A4
**Harley St. W1 16 D2**
Harley St. W1 110 B4
Harleyford, Brom. 191 H1
**Harleyford Rd. SE11 34 C5**
Harleyford Rd. SE11 131 F6
**Harleyford St. SE11 34 E6**
Harleyford St. SE11 131 G6
Harlinger St. SE18 136 B3
Harlington Cl., Hayes 121 F7
*New Rd.*
Harlington Rd., Bexh. 159 E3
Harlington Rd., Houns. 141 J4
Harlington Rd. E., Felt. 142 B7
Harlington Rd. W., Felt 142 B6
Harlow Rd. N13 60 A3
Harlyn Dr., Pnr. 66 B3
Harman Av., Wdf.Grn. 63 F7
Harman Cl. E4 62 D4
Harman Cl. NW2 90 B3
Harman Dr. NW2 90 B3
Harman Dr., Sid. 157 J6
Harman Rd., Enf. 44 C5
Harmondsworth La., West Dr. 120 B6
Harmondsworth Rd., West Dr. 120 B5
Harmony Cl. NW11 72 B5
Harmony Way NW4 71 J4
*Victoria Rd.*
Harmood Gro. NW1 92 B7
*Clarence Way*
Harmood Pl. NW1 92 B7
*Harmood St.*
Harmood St. NW1 92 B7
**Harmsworth Ms. SE11 27 G6**
**Harmsworth St. SE17 35 G4**
Harmsworth St. SE17 131 H5
Harmsworth Way N20 56 C1
Harness Rd. SE28 138 A2
Harold Av., Belv. 139 F5
Harold Av., Hayes 121 J3
**Harold Est. SE1 28 E6**
Harold Est. SE1 132 B3
Harold Gibbons Ct. SE7 135 J6
*Victoria Way*
**Harold Pl. SE11 34 E4**
Harold Pl. SE11 131 G5
Harold Rd. E4 62 C4
Harold Rd. E11 96 E1
Harold Rd. E13 115 H1
Harold Rd. N8 75 F5
Harold Rd. N15 76 C5
Harold Rd. NW10 106 D3
Harold Rd. SE19 170 A7
Harold Rd., Sutt. 199 G4
Harold Rd., Wdf.Grn. 79 G1
Haroldstone Rd. E17 77 G5
**Harp All. EC4 19 G3**
Harp Island Cl. NW10 88 D2
**Harp La. EC3 20 D6**
Harp Rd. W7 104 C4
Harpenden Rd. E12 97 J2
Harpenden Rd. SE27 169 H3
Harper Cl. N14 42 C5
*Alexandra Ct.*
Harper Rd. E6 116 C6
**Harper Rd. SE1 27 J5**
Harper Rd. SE1 131 J3
Harpers Yd. N17 76 C1
*Ruskin Rd.*
Harpley Sq. E1 113 F3
Harpour Rd., Bark. 99 F6
Harpsden St. SW11 150 A1
**Harpur Ms. WC1 18 C1**
**Harpur St. WC1 18 C1**
Harpur St. WC1 111 F5
Harraden Rd. SE3 155 J1
Harrap St. E14 114 C7
Harrier Av. E11 79 H6
*Eastern Av.*
Harrier Ms. SE28 137 G3
Harrier Rd. NW9 71 E2
Harrier Way E6 116 C5
Harriers Cl. W5 105 H7
Harries Rd., Hayes 102 C4
Harriet Cl. E8 112 D1
Harriet Gdns., Croy. 202 D2
**Harriet St. SW1 24 A4**
Harriet Tubman Cl. SW2 151 G7
**Harriet Wk. SW1 24 A4**
Harriet Wk. SW1 129 J2
Harringay Gdns. N8 75 H4
Harringay Rd. N15 75 H5
Harrington Cl. NW10 88 D3
Harrington Cl., Croy. 200 E2
Harrington Ct. W10 108 C3
*Dart St.*
**Harrington Gdns. SW7 30 B2**
Harrington Gdns. SW7 129 E4
Harrington Hill E5 95 E1
Harrington Rd. E11 97 E1
Harrington Rd. SE25 188 E4
**Harrington Rd. SW7 30 E1**
Harrington Rd. SW7 129 G4
**Harrington Sq. NW1 9 F2**
Harrington Sq. NW1 110 C2
**Harrington St. NW1 9 F3**
Harrington St. NW1 110 C3
Harrington Way SE18 136 A3
Harriott Cl. SE10 135 F4
Harris Cl., Enf. 43 H1
Harris Cl., Houns. 143 G1
Harris Rd., Bexh. 159 E1
Harris Rd., Dag. 101 F5
Harris St. E17 77 J7
Harris St. SE5 132 A7
Harrison Cl. N20 57 H1
Harrison Rd., Dag. 101 H6
**Harrison St. WC1 10 B4**
Harrison St. WC1 111 E3
Harrisons Ri., Croy. 201 H3
Harrogate Rd., Wat. 50 C3
Harrold Rd., Dag. 100 B5
Harrow Av., Enf. 44 C6
Harrow Cl., Chess. 195 G7
Harrow Dr. N9 60 C1
Harrow Flds. Gdns., Har. 86 B3
Harrow Grn. E11 96/97 E3
*Harrow Rd.*
Harrow La. E14 114 C7
Harrow Manorway SE2 138 C1
Harrow Pk., Har. 86 B2
Harrow Pas., Kings.T. 181 G2
*Market Pl.*
**Harrow Pl. E1 21 E3**
Harrow Pl. E1 112 B6
Harrow Rd. E6 116 B1
Harrow Rd. E11 97 E3
Harrow Rd. NW10 107 H3
**Harrow Rd. W2 14 A2**
Harrow Rd. W2 108 C4
Harrow Rd. W9 108 C4
Harrow Rd. W10 108 A4
Harrow Rd., Bark. 117 H1
Harrow Rd., Cars. 199 H5
Harrow Rd., Ilf. 99 F4
Harrow Rd., Wem. 87 F5
Harrow Rd. (Tokyngton), Wem. 88 B6
Harrow Vw., Har. 68 A4
Harrow Vw., Hayes 102 A6
Harrow Vw. Rd. W5 105 E4
Harrow Way, Wat. 50 E3
Harrow Weald Pk., Har. 52 A6
Harroway Rd. SW11 149 G2
**Harrowby St. W1 15 H3**
Harrowby St. W1 109 H6
Harrowdene Cl., Wem. 87 G4
Harrowdene Gdns., Tedd. 162 D6
Harrowdene Rd., Wem. 87 G3
Harrowes Meade, Edg. 54 A3
Harrowgate Rd. E9 95 H6
Hart Cres., Chig. 65 J5
Hart Gro. W5 126 A1
Hart Gro., Sthl. 103 G5
**Hart St. EC3 20 E5**
Harte Rd., Houns. 143 F2
Hartfield Av., Borwd. 38 A5
Hartfield Av., Nthlt. 102 B2
Hartfield Cl., Borwd. 38 A5
Hartfield Cres. SW19 166 C7
Hartfield Cres., W.Wick. 205 G3
Hartfield Gro. SE20 189 E1
Hartfield Rd. SW19 166 C7
Hartfield Rd., Chess. 195 G5
Hartfield Rd., W.Wick. 205 G4
Hartfield Ter. E3 114 A2
Hartford Av., Har. 68 D3
Hartford Rd., Bex. 159 G6
Hartford Rd., Epsom 196 A6
Hartforde Rd., Borwd. 38 A2
Hartham Cl. N7 93 E5
Hartham Cl., Islw. 144 D1
Hartham Rd. N7 92 E5
Hartham Rd. N17 76 C2
Hartham Rd., Islw. 144 C1
Harting Rd. SE9 174 B4
Hartington Cl., Har. 86 B4
Hartington Ct. W4 126 B7
Hartington Rd. E16 115 H6
Hartington Rd. E17 77 H6
Hartington Rd. SW8 150 E1
Hartington Rd. W4 126 B7
Hartington Rd. W13 105 E7
Hartington Rd., Sthl. 122 E2
Hartington Rd., Twick. 144 E7
Hartismere Rd. SW6 128 C7
Hartlake Rd. E9 95 G6
Hartland Cl. N21 43 J6
*Elmscott Gdns.*
Hartland Cl., Edg. 54 A2
Hartland Dr., Edg. 54 A2
Hartland Dr., Ruis. 84 B3
Hartland Rd. E15 97 F7
Hartland Rd. N11 57 J5
Hartland Rd. NW1 92 B7
Hartland Rd. NW6 108 C2
Hartland Rd., Hmptn. 161 H4
Hartland Rd., Islw. 144 D3
Hartland Rd., Mord. 184 D7
Hartland Way, Croy. 203 H2
Hartland Way, Mord. 184 C7
Hartlands Cl., Bex. 159 F6
Hartlepool Ct. E16 136/137 E2
*Barge Ho. Rd.*
Hartley Av. E6 116 B1
Hartley Av. NW7 55 F5
Hartley Cl. NW7 55 F5
Hartley Cl., Brom. 192 C2
Hartley Rd. E11 97 F1
Hartley Rd., Croy. 187 H7
Hartley Rd., Well. 138 C7
Hartley St. E2 113 F3
Hartmann Rd. E16 136 A1
Hartnoll St. N7 93 F5
*Eden Gro.*
Harton Cl., Brom. 192 A1
Harton Rd. N9 61 E2
Harton St. SE8 154 A1
Harts Gro., Wdf.Grn. 63 G5
Harts La. SE14 133 H7
Harts La., Bark. 98 E6
Hartsbourne Av., Bushey 51 J2
Hartsbourne Cl., Bushey 52 A2
Hartsbourne Rd., Bushey 52 A2
**Hartshorn All. EC3 21 E4**
Hartshorn Gdns. E6 116 D4
Hartslock Dr. SE2 138 D2
Hartsmead Rd. SE9 174 C2
Hartsway, Enf. 45 F4
Hartswood Gdns. W12 127 F3
Hartswood Grn., Bushey 52 A2
Hartswood Rd. W12 127 F2
Hartsworth Cl. E13 115 F2
Hartville Rd. SE18 137 H4
Hartwell Dr. E4 62 C6
Hartwell St. E8 94 C6
*Dalston La.*
Harvard Hill W4 126 B6
Harvard La. W4 126 B5
Harvard Rd. SE13 154 C5
Harvard Rd. W4 126 B5
Harvard Rd., Islw. 144 B1
Harvel Cres. SE2 138 D5
Harvest Bank Rd., W.Wick. 205 F3
Harvest La., Loug. 47 J7
*Fallow Flds.*
Harvest La., T.Ditt. 180 D6
Harvest Rd., Felt. 160 A4
Harvesters Cl., Islw. 144 A5
Harvey Dr., Hmptn. 179 H1
Harvey Gdns. E11 97 F1
*Harvey Rd.*
Harvey Gdns. SE7 136 A4
Harvey Gdns., Loug. 49 E3
Harvey Ho., Brent. 125 H5
*Green Dragon La.*
Harvey Pt. E16 115 H5
*Fife Rd.*
Harvey Rd. E11 97 F1
Harvey Rd. N8 75 F5
Harvey Rd. SE5 152 A1
Harvey Rd., Houns. 143 F7
Harvey Rd., Ilf. 99 E5
Harvey Rd., Nthlt. 84 C7
Harvey Rd., Walt. 178 A7
Harvey St. N1 112 A1
Harvill Rd., Sid. 176 D5
Harvington Wk. E8 94 D7
*Wilman Gro.*
Harvist Est. N7 93 G4
Harvist Rd. NW6 108 A2
Harwater Dr., Loug. 48 C2
Harwell Pas. N2 73 J4
**Harwich La. EC2 20 E1**
Harwich La. EC2 112 B5
Harwood Av., Brom. 191 H2
Harwood Av., Mitch. 185 H3
Harwood Cl. N12 57 H6
*Summerfields Av.*
Harwood Cl., Wem. 87 G4
*Harrowdene Rd.*
Harwood Rd. SW6 128 D7
Harwood Ter. SW6 148 E1
Harwoods Yd. N21 43 G7
*Wades Hill*
Hascombe Ter. SE5 152 A2
Haselbury Rd. N9 60 B4
Haselbury Rd. N18 60 B4
Haseley End SE23 153 F7
*Tyson Rd.*
Haselrigge Rd. SW4 150 D4
Haseltine Rd. SE26 171 J4
Haselwood Dr., Enf. 43 H4
Haskard Rd., Dag. 100 D4
Haskell Ho. NW10 106 D1
**Hasker St. SW3 31 H1**
Hasker St. SW3 129 H4

Hayfield Pas. E1 113 F4
*Stepney Grn.*
Hayfield Yd. E1 113 F4
*Mile End Rd.*
Haygarth Pl. SW19 166 A5
Haygreen Cl., Kings.T. 164 B6
Hayland Cl. NW9 70 D4
**Hayles St. SE11 35 G1**
Hayles St. SE11 131 H4
Haylett Gdns., Kings.T. 181 G4
*Anglesea Rd.*
Hayling Av., Felt. 160 A3
Hayling Cl. N16 94 B5
*Pellerin Rd.*
Hayling Rd., Wat. 50 B2
Hayman St. N1 93 H7
*Cross St.*
**Haymarket SW1 17 H6**
Haymarket SW1 110 D7
**Haymarket Arc. SW1 17 H6**
Haymer Gdns., Wor.Pk. 197 G3
**Haymerle Rd. SE15 37 H6**
Haymerle Rd. SE15 132 D6
Haymill Cl., Grnf. 104 C3
Hayne Rd., Beck. 189 J2
**Hayne St. EC1 19 H1**
Haynes Cl. N11 58 A3
Haynes Cl. N17 60 E7
Haynes Cl. SE3 155 E3
Haynes La. SE19 170 B6
Haynes Rd., Wem. 87 H7
Haynt Wk. SW20 184 B3
**Hay's La. SE1 28 D2**
**Hay's Ms. W1 16 D6**
Hay's Ms. W1 110 B7
Haysleigh Gdns. SE20 188 D2
Hayter Rd. SW2 151 E5
Hayton Cl. E8 94 C6
*Buttermere Wk.*
Hayward Cl. SW19 185 E1
Hayward Gdns. SW15 147 J6
Hayward Rd. N20 57 F2
Hayward Rd., T.Ditt. 194 D1
Haywards Cl., Rom. 82 B5
**Hayward's Pl. EC1 11 G5**
Haywood Cl., Pnr. 66 D2
Haywood Ri., Orp. 207 H4
Haywood Rd., Brom. 192 A4
Hayworth Cl., Enf. 45 H2
*Green St.*
Hazel Av., West Dr. 120 D3
Hazel Cl. N13 60 A3
Hazel Cl. N19 92 C2
*Hargrave Pk.*
Hazel Cl. SE15 152 D2
Hazel Cl., Brent. 125 E7
Hazel Cl., Croy. 189 G7
Hazel Cl., Mitch. 186 D4
Hazel Cl., Twick. 143 J7
Hazel Gdns., Edg. 54 B4
Hazel Gro. SE26 171 G4
Hazel Gro., Enf. 44 D6
*Dimsdale Dr.*
Hazel Gro., Orp. 206 E2
Hazel Gro., Rom. 82 E3
Hazel Gro., Wem. 105 H1
*Carlyon Rd.*
Hazel Gro. Est. SE26 171 G4
Hazel La., Rich. 163 H2
Hazel Mead, Barn. 39 H5
Hazel Rd. E15 96/97 E5
*Wingfield Rd.*
Hazel Rd. NW10 107 J3
Hazel Wk., Brom. 192 D6
Hazel Way E4 61 J6
**Hazel Way SE1 37 F1**
Hazelbank, Surb. 196 C1
Hazelbank Rd. SE6 172 D2
Hazelbourne Rd. SW12 150 B6
Hazelbrouck Gdns., Ilf. 65 G7
Hazelbury Cl. SW19 184 D2
Hazelbury Grn. N9 60 B3
Hazelbury La. N9 60 B3
Hazelcroft, Pnr. 51 G6
Hazeldean Rd. NW10 88 D7
Hazeldene Dr., Pnr. 66 C3
Hazeldene Rd., Ilf. 100 B2
Hazeldene Rd., Well. 158 C2
Hazeldon Rd. SE4 153 H5
Hazeleigh Gdns., Wdf.Grn. 64 B5
Hazelgreen Cl. N21 59 H1
Hazelhurst, Beck. 190 D1
Hazelhurst Rd. SW17 167 F4
Hazell Cres., Rom. 83 H1
Hazellville Rd. N19 74 D7
Hazelmere Cl., Felt. 141 G6
Hazelmere Cl., Nthlt. 103 F2
Hazelmere Dr., Nthlt. 103 F2
Hazelmere Rd. NW6 108 D1
Hazelmere Rd., Nthlt. 103 F2
Hazelmere Rd., Orp. 193 F4
Hazelmere Wk., Nthlt. 103 F2
Hazelmere Way, Brom. 191 G6
Hazeltree La., Nthlt. 103 E3
Hazelwood, Loug. 48 A5
Hazelwood Av., Mord. 185 E4
Hazelwood Cl. W5 125 H2
Hazelwood Cl., Har. 67 H4
Hazelwood Ct. NW10 88/89 E3
*Neasden La. N.*
Hazelwood Cres. N13 59 G4
Hazelwood Cft., Surb. 181 H6
Hazelwood Dr., Pnr. 66 B2
Hazelwood La. N13 59 G4
Hazelwood Pk. Cl., Chig. 65 H5
Hazelwood Rd. E17 77 H5
Hazelwood Rd., Enf. 44 C6
Hazlebury Rd. SW6 149 E2
Hazledean Rd., Croy. 202 A2
Hazledene Rd. W4 126 C6
Hazlemere Gdns., Wor.Pk. 197 H1
Hazlewell Rd. SW15 147 J5
Hazlewood Cl. E5 95 H3
*Mandeville St.*
Hazlewood Cres. W10 108 B4
Hazlitt Ms. W14 128 B3
*Hazlitt Rd.*
Hazlitt Rd. W14 128 B3
Head St. E1 113 G6
Headcorn Pl., Th.Hth. 187 F4
*Headcorn Rd.*
Headcorn Rd. N17 60 C7
Headcorn Rd., Brom. 173 F5
Headcorn Rd., Th.Hth. 187 F4
**Headfort Pl. SW1 24 C4**
Headfort Pl. SW1 130 A2
Headingley Cl., Ilf. 65 J6
Headington Rd. SW18 167 F2
Headlam Rd. SW4 150 D6
Headlam St. E1 113 E4
Headley App., Ilf. 80 D5
Headley Av., Wall. 201 F5
Headley Cl., Epsom 196 A6
Headley Ct. SE26 171 E5
Headley Dr., Croy. 204 B7
Headley Dr., Ilf. 80 E6
Head's Ms. W11 108 D6
*Artesian Rd.*
Headstone Dr., Har. 68 B3
Headstone Gdns., Har. 67 J4
Headstone La., Har. 67 H4
Headstone Rd., Har. 68 B5
Headway Cl., Rich. 163 F4
*Locksmeade Rd.*
Heald St. SE14 153 J1
Healey Dr., Orp. 207 J4
Healey St. NW1 92 B6
Heanor Ct. E5 95 G3
*Pedro St.*
Hearn Ri., Nthlt. 102 D1
**Hearn St. EC2 12 E6**
Hearn St. EC2 112 B4
Hearne Rd. W4 126 A6
**Hearn's Bldgs. SE17 36 C2**
Hearnville Rd. SW12 168 A1
Heath, The W7 124 B1
*Lower Boston Rd.*
Heath Av., Bexh. 138 D6
Heath Brow NW3 91 F3
*North End Way*
Heath Cl. NW11 72 E7
Heath Cl. W5 105 J4
Heath Cl., Hayes 121 G7
Heath Ct., Houns. 143 F4
Heath Dr. NW3 90 E4
Heath Dr. SW20 183 J4
Heath Gdns., Twick. 162 C1
Heath Gro. SE20 171 F7
*Maple Rd.*
Heath Hurst Rd. NW3 91 H4
Heath La. SE3 154 D2
Heath Mead SW19 166 A3
Heath Pk. Dr., Brom. 192 B3
Heath Pas. NW3 91 E2
Heath Ri. SW15 148 A6
Heath Ri., Brom. 191 F6
Heath Rd. SW8 150 B2
Heath Rd., Bex. 177 J1
Heath Rd., Har. 67 J7
Heath Rd., Houns. 143 H4
Heath Rd., Rom. 82 D7
Heath Rd., Th.Hth. 187 J3
Heath Rd., Twick. 162 C1
Heath Side NW3 91 G4
Heath Side, Orp. 207 F1
Heath St. NW3 91 F4
Heath Vw. N2 73 F4
Heath Vw. Cl. N2 73 F4
Heath Vil. SE18 137 J5
Heath Vil. SW18 167 F1
*Cargill Rd.*
Heath Way, Erith 159 J1
Heatham Pk., Twick. 144 C7
Heathbourne Rd., Bushey 52 B2
Heathbourne Rd., Stan. 52 B2
Heathcock Ct. WC2 110/111 E7
*Strand*
Heathcote Av., Ilf. 80 C2
Heathcote Gro. E4 62 C3
Heathcote Rd., Twick. 145 E6
**Heathcote St. WC1 10 C5**
Heathcote St. WC1 111 F4
Heathcote Way, West Dr. 120 A1
*Tavistock Rd.*
Heathcroft NW11 91 E1
Heathcroft W5 105 J4
Heathcroft Gdns. E17 78 D1
*Hale End Rd.*
Heathdale Av., Houns. 143 E3
Heathdene Dr., Belv. 139 H4
Heathdene Rd. SW16 169 F7
Heathdene Rd., Wall. 200 B7
Heathedge SE26 170 E2
Heather Cl. E6 116 E6
Heather Cl. SE13 154 D7
Heather Cl. SW8 150 B3
Heather Cl., Hmptn. 179 F1
Heather Cl., Islw. 144 A5
*Harvesters Cl.*
Heather Dr., Enf. 43 H2
*Chasewood Av.*
Heather Gdns. NW11 72 B6
Heather Gdns., Sutt. 198 D6
Heather Pk. Dr., Wem. 88 A7
Heather Rd. E4 61 J6
Heather Rd. NW2 89 F2
Heather Rd. SE12 173 G2
Heather Wk. W10 108 B4
*Droop St.*
Heather Wk., Edg. 54 B5
Heather Wk., Twick. 143 G7
*Stephenson Rd.*
Heather Way, Stan. 52 C6
Heatherbank SE9 156 C2
Heatherbank, Chis. 192 D2
Heatherdale Cl., Kings.T. 164 A6
Heatherdene Cl. N12 73 F1
*Bow La.*
Heatherdene Cl., Mitch. 185 H4
Heatherlands, Sun. 160 A6
Heatherley Dr., Ilf. 80 B3
Heathers, The, Stai. 140 C7
Heatherset Gdns. SW16 169 F7
Heatherside Rd., Epsom 196 D7
Heatherside Rd., Sid. 176 D3
*Wren Rd.*
Heatherwood Cl. E12 97 J2
Heathfield E4 62 C3
Heathfield, Chis. 175 F6
Heathfield Av. SW18 149 G7
*Heathfield Rd.*
Heathfield Cl. E16 116 A5
Heathfield Cl., Kes. 205 J5
Heathfield Dr., Mitch. 185 H1
Heathfield Gdns. NW11 72 A6
Heathfield Gdns. SW18 149 G6
*Heathfield Rd.*
Heathfield Gdns. W4 126 C5
Heathfield Gdns., Croy. 202 A4
*Coombe Rd.*
Heathfield La., Chis. 175 E6
Heathfield N., Twick. 144 C7
Heathfield Pk. NW2 89 J6
Heathfield Pk. Dr., Rom. 82 B5
Heathfield Rd. SW18 149 F6
Heathfield Rd. W3 126 B2
Heathfield Rd., Bexh. 159 F4
Heathfield Rd., Brom. 173 F7
Heathfield Rd., Croy. 202 A4
Heathfield Rd., Kes. 205 J5
Heathfield S., Twick. 144 C7
Heathfield Sq. SW18 149 G7
Heathfield St. W11 108 B7
*Portland Rd.*
Heathfield Ter. SE18 137 J6
Heathfield Ter. W4 126 C5
Heathfields Ct., Houns. 142/143 E5
*Frampton Rd.*
Heathgate NW11 72 E6
Heathgate Pl. NW3 91 J5
*Agincourt Rd.*
Heathland Rd. N16 94 B1
Heathlands Cl., Sun. 178 A2
Heathlands Cl., Twick. 162 C2
Heathlands Way, Houns. 142/143 E5
*Frampton Rd.*
Heathlee Rd. SE3 155 F4
Heathley End, Chis. 175 F6
Heathmans Rd. SW6 148 C1
Heathrow Interchange, Hayes 122 C1
Heathrow Int. Trd. Est., Houns. 142 B3
Heathrow Tunnel App., Houns. 140 E3
Heathrow Vehicle Tunnel, Houns. 140 E1
Heaths Cl., Enf. 44 B2
Heathside, Esher 194 B3
Heathside, Houns. 143 F7
Heathside Av., Bexh. 159 E1
Heathside Cl., Esher 194 B3
Heathstan Rd. W12 107 G6
Heathview Ct. SW19 166 A2
Heathview Dr. SE2 138 D6
Heathview Gdns. SW15 147 J7
Heathview Rd., Th.Hth. 187 G4
Heathville Rd. N19 74 E7
Heathwall St. SW11 149 J3
Heathway SE3 135 F7
Heathway, Croy. 203 J3
Heathway, Dag. 101 G7
Heathway, Wdf.Grn. 63 J4
Heathway Ind. Est., Dag. 101 H4
*Manchester Way*
Heathwood Gdns. SE7 136 B4
Heaton Cl. E4 62 C3
*Friars Cl.*
Heaton Rd. SE15 152 D3
Heaton Rd., Mitch. 168 A7
Heaver Rd. SW11 149 G3
*Wye St.*
Heavitree Cl. SE18 137 G5
Heavitree Rd. SE18 137 G5
Hebden Ct. E2 112 C1
*Laburnum St.*
Hebden Ter. N17 60 B6
*Commercial Rd.*
Hebdon Rd. SW17 167 H3
Heber Rd. NW2 90 A5
Heber Rd. SE22 152 C6
Hebron Rd. W6 127 H3
Hecham Cl. E17 77 H2
Heckfield Pl. SW6 128 D7
*Fulham Rd.*
Heckford St. E1 113 G7
*The Highway*
Hector St. SE18 137 H4
Heddington Gro. N7 93 F5
Heddon Cl., Islw. 144 D4
Heddon Ct. Av., Barn. 41 J5
Heddon Rd., Barn. 41 J5
**Heddon St. W1 17 F5**
Heddon St. W1 110 C7
Hedge Hill, Enf. 43 H1
Hedge La. N13 59 H3
Hedge Wk. SE6 172 B4
Hedgeley, Ilf. 80 C4
Hedgemans Rd., Dag. 100 D7
Hedgemans Way, Dag. 100 E6
**Hedger St. SE11 35 G1**
Hedgerley Gdns., Grnf. 103 J2
Hedgers Cl., Loug. 48 D4
*Newmans La.*
Hedgers Gro. E9 95 H6
Hedgewood Gdns., Ilf. 80 D5
Hedgley St. SE12 155 F5
Hedingham Cl. N1 93 J7
*Popham Rd.*
Hedingham Rd., Dag. 100 B5
Hedley Rd., Twick. 143 G7
Hedley Row N5 94 A5
*Poets Rd.*
Heenan Cl., Bark. 99 F6
*Glenny Rd.*
Heene Rd., Enf. 44 A1
Heidegger Cres. SW13 127 H6
*Trinity Ch. Rd.*
Heigham Rd. E6 98 A7
Heighton Gdns., Croy. 201 H5

Hildenborough Gdns., Brom. 173 E6
Hildenlea Pl., Brom. 190 E2
Hildreth St. SW12 168 B3
Hildyard Rd. SW6 128 D6
Hiley Rd. NW10 107 J3
Hilgrove Rd. NW6 91 F7
Hiliary Gdns., Stan. 69 F2
Hill Brow, Brom. 192 A1
Hill Cl. NW2 89 H3
Hill Cl. NW11 72 D6
Hill Cl., Barn. 39 J5
Hill Cl., Chis. 174 E5
Hill Cl., Har. 86 B3
Hill Cl., Stan. 52 E4
Hill Ct., Nthlt. 85 G5
Hill Cres. N20 56 E2
Hill Cres., Bex. 177 J1
Hill Cres., Har. 68 D5
Hill Cres., Surb. 181 J5
Hill Cres., Wor.Pk. 197 J2
Hill Crest, Sid. 158 A7
Hill Dr. NW9 88 C1
Hill Dr. SW16 187 F3
Hill End, Orp. 207 J2
*The App.*
Hill Fm. Rd. W10 107 J5
Hill Gro., Felt. 161 F2
*Watermill Way*
Hill Ho. Av., Stan. 52 C7
Hill Ho. Cl. N21 43 G7
Hill Ho. Dr., Hmptn. 179 G1
Hill Ho. Rd. SW16 169 F5
Hill Path SW16 169 F5
*Valley Rd.*
Hill Ri. N9 45 E6
Hill Ri. NW11 73 E4
Hill Ri. SE23 170/171 E4
*London Rd.*
Hill Ri., Esher 194 E2
Hill Ri., Grnf. 85 J7
Hill Ri., Rich. 145 G5
Hill Rd. N10 73 J1
**Hill Rd. NW8 6 D2**
Hill Rd. NW8 109 F2
Hill Rd., Cars. 199 H6
Hill Rd., Har. 68 D5
Hill Rd., Mitch. 186 B1
Hill Rd., Pnr. 66 E5
Hill Rd., Sutt. 199 E5
Hill Rd., Wem. 86 E3
**Hill St. W1 24 C1**
Hill St. W1 130 B1
Hill St., Rich. 145 G5
Hill Top NW11 73 E4
Hill Top, Loug. 48 D2
Hill Top, Mord. 184 D6
Hill Top, Sutt. 184 C7
Hill Top Cl., Loug. 48 D3
Hill Top Pl., Loug. 48 D3
Hill Top Vw., Wdf.Grn. 64 C6
Hill Vw. Cres., Orp. 207 J1
Hill Vw. Dr., Well. 157 H2
Hill Vw. Gdns. NW9 70 D5
Hill Vw. Rd., Esher 194 D7
Hill Vw. Rd., Orp. 207 J1
Hill Vw. Rd., Twick. 144 D6
Hillary Ri., Barn. 40 D4
Hillary Rd., Sthl. 123 G3
Hillbeck Cl. SE15 133 F7
Hillbeck Way, Grnf. 104 A1
Hillborne Cl., Hayes 122 A5
Hillborough Cl. SW19 167 F7
Hillbrook Rd. SW17 167 J3
Hillbrow, N.Mal. 183 F3
Hillbrow Rd., Brom. 172 E7
Hillbury Av., Har. 69 E5
Hillbury Rd. SW17 168 B3
Hillcote Av. SW16 169 G7
Hillcourt Av. N12 56 E6
Hillcourt Est. N16 94 A1
Hillcourt Rd. SE22 152 E6
Hillcrest N6 74 A7
Hillcrest N21 43 H7
Hillcrest Av. NW11 72 B5
Hillcrest Av., Edg. 54 B4
Hillcrest Av., Pnr. 66 D4
Hillcrest Cl. SE26 170 D4
Hillcrest Cl., Beck. 189 J5
Hillcrest Gdns. N3 72 B4
Hillcrest Gdns. NW2 89 G3
Hillcrest Gdns., Esher 194 C3
Hillcrest Rd. E17 78 D2
Hillcrest Rd. E18 79 F2
Hillcrest Rd. W3 126 A1
Hillcrest Rd. W5 105 H5
Hillcrest Rd., Brom. 173 G5
Hillcrest Rd., Loug. 48 A6
Hillcrest Vw., Beck. 189 J6
Hillcroft, Loug. 48 D2
Hillcroft Av., Pnr. 67 F6
Hillcroft Cres. W5 105 H6
Hillcroft Cres., Ruis. 84 D3
Hillcroft Cres., Wat. 50 D1

Hillcroft Cres., Wem. 87 J4
Hillcroft Rd. E6 116 E5
Hillcroome Rd., Sutt. 199 G6
Hillcross Av., Mord. 184 C5
Hilldale Rd., Sutt. 198 C4
Hilldown Rd. SW16 169 E7
Hilldown Rd., Brom. 205 E1
Hilldrop Est. N7 92 D5
Hilldrop La. N7 92 D5
Hilldrop Rd. N7 92 D5
Hilldrop Rd., Brom. 173 G6
Hillend SE18 156 D1
Hillersdon Av. SW13 147 G2
Hillersdon Av., Edg. 53 J5
**Hillery Cl. SE17 36 C2**
Hillfield Av. N8 75 E5
Hillfield Av. NW9 71 E5
Hillfield Av., Wem. 87 H7
Hillfield Cl., Har. 67 J4
Hillfield Ct. NW3 91 H5
Hillfield Par., Mord. 185 H6
Hillfield Pk. N10 74 B4
Hillfield Pk. N21 59 G2
Hillfield Pk. Ms. N10 74 B4
Hillfield Rd. NW6 90 C5
Hillfield Rd., Hmptn. 161 F7
Hillfoot Av., Rom. 83 J1
Hillfoot Rd., Rom. 83 J1
Hillgate Pl. SW12 150 B7
Hillgate Pl. W8 128 D1
Hillgate St. W8 128 D1
Hilliards Ct. E1 132/133 E1
*Wapping High St.*
Hillier Cl., Barn. 40 E6
Hillier Gdns., Croy. 201 G5
*Crowley Cres.*
Hillier Pl., Chess. 195 F6
Hillier Rd. SW11 149 J6
Hilliers La., Croy. 200 E3
Hillingdon Av., Bexh. 159 J2
**Hillingdon St. SE5 35 H6**
**Hillingdon St. SE17 35 H6**
Hillingdon St. SE17 131 H6
Hillington Gdns., Wdf.Grn. 80 A2
Hillman Dr. W10 107 J4
Hillman St. E8 95 E6
Hillmarton Rd. N7 92 E5
Hillmead Dr. SW9 151 H4
Hillmont Rd., Esher 194 B3
Hillmore Gro. SE26 171 G5
Hillreach SE18 136 C5
Hillrise Rd. N19 74 E7
Hills Ms. W5 105 H7
**Hills Pl. W1 17 F4**
Hills Rd., Buck.H. 63 H1
Hillsborough Grn., Wat. 50 A3
*Ashburnham Dr.*
Hillsborough Rd. SE22 152 B5
Hillsgrove, Well. 138 C7
Hillside NW9 70 D4
Hillside NW10 106 C1
Hillside SW19 166 A6
Hillside, Barn. 41 F5
Hillside Av. N11 57 J6
Hillside Av., Borwd. 38 B4
Hillside Av., Wem. 87 J4
Hillside Av., Wdf.Grn. 63 J5
**Hillside Cl. NW8 6 B1**
Hillside Cl., Mord. 184 B4
Hillside Cl., Wdf.Grn. 63 J5
Hillside Cres., Har. 85 J1
Hillside Cres., Nthwd. 66 A1
Hillside Dr., Edg. 54 A6
Hillside Est. N15 76 C6
Hillside Gdns. E17 78 D3
Hillside Gdns. N6 74 A6
Hillside Gdns. SW2 169 G2
Hillside Gdns., Barn. 40 B4
Hillside Gdns., Edg. 53 J4
Hillside Gdns., Har. 69 H7
Hillside Gdns., Nthwd. 50 A7
Hillside Gdns., Wall. 200 C7
Hillside Gro. N14 42 D7
Hillside Gro. NW7 55 G7
Hillside La., Brom. 205 G2
Hillside Pas. SW2 169 F2
Hillside Ri., Nthwd. 50 A7
Hillside Rd. N15 76 B7
Hillside Rd. SW2 169 G2
Hillside Rd. W5 105 H5
Hillside Rd., Brom. 191 F3
Hillside Rd., Croy. 201 H5
Hillside Rd., Nthwd. 50 A7
Hillside Rd., Pnr. 50 B7
Hillside Rd., Sthl. 103 G4
Hillside Rd., Surb. 181 J5
Hillside Rd., Sutt. 198 C7
Hillsleigh Rd. W8 128 C1

Hillstowe St. E5 95 F2
Hilltop Gdns. NW4 71 H1
*Great N. Way*
Hilltop Gdns., Orp. 207 H2
Hilltop Rd. NW6 90 D7
Hilltop Way, Stan. 52 D3
Hillview SW20 165 H7
Hillview, Mitch. 186 E4
Hillview Av., Har. 69 H5
Hillview Cl., Pnr. 51 F6
Hillview Cres., Ilf. 80 C6
Hillview Gdns. NW4 72 A4
Hillview Gdns., Har. 67 G3
Hillview Rd. NW7 56 A4
Hillview Rd., Chis. 174 D5
Hillview Rd., Pnr. 51 F7
Hillview Rd., Sutt. 199 F3
Hillway N6 92 A2
Hillway NW9 88 E1
Hillworth Rd. SW2 151 G7
Hilly Flds. Cres. SE4 154 A3
Hillyard Rd. W7 104 B5
Hillyard St. SW9 151 G1
Hillyfield E17 77 H3
Hillyfields, Loug. 48 D2
Hilsea St. E5 95 F4
Hilton Av. N12 57 G5
Hilversum Cres. SE22 152 B5
*East Dulwich Gro.*
Himley Rd. SW17 167 H5
Hinchcliffe Cl., Wall. 201 F7
Hinchley Cl., Esher 194 C3
Hinchley Dr., Esher 194 C3
Hinchley Way, Esher 194 D3
Hinckley Rd. SE15 152 D4
Hind Cl., Chig. 65 J5
**Hind Ct. EC4 19 F4**
Hind Gro. E14 114 A6
Hinde Ms. W1 110 A6
*Marylebone La.*
**Hinde St. W1 16 C3**
Hinde St. W1 110 A6
Hindes Rd., Har. 68 A5
Hindhead Cl. N16 94 B1
Hindhead Gdns. Nthlt. 102 E1
Hindhead Grn., Wat. 50 C5
Hindhead Way, Wall. 200 E5
Hindmans Rd. SE22 152 D5
Hindmans Way, Dag. 119 F4
**Hindmarsh Cl. E1 21 J5**
Hindrey Rd. E5 95 E5
Hindsley's Pl. SE23 171 F2
Hinkler Cl., Wall. 201 E7
Hinkler Rd., Har. 69 G3
Hinksey Path SE2 138 D3
Hinstock Rd. SE18 137 F6
Hinton Av., Houns. 142 D4
Hinton Cl. SE9 174 B1
Hinton Rd. N18 60 B4
Hinton Rd. SE24 151 H3
Hinton Rd., Wall. 200 C6
Hippodrome Ms. W11 108 B7
*Portland Rd.*
Hippodrome Pl. W11 108 B7
Hiscocks Ho. NW10 88 C7
Hitcham Rd. E17 77 J7
Hitchin Sq. E3 113 H2
Hither Fm. Rd. SE3 155 J3
Hither Grn. La. SE13 154 C5
Hitherbroom Rd., Hayes 122 A1
Hitherfield Rd. SW16 169 F2
Hitherfield Rd., Dag. 101 E2
Hitherlands SW12 168 B2
Hitherwell Dr., Har. 68 A1
Hitherwood Dr. SE19 170 C4
Hive Cl., Bushey 52 A2
Hive Rd., Bushey 52 A2
Hoadly Rd. SW16 168 D3
Hobart Cl. N20 57 H2
*Oakleigh Rd. N.*
Hobart Cl., Hayes 102 D4
Hobart Dr., Hayes 102 D4
Hobart Gdns., Th.Hth. 188 A3
Hobart La., Hayes 102 D4
**Hobart Pl. SW1 24 D5**
Hobart Pl. SW1 130 B3
Hobart Pl., Rich. 145 J6
*Chisholm Rd.*
Hobart Rd., Dag. 100 D4
Hobart Rd., Hayes 102 D4
Hobart Rd., Ilf. 81 F2
Hobart Rd., Wor.Pk. 197 H3
Hobbayne Rd. W7 104 A6
Hobbes Wk. SW15 147 H5
Hobbs Grn. N2 73 F3
Hobbs Ms., Ilf. 99 J2
*Ripley Rd.*
Hobbs Pl. Est. N1 112 B1
*Pitfield St.*
Hobbs Rd. SE27 169 J4
Hobday St. E14 114 B5
Hobill Wk., Surb. 181 J6

Hoblands End, Chis. 175 H6
**Hobsons Pl. E1 21 H1**
**Hobury St. SW10 30 D6**
Hobury St. SW10 129 F6
**Hocker St. E2 13 F4**
Hockett Cl. SE8 133 H4
Hockley Av. E6 116 B2
Hockley Ms., Bark. 117 H2
Hocroft Av. NW2 90 C3
Hocroft Rd. NW2 90 C4
Hocroft Wk. NW2 90 C3
Hodder Dr., Grnf. 104 C2
Hoddesdon Rd., Belv. 139 G5
Hodford Rd. NW11 90 C2
Hodgkin Cl. SE28 118 D7
*Fleming Way*
Hodister Cl. SE5 131 J7
*Badsworth Rd.*
Hodnet Gro. SE16 133 G4
Hodson Cl., Har. 85 F3
Hoe, The, Wat. 50 D2
Hoe St. E17 78 A4
Hofland Rd. W14 128 A3
**Hogan Ms. W2 14 E1**
Hogan Way E5 94 D2
*Geldeston Rd.*
Hogarth Cl. E16 116 A5
Hogarth Cl. W5 105 H5
**Hogarth Ct. EC3 20 E5**
Hogarth Ct. SE19 170 C4
*Fountain Dr.*
Hogarth Cres. SW19 185 G1
Hogarth Cres., Croy. 187 J7
Hogarth Gdns., Houns. 123 G7
Hogarth Hill NW11 72 C4
Hogarth La. W4 126 E6
**Hogarth Pl. SW5 30 A2**
Hogarth Reach, Loug. 48 C5
**Hogarth Rd. SW5 30 A2**
Hogarth Rd. SW5 128 E4
Hogarth Rd., Dag. 100 B5
Hogarth Rd., Edg. 70 A2
Hogarth Roundabout W4 127 E6
Hogarth Roundabout Flyover W4 126/127 E6
Hogarth Way, Hmptn. 179 J1
Hogg La., Borwd. 37 H3
Hogshead Pas. E1 112/113 E7
*Pennington St.*
Hogsmill Way, Epsom 196 C5
Holbeach Gdns., Sid. 157 H6
Holbeach Ms. SW12 168 B1
*Harberson Rd.*
Holbeach Rd. SE6 154 A7
Holbeck Row SE15 132 D7
**Holbein Ms. SW1 32 B3**
Holbein Ms. SW1 130 A5
**Holbein Pl. SW1 32 B2**
Holbein Pl. SW1 130 A4
Holbein Ter., Dag. 100 B4
*Marlborough Rd.*
Holberton Gdns. NW10 107 H3
**Holborn EC1 18 E2**
Holborn EC1 111 G5
**Holborn Circ. EC1 19 F2**
**Holborn Pl. WC1 18 C2**
Holborn Rd. E13 115 H4
**Holborn Viaduct EC1 19 F2**
Holborn Viaduct EC1 111 G5
Holborn Way, Mitch. 185 J2
Holbrook Cl. N19 92 B1
*Dartmouth Pk. Hill*
Holbrook Cl., Enf. 44 C1
Holbrook La., Chis. 175 G7
Holbrook Rd. E15 115 F2
Holbrook Way, Brom. 192 C6
Holbrooke Ct. N7 93 E4
Holbrooke Pl., Rich. 145 G5
*Hill Ri.*
Holburne Cl. SE3 155 J1
Holburne Gdns. SE3 156 A1
Holburne Rd. SE3 155 J1
Holcombe Hill NW7 55 G3
*Highwood Hill*
Holcombe Rd. N17 76 C3
Holcombe Rd., Ilf. 80 D7
Holcombe St. W6 127 H4
Holcote Cl., Belv. 138/139 E3
*Blakemore Way*
Holcroft Rd. E9 95 F7
Holden Av. N12 57 E5
Holden Av. NW9 88 C1
Holden Cl., Dag. 100 B3
Holden Pt. E15 96 D6
*Waddington Rd.*
Holden Rd. N12 56 E5
Holden St. SW11 150 A2
Holdenby Rd. SE4 153 H5
Holdenhurst Av. N12 57 E7
Holder Cl. N3 57 E7
Holderness Way SE27 169 H5

Holdernesse Cl., Islw. 144 D1
Holdernesse Rd. SW17 167 J3
Holders Hill Av. NW4 72 A2
Holders Hill Circ. NW7 56 B7
*Dollis Rd.*
Holders Hill Cres. NW4 72 A2
Holders Hill Dr. NW4 72 A3
Holders Hill Gdns. NW4 72 B2
Holders Hill Rd. NW4 72 A2
Holders Hill Rd. NW7 72 B1
Holdgate St. SE7 136 A3
*Westmoor St.*
**Holford Pl. WC1 10 D3**
Holford Rd. NW3 91 F3
**Holford St. WC1 10 E3**
Holford St. WC1 111 G3
Holgate Av. SW11 149 G3
Holgate Gdns., Dag. 101 G5
Holgate Rd., Dag. 101 G5
Holland Av. SW20 183 F1
Holland Cl., Barn. 41 G7
Holland Cl., Brom. 205 F2
Holland Cl., Rom. 83 J5
Holland Cl., Stan. 52 E5
Holland Dr. SE23 171 H3
Holland Gdns. W14 128 B3
Holland Gro. SW9 131 G7
Holland Pk. W8 128 C2
Holland Pk. W11 128 C2
Holland Pk. Av. W11 128 B2
Holland Pk. Av., Ilf. 81 H6
Holland Pk. Gdns. W14 128 B1
Holland Pk. Ms. W11 128 B1
Holland Pk. Rd. W14 128 C3
Holland Pas. N1 111 J1
*Basire St.*
**Holland Pl. W8 22 A3**
Holland Rd. E6 116 C1
Holland Rd. E15 115 E3
Holland Rd. NW10 107 G1
Holland Rd. SE25 188 D5
Holland Rd. W14 128 A2
Holland Rd., Wem. 87 G6
**Holland St. SE1 27 H1**
Holland St. SE1 131 H1
Holland St. W8 128 D2
Holland Vil. Rd. W14 128 B2
Holland Wk. N19 92 D1
*Duncombe Rd.*
Holland Wk. W8 128 C2
Holland Wk., Stan. 52 D5
Holland Way, Brom. 205 F2
Hollands, The, Felt. 160 D4
Hollands, The, Wor.Pk. 197 F1
Hollar Rd. N16 94 C3
*Stoke Newington High St.*
**Hollen St. W1 17 H3**
Hollen St. W1 110 C6
Holles Cl., Hmptn. 161 G6
**Holles St. W1 16 E3**
Holles St. W1 110 B6
Holley Rd. W3 127 E2
Hollickwood Av. N12 57 J6
Holliday Sq. SW11 149 G3
*Fowler Cl.*
Hollidge Way, Dag. 101 H6
Hollies, The E11 79 G5
Hollies, The N20 57 G1
*Oakleigh Pk. N.*
Hollies, The, Har. 68 D4
Hollies Av., Sid. 175 J2
Hollies Cl. SW16 169 G6
Hollies Cl., Twick. 162 C2
Hollies End NW7 55 H5
Hollies Rd. W5 125 F4
Hollies Way SW12 150 A7
*Bracken Av.*
Holligrave Rd., Brom. 191 G1
Hollingbourne Av., Bexh. 139 F7
Hollingbourne Gdns. W13 104 E5
Hollingbourne Rd. SE24 151 J5
Hollingsworth Rd., Croy. 203 E6
Hollington Cres., N.Mal. 183 F6
Hollington Rd. E6 116 C3
Hollington Rd. N17 76 D2
Hollingworth Cl., W.Mol. 179 F4
Hollingworth Rd., Orp. 192 E6
Hollman Gdns. SW16 169 H6
Hollow, The, Wdf.Grn. 63 F4
Hollow Wk., Rich. 125 H7
*Kew Rd.*
Holloway Cl., West Dr. 120 B5
Holloway La., West Dr. 120 B6
Holloway Rd. E6 116 C3
Holloway Rd. E11 96 E3
Holloway Rd. N7 93 G6
Holloway Rd. N19 92 D2
Holloway St., Houns. 143 H3
Hollowfield Wk., Nthlt. 84 E6
Hollows, The, Brent. 125 J6
*Kew Br. Rd.*
Holly Av., Stan. 69 H2
Holly Bush Hill NW3 91 F4
Holly Bush La., Hmptn. 161 F7
Holly Bush Steps NW3 91 F4
*Heath St.*
Holly Bush Vale NW3 91 F4
*Heath St.*
Holly Cl. NW10 88 E7
Holly Cl., Buck.H. 64 A3
Holly Cl., Felt. 160 E5
Holly Cl., Wall. 200 B7
Holly Cres., Beck. 189 J5
Holly Cres., Wdf.Grn. 62 D7
Holly Dr. E4 46 B7
Holly Dr., Brent. 124 D6
Holly Fm. Rd., Sthl. 122 E5
Holly Gdns., West Dr. 120 C2
Holly Gro. NW9 70 C7
Holly Gro. SE15 152 C2
Holly Gro., Pnr. 67 E1
Holly Hedge Ter. SE13 154 D5
Holly Hill N21 43 F6
Holly Hill NW3 91 F4
Holly Hill Rd., Belv. 139 H5
Holly Hill Rd., Erith 139 H5
Holly Lo. Gdns. N6 92 A2
**Holly Ms. SW10 30 D4**
Holly Mt. NW3 91 F4
*Holly Bush Hill*
Holly Pk. N3 72 C3
Holly Pk. N4 75 F7
Holly Pk. Est. N4 75 F7
*Blythwood Rd.*
Holly Pk. Gdns. N3 72 D3
Holly Pk. Rd. N11 58 A5
Holly Pk. Rd. W7 124 C1
Holly Pl. NW3 91 F4
*Holly Wk.*
Holly Rd. E11 79 F7
Holly Rd. W4 126 D4
*Dolman Rd.*
Holly Rd., Hmptn. 161 J6
Holly Rd., Houns. 143 H4
Holly Rd., Twick. 162 D1
Holly St. E8 94 C6
Holly St. Est. E8 94 C7
Holly Ter. N6 92 A1
*Highgate W. Hill*
Holly Ter. N20 57 F2
*Swan La.*
Holly Vw. Cl. NW4 71 G6
Holly Village N6 92 B2
*Swains La.*
Holly Wk. NW3 91 F4
Holly Wk., Enf. 44 A3
Holly Wk., Rich. 145 H2
Holly Way, Mitch. 186 D4
Hollybank Cl., Hmptn. 161 G5
Hollyberry La. NW3 91 F4
*Holly Wk.*
Hollybrake Cl., Chis. 175 G7
Hollybush Cl. E11 79 G5
Hollybush Cl., Har. 68 B1
Hollybush Gdns. E2 113 E3
Hollybush Hill E11 79 F6
Hollybush Pl. E2 112/113 E3
*Bethnal Grn. Rd.*
Hollybush Rd., Kings.T. 163 H5
Hollybush St. E13 115 H3
Hollybush Wk. SW9 151 H4
Hollycroft Av. NW3 90 D3
Hollycroft Av., Wem. 87 J2
Hollycroft Cl., S.Croy. 202 B5
Hollycroft Cl., West Dr. 120 D6
Hollycroft Gdns., West Dr. 120 D6
Hollydale Cl., Nthlt. 85 H4
*Dorchester Rd.*
Hollydale Dr., Brom. 206 C3
Hollydale Rd. SE15 153 F1
Hollydene SE15 152 E1
Hollydown Way E11 96 D3
Hollyfield Av. N11 57 J5
Hollyfield Rd., Surb. 181 J7
Hollymead, Cars. 199 J3
Hollymount Cl. SE10 154 C1
Hollytree Cl. SW19 166 A1
Hollywood Gdns., Hayes 102 B6
**Hollywood Ms. SW10 30 C5**
Hollywood Rd. E4 61 H5
**Hollywood Rd. SW10 30 C5**
Hollywood Rd. SW10 129 F6
Hollywood Way, Wdf.Grn. 62 D7
Holm Oak Cl. SW15 148 C6
*West Hill*
Holm Oak Ms. SW4 150/151 E5
*King's Av.*
Holm Wk. SE3 155 G2
*Blackheath Pk.*
Holman Rd. SW11 149 G2
Holman Rd., Epsom 196 C5
Holmbridge Gdns., Enf. 45 G4
Holmbrook Dr. NW4 72 A5
Holmbury Ct. SW17 167 J3
Holmbury Ct. SW19 167 H7
*Cavendish Rd.*
Holmbury Gdns., Hayes 121 J1
*Church Rd.*
Holmbury Gro., Croy. 203 J7
Holmbury Pk., Brom. 174 B7
Holmbury Vw. E5 95 E1
Holmbush Rd. SW15 148 B6
Holmcote Gdns. N5 93 J5
Holmcroft Way, Brom. 192 C5
Holmdale Gdns. NW4 72 A5
Holmdale Rd. NW6 90 D5
Holmdale Rd., Chis. 175 F5
Holmdale Ter. N15 76 B7
Holmdene Av. NW7 55 G6
Holmdene Av. SE24 151 J5
Holmdene Av., Har. 67 H3
Holmdene Cl., Beck. 190 C2
Holme Lacey Rd. SE12 155 F6
Holme Rd. E6 116 B1
Holme Way, Stan. 52 C6
Holmead Rd. SW6 129 E7
Holmebury Cl., Bushey 52 B2
Holmefield Ct. NW3 91 H6
Holmes Av. E17 77 J3
Holmes Av. NW7 56 B5
**Holmes Pl. SW10 30 D5**
Holmes Rd. NW5 92 B5
Holmes Rd. SW19 167 F7
Holmes Rd., Twick. 162 C2
**Holmes Ter. SE1 27 E3**
Holmes Ter. SE1 131 G2
Holmesdale Av. SW14 146 B3
Holmesdale Cl. SE25 188 C3
Holmesdale Rd. N6 74 B7
Holmesdale Rd. SE25 188 A5
Holmesdale Rd., Bexh. 158 D2
Holmesdale Rd., Croy. 188 A5
Holmesdale Rd., Rich. 145 J1
Holmesdale Rd., Tedd. 163 F6
Holmesley Rd. SE23 153 H6
Holmewood Gdns. SW2 151 F7
Holmewood Rd. SE25 188 B3
Holmewood Rd. SW2 151 E7
Holmfield Av. NW4 72 A5
Holmhurst Rd., Belv. 139 H5
Holmleigh Rd. N16 94 B1
Holmleigh Rd. Est. N16 94 C1
*Holmleigh Rd.*
**Holms St. E2 13 H1**
Holms St. E2 112 D2
Holmshaw Cl. SE26 171 H4
Holmside Ri., Wat. 50 B3
Holmside Rd. SW12 150 A6
Holmsley Cl., N.Mal. 183 F6
Holmstall Av., Edg. 70 C3
Holmwood Cl., Har. 67 J3
Holmwood Cl., Nthlt. 85 H6
Holmwood Gdns. N3 72 D2
Holmwood Gdns., Wall. 200 B6
Holmwood Gro. NW7 54 D5
Holmwood Rd., Chess. 195 G5
Holmwood Rd., Ilf. 99 H2
Holmwood Vil. SE7 135 G5
*Woolwich Rd.*
Holne Chase N2 73 F6
Holne Chase, Mord. 184 C6
Holness Rd. E15 97 F6
Holroyd Rd. SW15 147 J4
Holstein Way, Erith 138 E3
Holstock Rd., Ilf. 99 F3
Holsworth Cl., Har. 67 J5
**Holsworthy Sq. WC1 10 D6**
Holsworthy Way, Chess. 195 F5
Holt, The, Ilf. 65 F6
Holt, The, Wall. 200 C4
Holt Cl. N10 74 A4
Holt Cl. SE28 118 B7
Holt Cl., Chig. 65 J5
Holt Ct. E15 96 C5
*Clays La.*
Holt Rd. E16 136 B1
Holt Rd., Wem. 87 E3
Holt Way, Chig. 65 J5
Holton St. E1 113 G4
Holtwhite Av., Enf. 43 J2
Holtwhites Hill, Enf. 43 H1
Holwell Pl., Pnr. 66 E4
Holwood Pk. Av., Orp. 206 C4
Holwood Pl. SW4 150 D4
Holybourne Av. SW15 147 G7
Holyhead Cl. E3 114 A3
Holyhead Cl. E6 116 C5
*Valiant Way*
**Holyoak Rd. SE11 35 G1**
Holyoake Ct. SE16 133 J2
*Bryan Rd.*
Holyoake Wk. N2 73 F3
Holyoake Wk. W5 105 F4
Holyport Rd. SW6 127 J7
Holyrood Av., Har. 85 E4
Holyrood Gdns., Edg. 70 B3
Holyrood Ms. E16 135 G1
*Wesley Av.*
Holyrood Rd., Barn. 41 F6
**Holyrood St. SE1 28 D2**
Holywell Cl. SE3 135 G6
Holywell Cl. SE16 132/133 E5
*Masters Dr.*
**Holywell La. EC2 12 E5**
Holywell La. EC2 112 B4
**Holywell Row EC2 12 D6**
Holywell Row EC2 112 B4
Home Cl., Cars. 199 J2
Home Cl., Nthlt. 103 F3
Home Ct., Felt. 160 A1
Home Fm. Cl., T.Ditt. 180 C7
Home Gdns., Dag. 101 J3
Home Lea, Orp. 207 J5
Home Mead, Stan. 69 F1
Home Pk. Rd. SW19 166 D3
Home Pk. Wk., Kings.T. 181 G4
Home Rd. SW11 149 H2
Homecroft Gdns., Loug. 48 E4
Homecroft Rd. N22 75 J1
Homecroft Rd. SE26 171 F5
Homefarm Rd. W7 104 B6
Homefield Av., Ilf. 81 H5
Homefield Cl. NW10 88 C6
Homefield Cl., Hayes 102 C4
Homefield Gdns. N2 73 G3
Homefield Gdns., Mitch. 185 F2
Homefield Ms., Beck. 190 A1
Homefield Pk., Sutt. 198 E6
Homefield Rd. SW19 166 A6
Homefield Rd. W4 127 F4
Homefield Rd., Brom. 191 J1
Homefield Rd., Edg. 54 D6
Homefield Rd., Walt. 179 E7
Homefield Rd., Wem. 86 D4
**Homefield St. N1 12 D2**
Homefield St. N1 112 B2
Homelands Dr. SE19 170 B7
Homeleigh Rd. SE15 153 G5
Homemead SW12 168 C2
Homemead Rd., Brom. 192 C5
Homemead Rd., Croy. 186 C6
Homer Cl., Bexh. 159 J1
Homer Dr. E14 134 A4
Homer Rd. E9 95 H6
Homer Rd., Croy. 189 G6
**Homer Row W1 15 H2**
Homer Row W1 109 H5
**Homer St. W1 15 H2**
Homer St. W1 109 H5
Homersham Rd., Kings.T. 182 A2
Homerton Gro. E9 95 G5
Homerton High St. E9 95 F5
Homerton Rd. E9 95 H5
Homerton Row E9 95 F5
Homerton Ter. E9 95 F6
*Morning La.*
Homesdale Cl. E11 79 G5
Homesdale Rd., Brom. 191 J4
Homesdale Rd., Orp. 193 H7
Homesfield NW11 72 D5
Homestall Rd. SE22 153 F5
Homestead, The N11 58 B4
Homestead Gdns., Esher 194 B5

|  | | |
|---|---|---|
| Homestead Paddock N14 | 42 | B5 |
| Homestead Pk. NW2 | 89 | F3 |
| Homestead Rd. SW6 | 128 | C7 |
| Homestead Rd., Dag. | 101 | F2 |
| Homewillow Cl. N21 | 43 | H6 |
| Homewood Cl., Hmptn. | 161 | F6 |
| *Fearnley Cres.* | | |
| Homewood Cres., Chis. | 175 | H6 |
| **Honduras St. EC1** | 11 | J5 |
| Honey Cl., Dag. | 101 | H6 |
| **Honey La. EC2** | 20 | A4 |
| Honeybourne Rd. NW6 | 90 | E5 |
| Honeybourne Way, Orp. | 207 | G1 |
| Honeybrook Rd. SW12 | 150 | C7 |
| Honeycroft, Loug. | 48 | D4 |
| Honeyden Rd., Sid. | 177 | E6 |
| Honeyman Cl. NW6 | 90 | A7 |
| Honeypot Cl. NW9 | 69 | J4 |
| Honeypot La. NW9 | 69 | J3 |
| Honeypot La., Stan. | 69 | J3 |
| Honeysett Rd. N17 | 76 | C2 |
| *Reform Row* | | |
| Honeysuckle Cl., Sthl. | 102 | E7 |
| Honeysuckle Gdns., Croy. | 203 | G1 |
| *Primrose La.* | | |
| Honeywell Rd. SW11 | 149 | J6 |
| Honeywood Rd. NW10 | 107 | F2 |
| Honeywood Rd., Islw. | 144 | D4 |
| Honeywood Wk., Cars. | 199 | J4 |
| Honister Cl., Stan. | 69 | E1 |
| Honister Gdns., Stan. | 53 | E7 |
| Honister Pl., Stan. | 69 | E1 |
| Honiton Rd. NW6 | 108 | C2 |
| Honiton Rd., Well. | 157 | J2 |
| Honley Rd. SE6 | 154 | B7 |
| Honnor Gdns., Islw. | 143 | J3 |
| *London Rd.* | | |
| Honor Oak Pk. SE23 | 153 | F6 |
| Honor Oak Ri. SE23 | 153 | F6 |
| Honor Oak Rd. SE23 | 171 | F1 |
| Hood Av. N14 | 42 | B6 |
| Hood Av. SW14 | 146 | C5 |
| Hood Cl., Croy. | 201 | H1 |
| *Parson's Mead* | | |
| **Hood Ct. EC4** | 19 | F4 |
| Hood Rd. SW20 | 165 | F7 |
| Hood Wk., Rom. | 83 | H1 |
| Hoodcote Gdns. N21 | 43 | H7 |
| Hook, The, Barn. | 41 | G6 |
| Hook Fm. Rd., Brom. | 192 | A5 |
| Hook La., Well. | 157 | J3 |
| Hook Ri. N., Surb. | 196 | A3 |
| Hook Ri. S., Surb. | 196 | A3 |
| Hook Ri. S. Ind. Pk., Surb. | 196 | A3 |
| Hook Rd., Chess. | 195 | G5 |
| Hook Rd., Surb. | 195 | H3 |
| Hook Wk., Edg. | 54 | C6 |
| Hookers Ct. E17 | 77 | G3 |
| Hooking Grn., Har. | 67 | H5 |
| Hooks Cl. SE15 | 152/153 | E1 |
| *Woods Rd.* | | |
| Hooks Hall Dr., Dag. | 101 | J3 |
| Hooks Way SE22 | 170 | D1 |
| *Dulwich Common* | | |
| Hookstone Way, Wdf.Grn. | 64 | A7 |
| Hoop La. NW11 | 72 | C7 |
| Hooper St. E16 | 115 | G6 |
| **Hooper St. E1** | 21 | H5 |
| Hooper St. E1 | 112 | D6 |
| **Hooper's Ct. SW3** | 23 | A4 |
| **Hop Gdns. WC2** | 18 | A6 |
| Hope Cl. N1 | 93 | J6 |
| *Wallace Rd.* | | |
| Hope Cl. SE12 | 173 | H3 |
| Hope Cl., Sutt. | 199 | F5 |
| Hope Cl., Wdf.Grn. | 63 | J6 |
| *West Gro.* | | |
| Hope Pk., Brom. | 173 | F7 |
| Hope St. SW11 | 149 | G3 |
| Hope Wf. SE16 | 133 | F2 |
| *St. Marychurch St.* | | |
| Hopedale Rd. SE7 | 135 | H6 |
| Hopefield Av. NW6 | 108 | B2 |
| Hopes Cl., Houns. | 123 | G6 |
| *Old Cote Dr.* | | |
| **Hopetown St. E1** | 21 | G2 |
| Hopewell St. SE5 | 132 | A7 |
| Hopewell Yd. SE5 | 132 | A7 |
| *Hopewell St.* | | |
| Hopgood St. W12 | 127 | J1 |
| *Macfarlane Rd.* | | |
| Hopkins Cl. N10 | 58 | A7 |
| *Cromwell Rd.* | | |
| Hopkins Ms. E15 | 115 | F1 |
| *West Rd.* | | |
| **Hopkins St. W1** | 17 | G4 |
| Hopkinsons Pl. NW1 | 110 | A1 |
| *Fitzroy Rd.* | | |
| Hoppers Rd. N13 | 59 | G2 |
| Hoppers Rd. N21 | 59 | G2 |
| Hoppett Rd. E4 | 62 | E3 |
| Hopping La. N1 | 93 | H6 |
| *St. Mary's Gro.* | | |
| Hoppingwood Av., N.Mal. | 183 | E3 |
| **Hopton Gdns. SE1** | 27 | H1 |
| Hopton Gdns. SE1 | 131 | H1 |
| Hopton Gdns., N.Mal. | 183 | G6 |
| Hopton Rd. SW16 | 168 | E5 |
| **Hopton St. SE1** | 27 | H1 |
| Hopton St. SE1 | 131 | H1 |
| Hopwood Cl. SW17 | 167 | F3 |
| **Hopwood Rd. SE17** | 36 | C5 |
| Hopwood Rd. SE17 | 132 | A6 |
| Hopwood Wk. E8 | 94 | D7 |
| *Wilman Gro.* | | |
| Horace Av., Rom. | 101 | J1 |
| Horace Rd. E7 | 97 | H4 |
| Horace Rd., Ilf. | 81 | F3 |
| Horace Rd., Kings.T. | 181 | J3 |
| Horatio Ct. SE16 | 133 | F1 |
| *Rotherhithe St.* | | |
| Horatio Pl. E14 | 134 | C2 |
| *Cold Harbour* | | |
| Horatio Pl. SW19 | 166 | D7 |
| *Kingston Rd.* | | |
| **Horatio St. E2** | 13 | H2 |
| Horatio St. E2 | 112 | C2 |
| Horatius Way, Croy. | 201 | F5 |
| Horbury Cres. W11 | 108 | D7 |
| Horbury Ms. W11 | 108 | C7 |
| *Ladbroke Rd.* | | |
| Horder Rd. SW6 | 148 | B1 |
| **Hordle Prom. E. SE15** | 37 | G7 |
| **Hordle Prom. N. SE15** | 37 | E7 |
| **Hordle Prom. S. SE15** | 37 | E7 |
| **Hordle Prom. W. SE15** | 37 | E7 |
| Horizon Way SE7 | 135 | H4 |
| Horle Wk. SE5 | 151 | H2 |
| *Lilford Rd.* | | |
| Horley Cl., Bexh. | 159 | G5 |
| Horley Rd. SE9 | 174 | B4 |
| Hormead Rd. W9 | 108 | C4 |
| Horn La. SE10 | 135 | G4 |
| Horn La. W3 | 106 | C7 |
| Horn La., Wdf.Grn. | 63 | G6 |
| Horn Link Way SE10 | 135 | G4 |
| Horn Pk. Cl. SE12 | 155 | H5 |
| Horn Pk. La. SE12 | 155 | H5 |
| Hornbeam Cl. NW7 | 55 | F3 |
| *Marsh La.* | | |
| **Hornbeam Cl. SE11** | 34 | E1 |
| Hornbeam Cl., Borwd. | 38 | A1 |
| Hornbeam Cl., Buck.H. | 64 | A3 |
| *Hornbeam Rd.* | | |
| Hornbeam Cl., Ilf. | 99 | G5 |
| Hornbeam Cl., Nthlt. | 85 | F5 |
| Hornbeam Cres., Brent. | 125 | E7 |
| Hornbeam Gro. E4 | 63 | E3 |
| Hornbeam La. E4 | 47 | E5 |
| Hornbeam La., Bexh. | 159 | J1 |
| Hornbeam Rd., Buck.H. | 64 | A3 |
| Hornbeam Rd., Hayes | 102 | C5 |
| Hornbeam Ter., Cars. | 199 | H1 |
| Hornbeam Twr. E11 | 96 | D3 |
| *Hollydown Way* | | |
| Hornbeam Wk., Rich. | 163 | J3 |
| Hornbeam Way, Brom. | 192 | D6 |
| Hornbeams Ri. N11 | 58 | A6 |
| Hornblower Cl. SE16 | 133 | H4 |
| *Greenland Quay* | | |
| Hornbuckle Cl., Har. | 86 | A2 |
| Hornby Cl. NW3 | 91 | G7 |
| Horncastle Cl. SE12 | 155 | G7 |
| Horncastle Rd. SE12 | 155 | G7 |
| Hornchurch Cl., Kings.T. | 163 | G4 |
| Horndean Cl. SW15 | 165 | G1 |
| *Bessborough Rd.* | | |
| Horndon Cl., Rom. | 83 | J1 |
| Horndon Grn., Rom. | 83 | J1 |
| Horndon Rd., Rom. | 83 | J1 |
| Horne Way SW15 | 147 | J2 |
| Horner La., Mitch. | 185 | G2 |
| Hornfair Rd. SE7 | 135 | J6 |
| Horniman Dr. SE23 | 171 | E1 |
| Horning Cl. SE9 | 174 | B4 |
| Horns End Pl., Pnr. | 66 | C4 |
| Horns Rd., Ilf. | 81 | F6 |
| Hornsey La. N6 | 92 | B1 |
| Hornsey La. N19 | 74 | C7 |
| Hornsey La. Est. N19 | 74 | D7 |
| *Hornsey La.* | | |
| Hornsey La. Gdns. N6 | 74 | C7 |
| Hornsey Pk. Rd. N8 | 75 | F3 |
| Hornsey Ri. N19 | 74 | D7 |
| Hornsey Ri. Gdns. N19 | 74 | D7 |
| Hornsey Rd. N7 | 93 | E2 |
| Hornsey Rd. N19 | 93 | E2 |
| Hornsey St. N7 | 93 | F5 |
| Hornshay St. SE15 | 133 | F6 |
| **Hornton Pl. W8** | 22 | A4 |
| Hornton Pl. W8 | 128 | D2 |
| Hornton St. W8 | 128 | D2 |
| Horsa Cl., Wall. | 201 | E7 |
| Horsa Rd. SE12 | 155 | J7 |
| Horsa Rd., Erith | 139 | J7 |
| **Horse & Dolphin Yd. W1** | 17 | J5 |
| Horse Fair, Kings.T. | 181 | G2 |
| **Horse Guards Av. SW1** | 26 | A2 |
| Horse Guards Av. SW1 | 130 | E1 |
| **Horse Guards Rd. SW1** | 25 | J2 |
| Horse Guards Rd. SW1 | 130 | D1 |
| Horse Leaze E6 | 116 | D6 |
| **Horse Ride SW1** | 25 | H2 |
| Horse Ride SW1 | 130 | C1 |
| Horse Rd. E7 | 97 | H3 |
| *Centre Rd.* | | |
| Horse Shoe Cres. E6 | 103 | G2 |
| *Nthlt.* | | |
| Horse Shoe Grn., Sutt. | 198/199 | E2 |
| *Aultone Way* | | |
| Horse Yd. N1 | 111 | H1 |
| *Essex Rd.* | | |
| Horsebridge Cl., Dag. | 119 | E1 |
| Horsecroft Rd., Edg. | 54 | D7 |
| Horseferry Pl. SE10 | 134 | C6 |
| Horseferry Rd. E14 | 113 | H7 |
| **Horseferry Rd. SW1** | 25 | H6 |
| Horseferry Rd. SW1 | 130 | D4 |
| Horsell Rd. N5 | 93 | G5 |
| **Horselydown La. SE1** | 29 | F3 |
| Horselydown La. SE1 | 132 | C2 |
| Horsenden Av., Grnf. | 86 | B5 |
| Horsenden Cres., Grnf. | 86 | C5 |
| Horsenden La. N., Grnf. | 86 | C6 |
| Horsenden La. S., Grnf. | 104 | D2 |
| Horseshoe Cl. E14 | 134 | C5 |
| *Ferry St.* | | |
| Horseshoe Cl. NW2 | 89 | H2 |
| Horseshoe La. N20 | 56 | A1 |
| Horseshoe La., Enf. | 43 | J3 |
| *Chase Side* | | |
| Horsfeld Gdns. SE9 | 156 | B5 |
| Horsfeld Rd. SE9 | 156 | A5 |
| Horsford Rd. SW2 | 151 | F5 |
| Horsham Av. N12 | 57 | H5 |
| Horsham Rd., Bexh. | 159 | G5 |
| Horsham Rd., Felt. | 141 | F6 |
| Horsley Dr., Croy. | 204 | C7 |
| Horsley Dr., Kings.T. | 163 | G5 |
| Horsley Rd. E4 | 62 | C2 |
| Horsley Rd., Brom. | 191 | H1 |
| *Palace Rd.* | | |
| **Horsley St. SE17** | 36 | B5 |
| Horsley St. SE17 | 132 | A6 |
| Horsmonden Cl., Orp. | 193 | H7 |
| Horsmonden Rd. SE4 | 153 | J5 |
| **Hortensia Rd. SW10** | 30 | C7 |
| Hortensia Rd. SW10 | 129 | F7 |
| Horticultural Pl. W4 | 126 | D5 |
| *Heathfield Ter.* | | |
| Horton Av. NW2 | 90 | B4 |
| Horton Br. Rd., West Dr. | 120 | C1 |
| Horton Cl., West Dr. | 120 | C1 |
| Horton Ind. Pk., West Dr. | 120 | C1 |
| Horton Rd. E8 | 94 | E6 |
| Horton Rd., West Dr. | 120 | D1 |
| Horton St. SE13 | 154 | B3 |
| Horton Way, Croy. | 189 | G5 |
| Hortus Rd. E4 | 62 | C2 |
| Hortus Rd., Sthl. | 123 | F2 |
| Hosack Rd. SW17 | 167 | J2 |
| Hoser Av. SE12 | 173 | G2 |
| **Hosier La. EC1** | 19 | G2 |
| Hosier La. EC1 | 111 | H5 |
| Hoskins Cl. E16 | 115 | J6 |
| Hoskins Cl., Hayes | 121 | J5 |
| *Cranford Dr.* | | |
| Hoskins St. SE10 | 134 | D5 |
| Hospital Br. Rd., Twick. | 143 | H7 |
| *Homerton Row* | | |
| Hospital Rd. E9 | 95 | G5 |
| Hospital Rd., Houns. | 143 | G3 |
| Hotham Cl., W.Mol. | 179 | G3 |
| *Garrick Gdns.* | | |
| Hotham Rd. SW15 | 147 | J3 |
| Hotham Rd. SW19 | 167 | F7 |
| Hotham Rd. Ms. SW19 | 167 | F7 |
| *Haydons Rd.* | | |
| Hotham St. E15 | 114 | E1 |
| Hothfield Pl. SE16 | 133 | F3 |
| *Lower Rd.* | | |
| Hotspur Rd., Nthlt. | 103 | G2 |
| **Hotspur St. SE11** | 34 | E3 |
| Hotspur St. SE11 | 131 | G5 |
| Houblon Rd., Rich. | 145 | H5 |
| Houghton Cl. E8 | 94 | C6 |
| *Buttermere Wk.* | | |
| Houghton Rd. N15 | 76 | C5 |
| *West Grn. Rd.* | | |
| **Houghton St. WC2** | 18 | D4 |
| Houlder Cres., Croy. | 201 | H6 |
| Houndsden Rd. N21 | 43 | F6 |
| **Houndsditch EC3** | 20 | E3 |
| Houndsditch EC3 | 112 | B6 |
| Houndsfield Rd. N9 | 44 | E7 |
| Hounslow Av., Houns. | 143 | H5 |
| Hounslow Gdns., Houns. | 143 | H5 |
| Hounslow Rd. (Feltham), Felt. | 160 | B1 |
| Hounslow Rd. (Hanworth), Felt. | 160 | D4 |
| Hounslow Rd. (Whitton), Twick. | 143 | J6 |
| Houseman Way SE5 | 132 | A7 |
| *Hopewell St.* | | |
| Houston Pl., Esher | 194 | B1 |
| *Lime Tree Av.* | | |
| Houston Rd. SE23 | 171 | H2 |
| Houston Rd., Surb. | 181 | E6 |
| Hove Av. E17 | 77 | J5 |
| Hove Gdns., Sutt. | 199 | E1 |
| Hoveden Rd. NW2 | 90 | B5 |
| Hoveton Rd. SE28 | 118 | C6 |
| Howard Av., Bex. | 176 | C1 |
| Howard Cl. N11 | 58 | A2 |
| Howard Cl. NW2 | 90 | B4 |
| Howard Cl. W3 | 106 | B6 |
| Howard Cl., Hmptn. | 161 | J6 |
| Howard Cl., Loug. | 48 | B6 |
| Howard Dr., Borwd. | 38 | D4 |
| Howard Ms. N5 | 93 | H4 |
| *Hamilton Pk.* | | |
| **Howard Pl. SW1** | 25 | F6 |
| Howard Rd. E6 | 116 | C2 |
| Howard Rd. E11 | 97 | E3 |
| Howard Rd. E17 | 78 | A3 |
| Howard Rd. N15 | 76 | B6 |
| Howard Rd. N16 | 94 | A4 |
| Howard Rd. NW2 | 90 | A4 |
| Howard Rd. SE20 | 189 | F1 |
| Howard Rd. SE25 | 188 | D5 |
| Howard Rd., Bark. | 117 | G1 |
| Howard Rd., Brom. | 173 | G7 |
| Howard Rd., Ilf. | 99 | E4 |
| Howard Rd., Islw. | 144 | C3 |
| Howard Rd., N.Mal. | 183 | E3 |
| Howard Rd., Sthl. | 103 | H6 |
| Howard St., T.Ditt. | 181 | E7 |
| Howard Wk. N2 | 73 | F4 |
| Howard Way, Barn. | 40 | A5 |
| Howards Cl., Pnr. | 66 | B2 |
| Howards Crest Cl., Beck. | 190 | C2 |
| Howards La. SW15 | 147 | H4 |
| Howards Rd. E13 | 115 | G3 |
| Howarth Ct. E15 | 96 | C5 |
| *Clays La.* | | |
| Howarth Rd. SE2 | 138 | A5 |
| Howberry Cl., Edg. | 53 | G6 |
| Howberry Rd., Edg. | 53 | G6 |
| Howberry Rd., Stan. | 53 | G6 |
| Howberry Rd., Th.Hth. | 188 | A1 |
| Howbury Rd. SE15 | 153 | F3 |
| Howcroft Cres. N3 | 56 | D7 |
| Howcroft La., Grnf. | 104 | A3 |
| *Cowgate Rd.* | | |
| Howden Cl. SE28 | 118 | D7 |
| Howden Rd. SE25 | 188 | C2 |
| Howden St. SE15 | 152 | D3 |
| Howe Cl., Rom. | 83 | G1 |
| Howe Cl., Rom. | 82 | D5 |
| **Howell Wk. SE1** | 35 | H2 |
| Howes Cl. N3 | 72 | D3 |
| Howfield Pl. N17 | 76 | C3 |
| Howgate Rd. SW14 | 146 | D3 |

**Howick Pl. SW1** 25 G6
Howick Pl. SW1 130 C3
Howie St. SW11 129 H7
Howitt Cl. NW3 91 H6
*Howitt Rd.*
Howitt Rd. NW3 91 H6
Howland Est. SE16 133 F3
**Howland Ms. E. W1** 17 G1
**Howland St. W1** 17 F1
Howland St. W1 110 C5
Howland Way SE16 133 H2
Howletts Rd. SE24 151 J6
**Howley Pl. W2** 14 D1
Howley Pl. W2 109 F5
Howley Rd., Croy. 201 H3
**Hows St. E2** 13 F1
Hows St. E2 112 C2
Howsman Rd. SW13 127 G6
Howson Rd. SE4 153 H4
Howson Ter., Rich. 145 H6
Howton Pl., Bushey 52 A1
**Hoxton Mkt. N1** 12 D4
**Hoxton Sq. N1** 12 D4
Hoxton Sq. N1 112 B3
**Hoxton St. N1** 12 E4
Hoxton St. N1 112 B1
Hoy St. E16 115 F6
Hoylake Gdns., Mitch. 186 C3
Hoylake Gdns., Ruis. 84 B1
Hoylake Rd., Wat. 50 D4
Hoylake Rd. W3 107 E6
Hoyland Cl. SE15 132/133 E7
*Commercial Way*
Hoyle Rd. SW17 167 H5
Hubbard Dr., Chess. 195 F6
Hubbard Rd. SE27 169 J4
Hubbard St. E15 114 E1
Hubbinet Ind. Est., 83 J3
Rom.
Hubert Gro. SW9 151 E3
Hubert Rd. E6 116 A3
Huddart St. E3 114 A5
Huddleston Cl. E2 113 F2
Huddleston Rd. N7 92 D4
Huddlestone Rd. NW2 89 H6
Huddlestone Rd. E14 134 A5
*Napier Av.*
Hudson Ct. SW19 167 E7
Hudson Gdns., Orp. 207 J6
*Superior Dr.*
Hudson Pl. SE18 137 F5
Hudson Rd., Bexh. 159 F2
Hudson Rd., Hayes 121 G6
**Hudson's Pl. SW1** 33 E1
**Huggin Ct. EC4** 20 A5
**Huggin Hill EC4** 20 A5
Huggins Pl. SW2 169 F1
*Roupell Rd.*
Hugh Dalton Av. 128 C6
SW6
Hugh Gaitskell Cl. 128 C6
SW6
**Hugh Ms. SW1** 33 E2
**Hugh Pl. SW1** 33 H1
**Hugh St. SW1** 32 E2
Hugh St. SW1 130 B4
Hughan Rd. E15 96 D5
Hughenden Av., Har. 69 E5
Hughenden Gdns., 102 C3
Nthlt.
Hughenden Rd., 183 G7
Wor.Pk.
Hughenden Ter. E15 96 C4
*Westdown Rd.*
Hughes Rd., Hayes 102 B7
Hughes Wk., Croy. 187 J7
*St. Saviours Rd.*
Hugo Rd. N19 92 C4
Hugon Rd. SW6 148 E3
**Huguenot Pl. E1** 21 G1
Huguenot Pl. E1 112 C5
Huguenot Pl. SW18 149 F5
Huguenot Sq. 152/153 E3
SE15
*Scylla Rd.*
Hull Cl. SE16 133 G2
Hull Pl. E16 136/137 E2
*Barge Ho. Rd.*
**Hull St. EC1** 11 J4
Hullbridge Ms. N1 112 A1
*Sherborne St.*
Hulse Av., Bark. 99 G6
Hulse Av., Rom. 83 H1
Hulse Ter., Ilf. 99 F5
*Buttsbury Rd.*
Humber Cl., West 120 A1
Dr.
Humber Dr. W10 108 A4
Humber Rd. NW2 89 H2
Humber Rd. SE3 135 F6
Humberstone Rd. E13 115 J3
Humberton Cl. E9 95 H5
*Marsh Hill*

Humbolt Rd. W6 128 B6
Hume Ter. E16 115 J6
*Prince Regent La.*
Hume Way, Ruis. 66 A6
Humes Av. W7 124 B3
Humphrey Cl., Ilf. 80 C1
**Humphrey St. SE1** 37 F3
Humphrey St. SE1 132 C5
Humphries Cl., Dag. 101 F4
Hundred Acre NW9 71 F2
**Hungerford Br. SE1** 26 B1
Hungerford Br. SE1 131 E1
**Hungerford Br. WC2** 26 B1
Hungerford Br. WC2 131 E1
**Hungerford La. WC2** 26 A1
Hungerford Rd. N7 92 E5
Hungerford St. E1 112/113 E6
*Commercial Rd.*
Hunsdon Cl., Dag. 101 E6
Hunsdon Rd. SE14 133 G6
Hunslett St. E2 113 F2
*Royston St.*
Hunston Rd., Mord. 198 E1
Hunt Rd., Sthl. 123 G3
Hunt St. W11 128 A1
Hunt Way SE22 170 D1
*Dulwich Common*
**Hunter Cl. SE1** 28 C6
Hunter Cl. SW12 168 A1
*Balham Pk. Rd.*
Hunter Cl., Borwd. 38 C5
Hunter Ho., Felt. 160 A1
Hunter Rd. SW20 183 J1
Hunter Rd., Ilf. 99 E5
Hunter Rd., Th.Hth. 188 A3
**Hunter St. WC1** 10 B5
Hunter St. WC1 111 E4
Hunter Wk. E13 115 G2
Hunter Wk., Borwd. 38 C5
*Ashley Dr.*
Huntercrombe Gdns., 50 C4
Wat.
Hunters, The, Beck. 190 C1
Hunters Ct., Rich. 145 G5
*Friars La.*
Hunters Gro., Har. 69 F4
Hunters Gro., Hayes 122 A1
Hunters Gro., Orp. 207 E4
Hunters Hall Rd., 101 G4
Dag.
Hunters Hill, Ruis. 84 C3
Hunters Meadow 170 B4
SE19
*Dulwich Wd. Av.*
Hunters Rd., Chess. 195 H3
Hunters Sq., Dag. 101 G4
Hunters Way, Croy. 202 B4
*Brownlow Rd.*
Hunters Way, Enf. 43 G1
Hunting Gate Cl., 43 G3
Enf.
Hunting Gate Dr., 195 H7
Chess.
Hunting Gate Ms., 199 E3
Sutt.
Hunting Gate Ms., 162 B1
Twick.
*Colne Rd.*
Huntingdon Cl., 187 E3
Mitch.
Huntingdon Gdns. 126 C7
W4
Huntingdon Gdns., 197 J3
Wor.Pk.
Huntingdon Rd. N2 73 H3
Huntingdon Rd. N9 61 F1
Huntingdon St. E16 115 F6
Huntingdon St. N1 93 F7
Huntingfield, Croy. 203 J7
Huntingfield Rd. 147 G5
SW15
Huntings Rd., Dag. 101 G6
Huntley Dr. N3 56 D6
**Huntley St. WC1** 9 G6
Huntley St. WC1 110 C4
Huntley Way SW20 183 G2
Huntly Rd. SE25 188 B4
**Hunton St. E1** 13 H6
Hunton St. E1 112 D4
Hunt's Cl. SE3 155 G2
**Hunt's Ct. WC2** 17 J6
Hunts La. E15 114 C2
Hunts Mead, Enf. 45 G3
Hunts Mead Cl., 174 C7
Chis.
Hunts Slip Rd. SE21 170 B3
**Huntsman St. SE17** 36 C2
Huntsman St. SE17 132 A4
Huntsmans Cl., Felt. 160 B4
Huntsmoor Rd., 196 D5
Epsom
Huntspill St. SW17 167 F3
**Huntsworth Ms. NW1** 7 J6

Hurley Cres. SE16 133 G2
*Marlow Way*
**Hurley Rd. SE11** 35 F2
Hurley Rd. SE11 131 G4
Hurley Rd., Grnf. 103 H6
Hurlingham Ct. SW6 148 C3
Hurlingham Gdns. 148 C3
SW6
Hurlingham Rd. SW6 148 C2
Hurlingham Rd., 139 F7
Bexh.
Hurlingham Sq. 148/149 E3
SW6
*Peterborough Rd.*
Hurlock St. N5 93 H3
Hurlstone Rd. SE25 188 A5
Hurn Ct. Rd., Houns. 142 D2
*Renfrew Rd.*
Huron Cl., Orp. 207 J6
*Winnipeg Dr.*
Huron Rd. SW17 168 A2
Hurren Cl. SE3 154 E3
Hurry Cl. E15 97 E7
Hursley Rd., Chig. 65 J5
*Tufter Rd.*
Hurst Av. E4 62 A4
Hurst Av. N6 74 C6
Hurst Cl. E4 62 A3
Hurst Cl. NW11 72 E6
Hurst Cl., Brom. 205 F1
Hurst Cl., Chess. 196 A5
Hurst Cl., Nthlt. 85 F5
Hurst Est. SE2 138 D5
Hurst La. SE2 138 D5
Hurst La., E.Mol. 179 J4
Hurst Ri., Barn. 40 D3
Hurst Rd. E17 78 B3
Hurst Rd. N21 59 G1
Hurst Rd., Bex. 176 D1
Hurst Rd., Buck.H. 64 A1
Hurst Rd., Croy. 202 A5
Hurst Rd., E.Mol. 179 H3
Hurst Rd., Erith 139 J7
Hurst Rd., Sid. 176 B3
Hurst Rd., Walt. 178 C5
Hurst Rd., W.Mol. 179 E3
Hurst Springs, Bex. 177 E1
Hurst St. SE24 151 H6
Hurst Vw. Rd., 202 B7
S.Croy.
Hurst Way, S.Croy. 202 B6
Hurstbourne, Esher 194 C6
Hurstbourne Gdns., 99 H6
Bark.
Hurstbourne Rd. 171 H1
SE23
Hurstcourt Rd., Sutt. 198 E2
Hurstdene Av., 205 F1
Brom.
Hurstdene Gdns. N15 76 B7
Hurstfield, Brom. 191 G5
Hurstfield Rd., W.Mol. 179 G3
Hurstleigh Gdns., Ilf. 80 C1
Hurstmead Ct., Edg. 54 B4
Hurstway Wk. N11 108 A7
Hurstwood Av. E18 79 H4
Hurstwood Av., Bex. 176 E1
Hurstwood Dr., Brom. 192 C3
Hurstwood Rd. NW11 72 B4
Hurtwood Rd., Walt. 179 F7
Huson Cl. NW3 91 H7
Hussars Cl., Houns. 142 E3
Husseywell Cres., 205 G1
Brom.
Hutchings St. E14 134 A2
Hutchings Wk. NW11 73 E4
Hutchins Cl. E15 96 C7
*Gibbins Rd.*
Hutchins Rd. SE28 118 A7
Hutchinson Ter., Wem. 87 G3
Hutton Cl., Grnf. 86 A5
*Mary Peters Dr.*
Hutton Cl., Wdf.Grn. 63 H6
Hutton Gdns., Har. 51 J7
Hutton Gro. N12 57 E5
Hutton La., Har. 51 J7
Hutton Row, Edg. 54 C7
*Pavilion Way*
**Hutton St. EC4** 19 F4
Hutton Wk., Har. 51 J7
Huxbear St. SE4 153 J5
Huxley Cl., Nthlt. 103 E1
Huxley Dr., Rom. 82 B7
Huxley Gdns. NW10 105 J3
Huxley Par. N18 60 A5
Huxley Pl. N13 59 H4
Huxley Rd. E10 96 C2
Huxley Rd. N18 60 A4
Huxley Rd., Well. 157 J3
Huxley Sayze N18 60 A5
Huxley St. W10 108 B3
Hyacinth Cl., Hmptn. 161 G6
*Gresham Rd.*
Hyacinth Cl., Ilf. 98 E6

Hyacinth Ct., Pnr. 66 C3
*Tulip Ct.*
Hyacinth Rd. SW15 165 G1
Hycliffe Gdns., Chig. 65 F4
Hyde, The NW9 71 E5
Hyde Cl. E13 115 G2
Hyde Cl., Barn. 40 C3
Hyde Cl. N20 57 G3
Hyde Cres. NW9 71 E5
Hyde Est. Rd. NW9 71 F5
Hyde Ho. NW9 71 E5
Hyde La. SW11 149 H1
*Battersea Br. Rd.*
**Hyde Pk. SW7** 23 G1
Hyde Pk. SW7 129 J1
**Hyde Pk. W1** 23 G1
Hyde Pk. W1 129 J1
**Hyde Pk. W2** 23 G1
Hyde Pk. W2 129 J1
Hyde Pk. Av. N21 59 J2
**Hyde Pk. Cor. W1** 24 C3
Hyde Pk. Cor. W1 130 A2
**Hyde Pk. Cres. W2** 15 G4
Hyde Pk. Cres. W2 109 H6
Hyde Pk. Gdns. N21 59 J1
**Hyde Pk. Gdns. W2** 15 F5
Hyde Pk. Gdns. W2 109 G7
**Hyde Pk. Gdns. Ms.** 15 F5
**W2**
**Hyde Pk. Gate SW7** 22 D4
Hyde Pk. Gate SW7 129 F2
**Hyde Pk. Gate Ms.** 22 D4
**SW7**
**Hyde Pk. Pl. W2** 15 H5
Hyde Pk. Pl. W2 109 H7
**Hyde Pk. Sq. W2** 15 G4
Hyde Pk. Sq. W2 109 H6
**Hyde Pk. Sq. Ms. W2** 15 G4
**Hyde Pk. St. W2** 15 G4
Hyde Pk. St. W2 109 H6
Hyde Rd. N1 112 A1
Hyde Rd., Bexh. 159 F2
Hyde Rd., Rich. 145 J5
*Albert Rd.*
Hyde St. SE8 134 A6
*Deptford High St.*
Hyde Vale SE10 134 C7
Hyde Wk., Mord. 184 D7
Hyde Way N9 60 C2
Hyde Way, Hayes 121 J4
Hydefield Cl. N21 60 A1
Hydefield Ct. N9 60 B2
Hyderabad Way E15 96 E7
Hydes Pl. N1 93 H7
*Compton Av.*
Hydeside Gdns. N9 60 C2
Hydethorpe Av. N9 60 C2
Hydethorpe Rd. SW12 168 C1
Hylands Rd. E17 78 D2
Hylton St. SE18 137 J4
Hyndewood SE23 171 G3
Hyndman St. SE15 132 E6
Hynton Rd., Dag. 100 C2
Hyrstdene, S.Croy. 201 H4
Hyson Rd. SE16 132/133 E4
*Galleywall Rd.*
Hythe Av., Bexh. 139 F7
Hythe Cl. N18 60 D4
Hythe Path, Th.Hth. 188 A3
Hythe Rd. NW10 107 G4
Hythe Rd., Th.Hth. 188 A2
Hyver Hill NW7 38 D6

# I

Ian Sq., Enf. 45 G1
*Lansbury Rd.*
Ibbetson Path, Loug. 49 E3
Ibbotson Av. E16 115 F6
Ibbott St. E1 113 F4
*Mantus Rd.*
Iberian Av., Wall. 200 D4
Ibis La. W4 146 C1
Ibis Way, Hayes 102 D6
*Cygnet Way*
Ibscott Cl., Dag. 101 J6
Ibsley Gdns. SW15 165 G1
Ibsley Way, Barn. 41 H5
**Ice Wf. Marina N1** 10 B1
Iceland Rd. E3 114 A1
Iceni Ct. E3 113 J1
*Roman Rd.*
Ickburgh Est. E5 94/95 E3
*Ickburgh Rd.*
Ickburgh Rd. E5 94 E3
Ickleton Rd. SE9 174 B4
Icknield Dr., Ilf. 81 E5
Ickworth Pk. Rd. E17 77 H4
Ida Rd. N15 76 A5
Ida St. E14 114 C6
Iden Cl., Brom. 191 E3
Idlecombe Rd. SW17 168 A6
Idmiston Rd. E15 97 F5
Idmiston Rd. SE27 169 J3

Killyon Ter. SW8 150 C2
Kilmaine Rd. SW6 128 B7
Kilmarnock Gdns., Dag. 100 C3
*Lindsey Rd.*
Kilmarnock Rd., Wat. 50 D4
Kilmarsh Rd. W6 127 J4
Kilmartin Av. SW16 187 F3
Kilmartin Rd., Ilf. 100 A2
**Kilmeston Way SE15 37 F7**
Kilmington Rd. SW13 127 G6
Kilmorey Gdns., Twick. 144 E5
Kilmorey Rd., Twick. 144 E4
Kilmorie Rd. SE23 171 H1
Kiln Cl., Hayes 121 G6
*Brickfield La.*
Kiln Ms. SW17 167 G5
Kiln Pl. NW5 92 A5
Kilner St. E14 114 A5
Kilnside, Esher 194 D7
Kilpatrick Way, Hayes 103 E5
Kilravock St. W10 108 B3
Kilsby Wk., Dag. 100 B6
*Rugby Rd.*
Kilsha Rd., Walt. 178 B6
Kimbell Gdns. SW6 148 B1
Kimbell Pl. SE3 155 J4
*Tudway Rd.*
Kimber Rd. SW18 148 D7
Kimberley Av. E6 116 B2
Kimberley Av. SE15 153 E2
Kimberley Av., Ilf. 81 G7
Kimberley Av., Rom. 83 J6
Kimberley Dr., Sid. 176 D2
Kimberley Gdns. N4 75 H5
Kimberley Gdns., Enf. 44 C3
Kimberley Gate, Brom. 173 F7
*Oaklands Rd.*
Kimberley Rd. E4 62 E1
Kimberley Rd. E11 96 D2
Kimberley Rd. E16 115 F4
Kimberley Rd. E17 77 J1
Kimberley Rd. N17 76 D2
Kimberley Rd. N18 61 E6
Kimberley Rd. NW6 108 B1
Kimberley Rd. SW9 151 E2
Kimberley Rd., Beck. 189 G2
Kimberley Rd., Croy. 187 H6
Kimberley Way E4 63 E1
Kimble Rd. SW19 167 G6
Kimbolton Cl. SE12 155 F6
Kimbolton Grn., Borwd. 38 C4
**Kimbolton Row SW3 31 G2**
Kimmeridge Gdns. SE9 174 B4
Kimmeridge Rd. SE9 174 B4
Kimpton Rd. SE5 152 A1
Kimpton Rd., Sutt. 198 C2
Kimpton Trade Business Cen., Sutt. 198 C2
Kinburn St. SE16 133 G2
Kincaid Rd. SE15 132 E7
Kincardine Gdns. W9 108 C4
*Harrow Rd.*
Kinch Gro., Wem. 69 J7
Kinder Cl. SE28 118 D7
Kinder St. E1 112/113 E6
*Cannon St. Rd.*
Kinfauns Rd. SW2 169 G2
Kinfauns Rd., Ilf. 100 A1
King Alfred Av. SE6 172 A3
King & Queen Cl. SE9 174 B4
*St. Keverne Rd.*
**King & Queen St. SE17 36 A2**
King & Queen St. SE17 131 J5
King Arthur Cl. SE15 133 F7
King Charles Cres., Surb. 181 J7
King Charles Rd., Surb. 181 J5
**King Charles St. SW1 25 J3**
King Charles St. SW1 130 D2
King Charles Ter. E1 112/113 E7
*Sovereign Cl.*
King Charles Wk. SW19 166 B1
*Princes Way*
King David La. E1 113 F7
King Edward Dr., Chess. 195 H3
*Kelvin Gro.*
King Edward Ms. SW13 147 G1
King Edward Rd. E10 96 C1
King Edward Rd. E17 77 H3
King Edward Rd., Barn. 40 D4
**King Edward St. EC1 19 J3**
King Edward St. EC1 111 J6
King Edward III Ms. SE16 132/133 E2
*Paradise St.*
**King Edward Wk. SE1 27 F5**
King Edward Wk. SE1 131 G3
King Edward's Gdns. W3 126 A1
King Edwards Gro., Tedd. 163 E6
King Edward's Pl. W3 126 A1
*King Edward's Gdns.*
King Edwards Rd. E9 113 E1
King Edwards Rd. N9 44 E7
King Edwards Rd., Bark. 117 G1
King Edward's Rd., Enf. 45 G4
King Frederik IX Twr. SE16 133 J3
*Finland St.*
King Gdns., Croy. 201 H5
King George Av. E16 116 A6
King George Av., Ilf. 81 G5
King George Cl., Rom. 83 J3
King George VI Av., Mitch. 185 J4
King George Sq., Rich. 145 J6
King George St. SE10 134 C7
King Georges Dr., Sthl. 103 F5
King George's Trd. Est., Chess. 196 A4
King Harolds Way, Bexh. 138 D7
King Henry Ms., Orp. 207 J5
*Osgood Av.*
King Henry St. N16 94 B5
King Henry Ter. E1 112/113 E7
*Sovereign Cl.*
King Henry's Rd. NW3 91 H7
King Henry's Rd., Kings.T. 182 B3
King Henry's Wk. N1 94 B6
**King James St. SE1 27 H4**
King James St. SE1 131 H2
**King John Ct. EC2 12 E5**
King John St. E1 113 G5
King Johns Wk. SE9 174 A1
**King Sq. EC1 11 J4**
King Stairs Cl. SE16 132/133 E2
*Elephant La.*
King St. E13 115 G4
**King St. EC2 20 A4**
King St. EC2 111 J6
King St. N2 73 G3
King St. N17 76 C1
**King St. SW1 25 G2**
King St. SW1 130 C1
King St. W3 126 B1
King St. W6 127 G4
**King St. WC2 18 A5**
King St. WC2 110 E7
King St., Rich. 145 G5
King St., Sthl. 123 E3
King St., Twick. 162 D1
King William IV Gdns. SE20 171 F6
*St. John's Rd.*
King William La. SE10 134/135 E5
*Orlop St.*
**King William St. EC4 20 C6**
King William St. EC4 112 A7
King William Wk. SE10 134 C6
Kingcup Cl., Croy. 203 G1
*Primrose La.*
Kingdon Rd. NW6 90 D6
Kingfield Rd. W5 105 G4
Kingfield St. E14 134 C4
Kingfisher Av. E11 79 H6
*Eastern Av.*
Kingfisher Cl. SE28 118 C7
Kingfisher Cl., Har. 52 C7
Kingfisher Ct. SW19 166 B2
*Queensmere Rd.*
Kingfisher Ct., Sutt. 198 B2
*Gander Grn. La.*
Kingfisher Dr., Rich. 163 E4
Kingfisher Sq. SE8 133 J6
Kingfisher St. E6 116 B5
Kingfisher Wk. NW9 70/71 E2
*Eagle Dr.*
Kingfisher Way NW10 88 D6
Kingfisher Way, Beck. 189 G5
Kingham Cl. SW18 149 F7
Kingham Cl. W11 128 B2
**Kinghorn St. EC1 19 J2**
**Kinglake Est. SE17 37 E3**
**Kinglake St. SE17 36 D4**
Kinglake St. SE17 132 B5
**Kingly Ct. W1 17 F5**
**Kingly St. W1 17 F4**
Kingly St. W1 110 C6
Kings Arbour, Sthl. 122 E5
**Kings Arms Ct. E1 21 H2**
**Kings Arms Yd. EC2 20 B3**
Kings Av. N10 74 A3
Kings Av. N21 59 H1
King's Av. SW4 150 D7
King's Av. SW12 168 D1
Kings Av. W5 105 G6
Kings Av., Brom. 173 F6
Kings Av., Buck.H. 64 A2
Kings Av., Cars. 199 H7
Kings Av., Grnf. 103 H6
Kings Av., Houns. 143 H1
Kings Av., N.Mal. 183 E4
Kings Av., Rom. 83 F6
Kings Av., Wdf.Grn. 63 H5
**Kings Bench St. SE1 27 H3**
**Kings Bench Wk. EC4 19 F4**
Kings Chace Vw., Enf. 43 G2
*Crofton Way*
Kings Chase, E.Mol. 179 J3
Kings Cl. E10 78 B7
Kings Cl. NW4 72 A4
Kings Cl., T.Ditt. 180 D6
Kings College Rd. NW3 91 H7
Kings Ct. E13 115 H1
Kings Ct. W6 127 G4
*King St.*
Kings Ct., Wem. 88 B2
Kings Cres. N4 93 J3
Kings Cres. Est. N4 93 J2
**King's Cross Br. N1 10 B3**
**King's Cross Rd. WC1 10 D3**
King's Cross Rd. WC1 111 F3
Kings Dr., Edg. 53 J4
Kings Dr., Surb. 182 A7
Kings Dr., Tedd. 162 A5
Kings Dr., T.Ditt. 180 E6
Kings Dr., Wem. 88 B2
Kings Fm. Av., Rich. 146 A4
Kings Gdns. NW6 90 D7
*West End La.*
Kings Gdns., Ilf. 99 G1
King's Garth Ms. SE23 171 F2
*London Rd.*
Kings Grn., Loug. 48 B3
Kings Gro. SE15 133 E7
Kings Hall Rd., Beck. 171 H7
Kings Head Hill E4 46 B7
**Kings Head Yd. SE1 28 B2**
Kings Highway SE18 137 H6
Kings Hill, Loug. 48 B2
Kings Keep, Kings.T. 181 H4
*Beaufort Rd.*
Kings La., Sutt. 199 G6
Kings Mead Pk., Esher 194 B7
Kings Ms. SW4 150/151 E5
*King's Av.*
**King's Ms. WC1 10 D6**
King's Ms. WC1 111 F5
Kings Ms., Chig. 65 F2
Kings Oak, Rom. 83 G3
King's Orchard SE9 156 B6
Kings Paddock, Hmptn. 179 J1
Kings Par., Cars. 199 H3
*Wrythe La.*
King's Pas. E11 78 E7
Kings Pas., Kings.T. 181 G2
**Kings Pl. SE1 27 J4**
Kings Pl. W4 126 C5
Kings Pl., Buck.H. 63 J2
Kings Pl., Loug. 47 J7
*Fallow Flds.*
**King's Reach Twr. SE1 27 F1**
King's Reach Twr. SE1 131 G1
Kings Ride Gate, Rich. 146 A4
Kings Rd. E4 62 D1
Kings Rd. E6 115 J1
Kings Rd. E11 78 E7
King's Rd. N17 76 C1
Kings Rd. N18 60 D5
Kings Rd. N22 75 F1
Kings Rd. NW10 89 H7
Kings Rd. SE25 188 D3
**King's Rd. SW1 31 H3**
King's Rd. SW1 129 J5
**King's Rd. SW3 31 H3**
King's Rd. SW3 129 J5
King's Rd. SW6 148 E1
King's Rd. SW10 148 E1
Kings Rd. SW14 146 D3
Kings Rd. SW19 166 D6
Kings Rd. W5 105 G5
Kings Rd., Bark. 99 F7
*North St.*
Kings Rd., Barn. 39 J3
Kings Rd., Felt. 160 C1
Kings Rd., Har. 85 F2
Kings Rd., Kings.T. 163 H7
Kings Rd., Mitch. 186 A3
Kings Rd., Orp. 207 J4
Kings Rd., Rich. 145 J5
Kings Rd., Surb. 195 F1
Kings Rd., Tedd. 162 A5
Kings Rd., Twick. 145 E6
Kings Rd., West Dr. 120 C2
Kings Rd. Bungalows, Har. 85 F3
*Kings Rd.*
**King's Scholars' Pas. SW1 33 F1**
King's Ter. NW1 110 C1
*Plender St.*
Kings Ter., Islw. 144 D3
*Worple Rd.*
King's Wk., Kings.T. 181 G1
Kings Way, Har. 68 B4
Kingsand Rd. SE12 173 G2
Kingsash Dr., Hayes 102 E4
Kingsbridge Av. W3 125 J2
Kingsbridge Cres., Sthl. 103 F5
Kingsbridge Rd. W10 107 J6
Kingsbridge Rd., Bark. 117 G2
Kingsbridge Rd., Mord. 184 A7
Kingsbridge Rd., Sthl. 123 F4
Kingsbridge Rd., Walt. 178 B7
Kingsbury Circle NW9 70 A5
Kingsbury Rd. N1 94 B6
Kingsbury Rd. NW9 70 B5
Kingsbury Ter. N1 94 B6
Kingsbury Trd. Est. NW9 70 D6
Kingsclere Cl. SW15 147 G7
Kingsclere Pl., Enf. 43 J2
*Chase Side*
Kingscliffe Gdns. SW19 166 C1
Kingscote Rd. W4 126 D3
Kingscote Rd., Croy. 188 E7
Kingscote Rd., N.Mal. 182 D3
**Kingscote St. EC4 19 G5**
Kingscourt Rd. SW16 168 D3
Kingscroft Rd. NW2 90 C6
Kingsdale Gdns. W11 128 A1
Kingsdale Rd. SE18 137 J7
Kingsdale Rd. SE20 171 G7
Kingsdown Av. W3 107 E7
Kingsdown Av. W13 125 E2
Kingsdown Cl. SE16 132/133 E5
*Masters Dr.*
Kingsdown Cl. W10 108 A6
Kingsdown Rd. E11 97 E3
Kingsdown Rd. N19 92 E2
Kingsdown Rd., Sutt. 198 B5
Kingsdown Way, Brom. 191 G7
Kingsdowne Rd., Surb. 181 H7
Kingsfield Av., Har. 67 H4
Kingsfield Ho. SE9 174 A3
Kingsfield Rd., Har. 68 A7
Kingsford Av., Wall. 201 E7
Kingsford St. NW5 91 J5
Kingsford Way E6 116 C5
Kingsgate, Wem. 88 C3
Kingsgate Av. N3 72 D3
Kingsgate Cl., Bexh. 158 E1
Kingsgate Pl. NW6 90 D7
Kingsgate Rd. NW6 90 D7
Kingsgate Rd., Kings.T. 181 H1
Kingsground SE9 156 B7
Kingshall Ms. SE13 154 C3
*Lewisham Rd.*
Kingshill Av., Har. 69 E4
Kingshill Av., Nthlt. 102 A3
Kingshill Av., Wor.Pk. 183 G7
Kingshill Dr., Har. 68 E3
Kingshold Rd. E9 95 F7
Kingsholm Gdns. SE9 156 A4
Kingshurst Rd. SE12 155 G7
Kingsland NW8 109 H1
*Broxwood Way*
Kingsland Grn. E8 94 B6
Kingsland High St. E8 94 C5
Kingsland Pas. E8 94 B6
*Kingsland Grn.*
**Kingsland Rd. E2 13 E3**
Kingsland Rd. E2 112 B2
Kingsland Rd. E8 112 B2
Kingsland Rd. E13 115 J3
Kingslawn Cl. SW15 147 H5
*Howards La.*

Kingsleigh Pl., Mitch. 185 J3
*Chatsworth Pl.*
Kingsleigh Wk., Brom. 191 F4
*Stamford Dr.*
Kingsley Av. W13 104 D6
Kingsley Av., Houns. 143 J2
Kingsley Av., Sthl. 103 G7
Kingsley Av., Sutt. 199 G4
Kingsley Cl. N2 73 F5
Kingsley Cl., Dag. 101 H4
Kingsley Ct., Edg. 54 B2
Kingsley Dr., Wor.Pk. 197 F2
*Badgers Copse*
Kingsley Flats SE1 132 B4
*Old Kent Rd.*
Kingsley Gdns. E4 62 A5
Kingsley Ms. E1 112/113 E7
*Wapping La.*
**Kingsley Ms. W8 22 B6**
Kingsley Ms., Chis. 175 E6
Kingsley Pl. N6 74 A7
Kingsley Rd. E7 97 G7
Kingsley Rd. E17 78 C2
Kingsley Rd. N13 59 G4
Kingsley Rd. NW6 108 C1
Kingsley Rd. SW19 167 E5
Kingsley Rd., Croy. 201 G1
Kingsley Rd., Har. 85 J4
Kingsley Rd., Houns. 143 J2
Kingsley Rd., Ilf. 81 F1
Kingsley Rd., Loug. 49 G3
Kingsley Rd., Orp. 207 J7
Kingsley Rd., Pnr. 67 F4
Kingsley St. SW11 149 J3
Kingsley Way N2 73 F6
Kingsley Wd. Dr. SE9 174 C3
Kingslyn Cres. SE19 188 B1
Kingsman Par. SE18 136 C3
*Woolwich Ch. St.*
Kingsman St. SE18 136 C3
Kingsmead, Barn. 40 D4
Kingsmead, Rich. 145 J6
Kingsmead Av. N9 60 E1
Kingsmead Av. NW9 70 D7
Kingsmead Av., Mitch. 186 C3
Kingsmead Av., Sun. 178 C3
Kingsmead Av., Surb. 196 A2
Kingsmead Av., Wor.Pk. 197 H3
Kingsmead Cl., Epsom 196 D7
Kingsmead Cl., Sid. 176 A2
Kingsmead Cl., Tedd. 162 D6
Kingsmead Dr., Nthlt. 85 F7
Kingsmead Est. E9 95 H4
*Kingsmead Way*
Kingsmead Rd. SW2 169 G2
Kingsmead Way E9 95 H4
Kingsmere Cl. SW15 148 B3
*Felsham Rd.*
Kingsmere Pk. NW9 88 B1
Kingsmere Rd. SW19 166 A2
Kingsmill Gdns., Dag. 101 F5
Kingsmill Rd., Dag. 101 F5
**Kingsmill Ter. NW8 7 F1**
Kingsmill Ter. NW8 109 G2
Kingsnympton Pk., Kings.T. 164 B6
Kingspark Ct. E18 79 G3
Kingsridge SW19 166 B2
Kingsthorpe Rd. SE26 171 G4
Kingston Av., Felt. 141 H6
Kingston Av., Sutt. 198 B3
Kingston Br., Kings.T. 181 G2
Kingston Bypass SW15 165 E4
Kingston Bypass SW20 165 E4
Kingston Bypass, Esher 194 D3
Kingston Bypass, N.Mal. 183 F1
Kingston Bypass, Surb. 195 H3
Kingston Cl., Nthlt. 103 F1
Kingston Cl., Rom. 82 E3
Kingston Cl., Tedd. 162 E6
Kingston Ct. N4 75 J6
*Wiltshire Gdns.*
Kingston Cres., Beck. 189 J1
Kingston Gdns., Croy. 200/201 E3
*Wandle Rd.*
Kingston Hall Rd., Kings.T. 181 G3
Kingston Hill, Kings.T. 164 C6
Kingston Hill Av., Rom. 83 E3
Kingston Hill Pl., Kings.T. 164 C4
Kingston La., Tedd. 162 D5
Kingston La., West Dr. 120 C2
Kingston Pk. Est., Kings.T. 164 B6
Kingston Pl., Har. 52 C7
*Richmond Gdns.*
Kingston Rd. N9 60 D2
Kingston Rd. SW15 165 G1
Kingston Rd. SW19 184 C1
Kingston Rd. SW20 184 A2
Kingston Rd., Barn. 41 G5
Kingston Rd., Epsom 197 E5
Kingston Rd., Ilf. 99 E4
Kingston Rd., Kings.T. 182 B3
Kingston Rd., N.Mal. 182 D4
Kingston Rd., Sthl. 123 F2
Kingston Rd., Surb. 196 B2
Kingston Rd., Tedd. 162 E5
Kingston Rd., Wor.Pk. 196 B2
Kingston Sq. SE19 170 A5
Kingston Vale SW15 164 D4
Kingstown St. NW1 110 A1
Kingswater Pl. SW11 129 H7
*Battersea Ch. Rd.*
Kingsway N12 57 F6
Kingsway SW14 146 B3
**Kingsway WC2 18 C3**
Kingsway WC2 111 F6
Kingsway, Croy. 201 F5
Kingsway, Enf. 45 E5
Kingsway, N.Mal. 183 J4
Kingsway, Orp. 193 H5
Kingsway, Wem. 87 H4
Kingsway, W.Wick. 205 E3
Kingsway, Wdf.Grn. 63 J5
Kingsway Business Pk., Hmptn. 179 F1
Kingsway Cres., Har. 67 J4
Kingsway Rd., Sutt. 198 B7
Kingswear Rd. NW5 92 B3
Kingswear Rd., Ruis. 84 A2
Kingswood Av. NW6 108 B1
Kingswood Av., Belv. 139 F4
Kingswood Av., Brom. 190 E3
Kingswood Av., Hmptn. 161 H6
Kingswood Av., Houns. 143 F1
Kingswood Av., Th.Hth. 187 G5
Kingswood Cl. N20 41 F6
Kingswood Cl. SW8 131 E7
Kingswood Cl., Enf. 44 B5
Kingswood Cl., N.Mal. 183 F6
*Motspur Pk.*
Kingswood Cl., Orp. 193 G7
Kingswood Cl., Surb. 181 H7
Kingswood Dr. SE19 170 B4
Kingswood Dr., Cars. 199 J1
Kingswood Est. SE21 170 B4
*Bowen Dr.*
Kingswood Pk. N3 72 C2
Kingswood Pl. SE13 155 E4
Kingswood Rd. E11 96 D2
*Grove Grn. Rd.*
Kingswood Rd. SE20 171 F6
Kingswood Rd. SW2 150 E6
Kingswood Rd. SW19 166 C7
Kingswood Rd. W4 126 C3
Kingswood Rd., Brom. 190 D4
Kingswood Rd., Ilf. 100 A1
Kingswood Rd., Wem. 88 A3
Kingswood Ter. W4 126 C3
*Kingswood Rd.*
Kingswood Way, Wall. 201 E5
Kingsworth Cl., Beck. 189 H5
Kingsworthy Cl., Kings.T. 181 J3
Kingthorpe Rd. NW10 88 D7
Kingthorpe Ter. NW10 88 D6
Kingwood Rd. SW6 148 B1
Kinlet Rd. SE18 157 F1
Kinloch Dr. NW9 70 E7
Kinloch St. N7 93 F3
*Hornsey Rd.*
Kinloss Ct. N3 72 C4
*Haslemere Gdns.*
Kinloss Gdns. N3 72 C4
Kinloss Rd., Cars. 185 F7
Kinnaird Av. W4 126 C7
Kinnaird Av., Brom. 173 F6
Kinnaird Cl., Brom. 173 F6
Kinnaird Way, Wdf.Grn. 64 C6
Kinnear Rd. W12 127 F2
**Kinnerton Pl. N. SW1 24 A4**
**Kinnerton Pl. S. SW1 24 A4**
**Kinnerton St. SW1 24 B4**
Kinnerton St. SW1 130 A2
**Kinnerton Yd. SW1 24 A4**
Kinnoul Rd. W6 128 B6
Kinross Av., Wor.Pk. 197 G2
Kinross Cl., Edg. 54 B2
*Tayside Dr.*
Kinross Cl., Har. 69 J5
Kinsale Rd. SE15 152 D3
**Kintore Way SE1 37 F1**
Kintyre Cl. SW16 187 F3
Kinveachy Gdns. SE7 136 B5
Kinver Rd. SE26 171 F4
Kipling Dr. SW19 167 G6
**Kipling Est. SE1 28 C4**
Kipling Est. SE1 132 A2
Kipling Pl., Stan. 52 C6
*Uxbridge Rd.*
Kipling Rd., Bexh. 159 E1
**Kipling St. SE1 28 C4**
Kipling St. SE1 132 A2
Kipling Ter. N9 60 A3
Kippington Dr. SE9 174 A1
Kirby Cl., Epsom 197 F5
Kirby Cl., Ilf. 65 H6
Kirby Cl., Loug. 48 B7
Kirby Est. SE16 132 E3
**Kirby Gro. SE1 28 D3**
Kirby Gro. SE1 132 B2
**Kirby St. EC1 19 F1**
Kirby Way, Walt. 178 C6
Kirchen Rd. W13 104 E7
Kirk La. SE18 137 F6
Kirk Ri., Sutt. 199 E3
Kirk Rd. E17 77 J6
Kirkby Cl. N11 58 A6
*Coverdale Rd.*
Kirkcaldy Grn., Wat. 50 C3
*Trevose Way*
Kirkdale SE26 170 E2
Kirkdale Rd. E11 97 E1
Kirkfield Cl. W13 124/125 E1
*Broomfield Rd.*
Kirkham Rd. E6 116 B6
Kirkham St. SE18 137 H6
Kirkland Av., Ilf. 80 D2
Kirkland Cl., Sid. 157 H6
Kirkland Wk. E8 94 C6
Kirkleas Rd., Surb. 195 H1
Kirklees Rd., Dag. 100 C5
Kirklees Rd., Th.Hth. 187 G5
Kirkley Rd. SW19 184 D1
**Kirkman Pl. W1 17 H2**
Kirkmichael Rd. E14 114 C6
*Dee St.*
Kirks Pl. E14 113 J5
*Rhodeswell Rd.*
Kirkside Rd. SE3 135 G6
Kirkstall Av. N17 76 A4
Kirkstall Gdns. SW2 168 E1
Kirkstall Rd. SW2 168 D1
Kirkstead Ct. E5 95 H3
*Mandeville St.*
Kirksted Rd., Mord. 198 E1
Kirkstone Way, Brom. 173 E7
Kirkton Rd. N15 76 B4
Kirkwall Pl. E2 113 F3
Kirkwood Rd. SE15 153 E2
Kirn Rd. W13 104/105 E7
*Kirchen Rd.*
Kirrane Cl., N.Mal. 183 F5
Kirtley Rd. SE26 171 H4
**Kirtling St. SW8 33 F7**
Kirtling St. SW8 130 C7
Kirton Cl. W4 126 D4
*Dolman Rd.*
**Kirton Gdns. E2 13 G4**
Kirton Rd. E13 115 J2
Kirton Wk., Edg. 54 C7
**Kirwyn Way SE5 35 H7**
Kirwyn Way SE5 131 H7
Kitcat Ter. E3 114 A3
Kitchener Rd. E7 97 H6
Kitchener Rd. E17 78 B1
Kitchener Rd. N2 73 H3
Kitchener Rd. N17 76 A3
Kitchener Rd., Dag. 101 H6
Kitchener Rd., Th.Hth. 188 A3
**Kite Pl. E2 13 J3**
Kite Yd. SW11 149 J1
*Cambridge Rd.*
Kitley Gdns. SE19 188 C1
**Kitson Rd. SE5 36 A7**
Kitson Rd. SE5 132 A7
Kitson Rd. SW13 147 G1
Kittiwake Pl., Sutt. 198 B2
*Gander Grn. La.*
Kittiwake Rd., Nthlt. 102 D3
Kittiwake Way, Hayes 102 D5
Kitto Rd. SE14 153 G2
Kiver Rd. N19 92 D2
Kiwi Cl., Twick. 144/145 E6
*Crown Rd.*
Klea Av. SW4 150 C6
Knapdale Cl. SE23 171 E2
Knapmill Rd. SE6 172 A2
Knapmill Way SE6 172 B2
Knapp Cl. NW10 89 E6
Knapp Rd. E3 114 A4
Knapton Ms. SW17 168 A6
*Seely Rd.*
Knaresborough Dr. SW18 166 E1
**Knaresborough Pl. SW5 30 A1**
Knaresborough Pl. SW5 128 E4
Knatchbull Rd. NW10 106 D1
Knatchbull Rd. SE5 151 J1
Knebworth Av. E17 78 A1
Knebworth Path, Borwd. 38 D4
Knebworth Rd. N16 94 B4
*Nevill Rd.*
Knee Hill SE2 138 C4
Knee Hill Cres. SE2 138 C4
Kneller Gdns., Islw. 144 A5
Kneller Rd. SE4 153 H4
Kneller Rd., N.Mal. 182 E7
Kneller Rd., Twick. 143 J6
**Knighten St. E1 29 J2**
Knighten St. E1 132 D1
Knightland Rd. E5 94 E2
Knighton Cl., S.Croy. 201 H7
Knighton Cl., Wdf.Grn. 63 H4
Knighton Dr., Wdf.Grn. 63 G4
Knighton La., Buck.H. 63 H2
Knighton Pk. Rd. SE26 171 G5
Knighton Rd. E7 97 G3
Knighton Rd., Rom. 83 J6
**Knightrider Ct. EC4 19 J5**
Knightrider St. EC4 111 J7
*Godliman St.*
**Knights Arc. SW1 23 J4**
Knights Av. W5 125 H2
Knights Cl. E9 95 F5
*Churchill Wk.*
Knights Ct., Kings.T. 181 H3
Knights Ct., Rom. 83 E6
Knights Hill SE27 169 H5
Knights Hill Sq. SE27 169 H4
*Knights Hill*
Knights La. N9 60 D3
Knights Pk., Kings.T. 181 H3
Knights Rd. E16 135 G2
Knights Rd., Stan. 53 F4
**Knights Wk. SE11 35 G2**
Knights Way, Ilf. 65 F6
**Knightsbridge SW1 24 A4**
Knightsbridge SW1 129 J2
**Knightsbridge SW7 23 H4**
Knightsbridge SW7 129 H2
**Knightsbridge Grn. SW1 23 J4**
Knightsbridge Grn. SW1 129 J2
Knightswood Cl., Edg. 54 C2
Knightwood Cres., N.Mal. 182 E6
Knivet Rd. SW6 128 D6
Knobs Hill Rd. E15 114 B1
Knockholt Rd. SE9 156 A5
Knole, The SE9 174 D4
Knole Cl., Croy. 189 F6
*Stockbury Rd.*
Knole Gate, Sid. 175 H3
*Woodside Cres.*
Knoll, The W13 105 F5
Knoll, The, Beck. 190 B1
Knoll, The, Brom. 205 G2
Knoll Ct. SE19 170 C5
Knoll Dr. N14 42 A7
Knoll Ri., Orp. 207 J1
Knoll Rd. SW18 149 F5
Knoll Rd., Bex. 159 G7
Knoll Rd., Sid. 176 B5
Knollmead, Surb. 196 C1
Knolls Cl., Wor.Pk. 197 H3
Knollys Cl. SW16 169 G3
Knollys Rd. SW16 169 G3
Knottisford St. E2 113 F3
Knotts Grn. Ms. E10 78 B6
Knotts Grn. Rd. E10 78 B6
Knowle Av., Bexh. 139 E7
Knowle Cl. SW9 151 G3
Knowle Rd., Brom. 206 B2
Knowle Rd., Twick. 162 B1
Knowles Cl., West Dr. 120 B1
Knowles Hill Cres. SE13 154 D5
Knowles Wk. SW4 150 C3
Knowlton Grn., Brom. 191 F5
Knowsley Av., Sthl. 123 G1
Knowsley Rd. SW11 149 J2
Knox Rd. E7 97 F6
**Knox St. W1 15 J1**
Knox St. W1 109 J5
Knoyle St. SE14 133 H6
*Chubworthy St.*

Lancaster W. W11 108 A7
*Grenfell Rd.*
Lanco Rd., Har. 67 J7
Lancefield St. W10 108 C3
Lancell St. N16 94 B2
*Stoke Newington Ch. St.*
Lancelot Av., Wem. 87 G4
Lancelot Cres., Wem. 87 G4
Lancelot Gdns., Barn. 42 A7
**Lancelot Pl. SW7 23 J4**
Lancelot Pl. SW7 129 J2
Lancelot Rd., Ilf. 65 H6
Lancelot Rd., Well. 158 A4
Lancelot Rd., Wem. 87 G5
**Lancer Sq. W8 22 A3**
Lancey Cl. SE7 136 A4
*Cleveley Cl.*
Lanchester Rd. N6 73 J5
Lancing Gdns. N9 60 C1
Lancing Rd. W13 104/105 E7
*Drayton Grn. Rd.*
Lancing Rd., Croy. 187 F6
Lancing Rd., Ilf. 81 G6
**Lancing St. NW1 9 H4**
Lancresse Ct. N1 112 B1
Landcroft Rd. SE22 152 C6
Landells Rd. SE22 152 C6
Landford Rd. SW15 147 J3
Landgrove Rd. SW19 166 D5
Landmann Way SE14 133 G5
**Landon Pl. SW1 23 J5**
Landon Pl. SW1 129 J3
Landon Wk. E14 114 B7
*Cottage St.*
Landons Cl. E14 134 C1
Landor Rd. SW9 150 E3
Landor Wk. W12 127 G2
**Landport Way SE15 37 G7**
Landra Gdns. N21 43 H6
Landridge Rd. SW6 148 C2
Landrock Rd. N8 75 E6
Landscape Rd., Wdf.Grn. 63 H7
Landseer Av. E12 98 D5
Landseer Cl. SW19 185 F1
*Brangwyn Cres.*
Landseer Cl., Edg. 70 A2
Landseer Rd. N19 92 E3
Landseer Rd., Enf. 44 D5
Landseer Rd., N.Mal. 182 D7
Landseer Rd., Sutt. 198 D6
Landstead Rd. SE18 137 G7
**Lane, The NW8 6 C1**
Lane, The SE3 155 G3
Lane App. NW7 56 B5
Lane Cl. NW2 89 H3
Lane End, Bexh. 159 H3
Lane Ms. E12 98 C3
*Colchester Av.*
Lanercost Cl. SW2 169 G2
Lanercost Gdns. N14 42 E7
Lanercost Rd. SW2 169 G2
**Lanesborough Pl. SW1 24 B3**
Laneside, Chis. 175 E5
Laneside, Edg. 54 C5
Laneside Av., Dag. 83 F7
Laneway SW15 147 H5
Lanfranc Rd. E3 113 H2
Lanfrey Pl. W14 128 C5
*North End Rd.*
Lang St. E1 113 F4
Langbourne Av. N6 92 A2
Langbourne Pl. E14 134 A2
*Westferry Rd.*
Langbourne Way, Esher 194 D6
Langbrook Rd. SE3 156 A3
Langcroft Cl., Cars. 199 J3
Langdale Av., Mitch. 185 J3
**Langdale Cl. SE17 35 J5**
Langdale Cl. SE17 131 J6
Langdale Cl. SW14 146 B4
*Clifford Av.*
Langdale Cl., Dag. 100 C1
Langdale Cl., Orp. 206/207 E3
*Grasmere Rd.*
Langdale Cres., Bexh. 139 G7
Langdale Gdns., Grnf. 105 E3
Langdale Rd. SE10 134 C7
Langdale Rd., Th.Hth. 187 G4
Langdale St. E1 112/113 E6
*Burslem St.*
Langdon Ct. NW10 106 E1
Langdon Cres. E6 116 D2
Langdon Dr. NW9 88 C1
Langdon Pk. Rd. N6 74 C7
Langdon Pl. SW14 146 C3
*Rosemary La.*
Langdon Rd. E6 116 D1
Langdon Rd., Brom. 191 H3
Langdon Rd., Mord. 185 F5
Langdon Shaw, Sid. 175 J5
Langdon Wk., Mord. 185 F5
**Langdon Way SE1 37 J2**
Langdons Ct., Sthl. 123 G3
Langford Cl. E8 94 D5
Langford Cl. N15 76 B6
**Langford Cl. NW8 6 D1**
**Langford Ct. NW8 6 C2**
Langford Ct. NW8 109 F2
Langford Cres., Barn. 41 J4
Langford Grn. SE5 152 B3
**Langford Pl. NW8 6 D1**
Langford Pl. NW8 109 F2
Langford Pl., Sid. 176 A3
Langford Rd. SW6 149 E2
Langford Rd., Barn. 41 H4
Langford Rd., Wdf.Grn. 63 J6
Langfords, Buck.H. 64 A2
Langham Cl. N15 75 H3
*Langham Rd.*
Langham Dr., Rom. 82 B6
Langham Gdns. N21 43 G5
Langham Gdns. W13 105 E7
Langham Gdns., Edg. 54 C7
Langham Gdns., Rich. 163 F4
Langham Gdns., Wem. 87 F2
Langham Ho. Cl., Rich. 163 G4
Langham Pl. N15 75 H3
**Langham Pl. W1 16 E2**
Langham Pl. W1 110 B5
Langham Pl. W4 126/127 E6
*Hogarth Roundabout*
Langham Rd. N15 75 H3
Langham Rd. SW20 183 J1
Langham Rd., Edg. 54 C6
Langham Rd., Tedd. 162 E5
**Langham St. W1 17 E2**
Langham St. W1 110 B5
Langhedge Cl. N18 60 C6
*Langhedge La.*
Langhedge La. N18 60 C5
Langhedge La. Ind. Est. N18 60 C6
Langholm Cl. SW12 150 D7
*King's Av.*
Langholme, Bushey 51 J1
Langhorne Rd., Dag. 101 G7
Langland Cres., Stan. 69 H3
Langland Dr., Pnr. 50 E7
Langland Gdns. NW3 91 E5
Langland Gdns., Croy. 203 J2
Langler Rd. NW10 107 J2
Langley Av., Ruis. 84 B1
Langley Av., Surb. 195 G1
Langley Av., Wor.Pk. 198 A2
Langley Ct. SE9 156 D6
**Langley Ct. WC2 18 A5**
Langley Ct., Beck. 190 B5
Langley Cres. E11 79 J7
Langley Cres., Dag. 100 C7
Langley Cres., Edg. 54 C3
Langley Cres., Hayes 121 J7
Langley Dr. E11 79 H7
Langley Dr. W3 126 B2
Langley Gdns., Brom. 191 J4
Langley Gdns., Dag. 100 D7
Langley Gdns., Orp. 193 E6
Langley Gro., N.Mal. 182 E2
**Langley La. SW8 34 B5**
Langley La. SW8 131 F6
Langley Meadow, Loug. 49 G2
Langley Pk. NW7 54 E6
Langley Pk. Rd., Sutt. 199 F5
Langley Rd. SW19 184 C1
Langley Rd., Beck. 189 H4
Langley Rd., Islw. 144 C2
Langley Rd., Surb. 181 H7
Langley Rd., Well. 138 C6
Langley Row, Barn. 40 C1
**Langley St. WC2 18 A4**
Langley St. WC2 110 E6
Langley Way, W.Wick. 204 D1
Langmead Dr., Bushey 52 A1
Langmead St. SE27 169 H4
*Beadman St.*
Langmore Ct., Bexh. 158 D3
*Regency Way*
Langridge Ms., Hmptn. 161 F6
*Oak Av.*
Langroyd Rd. SW17 167 J2
Langside Av. SW15 147 G4
Langside Cres. N14 58 D3
Langston Hughes Cl. SE24 151 H4
*Shakespeare Rd.*
Langston Rd., Loug. 49 F5
**Langthorn Ct. EC2 20 B3**
Langthorne Rd. E11 96 C3
Langthorne St. SW6 128 A7
Langton Av. E6 116 D3
Langton Av. N20 41 F7
**Langton Cl. WC1 10 D4**
Langton Pl. SW18 166 D1
*Merton Rd.*
Langton Ri. SE23 152 E7
Langton Rd. NW2 89 J3
Langton Rd. SW9 131 H7
Langton Rd., Har. 51 J7
Langton Rd., W.Mol. 179 J4
**Langton St. SW10 30 D6**
Langton St. SW10 129 F6
Langton Way SE3 155 F1
Langton Way, Croy. 202 B4
Langtry Rd. NW8 108 E1
Langtry Rd., Nthlt. 102 D2
Langtry Wk. NW8 91 F7
*Alexandra Pl.*
Langwood Chase, Tedd. 163 F6
Langworth Dr., Hayes 102 A6
Lanhill Rd. W9 108 D4
Lanier Rd. SE13 154 C6
Lanigan Dr., Houns. 143 H5
Lankaster Gdns. N2 73 G1
Lankers Dr., Har. 67 F6
Lankton Cl., Beck. 190 C1
Lannock Rd., Hayes 121 H1
Lannoy Rd. SE9 175 F1
Lanrick Rd. E14 114 D6
Lanridge Rd. SE2 138 D3
Lansbury Av. N18 60 A5
Lansbury Av., Bark. 100 A7
Lansbury Av., Felt. 142 B6
Lansbury Av., Rom. 83 E5
Lansbury Cl. NW10 88 C5
Lansbury Est. E14 114 B6
Lansbury Gdns. E14 114 D6
Lansbury Rd., Enf. 45 G1
Lansbury Way N18 60 B5
Lanscombe Wk. SW8 150 E1
Lansdell Rd., Mitch. 186 A2
Lansdown Rd. E7 97 J7
Lansdown Rd., Sid. 176 B3
Lansdowne Av., Bexh. 138 D7
Lansdowne Av., Orp. 207 E1
Lansdowne Cl. SW20 166 A7
Lansdowne Cl., Surb. 196 B2
*Kingston Rd.*
Lansdowne Cl., Twick. 162 C1
*Lion Rd.*
Lansdowne Ct., Wor.Pk. 197 G2
*The Av.*
Lansdowne Cres. W11 108 B7
Lansdowne Dr. E8 94 D6
Lansdowne Gdns. SW8 150 E1
Lansdowne Grn. SW8 150/151 E1
*Hartington Rd.*
Lansdowne Gro. NW10 89 E4
Lansdowne Hill SE27 169 H3
Lansdowne La. SE7 136 A6
Lansdowne Ms. SE7 136 A5
Lansdowne Ms. W11 128 C1
*Lansdowne Rd.*
**Lansdowne Pl. SE1 28 C6**
Lansdowne Pl. SE19 170 C7
Lansdowne Ri. W11 108 B7
Lansdowne Rd. E4 62 A2
Lansdowne Rd. E11 97 F2
Lansdowne Rd. E17 78 A5
Lansdowne Rd. E18 79 G3
Lansdowne Rd. N3 56 C7
Lansdowne Rd. N10 74 C2
Lansdowne Rd. N17 76 C1
Lansdowne Rd. SW20 165 J7
Lansdowne Rd. W11 108 B7
Lansdowne Rd., Brom. 173 G7
Lansdowne Rd., Croy. 202 A2
Lansdowne Rd., Epsom 196 C7
Lansdowne Rd., Har. 68 B7
Lansdowne Rd., Houns. 143 H3
Lansdowne Rd., Ilf. 99 J1
Lansdowne Rd., Stan. 53 F6
**Lansdowne Row W1 24 E1**
**Lansdowne Ter. WC1 10 B6**
Lansdowne Ter. WC1 111 E4
Lansdowne Wk. W11 128 B1
Lansdowne Way SW8 150 E1
Lansdowne Wd. Cl. SE27 169 H3
Lansfield Av. N18 60 D4
**Lant St. SE1 27 J3**
Lant St. SE1 131 J2
Lantern Cl. SW15 147 G4
Lantern Cl., Wem. 87 G5
Lantern Way, West Dr. 120 B2
*Warwick Rd.*
Lanterns Ct. E14 134 A2
Lanvanor Rd. SE15 153 F2
Lapford Cl. W9 108 C4
Lapponum Wk., Hayes 102 D5
*Lochan Cl.*
Lapse Wd. Wk. SE23 170 E1
Lapstone Gdns., Har. 69 F6
Lapwing Ct., Surb. 196 A3
*Chaffinch Cl.*
Lapwing Way, Hayes 102 D6
Lara Cl. SE13 154 C6
Lara Cl., Chess. 195 H7
Larbert Rd. SW16 186 C1
Larch Av. W3 126 E1
Larch Cl. E13 115 H4
Larch Cl. N11 58 A7
Larch Cl. N19 92 C2
*Bredgar Rd.*
Larch Cl. SE8 133 J6
*Clyde St.*
Larch Cl. SW12 168 B2
Larch Cres., Epsom 196 B6
Larch Cres., Hayes 102 C4
Larch Dr. W4 126 A5
*Gunnersbury Av.*
Larch Grn. NW9 70/71 E1
*Clayton Fld.*
Larch Gro., Sid. 175 J1
Larch Ms. N19 92 C2
*Bredgar Rd.*
Larch Rd. E10 96 A2
*Walnut Rd.*
Larch Rd. NW2 89 J4
Larch Tree Way, Croy. 204 A3
Larch Way, Brom. 192 D7
Larchdene, Orp. 206 D2
Larches, The N13 59 J3
Larches Av. SW14 146 D4
Larchwood Rd. SE9 175 E2
**Larcom St. SE17 36 A2**
Larcom St. SE17 131 J4
Larcombe Cl., Croy. 202 C4
Larden Rd. W3 127 E1
Largewood Av., Surb. 196 A2
**Larissa St. SE17 36 C3**
Lark Row E2 113 F1
Lark Way, Cars. 185 H7
Larkbere Rd. SE26 171 H4
Larken Dr., Bushey 51 J1
Larkfield Av., Har. 69 E3
Larkfield Cl., Brom. 205 F2
Larkfield Rd., Rich. 145 H4
Larkfield Rd., Sid. 175 J3
Larkhall La. SW4 150 D2
Larkhall Ri. SW4 150 C3
Larkhill Ter. SE18 136 D7
Larks Gro., Bark. 99 H7
Larksfield Gro., Enf. 45 E1
Larkshall Ct., Rom. 83 J2
Larkshall Cres. E4 62 C4
Larkshall Rd. E4 62 C5
Larkspur Cl. E6 116 B5
Larkspur Cl. N17 60 A7
*Fryatt Rd.*
Larkspur Cl. NW9 70 B5
Larkspur Gro., Edg. 54 C4
Larkspur Way, Epsom 196 C5
Larkswood Ct. E4 62 D5
Larkswood Ri., Pnr. 66 C4
Larkswood Rd. E4 62 A4
Larkway Cl. NW9 70 D4
Larnach Rd. W6 128 A6
Larpent Av. SW15 147 J5
Larwood Cl., Grnf. 86 A5
Lascelles Av., Har. 68 A7
Lascelles Cl. E11 96 D2
Lascotts Rd. N22 59 F6
Lassa Rd. SE9 156 B5
Lassell St. SE10 134 D5
Lasseter Pl. SE3 135 F6
*Vanbrugh Hill*
Latchett Rd. E18 79 H1
Latchingdon Ct. E17 77 G4
Latchingdon Gdns., Wdf.Grn. 64 B6
Latchmere Cl., Rich. 163 H5
Latchmere La., Kings.T. 163 J6
Latchmere Pas. SW11 149 H2
*Cabul Rd.*
Latchmere Rd. SW11 149 J2
Latchmere Rd., Kings.T. 163 H7
Latchmere St. SW11 149 J2
Lateward Rd., Brent. 125 G6
Latham Cl. E6 116 B6
*Oliver Gdns.*
Latham Cl., Twick. 144 D7
Latham Ho. E1 113 G6

Lodge Av., Har. 69 H4
Lodge Cl. N18 59 J5
Lodge Cl., Edg. 53 J6
Lodge Cl., Islw. 144 E1
Lodge Cl., Wall. 200 A1
Lodge Ct., Wem. 87 H5
Lodge Dr. N13 59 G4
Lodge Gdns., Beck. 189 J5
Lodge Hill SE2 138 B7
Lodge Hill, Ilf. 80 B4
Lodge Hill, Well. 138 B7
Lodge La. N12 57 F5
Lodge La., Bex. 158 D6
Lodge La., Croy. 204 A6
Lodge Pl., Sutt. 199 E5
Lodge Rd. NW4 71 J4
**Lodge Rd. NW8 7 F4**
Lodge Rd. NW8 109 G3
Lodge Rd., Brom. 173 H7
Lodge Rd., Croy. 187 H6
Lodge Rd., Sutt. 198/199 E5
*Throwley Way*
Lodge Rd., Wall. 200 B5
Lodge Vil., Wdf.Grn. 63 F7
Lodgehill Pk. Cl., Har. 85 H2
Lodore Gdns. NW9 70 E5
Lodore St. E14 114 C6
Lofthouse Pl., Chess. 195 F6
**Loftie St. SE16 29 J4**
Loftie St. SE16 132 D2
Lofting Rd. N1 93 F7
Loftus Rd. W12 127 H1
Logan Cl., Enf. 45 G1
Logan Cl., Houns. 143 F3
Logan Ms. W8 128 D4
Logan Pl. W8 128 D4
Logan Rd. N9 61 E2
Logan Rd., Wem. 87 H2
Loggetts, The SE21 170 B2
Logs Hill, Brom. 174 B7
Logs Hill, Chis. 174 B7
Logs Hill Cl., Chis. 192 B1
**Lolesworth Cl. E1 21 G2**
**Lollard St. SE11 34 D1**
Lollard St. SE11 131 F4
**Loman St. SE1 27 H3**
Loman St. SE1 131 H2
Lomas Cl., Croy. 204 C7
Lomas Ct. E8 94 C7
**Lomas St. E1 21 J1**
Lomas St. E1 112 D5
Lombard Av., Enf. 45 F1
Lombard Av., Ilf. 99 H1
Lombard Business Pk. SW19 185 F2
**Lombard Ct. EC3 20 C5**
Lombard Ct. W3 126 B1
*Crown St.*
**Lombard La. EC4 19 F4**
Lombard Rd. N11 58 B5
Lombard Rd. SW11 149 G2
Lombard Rd. SW19 185 E2
**Lombard St. EC3 20 C4**
Lombard St. EC3 112 A6
Lombard Wall SE7 135 H3
**Lombardy Pl. W2 14 A6**
Lomond Cl. N15 76 B4
Lomond Cl., Wem. 87 J7
Lomond Gdns., S.Croy. 203 H7
**Lomond Gro. SE5 36 B7**
Lomond Gro. SE5 132 A7
**Loncroft Rd. SE5 37 E5**
Loncroft Rd. SE5 132 B6
Londesborough Rd. N16 94 B4
**London Br. EC4 28 C1**
London Br. EC4 132 A1
**London Br. SE1 28 C1**
London Br. SE1 132 A1
**London Br. St. SE1 28 B2**
London Br. St. SE1 132 A1
**London Br. Wk. SE1 28 C1**
London Br. Wk. SE1 132 B1
London City Airport E16 136 C1
London Flds. E8 94 E7
London Flds. E. Side E8 94 E7
London Flds. W. Side E8 94 D7
London La. E8 95 E7
London La., Brom. 173 F7
**London Ms. W2 15 F4**
London Rd. E13 115 G2
**London Rd. SE1 27 G5**
London Rd. SE1 131 H3
London Rd. SE23 170 D1
London Rd. SW16 187 F1
London Rd. SW17 185 J2
London Rd., Bark. 98 E7
London Rd., Brent. 125 F7
London Rd., Brom. 173 F7
London Rd., Croy. 187 H7
London Rd., Enf. 44 A3
London Rd., Har. 86 B2
London Rd., Houns. 144 A3
London Rd., Islw. 144 C2
London Rd., Kings.T. 181 J2
London Rd., Mitch. 185 J2
London Rd. (Beddington Cor.), Mitch. 186 A7
London Rd., Mord. 184 D5
London Rd., Rom. 83 G6
London Rd. (Abridge), Rom. 49 J4
London Rd., Stan. 53 F5
London Rd., Sutt. 198 A3
London Rd., Th.Hth. 187 G5
London Rd., Twick. 144 D5
London Rd., Wall. 200 B4
London Rd., Wem. 87 H6
London Stile W4 126 A5
*Wellesley Rd.*
**London St. EC3 20 E5**
**London St. W2 15 F4**
London St. W2 109 G6
**London Wall EC2 20 A2**
London Wall EC2 111 J5
**London Wall Bldgs. EC2 20 C2**
Lonesome Way SW16 186 B1
**Long Acre WC2 18 A5**
Long Acre WC2 110 E7
Long Deacon Rd. E4 62 E1
Long Dr. W3 106 E6
Long Dr., Grnf. 103 H1
Long Dr., Ruis. 84 D4
Long Elmes, Har. 67 H1
Long Fld. NW9 55 E7
Long Grn., Chig. 65 H4
Long Hedges, Houns. 143 G1
**Long La. EC1 19 H1**
Long La. EC1 111 H5
Long La. N2 73 F2
Long La. N3 73 F2
**Long La. SE1 28 B4**
Long La. SE1 132 A2
Long La., Bexh. 138 D7
Long La., Croy. 189 F5
Long Leys E4 62 B6
Long Mark Rd. E16 116 A5
*Fulmer Rd.*
Long Mead NW9 71 F1
Long Meadow NW5 92 D5
*Torriano Av.*
Long Meadow Cl., W.Wick. 190 C7
Long Pond Rd. SE3 154 E1
Long Reach Ct., Bark. 117 G2
Long Rd. SW4 150 C4
**Long St. E2 13 F3**
Long St. E2 112 C3
**Long Wk. SE1 29 E5**
Long Wk. SE18 136 E6
Long Wk. SW13 147 E2
Long Wk., N.Mal. 182 C3
**Long Yd. WC1 10 C6**
Long Yd. WC1 111 F4
Longacre Pl., Cars. 200 A6
*Beddington Gdns.*
Longacre Rd. E17 78 D1
Longbeach Rd. SW11 149 J3
Longberrys NW2 90 C3
Longboat Row, Sthl. 103 F6
Longbridge Rd., Bark. 99 F7
Longbridge Rd., Dag. 100 A4
Longbridge Way SE13 154 C5
Longcliffe Path, Wat. 50 A3
*Gosforth La.*
Longcroft SE9 174 C3
Longcroft Ri., Loug. 48 D5
Longcrofte Rd., Edg. 53 G7
Longdon Wd., Kes. 206 B4
Longdown Rd. SE6 172 A4
Longfellow Rd. E17 77 J6
Longfellow Rd., Wor.Pk. 197 G2
**Longfellow Way SE1 37 G2**
Longfield, Brom. 191 F1
Longfield, Loug. 47 J5
Longfield Av. E17 77 H4
Longfield Av. NW7 55 G7
Longfield Av. W5 105 F7
Longfield Av., Wall. 200 A1
Longfield Av., Wem. 87 H1
Longfield Cres. SE26 171 F3
Longfield Dr. SW14 146 B5
Longfield Dr., Mitch. 167 H7
**Longfield Est. SE1 37 G2**
Longfield Est. SE1 132 C4
Longfield Rd. W5 105 F7
Longfield St. SW18 148 D7
Longfield Wk. W5 105 F6
Longford Av., Felt. 141 H6
Longford Av., Sthl. 103 G7
Longford Cl., Hmptn. 161 G4
Longford Cl., Hayes 102 D7
*Longford Gdns.*
Longford Ct. E5 95 G4
*Pedro St.*
Longford Ct. NW4 72 A4
Longford Ct., Epsom 196 C4
Longford Gdns., Hayes 102 D7
Longford Gdns., Sutt. 199 F3
Longford Rd., Twick. 161 G1
**Longford St. NW1 8 E5**
Longford St. NW1 110 B4
Longford Wk. SW2 151 G7
Longhayes Av., Rom. 82 D4
Longhayes Ct., Rom. 82 D4
*Longhayes Av.*
Longheath Gdns., Croy. 189 F5
Longhedge Ho. SE26 170 C4
Longhedge St. SW11 150 A2
Longhill Rd. SE6 172 D2
Longhook Gdns., Nthlt. 102 A2
**Longhope Cl. SE15 37 E6**
Longhope Cl. SE15 132 B6
Longhurst Rd. SE13 154 D5
Longhurst Rd., Croy. 189 E6
**Longland Ct. SE1 37 H3**
Longland Dr. N20 56 E3
Longlands Ct. W11 108 C7
*Portobello Rd.*
Longlands Ct., Mitch. 186 A1
*Summerhill Way*
Longlands Pk. Cres., Sid. 175 H3
Longlands Rd., Sid. 175 H3
Longleat Rd., Enf. 44 B5
Longleat Way, Felt. 141 G7
Longleigh La. SE2 138 C6
Longleigh La., Bexh. 138 C6
Longlents Ho. NW10 106 D1
Longley Av., Wem. 105 J1
Longley Rd. SW17 167 H6
Longley Rd., Croy. 187 H7
Longley Rd., Har. 67 J5
**Longley St. SE1 37 H2**
Longley St. SE1 132 D4
Longley Way NW2 89 J3
Longmead, Chis. 192 D2
Longmead Dr., Sid. 176 D2
Longmead Rd. SW17 167 J5
Longmead Rd., T.Ditt. 180 B7
Longmeadow Rd., Sid. 175 H1
Longmoor Pt. SW15 165 H1
*Norley Vale*
**Longmoore St. SW1 33 F2**
Longmoore St. SW1 130 C4
Longmore Av., Barn. 41 F6
Longnor Rd. E1 113 G3
Longreach Rd., Bark. 117 J4
Longridge La., Sthl. 103 H7
Longridge Rd. SW5 128 D4
**Long's Ct. WC2 17 H5**
Long's Ct. WC2 110 D7
Longs Ct., Rich. 145 J4
*Crown Ter.*
Longshaw Rd. E4 62 D3
Longshore SE8 133 J4
Longstaff Cres. SW18 148 D6
Longstaff Rd. SW18 148 D6
Longstone Av. NW10 89 F7
Longstone Rd. SW17 168 B5
Longthornton Rd. SW16 186 C2
Longton Av. SE26 170 D4
Longton Gro. SE26 170 E4
**Longville Rd. SE11 35 G1**
Longwalk Rd., Uxb. 121 E1
Longwood Dr. SW15 147 G6
Longwood Gdns., Ilf. 80 C4
Longworth Cl. SE28 118 D6
Loning, The NW9 71 E4
Lonsdale Av. E6 116 A4
Lonsdale Av., Rom. 83 J6
Lonsdale Av., Wem. 87 H5
Lonsdale Cl. E6 116 B4
*Lonsdale Av.*
Lonsdale Cl. SE9 174 A3
Lonsdale Cl., Edg. 53 J5
*Orchard Dr.*
Lonsdale Cl., Pnr. 51 E7
Lonsdale Cres., Ilf. 80 E6
Lonsdale Dr., Enf. 43 E5
Lonsdale Gdns., Th.Hth. 187 F4
Lonsdale Ms., Rich. 146 A1
*Elizabeth Cotts.*
Lonsdale Pl. N1 93 G7
*Barnsbury St.*
Lonsdale Rd. E11 79 F7
Lonsdale Rd. NW6 108 C2
Lonsdale Rd. SE25 188 E4
Lonsdale Rd. SW13 127 G6
Lonsdale Rd. W4 127 F4
Lonsdale Rd. W11 108 C6
Lonsdale Rd., Bexh. 159 F2
Lonsdale Rd., Sthl. 122 D3
Lonsdale Sq. N1 93 G7
Loobert Rd. N15 76 B3
Looe Gdns., Ilf. 81 E3
**Loom Ct. E1 13 E6**
Loop Rd., Chis. 175 F6
Lopen Rd. N18 60 B4
Loraine Cl., Enf. 45 F5
Loraine Rd. N7 93 F4
Loraine Rd. W4 126 B6
Lord Amory Way E14 134 C2
Lord Av., Ilf. 80 C4
Lord Chancellor Wk., Kings.T. 182 C1
Lord Gdns., Ilf. 80 B4
**Lord Hills Br. W2 14 B2**
**Lord Hills Rd. W2 14 B1**
Lord Hills Rd. W2 109 E5
Lord Holland La. SW9 151 G1
*Myatt's Flds. S.*
Lord Knyvett Cl., Stai. 140 A6
Lord Napier Pl. W6 127 G5
*Upper Mall*
**Lord N. St. SW1 26 A6**
Lord N. St. SW1 130 E3
Lord Roberts Ms. SW6 128/129 E7
*Moore Pk. Rd.*
Lord Roberts Ter. SE18 136 D5
Lord St. E16 136 B1
Lord Warwick St. SE18 136 C3
Lordell Pl. SW19 165 J6
**Lorden Wk. E2 13 H4**
Lorden Wk. E2 112 D3
Lord's Cl. SE21 169 J2
Lords Cl., Felt. 161 E2
**Lord's Vw. NW8 7 F4**
Lordship Gro. N16 94 A2
Lordship La. N17 75 J1
Lordship La. N22 75 G2
Lordship La. SE22 152 C6
Lordship La. Est. SE22 170 D1
Lordship Pk. N16 93 J2
Lordship Pk. Ms. N16 93 J2
*Allerton Rd.*
**Lordship Pl. SW3 31 G6**
Lordship Rd. N16 94 A2
Lordship Rd., Nthlt. 84 E7
Lordship Ter. N16 94 A2
Lordsmead Rd. N17 76 B1
**Lorenzo St. WC1 10 C3**
Lorenzo St. WC1 111 F3
Loretto Gdns., Har. 69 H4
Lorian Cl. N12 56 E4
Loring Rd. N20 57 H2
Loring Rd., Islw. 144 C2
Loris Rd. W6 127 J3
Lorn Ct. SW9 151 G2
Lorn Rd. SW9 151 F2
Lorne Av., Croy. 189 G7
**Lorne Cl. NW8 7 H4**
Lorne Gdns. E11 79 J4
Lorne Gdns. W11 128 A2
Lorne Gdns., Croy. 189 H7
Lorne Rd. E7 97 H4
Lorne Rd. E17 78 A5
Lorne Rd. N4 93 F1
Lorne Rd., Har. 68 C2
Lorne Rd., Rich. 145 J5
*Albert Rd.*
Lorraine Pk., Har. 52 B7
**Lorrimore Rd. SE17 35 H5**
Lorrimore Rd. SE17 131 H6
**Lorrimore Sq. SE17 35 H5**
Lorrimore Sq. SE17 131 H6
Loseberry Rd., Esher 194 A5
Lothair Rd. W5 125 G2
Lothair Rd. N. N4 75 H6
Lothair Rd. S. N4 75 G7
**Lothbury EC2 20 B3**
Lothbury EC2 112 A6
Lothian Av., Hayes 102 B5
Lothian Cl., Wem. 86 D4
Lothian Rd. SW9 151 H1
Lothrop St. W10 108 B3
Lots Rd. SW10 129 F7
Lotus Cl. SE21 169 J3
Loubet St. SW17 167 J6
Loudoun Av., Ilf. 81 E5

Luton St. NW8 109 G4
Lutton Ter. NW3 91 G4
*Flask Wk.*
Luttrell Av. SW15 147 H5
Lutwyche Rd. SE6 171 J2
Luxborough La., Chig. 64 B3
**Luxborough St. W1 16 B1**
Luxborough St. W1 110 A4
Luxemburg Gdns. W6 128 A4
Luxfield Rd. SE9 174 B1
Luxford St. SE16 133 G4
Luxmore St. SE4 153 J1
Luxor St. SE5 151 J3
Lyal Rd. E3 113 H2
Lyall Av. SE21 170 B3
**Lyall Ms. SW1 24 B6**
Lyall Ms. SW1 130 A3
**Lyall Ms. W. SW1 24 B6**
**Lyall St. SW1 24 B6**
Lyall St. SW1 130 A3
Lycett Pl. W12 127 G2
*Becklow Rd.*
Lyconby Gdns., Croy. 189 H7
Lydd Cl., Sid. 175 H3
Lydd Rd., Bexh. 139 F7
Lydden Ct. SE9 157 H6
Lydden Gro. SW18 148 E7
Lydden Rd. SW18 148 E7
Lydeard Rd. E6 98 C7
Lydford Cl. N16 94 B5
*Pellerin Rd.*
Lydford Rd. N15 76 A5
Lydford Rd. NW2 90 A6
Lydford Rd. W9 108 C4
Lydhurst Av. SW2 169 F2
**Lydney Cl. SE15 36 E7**
Lydney Cl. SE15 132 B7
Lydney Cl. SW19 166 B2
*Princes Way*
Lydon Rd. SW4 150 C3
Lydstep Rd., Chis. 174 D4
Lyford Rd. SW18 149 G7
**Lygon Pl. SW1 24 D6**
Lyham Cl. SW2 151 E6
Lyham Rd. SW2 150 E5
Lyle Cl., Mitch. 186 A7
Lyme Fm. Rd. SE12 155 G4
Lyme Gro. E9 95 F7
*St. Thomas's Sq.*
Lyme Rd., Well. 158 B1
Lyme St. NW1 92 C7
Lyme Ter. NW1 92 C7
*Royal College St.*
Lymer Av. SE19 170 C5
Lymescote Gdns., Sutt. 198 D2
Lyminge Cl., Sid. 175 J4
Lyminge Gdns. SW18 167 H1
Lymington Av. N22 75 G2
Lymington Cl. E6 116 C5
*Valiant Way*
Lymington Cl. SW16 186 D2
Lymington Gdns., Epsom 197 F5
Lymington Rd. NW6 90 E6
Lymington Rd., Dag. 100 D1
**Lympstone Gdns. SE15 37 J7**
Lympstone Gdns. SE15 132 D7
Lyn Ms. E3 113 J3
*Tredegar Sq.*
Lynbridge Gdns. N13 59 H4
**Lynbrook Cl. SE15 36 E7**
Lynch Wk. SE8 133 J6
*Prince St.*
Lynchen Cl., Houns. 142 A1
*The Av.*
Lyncott Cres. SW4 150 B4
Lyncroft Av., Pnr. 66 E5
Lyncroft Gdns. NW6 90 D5
Lyncroft Gdns. W13 125 F2
Lyncroft Gdns., Houns. 143 J4
Lyndale NW2 90 C4
Lyndale Av. NW2 90 C3
Lyndale Cl. SE3 135 F6
Lyndhurst Av. N12 57 J6
Lyndhurst Av. NW7 54 E6
Lyndhurst Av. SW16 186 D2
Lyndhurst Av., Pnr. 66 B1
Lyndhurst Av., Sthl. 123 H1
Lyndhurst Av., Sun. 178 A3
Lyndhurst Av., Surb. 196 B1
Lyndhurst Av., Twick. 161 F1
Lyndhurst Cl. NW10 88 D3
Lyndhurst Cl., Bexh. 159 H3
Lyndhurst Cl., Croy. 202 C3
Lyndhurst Cl., Orp. 207 E4
Lyndhurst Dr. E10 78 C7
Lyndhurst Dr., N.Mal. 183 E6
Lyndhurst Gdns. N3 72 B1
Lyndhurst Gdns. NW3 91 G5
Lyndhurst Gdns., Bark. 99 H6
Lyndhurst Gdns., Enf. 44 B4
Lyndhurst Gdns., Ilf. 81 G6
Lyndhurst Gdns., Pnr. 66 B1
Lyndhurst Gro. SE15 152 B2
Lyndhurst Ri., Chig. 64 D4
Lyndhurst Rd. E4 62 C7
Lyndhurst Rd. N18 60 D4
Lyndhurst Rd. N22 59 F6
Lyndhurst Rd. NW3 91 G5
Lyndhurst Rd., Bexh. 159 H3
Lyndhurst Rd., Grnf. 103 H4
Lyndhurst Rd., Th.Hth. 187 G4
Lyndhurst Sq. SE15 152 C1
Lyndhurst Ter. NW3 91 G5
Lyndhurst Way SE15 152 C1
Lyndhurst Way, Sutt. 198 D7
Lyndon Av., Pnr. 51 E6
Lyndon Av., Sid. 157 J5
Lyndon Av., Wall. 200 A3
Lyndon Rd., Belv. 139 G4
Lyne Cres. E17 77 J1
Lyneham Wk. E5 95 H5
Lynett Rd., Dag. 100 D2
Lynette Av. SW4 150 B6
Lynford Cl., Barn. 39 F5
*Rowley La.*
Lynford Cl., Edg. 54 C7
Lynford Gdns., Edg. 54 B3
Lynford Gdns., Ilf. 99 J2
Lynmere Rd., Well. 158 B2
Lynmouth Av., Enf. 44 C6
Lynmouth Av., Mord. 184 A7
Lynmouth Dr., Ruis. 84 B2
Lynmouth Gdns., Grnf. 105 E1
Lynmouth Gdns., Houns. 142 D1
Lynmouth Rd. E17 77 H6
Lynmouth Rd. N2 73 J3
Lynmouth Rd. N16 94 C1
Lynmouth Rd., Grnf. 105 E1
Lynn Cl., Har. 68 A2
Lynn Ms. E11 96/97 E2
*Lynn Rd.*
Lynn Rd. E11 96 E2
Lynn Rd. SW12 150 B7
Lynn Rd., Ilf. 81 G7
Lynn St., Enf. 44 A1
Lynne Cl., Orp. 207 J6
Lynne Way NW10 88 E6
Lynne Way, Nthlt. 102 D2
Lynsted Cl., Bexh. 159 H5
Lynsted Cl., Brom. 191 J2
Lynsted Ct., Beck. 189 H2
*Churchfields Rd.*
Lynsted Gdns. SE9 156 A3
Lynton Av. N12 57 G4
Lynton Av. NW9 71 F4
Lynton Av. W13 104 D6
Lynton Av., Rom. 83 G1
Lynton Cl. NW10 88 E5
Lynton Cl., Chess. 195 H4
Lynton Cl., Islw. 144 C4
Lynton Cres., Ilf. 80 E6
**Lynton Est. SE1 37 H2**
Lynton Gdns. N11 58 D6
Lynton Gdns., Enf. 44 B7
Lynton Mead N20 56 D3
Lynton Rd. E4 62 B5
Lynton Rd. N8 74 D5
Lynton Rd. NW6 108 C1
**Lynton Rd. SE1 37 G2**
Lynton Rd. SE1 132 C4
Lynton Rd. W3 106 A7
Lynton Rd., Croy. 187 G6
Lynton Rd., Har. 85 E2
Lynton Rd., N.Mal. 182 D5
Lynton Ter. W3 106 C6
*Lynton Rd.*
Lynwood Cl. E18 79 J1
Lynwood Cl., Har. 85 E3
Lynwood Dr., Wor.Pk. 197 G2
Lynwood Gdns., Croy. 201 F4
Lynwood Gdns., Sthl. 103 F6
Lynwood Gro. N21 59 G1
Lynwood Gro., Orp. 193 H7
Lynwood Rd. SW17 167 J3
Lynwood Rd. W5 105 H4
Lynwood Rd., T.Ditt. 194 C2
Lyon Business Pk., Bark. 117 H2
Lyon Meade, Stan. 69 F1
Lyon Pk. Av., Wem. 87 H6
Lyon Rd. SW19 185 F1
Lyon Rd., Har. 68 C6
Lyon St. N1 93 F7
*Caledonian Rd.*
Lyon Way, Grnf. 104 B1
**Lyons Pl. NW8 7 E5**
Lyons Pl. NW8 109 G4
Lyons Wk. W14 128 B4
Lyonsdown Av., Barn. 41 F6
Lyonsdown Rd., Barn. 41 F6
Lyoth Rd., Orp. 207 F2
Lyric Dr., Grnf. 103 H4
Lyric Rd. SW13 147 F1
Lysander Gdns., Surb. 181 J6
*Ewell Rd.*
Lysander Gro. N19 92 D1
Lysander Rd., Croy. 201 F6
Lysander Way, Orp. 207 F3
Lysia St. SW6 128 A7
Lysias Rd. SW12 150 A6
Lysons Wk. SW15 147 G5
*Swinburne Rd.*
Lytchet Rd., Brom. 173 H7
Lytchet Way, Enf. 45 F1
Lytchgate Cl., S.Croy. 202 B7
Lytcott Dr., W.Mol. 179 F3
*Freeman Dr.*
Lytcott Gro. SE22 152 C5
Lyte St. E2 113 F2
*Bishops Way*
Lytham Av., Wat. 50 D5
Lytham Gro. W5 105 H3
**Lytham St. SE17 36 B4**
Lytham St. SE17 132 A5
Lyttelton Cl. NW3 91 H7
Lyttelton Rd. E10 96 B3
Lyttelton Rd. N2 73 F5
Lyttleton Rd. N8 75 G3
Lytton Av. N13 59 G2
Lytton Cl. N2 73 G5
Lytton Cl., Loug. 49 G3
Lytton Cl., Nthlt. 85 F7
Lytton Gdns., Wall. 200 D4
Lytton Gro. SW15 148 A5
Lytton Rd. E11 78 E7
Lytton Rd., Barn. 41 F4
Lytton Rd., Pnr. 50 E7
Lytton Strachey Path SE28 118 B7
*Titmuss Av.*
Lyveden Rd. SE3 135 H7
Lyveden Rd. SW17 167 H6


## M


Maberley Cres. SE19 170 D7
Maberley Rd. SE19 188 C1
Maberley Rd., Beck. 189 G3
**Mabledon Pl. WC1 9 J4**
Mabledon Pl. WC1 110 D3
Mablethorpe Rd. SW6 128 B7
Mabley St. E9 95 H6
Macaret Cl. N20 41 E7
MacArthur Cl. E7 97 G6
MacArthur Ter. SE7 136 B6
Macaulay Av., Esher 194 C2
Macaulay Ct. SW4 150 B3
Macaulay Rd. E6 116 A2
Macaulay Rd. SW4 150 B3
Macaulay Sq. SW4 150 B4
Macaulay Way SE28 118 B7
*Booth Cl.*
Macauley Ms. SE13 154 C2
Macbean St. SE18 136 D3
Macbeth St. W6 127 H5
**Macclesfield Br. NW1 7 H1**
Macclesfield Br. NW1 109 H2
**Macclesfield Rd. EC1 11 J3**
Macclesfield Rd. EC1 111 J3
Macclesfield Rd. SE25 189 E5
**Macclesfield St. W1 17 J5**
Macclesfield St. W1 110 D7
Macdonald Av., Dag. 101 H3
Macdonald Rd. E7 97 G4
Macdonald Rd. E17 78 C2
Macdonald Rd. N11 57 J5
Macdonald Rd. N19 92 C2
Macduff Rd. SW11 150 A1
Mace Cl. E1 132/133 E1
*Kennet St.*
Mace St. E2 113 G2
MacFarlane La., Islw. 124 C6
Macfarlane Rd. W12 127 J1
**Macfarren Pl. NW1 8 C6**
Macgregor Rd. E16 115 J5
Machell Rd. SE15 153 F3
Mackay Rd. SW4 150 B3
**Mackennal St. NW8 7 H2**
Mackennal St. NW8 109 H2
Mackenzie Rd. N7 93 F6
Mackenzie Rd., Beck. 189 F2
Mackenzie Wk. E14 134 A1
Mackeson Rd. NW3 91 J4
Mackie Rd. SW2 151 G7
Mackintosh La. E9 95 G5
*Homerton High St.*
**Macklin St. WC2 18 B3**
Macklin St. WC2 111 E6
Mackrow Wk. E14 114 C7
*Robin Hood La.*
**Macks Rd. SE16 37 J1**
Macks Rd. SE16 132 D4
**Mackworth St. NW1 9 F3**
Mackworth St. NW1 110 C3
Maclaren Ms. SW15 147 J4
*Clarendon Dr.*
Maclean Rd. SE23 153 H6
Macleod Rd. N21 43 E5
**Macleod St. SE17 36 A4**
Macleod St. SE17 131 J5
Maclise Rd. W14 128 B3
Macoma Rd. SE18 137 G6
Macoma Ter. SE18 137 G6
Maconochies Rd. E14 134 B5
Macquarie Way E14 134 B4
Macready Pl. N7 92/93 E4
*Warlters Rd.*
Macroom Rd. W9 108 C3
Mada Rd., Orp. 206 E3
Maddams St. E3 114 B4
Maddison Cl., Tedd. 162 C6
**Maddock Way SE17 35 H6**
Maddock Way SE17 131 H6
Maddocks Cl., Sid. 176 E5
**Maddox St. W1 17 E5**
Maddox St. W1 110 B7
Madeira Av., Brom. 173 E7
Madeira Gro., Wdf.Grn. 63 J6
Madeira Rd. E11 96 D1
Madeira Rd. N13 59 H4
Madeira Rd. SW16 169 E5
Madeira Rd., Mitch. 185 J4
Madeley Rd. W5 105 H6
Madeline Gro., Ilf. 99 G5
Madeline Rd. SE20 188 D1
Madge Gill Way E6 116 B1
*Ron Leighton Way*
Madinah Rd. E8 94 D6
Madison Cres., Bexh. 138 C7
Madison Gdns., Bexh. 138 C7
Madison Gdns., Brom. 191 F3
Madras Pl. N7 93 G6
Madras Rd., Ilf. 99 E4
Madrid Rd. SW13 147 G1
Madrigal La. SE5 131 H7
**Madron St. SE17 37 E3**
Madron St. SE17 132 B5
Mafeking Av. E6 116 A2
Mafeking Av., Brent. 125 H6
Mafeking Av., Ilf. 81 G7
Mafeking Rd. E16 115 F4
Mafeking Rd. N17 76 D2
Mafeking Rd., Enf. 44 C3
Magdala Av. N19 92 B2
Magdala Rd., Islw. 144 D3
Magdala Rd., S.Croy. 202 A7
*Napier Rd.*
**Magdalen Pas. E1 21 G5**
Magdalen Rd. SW18 167 F1
**Magdalen St. SE1 28 D2**
Magdalen St. SE1 132 B1
Magdalene Cl. SE15 152/153 E2
*Heaton Rd.*
Magdalene Gdns. E6 116 D4
**Magee St. SE11 35 E5**
Magee St. SE11 131 G6
Magellan Pl. E14 134 A5
*Napier Av.*
**Maggie Blake's Cause SE1 29 F2**
Magnet Rd., Wem. 87 G2
Magnin Cl. E8 112 D1
*Wilde Cl.*
Magnolia Cl. E10 96 A2
Magnolia Cl., Kings.T. 164 C6
Magnolia Ct., Har. 69 J7
Magnolia Ct., Rich. 146 B1
*West Hall Rd.*
Magnolia Gdns., Edg. 54 C4
*Ash Cl.*
Magnolia Pl. SW4 150 E5
Magnolia Pl. W5 105 H5
*Montpelier Rd.*
Magnolia Rd. W4 126 B6
Magnolia St., West Dr. 120 A4
Magnolia Way, Epsom 196 C5
**Magpie All. EC4 19 F4**
Magpie Cl. E7 97 F5

| Name | No. | Grid |
|---|---|---|
| Manor Hall Dr. NW4 | 72 | A2 |
| Manor Ho. Dr. NW6 | 90 | A7 |
| Manor Ho. Est., Stan. | 52/53 | E6 |
| *Old Ch. La.* | | |
| Manor Ho. Way, Islw. | 144 | E3 |
| Manor La. SE12 | 155 | E6 |
| Manor La. SE13 | 154 | E4 |
| Manor La., Felt. | 160 | A2 |
| Manor La., Hayes | 121 | G6 |
| Manor La., Sun. | 178 | A2 |
| Manor La., Suth. | 199 | F5 |
| Manor La. Ter. SE13 | 154 | E4 |
| Manor Ms. NW6 | 108 | D2 |
| *Cambridge Av.* | | |
| Manor Ms. SE4 | 154 | A2 |
| Manor Mt. SE23 | 171 | F1 |
| Manor Par. NW10 | 107 | F2 |
| *Station Rd.* | | |
| Manor Pk. SE13 | 154 | D4 |
| Manor Pk., Chis. | 193 | G2 |
| Manor Pk., Rich. | 145 | J4 |
| Manor Pk. Cl., W.Wick. | 204 | B1 |
| Manor Pk. Cres., Edg. | 54 | A6 |
| Manor Pk. Dr., Har. | 67 | H3 |
| Manor Pk. Gdns., Edg. | 54 | A5 |
| Manor Pk. Par. SE13 | 154 | D4 |
| *Lee High Rd.* | | |
| Manor Pk. Rd. E12 | 98 | A4 |
| Manor Pk. Rd. N2 | 73 | G3 |
| Manor Pk. Rd. NW10 | 107 | F1 |
| Manor Pk. Rd., Chis. | 193 | F1 |
| Manor Pk. Rd., Sutt. | 199 | F5 |
| Manor Pk. Rd., W.Wick. | 204 | B1 |
| Manor Pl. SE17 | 35 | H4 |
| Manor Pl. SE17 | 131 | H5 |
| Manor Pl., Chis. | 193 | G1 |
| Manor Pl., Felt. | 160 | A1 |
| Manor Pl., Mitch. | 186 | C3 |
| Manor Pl., Sutt. | 199 | E4 |
| Manor Rd. E10 | 78 | A7 |
| Manor Rd. E15 | 114 | E2 |
| Manor Rd. E16 | 114 | E3 |
| Manor Rd. E17 | 77 | H2 |
| Manor Rd. N16 | 94 | A1 |
| Manor Rd. N17 | 76 | D1 |
| Manor Rd. N22 | 59 | E6 |
| Manor Rd. SE25 | 188 | D4 |
| Manor Rd. SW20 | 184 | C2 |
| Manor Rd. W13 | 104 | D7 |
| Manor Rd., Bark. | 99 | G6 |
| Manor Rd., Barn. | 40 | B5 |
| Manor Rd., Beck. | 190 | B2 |
| Manor Rd., Bex. | 177 | H1 |
| Manor Rd., Chig. | 64 | E5 |
| Manor Rd., Dag. | 101 | J6 |
| Manor Rd., E.Mol. | 180 | A4 |
| Manor Rd., Enf. | 44 | A2 |
| Manor Rd., Har. | 68 | D6 |
| Manor Rd., Hayes | 102 | A6 |
| Manor Rd., Loug. | 47 | H3 |
| Manor Rd., Mitch. | 186 | C4 |
| Manor Rd., Rich. | 145 | J3 |
| Manor Rd., (Chadwell Heath), Rom. | 82 | D6 |
| Manor Rd., Sid. | 175 | J3 |
| Manor Rd., Sutt. | 198 | C7 |
| Manor Rd., Tedd. | 162 | E5 |
| Manor Rd., Twick. | 161 | J2 |
| Manor Rd., Wall. | 200 | B4 |
| Manor Rd., W.Wick. | 204 | B2 |
| Manor Rd., Wdf.Grn. | 64 | C6 |
| Manor Rd. N., Esher | 194 | D1 |
| Manor Rd. N., T.Ditt. | 194 | D2 |
| Manor Rd. N., Wall. | 200 | B4 |
| Manor Rd. S., Esher | 194 | B4 |
| Manor Sq., Dag. | 100 | D2 |
| Manor Vale, Brent. | 125 | F5 |
| Manor Vw. N3 | 72 | E2 |
| Manor Way E4 | 62 | D4 |
| Manor Way NW9 | 70 | E3 |
| Manor Way SE3 | 155 | F4 |
| Manor Way SE28 | 138 | C1 |
| Manor Way, Beck. | 190 | A2 |
| Manor Way, Bex. | 177 | G1 |
| Manor Way, Borwd. | 38 | C4 |
| Manor Way, Brom. | 192 | B6 |
| Manor Way, Har. | 67 | G5 |
| Manor Way, Mitch. | 186 | C3 |
| Manor Way, Orp. | 193 | F4 |
| Manor Way, S.Croy. | 202 | B6 |
| Manor Way, Sthl. | 122 | D4 |
| Manor Way, Wor.Pk. | 197 | E1 |
| Manor Way, The, Wall. | 200 | B4 |
| Manorbrook SE3 | 155 | G4 |
| Manordene Cl., T.Ditt. | 194 | D1 |
| Manordene Rd. SE28 | 118 | C6 |
| Manorfield Cl. N19 | 92 | C4 |
| *Tufnell Pk. Rd.* | | |
| Manorfields Cl., Chis. | 193 | J3 |
| Manorgate Rd., Kings.T. | 182 | A1 |
| Manorhall Gdns. E10 | 96 | A1 |
| Manorside, Barn. | 40 | B4 |
| Manorside Cl. SE2 | 138 | C4 |
| Manorway, Enf. | 44 | B7 |
| Manorway, Wdf.Grn. | 63 | J5 |
| Manpreet Ct. E12 | 98 | C5 |
| *Morris Av.* | | |
| Manresa Rd. SW3 | 31 | G4 |
| Manresa Rd. SW3 | 129 | H5 |
| Mansard Beeches SW17 | 168 | A5 |
| Mansard Cl., Pnr. | 66 | D3 |
| Manse Cl., Hayes | 121 | G6 |
| Manse Rd. N16 | 94 | C3 |
| Mansel Gro. E17 | 78 | A1 |
| Mansel Rd. SW19 | 166 | B6 |
| Mansell Rd. W3 | 126 | D2 |
| Mansell Rd., Grnf. | 103 | H5 |
| Mansell St. E1 | 21 | G6 |
| Mansell St. E1 | 112 | C6 |
| Mansergh Cl. SE18 | 136 | B7 |
| Mansfield Av. N15 | 76 | A4 |
| Mansfield Av., Barn. | 41 | J6 |
| Mansfield Av., Ruis. | 84 | B1 |
| Mansfield Cl. N9 | 44 | D6 |
| Mansfield Hill E4 | 62 | B1 |
| Mansfield Ms. W1 | 16 | D2 |
| *New End* | | |
| Mansfield Pl. NW3 | 91 | F4 |
| Mansfield Rd. E11 | 79 | H6 |
| Mansfield Rd. E17 | 77 | J4 |
| Mansfield Rd. NW3 | 91 | J5 |
| Mansfield Rd. W3 | 106 | B4 |
| Mansfield Rd., Chess. | 195 | F5 |
| Mansfield Rd., Ilf. | 98 | D2 |
| Mansfield Rd., S.Croy. | 202 | A6 |
| Mansfield St. W1 | 16 | D2 |
| Mansfield St. W1 | 110 | B5 |
| Mansford St. E2 | 13 | J2 |
| Mansford St. E2 | 112 | D2 |
| Manship Rd., Mitch. | 168 | A7 |
| Mansion Cl. SW9 | 151 | G1 |
| *Cowley Rd.* | | |
| Mansion Gdns. NW3 | 91 | E3 |
| Mansion Ho. EC4 | 20 | B4 |
| Mansion Ho. EC4 | 112 | A6 |
| Mansion Ho. Pl. EC4 | 20 | B4 |
| Mansion Ho. St. EC4 | 20 | B4 |
| Manson Ms. SW7 | 30 | D2 |
| Manson Ms. SW7 | 129 | F4 |
| Manson Pl. SW7 | 30 | E2 |
| Manson Pl. SW7 | 129 | G4 |
| Mansted Gdns., Rom. | 82 | C7 |
| Manston Av., Sthl. | 123 | G4 |
| Manston Cl. SE20 | 189 | F1 |
| *Garden Rd.* | | |
| Manston Gro., Kings.T. | 163 | G5 |
| Manstone Rd. NW2 | 90 | B5 |
| Manthorp Rd. SE18 | 137 | F5 |
| Mantilla Rd. SW17 | 168 | A4 |
| Mantle Rd. SE4 | 153 | H3 |
| Mantle Way E15 | 96/97 | E7 |
| *Romford Rd.* | | |
| Mantlet Cl. SW16 | 168 | C7 |
| Manton Av. W7 | 124 | C2 |
| Manton Rd. SE2 | 138 | A4 |
| Mantua St. SW11 | 149 | G3 |
| Mantus Cl. E1 | 113 | F4 |
| *Mantus Rd.* | | |
| Mantus Rd. E1 | 113 | F4 |
| Manus Way N20 | 57 | F2 |
| *Blakeney Cl.* | | |
| Manville Gdns. SW17 | 168 | B2 |
| Manville Rd. SW17 | 168 | A2 |
| Manwood Rd. SE4 | 153 | J5 |
| Manwood St. E16 | 136 | C1 |
| Manygates SW12 | 168 | B2 |
| Mape St. E2 | 112 | E4 |
| Mapesbury Rd. NW2 | 90 | B6 |
| Mapeshill Pl. NW2 | 89 | J6 |
| Maple Av. E4 | 61 | J5 |
| Maple Av. W3 | 127 | E1 |
| Maple Av., Har. | 85 | H2 |
| Maple Cl. N3 | 56 | D6 |
| Maple Cl. N16 | 76 | D6 |
| Maple Cl. SW4 | 150 | D6 |
| Maple Cl., Buck.H. | 64 | A3 |
| Maple Cl., Hmptn. | 161 | F6 |
| Maple Cl., Hayes | 102 | D3 |
| Maple Cl., Ilf. | 65 | H5 |
| Maple Cl., Mitch. | 186 | B1 |
| Maple Cl., Orp. | 193 | G5 |
| Maple Cl., Ruis. | 66 | B6 |
| Maple Cl., N.Mal. | 182 | E3 |
| Maple Cres., Sid. | 158 | A6 |
| Maple Gdns., Edg. | 54 | E7 |
| Maple Gate, Loug. | 48 | D2 |
| Maple Gro. NW9 | 70 | C7 |
| Maple Gro. W5 | 125 | G3 |
| Maple Gro., Brent. | 124 | E7 |
| Maple Gro., Sthl. | 103 | F5 |
| Maple Ind. Est., Felt. | 160 | A3 |
| *Maple Way* | | |
| Maple Leaf Dr., Sid. | 175 | J1 |
| Maple Leaf Sq. SE16 | 133 | G2 |
| *St. Elmos Rd.* | | |
| Maple Ms. NW6 | 6 | A1 |
| Maple Ms. SW16 | 169 | F5 |
| Maple Pl. W1 | 9 | G6 |
| Maple Rd. E11 | 79 | E6 |
| Maple Rd. SE20 | 189 | E1 |
| Maple Rd., Hayes | 102 | C3 |
| Maple Rd., Surb. | 181 | H5 |
| Maple St. W1 | 17 | F1 |
| Maple St. W1 | 110 | C5 |
| Maple St., Rom. | 83 | J4 |
| Maple Wk. W10 | 108 | A4 |
| *Droop St.* | | |
| Maple Way, Felt. | 160 | B3 |
| Maplecroft Cl. E6 | 116 | B6 |
| *Allhallows Rd.* | | |
| Mapledale Av., Croy. | 202 | D2 |
| Mapledene, Chis. | 175 | F5 |
| *Kemnal Rd.* | | |
| Mapledene Rd. E8 | 94 | C7 |
| Maplehurst Cl., Kings.T. | 181 | H4 |
| Mapleleafe Gdns., Ilf. | 80 | E3 |
| Maples Pl. E1 | 112/113 | E5 |
| *Raven Row* | | |
| Maplestead Rd. SW2 | 151 | F7 |
| Maplestead Rd., Dag. | 118 | B1 |
| Maplethorpe Rd., Th.Hth. | 187 | H4 |
| Mapleton Cl., Brom. | 191 | G6 |
| Mapleton Cres. SW18 | 148 | E6 |
| Mapleton Rd. E4 | 62 | C3 |
| Mapleton Rd. SW18 | 148 | E6 |
| Mapleton Rd., Enf. | 45 | E2 |
| Maplin Cl. N21 | 43 | F6 |
| Maplin Ho. SE2 | 138 | D2 |
| *Wolvercote Rd.* | | |
| Maplin Rd. E16 | 115 | G6 |
| Maplin St. E3 | 113 | J3 |
| Mapperley Dr., Wdf.Grn. | 62/63 | E7 |
| *Forest Dr.* | | |
| Maran Way, Erith | 138 | D2 |
| Marban Rd. W9 | 108 | C3 |
| Marble Arch W1 | 16 | A5 |
| Marble Arch W1 | 109 | J7 |
| Marble Cl. W3 | 126 | B1 |
| Marble Dr. NW2 | 72 | A7 |
| Marble Hill Cl., Twick. | 145 | E7 |
| Marble Hill Gdns., Twick. | 144 | E7 |
| Marble Ho. SE18 | 137 | J5 |
| *Felspar Cl.* | | |
| Marble Quay E1 | 29 | H1 |
| Marble Quay E1 | 132 | D1 |
| Marbrook Ct. SE12 | 173 | J3 |
| Marcellina Way, Orp. | 207 | H3 |
| March Rd., Twick. | 144 | D7 |
| Marchant Rd. E11 | 96 | D2 |
| Marchant St. SE14 | 133 | H6 |
| *Sanford St.* | | |
| Marchbank Rd. W14 | 128 | C6 |
| Marchmont Gdns., Rich. | 145 | J5 |
| *Marchmont Rd.* | | |
| Marchmont Rd., Rich. | 145 | J5 |
| Marchmont Rd., Wall. | 200 | C7 |
| Marchmont St. WC1 | 10 | A5 |
| Marchmont St. WC1 | 110 | E4 |
| Marchside Cl., Houns. | 142 | D1 |
| *Springwell Rd.* | | |
| Marchwood Cl. SE5 | 152 | B7 |
| Marchwood Cres. W5 | 105 | F6 |
| Marcia Rd. SE1 | 37 | E2 |
| Marcia Rd. SE1 | 132 | B4 |
| Marcilly Rd. SW18 | 149 | G5 |
| Marco Rd. W6 | 127 | J3 |
| Marcon Pl. E8 | 94 | E6 |
| Marconi Rd. E10 | 96 | A1 |
| Marconi Way, Sthl. | 103 | H6 |
| Marcourt Lawns W5 | 105 | H4 |
| Marcus Ct. E15 | 115 | E1 |
| Marcus Garvey Ms. SE22 | 152/153 | E5 |
| *St. Aidan's Rd.* | | |
| Marcus Garvey Way SE24 | 151 | G4 |
| Marcus St. E15 | 115 | F1 |
| Marcus St. SW18 | 149 | E6 |
| Marcus Ter. SW18 | 149 | E6 |
| Mardale Dr. NW9 | 70 | D5 |
| Mardell Rd., Croy. | 189 | G5 |
| Marden Av., Brom. | 191 | G6 |
| Marden Cres., Bex. | 159 | J5 |
| Marden Cres., Croy. | 187 | F6 |
| Marden Rd. N17 | 76 | B3 |
| Marden Rd., Croy. | 187 | F6 |
| Marden Sq. SE16 | 132 | E3 |
| Marder Rd. W13 | 124 | D2 |
| Mare St. E8 | 113 | E1 |
| Marechal Niel Av., Sid. | 175 | G3 |
| Maresfield, Croy. | 202 | B3 |
| Maresfield Gdns. NW3 | 91 | F5 |
| Marfleet Cl., Cars. | 199 | H2 |
| Margaret Av. E4 | 46 | B6 |
| Margaret Bondfield Av., Bark. | 100 | A7 |
| Margaret Bldgs. N16 | 94 | C1 |
| *Margaret Rd.* | | |
| Margaret Ct. W1 | 17 | F3 |
| Margaret Gardner Dr. SE9 | 174 | C2 |
| Margaret Ingram Cl. SW6 | 128 | C6 |
| *John Smith Av.* | | |
| Margaret Lockwood Cl., Kings.T. | 181 | J4 |
| Margaret Rd. N16 | 94 | C1 |
| Margaret Rd., Barn. | 41 | G4 |
| Margaret Rd., Bex. | 158 | D6 |
| Margaret St. W1 | 17 | E3 |
| Margaret St. W1 | 110 | B6 |
| Margaret Way, Ilf. | 80 | B6 |
| Margaretta Ter. SW3 | 31 | G4 |
| Margaretta Ter. SW3 | 129 | H6 |
| Margaretting Rd. E12 | 97 | J1 |
| Margate Rd. SW2 | 150 | E5 |
| Margeholes, Wat. | 50 | E2 |
| Margery Pk. Rd. E7 | 97 | G6 |
| Margery Rd., Dag. | 100 | D3 |
| Margery St. WC1 | 10 | E4 |
| Margery St. WC1 | 111 | G3 |
| Margin Dr. SW19 | 166 | A5 |
| Margravine Gdns. W6 | 128 | A5 |
| Margravine Rd. W6 | 128 | A4 |
| Marham Gdns. SW18 | 167 | H1 |
| Marham Gdns., Mord. | 185 | F6 |
| Maria Ter. E1 | 113 | G4 |
| Maria Theresa Cl., N.Mal. | 182 | D5 |
| Marian Cl., Hayes | 102 | D4 |
| Marian Ct., Sutt. | 198 | E5 |
| Marian Pl. E2 | 112 | E2 |
| Marian Rd. SW16 | 186 | C1 |
| Marian Sq. E2 | 13 | J1 |
| Marian St. E2 | 112/113 | E2 |
| *Hackney Rd.* | | |
| Marian Way NW10 | 89 | F7 |
| Maricas Av., Har. | 68 | A1 |
| Marie Lloyd Gdns. N19 | 74/75 | E7 |
| *Hornsey Ri. Gdns.* | | |
| Marie Lloyd Wk. E8 | 94 | D6 |
| *Forest Rd.* | | |
| Marigold All. SE1 | 19 | G6 |
| Marigold Cl., Sthl. | 102/103 | E7 |
| *Lancaster Rd.* | | |
| Marigold Rd. N17 | 61 | F7 |
| Marigold St. SE16 | 132 | E2 |
| Marigold Way E4 | 61 | J6 |
| *Silver Birch Av.* | | |
| Marigold Way, Croy. | 203 | G1 |
| Marina App., Hayes | 103 | E5 |
| Marina Av., N.Mal. | 183 | H5 |
| Marina Cl., Brom. | 191 | G3 |
| Marina Dr., Well. | 157 | H2 |
| Marina Gdns., Rom. | 83 | J5 |
| Marina Way, Tedd. | 163 | G7 |
| *Fairways* | | |
| Marine Dr. SE18 | 136 | C4 |
| Marine Dr., Bark. | 117 | H3 |
| *Thames Rd.* | | |
| Marine St. SE16 | 29 | H5 |
| Marinefield Rd. SW6 | 149 | E2 |
| Mariner Gdns., Rich. | 163 | F3 |
| Mariner Rd. E12 | 98 | C4 |
| *Dersingham Av.* | | |
| Mariners Ms. E14 | 134 | D4 |
| Marion Cl., Ilf. | 65 | G7 |
| Marion Gro., Wdf.Grn. | 63 | E5 |
| Marion Rd. NW7 | 55 | G5 |
| Marion Rd., Th.Hth. | 187 | J5 |
| Marischal Rd. SE13 | 154 | D3 |
| Maritime Quay E14 | 134 | A5 |
| Maritime St. E3 | 113 | J4 |

| | | |
|---|---|---|
| Marius Pas. SW17 | 168 | A2 |
| *Marius Rd.* | | |
| Marius Rd. SW17 | 168 | A2 |
| Marjorams Av., | 48 | C2 |
| Loug. | | |
| Marjorie Gro. SW11 | 149 | J4 |
| Marjorie Ms. E1 | 113 | G6 |
| *Arbour Sq.* | | |
| Mark Av. E4 | 46 | B6 |
| Mark Cl., Bexh. | 158 | E1 |
| Mark Cl., Sthl. | 123 | H1 |
| *Longford Av.* | | |
| **Mark La. EC3** | **20** | **E5** |
| Mark La. EC3 | 112 | B7 |
| Mark Rd. N22 | 75 | H2 |
| **Mark Sq. EC2** | **12** | **D5** |
| Mark St. E15 | 96 | E7 |
| **Mark St. EC2** | **12** | **D5** |
| Marke Cl., Kes. | 206 | B4 |
| Markeston Grn., Wat. | 50 | D4 |
| **Market Ct. W1** | **17** | **F3** |
| Market Est. N7 | 92 | E6 |
| Market Hill SE18 | 136 | D3 |
| Market La., Edg. | 70 | C1 |
| **Market Ms. W1** | **24** | **D2** |
| Market Ms. W1 | 130 | B1 |
| Market Par. SE15 | 152 | D2 |
| *Rye La.* | | |
| Market Pl. N2 | 73 | H3 |
| Market Pl. NW11 | 73 | F4 |
| **Market Pl. SE16** | **37** | **J1** |
| **Market Pl. W1** | **17** | **F3** |
| Market Pl. W1 | 110 | C6 |
| Market Pl. W3 | 126 | C1 |
| Market Pl., Bexh. | 159 | G4 |
| Market Pl., Brent. | 125 | F7 |
| Market Pl., Enf. | 44 | A3 |
| *The Town* | | |
| Market Pl., Kings.T. | 181 | G2 |
| Market Rd. N7 | 92 | E6 |
| Market Rd., Rich. | 146 | A3 |
| Market Row SW9 | 151 | G4 |
| *Atlantic Rd.* | | |
| **Market Sq. E2** | **13** | **F3** |
| Market Sq. E14 | 114 | B6 |
| *Chrisp St.* | | |
| Market Sq. N9 | 60 | D2 |
| *New Rd.* | | |
| Market Sq., Brom. | 191 | G2 |
| Market St. E6 | 116 | C2 |
| Market St. SE18 | 136 | D4 |
| Market Way E14 | 114 | B6 |
| *Kerbey St.* | | |
| Market Way, Wem. | 87 | H5 |
| *Turton Rd.* | | |
| Markfield Gdns. E4 | 46 | B7 |
| Markfield Rd. N15 | 76 | D4 |
| **Markham Pl. SW3** | **31** | **J3** |
| **Markham Sq. SW3** | **31** | **J3** |
| Markham Sq. SW3 | 129 | J5 |
| **Markham St. SW3** | **31** | **H3** |
| Markham St. SW3 | 129 | H5 |
| Markhole Cl., Hmptn. | 161 | F7 |
| *Priory Rd.* | | |
| Markhouse Av. E17 | 77 | H6 |
| Markhouse Rd. E17 | 77 | J5 |
| Markmanor Av. E17 | 77 | H7 |
| Marks Rd., Rom. | 83 | J5 |
| Marksbury Av., Rich. | 146 | A3 |
| Markway, Sun. | 178 | C2 |
| Markwell Cl. | 170/171 | E4 |
| SE26 | | |
| *Longton Gro.* | | |
| Markyate Rd., Dag. | 100 | B5 |
| Marl Rd. SW18 | 149 | E4 |
| Marl St. SW18 | 149 | F4 |
| *Marl Rd.* | | |
| Marlands Rd., Ilf. | 80 | B3 |
| Marlborough Av. E8 | 112 | D1 |
| Marlborough Av. | 58 | C3 |
| N14 | | |
| Marlborough Av., | 54 | B3 |
| Edg. | | |
| **Marlborough Bldgs.** | **31** | **H1** |
| **SW3** | | |
| Marlborough Bldgs. | 129 | H4 |
| SW3 | | |
| Marlborough Cl. N20 | 57 | J3 |
| *Marlborough Gdns.* | | |
| **Marlborough Cl.** | **35** | **H2** |
| **SE17** | | |
| Marlborough Cl. | 167 | H6 |
| SW19 | | |
| Marlborough Cl., | 193 | J7 |
| Orp. | | |
| *Aylesham Rd.* | | |
| **Marlborough Ct. W1** | **17** | **F4** |
| Marlborough Ct. W8 | 128 | D4 |
| Marlborough Ct., | 200 | C7 |
| Wall. | | |
| *Cranley Gdns.* | | |
| Marlborough Cres. | 126 | D3 |
| W4 | | |
| Marlborough Dr., Ilf. | 80 | B3 |

| | | |
|---|---|---|
| Marlborough Gdns. | 57 | J3 |
| N20 | | |
| **Marlborough Gate** | **14** | **E5** |
| **Ho. W2** | | |
| **Marlborough Gro.** | **37** | **H4** |
| **SE1** | | |
| Marlborough Gro. | 132 | D5 |
| SE1 | | |
| Marlborough Hill | 109 | F1 |
| NW8 | | |
| Marlborough Hill, | 68 | C4 |
| Har. | | |
| Marlborough La. | 135 | J6 |
| SE7 | | |
| Marlborough Pk. Av., | 158 | A7 |
| Sid. | | |
| **Marlborough Pl.** | **6** | **C2** |
| **NW8** | | |
| Marlborough Pl. | 109 | F2 |
| NW8 | | |
| Marlborough Rd. E4 | 62 | A6 |
| Marlborough Rd. E7 | 97 | J7 |
| E15 | | |
| *Borthwick Rd.* | | |
| Marlborough Rd. E18 | 79 | G3 |
| Marlborough Rd. N9 | 60 | C1 |
| Marlborough Rd. N19 | 92 | D2 |
| Marlborough Rd. N22 | 59 | E7 |
| **Marlborough Rd.** | **25** | **G2** |
| **SW1** | | |
| Marlborough Rd. | 130 | C1 |
| SW1 | | |
| Marlborough Rd. | 167 | G6 |
| SW19 | | |
| Marlborough Rd. W4 | 126 | C5 |
| Marlborough Rd. W5 | 125 | G2 |
| Marlborough Rd., | 158 | D3 |
| Bexh. | | |
| Marlborough Rd., | 191 | J4 |
| Brom. | | |
| Marlborough Rd., | 100 | B4 |
| Dag. | | |
| Marlborough Rd., | 160 | D2 |
| Felt. | | |
| Marlborough Rd., | 161 | G6 |
| Hmptn. | | |
| Marlborough Rd., | 144 | E1 |
| Islw. | | |
| Marlborough Rd., | 145 | H6 |
| Rich. | | |
| Marlborough Rd., | 83 | G4 |
| Rom. | | |
| Marlborough Rd., | 201 | J7 |
| S.Croy. | | |
| Marlborough Rd., | 122 | C3 |
| Sthl. | | |
| Marlborough Rd., | 198 | D3 |
| Sutt. | | |
| **Marlborough St.** | **31** | **G2** |
| **SW3** | | |
| Marlborough St. | 129 | H4 |
| SW3 | | |
| Marlborough Yd. | 92 | D2 |
| N19 | | |
| *Marlborough Rd.* | | |
| Marlescroft Way, | 48 | E5 |
| Loug. | | |
| Marley Av., Bexh. | 138 | D6 |
| Marley Cl. N15 | 75 | H4 |
| *Stanmore Rd.* | | |
| Marley Cl., Grnf. | 103 | G3 |
| *Lennon Rd.* | | |
| Marlingdene Cl., | 161 | G6 |
| Hmptn. | | |
| Marlings Cl., Chis. | 193 | H4 |
| Marlings Pk. Av., | 193 | H4 |
| Chis. | | |
| Marlins Cl., Sutt. | 199 | F5 |
| *Turnpike La.* | | |
| Marloes Cl., Wem. | 87 | G4 |
| **Marloes Rd. W8** | **22** | **A6** |
| Marloes Rd. W8 | 128 | E3 |
| Marlow Cl. SE20 | 189 | E3 |
| Marlow Cl. NW6 | 90 | A7 |
| Marlow Cl. NW9 | 71 | F3 |
| Marlow Cres., Twick. | 144 | C6 |
| Marlow Dr., Sutt. | 198 | A2 |
| Marlow Gdns. | 121 | G3 |
| Hayes | | |
| Marlow Rd. E6 | 116 | C3 |
| Marlow Rd. SE20 | 189 | E3 |
| Marlow Rd., Sthl. | 123 | F3 |
| Marlow Way SE16 | 133 | G2 |
| Marlowe Cl., Chis. | 175 | G6 |
| Marlowe Cl., Ilf. | 81 | F1 |
| Marlowe Gdns. SE9 | 156 | D6 |
| Marlowe Rd. E17 | 78 | C4 |
| Marlowe Sq., Mitch. | 186 | C4 |
| Marlowe Way, Croy. | 201 | E2 |
| Marlowes, The | 109 | G1 |
| NW8 | | |

| | | |
|---|---|---|
| Marlton St. SE10 | 135 | F5 |
| *Woolwich Rd.* | | |
| Marlwood Cl., Sid. | 175 | H2 |
| Marmadon Rd. SE18 | 137 | J4 |
| Marmion App. E4 | 62 | A4 |
| Marmion Av. E4 | 61 | J4 |
| Marmion Cl. E4 | 61 | J4 |
| Marmion Ms. SW11 | 150 | A3 |
| *Taybridge Rd.* | | |
| Marmion Rd. SW11 | 150 | A4 |
| Marmont Rd. SE15 | 152 | D1 |
| Marmora Rd. SE22 | 153 | F6 |
| Marmot Rd., Houns. | 142 | D3 |
| Marne Av. N11 | 58 | B4 |
| Marne Av., Well. | 158 | A3 |
| Marne St. W10 | 108 | B3 |
| Marnell Way, Houns. | 142 | D3 |
| Marney Rd. SW11 | 150 | A4 |
| Marnfield Cres. | 151 | F7 |
| SW2 | | |
| Marnham Av. NW2 | 90 | B4 |
| Marnham Cres., | 103 | H3 |
| Grnf. | | |
| Marnock Rd. SE4 | 153 | H5 |
| Maroon St. E14 | 113 | H5 |
| Maroons Way SE6 | 172 | A5 |
| Marquess Rd. N1 | 94 | A6 |
| Marquis Cl., Wem. | 87 | J7 |
| Marquis Rd. N4 | 93 | F1 |
| Marquis Rd. N22 | 59 | F6 |
| Marquis Rd. NW1 | 92 | D6 |
| Marrabon Cl., Sid. | 176 | A1 |
| Marrick Cl. SW15 | 147 | G4 |
| Marriots Cl. NW9 | 71 | F6 |
| Marriott Cl., Felt. | 141 | G6 |
| Marriott Rd. E15 | 114 | E1 |
| Marriott Rd. N4 | 93 | F1 |
| Marriott Rd. N10 | 73 | J1 |
| Marriott Rd., Barn. | 40 | A3 |
| Marryat Pl. SW19 | 166 | B4 |
| Marryat Rd. SW19 | 166 | A5 |
| Marryat Sq. SW6 | 148 | B1 |
| Marsala Rd. SE13 | 154 | B4 |
| Marsden Rd. N9 | 60 | E2 |
| Marsden Rd. SE15 | 152 | C3 |
| Marsden St. NW5 | 92 | A6 |
| Marsden Way, Orp. | 207 | J4 |
| Marsh Av., Mitch. | 186 | A2 |
| Marsh Cl. NW7 | 55 | F3 |
| Marsh Ct. SW19 | 185 | F1 |
| Marsh Dr. NW9 | 71 | F6 |
| Marsh Fm. Rd., | 162 | C1 |
| Twick. | | |
| Marsh Grn. Rd., Dag. | 119 | G1 |
| Marsh Hill E9 | 95 | H5 |
| Marsh La. E10 | 96 | A2 |
| Marsh La. N17 | 61 | E7 |
| Marsh La. NW7 | 54 | E4 |
| Marsh La., Stan. | 53 | F5 |
| Marsh Rd., Pnr. | 66 | E4 |
| Marsh Rd., Wem. | 105 | G2 |
| Marsh St. E14 | 134 | B4 |
| *Harbinger Rd.* | | |
| Marsh Wall E14 | 134 | A1 |
| Marshall Cl. SW18 | 149 | F6 |
| *Allfarthing La.* | | |
| Marshall Cl., Har. | 68 | A7 |
| *Bowen Rd.* | | |
| Marshall Cl., Houns. | 143 | F5 |
| Marshall Path SE28 | 118 | B7 |
| *Attlee Rd.* | | |
| Marshall Rd. E10 | 96 | B3 |
| Marshall Rd. N17 | 76 | A1 |
| Marshall St. W1 | 110 | C6 |
| Marshalls Cl. N11 | 58 | B4 |
| Marshall's Gro. SE18 | 136 | B4 |
| **Marshalls Pl. SE16** | **29** | **G6** |
| Marshalls Rd., Sutt. | 198 | E4 |
| **Marshalsea Rd. SE1** | **28** | **A3** |
| Marshalsea Rd. SE1 | 131 | J2 |
| Marsham Cl., Chis. | 174 | E5 |
| **Marsham St. SW1** | **25** | **J6** |
| Marsham St. SW1 | 130 | D3 |
| Marshbrook Cl. SE3 | 156 | A3 |
| Marshfield St. E14 | 134 | C3 |
| Marshgate La. E15 | 114 | B1 |
| Marshgate Path | 137 | F3 |
| SE28 | | |
| *Tom Cribb Rd.* | | |
| Marshgate Sidings | 96 | B7 |
| E15 | | |
| *Marshgate La.* | | |
| Marshside Cl. N9 | 61 | F1 |
| **Marsland Cl. SE17** | **35** | **H4** |
| Marsland Cl. SE17 | 131 | H5 |
| Marston Av., Chess. | 195 | H6 |
| Marston Av., Dag. | 101 | G2 |
| Marston Cl. NW6 | 91 | F7 |
| *Fairfax Rd.* | | |
| Marston Cl., Dag. | 101 | G3 |
| Marston Rd., Ilf. | 80 | B1 |
| Marston Rd., Tedd. | 162 | E5 |
| Marston Way SE19 | 169 | H7 |

| | | |
|---|---|---|
| Marsworth Av., Pnr. | 66 | D1 |
| Marsworth Cl., | 103 | E5 |
| Hayes | | |
| **Mart St. WC2** | **18** | **B4** |
| Martaban Rd. N16 | 94 | B2 |
| Martel Pl. E8 | 94 | C6 |
| *Dalston La.* | | |
| Martell Rd. SE21 | 170 | A3 |
| Martello St. E8 | 94 | E7 |
| Martello Ter. E8 | 94 | E7 |
| Marten Rd. E17 | 78 | A2 |
| Martens Av., Bexh. | 159 | J4 |
| Martens Cl., Bexh. | 159 | J4 |
| Martha Ct. E2 | 112/113 | E2 |
| *Cambridge Heath Rd.* | | |
| Martha Rd. E4 | 61 | J6 |
| Martha Rd. E15 | 97 | E6 |
| Martha St. E1 | 113 | E6 |
| Martham Cl. SE28 | 118 | D7 |
| Marthorne Cres., Har. | 68 | A2 |
| Martin Bowes Rd. | 156 | C3 |
| SE9 | | |
| Martin Cl. N9 | 61 | G1 |
| Martin Cres., Croy. | 201 | G1 |
| Martin Dene, Bexh. | 159 | F5 |
| Martin Dr., Nthlt. | 85 | F5 |
| Martin Gdns., Dag. | 100 | C4 |
| Martin Gro., Mord. | 184 | D3 |
| **Martin La. EC4** | **20** | **C5** |
| Martin Ri., Bexh. | 159 | F5 |
| Martin Rd., Dag. | 100 | C4 |
| Martin St. SE28 | 137 | H1 |
| *Merbury Rd.* | | |
| Martin Way SW20 | 184 | B3 |
| Martin Way, Mord. | 184 | B3 |
| Martinbridge Ind. | 44 | D5 |
| Est., Enf. | | |
| Martindale SW14 | 146 | C5 |
| Martindale Av. E16 | 115 | G7 |
| Martindale Rd. SW12 | 150 | B7 |
| Martindale Rd., | 142 | E3 |
| Houns. | | |
| Martineau Cl., Esher | 194 | A4 |
| Martineau Ms. N5 | 93 | H4 |
| *Martineau Rd.* | | |
| Martineau Rd. N5 | 93 | H4 |
| Martineau St. E1 | 113 | F7 |
| Martingale Cl., Sun. | 178 | A4 |
| Martingales Cl., | 163 | G3 |
| Rich. | | |
| Martins Cl., W.Wick. | 204 | D1 |
| Martins Mt., Barn. | 40 | D4 |
| Martins Rd., Brom. | 191 | E2 |
| Martins Wk. N10 | 74 | A1 |
| Martins Wk., Borwd. | 38 | A4 |
| *Siskin Cl.* | | |
| Martinsfield Cl., Chig. | 65 | H4 |
| Martlet Gro., Nthlt. | 102 | D3 |
| *Javelin Way* | | |
| **Martlett Ct. WC2** | **18** | **B4** |
| Martley Dr., Ilf. | 80 | E5 |
| Martock Cl., Har. | 68 | D4 |
| Marton Cl. SE6 | 172 | A3 |
| Marton Rd. N16 | 94 | B2 |
| Martys Yd. NW3 | 91 | G4 |
| *Hampstead High St.* | | |
| Marvell Av., Hayes | 102 | A5 |
| Marvels Cl. SE12 | 173 | H2 |
| Marvels La. SE12 | 173 | H2 |
| Marville Rd. SW6 | 128 | C7 |
| Marvin St. E8 | 94/95 | E6 |
| *Sylvester Rd.* | | |
| Marwell Cl., W.Wick. | 205 | F2 |
| *Deer Pk. Way* | | |
| Marwood Cl., Well. | 158 | B3 |
| Mary Adelaide Cl. | 164 | E4 |
| SW15 | | |
| Mary Ann Gdns. SE8 | 134 | A6 |
| Mary Cl., Stan. | 69 | J4 |
| Mary Datchelor Cl. | 152 | A1 |
| SE5 | | |
| Mary Grn. NW8 | 109 | E1 |
| Mary Kingsley Ct. | 74/75 | E7 |
| N19 | | |
| *Hillrise Rd.* | | |
| Mary Lawrenson Pl. | 135 | F7 |
| SE3 | | |
| Mary Macarthur Ho. | 128 | B6 |
| W6 | | |
| *Field Rd.* | | |
| Mary Peters Dr., Grnf. | 86 | A5 |
| Mary Pl. W11 | 108 | B7 |
| Mary Rose Cl., | 179 | G1 |
| Hmptn. | | |
| *Ashley Rd.* | | |
| Mary Rose Mall E6 | 116 | D5 |
| *Frobisher Rd.* | | |
| Mary Seacole Cl. E8 | 112 | C1 |
| *Clarissa St.* | | |
| Mary St. E16 | 115 | F5 |
| *Barking Rd.* | | |
| Mary St. N1 | 111 | J1 |
| Mary Ter. NW1 | 110 | B1 |
| Maryatt Av., Har. | 85 | H2 |

Mendip Cl. SW19 166 B2
*Queensmere Rd.*
Mendip Cl., Hayes 121 G7
Mendip Cl., Wor.Pk. 197 J1
Mendip Dr. NW2 90 A2
Mendip Rd. SW11 149 F3
Mendip Rd., Ilf. 81 H5
Mendora Rd. SW6 128 B7
Menelik Rd. NW2 90 B4
Menlo Gdns. SE19 170 A7
**Menotti St. E2 13 J5**
Mentmore Cl., Har. 69 F6
Mentmore Ter. E8 95 E7
Meon Ct., Islw. 144 B2
Meon Rd. W3 126 C2
Meopham Rd., Mitch. 186 C1
Mepham Cres., Har. 51 J7
Mepham Gdns., Har. 51 J7
**Mepham St. SE1 26 D2**
Mepham St. SE1 131 F1
Mera Dr., Bexh. 159 G4
Merantun Way SW19 185 F1
Merbury Cl. SE13 154 C5
Merbury Rd. SE28 137 H2
Mercator Pl. E14 134 A5
*Napier Av.*
Mercator Rd. SE13 154 D4
Mercer Cl., T.Ditt. 180 C7
Mercer Pl., Pnr. 66 C2
*Crossway*
**Mercer St. WC2 18 A4**
Mercer St. WC2 110 E6
Merceron St. E1 112 E4
Mercers Cl. SE10 135 F4
Mercers Pl. W6 127 J4
Mercers Rd. N19 92 D3
Merchant St. E3 113 J3
Merchiston Rd. SE6 172 D2
Merchland Rd. SE9 175 F1
Mercia Gro. SE13 154 C4
Mercier Rd. SW15 148 B5
Mercury Cen., Felt. 142 B5
Mercury Way SE14 133 G6
Mercy Ter. SE13 154 B4
Mere Cl. SW15 148 A7
Mere Cl., Orp. 206 E2
Mere End, Croy. 189 G7
Mere Side, Orp. 206 D2
Merebank La., Croy. 201 F5
Meredith Av. NW2 89 J5
Meredith Cl., Pnr. 50 D7
Meredith St. E13 115 G3
**Meredith St. EC1 11 G4**
Meredyth Rd. SW13 147 G2
Meretone Cl. SE4 153 H4
Merevale Cres., Mord. 185 F6
Mereway Rd., Twick. 162 A1
Merewood Cl., Brom. 192 D2
Merewood Rd., Bexh. 159 J2
Mereworth Cl., Brom. 191 F5
Mereworth Dr. SE18 137 F7
Merganser Gdns. SE28 137 G3
*Avocet Ms.*
Meriden Cl., Brom. 174 A7
Meriden Cl., Ilf. 81 F1
Meridian Gate E14 134 C2
Meridian Pl. E14 134 B2
Meridian Rd. SE7 136 A7
Meridian Trd. Est. SE7 135 H4
Meridian Wk. N17 60 B6
*Commercial Rd.*
Meridian Way N9 61 F5
Meridian Way N18 61 F6
Meridian Way, Enf. 45 G6
Merifield Rd. SE9 155 J4
Merino Cl. E11 79 J4
Merino Pl., Sid. 158 A6
*Blackfen Rd.*
Merivale Rd. SW15 148 B4
Merivale Rd., Har. 67 J7
Merlewood Dr., Chis. 192 C1
Merley Ct. NW9 88 C1
Merlin Cl., Croy. 202 B4
*Minster Dr.*
Merlin Cl., Mitch. 185 H3
Merlin Cl., Nthlt. 102 C3
Merlin Cres., Edg. 69 J1
Merlin Gdns., Brom. 173 G3
Merlin Gro., Beck. 189 J4
Merlin Gro., Ilf. 65 E7
Merlin Rd. E12 98 A2
Merlin Rd., Well. 158 A4
Merlin Rd. N., Well. 158 A4
**Merlin St. WC1 11 E4**
Merling Cl., Chess. 195 G5
*Coppard Gdns.*
Merlins Av., Har. 85 F3
**Mermaid Ct. SE1 28 B3**
Mermaid Ct. SE1 132 A2
Mermaid Ct. SE16 133 J1
Merredene St. SW2 151 F6
Merriam Cl. E4 62 C5
Merrick Rd., Sthl. 123 F2
**Merrick Sq. SE1 28 A5**
Merrick Sq. SE1 131 J3
Merridene N21 43 H6
Merrielands Cres., Dag. 119 F1
Merrilands Rd., Wor.Pk. 197 J1
Merrilees Rd., Sid. 157 H7
Merrilyn Cl., Esher 194 D6
Merriman Rd. SE3 155 J1
Merrington Rd. SW6 128 D6
Merrion Av., Stan. 53 G5
Merrion Wk. SE17 132 A5
*Dawes St.*
Merritt Gdns., Chess. 195 F6
Merritt Rd. SE4 153 J5
Merrivale N14 42 D6
Merrivale Av., Ilf. 80 A4
**Merrow St. SE17 36 C4**
Merrow St. SE17 131 J6
**Merrow Wk. SE17 36 C3**
Merrow Way, Croy. 204 C6
Merry Hill Mt., Bushey 51 H1
Merry Hill Rd., Bushey 51 H1
Merrydown Way, Chis. 192 B1
Merryfield SE3 155 F2
Merryfield Gdns., Stan. 53 F5
Merryfields Way SE6 154 B7
Merryhill Cl. E4 46 B7
Merryhills Ct. N14 42 C5
Merryhills Dr., Enf. 42 D4
Mersea Ho., Bark. 98 E6
Mersey Rd. E17 77 J3
Mersey Wk., Nthlt. 103 G2
*Brabazon Rd.*
Mersham Dr. NW9 70 A5
Mersham Pl. SE20 189 E1
Mersham Rd., Th.Hth. 188 A3
Merten Rd., Rom. 83 E7
Merthyr Ter. SW13 127 H6
Merton Av. W4 127 F4
Merton Av., Nthlt. 85 J5
Merton Gdns., Orp. 193 E5
Merton Hall Gdns. SW20 184 B1
Merton Hall Rd. SW19 184 B1
Merton High St. SW19 167 E7
Merton Ind. Pk. SW19 185 F1
Merton La. N6 91 J2
Merton Mans. SW20 184 A2
Merton Pk. Par. SW19 184 C1
*Kingston Rd.*
Merton Ri. NW3 91 H7
Merton Rd. E17 78 C5
Merton Rd. SE25 188 D5
Merton Rd. SW18 148 D6
Merton Rd. SW19 166 E7
Merton Rd., Bark. 99 J7
Merton Rd., Har. 85 J1
Merton Rd., Ilf. 81 J7
Merton Way, W.Mol. 179 H4
Merttins Rd. SE15 153 G5
Meru Cl. NW5 92 A4
Mervan Rd. SW2 151 G4
Mervyn Av. SE9 175 F3
Mervyn Rd. W13 124 D3
Messaline Av. W3 106 C6
Messent Rd. SE9 155 J5
Messeter Pl. SE9 156 D6
Messina Av. NW6 90 D7
Metcalf Wk., Felt. 160/161 E4
*Gabriel Cl.*
Meteor St. SW11 150 A4
Meteor Way, Wall. 200 E7
Metheringham Way NW9 70 E1
**Methley St. SE11 35 F4**
Methley St. SE11 131 G5
Methuen Cl., Edg. 54 A7
Methuen Pk. N10 74 B2
Methuen Rd., Belv. 139 H4
Methuen Rd., Bexh. 159 F1
Methuen Rd., Edg. 54 A7
Methwold Rd. W10 108 A5
Metro Cen., The, Islw. 144 B2
Metropolitan Cen., The, Grnf. 103 H1
Metropolitan Cl. E14 114 A5
*Broomfield St.*
Mews, The N1 111 J1
*St. Paul St.*
Mews, The, Ilf. 80 A5
Mews, The, Twick. 144/145 E6
*Bridge Rd.*
Mews Deck E1 113 E7
Mews Pl., Wdf.Grn. 63 G4
**Mews St. E1 29 H1**
Mews St. E1 132 D1
Mexfield Rd. SW15 148 C5
Meyer Rd., Erith 139 J6
**Meymott St. SE1 27 G2**
Meymott St. SE1 131 H1
Meynell Cres. E9 95 G7
Meynell Gdns. E9 95 G7
Meynell Rd. E9 95 G7
Meyrick Rd. NW10 89 G6
Meyrick Rd. SW11 149 G3
Miah Ter. E1 132 D1
*Wapping High St.*
Miall Wk. SE26 171 H4
**Micawber St. N1 12 A3**
Micawber St. N1 111 J3
**Michael Faraday Ho. SE17 36 C4**
Michael Gaynor Cl. W7 124 C1
Michael Rd. E11 97 E1
Michael Rd. SE25 188 B3
Michael Rd. SW6 149 E1
Michaelmas Cl. SW20 183 J3
Michaels Cl. SE13 154 E4
Micheldever Rd. SE12 155 E6
Michelham Gdns., Twick. 162 C3
Michels Row, Rich. 145 H4
*Kew Foot Rd.*
Michigan Av. E12 98 B4
Michleham Down N12 56 C4
Mickleham Cl., Orp. 193 J2
Mickleham Gdns., Sutt. 198 B6
Mickleham Rd., Orp. 193 J1
Mickleham Way, Croy. 204 D7
Micklethwaite Rd. SW6 128 D6
Midas Metropolitan Ind. Est., The, Mord. 198 A1
*Garth Rd.*
Middle Dene NW7 54 D3
Middle Fld. NW8 109 G1
Middle Grn. Cl., Surb. 181 J6
*Alpha Rd.*
Middle La. N8 74 E5
Middle La., Tedd. 162 C6
Middle La. Ms. N8 74/75 E5
*Middle La.*
Middle Pk. Av. SE9 156 A6
Middle Path, Har. 86 A1
*Middle Rd.*
Middle Rd. E13 115 G2
*London Rd.*
Middle Rd. SW16 186 D2
Middle Rd., Barn. 41 H6
Middle Rd., Har. 86 A2
Middle Row W10 108 B4
**Middle St. EC1 19 J1**
Middle St., Croy. 201 J3
*Surrey St.*
**Middle Temple EC4 19 E5**
**Middle Temple La. EC4 19 E4**
Middle Temple La. EC4 111 G6
Middle Way SW16 186 D2
Middle Way, Erith 138 E3
Middle Way, Hayes 102 C4
Middle Way, The, Har. 68 C2
**Middle Yd. SE1 28 C1**
Middlefield Gdns., Ilf. 81 E6
Middlefielde W13 104 E5
Middleham Gdns. N18 60 D6
Middleham Rd. N18 60 D6
Middlesborough Rd. N18 60 D6
Middlesex Business Cen., Sthl. 123 G2
Middlesex Ct. W4 127 F4
*British Gro.*
**Middlesex Pas. EC1 19 H2**
Middlesex Rd., Mitch. 186 E5
**Middlesex St. E1 21 E2**
Middlesex St. E1 112 B5
Middlesex Wf. E5 95 F2
Middleton Av. E4 61 J4
Middleton Av., Grnf. 104 A2
Middleton Av., Sid. 176 C6
**Middleton Bldgs. W1 17 F2**
Middleton Cl. E4 61 J3
Middleton Dr. SE16 133 G2
Middleton Dr., Pnr. 66 A3
Middleton Gdns., Ilf. 81 E6
Middleton Gro. N7 92 E5
Middleton Ms. N7 92/93 E5
*Middleton Gro.*
Middleton Rd. E8 94 C7
Middleton Rd. NW11 72 D7
Middleton Rd., Cars. 185 H7
Middleton Rd., Mord. 185 F6
Middleton St. E2 112 E3
Middleton Way SE13 154 D4
Middleway NW11 73 E5
Midfield Av., Bexh. 159 J3
Midfield Par., Bexh. 159 J3
**Midford Pl. W1 9 G6**
Midholm NW11 72 E4
Midholm, Wem. 88 A1
Midholm Cl. NW11 72 E4
Midholm Rd., Croy. 203 H2
**Midhope St. WC1 10 B4**
Midhurst Av. N10 74 A3
Midhurst Av., Croy. 187 G7
Midhurst Hill, Bexh. 159 G6
Midhurst Rd. W13 124 D2
Midland Cres. NW3 91 F6
*Finchley Rd.*
Midland Pl. E14 134 C5
*Ferry St.*
Midland Rd. E10 78 C7
**Midland Rd. NW1 9 J2**
Midland Rd. NW1 110 D2
Midland Ter. NW2 90 A3
*Kara Way*
Midland Ter. NW10 107 E4
Midleton Rd., N.Mal. 182 C3
Midlothian Rd. E3 113 J5
Midmoor Rd. SW12 168 C1
Midmoor Rd. SW19 184 A1
Midship Cl. SE16 133 G1
*Surrey Water Rd.*
Midship Pt. E14 134 A2
Midstrath Rd. NW10 89 E4
Midsummer Av., Houns. 143 F4
Midway, Sutt. 184 C7
Midwinter Cl., Well. 158 A3
*Hook La.*
Midwood Cl. NW2 89 H3
Miers Cl. E6 116 D1
Mighell Av., Ilf. 80 A5
Milan Rd., Sthl. 123 F2
**Milborne Gro. SW10 30 D4**
Milborne Gro. SW10 129 F5
Milborne St. E9 95 F6
Milborough Cres. SE12 155 E6
**Milcote St. SE1 27 G4**
Milcote St. SE1 131 H2
Mildenhall Rd. E5 95 F4
Mildmay Av. N1 94 A6
Mildmay Gro. N. N1 94 A5
Mildmay Gro. S. N1 94 A5
Mildmay Pk. N1 94 A5
Mildmay Pl. N16 94 B5
*Boleyn Rd.*
Mildmay Rd. N1 94 B5
Mildmay Rd., Ilf. 98/99 E3
*Winston Way*
Mildmay Rd., Rom. 83 J5
Mildmay St. N1 94 A6
Mildred Av., Borwd. 38 A4
Mildred Av., Hayes 121 G4
Mildred Av., Nthlt. 85 H5
Mile End, The E17 77 G1
Mile End Pl. E1 113 G4
Mile End Rd. E1 113 F5
Mile End Rd. E3 113 F5
Mile Rd., Wall. 200 C1
Miles Dr. SE28 137 H1
*Merbury Rd.*
**Miles Pl. NW1 15 F1**
Miles Pl., Surb. 181 J4
*Villiers Av.*
Miles Rd. N8 75 E3
Miles Rd., Mitch. 185 H3
**Miles St. SW8 34 B6**
Miles St. SW8 131 E6
Miles Way N20 57 H2
Milespit Hill NW7 55 H5
Milestone Cl. N9 60 D2
*Chichester Rd.*
Milestone Cl., Sutt. 199 G6
Milestone Rd. SE19 170 C6
Milfoil St. W12 107 G7
Milford Cl. SE2 139 E6

316 Mou–Nas

Mount Rd., Bexh. 158 D5
Mount Rd., Chess. 195 J5
Mount Rd., Dag. 101 F1
Mount Rd., Felt. 160 E3
Mount Rd., Hayes 122 A2
Mount Rd., Ilf. 98 E5
Mount Rd., Mitch. 185 H2
Mount Rd., N.Mal. 182 D3
**Mount Row W1 16 D6**
Mount Row W1 110 B7
Mount Sq., The NW3 91 F3
*Heath St.*
Mount Stewart Av., Har. 69 G6
**Mount St. W1 16 C6**
Mount St. W1 110 A7
Mount Ter. E1 112/113 E5
*New Rd.*
Mount Vernon NW3 91 F4
Mount Vw. NW7 54 D3
Mount Vw. W5 105 G4
Mount Vw. Rd. E4 46 C7
Mount Vw. Rd. N4 75 E7
Mount Vw. Rd. NW9 70 D4
Mount Vil. SE27 169 H3
Mountacre Cl. SE26 170 C4
Mountague Pl. E14 114 C7
Mountbatten Cl. SE18 137 H6
Mountbatten Cl. SE19 170 B5
Mountbatten Ct. SE16 133 F1
*Rotherhithe St.*
Mountbatten Ct., Buck.H. 64 A2
Mountbatten Gdns., Beck. 189 H4
*Balmoral Av.*
Mountbatten Ms. SW18 167 F1
*Inman Rd.*
Mountbel Rd., Stan. 68 D1
Mountcombe Cl., Surb. 181 H7
Mountearl Gdns. SW16 169 F3
Mountfield Cl. SE6 154 D7
Mountfield Rd. E6 116 D2
Mountfield Rd. N3 72 D3
Mountfield Rd. W5 105 G6
**Mountford St. E1 21 H3**
Mountfort Cres. N1 93 G7
*Barnsbury Sq.*
Mountfort Ter. N1 93 G7
*Barnsbury Sq.*
Mountgrove Rd. N5 93 H3
Mounthurst Rd., Brom. 191 F7
Mountington Pk. Cl., Har. 69 G6
Mountjoy Cl. SE2 138 B2
Mounts Pond Rd. SE3 154 D2
Mountsfield Ct. SE13 154 D6
Mountside, Felt. 160/161 E3
*Hampton Rd. W.*
Mountside, Stan. 68 C1
Mountview Ct. N8 75 H4
*Green Las.*
Mountview Rd., Esher 194 E7
Mountwood, W.Mol. 179 G3
Movers La., Bark. 117 H2
Mowatt Cl. N19 92 D1
Mowbray Rd. NW6 90 B7
Mowbray Rd. SE19 188 C1
Mowbray Rd., Barn. 41 F4
Mowbray Rd., Edg. 54 A4
Mowbray Rd., Rich. 163 F3
Mowbrays Cl., Rom. 83 J1
Mowbrays Rd., Rom. 83 J2
Mowbrey Gdns., Loug. 49 F2
Mowlem St. E2 113 E2
Mowlem Trd. Est. N17 61 F7
Mowll St. SW9 131 G7
Moxon Cl. E13 115 F2
*Whitelegg Rd.*
**Moxon St. W1 16 B2**
Moxon St. W1 110 A5
Moxon St., Barn. 40 C3
**Moye Cl. E2 13 J1**
Moyers Rd. E10 78 C7
Moylan Rd. W6 128 B6
Moyne Pl. NW10 106 A2
Moynihan Dr. N21 43 E5
Moys Cl., Croy. 186 E6
Moyser Rd. SW16 168 B5
Mozart St. W10 108 C3
**Mozart Ter. SW1 32 C2**
Mozart Ter. SW1 130 A4
Muchelney Rd., Mord. 185 F6
Mud La. W5 105 G5
Mudlarks Way SE7 135 G3
Mudlarks Way SE10 135 G3
Muggeridge Cl., S.Croy. 202 A5
Muggeridge Rd., Dag. 101 H4
Muir Dr. SW18 149 G6
Muir Rd. E5 94 D4
Muir St. E16 136 C1
*Newland St.*
Muirdown Av. SW14 146 D4
Muirfield W3 107 E6
Muirfield Cl. SE16 132/133 E5
*Ryder Dr.*
Muirfield Cl., Wat. 50 C4
Muirfield Cres. E14 134 B3
*Millharbour*
Muirfield Grn., Wat. 50 C4
Muirfield Rd., Wat. 50 D4
Muirkirk Rd. SE6 172 C1
Mulberry Cl. E4 62 A2
Mulberry Cl. N8 74 E5
Mulberry Cl. NW3 91 G4
*Hampstead High St.*
Mulberry Cl. NW4 71 J3
Mulberry Cl. SE7 136 A6
Mulberry Cl. SE22 152 D5
Mulberry Cl. SW3 129 G6
*Beaufort St.*
Mulberry Cl. SW16 168 C4
Mulberry Cl., Barn. 41 G4
Mulberry Cl., Nthlt. 102/103 E2
*Parkfield Av.*
Mulberry Ct., Bark. 99 J7
*Westrow Dr.*
Mulberry Cres., Brent. 125 E7
Mulberry Cres., West Dr. 120 D2
Mulberry La., Croy. 202 C1
Mulberry Ms., Wall. 200 C6
*Ross Rd.*
Mulberry Par., West Dr. 120 D3
Mulberry Pl. W6 127 G5
*Chiswick Mall*
Mulberry Rd. E8 94 C7
**Mulberry St. E1 21 H3**
**Mulberry Wk. SW3 31 F5**
Mulberry Wk. SW3 129 G6
Mulberry Way E18 79 H2
Mulberry Way, Belv. 139 J2
Mulberry Way, Ilf. 81 F4
Mulgrave Rd. NW10 89 F4
Mulgrave Rd. SW6 128 C6
Mulgrave Rd. W5 105 G3
Mulgrave Rd., Croy. 202 A3
Mulgrave Rd., Har. 86 D2
Mulgrave Rd., Sutt. 198 D6
Mulholland Cl., Mitch. 186 B2
Mulkern Rd. N19 92 D1
Mull Wk. N1 93 J6
*Clephane Rd.*
Mullards Cl., Mitch. 199 J1
Muller Rd. SW4 150 D6
**Mullet Gdns. E2 13 J2**
Mullins Path SW14 146 D3
Mullion Cl., Har. 67 H1
Mullion Wk., Wat. 50 D4
*Ormskirk Rd.*
**Mulready St. NW8 7 G6**
Multi Way W3 126/127 E2
*Valetta Rd.*
Multon Rd. SW18 149 G7
**Mulvaney Way SE1 28 C4**
Mulvaney Way SE1 132 A2
**Mumford Ct. EC2 20 A3**
Mumford Rd. SE24 151 H5
*Railton Rd.*
Muncaster Rd. SW11 149 J5
Muncies Ms. SE6 172 C2
Mund St. W14 128 C5
Mundania Rd. SE22 153 E6
Munday Rd. E16 115 G6
Munden St. W14 128 B4
Mundesley Cl., Wat. 50 C4
Mundford Rd. E5 95 F2
Mundon Gdns., Ilf. 99 G1
**Mundy St. N1 12 D3**
Mundy St. N1 112 B3
Mungo Pk. Cl., Bushey 51 J2
Munnery Way, Orp. 206 D3
Munnings Gdns., Islw. 144 A5
Munro Dr. N11 58 C6
Munro Ms. W10 108 B5
**Munro Ter. SW10 31 E7**
Munro Ter. SW10 129 G7
Munslow Gdns., Sutt. 199 G4
Munster Av., Houns. 143 F4
Munster Ct., Tedd. 163 F6
Munster Gdns. N13 59 H4
Munster Ms. SW6 128 B7
*Munster Rd.*
Munster Rd. SW6 148 C1
Munster Rd., Tedd. 163 F6
**Munster Sq. NW1 9 E5**
Munster Sq. NW1 110 B3
**Munton Rd. SE17 36 A1**
Munton Rd. SE17 131 J4
Murchison Av., Bex. 176 D1
Murchison Rd. E10 96 C2
Murdock Cl. E16 115 F6
*Rogers Rd.*
Murdock St. SE15 132 E6
Murfett Cl. SW19 166 B2
**Muriel St. N1 10 D1**
Muriel St. N1 111 F2
Murillo Rd. SE13 154 D4
**Murphy St. SE1 27 E4**
Murphy St. SE1 131 G2
Murray Av., Brom. 191 H2
Murray Av., Houns. 143 H5
Murray Cres., Pnr. 66 D1
**Murray Gro. N1 12 B2**
Murray Gro. N1 111 J2
Murray Ms. NW1 92 D7
Murray Rd. SW19 166 A6
Murray Rd. W5 125 F4
Murray Rd., Rich. 163 E2
Murray Sq. E16 115 G6
Murray St. NW1 92 D7
Murray Ter. NW3 91 G4
*Flask Wk.*
Murray Ter. W5 125 G4
*Murray Rd.*
Mursell Est. SW8 151 F1
Murtwell Dr., Chig. 65 F6
Musard Rd. W6 128 B6
Musard Rd. W14 128 B6
Musbury St. E1 113 F6
Muscal W6 128 B6
Muscatel Pl. SE5 152 B1
*Dalwood St.*
Muschamp Rd. SE15 152 C3
Muschamp Rd., Cars. 199 H2
Muscovy Ho., Erith 138/139 E2
*Kale Rd.*
**Muscovy St. EC3 21 E6**
**Museum La. SW7 23 E6**
Museum Pas. E2 112/113 E3
*Victoria Pk. Sq.*
**Museum St. WC1 18 A2**
Museum St. WC1 110 E6
Musgrave Cl., Barn. 41 F1
Musgrave Cres. SW6 148 D1
Musgrave Rd., Islw. 144 C1
Musgrove Rd. SE14 153 G1
Musjid Rd. SW11 149 G2
*Kambala Rd.*
Musket Cl., Barn. 41 G5
*East Barnet Rd.*
Musquash Way, Houns. 142 C2
Muston Rd. E5 94 E2
Mustow Pl. SW6 148 C2
*Munster Rd.*
Muswell Av. N10 74 B2
Muswell Hill N10 74 B3
Muswell Hill Bdy. N10 74 B3
Muswell Hill Pl. N10 74 B4
Muswell Hill Rd. N6 74 A6
Muswell Hill Rd. N10 74 A4
Muswell Ms. N10 74 B3
*Muswell Rd.*
Muswell Rd. N10 74 B3
Mutrix Rd. NW6 108 D1
Mutton Pl. NW1 92 B6
*Harmood St.*
Muybridge Rd., N.Mal. 182 C2
Myatt Rd. SW9 151 H1
Myatt's Flds. N. SW9 151 G1
*Eythorne Rd.*
Myatt's Flds. S. SW9 151 G2
Mycenae Rd. SE3 135 G7
Myddelton Cl., Enf. 44 C1
Myddelton Gdns. N21 43 H7
Myddelton Pk. N20 57 G3
**Myddelton Pas. EC1 11 F3**
Myddelton Rd. N8 75 E4
**Myddelton Sq. EC1 11 F3**
Myddelton Sq. EC1 111 G3
**Myddelton St. EC1 11 F4**
Myddelton St. EC1 111 G3
Myddleton Av. N4 93 J2
Myddleton Ms. N22 59 E7
Myddleton Rd. N22 59 E7
Myers La. SE14 133 G6
Mylis Cl. SE26 171 E4
Mylius Cl. SE14 153 F1
*Kender St.*
**Mylne St. EC1 11 E2**
Mylne St. EC1 111 G3
Myra St. SE2 138 A4
**Myrdle St. E1 21 J2**
Myrdle St. E1 112 D5
Myrna Cl. SW19 167 H7
Myron Pl. SE13 154 C3
Myrtle Av., Felt. 141 H4
Myrtle Av., Ruis. 66 A7
Myrtle Cl., Barn. 57 J1
Myrtle Cl., West Dr. 120 C3
Myrtle Gdns. W7 124 B1
Myrtle Gro., N.Mal. 182 C2
Myrtle Rd. E6 116 B1
Myrtle Rd. E17 77 H6
Myrtle Rd. N13 59 J3
Myrtle Rd. W3 126 C1
Myrtle Rd., Croy. 204 A3
Myrtle Rd., Hmptn. 161 J6
Myrtle Rd., Houns. 143 J2
Myrtle Rd., Ilf. 99 E2
Myrtle Rd., Sutt. 199 F5
**Myrtle Wk. N1 12 D2**
Myrtle Wk. N1 112 B2
Myrtleberry Cl. E8 94 C6
*Beechwood Rd.*
Myrtledene Rd. SE2 138 A5
Mysore Rd. SW11 149 J3
Myton Rd. SE21 170 A3

## N

Nadine St. SE7 135 J5
Nafferton Ri., Loug. 48 A5
Nagle Cl. E17 78 D2
**Nag's Head Ct. EC1 11 J6**
Nags Head La., Well. 158 B3
Nags Head Rd., Enf. 45 F4
Nairn Grn., Wat. 50 A3
Nairn Rd., Ruis. 84 C6
Nairn St. E14 114 C5
Nairne Gro. SE24 152 A5
Naish Ct. N1 111 E1
Nallhead Rd., Felt. 160 C5
Namba Roy Cl. SW16 169 F4
*Valley Rd.*
Namton Dr., Th.Hth. 187 F4
Nan Clark's La. NW7 55 F2
Nankin St. E14 114 A6
Nansen Rd. SW11 150 A4
Nant Rd. NW2 90 C2
Nant St. E2 112/113 E3
*Cambridge Heath Rd.*
Nantes Cl. SW18 149 F4
**Nantes Pas. E1 21 F1**
**Naoroji St. WC1 11 E4**
Napier Av. E14 134 A5
Napier Av. SW6 148 C3
Napier Cl. SE8 133 J7
*Amersham Vale*
Napier Cl. W14 128 C3
*Napier Rd.*
Napier Cl., West Dr. 120 C3
Napier Ct. SW6 148 C3
*Ranelagh Gdns.*
**Napier Gro. N1 12 A2**
Napier Gro. N1 111 J2
Napier Pl. W14 128 C3
Napier Rd. E6 116 D1
Napier Rd. E11 96 E4
Napier Rd. E15 115 E2
Napier Rd. N17 76 B3
Napier Rd. NW10 107 H3
Napier Rd. SE25 188 E4
Napier Rd. W14 128 C3
Napier Rd., Belv. 139 F4
Napier Rd., Brom. 191 H4
Napier Rd., Enf. 45 G5
Napier Rd., Houns. 140 A1
Napier Rd., Islw. 144 D4
Napier Rd., S.Croy. 202 A7
Napier Rd., Wem. 87 G5
Napier Ter. N1 93 H7
Napoleon Rd. E5 94 E3
Napoleon Rd., Twick. 145 E7
Napton Cl., Hayes 102/103 E4
*Kingsash Dr.*
Narbonne Av. SW4 150 C5
Narborough St. SW6 148 E2
Narcissus Rd. NW6 90 D5
Naresby Fold, Stan. 53 F6
*Bernays Cl.*
Narford Rd. E5 94 D3
Narrow St. E14 113 H7
Narrow Way, Brom. 192 B6
Nascot St. W12 107 J6
Naseby Cl. NW6 91 F7
*Fairfax Rd.*
Naseby Cl., Islw. 144 B1
Naseby Rd. SE19 170 A6
Naseby Rd., Dag. 101 G3

Naseby Rd., Ilf. 80 C1
Nash Cl., Sutt. 199 G3
Nash Grn., Brom. 173 G6
Nash La., Kes. 205 G5
Nash Pl. E14 134 B1
*South Colonnade*
Nash Rd. N9 61 F2
Nash Rd. SE4 153 H4
Nash Rd., Rom. 82 D4
**Nash St. NW1 8 E4**
Nash Way, Har. 69 E6
Nasmyth St. W6 127 H3
Nassau Path SE28 138 C1
*Disraeli Cl.*
Nassau Rd. SW13 147 F1
**Nassau St. W1 17 F2**
Nassau St. W1 110 C5
Nassington Rd. NW3 91 H4
Natal Rd. N11 58 E6
Natal Rd. SW16 168 D6
Natal Rd., Ilf. 98 E4
Natal Rd., Th.Hth. 188 A3
Natalie Cl., Felt. 141 G7
Natalie Ms., Twick. 162 A3
*Sixth Cross Rd.*
Nathan Way SE28 137 H4
**Nathaniel Cl. E1 21 G2**
Nathans Rd., Wem. 87 F1
Nation Way E4 62 C1
Naval Row E14 114 C7
Naval Wk., Brom. 191 G3
*High St.*
Navarino Gro. E8 94 D6
Navarino Rd. E8 94 D6
Navarre Rd. E6 116 B2
**Navarre St. E2 13 F5**
Navarre St. E2 112 C4
Navenby Wk. E3 114 A4
*Rounton Rd.*
Navestock Cl. E4 62 C3
*Mapleton Rd.*
Navestock Cres., Wdf.Grn. 79 J1
Navestock Ho., Bark. 118 B2
Navigator Dr., Sthl. 123 J2
Navy St. SW4 150 D3
Naylor Gro., Enf. 45 G5
*South St.*
Naylor Rd. N20 57 F2
Naylor Rd. SE15 132 E7
Nazareth Gdns. SE15 152 E2
**Nazrul St. E2 13 F3**
Nazrul St. E2 112 C3
Neagle Cl., Borwd. 38 C1
*Balcon Way*
Neal Av., Sthl. 103 F4
Neal Cl., Nthwd. 66 A1
**Neal St. WC2 18 A4**
Neal St. WC2 110 E6
Nealden St. SW9 151 F3
Neale Cl. N2 73 F3
**Neal's Yd. WC2 18 A4**
Near Acre NW9 71 F1
Neasden Cl. NW10 89 E5
Neasden La. NW10 89 E4
Neasden La. N. NW10 88 D3
Neasham Rd., Dag. 100 B5
**Neate St. SE5 37 F5**
Neate St. SE5 132 C6
Neath Gdns., Mord. 185 F6
**Neathouse Pl. SW1 33 F1**
Neatscourt Rd. E6 116 A5
**Nebraska St. SE1 28 B4**
Nebraska St. SE1 132 A2
**Neckinger SE16 29 G5**
Neckinger SE16 132 C3
**Neckinger Est. SE16 29 G5**
Neckinger Est. SE16 132 C3
**Neckinger St. SE1 29 G4**
Neckinger St. SE1 132 C2
Nectarine Way SE13 154 B2
Needham Rd. W11 108 D6
*Westbourne Gro.*
Needham Ter. NW2 90 A3
Needleman St. SE16 133 G2
Neeld Cres. NW4 71 H5
Neeld Cres., Wem. 88 A5
Neeld Par., Wem. 88 A5
*Harrow Rd.*
Neil Wates Cres. SW2 169 G1
Nelgarde Rd. SE6 154 A7
Nella Rd. W6 128 A6
Nelldale Rd. SE16 133 F4
Nello James Gdns. SE27 170 A4
Nelson Cl., Croy. 201 H1
Nelson Cl., Rom. 83 H1
Nelson Ct. SE16 133 F1
*Brunel Rd.*
**Nelson Gdns. E2 13 J3**
Nelson Gdns. E2 112 D3
Nelson Gdns., Houns. 143 G6
Nelson Gro. Rd. SW19 185 E1
Nelson Mandela Cl. N10 74 A2
Nelson Mandela Rd. SE3 155 J3
**Nelson Pas. EC1 12 A4**
**Nelson Pl. N1 11 H2**
Nelson Pl. N1 111 H2
Nelson Pl., Sid. 176 A4
Nelson Rd. E4 62 B6
Nelson Rd. E11 79 G4
Nelson Rd. N8 75 F5
Nelson Rd. N9 61 E2
Nelson Rd. N15 76 B4
Nelson Rd. SE10 134 C6
Nelson Rd. SW19 167 E7
Nelson Rd., Belv. 139 F5
Nelson Rd., Brom. 191 J4
Nelson Rd., Enf. 45 G6
Nelson Rd., Har. 86 A1
Nelson Rd., Houns. 143 J7
Nelson Rd. (Heathrow Airport), Houns. 140 C1
Nelson Rd., N.Mal. 182 D5
Nelson Rd., Sid. 176 A4
Nelson Rd., Stan. 53 F6
Nelson Rd., Twick. 143 J6
**Nelson Sq. SE1 27 G3**
Nelson Sq. SE1 131 H2
Nelson St. E1 112 E6
Nelson St. E6 116 C2
Nelson St. E16 115 F7
*Huntingdon St.*
**Nelson Ter. N1 11 H2**
Nelson Ter. N1 111 H2
Nelson Trd. Est. SW19 184 E1
Nelson Wk. SE16 133 H1
*Rotherhithe St.*
Nelson's Row SW4 150 D4
**Nelsons Yd. NW1 9 F1**
Nemoure Rd. W3 106 C7
Nene Gdns., Felt. 161 F2
Nene Rd., Houns. 141 E1
Nepaul Rd. SW11 149 H2
Nepean St. SW15 147 G6
Neptune Rd., Har. 68 A6
Neptune Rd. (Heathrow Airport), Houns. 141 G1
Neptune St. SE16 133 F3
Nesbit Rd. SE9 156 A4
Nesbitt Cl. SE3 154/155 E3
*Hurren Cl.*
Nesbitt Sq. SE19 170 B7
*Coxwell Rd.*
Nesbitts All., Barn. 40 C3
*Bath Pl.*
**Nesham St. E1 29 H1**
Nesham St. E1 132 D1
**Ness St. SE16 29 H5**
Nesta Rd., Wdf.Grn. 63 E6
Nestles Av., Hayes 121 J3
Nestor Av. N21 43 H6
Nether Cl. N3 56 D7
Nether St. N3 72 D1
Nether St. N12 56 D7
Netheravon Rd. W4 127 F4
Netheravon Rd. W7 124 C1
Netheravon Rd. S. W4 127 F5
Netherbury Rd. W5 125 G3
Netherby Gdns., Enf. 42 E4
Netherby Rd. SE23 153 F7
Nethercourt Av. N3 56 D6
Netherfield Gdns., Bark. 99 G6
Netherfield Rd. N12 57 E5
Netherfield Rd. SW17 168 A3
Netherford Rd. SW4 150 C2
Netherhall Gdns. NW3 91 F6
Netherhall Way NW3 91 F5
*Netherhall Gdns.*
Netherlands Rd., Barn. 41 G6
Netherleigh Cl. N6 92 B1
**Netherton Gro. SW10 30 D6**
Netherton Gro. SW10 129 F6
Netherton Rd. N15 76 A6
Netherton Rd., Twick. 144 E5
Netherwood N2 73 G2
Netherwood Pl. W14 128 A3
*Netherwood Rd.*
Netherwood Rd. W14 128 A3
Netherwood St. NW6 90 C7
Netley Cl., Croy. 204 C7
Netley Cl., Sutt. 198 A5
Netley Dr., Walt. 179 F7
Netley Gdns., Mord. 185 F7
Netley Rd. E17 77 J5
Netley Rd., Brent. 125 H6
Netley Rd. (Heathrow Airport), Houns. 141 G1
Netley Rd., Ilf. 81 G5
Netley Rd., Mord. 185 F7
**Netley St. NW1 9 F4**
Nettleden Av., Wem. 88 A6
Nettlefold Pl. SE27 169 H3
Nettlestead Cl., Beck. 171 J7
*Copers Cope Rd.*
Nettleton Rd. SE14 153 G1
Nettleton Rd., Houns. 141 E1
Nettlewood Rd. SW16 168 D7
Neuchatel Rd. SE6 171 J2
Nevada Cl., N.Mal. 182 C4
*Georgia Rd.*
Nevada St. SE10 134 C6
Nevern Pl. SW5 128 D4
Nevern Rd. SW5 128 D4
Nevern Sq. SW5 128 D5
Nevill Rd. N16 94 B4
Nevill Way, Loug. 48 B7
*Valley Hill*
Neville Av., N.Mal. 182 D1
Neville Cl. E11 97 F3
**Neville Cl. NW1 9 J2**
Neville Cl. NW6 108 C2
Neville Cl. SE15 132 D7
Neville Cl. W3 126 C2
*Acton La.*
Neville Cl., Houns. 143 H2
Neville Cl., Sid. 175 J4
Neville Dr. N2 73 F6
Neville Gdns., Dag. 100 D3
Neville Gill Cl. SW18 148 D6
Neville Pl. N22 75 F1
Neville Rd. E7 97 G7
Neville Rd. NW6 108 C2
Neville Rd. W5 105 G4
Neville Rd., Croy. 188 A7
Neville Rd., Dag. 100 D2
Neville Rd., Ilf. 81 F1
Neville Rd., Kings.T. 182 A2
Neville Rd., Rich. 163 F3
**Neville St. SW7 31 E3**
Neville St. SW7 129 G5
**Neville Ter. SW7 31 E3**
Neville Ter. SW7 129 G5
Neville Wk., Cars. 185 H7
*Green Wrythe La.*
Nevilles Ct. NW2 89 G3
Nevin Dr. E4 62 B1
Nevinson Cl. SW18 149 G6
Nevis Rd. SW17 168 A2
New Ash Cl. N2 73 G3
*Oakridge Dr.*
New Barn St. E13 115 G4
New Barns Av., Mitch. 186 D4
New Barns Way, Chig. 64 E3
**New Bond St. W1 17 E5**
New Bond St. W1 110 B7
New Brent St. NW4 71 J5
**New Br. St. EC4 19 G4**
New Br. St. EC4 111 H6
**New Broad St. EC2 20 D2**
New Broad St. EC2 112 B5
New Bdy. W5 105 G7
New Bdy., Hmptn. 162 A5
*Hampton Rd.*
**New Burlington Ms. W1 17 F5**
**New Burlington Pl. W1 17 F5**
**New Burlington St. W1 17 F5**
New Burlington St. W1 110 C7
New Butt La. SE8 134 A7
New Butt La. N. SE8 134 A7
*Reginald Rd.*
**New Cavendish St. W1 17 E1**
New Cavendish St. W1 110 A5
**New Change EC4 19 J4**
New Change EC4 111 J6
New Chapel Sq., Felt. 160 B1
**New Charles St. EC1 11 H3**
**New Ch. Rd. SE5 36 A7**
New Ch. Rd. SE5 131 J7
New City Rd. E13 115 J3
New Cl. SW19 185 F3
New Cl., Felt. 160 E5
New College Ct. NW3 91 F7
*College Cres.*
New College Ms. N1 93 G7
*Islington Pk. St.*
New College Par. NW3 91 G6
*College Cres.*
**New Compton St. WC2 17 J4**
New Compton St. WC2 110 D6
**New Ct. EC4 18 E5**
New Covent Gdn. Mkt. SW8 130 D7
**New Coventry St. W1 17 J6**
New Crane Pl. E1 133 F1
*Garnet St.*
New Cross Rd. SE14 133 F7
New End NW3 91 F4
New End Sq. NW3 91 G4
New Era Est. N1 112 B1
*Phillipp St.*
New Fm. Av., Brom. 191 G4
New Ferry App. SE18 136 D3
**New Fetter La. EC4 19 F3**
New Fetter La. EC4 111 G6
New Forest La., Chig. 64 D6
New Gdn. Dr., West Dr. 120 B2
*Drayton Gdns.*
**New Globe Wk. SE1 27 J1**
New Globe Wk. SE1 131 J1
**New Goulston St. E1 21 F3**
New Grn. Pl. SE19 170 B6
*Hawke Rd.*
New Heston Rd., Houns. 123 F7
New Horizons Ct., Brent. 124 D6
*Shield Dr.*
**New Inn Bdy. EC2 12 E5**
**New Inn Pas. WC2 18 D4**
**New Inn St. EC2 12 E5**
**New Inn Yd. EC2 12 E5**
New Inn Yd. EC2 112 B4
New James Ct. SE15 152/153 E3
*Nunhead La.*
**New Kent Rd. SE1 27 J6**
New Kent Rd. SE1 131 J3
New King St. SE8 134 A6
New Kings Rd. SW6 148 C2
**New London St. EC3 21 E5**
New Lydenburg St. SE7 135 J3
New Mt. St. E15 96 D7
*Bridge Rd.*
**New N. Pl. EC2 12 D6**
**New N. Rd. N1 12 C2**
New N. Rd. N1 112 A2
New N. Rd., Ilf. 65 G7
**New N. St. WC1 18 C1**
New N. St. WC1 111 F5
New Oak Rd. N2 73 F2
New Orleans Wk. N19 74 D7
**New Oxford St. WC1 17 J3**
New Oxford St. WC1 110 D6
New Pk. Av. N13 59 J3
New Pk. Cl., Nthlt. 84 E6
New Pk. Ct. SW2 151 E7
New Pk. Par. SW2 150/151 E6
*Doverfield Rd.*
New Pk. Rd. SW2 168 D1
New Pl. Sq. SE16 132 E3
New Plaistow Rd. E15 115 E1
New Printing Ho. Sq WC1 111 F4
*Gray's Inn Rd.*
New Priory Ct. NW6 90 D7
*Mazenod Av.*
**New Quebec St. W1 16 A4**
New Quebec St. W1 109 J6
**New Ride SW7 23 J3**
New Ride SW7 129 H2
New River Cres. N13 59 H4
New River Wk. N1 93 J6
New River Way N4 76 A7
New Rd. E1 112 E5
New Rd. E4 62 B4
New Rd. N8 74 E5
New Rd. N9 60 D3
New Rd. N17 76 C1
New Rd. N22 75 J1
New Rd. NW7 56 B7
New Rd. (Barnet Gate) NW7 39 F7
New Rd. SE2 138 D4
New Rd., Brent. 125 G6
New Rd., Dag. 119 G1
New Rd., Felt. 141 G6
New Rd. (East Bedfont), Felt. 160 B1
New Rd. (Hanworth), Felt. 160 E5
New Rd., Har. 86 C4
New Rd., Hayes 121 F7
New Rd., Houns. 143 H4
*Station Rd.*
New Rd., Ilf. 99 H2
New Rd., Kings.T. 164 A7

| Entry | Page | Ref |
|---|---|---|
| New Rd., Mitch. | 199 | J1 |
| New Rd., Rich. | 163 | F4 |
| New Rd., Well. | 158 | B2 |
| New Rd., W.Mol. | 179 | G3 |
| **New Row WC2** | 18 | A5 |
| New Row W2 | 110 | E7 |
| **New Spring Gdns. Wk. SE11** | 34 | B4 |
| New Sq. WC2 | 18 | D3 |
| New Sq. WC2 | 111 | F6 |
| New Sq. Pas. WC2 | 111 | F6 |
| *New Sq.* | | |
| New St. EC2 | 20 | E2 |
| New St. EC2 | 112 | B5 |
| New St. Hill, Brom. | 173 | H5 |
| **New St. Sq. EC4** | 19 | F3 |
| New Trinity Rd. N2 | 73 | G3 |
| **New Turnstile WC1** | 18 | C2 |
| New Union Cl. E14 | 134 | C3 |
| **New Union St. EC2** | 20 | B2 |
| New Union St. EC2 | 112 | A5 |
| New Wanstead E11 | 79 | F6 |
| New Way Rd. NW9 | 71 | F4 |
| **New Wf. Rd. N1** | 10 | B1 |
| New Wf. Rd. N1 | 111 | E2 |
| New Zealand Way W12 | 107 | H7 |
| Newall Rd., Houns. | 141 | F1 |
| Newark Cres. NW10 | 106 | D3 |
| Newark Grn., Borwd. | 38 | D3 |
| Newark Knok E6 | 116 | D6 |
| Newark Par. NW4 | 71 | G3 |
| *Greyhound Hill* | | |
| Newark Rd., S.Croy. | 202 | A6 |
| Newark St. E1 | 112 | E5 |
| Newark Way NW4 | 71 | G4 |
| Newbiggin Path, Wat. | 50 | C4 |
| Newbolt Av., Sutt. | 197 | J5 |
| Newbolt Rd., Stan. | 52 | C6 |
| Newborough Grn., N.Mal. | 182 | D4 |
| Newburgh Rd. W3 | 126 | C1 |
| **Newburgh St. W1** | 17 | F4 |
| Newburgh St. W1 | 110 | C6 |
| **Newburn St. SE11** | 34 | D3 |
| Newburn St. SE11 | 131 | F5 |
| Newbury Cl., Nthlt. | 85 | F6 |
| Newbury Gdns., Epsom | 197 | F4 |
| Newbury Ho. N22 | 75 | E1 |
| Newbury Ms. NW5 | 92 | A6 |
| *Malden Rd.* | | |
| Newbury Rd. E4 | 62 | C6 |
| Newbury Rd., Brom. | 191 | G3 |
| Newbury Rd., Houns. | 140 | C1 |
| Newbury Rd., Ilf. | 81 | H6 |
| **Newbury St. EC1** | 19 | J2 |
| Newbury Way, Nthlt. | 85 | E6 |
| Newby Pl. E14 | 114 | C7 |
| Newby St. SW8 | 150 | B3 |
| **Newcastle Cl. EC4** | 19 | G3 |
| **Newcastle Pl. W2** | 15 | F2 |
| Newcastle Pl. W2 | 109 | G5 |
| **Newcastle Row EC1** | 11 | F5 |
| Newcombe Gdns. SW16 | 169 | E4 |
| Newcombe Pk. NW7 | 55 | E5 |
| Newcombe Pk., Wem. | 105 | J1 |
| Newcombe St. W8 | 128 | D1 |
| *Kensington Pl.* | | |
| Newcomen Rd. E11 | 97 | F3 |
| Newcomen Rd. SW11 | 149 | G3 |
| **Newcomen St. SE1** | 28 | B3 |
| Newcomen St. SE1 | 132 | A2 |
| **Newcourt St. NW8** | 7 | G2 |
| Newcourt St. NW8 | 109 | H2 |
| Newdales Cl. N9 | 60 | D2 |
| *Balham Rd.* | | |
| Newdene Av., Nthlt. | 102 | D2 |
| Newell St. E14 | 113 | J6 |
| **Newent Cl. SE15** | 36 | D7 |
| Newent Cl. SE15 | 132 | B7 |
| Newent Cl., Cars. | 199 | J1 |
| Newfield Cl., Hmptn. | 179 | G1 |
| *Percy Rd.* | | |
| Newfield Ri. NW2 | 89 | H3 |
| Newgale Gdns., Edg. | 69 | J1 |
| Newgate, Croy. | 201 | J1 |
| Newgate Cl., Felt. | 161 | E2 |
| Newgate St. E4 | 63 | F3 |
| **Newgate St. EC1** | 19 | H3 |
| Newgate St. EC1 | 111 | H6 |
| Newham Way E6 | 115 | J5 |
| Newham Way E16 | 115 | J5 |
| **Newhams Row SE1** | 28 | E4 |
| Newhaven Cl., Hayes | 171 | I4 |
| Newhaven Gdns. SE9 | 156 | A4 |
| Newhaven La. E16 | 115 | F4 |
| Newhaven Rd. SE25 | 188 | A5 |
| Newhouse Av., Rom. | 82 | D3 |
| Newhouse Cl., N.Mal. | 183 | E7 |
| Newhouse Wk., Mord. | 185 | F7 |
| Newick Cl., Bex. | 159 | H6 |
| Newick Rd. E5 | 95 | E3 |
| Newing Grn., Brom. | 174 | A7 |
| Newington Barrow Way N7 | 93 | F3 |
| **Newington Butts SE1** | 35 | H2 |
| Newington Butts SE1 | 131 | H4 |
| **Newington Butts SE11** | 35 | H2 |
| Newington Butts SE1 | 131 | H4 |
| **Newington Causeway SE1** | 27 | H6 |
| Newington Causeway SE1 | 131 | H3 |
| Newington Grn. N1 | 94 | A5 |
| Newington Grn. N16 | 94 | A5 |
| Newington Grn. Rd. N1 | 94 | A6 |
| Newington Way N7 | 93 | F2 |
| *Hornsey Rd.* | | |
| Newland Cl., Pnr. | 51 | E6 |
| Newland Ct., Wem. | 88 | A2 |
| *Forty Av.* | | |
| Newland Dr., Enf. | 44 | E1 |
| Newland Gdns. W13 | 124 | D2 |
| Newland Rd. N8 | 74 | E3 |
| Newland St. E16 | 136 | B1 |
| Newlands, The, Wall. | 200 | C7 |
| Newlands Av., T.Ditt. | 194 | B1 |
| Newlands Cl., Edg. | 53 | H3 |
| Newlands Cl., Sthl. | 122 | E5 |
| Newlands Cl., Wem. | 87 | F6 |
| Newlands Ct. SE9 | 156 | D6 |
| Newlands Pk. SE26 | 171 | G5 |
| Newlands Pl., Barn. | 40 | A5 |
| Newlands Quay E1 | 113 | F7 |
| Newlands Rd. SW16 | 187 | E2 |
| Newlands Rd., Wdf.Grn. | 63 | F2 |
| Newlands Way, Chess. | 195 | F5 |
| Newling Cl. E6 | 116 | C6 |
| *Porter Rd.* | | |
| Newlyn Gdns., Har. | 67 | F7 |
| Newlyn Rd. N17 | 76 | C1 |
| Newlyn Rd. NW2 | 89 | J1 |
| *Tilling Rd.* | | |
| Newlyn Rd., Barn. | 40 | C4 |
| Newlyn Rd., Well. | 157 | J2 |
| **Newman Pas. W1** | 17 | G2 |
| Newman Rd. E13 | 115 | H3 |
| Newman Rd. E17 | 77 | G5 |
| *Southcote Rd.* | | |
| Newman Rd., Brom. | 191 | G1 |
| Newman Rd., Croy. | 201 | F1 |
| Newman Rd., Hayes | 102 | B7 |
| **Newman St. W1** | 17 | G2 |
| Newman St. W1 | 110 | C5 |
| **Newman Yd. W1** | 17 | H3 |
| **Newman's Ct. EC3** | 20 | C4 |
| Newmans La., Loug. | 48 | D3 |
| Newmans La., Surb. | 181 | G6 |
| **Newman's Row WC2** | 18 | D2 |
| Newmans Way, Barn. | 41 | F1 |
| Newmarket Av., Nthlt. | 85 | G5 |
| Newmarket Grn. SE9 | 156 | A7 |
| *Middle Pk. Av.* | | |
| Newminster Rd., Mord. | 185 | F6 |
| Newnes Path SW15 | 147 | H4 |
| *Putney Pk. La.* | | |
| Newnham Av., Ruis. | 84 | C1 |
| Newnham Cl., Loug. | 48 | A6 |
| Newnham Cl., Nthlt. | 85 | J5 |
| Newnham Cl., Th.Hth. | 187 | J2 |
| Newnham Gdns., Nthlt. | 85 | J5 |
| Newnham Ms. N22 | 75 | F1 |
| *Newnham Rd.* | | |
| Newnham Rd. N22 | 75 | F1 |
| **Newnham Ter. SE1** | 26 | E5 |
| Newnham Way, Har. | 69 | H5 |
| Newnhams Cl., Brom. | 192 | C3 |
| Newnton Cl. N4 | 76 | A7 |
| Newpiece, Loug. | 48 | E3 |
| Newport Av. E13 | 115 | H4 |
| Newport Av. E14 | 114 | D7 |
| **Newport Ct. WC2** | 17 | J5 |
| Newport Mead, Wat. | 50 | D4 |
| *Kilmarnock Rd.* | | |
| **Newport Pl. WC2** | 17 | J5 |
| Newport Pl. WC2 | 110 | D7 |
| Newport Rd. E10 | 96 | C2 |
| Newport Rd. E17 | 77 | H4 |
| Newport Rd. SW13 | 147 | G1 |
| Newport Rd., Houns. | 140 | D1 |
| **Newport St. SE11** | 34 | C2 |
| Newport St. SE11 | 131 | F4 |
| Newquay Cres., Har. | 85 | E2 |
| Newquay Gdns., Wat. | 50 | B2 |
| *Fulford Gro.* | | |
| Newquay Rd. SE6 | 172 | B2 |
| Newry Rd., Twick. | 144 | D4 |
| Newsam Av. N15 | 76 | A5 |
| Newsholme Dr. N21 | 43 | F5 |
| Newstead Av., Orp. | 207 | G3 |
| Newstead Rd. SE12 | 155 | E7 |
| Newstead Wk., Cars. | 185 | F7 |
| Newstead Way SW19 | 166 | A4 |
| Newton Av. N10 | 74 | A1 |
| Newton Av. W3 | 126 | C2 |
| Newton Cl. E17 | 77 | H6 |
| Newton Cl., Har. | 85 | G2 |
| Newton Cres., Borwd. | 38 | C4 |
| Newton Gro. W4 | 126 | E4 |
| Newton Rd. E15 | 96 | D5 |
| Newton Rd. N15 | 76 | C5 |
| Newton Rd. NW2 | 89 | J3 |
| Newton Rd. SW19 | 166 | B7 |
| **Newton Rd. W2** | 14 | A4 |
| Newton Rd. W2 | 108 | D6 |
| Newton Rd., Har. | 68 | B2 |
| Newton Rd., Islw. | 144 | C2 |
| Newton Rd., Well. | 158 | A3 |
| Newton Rd., Wem. | 87 | J7 |
| **Newton St. WC2** | 18 | B3 |
| Newton St. WC2 | 111 | E6 |
| Newton Wk., Edg. | 70 | B1 |
| *North Rd.* | | |
| Newton Way N18 | 59 | J5 |
| Newtons Yd. SW18 | 148/149 | E5 |
| *Wandsworth High St.* | | |
| Newtown St. SW11 | 150 | B1 |
| *Strasburg Rd.* | | |
| Niagara Av. W5 | 125 | F4 |
| Nibthwaite Rd., Har. | 68 | B5 |
| Nichol Cl. N14 | 58 | D1 |
| Nichol La., Brom. | 173 | G7 |
| Nicholas Cl., Grnf. | 103 | H2 |
| Nicholas Ct. E13 | 115 | H3 |
| *Tunmarsh La.* | | |
| Nicholas Gdns. W5 | 125 | G2 |
| **Nicholas La. EC4** | 20 | C5 |
| **Nicholas Pas. EC4** | 20 | C5 |
| Nicholas Rd. E1 | 113 | F4 |
| Nicholas Rd., Croy. | 201 | E4 |
| Nicholas Rd., Dag. | 101 | F2 |
| Nicholay Rd. N19 | 92 | D1 |
| Nicholes Rd., Houns. | 143 | G4 |
| Nicholl St. E2 | 112 | D1 |
| Nichollsfield Wk. N7 | 93 | F5 |
| *Hillmarton Rd.* | | |
| Nichols Cl. N4 | 93 | G1 |
| *Osborne Rd.* | | |
| Nichols Cl., Chess. | 195 | F6 |
| *Merritt Gdns.* | | |
| Nichols Grn. W5 | 105 | H5 |
| *Montpelier Rd.* | | |
| Nicholson Rd., Croy. | 202 | C1 |
| **Nicholson St. SE1** | 27 | G2 |
| Nicholson St. SE1 | 131 | H1 |
| Nickleby Cl. SE28 | 118 | C6 |
| Nicol Cl., Twick. | 144/145 | E6 |
| *Cassilis Rd.* | | |
| Nicola Cl., Har. | 68 | A2 |
| Nicola Cl., S.Croy. | 201 | J6 |
| Nicola Ms., Ilf. | 65 | E7 |
| Nicoll Pl. NW4 | 71 | H6 |
| Nicoll Rd. NW10 | 107 | E1 |
| Nicoll Way, Borwd. | 38 | D5 |
| Nicolson Dr., Bushey | 51 | J1 |
| Nicosia Rd. SW18 | 149 | H7 |
| Niederwald Rd. SE26 | 171 | H4 |
| Nield Rd., Hayes | 121 | J2 |
| Nigel Cl., Nthlt. | 102/103 | E1 |
| *Church Rd.* | | |
| Nigel Fisher Way, Chess. | 195 | G6 |
| *Ashlyns Way* | | |
| Nigel Ms., Ilf. | 98 | E4 |
| Nigel Playfair Av. W6 | 127 | H4 |
| *King St.* | | |
| Nigel Rd. E7 | 97 | J5 |
| Nigel Rd. SE15 | 152 | D3 |
| Nigeria Rd. SE7 | 135 | J7 |
| Nightingale Av. E4 | 62 | E5 |
| Nightingale Cl. E4 | 62 | F4 |
| Nightingale Cl. W4 | 126 | C6 |
| *Grove Pk. Ter.* | | |
| Nightingale Cl., Cars. | 200 | A2 |
| Nightingale Cl., Pnr. | 66 | C5 |
| Nightingale Dr., Epsom | 196 | B6 |
| Nightingale Est. E5 | 94 | D3 |
| Nightingale Gro. SE13 | 154 | D5 |
| Nightingale La. E11 | 79 | H5 |
| Nightingale La. N6 | 91 | H1 |
| Nightingale La. N8 | 74 | E4 |
| Nightingale La. SW4 | 149 | J7 |
| Nightingale La. SW12 | 149 | J7 |
| Nightingale La., Brom. | 191 | J2 |
| Nightingale La., Rich. | 145 | H7 |
| Nightingale Ms. E3 | 113 | H2 |
| *Chisenhale Rd.* | | |
| Nightingale Ms., Kings.T. | 181 | G3 |
| *South La.* | | |
| Nightingale Pl. SE18 | 136 | D6 |
| **Nightingale Pl. SW10** | 30 | D5 |
| Nightingale Rd. E5 | 95 | E4 |
| Nightingale Rd. N9 | 45 | F6 |
| Nightingale Rd. N22 | 75 | E1 |
| Nightingale Rd. NW10 | 107 | F2 |
| Nightingale Rd. W7 | 124 | C1 |
| Nightingale Rd., Cars. | 199 | J3 |
| Nightingale Rd., Hmptn. | 161 | G5 |
| Nightingale Rd., Orp. | 193 | F6 |
| Nightingale Rd., Walt. | 178 | B7 |
| Nightingale Rd., W.Mol. | 179 | H5 |
| Nightingale Sq. SW12 | 150 | A7 |
| Nightingale Vale SE18 | 136 | D6 |
| Nightingale Wk. SW4 | 150 | B6 |
| Nightingale Way E6 | 116 | B5 |
| Nightingales, The, Stai. | 140 | C7 |
| Nile Path SE18 | 136 | D6 |
| *Jackson St.* | | |
| Nile Rd. E13 | 115 | J2 |
| **Nile St. N1** | 12 | A3 |
| Nile St. N1 | 112 | A3 |
| **Nile Ter. SE15** | 37 | F4 |
| Nile Ter. SE15 | 132 | C5 |
| Nimegen Way SE22 | 152 | B5 |
| Nimrod Cl., Nthlt. | 102 | D3 |
| *Britannia Cl.* | | |
| Nimrod Pas. N1 | 94 | B6 |
| *Tottenham Rd.* | | |
| Nimrod Rd. SW16 | 168 | B6 |
| Nina Mackay Cl. E15 | 114/115 | E1 |
| *Arthingworth St.* | | |
| Nine Acres Cl. E12 | 98 | B5 |
| **Nine Elms La. SW8** | 33 | G7 |
| Nine Elms La. SW8 | 130 | C6 |
| Nineteenth Rd., Mitch. | 186 | E4 |
| Ninhams Wd., Orp. | 206 | D4 |
| Ninth Av., Hayes | 102 | A7 |
| Nisbet Ho. E9 | 95 | G5 |
| *Homerton High St.* | | |
| Nithdale Rd. SE18 | 137 | E7 |
| Niton Cl., Barn. | 40 | A6 |
| Niton Rd., Rich. | 146 | A3 |
| Niton St. SW6 | 128 | A7 |
| Niven Cl., Borwd. | 38 | C1 |
| Nobel Dr., Hayes | 121 | G7 |
| Nobel Rd. N18 | 61 | F5 |
| **Noble St. EC2** | 19 | J3 |
| Noble St. EC2 | 111 | J6 |
| Noel Pk. Rd. N22 | 75 | G2 |
| Noel Rd. E6 | 116 | B4 |
| **Noel Rd. N1** | 11 | G1 |
| Noel Rd. N1 | 111 | H2 |
| Noel Rd. W3 | 106 | B6 |
| Noel Sq., Dag. | 100 | C4 |
| **Noel St. W1** | 17 | G4 |
| Noel St. W1 | 110 | C6 |
| Noel Ter. SE23 | 171 | F2 |
| *Dartmouth Rd.* | | |
| Nolan Way E5 | 94 | D4 |
| Nolton Pl., Edg. | 69 | J1 |
| Nonsuch Cl., Ilf. | 65 | E6 |
| Nora Gdns. NW4 | 72 | A4 |
| Norbiton Av., Kings.T. | 182 | A2 |
| Norbiton Common Rd., Kings.T. | 182 | B3 |
| Norbiton Rd. E14 | 113 | J6 |
| Norbreck Gdns. NW10 | 105 | J3 |
| *Lytham Gro.* | | |
| Norbreck Par. NW10 | 105 | J3 |
| *Lytham Gro.* | | |
| Norburn St. W10 | 108 | B5 |
| *Chesterton Rd.* | | |
| Norbury Av. SW16 | 187 | F1 |
| Norbury Av., Houns. | 144 | A5 |
| Norbury Av., Th.Hth. | 187 | G2 |
| Norbury Cl. SW16 | 187 | G1 |

| Name | Page | Grid |
|---|---|---|
| Norbury Ct. Rd. SW16 | 186 | E2 |
| Norbury Cres. SW16 | 187 | F1 |
| Norbury Cross SW16 | 186 | E2 |
| Norbury Gdns., Rom. | 82 | D5 |
| Norbury Gro. NW7 | 54 | E3 |
| Norbury Hill SW16 | 169 | G7 |
| Norbury Ri. SW16 | 186 | E3 |
| Norbury Rd. E4 | 62 | A5 |
| Norbury Rd., Th.Hth. | 187 | J2 |
| Norcombe Gdns., Har. | 69 | F6 |
| Norcott Cl., Hayes | 102 | C4 |
| *Willow Tree La.* | | |
| Norcott Rd. N16 | 94 | D2 |
| Norcroft Gdns. SE22 | 152 | D7 |
| Norcutt Rd., Twick. | 162 | B1 |
| Norfield Rd., Dart. | 177 | J4 |
| Norfolk Av. N13 | 59 | H6 |
| Norfolk Av. N15 | 76 | C6 |
| Norfolk Cl. N2 | 73 | H3 |
| *Park Rd.* | | |
| Norfolk Cl. N13 | 59 | H6 |
| Norfolk Cl., Barn. | 42 | A4 |
| Norfolk Cl., Twick. | 144/145 | E6 |
| *Cassilis Rd.* | | |
| **Norfolk Cres. W2** | **15** | **H3** |
| Norfolk Cres. W2 | 109 | H6 |
| Norfolk Cres., Sid. | 157 | H7 |
| Norfolk Gdns., Bexh. | 159 | F1 |
| Norfolk Gdns., Borwd. | 38 | D4 |
| Norfolk Ho. SE3 | 135 | E6 |
| Norfolk Ho. Rd. SW16 | 168 | D3 |
| Norfolk Ms. W10 | 108 | C5 |
| *Blagrove Rd.* | | |
| **Norfolk Pl. W2** | **15** | **F3** |
| Norfolk Pl. W2 | 109 | G6 |
| Norfolk Pl., Well. | 158 | A2 |
| Norfolk Rd. E6 | 116 | C1 |
| Norfolk Rd. E17 | 77 | G2 |
| Norfolk Rd. NW8 | 109 | G1 |
| Norfolk Rd. NW10 | 88 | E7 |
| Norfolk Rd. SW19 | 167 | H7 |
| Norfolk Rd., Bark. | 99 | H7 |
| Norfolk Rd., Barn. | 40 | D3 |
| Norfolk Rd., Dag. | 101 | H5 |
| Norfolk Rd., Enf. | 45 | E6 |
| Norfolk Rd., Esher | 194 | B5 |
| Norfolk Rd., Felt. | 160 | C1 |
| Norfolk Rd., Har. | 67 | H5 |
| Norfolk Rd., Ilf. | 99 | H1 |
| Norfolk Rd., Rom. | 83 | J6 |
| Norfolk Rd., Th.Hth. | 187 | J3 |
| **Norfolk Row SE1** | **34** | **C1** |
| **Norfolk Sq. W2** | **15** | **F4** |
| Norfolk Sq. W2 | 109 | G6 |
| **Norfolk Sq. Ms. W2** | **15** | **F4** |
| Norfolk St. E7 | 97 | G4 |
| Norfolk Ter. W6 | 128 | B5 |
| Norgrove St. SW12 | 150 | A7 |
| Norhyrst Av. SE25 | 188 | C3 |
| Norland Pl. W11 | 128 | B1 |
| Norland Rd. W11 | 128 | A1 |
| Norland Sq. W11 | 128 | B1 |
| Norlands Cres., Chis. | 192 | E1 |
| Norlands Gate, Chis. | 193 | E1 |
| Norley Vale SW15 | 165 | G1 |
| Norlington Rd. E10 | 96 | C1 |
| Norlington Rd. E11 | 96 | C1 |
| Norman Av. N22 | 75 | H1 |
| Norman Av., Felt. | 161 | E2 |
| Norman Av., Sthl. | 103 | E7 |
| Norman Av., Twick. | 145 | E7 |
| Norman Cl., Orp. | 207 | F3 |
| Norman Cl., Rom. | 83 | H2 |
| Norman Cl., Ilf. | 81 | G7 |
| Norman Cres., Houns. | 142 | D1 |
| Norman Cres., Pnr. | 66 | C1 |
| Norman Gro. E3 | 113 | H2 |
| Norman Rd. E6 | 116 | C4 |
| Norman Rd. E11 | 96 | D2 |
| Norman Rd. N15 | 76 | C5 |
| Norman Rd. SE10 | 134 | B7 |
| Norman Rd. SW19 | 167 | F7 |
| Norman Rd., Belv. | 139 | H3 |
| Norman Rd., Ilf. | 99 | E5 |
| Norman Rd., Sutt. | 198 | D5 |
| Norman Rd., Th.Hth. | 187 | H5 |
| **Norman St. EC1** | **11** | **J4** |
| Norman Way N14 | 58 | E2 |
| Norman Way W3 | 106 | B5 |
| Normanby Cl. SW15 | 148 | C5 |
| *Manfred Rd.* | | |
| Normanby Rd. NW10 | 89 | F4 |
| Normand Gdns. W14 | 128 | B6 |
| *Greyhound Rd.* | | |
| Normand Ms. W14 | 128 | B6 |
| *Normand Rd.* | | |
| Normand Rd. W14 | 128 | C6 |
| Normandy Av., Barn. | 40 | C5 |
| Normandy Rd. SW9 | 151 | G1 |
| Normandy Ter. E16 | 115 | H6 |
| Normanhurst Av., Bexh. | 158 | D1 |
| Normanhurst Dr., Twick. | 144/145 | E5 |
| *St. Margarets Rd.* | | |
| Normanhurst Rd. SW2 | 169 | F2 |
| Norman's Bldgs. EC1 | 111 | J3 |
| *Ironmonger Row* | | |
| Normans Cl. NW10 | 88 | D6 |
| Normans Mead NW10 | 88 | D6 |
| Normansfield Av., Tedd. | 163 | F7 |
| Normanshire Av. E4 | 62 | C4 |
| Normanshire Dr. E4 | 62 | A4 |
| Normanton Av. SW19 | 166 | D2 |
| Normanton Pk. E4 | 62 | E3 |
| Normanton Rd., S.Croy. | 202 | B6 |
| Normanton St. SE23 | 171 | G2 |
| Normington Cl. SW16 | 169 | G5 |
| Norrice Lea N2 | 73 | G5 |
| **Norris St. SW1** | **17** | **H6** |
| Norroy Rd. SW15 | 148 | A4 |
| Norrys Cl., Barn. | 41 | J5 |
| Norrys Rd., Barn. | 41 | J4 |
| Norseman Cl., Ilf. | 100 | B1 |
| Norseman Way, Grnf. | 103 | H1 |
| *Olympic Way* | | |
| Norstead Pl. SW15 | 165 | G2 |
| North Access Rd. E17 | 77 | G6 |
| North Acre NW9 | 71 | E1 |
| North Acton Rd. NW10 | 106 | D2 |
| **North Audley St. W1** | **16** | **B4** |
| North Audley St. W1 | 110 | A6 |
| North Av. N18 | 60 | D4 |
| North Av. W13 | 104 | E6 |
| North Av., Cars. | 199 | J7 |
| North Av., Har. | 67 | H6 |
| North Av., Hayes | 102 | A7 |
| North Av., Rich. | 146 | A1 |
| *Sandycombe Rd.* | | |
| North Av., Sthl. | 103 | F7 |
| **North Bank NW8** | **7** | **G4** |
| North Bank NW8 | 109 | H3 |
| North Birkbeck Rd. E11 | 96 | D3 |
| North Branch Av. W10 | 107 | J3 |
| *Harrow Rd.* | | |
| **North Carriage Dr. W2** | **15** | **G5** |
| North Carriage Dr. W2 | 109 | G7 |
| North Circular Rd. E4 | 61 | J7 |
| North Circular Rd. E18 | 79 | J2 |
| North Circular Rd. N3 | 72 | E3 |
| North Circular Rd. N12 | 73 | G1 |
| North Circular Rd. N13 | 59 | G5 |
| North Circular Rd. NW2 | 88 | E3 |
| North Circular Rd. NW10 | 88 | C7 |
| North Circular Rd. NW11 | 72 | B4 |
| North Cl., Barn. | 39 | J5 |
| North Cl., Bexh. | 158 | D4 |
| North Cl., Dag. | 119 | G1 |
| North Cl., Felt. | 141 | G6 |
| *North Rd.* | | |
| North Cl., Mord. | 184 | B4 |
| North Colonnade E14 | 134 | A1 |
| North Common Rd. W5 | 105 | H7 |
| North Countess Rd. E17 | 77 | J1 |
| **North Ct. W1** | **17** | **G1** |
| North Cray Rd., Bex. | 177 | F3 |
| North Cray Rd., Sid. | 176 | E6 |
| North Cres. E16 | 114 | D4 |
| North Cres. N3 | 72 | C2 |
| **North Cres. WC1** | **17** | **H1** |
| North Cres. WC1 | 110 | D5 |
| North Cross Rd. SE22 | 152 | C5 |
| North Cross Rd., Ilf. | 81 | F4 |
| North Dene NW7 | 54 | D3 |
| North Dene, Houns. | 143 | H1 |
| North Dr. SW16 | 168 | C4 |
| North Dr., Houns. | 143 | J2 |
| North Dr., Orp. | 207 | H4 |
| North End NW3 | 91 | F2 |
| North End, Buck.H. | 47 | J7 |
| North End, Croy. | 201 | J2 |
| North End Av. NW3 | 91 | F2 |
| North End Cres. W14 | 128 | C4 |
| North End Ho. W14 | 128 | B4 |
| North End Par. W14 | 128 | B4 |
| *North End Rd.* | | |
| North End Rd. NW11 | 90 | D1 |
| North End Rd. SW6 | 128 | C6 |
| North End Rd. W14 | 128 | B4 |
| North End Rd., Wem. | 88 | A3 |
| North Eyot Gdns. W6 | 127 | F5 |
| *St. Peter's Sq.* | | |
| **North Flockton St. SE16** | **29** | **H3** |
| North Gdn. E14 | 133 | J1 |
| *Westferry Circ.* | | |
| North Gdns. SW19 | 167 | G7 |
| North Glade, The, Bex. | 159 | F7 |
| **North Gower St. NW1** | **9** | **G4** |
| North Gower St. NW1 | 110 | C3 |
| North Grn. NW9 | 54/55 | E7 |
| *Clayton Fld.* | | |
| North Gro. N6 | 74 | A7 |
| North Gro. N15 | 76 | A5 |
| North Hatton Rd. (Heathrow Airport), Houns. | 141 | G1 |
| North Hill N6 | 73 | J6 |
| North Hill Av. N6 | 74 | A6 |
| North Hyde Gdns. Hayes | 122 | A4 |
| North Hyde La. Houns. | 123 | E5 |
| North Hyde La., Sthl. | 123 | E5 |
| North Hyde Rd., Hayes | 121 | J3 |
| North La., Tedd. | 162 | C6 |
| North Lo. Cl. SW15 | 148 | A5 |
| *Westleigh Av.* | | |
| North Mall N9 | 60/61 | E2 |
| *St. Martins Rd.* | | |
| **North Ms. WC1** | **10** | **D6** |
| North Ms. WC1 | 111 | F4 |
| North Par., Chess. | 195 | H5 |
| North Pk. SE9 | 156 | C6 |
| North Pas. SW18 | 148 | D4 |
| **North Peckham Est. SE15** | **37** | **E7** |
| North Peckham Est. | 132 | C7 |
| North Pl., Mitch. | 167 | J7 |
| North Pl., Tedd. | 162 | C6 |
| North Pole La., Kes. | 205 | F6 |
| North Pole Rd. W10 | 107 | J5 |
| **North Ride W2** | **15** | **G6** |
| North Ride W2 | 109 | H7 |
| North Rd. N6 | 74 | A7 |
| North Rd. N7 | 92 | E6 |
| North Rd. N9 | 60 | E1 |
| North Rd. SE18 | 137 | H4 |
| North Rd. SW19 | 167 | F6 |
| North Rd. W5 | 125 | G3 |
| North Rd., Belv. | 139 | H3 |
| North Rd., Brent. | 125 | H6 |
| North Rd., Brom. | 191 | H1 |
| North Rd., Edg. | 70 | B1 |
| North Rd., Felt. | 141 | G6 |
| North Rd., Ilf. | 99 | H2 |
| North Rd., Rich. | 146 | A3 |
| North Rd., Rom. | 82 | E5 |
| North Rd., Sthl. | 103 | G7 |
| North Rd., Surb. | 181 | G6 |
| North Rd., West Dr. | 120 | C3 |
| North Rd., W.Wick. | 204 | B1 |
| **North Row W1** | **16** | **A5** |
| North Row W1 | 109 | J7 |
| North Several SE3 | 154 | D2 |
| *Orchard Dr.* | | |
| North Side Wandsworth Common SW18 | 149 | G5 |
| North Sq. N9 | 60/61 | E2 |
| *St. Martins Rd.* | | |
| North Sq. NW11 | 72 | D5 |
| North St. E13 | 115 | H2 |
| North St. NW4 | 71 | J5 |
| North St. SW4 | 150 | C3 |
| North St., Bark. | 99 | E6 |
| North St., Bexh. | 159 | G4 |
| North St., Brom. | 191 | G1 |
| North St., Cars. | 199 | J3 |
| North St., Islw. | 144 | D3 |
| North St. Pas. E13 | 115 | H2 |
| **North Tenter St. E1** | **21** | **G4** |
| North Tenter St. E1 | 112 | C6 |
| **North Ter. SW3** | **23** | **G6** |
| North Ter. SW3 | 129 | H3 |
| North Verbena Gdns. W6 | 127 | G5 |
| *St. Peter's Sq.* | | |
| North Vw. SW19 | 165 | H5 |
| North Vw. W5 | 105 | F4 |
| North Vw., Pnr. | 66 | C7 |
| North Vw. Dr., Wdf.Grn. | 80 | A2 |
| North Vw. Rd. N8 | 74 | D3 |
| North Vil. NW1 | 92 | D6 |
| **North Wk. W2** | **14** | **C6** |
| North Wk., Croy. | 204 | B5 |
| North Way N9 | 61 | F2 |
| North Way N11 | 58 | C6 |
| North Way NW9 | 70 | B3 |
| North Way, Pnr. | 66 | C3 |
| **North Wf. Rd. W2** | **14** | **E2** |
| North Wf. Rd. W2 | 109 | G5 |
| North Woolwich Rd. E16 | 135 | G1 |
| North Woolwich Roundabout E16 | 136 | A1 |
| *North Woolwich Rd.* | | |
| North Worple Way SW14 | 146 | D3 |
| Northall Rd., Bexh. | 159 | J2 |
| Northampton Gro. N1 | 94 | A5 |
| Northampton Pk. N1 | 93 | J6 |
| **Northampton Rd. EC1** | **11** | **F5** |
| Northampton Rd. EC1 | 111 | G4 |
| Northampton Rd., Croy. | 202 | D2 |
| Northampton Rd., Enf. | 45 | H4 |
| **Northampton Sq. EC1** | **11** | **G4** |
| Northampton Sq. EC1 | 111 | H3 |
| Northampton St. N1 | 93 | J7 |
| Northanger Rd. SW16 | 168 | E6 |
| Northbank Rd. E17 | 78 | C2 |
| Northborough Rd. SW16 | 186 | D3 |
| Northbourne, Brom. | 191 | G3 |
| Northbourne Rd. SW4 | 150 | D4 |
| Northbrook Rd. N22 | 59 | E7 |
| Northbrook Rd. SE13 | 154 | D5 |
| Northbrook Rd., Barn. | 40 | B6 |
| Northbrook Rd., Croy. | 188 | A5 |
| Northbrook Rd., Ilf. | 98 | D2 |
| **Northburgh St. EC1** | **11** | **H5** |
| Northburgh St. EC1 | 111 | H4 |
| **Northchurch SE17** | **36** | **C3** |
| Northchurch Rd. N1 | 94 | A7 |
| Northchurch Rd., Wem. | 87 | J6 |
| Northchurch Ter. N1 | 94 | B7 |
| Northcliffe Cl., Wor.Pk. | 197 | E3 |
| Northcliffe Dr. N20 | 56 | C2 |
| Northcote, Pnr. | 66 | C2 |
| Northcote Av. W5 | 105 | H7 |
| Northcote Av., Islw. | 144 | D5 |
| Northcote Av., Sthl. | 103 | E7 |
| Northcote Av., Surb. | 182 | A7 |
| Northcote Rd. E17 | 77 | H4 |
| Northcote Rd. NW10 | 89 | E7 |
| Northcote Rd. SW11 | 149 | H4 |
| Northcote Rd., Croy. | 188 | A6 |
| Northcote Rd., N.Mal. | 182 | C3 |
| Northcote Rd., Sid. | 175 | H4 |
| Northcote Rd., Twick. | 144 | D5 |
| Northcott Av. N22 | 75 | E1 |
| Northcroft Rd. W13 | 124 | E2 |
| Northcroft Rd., Epsom | 196 | D7 |
| Northcroft Ter. W13 | 124/125 | E2 |
| *Northcroft Rd.* | | |
| Northdene, Chig. | 65 | G5 |
| Northdene Gdns. N15 | 76 | C6 |
| Northdown Gdns., Ilf. | 81 | H5 |
| Northdown Rd., Well. | 158 | B2 |
| **Northdown St. N1** | **10** | **B1** |
| Northern Av. N9 | 60 | C2 |
| Northern Perimeter Rd., Houns. | 141 | F1 |
| Northern Perimeter Rd. W., Houns. | 140 | A1 |
| Northern Relief Rd., Bark. | 99 | E7 |
| Northern Rd. E13 | 115 | H1 |
| Northern Service Rd., Barn. | 40 | B3 |
| Northernhay Wk. Mord. | 184 | B4 |
| Northey St. E14 | 113 | H7 |
| Northfield, Loug. | 48 | A4 |
| Northfield Av. W5 | 125 | E2 |
| Northfield Av. W13 | 125 | E2 |
| Northfield Av., Pnr. | 66 | D4 |
| Northfield Cl., Brom. | 192 | B1 |
| Northfield Cl., Hayes | 121 | J3 |
| Northfield Cres., Sutt. | 198 | B4 |

322 Old–Orc

**Old Compton St. W1 17 H5**
Old Compton St. W1 110 D7
Old Cote Dr., Houns. 123 G6
**Old Ct. Pl. W8 22 A3**
Old Ct. Pl. W8 128 E2
Old Deer Pk. Gdns., Rich. 145 H3
Old Devonshire Rd. SW12 150 B7
Old Dock Cl., Rich. 126 A6
*Watcombe Cotts.*
Old Dover Rd. SE3 135 H7
Old Fm. Av. N14 42 C7
Old Fm. Av., Sid. 175 G1
Old Fm. Cl., Houns. 143 F4
Old Fm. Pas., Hmptn. 179 J1
Old Fm. Rd. N2 73 G1
Old Fm. Rd., Hmptn. 161 F6
Old Fm. Rd., West Dr. 120 A2
Old Fm. Rd. E., Sid. 176 A2
Old Fm. Rd. W., Sid. 175 J2
**Old Fish St. Hill EC4 19 J5**
**Old Fleet La. EC4 19 G3**
Old Fold Cl., Barn. 40 C1
*Old Fold La.*
Old Fold La., Barn. 40 C1
Old Fold Vw., Barn. 39 J3
Old Ford Rd. E2 113 F2
Old Ford Rd. E3 113 H2
Old Forge Cl., Stan. 52 D4
Old Forge Ms. W12 127 H2
*Goodwin Rd.*
Old Forge Way, Sid. 176 B4
Old Fox Footpath, S.Croy. 202 B7
*Essenden Rd.*
**Old Gloucester St. WC1 18 B1**
Old Gloucester St. WC1 111 E5
Old Hall Cl., Pnr. 67 E1
Old Hall Dr., Pnr. 66 E1
Old Hill, Chis. 192 D1
Old Hill, Orp. 207 G6
Old Homesdale Rd., Brom. 191 J4
Old Hospital Cl. SW12 167 J1
Old Ho. Cl. SW19 166 B5
Old Ho. Gdns., Twick. 145 F5
**Old Jamaica Rd. SE16 29 H5**
Old Jamaica Rd. SE16 132 D3
Old James St. SE15 152 E3
**Old Jewry EC2 20 B4**
Old Jewry EC2 112 A6
**Old Kent Rd. SE1 36 D1**
Old Kent Rd. SE1 132 B4
Old Kent Rd. SE15 132 B4
Old Kenton La. NW9 70 B5
Old Kingston Rd., Wor.Pk. 196 C3
Old Lo. Pl., Twick. 144/145 E6
*St. Margarets Rd.*
Old Lo. Way, Stan. 52 D5
Old Maidstone Rd., Sid. 177 F7
Old Malden La., Wor.Pk. 196 D2
Old Manor Dr., Islw. 143 J6
Old Manor Way, Chis. 174 C5
**Old Marylebone Rd. NW1 15 H2**
Old Marylebone Rd. NW1 109 H5
Old Ms., Har. 68 B5
*Hindes Rd.*
Old Mill Ct. E18 79 J3
Old Mill Rd. SE18 137 G6
Old Mitre Ct. EC4 111 G6
*Fleet St.*
**Old Montague St. E1 21 H2**
Old Montague St. E1 112 D5
**Old Nichol St. E2 13 F5**
Old Nichol St. E2 112 C4
**Old N. St. WC1 18 C1**
Old Oak Cl., Chess. 195 J4
Old Oak Common La. NW10 107 E4
Old Oak Common La. W3 107 E5
Old Oak La. NW10 107 E3
Old Oak Rd. W3 107 F7
Old Orchard, Sun. 178 C2
Old Orchard, The NW3 91 J4
*Nassington Rd.*
Old Palace La., Rich. 145 F5
Old Palace Rd., Croy. 201 H3
Old Palace Ter., Rich. 145 G5
*King St.*
**Old Palace Yd. SW1 26 A5**
Old Palace Yd. SW1 130 E3
Old Palace Yd., Rich. 145 F5
**Old Paradise St. SE11 34 C1**
Old Paradise St. SE11 131 F4
Old Pk. Av. SW12 150 A6
Old Pk. Av., Enf. 43 J4
Old Pk. Gro., Enf. 43 J4
**Old Pk. La. W1 24 C2**
Old Pk. La. W1 130 A1
Old Pk. Ms., Houns. 123 F7
Old Pk. Ridings N21 43 H6
Old Pk. Rd. N13 59 F4
Old Pk. Rd. SE2 138 A5
Old Pk. Rd., Enf. 43 H3
Old Pk. Rd. S., Enf. 43 H4
Old Pk. Vw., Enf. 43 G3
Old Perry St., Chis. 175 H7
Old Pound Cl., Islw. 144 D1
**Old Pye St. SW1 25 H5**
Old Pye St. SW1 130 D3
**Old Quebec St. W1 16 A4**
Old Quebec St. W1 109 J6
**Old Queen St. SW1 25 J4**
Old Queen St. SW1 130 D2
Old Rectory Gdns., Edg. 54 A6
Old Redding, Har. 51 J4
Old Rd. SE13 155 E4
Old Rd., Enf. 45 F1
Old Rope Wk., Sun. 178 B3
*The Av.*
Old Royal Free Pl. N1 111 G1
*Liverpool Rd.*
Old Royal Free Sq. N1 111 G1
Old Ruislip Rd., Nthlt. 102 D2
Old Savill's Cotts., Chig. 65 F4
*The Chase*
Old Sch. Cl. SW19 184 D2
Old Sch. Cl., Beck. 189 G2
Old Sch. Cres. E7 97 F6
Old Sch. Sq., T.Ditt. 180 C6
**Old Seacoal La. EC4 19 G3**
Old S. Cl., Pnr. 66 D1
**Old S. Lambeth Rd. SW8 34 B7**
Old S. Lambeth Rd. SW8 131 E7
**Old Spitalfields Mkt. E1 21 F1**
Old Spitalfields Mkt. E1 112 C5
**Old Sq. WC2 18 D3**
Old Sq. WC2 111 F6
Old Sta. Rd., Hayes 121 J3
Old Sta. Rd., Loug. 48 B5
Old Stockley Rd., West Dr. 120 E2
Old St. E13 115 H2
**Old St. EC1 11 J5**
Old St. EC1 111 J4
Old Swan Yd., Cars. 199 J4
Old Town SW4 150 C3
Old Town, Croy. 201 H3
Old Tram Yd. SE18 137 H4
*Lakedale Rd.*
Old Woolwich Rd. SE10 134 D6
Old York Rd. SW18 149 E5
Oldacre Ms. SW12 150 B7
*Balham Gro.*
Oldberry Rd., Edg. 54 D6
Oldborough Rd., Wem. 87 F2
**Oldbury Pl. W1 16 C1**
Oldbury Pl. W1 110 A4
Oldbury Rd., Enf. 44 D2
Oldfield Cl., Brom. 192 C4
Oldfield Cl., Grnf. 86 B5
Oldfield Cl., Stan. 52 D5
Oldfield Fm. Gdns., Grnf. 104 A1
Oldfield Gro. SE16 133 G4
Oldfield La. N., Grnf. 86 B6
Oldfield La. S., Grnf. 103 J4
Oldfield Ms. N6 74 C7
Oldfield Rd. N16 94 B3
Oldfield Rd. NW10 89 F7
Oldfield Rd. SW19 166 B6
Oldfield Rd. W3 127 F2
*Valetta Rd.*
Oldfield Rd., Bexh. 159 E2
Oldfield Rd., Brom. 192 C4
Oldfield Rd., Hmptn. 179 F1
Oldfields Circ., Nthlt. 85 J6
Oldfields Rd., Sutt. 198 C3
Oldfields Trd. Est., Sutt. 198 D3
*Oldfields Rd.*
Oldham Ter. W3 126 C1
Oldhill St. N16 94 D1
Oldridge Rd. SW12 150 A7
Oldstead Rd., Brom. 172 D4
Oleander Cl., Orp. 207 G5
O'Leary Sq. E1 113 F5
Olinda Rd. N16 76 C6
Oliphant St. W10 108 A3
Olive Rd. E13 115 J3
Olive Rd. NW2 89 J4
Olive Rd. SW19 167 F7
*Norman Rd.*
Olive Rd. W5 125 G3
Oliver Av. SE25 188 C3
Oliver Cl. E10 96 B2
*Oliver Rd.*
Oliver Cl. W4 126 B6
Oliver Gdns. E6 116 B6
Oliver Gro. SE25 188 C4
Oliver Rd. E10 96 B2
Oliver Rd. E17 78 C5
Oliver Rd., N.Mal. 182 C2
Oliver Rd., Sutt. 199 G4
Oliver-Goldsmith Est. SE15 152 D1
**Olivers Yd. EC1 12 C5**
Olivette St. SW15 148 A4
Ollards Gro., Loug. 48 A4
Ollerton Grn. E3 113 J1
Ollerton Rd. N11 58 D5
Olley Cl., Wall. 200 E7
Ollgar Cl. W12 127 F1
Olliffe St. E14 134 C3
**Olmar St. SE1 37 H5**
Olmar St. SE1 132 D6
**Olney Rd. SE17 35 J5**
Olney Rd. SE17 131 H6
Olron Cres., Bexh. 158 D5
Olven Rd. SE18 137 F7
Olveston Wk., Cars. 185 G6
Olwen Ms., Pnr. 66 D2
Olyffe Av., Well. 158 A2
Olyffe Dr., Beck. 190 C1
**Olympia Ms. W2 14 B6**
Olympia Way W14 128 B3
Olympic Retail Pk., Wem. 88 B4
Olympic Way, Grnf. 103 H1
Olympic Way, Wem. 88 A4
Olympus Sq. E5 94 D4
*Nolan Way*
Oman Av. NW2 89 J4
**O'Meara St. SE1 28 A2**
O'Meara St. SE1 131 J1
Omega Cl. E14 134 B3
*Tiller Rd.*
**Omega Pl. N1 10 B2**
Omega St. SE14 154 A1
Ommaney Rd. SE14 153 G1
Omnibus Way E17 78 A2
On The Hill, Wat. 50 E2
Ondine Rd. SE15 152 C4
One Tree Cl. SE23 153 F6
Onega Gate SE16 133 H3
O'Neill Path SE18 136 D6
*Kempt St.*
Ongar Cl., Rom. 82 C5
Ongar Rd. SW6 128 D6
Onra Rd. E17 78 A7
Onslow Av., Rich. 145 H5
Onslow Cl. E4 62 C2
Onslow Cl., T.Ditt. 194 B1
Onslow Cres., Chis. 192 E1
Onslow Dr., Sid. 176 D2
Onslow Gdns. E18 79 H3
Onslow Gdns. N10 74 B5
Onslow Gdns. N21 43 G5
**Onslow Gdns. SW7 31 E3**
Onslow Gdns. SW7 129 G5
Onslow Gdns., T.Ditt. 194 B1
Onslow Gdns., Wall. 200 C6
**Onslow Ms. E. SW7 31 E2**
**Onslow Ms. W. SW7 30 E2**
Onslow Rd., Croy. 187 F7
Onslow Rd., N.Mal. 183 G4
Onslow Rd., Rich. 145 H5
**Onslow Sq. SW7 31 F1**
Onslow Sq. SW7 129 G4
**Onslow St. EC1 11 F6**
Onslow Way, T.Ditt. 194 B1
**Ontario St. SE1 27 H6**
Ontario St. SE1 131 H3
Ontario Way E14 114 A7
Opal Cl. E16 116 A6
Opal Ms. NW6 108 C1
*Priory Pk. Rd.*
Opal Ms., Ilf. 98/99 E2
*Ley St.*
**Opal St. SE11 35 G2**
Opal St. SE11 131 H4
Openshaw Rd. SE2 138 B4
Openview SW18 167 F1
Ophelia Gdns. NW2 90 B3
*The Vale*
Ophir Ter. SE15 152 D1
Opossum Way, Houns. 142 C2
Oppenheim Rd. SE13 154 C2
Oppidans Ms. NW3 91 J7
*Meadowbank*
Oppidans Rd. NW3 91 J7
**Orange Ct. E1 29 J2**
Orange Gro. E11 96 E3
Orange Gro., Chig. 65 F6
Orange Hill Rd., Edg. 54 C7
Orange Pl. SE16 133 F3
*Lower Rd.*
**Orange St. WC2 17 H6**
Orange St. WC2 110 D7
**Orange Yd. W1 17 J4**
Orangery, The, Rich. 163 F2
Orangery La. SE9 156 C5
**Oratory La. SW3 31 F3**
**Orb St. SE17 36 B2**
Orb St. SE17 132 A4
Orbain Rd. SW6 128 B7
Orbel St. SW11 149 H1
Orchard, The N14 42 B5
Orchard, The N21 44 A6
Orchard, The NW11 72 D5
Orchard, The SE3 154 D2
Orchard, The W4 126 D4
Orchard, The W5 105 G5
Orchard, The, Epsom 197 F7
Orchard, The, Houns. 143 J2
Orchard Av. N3 72 D3
Orchard Av. N14 42 C6
Orchard Av. N20 57 G2
Orchard Av., Belv. 139 E6
Orchard Av., Croy. 189 H7
Orchard Av., Felt. 141 G5
Orchard Av., Houns. 123 E7
Orchard Av., Mitch. 200 A1
Orchard Av., N.Mal. 183 E2
Orchard Av., Sthl. 123 E1
Orchard Av., T.Ditt. 194 D1
Orchard Cl. E4 62 A4
*Chingford Mt. Rd.*
Orchard Cl. E11 79 H4
Orchard Cl. N1 93 J7
*Morton Rd.*
Orchard Cl. NW2 89 G3
Orchard Cl. SE23 153 F6
*Brenchley Gdns.*
Orchard Cl. SW20 183 J4
*Grand Dr.*
Orchard Cl. W10 108 B5
Orchard Cl., Bexh. 158 E1
Orchard Cl., Bushey 52 A1
Orchard Cl., Edg. 53 H6
Orchard Cl., Epsom 196 B6
Orchard Cl., Nthlt. 85 J5
Orchard Cl., Surb. 181 E7
Orchard Cl., Walt. 178 B7
*Garden Rd.*
Orchard Cl., Wem. 105 H1
Orchard Ct., Islw. 144 A1
*Thornbury Av.*
Orchard Ct., Twick. 162 A2
Orchard Ct., Wor.Pk. 197 G1
*The Av.*
Orchard Cres., Edg. 54 C5
Orchard Cres., Enf. 44 C1
Orchard Dr. SE3 154 E2
Orchard Dr., Edg. 53 J5
Orchard Gdns., Chess. 195 H4
Orchard Gdns., Sutt. 198 D5
Orchard Gate NW9 70 E4
Orchard Gate, Esher 194 A1
Orchard Gate, Grnf. 86 E6
Orchard Grn., Orp. 207 H2
Orchard Gro. SE20 170 D7
Orchard Gro., Croy. 189 H7
Orchard Gro., Edg. 70 A1
Orchard Gro., Har. 69 J5
Orchard Gro., Orp. 207 J2
Orchard Hill SE13 154 B2
*Coldbath St.*
Orchard Hill, Cars. 199 J5
Orchard La. SW20 183 H1
Orchard La., E.Mol. 180 A6
Orchard La., Wdf.Grn. 63 J4
Orchard Ms. N1 94 A7
*Southgate Gro.*
Orchard Pl. E14 115 E7
Orchard Pl. N17 60 C7
Orchard Ri., Croy. 203 H1
Orchard Ri., Kings.T. 182 C1
Orchard Ri., Rich. 146 B4
Orchard Ri. E., Sid. 157 J5
Orchard Ri. W., Sid. 157 H5
Orchard Rd. N6 74 B7
Orchard Rd. SE3 154/155 E2
*Eliot Pl.*
Orchard Rd. SE18 137 G4
Orchard Rd., Barn. 40 C4
Orchard Rd., Belv. 139 G4
Orchard Rd., Brent. 125 F6
Orchard Rd., Brom. 191 J1
Orchard Rd., Chess. 195 H4
Orchard Rd., Dag. 119 G1

Orchard Rd., Enf. 45 F5
Orchard Rd., Hmptn. 161 F7
Orchard Rd., Hayes 102 A7
Orchard Rd., Houns. 143 F5
Orchard Rd., Kings.T. 181 H2
Orchard Rd., Mitch. 200 A1
Orchard Rd. (Farnborough), Orp. 207 E5
Orchard Rd., Rich. 146 A3
Orchard Rd., Rom. 83 H1
Orchard Rd., Sid. 175 H4
Orchard Rd., Sun. 160 B7
*Hanworth Rd.*
Orchard Rd., Sutt. 198 D5
Orchard Rd., Twick. 144 D5
Orchard Rd., Well. 158 B3
Orchard Sq. W14 128 C5
*Sun Rd.*
Orchard St. E17 77 H4
**Orchard St. W1 16 B4**
Orchard St. W1 110 A6
Orchard Ter., Enf. 44 D6
*Great Cambridge Rd.*
Orchard Way, Beck. 189 H5
Orchard Way, Croy. 189 H7
Orchard Way, Enf. 44 B3
Orchard Way, Sutt. 199 G4
Orchardleigh Av., Enf. 45 F2
Orchardmede N21 44 A6
**Orchardson St. NW8 7 E6**
Orchardson St. NW8 109 G4
Orchid Cl. E6 116 B5
Orchid Cl., Sthl. 103 E6
Orchid Rd. N14 42 C7
Orchid St. W12 107 G7
**Orde Hall St. WC1 10 C6**
Orde Hall St. WC1 111 F4
Ordell Rd. E3 113 J2
Ordnance Cl., Felt. 160 A3
Ordnance Cres. SE10 134 D2
Ordnance Hill NW8 109 G1
**Ordnance Ms. NW8 7 F1**
Ordnance Rd. E16 115 F5
Ordnance Rd. SE18 136 D6
Oregano Dr. E14 114 D6
Oregon Av. E12 98 C4
Oregon Cl., N.Mal. 182 C4
*Georgia Rd.*
Oregon Sq., Orp. 207 G1
Orestes Ms. NW6 90 D5
*Aldred Rd.*
Orford Ct. SE27 169 H2
Orford Gdns., Twick. 162 C2
Orford Rd. E17 78 A5
Orford Rd. E18 79 H3
Orford Rd. SE6 172 B3
Organ La. E4 62 C2
Oriel Cl., Mitch. 186 D4
Oriel Ct. NW3 91 F4
*Heath St.*
Oriel Dr. SW13 127 H6
Oriel Gdns., Ilf. 80 C3
Oriel Pl. NW3 91 F4
*Heath St.*
Oriel Rd. E9 95 G6
Oriel Way, Nthlt. 85 H7
Orient Ind. Pk. E10 96 A2
**Orient St. SE11 35 G1**
Orient Way E5 95 G3
Orient Way E10 95 H2
Oriental Rd. E16 136 A1
Oriental St. E14 114 A7
*Morant St.*
Oriole Way SE28 118 B7
Orion Rd. N11 58 B6
Orissa Rd. SE18 137 H5
Orkney St. SW11 150 A2
Orlando Rd. SW4 150 C3
Orleans Cl., Esher 194 A2
Orleans Rd. SE19 170 A6
Orleans Rd., Twick. 145 E7
Orleston Ms. N7 93 G6
Orleston Rd. N7 93 G6
Orley Fm. Rd., Har. 86 B3
Orlop St. SE10 134 E5
Ormanton Rd. SE26 170 D4
**Orme Ct. W2 14 A6**
Orme Ct. W2 108 E7
**Orme Ct. Ms. W2 14 B6**
**Orme La. W2 14 A6**
Orme La. W2 108 E7
Orme Rd., Kings.T. 182 B2
**Orme Sq. W2 14 A6**
Ormeley Rd. SW12 168 B1
Ormerod Gdns., Mitch. 186 A2
Ormesby Cl. SE28 118 D7
*Wroxham Rd.*
Ormesby Way, Har. 69 J6
Ormiston Gro. W12 127 H1
Ormiston Rd. SE10 135 G5
Ormond Av., Hmptn. 179 H1
Ormond Av., Rich. 145 G5
*Ormond Rd.*
**Ormond Cl. WC1 18 B1**
Ormond Cres., Hmptn. 179 H1
Ormond Dr., Hmptn. 161 H7
**Ormond Ms. WC1 10 B6**
Ormond Rd. N19 93 E1
Ormond Rd., Rich. 145 G5
**Ormond Yd. SW1 25 G1**
Ormonde Av., Orp. 207 F2
**Ormonde Gate SW3 32 A4**
Ormonde Gate SW3 129 J5
**Ormonde Pl. SW1 32 B2**
Ormonde Ri., Buck.H. 63 J1
Ormonde Rd. SW14 146 B3
Ormonde Ter. NW8 109 J1
Ormsby Gdns., Grnf. 103 J2
Ormsby Pl. N16 94 C3
*Victorian Gro.*
Ormsby Pt. SE18 136/137 E4
*Troy Ct.*
**Ormsby St. E2 13 F1**
Ormsby St. E2 112 C2
Ormside St. SE15 133 F6
Ormskirk Rd., Wat. 50 D4
Ornan Rd. NW3 91 H5
Oronsay Wk. N1 93 J6
*Clephane Rd.*
Orpen Wk. N16 94 B3
Orpheus St. SE5 152 A1
Orpington Gdns. N18 60 B3
Orpington Rd. N21 59 H1
Orpington Rd., Chis. 193 H3
Orpwood Cl., Hmptn. 161 F5
**Orsett St. SE11 34 D3**
Orsett St. SE11 131 F5
**Orsett Ter. W2 14 B3**
Orsett Ter. W2 109 F6
Orsett Ter., Wdf.Grn. 79 J1
Orsman Rd. N1 112 B1
**Orton St. E1 29 H2**
Orville Rd. SW11 149 G2
Orwell Ct. N5 93 J4
Orwell Rd. E13 115 J2
Osbaldeston Rd. N16 94 D2
**Osbert St. SW1 33 H2**
Osberton Rd. SE12 155 G5
Osborn Cl. E8 112 D1
Osborn Gdns. NW7 56 A7
Osborn La. SE23 153 H7
**Osborn St. E1 21 G2**
Osborn St. E1 112 C5
Osborn Ter. SE3 155 F4
*Lee Rd.*
Osborne Cl., Barn. 41 J3
Osborne Cl., Beck. 189 H4
Osborne Cl., Felt. 160 D5
Osborne Gdns., Th.Hth. 187 J2
Osborne Gro. E17 77 J4
Osborne Gro. N4 93 G1
Osborne Ms. E17 77 J4
*Osborne Gro.*
Osborne Pl., Sutt. 199 G5
Osborne Rd. E7 97 H5
Osborne Rd. E9 95 J6
Osborne Rd. E10 96 B3
Osborne Rd. N4 93 G1
Osborne Rd. N13 59 G3
Osborne Rd. NW2 89 H6
Osborne Rd. W3 126 B3
Osborne Rd., Belv. 139 F5
Osborne Rd., Buck.H. 63 H1
Osborne Rd., Dag. 101 F5
Osborne Rd., Enf. 45 H2
Osborne Rd., Houns. 143 F3
Osborne Rd., Kings.T. 163 H7
Osborne Rd., Sthl. 103 J6
Osborne Rd., Th.Hth. 187 J2
Osborne Sq., Dag. 101 F4
Osborne Ter. SW17 168 A5
*Church La.*
Oscar St. SE8 154 A1
Oseney Cres. NW5 92 C6
Osgood Av., Orp. 207 J5
Osgood Gdns., Orp. 207 J5
O'Shea Gro. E3 113 J1
Osidge La. N14 58 A1
Osier Ms. W4 127 F6
Osier St. E1 113 F4
Osier Way E10 96 B3
Osier Way, Mitch. 185 H5
Osiers Rd. SW18 148 D4
Oslac Rd. SE6 172 B5
**Oslo Ct. NW8 7 G2**
Oslo Sq. SE16 133 H3
*Norway Gate*
Osman Cl. N15 76 A6
*Tewkesbury Rd.*
Osman Rd. N9 60 D3
Osman Rd. W6 127 J3
*Batoum Gdns.*
Osmond Cl., Har. 85 J2
Osmond Gdns., Wall. 200 C5
Osmund St. W12 107 F6
*Braybrook St.*
**Osnaburgh St. NW1 9 E6**
Osnaburgh St. NW1 110 B4
**Osnaburgh Ter. NW1 8 E5**
Osney Ho. SE2 138 D2
*Hartslock Dr.*
Osney Wk., Cars. 185 G6
Osprey Cl. E6 116 B5
*Dove App.*
Osprey Cl. E11 79 G4
Osprey Cl. E17 61 H7
Osprey Cl., Sutt. 198 B2
*Gander Grn. La.*
Osprey Cl., West Dr. 120 B2
Osprey Ms., Enf. 45 E5
Ospringe Cl. SE20 171 F7
Ospringe Ct. SE9 157 G6
*Alderwood Rd.*
Ospringe Rd. NW5 92 C4
Osram Rd., Wem. 87 G3
**Osric Path N1 12 D2**
Osric Path N1 112 B2
Ossian Ms. N4 75 F7
Ossian Rd. N4 75 F7
**Ossington Bldgs. W1 16 B1**
**Ossington St. W2 14 A6**
Ossington St. W2 108 E7
**Ossory Rd. SE1 37 H4**
Ossory Rd. SE1 132 D5
**Ossulston St. NW1 9 H2**
Ossulston St. NW1 110 D3
Ossulton Pl. N2 73 F3
*East End Rd.*
Ossulton Way N2 73 F4
Ostade Rd. SW2 151 F7
**Osten Ms. SW7 22 B6**
Oster Ter. E17 77 G5
*Southcote Rd.*
Osterley Av., Islw. 124 A7
Osterley Ct., Islw. 144 A1
Osterley Cres., Islw. 144 B1
Osterley Gdns., Th.Hth. 187 J2
Osterley Ho. E14 114 B6
*Giraud St.*
Osterley La., Islw. 124 B5
Osterley La., Sthl. 123 G5
Osterley Pk., Islw. 124 A5
Osterley Pk. Rd., Sthl. 123 F3
Osterley Pk. Vw. Rd. W7 124 B2
Osterley Rd. N16 94 B4
Osterley Rd., Islw. 124 B7
Osterley Views, Sthl. 123 J1
*West Pk. Rd.*
Ostliffe Rd. N13 59 H5
Oswald Rd., Sthl. 123 E1
Oswald St. E5 95 G3
Oswald Ter. NW2 89 J3
*Temple Rd.*
Oswald's Mead E9 95 H4
*Lindisfarne Way*
Osward Pl. N9 60 E2
Osward Rd. SW17 167 J2
Oswell Ho. E1 133 E1
**Oswin St. SE11 35 H1**
Oswin St. SE11 131 H4
Oswyth Rd. SE5 152 B2
Otford Cl. SE20 189 F1
Otford Cl., Bex. 159 H6
*Southwold Rd.*
Otford Cl., Brom. 192 D3
Otford Cres. SE4 153 J6
**Othello Cl. SE11 35 G3**
Otis St. E3 114 C3
Otley App., Ilf. 81 E6
Otley Dr., Ilf. 80 E5
Otley Rd. E16 115 J6
Otley Ter. E5 95 G2
Otley Way, Wat. 50 C3
Ottaway St. E5 94 D3
*Stellman Cl.*
Ottenden Cl., Orp. 207 H4
*Southfleet Rd.*
Otter Rd., Grnf. 103 J4
Otterbourne Rd. E4 62 D3
Otterbourne Rd., Croy. 201 J2
Otterburn Gdns., Islw. 124 D7
**Otterburn Ho. SE5 35 J7**
Otterburn Ho. SE5 131 J7
Otterburn St. SW17 167 J6
Otterden St. SE6 172 A4
Otto Cl. SE26 170 E3
**Otto St. SE17 35 G6**
Otto St. SE17 131 H6
Oulton Cl. E5 95 F2
*Mundford Rd.*
Oulton Cl. SE28 118 C6
*Rollesby Way*
Oulton Cres., Bark. 99 J6
Oulton Rd. N15 76 A5
Oulton Way, Wat. 51 E4
Ouseley Rd. SW12 167 J1
**Outer Circle NW1 8 B6**
Outer Circle NW1 110 B2
Outgate Rd. NW10 89 F7
Outram Pl. N1 111 E1
Outram Rd. E6 116 B1
Outram Rd. N22 74 D1
Outram Rd., Croy. 202 C1
**Outwich St. EC3 20 E3**
Oval, The E2 112 E2
Oval, The, Sid. 158 A7
**Oval Pl. SW8 34 C7**
Oval Pl. SW8 131 F7
Oval Rd. NW1 110 B1
Oval Rd., Croy. 202 B1
Oval Rd. N., Dag. 119 H1
Oval Rd. S., Dag. 119 H2
**Oval Way SE11 34 D4**
Oval Way SE11 131 F5
Overbrae, Beck. 172 A6
Overbrook Wk., Edg. 54 A7
Overbury Av., Beck. 190 B3
Overbury Rd. N15 76 A6
Overbury St. E5 95 G4
Overcliff Rd. SE13 154 A3
Overcourt Cl., Sid. 158 B6
Overdale Av., N.Mal. 182 C2
Overdale Rd. W5 125 F3
Overdown Rd. SE6 172 A4
Overhill Rd. SE22 152 D7
Overhill Way, Beck. 190 D5
Overlea Rd. E5 76 D7
Overmead, Sid. 157 G7
Oversley Ho. W2 108 D5
Overstand Cl., Beck. 190 A5
Overstone Gdns., Croy. 189 J7
Overstone Rd. W6 127 J3
Overton Cl. NW10 88 C6
Overton Cl., Islw. 144 C1
*Avenue Rd.*
Overton Ct. E11 79 G7
Overton Dr. E11 79 H7
Overton Dr., Rom. 82 C7
Overton Rd. E10 95 H1
Overton Rd. N14 42 E5
Overton Rd. SE2 138 C3
Overton Rd. SW9 151 G2
Overton Rd., Sutt. 198 D6
Overton Rd. E. SE2 138 D3
Overtons Yd., Croy. 201 J3
Ovesdon Av., Har. 85 F1
Ovett Cl. SE19 170 B6
Ovex Cl. E14 134 C2
**Ovington Gdns. SW3 23 H6**
Ovington Gdns. SW3 129 H3
**Ovington Ms. SW3 23 H6**
Ovington Ms. SW3 129 H3
**Ovington Sq. SW3 23 H6**
Ovington Sq. SW3 129 H3
**Ovington St. SW3 23 H6**
Ovington St. SW3 129 H3
Owen Cl. SE28 138 C1
Owen Cl., Croy. 188 A6
Owen Cl., Hayes 102 B3
Owen Gdns., Wdf.Grn. 64 B6
Owen Rd. N13 59 J5
Owen Rd., Hayes 102 B3
**Owen St. EC1 11 G2**
Owen Wk. SE20 170 D7
*Sycamore Gro.*
Owen Waters Ho., Ilf. 80 C1
Owen Way NW10 88 C6
Owenite St. SE2 138 B4
**Owen's Ct. EC1 11 G3**
**Owen's Row EC1 11 G3**
Owens Way SE23 153 H7
Owgan Cl. SE5 132 A7
*Benhill Rd.*
Owl Pk., Loug. 47 F2
Oxberry Av. SW6 148 B2
**Oxendon St. SW1 17 H6**
Oxendon St. SW1 110 D7
Oxenford St. SE15 152 C3
**Oxenholme NW1 9 G2**
Oxenholme NW1 110 C2
Oxenpark Av., Wem. 69 H7
Oxestalls Rd. SE8 133 H5
Oxford Av. SW20 184 B2
Oxford Av., Hayes 121 J7
Oxford Av., Houns. 123 G5
**Oxford Circ. Av. W1 17 F4**
Oxford Cl. N9 60 E2
Oxford Cl., Mitch. 186 C3
**Oxford Ct. EC4 20 B5**
Oxford Ct. W3 106 A6

Parr Cl. N9 60 E4
Parr Cl. N18 60 E4
Parr Ct., Felt. 160 C4
Parr Rd. E6 116 A1
Parr Rd., Stan. 69 G1
**Parr St. N1 12 B1**
Parr St. N1 112 A2
Parrs Pl., Hmptn. 161 G7
Parry Av. E6 116 C6
Parry Cl., Epsom 197 G7
Parry Pl. SE18 137 E4
Parry Rd. SE25 188 B3
Parry Rd. W10 108 B3
**Parry St. SW8 34 A5**
Parry St. SW8 130 E6
Parsifal Rd. NW6 90 D5
Parsley Gdns., Croy. 203 G1
*Primrose La.*
Parsloes Av., Dag. 100 D4
Parson St. NW4 71 J4
Parsonage Gdns., Enf. 43 J2
Parsonage La., Enf. 44 A2
Parsonage La., Sid. 177 F4
Parsonage Manorway, Belv. 139 G6
Parsonage St. E14 134 C4
Parsons Cres., Edg. 54 A3
Parsons Grn. SW6 148 D1
Parsons Grn. La. SW6 148 D1
Parsons Gro., Edg. 54 A3
Parsons Hill SE18 136 D3
*Powis St.*
**Parson's Ho. W2 7 E6**
Parson's Ho. W2 109 G4
Parson's Mead, Croy. 201 H1
Parsons Mead, E.Mol. 179 J3
Parsons Rd. E13 115 J2
*Old St.*
Parthenia Rd. SW6 148 D1
Partingdale La. NW7 56 A5
Partington Cl. N19 92 D1
Partridge Cl. E16 116 A5
*Fulmer Rd.*
Partridge Cl., Barn. 39 J6
Partridge Cl., Bushey 51 H1
Partridge Cl., Stan. 53 H4
Partridge Ct. EC1 111 H4
*Percival St.*
Partridge Dr., Orp. 207 F3
Partridge Grn. SE9 174 D3
Partridge Rd., Hmptn. 161 F6
Partridge Rd., Sid. 175 H3
Partridge Sq. E6 116 B5
*Nightingale Way*
Partridge Way N22 75 E1
Parvin St. SW8 150 D1
Pasadena Cl., Hayes 122 B2
Pasadena Cl. Trd. Est., Hayes 122 B2
*Pasadena Cl.*
**Pascal St. SW8 33 J7**
Pascal St. SW8 130 D7
Pascoe Rd. SE13 154 D5
**Pasley Cl. SE17 35 J4**
Pasquier Rd. E17 77 H3
Passey Pl. SE9 156 C6
Passfield Dr. E14 114 B5
*Uamvar St.*
Passfield Path SE28 118 B7
*Booth Cl.*
**Passing All. EC1 11 H6**
Passmore Gdns. N11 58 D6
**Passmore St. SW1 32 B2**
Passmore St. SW1 130 A4
Pasteur Cl. NW9 71 E2
Pasteur Gdns. N18 59 H5
Paston Cl. E5 95 G3
*Caldecott Way*
Paston Cl., Wall. 200 C3
Paston Cres. SE12 155 H7
**Pastor St. SE11 35 H1**
Pastor St. SE11 131 H4
Pasture Cl., Wem. 86 E3
Pasture Rd. SE6 173 F1
Pasture Rd., Dag. 101 F4
Pasture Rd., Wem. 86 E2
Pastures, The N20 56 C1
Patcham Ter. SW8 150 B1
Pater St. W8 128 D3
**Paternoster Row EC4 19 J4**
**Paternoster Sq. EC4 19 H3**
Pates Manor Dr., Felt. 141 G7
Path, The SW19 184 E1
Pathfield Rd. SW16 168 D6
Pathway, The, Wat. 50 D1
*Anthony Cl.*
Patience Rd. SW11 149 H2
Patio Cl. SW4 150 D6
Patmore Est. SW8 150 C1
Patmore St. SW8 150 C1
Patmos Rd. SW9 131 H7
Paton Cl. E3 114 A3
**Paton St. EC1 11 J4**
Patricia Ct., Chis. 193 G1
*Manor Pk. Rd.*
Patricia Ct., Well. 138 B7
Patrick Connolly Gdns. E3 114 B3
*Talwin St.*
Patrick Pas. SW11 149 H2
Patrick Rd. E13 115 J3
Patriot Sq. E2 113 E2
Patrol Pl. SE6 154 B6
Patshull Pl. NW5 92 C6
*Patshull Rd.*
Patshull Rd. NW5 92 C6
Patten All., Rich. 145 G5
*The Hermitage*
Patten Rd. SW18 149 H7
Pattenden Rd. SE6 171 J1
Patterdale Cl., Brom. 173 F6
Patterdale Rd. SE15 133 F7
Patterson Ct. SE19 170 C7
Patterson Rd. SE19 170 C6
Pattina Wk. SE16 133 J1
Pattison Pt. E16 115 G5
*Fife Rd.*
Pattison Rd. NW2 90 D3
Pattison Wk. SE18 137 F5
Paul Cl. E15 96/97 E7
*Paul St.*
Paul Gdns., Croy. 202 C2
Paul Julius Cl. E14 114 D7
Paul Robeson Cl. E6 116 D3
*Eastbourne Rd.*
Paul St. E15 114 D1
**Paul St. EC2 12 C6**
Paul St. EC2 112 A4
Paulet Rd. SE5 151 H2
Paulhan Rd., Har. 69 G4
Paulin Dr. N21 43 G7
Pauline Cres., Twick. 161 J1
**Paul's Wk. EC4 19 H5**
Paul's Wk. EC4 111 J7
**Paultons Sq. SW3 31 F5**
Paultons Sq. SW3 129 G6
**Paultons St. SW3 31 F6**
Paultons St. SW3 129 G6
Pauntley St. N19 92 C1
Paved Ct., Rich. 145 G5
Paveley Dr. SW11 129 H7
**Paveley St. NW8 7 H5**
Paveley St. NW8 109 H4
Pavement, The SW4 150 C4
Pavement, The W5 125 H3
*Popes La.*
Pavement Ms., Rom. 82 D7
*Clarissa Rd.*
Pavement Sq., Croy. 202 D1
Pavet Cl., Dag. 101 H6
Pavilion Ms. N3 72 D2
*Windermere Av.*
**Pavilion Rd. SW1 24 A6**
Pavilion Rd. SW1 129 J2
Pavilion Rd., Ilf. 80 C7
**Pavilion St. SW1 24 A6**
Pavilion Ter., E.Mol. 180 C4
Pavilion Ter., Ilf. 81 H5
*Southdown Cres.*
Pavilion Way, Edg. 54 B7
Pavilion Way, Ruis. 84 C2
Pawleyne Cl. SE20 171 F7
Pawsey Cl. E13 115 G1
*Plashet Rd.*
Pawson's Rd., Croy. 187 J6
Paxford Rd., Wem. 86 E2
Paxton Cl., Rich. 145 J2
Paxton Cl., Walt. 178 C7
*Shaw Dr.*
Paxton Pl. SE27 170 B4
Paxton Rd. N17 60 C7
Paxton Rd. SE23 171 H3
Paxton Rd. W4 126 E6
Paxton Rd., Brom. 173 G7
**Paxton Ter. SW1 33 E5**
Paxton Ter. SW1 130 B6
Payne Rd. E3 114 B2
Payne St. SE8 133 J6
Paynell Ct. SE3 154/155 E3
*Lawn Ter.*
Paynes Wk. W6 128 B6
Paynesfield Av. SW14 146 D3
**Peabody Av. SW1 32 D3**
Peabody Cl. SE10 154 B1
*Devonshire Dr.*
Peabody Cl., Croy. 203 F1
*Shirley Rd.*
**Peabody Dws. WC1 10 A5**
**Peabody Est. EC1 12 A6**
Peabody Est. N17 76 B1
**Peabody Est. SE1 27 F2**
Peabody Est. SE24 151 J7
**Peabody Est. SW3 31 H5**
Peabody Est. W6 127 J5
*The Sq.*
Peabody Est. W10 107 J5
Peabody Hill SE21 169 H1
Peabody Hill Est. SE21 151 H7
Peabody Sq. N1 111 H1
*Essex Rd.*
**Peabody Sq. SE1 27 G4**
Peabody Sq. SE1 131 H2
**Peabody Trust SE1 27 J2**
Peabody Trust SE1 131 J1
Peabody Yd. N1 111 J1
*Greenman St.*
Peace Cl. N14 42 B5
Peace Cl. SE25 188 B4
Peace Gro., Wem. 88 B3
Peace St. SE18 136/137 E6
*Nightingale Vale*
Peach Rd. W10 108 A3
Peaches Cl., Sutt. 198 B7
Peachum Rd. SE3 135 F6
**Peacock St. SE17 35 H2**
Peacock Wk. E16 115 H6
**Peacock Yd. SE17 35 H2**
Peak, The SE26 171 F3
Peak Hill SE26 171 F4
Peak Hill Av. SE26 171 F4
Peak Hill Gdns. SE26 171 F4
Peaketon Av., Ilf. 80 A4
Peal Gdns. W13 104 D4
*Ruislip Rd. E.*
Peall Rd., Croy. 187 F6
Pear Cl. NW9 70 D4
Pear Cl. SE14 133 H7
*Southerngate Way*
**Pear Pl. SE1 27 E3**
Pear Rd. E11 96 D3
Pear Tree Cl. E2 112 C1
Pear Tree Cl., Chess. 196 A5
Pear Tree Cl., Mitch. 185 H2
**Pear Tree Ct. EC1 11 F5**
Pear Tree Ct. EC1 111 G4
**Pear Tree St. EC1 11 H5**
Pear Tree St. EC1 111 H4
Pearce Cl., Mitch. 186 A2
Pearce Rd., W.Mol. 179 H3
Pearcefield Av. SE23 171 F1
Pearcroft Rd. E11 96 D2
Peardon St. SW8 150 B2
Peareswood Gdns., Stan. 69 G1
Pearfield Rd. SE23 171 H3
Pearl Cl. E6 116 D6
Pearl Cl. NW2 72 A7
*Marble Dr.*
Pearl Rd. E17 78 A3
Pearl St. E1 132/133 E1
*Penang St.*
**Pearman St. SE1 27 F5**
Pearman St. SE1 131 G2
Pears Rd., Houns. 143 J3
Pearscroft Ct. SW6 149 E1
Pearscroft Rd. SW6 149 E1
**Pearse St. SE15 36 E6**
Pearson Ms. SW4 150 D3
*Edgeley Rd.*
**Pearson St. E2 13 E1**
Pearson St. E2 112 C2
Pearsons Av. SE14 154 A1
*Tanners Hill*
Peartree Av. SW17 167 F3
Peartree Gdns., Dag. 100 B4
Peartree Gdns., Rom. 83 H2
Peartree La. E1 113 F7
*Glamis Rd.*
Peartree Rd., Enf. 44 B3
Peartree Way SE10 135 G4
Peary Pl. E2 113 F3
*Kirkwall Pl.*
Peatfield Cl., Sid. 175 H3
*Woodside Rd.*
Pebble Way W3 126 B1
Pebworth Rd., Har. 86 D2
Peckarmans Wd. SE26 170 D3
Peckett Sq. N5 93 J4
*Highbury Gra.*
Peckford Pl. SW9 151 G2
**Peckham Gro. SE15 36 E7**
Peckham Gro. SE15 132 B7
Peckham High St. SE15 152 D1
**Peckham Hill St. SE15 37 H7**
Peckham Hill St. SE15 132 D7
**Peckham Pk. Rd. SE15 37 J7**
Peckham Pk. Rd. SE15 132 D7
Peckham Rd. SE5 152 B1
Peckham Rd. SE15 152 B1
Peckham Rye SE15 152 D3
Peckham Rye SE22 152 D4
**Pecks Yd. E1 21 F1**
Peckwater St. NW5 92 C5
Pedlars Wk. N7 93 E6
Pedley Rd., Dag. 100 C1
**Pedley St. E1 13 G6**
Pedley St. E1 112 C4
Pedro St. E5 95 G3
Pedworth Gdns. SE16 133 F4
*Rotherhithe New Rd.*
Peek Cres. SW19 166 A5
Peel Cl. E4 62 B2
Peel Cl. N9 60 D3
*Plevna Rd.*
Peel Dr. NW9 71 F3
Peel Dr., Ilf. 80 B3
Peel Gro. E2 113 F2
Peel Pas. W8 128 D1
*Peel St.*
Peel Pl., Ilf. 80 B2
Peel Prec. NW6 108 D2
Peel Rd. E18 79 F1
Peel Rd. NW6 108 C3
Peel Rd., Har. 68 C3
Peel Rd., Orp. 207 F5
Peel Rd., Wem. 87 G3
Peel St. W8 128 D1
**Peerless St. EC1 12 B4**
Peerless St. EC1 112 A3
Pegamoid Rd. N18 61 F3
Pegasus Cl. N16 94 A4
*Green Las.*
**Pegasus Pl. SE11 35 E5**
Pegasus Way N11 58 B6
Pegg Rd., Houns. 122 D7
Pegley Gdns. SE12 173 G2
Pegwell St. SE18 137 H7
Pekin Cl. E14 114 A6
*Pekin St.*
Pekin St. E14 114 A6
Peldon Ct., Rich. 145 J4
Peldon Pas., Rich. 145 J4
*Worple Way*
Peldon Wk. N1 111 H1
*Britannia Row*
Pelham Av., Bark. 117 J1
Pelham Cl. SE5 152 B2
**Pelham Cres. SW7 31 G2**
Pelham Cres. SW7 129 H4
**Pelham Pl. SW7 31 G2**
Pelham Pl. SW7 129 H4
Pelham Rd. E18 79 H3
Pelham Rd. N15 76 C4
Pelham Rd. N22 75 G2
Pelham Rd. SW19 166 D7
Pelham Rd., Beck. 189 F2
Pelham Rd., Bexh. 159 G3
Pelham Rd., Ilf. 99 G2
**Pelham St. SW7 31 F1**
Pelham St. SW7 129 H4
Pelican Est. SE15 152 C1
Pelican Pas. E1 113 F4
*Cambridge Heath Rd.*
Pelican Wk. SW9 151 H4
*Loughborough Pk.*
**Pelier St. SE17 36 A5**
Pelinore Rd. SE6 172 E2
Pellant Rd. SW6 128 B7
Pellatt Gro. N22 75 G1
Pellatt Rd. SE22 152 C5
Pellatt Rd., Wem. 87 G2
Pellerin Rd. N16 94 B5
Pelling St. E14 114 A6
Pellipar Cl. N13 59 G3
Pellipar Gdns. SE18 136 C5
Pelly Rd. E13 115 G2
**Pelter St. E2 13 F3**
Pelter St. E2 112 C3
Pelton Rd. SE10 134 E5
Pembar Av. E17 77 H3
Pember Rd. NW10 108 A3
Pemberley Chase (West Ewell), Epsom 196 B5
Pemberley Cl. (West Ewell), Epsom 196 B5
*Ruxley Cl.*
Pemberton Gdns. N19 92 C3
Pemberton Gdns., Rom. 82 E5
Pemberton Ho. SE26 170 D4
*High Level Dr.*
Pemberton Pl. E8 94/95 E7
*Mare St.*
Pemberton Rd. N4 75 G5
Pemberton Rd., E.Mol. 179 J4
**Pemberton Row EC4 19 F3**
Pemberton Ter. N19 92 C3
Pembridge Av., Twick. 161 F1
Pembridge Cres. W11 108 D7
Pembridge Gdns. W2 108 D7
Pembridge Ms. W11 108 D7
Pembridge Pl. SW15 148 D5
*Oakhill Rd.*
Pembridge Pl. W2 108 D7

Ronart St., Har. 68 C3
*Stuart Rd.*
Rondu Rd. NW2 90 B5
Ronelean Rd., Surb. 195 J3
Ronver Rd. SE12 155 F7
**Rood La. EC3** 20 D5
Rood La. EC3 112 B7
Rook Wk. E6 116 B6
*Allhallows Rd.*
Rookby St. N21 59 H2
*Carpenter Gdns.*
Rooke Way SE10 135 F5
Rookeries Cl., Felt. 160 B3
Rookery Cl. NW9 71 F5
Rookery Cres., Dag. 101 H7
Rookery Dr., Chis. 192 D1
Rookery La., Brom. 192 A6
Rookery Rd. SW4 150 C4
Rookery Way NW9 71 F5
Rookfield Av. N10 74 C4
Rookfield Cl. N10 74 C4
*Cranmore Way*
Rookstone Rd. SW17 167 J5
Rookwood Av., Loug. 49 F3
Rookwood Av., 183 G4
N.Mal.
Rookwood Av., Wall. 200 D4
Rookwood Gdns. E4 63 F1
*Whitehall Rd.*
Rookwood Gdns., 49 F3
Loug.
Rookwood Ho., Bark. 117 G2
*St. Marys*
Rookwood Rd. N16 76 C7
Rootes Dr. W10 108 A4
Rope St. SE16 133 H4
Rope Wk., Sun. 178 C3
**Rope Wk. Gdns. E1** 21 J4
Rope Yd. Rails SE18 136 E3
Ropemaker Rd. SE16 133 H3
**Ropemaker St. EC2** 20 B1
Ropemaker St. EC2 112 A5
Ropemakers Flds. E14 113 J7
*Narrow St.*
**Roper La. SE1** 29 E4
Roper St. SE9 156 C6
Roper Way, Mitch. 186 A2
Ropers Av. E4 62 C5
Ropers Wk. SW2 151 G7
*Brockwell Pk. Gdns.*
Ropery St. E3 113 J4
**Ropley St. E2** 13 H2
Ropley St. E2 112 D2
Rosa Alba Ms. N5 93 J4
*Kelross Rd.*
Rosaline Rd. SW6 128 B7
Rosamond St. SE26 170 E3
Rosamun St., Sthl. 123 E4
Rosamund Cl., 202 A4
S.Croy.
*Rosary Cl., Houns.* 142 E2
**Rosary Gdns. SW7** 30 C2
Rosary Gdns. SW7 129 F4
Rosaville Rd. SW6 128 C7
**Roscoe St. EC1** 12 A6
Roscoff Cl., Edg. 70 C1
**Rose All. SE1** 28 A1
Rose All. SE1 131 J1
**Rose & Crown Ct.** 19 J3
EC2
**Rose & Crown Yd.** 25 G1
SW1
Rose Av. E18 79 H2
Rose Av., Mitch. 185 J1
Rose Av., Mord. 185 F5
Rose Bates Dr. NW9 70 A4
Rose Ct. E1 112 B5
*Sandy's Row*
Rose Ct. SE26 170 E2
Rose Ct., Pnr. 66 C3
*Nursery Rd.*
Rose Dale, Orp. 207 E3
Rose End, Wor.Pk. 198 A1
Rose Gdn. Cl., Edg. 53 H6
Rose Gdns. W5 125 G3
Rose Gdns., Felt. 160 A2
Rose Gdns., Sthl. 103 G4
Rose Gdns., Stai. 140 A7
*Diamedes Av.*
Rose Glen NW9 70 D4
Rose Hill, Sutt. 199 E2
Rose La., Rom. 82 D3
Rose Lawn, Bushey 51 J1
**Rose Sq. SW3** 31 F3
Rose Sq. SW3 129 G5
**Rose St. WC2** 18 A5
Rose Wk., Surb. 182 B5
Rose Wk., W.Wick. 204 D2
Rose Way SE12 155 G5
Rose Way, Edg. 54 C4
*Stoneyfields La.*
Roseacre Cl. W13 104/105 E5
*Middlefielde*
Roseacre Rd., Well. 158 B3

Roseary Cl., West Dr. 120 A4
Rosebank SE20 170 E7
Rosebank Av., Wem. 86 C4
Rosebank Cl. N12 57 H5
Rosebank Cl., Tedd. 162 D6
Rosebank Gdns. E3 113 J2
Rosebank Gro. E17 77 J3
Rosebank Rd. E17 78 B6
Rosebank Rd. W7 124 B2
Rosebank Vil. E17 78 A4
Rosebank Wk. NW1 92 D7
*Maiden La.*
Rosebank Wk. SE18 136 B4
*Woodhill*
Rosebank Way W3 106 D6
Roseberry Gdns. N4 75 H6
Roseberry Gdns., 207 H3
Orp.
Roseberry Pl. E8 94 C6
Roseberry St. SE16 132 E4
Roseberry Av. E12 98 B6
**Rosebery Av. EC1** 10 E6
Rosebery Av. EC1 111 G4
Rosebery Av. N17 76 D2
Rosebery Av., Har. 85 F4
Rosebery Av., N.Mal. 183 F2
Rosebery Av., Sid. 157 H7
Rosebery Av., 187 J2
Th.Hth.
Rosebery Cl., Mord. 184 A6
Rosebery Ct. EC1 111 G4
*Rosebery Av.*
Rosebery Gdns. N8 74 E5
Rosebery Gdns. W13 104 D6
Rosebery Gdns., Sutt. 199 E4
Rosebery Ms. N10 74 C2
Rosebery Ms. 150/151 E6
SW2
*Rosebery Rd.*
Rosebery Rd. N9 60 D3
Rosebery Rd. N10 74 C2
Rosebery Rd. SW2 150 E6
Rosebery Rd., Houns. 143 J5
Rosebery Rd., 182 B2
Kings.T.
Rosebery Rd., Sutt. 198 C6
**Rosebery Sq. EC1** 10 E6
Rosebery Sq., 182 A2
Kings.T.
Rosebine Av., 144 A7
Twick.
Rosebury Rd. SW6 149 E2
Rosecourt Rd., Croy. 187 F6
Rosecroft Av. NW3 90 D3
Rosecroft Gdns. NW2 89 G3
Rosecroft Gdns., 162 A1
Twick.
Rosecroft Rd., Sthl. 103 G4
Rosecroft Wk., Pnr. 66 D5
Rosecroft Wk., Wem. 87 G5
Rosedale Cl. SE2 138 B3
*Finchale Rd.*
Rosedale Cl. W7 124 C2
*Boston Rd.*
Rosedale Cl., Stan. 53 E6
Rosedale Cl. N5 93 H4
Rosedale Gdns., Dag. 100 B7
Rosedale Rd. E7 97 J5
Rosedale Rd., Dag. 100 B7
Rosedale Rd., Epsom 197 G5
Rosedale Rd., Rich. 145 H4
Rosedale Ter. W6 127 H3
*Dalling Rd.*
Rosedene NW6 108 A1
*Christchurch Av.*
Rosedene Av. SW16 169 F3
Rosedene Av., Croy. 187 F7
Rosedene Av., Grnf. 103 G3
Rosedene Av., Mord. 184 D5
Rosedene Gdns., Ilf. 80 D4
Rosedene Ter. E10 96 B2
Rosedew Rd. W6 128 A6
Rosefield Cl., Cars. 199 H5
*Alma Rd.*
Rosefield Gdns. E14 114 A7
Roseford Ct. W12 128 A2
Rosehart Ms. W11 108 D6
*Westbourne Gro.*
Rosehatch Av., Rom. 82 D3
Roseheath Rd., 143 F5
Houns.
Rosehill, Esher 194 D6
Rosehill, Hmptn. 179 G1
Rosehill Av., Sutt. 199 F1
Rosehill Gdns., Grnf. 86 C5
Rosehill Gdns., Sutt. 199 E2
Rosehill Pk. W., Sutt. 199 F1
Rosehill Rd. SW18 149 F6
Roseland Cl. N17 60 A7
*Cavell Rd.*
Roseleigh Av. N5 93 H4
Roseleigh Cl., Twick. 145 G6
Rosemary Av. N3 73 E2

Rosemary Av. N9 60 E1
Rosemary Av., Enf. 44 A1
Rosemary Av., Houns. 142 D2
Rosemary Av., W.Mol. 179 G3
Rosemary Cl., Croy. 186 E6
Rosemary Dr. E14 114 D6
Rosemary Dr., Ilf. 80 A5
Rosemary Gdns. 146 C3
SW14
*Rosemary La.*
Rosemary Gdns., 195 H4
Chess.
Rosemary Gdns., Dag. 101 F1
Rosemary La. SW14 146 C3
**Rosemary Rd. SE15** 37 G7
Rosemary Rd. SE15 132 C7
Rosemary Rd. SW17 167 F3
Rosemary Rd., Well. 157 J1
Rosemary St. N1 112 A1
*Shepperton Rd.*
Rosemead NW9 71 F7
Rosemead Av., Mitch. 186 C2
Rosemead Av., Wem. 87 H5
Rosemont Av. N12 57 F6
Rosemont Rd. NW3 91 F6
Rosemont Rd. W3 106 B7
Rosemont Rd., N.Mal. 182 C3
Rosemont Rd., Rich. 145 H6
Rosemont Rd., Wem. 105 H1
**Rosemoor St. SW3** 31 J2
Rosemoor St. SW3 129 J4
Rosemount Cl., 64 C6
Wdf.Grn.
*Chapelmount Rd.*
Rosemount Dr., 192 C4
Brom.
Rosemount Rd. W13 104 D6
Rosenau Cres. SW11 149 H1
Rosenau Rd. SW11 149 H1
Rosendale Rd. SE21 151 J7
Rosendale Rd. SE24 151 J7
Roseneath Av. N21 59 H1
Roseneath Rd. SW11 150 A6
Roseneath Wk., Enf. 44 B4
Roseness Wk., Edg. 54 B3
Rosenthal Rd. SE6 154 B6
Rosenthorpe Rd. 153 G5
SE15
Roserton St. E14 134 C2
Rosery, The, Croy. 189 G6
Roses, The, Wdf.Grn. 63 F7
Rosethorn Cl. SW12 150 C7
Rosetta Cl. SW8 131 E7
Rosetti Ter., Dag. 100 B4
*Marlborough Rd.*
Roseveare Rd. SE12 173 J4
Roseville Av., Houns. 143 G5
Roseville Rd., Hayes 122 A5
Rosevine Rd. SW20 183 J1
Roseway SE21 152 A6
Rosewell Cl. SE20 170 E7
Rosewood, Esher 194 D2
Rosewood Av., Grnf. 86 D5
Rosewood Cl., Sid. 176 C3
Rosewood Ct., Brom. 191 J1
Rosewood Ct., Rom. 82 C5
Rosewood Gdns. 154 C2
SE13
*Lewisham Rd.*
Rosewood Gro., Sutt. 199 F2
Rosewood Sq. W12 107 G6
*Primula St.*
Rosewood Ter. SE20 171 F7
*Laurel Gro.*
Rosher Cl. E15 96 D7
Rosina St. E9 95 G5
Roskell Rd. SW15 148 A3
Roslin Rd. W3 126 B3
Roslin Way, Brom. 173 G5
Roslyn Cl., Mitch. 185 G2
Roslyn Rd. N15 76 A5
Rosmead Rd. W11 108 B7
**Rosoman Pl. EC1** 11 F4
Rosoman St. EC1 111 G3
Ross Av. NW7 56 B5
Ross Av., Dag. 101 F2
Ross Cl., Har. 51 J7
Ross Cl., Hayes 121 G4
Ross Ct. SW15 148 A7
Ross Par., Wall. 200 B6
Ross Rd. SE25 188 A3
Ross Rd., Twick. 161 H1
Ross Rd., Wall. 200 C5
Ross Way SE9 156 B3
Rossall Cres. NW10 105 J3
Rossdale, Sutt. 199 H5
Rossdale Dr. N9 45 F6
Rossdale Dr. NW9 88 C1
Rossdale Rd. SW15 147 J4
Rosse Ms. SE3 155 H1
Rossendale St. E5 94 E2
Rossendale Way NW1 92 C7

Rossetti Rd. SE16 132 E5
Rossignol Gdns., 200 A2
Cars.
Rossindel Rd., Houns. 143 G5
Rossington St. E5 94 D2
Rossiter Flds., Barn. 40 B6
Rossiter Rd. SW12 168 B1
Rossland Cl., Bexh. 159 H5
Rosslyn Av. E4 63 F2
Rosslyn Av. SW13 147 E3
Rosslyn Av., Barn. 41 H6
Rosslyn Av., Dag. 83 F7
Rosslyn Av., Felt. 142 A6
Rosslyn Cl., W.Wick. 205 F3
Rosslyn Cres., Har. 68 C5
Rosslyn Cres., Wem. 87 H4
Rosslyn Gdns., Wem. 87 H3
*Rosslyn Cres.*
Rosslyn Hill NW3 91 G4
Rosslyn Ms. NW3 91 G4
*Rosslyn Hill*
Rosslyn Pk. Ms. NW3 91 G5
*Lyndhurst Rd.*
Rosslyn Rd. E17 78 C4
Rosslyn Rd., Bark. 99 G7
Rosslyn Rd., Twick. 145 F6
**Rossmore Rd. NW1** 7 H6
Rossmore Rd. NW1 109 H4
Rosswood Gdns., 200 C6
Wall.
Rostella Rd. SW17 167 G4
Rostrevor Av. N15 76 C6
Rostrevor Gdns., 121 H1
Hayes
Rostrevor Gdns., 123 E5
Sthl.
Rostrevor Ms. SW6 148 C1
Rostrevor Rd. SW6 148 C1
Rostrevor Rd. SW19 166 D5
**Rotary St. SE1** 27 G5
Roth Wk. N7 93 F3
*Durham Rd.*
Rothbury Gdns., Islw. 124 D7
Rothbury Rd. E9 95 J7
Rothbury Wk. N17 60 D7
Rotherfield Rd., Cars. 200 A4
Rotherfield St. N1 93 J7
**Rotherham Wk. SE1** 27 G2
**Rotherhithe New Rd.** 37 J4
SE16
Rotherhithe New Rd. 132 D5
SE16
Rotherhithe Old Rd. 133 G4
SE16
Rotherhithe St. SE16 133 F2
Rotherhithe Tunnel E1 133 F1
Rotherhithe Tunnel 133 F2
App. E14
Rotherhithe Tunnel 133 F2
App. SE16
Rothermere Rd., 201 F5
Croy.
Rotherwick Hill W5 105 J4
Rotherwick Rd. NW11 72 D7
Rotherwood Cl. 184 B1
SW20
Rotherwood Rd. 148 A3
SW15
Rothery St. N1 111 H1
*Gaskin St.*
Rothery Ter. SW9 131 H7
Rothesay Av. SW20 184 B2
Rothesay Av., Grnf. 86 A6
Rothesay Av., Rich. 146 B4
Rothesay Rd. SE25 188 B4
Rothesay Rd. E7 97 J6
**Rothsay Rd. SE1** 28 D5
Rothsay St. SE1 132 B3
Rothsay Wk. E14 134 A4
*Charnwood Gdns.*
Rothschild Rd. W4 126 C4
Rothschild St. SE27 169 H4
Rothwell Gdns., Dag. 100 C7
Rothwell Rd., Dag. 118 C1
Rothwell St. NW1 109 J1
**Rotten Row SW1** 24 B3
Rotten Row SW1 129 J2
**Rotten Row SW7** 23 G3
Rotten Row SW7 129 H2
Rotterdam Dr. E14 134 C3
**Rouel Rd. SE16** 29 H6
Rouel Rd. SE16 132 D3
Rougemont Av., 184 D6
Mord.
Round Gro., Croy. 189 G7
Round Hill SE26 171 F2
Roundacre SW19 166 A2
*Inner Pk. Rd.*
Roundaway Rd., Ilf. 80 C2
Roundel Cl. SE4 153 J4
*Adelaide Av.*
Roundhay Cl. SE23 171 G2
Roundhill Dr., Enf. 43 F4

| Entry | Page | Grid |
|---|---|---|
| St. Alphage | 112 | A5 |
| Highwalk EC2 | | |
| *London Wall* | | |
| St. Alphage Wk., Edg. | 70 | C2 |
| St. Alphege Rd. N9 | 45 | F7 |
| St. Alphonsus Rd. | 150 | C4 |
| SW4 | | |
| St. Amunds Cl. SE6 | 172 | A4 |
| **St. Andrew St. EC4** | **19** | **F2** |
| St. Andrew St. EC4 | 111 | G5 |
| St. Andrews Av. | 86 | D4 |
| Wem. | | |
| St. Andrew's Cl. N12 | 57 | F4 |
| *Woodside Av.* | | |
| St. Andrews Cl. NW2 | 89 | H3 |
| St. Andrews Cl. | 132/133 | E5 |
| SE16 | | |
| *Ryder Dr.* | | |
| St. Andrew's Cl., Islw. | 144 | A1 |
| St. Andrews Cl., Ruis. | 84 | D2 |
| St. Andrews Cl., Stan. | 69 | F2 |
| St. Andrew's Ct. | 167 | F2 |
| SW18 | | |
| *Waynflete St.* | | |
| St. Andrews Dr., | 69 | F1 |
| Stan. | | |
| St. Andrew's Gro. | 94 | A1 |
| N16 | | |
| **St. Andrew's Hill EC4** | **19** | **H5** |
| St. Andrew's Hill EC4 | 111 | H7 |
| St. Andrew's Ms. N16 | 94 | B1 |
| St. Andrews Ms. SE3 | 135 | G7 |
| *Mycenae Rd.* | | |
| **St. Andrews Pl. NW1** | **8** | **E5** |
| St. Andrews Pl. NW1 | 110 | B4 |
| St. Andrews Rd. E11 | 78 | E6 |
| St. Andrews Rd. E13 | 115 | H3 |
| St. Andrews Rd. E17 | 77 | G2 |
| St. Andrews Rd. N9 | 45 | F7 |
| St. Andrews Rd. NW9 | 88 | D1 |
| St. Andrews Rd. | 89 | H6 |
| NW10 | | |
| St. Andrews Rd. | 72 | C6 |
| NW11 | | |
| St. Andrews Rd. W3 | 107 | E7 |
| St. Andrews Rd. W7 | 124 | B2 |
| *Church Rd.* | | |
| St. Andrews Rd. | 128 | B6 |
| W14 | | |
| St. Andrews Rd., | 199 | H3 |
| Cars. | | |
| St. Andrews Rd., | 201 | J4 |
| Croy. | | |
| *Lower Coombe St.* | | |
| St. Andrews Rd., Enf. | 44 | A3 |
| St. Andrews Rd., Ilf. | 80 | C7 |
| St. Andrews Rd., Sid. | 176 | D3 |
| St. Andrew's Rd., | 181 | G6 |
| Surb. | | |
| *St. Marks Rd.* | | |
| St. Andrews Sq. W11 | 108 | B6 |
| St. Andrew's Sq., | 181 | G6 |
| Surb. | | |
| St. Andrews Twr., | 103 | J7 |
| Sthl. | | |
| St. Andrews Way E3 | 114 | B4 |
| St. Anna Rd., Barn. | 40 | A5 |
| *Sampson Av.* | | |
| St. Anne St. E14 | 113 | J6 |
| *Commercial Rd.* | | |
| St. Annes Av., Stai. | 140 | A7 |
| St. Anne's Cl. N6 | 92 | A3 |
| *Highgate W. Hill* | | |
| St. Anne's Cl., Wat. | 50 | C4 |
| **St. Anne's Ct. W1** | **17** | **H4** |
| St. Annes Gdns. | 105 | J3 |
| NW10 | | |
| St. Annes Pas. E14 | 113 | J6 |
| *Newell St.* | | |
| St. Anne's Rd. E11 | 96 | D2 |
| St. Anne's Rd., Wem. | 87 | G5 |
| St. Anne's Row E14 | 113 | J6 |
| *Commercial Rd.* | | |
| St. Ann's, Bark. | 117 | F1 |
| St. Ann's Cres. SW18 | 149 | F6 |
| St. Ann's Gdns. NW5 | 92 | A6 |
| *Queens Cres.* | | |
| St. Ann's Hill SW18 | 149 | E5 |
| **St. Ann's La. SW1** | **25** | **J5** |
| St. Ann's Pk. Rd. | 149 | F6 |
| SW18 | | |
| St. Ann's Pas. SW13 | 147 | E3 |
| St. Anns Rd. N9 | 60 | C2 |
| St. Ann's Rd. N15 | 75 | H5 |
| St. Ann's Rd SW13 | 147 | F2 |
| St. Anns Rd. W11 | 108 | A7 |
| St. Ann's Rd., Bark. | 117 | F1 |
| *Axe St.* | | |
| St. Ann's Rd., Har. | 68 | B6 |
| **St. Ann's St. SW1** | **25** | **J5** |
| **St. Ann's Ter. NW8** | **7** | **F1** |
| St. Ann's Ter. NW8 | 109 | G2 |
| St. Anns Vil. W11 | 128 | A1 |
| St. Anns Way, | 201 | H6 |
| S.Croy. | | |
| **St. Anselm's Pl. W1** | **16** | **D4** |
| St. Anselms Rd., | 121 | J2 |
| Hayes | | |
| St. Anthonys Av., | 63 | J6 |
| Wdf.Grn. | | |
| **St. Anthonys Cl. E1** | **29** | **H1** |
| St. Anthonys Cl. E1 | 132 | D1 |
| St. Anthonys Cl. | 167 | H2 |
| SW17 | | |
| *College Gdns.* | | |
| St. Anthony's Way, | 141 | J4 |
| Felt. | | |
| St. Antony's Rd. E7 | 97 | H7 |
| St. Arvans Cl., Croy. | 202 | B3 |
| St. Asaph Rd. SE4 | 153 | G3 |
| St. Aubyn's Av. | 166 | C5 |
| SW19 | | |
| St. Aubyns Av., | 143 | G5 |
| Houns. | | |
| St. Aubyns Cl., Orp. | 207 | J3 |
| St. Aubns Gdns., | 207 | J2 |
| Orp. | | |
| St. Aubyn's Rd. | 170 | C6 |
| SE19 | | |
| St. Audrey Av., Bexh. | 159 | G2 |
| St. Augustine's Av. | 105 | H2 |
| W5 | | |
| St. Augustines Av., | 192 | B5 |
| Brom. | | |
| St. Augustine's Av., | 201 | J6 |
| S.Croy. | | |
| St. Augustines Av., | 87 | H3 |
| Wem. | | |
| St. Augustine's Path | 93 | H5 |
| N5 | | |
| St. Augustines Rd. | 92 | D7 |
| NW1 | | |
| St. Augustine's Rd., | 139 | F4 |
| Belv. | | |
| St. Austell Cl., Edg. | 69 | J2 |
| St. Austell Rd. SE13 | 154 | C2 |
| St. Awdry's Rd., Bark. | 99 | G7 |
| St. Awdry's Wk., Bark. | 99 | F7 |
| *Station Par.* | | |
| St. Barnabas Cl. | 152 | B5 |
| SE22 | | |
| *East Dulwich Gro.* | | |
| St. Barnabas Cl., | 190 | C2 |
| Beck. | | |
| St. Barnabas Ct., Har. | 67 | J1 |
| St. Barnabas Gdns., | 179 | G5 |
| W.Mol. | | |
| St. Barnabas Rd. E17 | 78 | A6 |
| St. Barnabas Rd., | 168 | A7 |
| Mitch. | | |
| St. Barnabas Rd., | 199 | G5 |
| Sutt. | | |
| St. Barnabas Rd., | 79 | H1 |
| Wdf.Grn. | | |
| **St. Barnabas St. SW1** | **32** | **C3** |
| St. Barnabas St. SW1 | 130 | A5 |
| St. Barnabas Ter. E9 | 95 | G5 |
| St. Barnabas Vil. SW8 | 151 | E1 |
| St. Bartholomews Cl. | 171 | F4 |
| SE26 | | |
| St. Bartholomew's Rd. | 116 | B1 |
| E6 | | |
| St. Benedict's Cl. | 168 | A5 |
| SW17 | | |
| *Church La.* | | |
| St. Benet's Cl. SW17 | 167 | H2 |
| *College Gdns.* | | |
| St. Benet's Gro. | 185 | F7 |
| Cars. | | |
| **St. Benet's Pl. EC3** | **20** | **C5** |
| St. Bernards, Croy. | 202 | B3 |
| St. Bernard's Cl. | 170 | A4 |
| SE27 | | |
| *St. Gothard Rd.* | | |
| St. Bernard's Rd. E6 | 116 | A1 |
| St. Blaise Av., Brom. | 191 | H2 |
| **St. Botolph Row EC3** | **21** | **F4** |
| **St. Botolph St. EC3** | **21** | **F4** |
| St. Botolph St. EC3 | 112 | C6 |
| **St. Bride St. EC4** | **19** | **G3** |
| St. Bride St. EC4 | 111 | H6 |
| St. Bride's Av. EC4 | 111 | H6 |
| *New Br. St.* | | |
| St. Brides Av., Edg. | 69 | J1 |
| St. Brides Cl., Erith | 138 | D2 |
| *St. Katherines Rd.* | | |
| **St. Bride's Pas. EC4** | **19** | **G4** |
| St. Catherines Cl. | 167 | H2 |
| SW17 | | |
| *College Gdns.* | | |
| St. Catherines Dr. | 153 | G2 |
| SE14 | | |
| *Kitto Rd.* | | |
| **St. Catherine's Ms.** | **31** | **J1** |
| **SW3** | | |
| St. Catherines Rd. E4 | 62 | A2 |
| St. Chads Cl., Surb. | 181 | F7 |
| St. Chad's Gdns., | 82 | E7 |
| Rom. | | |
| **St. Chad's Pl. WC1** | **10** | **B3** |
| St. Chad's Pl. WC1 | 111 | E3 |
| St. Chad's Rd., Rom. | 82 | E6 |
| **St. Chad's Rd. WC1** | **10** | **B3** |
| St. Chad's St. WC1 | 111 | E3 |
| St. Charles Pl. W10 | 108 | B5 |
| *Chesterton Rd.* | | |
| St. Charles Sq. W10 | 108 | A5 |
| St. Christopher's Cl. | 144 | B1 |
| Islw. | | |
| St. Christopher's Dr., | 102 | B7 |
| Hayes | | |
| St. Christophers | 187 | G3 |
| Gdns., Th.Hth. | | |
| St. Christophers Ms., | 200 | C5 |
| Wall. | | |
| St. Clements Hts. | 170 | D3 |
| SE26 | | |
| **St. Clement's La. WC2** | **18** | **D4** |
| St. Clements St. N7 | 93 | G6 |
| St. Cloud Rd. SE27 | 169 | J4 |
| St. Crispins Cl. NW3 | 91 | H4 |
| St. Crispins Cl., Sthl. | 103 | F6 |
| **St. Cross St. EC1** | **19** | **F1** |
| St. Cross St. EC1 | 111 | G5 |
| St. Cuthberts Gdns., | 51 | F7 |
| Pnr. | | |
| *Westfield Pk.* | | |
| St. Cuthberts Rd. N13 | 59 | G6 |
| St. Cuthberts Rd. | 90 | C6 |
| NW2 | | |
| St. Cyprian's St. | 167 | J4 |
| SW17 | | |
| St. Davids Cl. | 132/133 | E5 |
| SE16 | | |
| *Masters Dr.* | | |
| St. Davids Cl., Wem. | 88 | C3 |
| St. David's Cl., | 190 | B7 |
| W.Wick. | | |
| St. David's Cl. E17 | 78 | C3 |
| St. Davids Dr., Edg. | 69 | J1 |
| St. Davids Pl. NW4 | 71 | H7 |
| St. Davids Sq. E14 | 134 | B5 |
| St. Denis Rd. SE27 | 170 | A4 |
| St. Dionis Rd. SW6 | 148 | C2 |
| St. Donatts Rd. SE14 | 153 | J1 |
| **St. Dunstan's All. EC3** | **20** | **D5** |
| St. Dunstans Av. W3 | 106 | D7 |
| St. Dunstans Cl., | 121 | J4 |
| Hayes | | |
| St. Dunstan's Ct. EC4 | 111 | G6 |
| *Fleet St.* | | |
| St. Dunstans Gdns. | 106 | D7 |
| W3 | | |
| *St. Dunstans Av.* | | |
| **St. Dunstan's Hill EC3** | **20** | **D6** |
| St. Dunstan's Hill EC3 | 112 | B7 |
| St. Dunstan's Hill, | 198 | B5 |
| Sutt. | | |
| **St. Dunstan's La. EC3** | **20** | **D6** |
| St. Dunstan's La., | 190 | C6 |
| Beck. | | |
| St. Dunstans Rd. E7 | 97 | J6 |
| St. Dunstans Rd. | 188 | C4 |
| SE25 | | |
| St. Dunstans Rd. W6 | 128 | A5 |
| St. Dunstans Rd. W7 | 124 | B2 |
| St. Dunstans Rd., | 142 | C2 |
| Houns. | | |
| St. Edmunds Cl. NW8 | 109 | J1 |
| *St. Edmunds Ter.* | | |
| St. Edmunds Cl. | 167 | H2 |
| SW17 | | |
| *College Gdns.* | | |
| St. Edmunds Cl., | 138 | D2 |
| Erith | | |
| *St. Katherines Rd.* | | |
| St. Edmunds Dr., Stan. | 68 | D1 |
| St. Edmund's La., | 143 | H7 |
| Twick. | | |
| St. Edmunds Rd. N9 | 44 | D7 |
| St. Edmunds Rd., Ilf. | 80 | C6 |
| St. Edmunds Sq. | 127 | J6 |
| SW13 | | |
| **St. Edmunds Ter.** | **7** | **H1** |
| **NW8** | | |
| St. Edmunds Ter. | 109 | H1 |
| NW8 | | |
| St. Edwards Cl. | 72 | D6 |
| NW11 | | |
| St. Egberts Way F4 | 62 | C1 |
| St. Elmo Rd. W12 | 127 | F1 |
| St. Elmos Rd. SE16 | 133 | H2 |
| St. Erkenwald Ms. | 117 | G1 |
| Bark. | | |
| *St. Erkenwald Rd.* | | |
| St. Erkenwald Rd. | 117 | G1 |
| Bark. | | |
| **St. Ermin's Hill SW1** | **25** | **H5** |
| St. Ervans Rd. W10 | 108 | B5 |
| St. Fabian Twr. E4 | 61 | J6 |
| *Iris Way* | | |
| St. Faiths Cl., Enf. | 43 | J1 |
| St. Faith's Rd. SE21 | 169 | H1 |
| St. Fillans Rd. SE6 | 172 | C1 |
| St. Francis Cl., Orp. | 193 | H6 |
| St. Francis Cl., Wat. | 50 | B1 |
| St. Francis Rd. SE22 | 152 | B4 |
| St. Francis Twr. E4 | 61 | J6 |
| *Iris Way* | | |
| St. Francis Way, Ilf. | 99 | H4 |
| St. Frideswides Ms. | 114 | C6 |
| E14 | | |
| *Lodore St.* | | |
| St. Gabriel's Cl. E11 | 97 | H1 |
| St. Gabriels Rd. NW2 | 90 | A5 |
| **St. George St. W1** | **17** | **E4** |
| St. George St. W1 | 110 | B6 |
| St. Georges Av. E7 | 97 | H7 |
| St. Georges Av. N7 | 92 | D4 |
| St. Georges Av. NW9 | 70 | C4 |
| St. George's Av. W5 | 125 | G2 |
| St. Georges Av., | 103 | F7 |
| Sthl. | | |
| **St. Georges Circ. SE1** | **27** | **G5** |
| St. Georges Circ. SE1 | 131 | H3 |
| St. Georges Cl. | 72 | C6 |
| NW11 | | |
| St. George's Cl. SW8 | 150 | C1 |
| *Patmore Est.* | | |
| St. Georges Cl., | 86 | D3 |
| Wem. | | |
| St. Georges Ct. E6 | 116 | C4 |
| **St. Georges Ct. EC4** | **19** | **G3** |
| **St. Georges Ct. SW7** | **22** | **C5** |
| **St. George's Dr. SW1** | **33** | **F3** |
| St. George's Dr. SW1 | 130 | B4 |
| St. Georges Dr., Wat. | 50 | E3 |
| **St. Georges Flds. W2** | **15** | **H4** |
| St. Georges Flds. W2 | 109 | H6 |
| St. George's Gdns., | 196 | B2 |
| Surb. | | |
| *Hamilton Av.* | | |
| St. Georges Gro. | 167 | G3 |
| SW17 | | |
| St. Georges Gro. Est. | 167 | G3 |
| SW17 | | |
| St. Georges Ind. Est., | 163 | G5 |
| Kings.T. | | |
| **St. Georges La. EC3** | **20** | **D5** |
| St. Georges Ms. NW1 | 91 | J7 |
| *Regents Pk. Rd.* | | |
| St. Georges Pl., | 162 | D1 |
| Twick. | | |
| *Church St.* | | |
| St. Georges Rd. E7 | 97 | H6 |
| St. Georges Rd. E10 | 96 | C3 |
| St. Georges Rd. N9 | 60 | D3 |
| St. Georges Rd. N13 | 59 | F3 |
| St. Georges Rd. | 72 | C6 |
| NW11 | | |
| **St. Georges Rd. SE1** | **27** | **F5** |
| St. Georges Rd. SE1 | 131 | G3 |
| St. George's Rd. | 166 | C6 |
| SW19 | | |
| St. Georges Rd. W4 | 126 | E2 |
| St. Georges Rd. W7 | 124 | C1 |
| St. George's Rd., | 190 | B1 |
| Beck. | | |
| St. Georges Rd., | 192 | C2 |
| Brom. | | |
| St. Georges Rd., Dag. | 100 | E5 |
| St. George's Rd., Felt. | 160 | D4 |
| St. Georges Rd., Ilf. | 80 | C7 |
| St. George's Rd., | 164 | A7 |
| Kings.T. | | |
| St. George's Rd., | 186 | B3 |
| Mitch. | | |
| St. George's Rd., Orp. | 193 | G6 |
| St. George's Rd., Rich. | 145 | J3 |
| St. George's Rd., Sid. | 176 | D6 |
| St. George's Rd., | 145 | E5 |
| Twick. | | |
| St. Georges Rd., Wall. | 200 | B5 |
| St. Georges Rd. W., | 192 | B1 |
| Brom. | | |
| St. Georges Sq. E7 | 97 | H7 |
| St. Georges Sq. E14 | 113 | H7 |
| *Narrow St.* | | |
| St. Georges Sq. SE8 | 133 | J4 |
| **St. George's Sq. SW1** | **33** | **H3** |
| St. George's Sq. SW1 | 130 | D5 |

| Entry | Page | Grid |
|---|---|---|
| St. George's Sq., N.Mal. | 182/183 | E3 |
| *High St.* | | |
| **St. George's Sq. Ms. SW1** | 33 | H4 |
| St. George's Sq. Ms. SW1 | 130 | D5 |
| St. Georges Ter. NW1 | 91 | J7 |
| *Regents Pk. Rd.* | | |
| St. Georges Wk., Croy. | 201 | J3 |
| **St. Georges Way SE15** | 36 | D6 |
| St. Georges Way SE15 | 132 | B6 |
| St. Gerards Cl. SW4 | 150 | C5 |
| St. German's Pl. SE3 | 155 | G1 |
| St. Germans Rd. SE23 | 171 | H1 |
| St. Giles Av., Dag. | 101 | H7 |
| St. Giles Cl., Dag. | 101 | H7 |
| *St. Giles Av.* | | |
| St. Giles Cl., Orp. | 207 | G5 |
| **St. Giles High St. WC2** | 17 | J3 |
| St. Giles High St. WC2 | 110 | D6 |
| **St. Giles Pas. WC2** | 17 | J4 |
| St. Giles Rd. SE5 | 132 | B7 |
| St. Gilles Ho. E2 | 113 | G2 |
| St. Gothard Rd. SE27 | 170 | A4 |
| St. Gregory Cl., Ruis. | 84 | C4 |
| St. Helena Rd. SE16 | 133 | G4 |
| **St. Helena St. WC1** | 10 | E4 |
| St. Helens Cres. SW16 | 187 | F1 |
| *St. Helens Rd.* | | |
| St. Helens Gdns. W10 | 108 | A6 |
| **St. Helens Pl. EC3** | 20 | D3 |
| St. Helens Rd. SW16 | 187 | F1 |
| St. Helen's Rd. W13 | 124/125 | E1 |
| *Dane Rd.* | | |
| St. Helens Rd., Erith | 138 | D2 |
| St. Helens Rd., Ilf. | 80 | C6 |
| St. Helier Av., Mord. | 185 | F7 |
| St. Heliers Av., Houns. | 143 | G5 |
| St. Heliers Rd. E10 | 78 | C6 |
| St. Hildas Cl. NW6 | 90 | A7 |
| St. Hildas Cl. SW17 | 167 | H2 |
| St. Hilda's Rd. SW13 | 127 | H6 |
| St. Hughe's Cl. SW17 | 167 | H2 |
| *College Gdns.* | | |
| St. Hughs Rd. SE20 | 188/189 | E1 |
| *Ridsdale Rd.* | | |
| St. James Av. N20 | 57 | H3 |
| St. James Av. W13 | 124 | D1 |
| St. James Av., Sutt. | 198 | D5 |
| St. James Cl. N20 | 57 | H3 |
| St. James Cl. SE18 | 137 | F5 |
| *Congleton Gro.* | | |
| St. James Cl., Barn. | 41 | G4 |
| St. James Cl., N.Mal. | 183 | F5 |
| St. James Cl., Ruis. | 84 | C2 |
| St. James Gdns., Wem. | 87 | G7 |
| St. James Gate NW1 | 92 | D7 |
| *St. Paul's Cres.* | | |
| St. James Gro. SW11 | 149 | J2 |
| *Reform St.* | | |
| St. James Ms. E14 | 134 | C3 |
| St. James Ms. E17 | 77 | H5 |
| *St. James's St.* | | |
| St. James Rd. E15 | 97 | F5 |
| St. James Rd. N9 | 60/61 | E2 |
| *Queens Rd.* | | |
| St. James Rd., Cars. | 199 | H3 |
| St. James Rd., Kings.T. | 181 | H2 |
| St. James Rd., Mitch. | 168 | A7 |
| St. James Rd., Surb. | 181 | G6 |
| St. James Rd., Sutt. | 198 | D5 |
| St. James St. W6 | 127 | J5 |
| St. James Wk. SE15 | 132 | C7 |
| *Commercial Way* | | |
| St. James Way, Sid. | 177 | E5 |
| St. James's Av. E14 | 153 | H1 |
| St. James's Av. E2 | 113 | F2 |
| St. James's Av., Beck. | 189 | H3 |
| St. James's Av., Hmptn. | 161 | J5 |
| St. James's Cl. SW17 | 167 | J2 |
| *St. James's Dr.* | | |
| St. James's Cotts., Rich. | 145 | G5 |
| *Paradise Rd.* | | |
| **St. James's Ct. SW1** | 25 | G5 |
| St. James's Ct. SW1 | 130 | C3 |
| St. James's Cres. SW9 | 151 | G3 |
| St. James's Dr. SW12 | 167 | J1 |
| St. James's Dr. SW17 | 167 | J1 |
| St. James's Gdns. W11 | 128 | B1 |
| St. James's La. N10 | 74 | B4 |
| **St. James's Mkt. SW1** | 17 | H6 |
| **St. James's Palace SW1** | 25 | G3 |
| St. James's Palace SW1 | 130 | C1 |
| **St. James's Pk. SW1** | 25 | H3 |
| St. James's Pk. SW1 | 130 | D2 |
| St. James's Pk., Croy. | 187 | J7 |
| **St. James's Pas. EC3** | 21 | E4 |
| **St. James's Pl. SW1** | 25 | F2 |
| St. James's Rd. SE1 | 130 | C1 |
| **St. James's Rd. SE1** | 37 | J3 |
| St. James's Rd. SE16 | 132 | D5 |
| **St. James's Rd. SE16** | 29 | J5 |
| St. James's Rd., Croy. | 132 | D3 |
| St. James's Rd., Hmptn. | 187 | H7 |
| **St. James's Row EC1** | 11 | F5 |
| **St. James's Sq. SW1** | 25 | G1 |
| St. James's Sq. SW1 | 130 | C1 |
| St. James's St. E17 | 77 | H5 |
| **St. James's St. SW1** | 25 | F1 |
| St. James's St. SW1 | 130 | C1 |
| **St. James's Ter. NW8** | 7 | J1 |
| St. James's Ter. Ms. NW8 | 109 | J1 |
| **St. James's Wk. EC1** | 11 | G5 |
| St. James's Wk. EC1 | 111 | H4 |
| St. Joans Rd. N9 | 60 | C1 |
| St. John Fisher Rd., Erith | 138 | D3 |
| **St. John St. EC1** | 11 | H6 |
| St. John St. EC1 | 111 | H4 |
| St. Johns Av. N11 | 57 | J5 |
| St. John's Av. NW10 | 107 | F1 |
| St. John's Av. SW15 | 148 | A5 |
| St. John's Ch. Rd. E9 | 95 | F5 |
| St. Johns Cl. N14 | 42 | C6 |
| *Chase Rd.* | | |
| St. John's Cl. SW6 | 128 | D7 |
| *Dawes Rd.* | | |
| St. John's Cl., Wem. | 87 | H5 |
| St. John's Cotts. SE20 | 171 | F7 |
| *Maple Rd.* | | |
| St. Johns Cotts., Rich. | 145 | H4 |
| *Kew Foot Rd.* | | |
| St. John's Ct., Buck.H. | 63 | H1 |
| St. John's Ct., Islw. | 144 | C2 |
| St. John's Cres. SW9 | 151 | G3 |
| St. Johns Dr. SW18 | 166 | E1 |
| **St. John's Est. N1** | 12 | C2 |
| St. John's Est. N1 | 112 | A2 |
| **St. John's Est. SE1** | 29 | F3 |
| St. John's Gdns. W11 | 108 | C7 |
| St. Johns Gro. N19 | 92 | C2 |
| St. Johns Gro. SW13 | 147 | F2 |
| *Terrace Gdns.* | | |
| St. Johns Gro., Rich. | 145 | H4 |
| *Kew Foot Rd.* | | |
| **St. John's Hill SW11** | 149 | G4 |
| St. John's Hill Gro. SW11 | 149 | G4 |
| **St. John's La. EC1** | 11 | G6 |
| St. John's La. EC1 | 111 | H4 |
| St. John's Ms. W11 | 108 | D6 |
| *Ledbury Rd.* | | |
| St. Johns Par., Sid. | 176 | A4 |
| *Church Rd.* | | |
| St. John's Pk. SE3 | 135 | F7 |
| St. Johns Pas. SE23 | 171 | F1 |
| *Davids Rd.* | | |
| St. John's Pas. SW19 | 166 | B6 |
| *Ridgway Pl.* | | |
| **St. John's Path EC1** | 11 | G6 |
| St. Johns Pathway SE23 | 171 | F1 |
| *Devonshire Rd.* | | |
| **St. John's Pl. EC1** | 11 | G6 |
| St. John's Rd. E4 | 62 | B3 |
| St. John's Rd. E6 | 116 | B1 |
| *Ron Leighton Way* | | |
| St. Johns Rd. E16 | 115 | G6 |
| St. Johns Rd. E17 | 78 | B2 |
| St. John's Rd. N15 | 76 | B6 |
| St. Johns Rd. NW11 | 72 | C6 |
| St. John's Rd. SE20 | 171 | F7 |
| St. John's Rd. SW11 | 149 | H4 |
| St. John's Rd. SW19 | 166 | B7 |
| St. John's Rd., Bark. | 117 | H1 |
| St. John's Rd., Cars. | 199 | H3 |
| St. Johns Rd., Croy. | 201 | H3 |
| *Sylverdale Rd.* | | |
| St. John's Rd., E.Mol. | 180 | A4 |
| St. John's Rd., Felt. | 161 | E4 |
| St. John's Rd., Har. | 68 | C6 |
| St. Johns Rd., Ilf. | 81 | G7 |
| St. John's Rd., Islw. | 144 | C2 |
| St. John's Rd., Kings.T. | 181 | F2 |
| St. Johns Rd., Loug. | 48 | C2 |
| St. John's Rd., N.Mal. | 182 | C3 |
| St. John's Rd., Orp. | 193 | G6 |
| St. John's Rd., Rich. | 145 | H4 |
| St. John's Rd., Sid. | 176 | B4 |
| St. John's Rd., Sthl. | 122 | E3 |
| St. John's Rd., Sutt. | 198 | D2 |
| St. John's Rd., Well. | 158 | B3 |
| St. John's Rd., Wem. | 87 | G4 |
| **St. John's Sq. EC1** | 11 | G6 |
| St. Johns Ter. E7 | 97 | H6 |
| St. Johns Ter. SE18 | 137 | F6 |
| St. Johns Ter. SW15 | 164 | D4 |
| *Kingston Vale* | | |
| St. Johns Ter. W10 | 108 | A4 |
| *Harrow Rd.* | | |
| St. Johns Vale SE8 | 154 | A2 |
| St. Johns Vil. N19 | 92 | D1 |
| **St. John's Vil. W8** | 22 | B6 |
| St. Johns Way N19 | 92 | D1 |
| **St. John's Wd. Ct. NW8** | 7 | F4 |
| **St. John's Wd. High St. NW8** | 7 | F2 |
| St. John's Wd. High St. NW8 | 109 | G2 |
| St. John's Wd. Pk. NW8 | 109 | G1 |
| **St. John's Wd. Rd. NW8** | 6 | E5 |
| St. John's Wd. Rd. NW8 | 109 | G4 |
| **St. John's Wd. Ter. NW8** | 7 | G1 |
| St. John's Wd. Ter. NW8 | 109 | G2 |
| St. Josephs Cl. W10 | 108 | B5 |
| *Bevington Rd.* | | |
| St. Joseph's Cl., Orp. | 207 | J4 |
| St. Joseph's Ct. SE7 | 135 | H6 |
| St. Josephs Dr., Sthl. | 123 | E1 |
| St. Josephs Gro. NW4 | 71 | H4 |
| St. Josephs Rd. N9 | 45 | E7 |
| St. Joseph's Vale SE3 | 154 | D2 |
| St. Jude St. N16 | 94 | B5 |
| St. Jude's Rd. E2 | 113 | E2 |
| St. Julian's Cl. SW16 | 169 | G4 |
| St. Julian's Fm. Rd. SE27 | 169 | G4 |
| St. Julian's Rd. NW6 | 90 | C7 |
| **St. Katharines Prec. NW1** | 8 | D1 |
| **St. Katharine's Way E1** | 29 | G1 |
| St. Katharine's Way E1 | 132 | C1 |
| St. Katherines Rd., Erith | 138 | D2 |
| **St. Katherine's Row EC3** | 21 | E4 |
| St. Katherine's Wk. W11 | 108 | A7 |
| *Hunt St.* | | |
| St. Keverne Rd. SE9 | 174 | B4 |
| St. Kilda Rd. W13 | 124 | D1 |
| St. Kilda Rd., Orp. | 207 | J1 |
| St. Kilda's Av. N16 | 94 | A1 |
| St. Kilda's Rd. N16 | 68 | B6 |
| St. Kilda's Rd., Har. | 68 | B6 |
| St. Kitts Ter. SE19 | 170 | B5 |
| St. Laurence Cl. NW6 | 108 | A1 |
| St. Lawrence Cl., Edg. | 53 | J7 |
| St. Lawrence Dr., Pnr. | 66 | B6 |
| St. Lawrence St. E14 | 134 | C1 |
| St. Lawrence Ter. W10 | 108 | B5 |
| St. Lawrence Way SW9 | 151 | G2 |
| St. Leonards Av. E4 | 62 | E6 |
| St. Leonards Av., Har. | 69 | G4 |
| St. Leonard's Cl., Well. | 158 | A3 |
| *Hook La.* | | |
| **St. Leonards Ct. N1** | 12 | A3 |
| St. Leonards Ct. N1 | 112 | A3 |
| St. Leonard's Gdns., Houns. | 122 | E7 |
| St. Leonards Gdns., Ilf. | 99 | F5 |
| St. Leonards Ri., Orp. | 207 | H4 |
| St. Leonards Rd. E14 | 114 | B5 |
| St. Leonards Rd. NW10 | 106 | D4 |
| St. Leonard's Rd. SW14 | 146 | B3 |
| St. Leonards Rd. W13 | 105 | F7 |
| St. Leonards Rd., Croy. | 201 | H3 |
| St. Leonards Rd., Esher | 194 | C6 |
| St. Leonard's Rd., Surb. | 181 | G5 |
| St. Leonards Rd., T.Ditt. | 180 | D6 |
| St. Leonards Sq. NW5 | 92 | A6 |
| St. Leonards Sq., Surb. | 181 | G5 |
| *St. Leonard's Rd.* | | |
| St. Leonards St. E3 | 114 | B3 |
| **St. Leonard's Ter. SW3** | 31 | J4 |
| St. Leonard's Ter. SW3 | 129 | J5 |
| St. Leonards Wk. SW16 | 169 | F7 |
| **St. Loo Av. SW3** | 31 | H5 |
| St. Loo Av. SW3 | 129 | H6 |
| St. Louis Rd. SE27 | 169 | J4 |
| St. Loy's Rd. N17 | 76 | B2 |
| St. Lucia Dr. E15 | 115 | F1 |
| St. Luke's Av. SW4 | 150 | D4 |
| St. Luke's Av., Ilf. | 99 | E5 |
| St. Lukes Cl. EC1 | 111 | J4 |
| *Old St.* | | |
| St. Luke's Cl. SE25 | 189 | E6 |
| **St. Luke's Est. EC1** | 12 | B4 |
| St. Luke's Est. EC1 | 112 | A3 |
| St. Lukes Ms. W11 | 108 | C6 |
| *Basing St.* | | |
| St. Lukes Pas., Kings.T. | 181 | J1 |
| St. Lukes Rd. W11 | 108 | C5 |
| St. Lukes Sq. E16 | 115 | F6 |
| **St. Luke's St. SW3** | 31 | G5 |
| St. Luke's St. SW3 | 129 | H5 |
| St. Luke's Yd. W9 | 108 | C2 |
| St. Malo Av. N9 | 61 | F3 |
| St. Margarets, Bark. | 117 | G1 |
| St. Margarets Av. N15 | 75 | H4 |
| St. Margarets Av. N20 | 57 | F2 |
| St. Margarets Av., Har. | 85 | J3 |
| St. Margarets Av., Sid. | 175 | G3 |
| St. Margarets Av., Sutt. | 198 | B3 |
| **St. Margaret's Ct. SE1** | 28 | A2 |
| St. Margarets Cres. SW15 | 147 | H5 |
| St. Margaret's Dr., Twick. | 144 | E5 |
| St. Margaret's Gro. E11 | 97 | F3 |
| St. Margaret's Gro. SE18 | 137 | F6 |
| St. Margaret's Gro., Twick. | 144 | D4 |
| **St. Margarets La. W8** | 22 | A6 |
| St. Margarets La. W8 | 128 | E3 |
| St. Margarets Pas. SE13 | 154/155 | E3 |
| *Church Ter.* | | |
| St. Margarets Rd. E12 | 97 | J2 |
| St. Margaret's Rd. N17 | 76 | B3 |
| St. Margaret's Rd. NW10 | 107 | J3 |
| St. Margarets Rd. SE4 | 153 | J4 |
| St. Margarets Rd. W7 | 124 | B2 |
| St. Margarets Rd., Edg. | 54 | B5 |
| St. Margarets Rd., Islw. | 144 | E4 |
| St. Margarets Rd., Twick. | 144 | E4 |
| St. Margarets Sq. SE4 | 153 | J4 |
| *Adelaide Av.* | | |
| **St. Margaret's St. SW1** | 26 | A4 |
| St. Margaret's St. SW1 | 130 | D4 |
| St. Margaret's Ter. SE18 | 137 | F5 |
| **St. Mark St. E1** | 21 | G4 |
| St. Mark St. E1 | 112 | C6 |
| St. Marks Cl. SE10 | 134 | C7 |
| *Ashburnham Gro.* | | |
| St. Marks Cl. N11 | 108 | B6 |
| *Lancaster Rd.* | | |
| St. Mark's Cl., Barn. | 40 | E3 |
| St. Marks Cres. NW1 | 110 | A1 |
| St. Marks Gate E9 | 95 | J7 |
| *Cadogan Ter.* | | |
| **St. Mark's Gro. SW10** | 30 | B7 |
| St. Mark's Gro. SW10 | 129 | E6 |
| St. Mark's Hill, Surb. | 181 | H6 |
| St. Mark's Pl. SW19 | 166 | C6 |
| *Wimbledon Hill Rd.* | | |

| | | |
|---|---|---|
| **St. Thomas St. SE1** | **28** | **B2** |
| St. Thomas St. SE1 | 132 | A1 |
| St. Thomas's Gdns. NW5 | 92 | A6 |
| *Queens Cres.* | | |
| St. Thomas's Pl. E9 | 95 | F7 |
| St. Thomas's Rd. N4 | 93 | G2 |
| St. Thomas's Rd. NW10 | 107 | E1 |
| St. Thomas's Sq. E9 | 95 | E7 |
| St. Thomas's Way SW6 | 128 | C7 |
| St. Timothy's Ms., Brom. | 191 | H1 |
| *Wharton Rd.* | | |
| St. Ursula Gro., Pnr. | 66 | D5 |
| St. Ursula Rd., Sthl. | 103 | G6 |
| St. Vincent Cl. SE27 | 169 | H5 |
| St. Vincent Rd., Twick. | 143 | J6 |
| **St. Vincent St. W1** | **16** | **C2** |
| St. Wilfrids Cl., Barn. | 41 | H5 |
| St. Wilfrids Rd., Barn. | 41 | G5 |
| St. Winefride's Av. E12 | 98 | C5 |
| St. Winifreds Cl., Chig. | 65 | F5 |
| St. Winifred's Rd., Tedd. | 163 | E6 |
| Saints Cl. SE27 | 169 | H4 |
| *Wolfington Rd.* | | |
| Saints Dr. E7 | 98 | A5 |
| **Salamanca Pl. SE1** | **34** | **C2** |
| **Salamanca St. SE1** | **34** | **B2** |
| Salamanca St. SE1 | 131 | F4 |
| Salamander Cl., Kings.T. | 163 | F5 |
| Salcombe Dr., Mord. | 198 | A1 |
| Salcombe Dr., Rom. | 83 | F6 |
| Salcombe Gdns. NW7 | 55 | J6 |
| Salcombe Pk., Loug. | 48 | A5 |
| *High Rd.* | | |
| Salcombe Rd. E17 | 77 | J7 |
| Salcombe Rd. N16 | 94 | B5 |
| Salcombe Way, Ruis. | 84 | A2 |
| Salcott Rd. SW11 | 149 | H5 |
| Salcott Rd., Croy. | 201 | E3 |
| **Sale Pl. W2** | **15** | **G2** |
| Sale Pl. W2 | 109 | H5 |
| **Sale St. E2** | **13** | **H5** |
| Salehurst Cl., Har. | 69 | H5 |
| Salehurst Rd. SE4 | 153 | J6 |
| Salem Pl., Croy. | 201 | J3 |
| **Salem Rd. W2** | **14** | **B5** |
| Salem Rd. W2 | 109 | E7 |
| Salford Rd. SW2 | 168 | D1 |
| Salhouse Cl. SE28 | 118 | C6 |
| *Rollesby Way* | | |
| Salisbury Av. N3 | 72 | C3 |
| Salisbury Av., Bark. | 99 | H7 |
| Salisbury Av., Sutt. | 198 | C6 |
| **Salisbury Cl. SE17** | **36** | **B1** |
| Salisbury Cl., Wor.Pk. | 197 | F3 |
| **Salisbury Ct. EC4** | **19** | **G4** |
| Salisbury Ct. EC4 | 111 | H6 |
| Salisbury Gdns. SW19 | 166 | B7 |
| Salisbury Gdns., Buck.H. | 64 | A2 |
| Salisbury Hall Gdns. E4 | 62 | A6 |
| Salisbury Ho. E14 | 114 | B6 |
| *Hobday St.* | | |
| Salisbury Ms. SW6 | 128 | C7 |
| *Dawes Rd.* | | |
| Salisbury Ms., Brom. | 192 | B5 |
| *Salisbury Rd.* | | |
| Salisbury Pl. SW9 | 131 | H7 |
| **Salisbury Pl. W1** | **15** | **J1** |
| Salisbury Pl. W1 | 109 | J5 |
| Salisbury Rd. E4 | 62 | A3 |
| Salisbury Rd. E7 | 97 | G6 |
| Salisbury Rd. E10 | 96 | C2 |
| Salisbury Rd. E12 | 98 | A5 |
| Salisbury Rd. E17 | 78 | C5 |
| Salisbury Rd. N4 | 75 | H5 |
| Salisbury Rd. N9 | 60 | D3 |
| Salisbury Rd. N22 | 75 | H1 |
| Salisbury Rd. SE25 | 188 | D6 |
| Salisbury Rd. SW19 | 166 | B7 |
| Salisbury Rd. W13 | 124 | D2 |
| Salisbury Rd., Barn. | 40 | B3 |
| Salisbury Rd., Bex. | 177 | G1 |
| Salisbury Rd., Brom. | 192 | B5 |
| Salisbury Rd., Cars. | 199 | J6 |
| Salisbury Rd., Dag. | 101 | H6 |
| Salisbury Rd., Felt. | 160 | C1 |
| Salisbury Rd., Har. | 68 | A5 |
| Salisbury Rd., Houns. | 142 | C3 |
| Salisbury Rd. (Heathrow Airport), Houns. | 141 | F5 |
| Salisbury Rd., Ilf. | 99 | H2 |
| Salisbury Rd., N.Mal. | 182 | D3 |
| Salisbury Rd., Pnr. | 66 | A4 |
| Salisbury Rd., Rich. | 145 | H4 |
| Salisbury Rd., Sthl. | 123 | E4 |
| Salisbury Rd., Wor.Pk. | 197 | F3 |
| **Salisbury Sq. EC4** | **19** | **F4** |
| **Salisbury St. NW8** | **7** | **G6** |
| Salisbury St. NW8 | 109 | H4 |
| Salisbury St. W3 | 126 | C2 |
| Salisbury Ter. SE15 | 153 | F3 |
| Salisbury Wk. N19 | 92 | C2 |
| Salix Cl., Sun. | 160 | B7 |
| *Oak Gro.* | | |
| Salliesfield, Twick. | 144 | A6 |
| Sally Murray Cl. E12 | 98 | D4 |
| *Grantham Rd.* | | |
| Salmen Rd. E13 | 115 | F2 |
| Salmon La. E14 | 113 | H6 |
| Salmon Rd., Belv. | 139 | G5 |
| Salmon St. E14 | 113 | J6 |
| *Salmon La.* | | |
| Salmon St. NW9 | 88 | B1 |
| Salmond Cl., Stan. | 52 | D6 |
| *Robb Rd.* | | |
| Salmons Rd. N9 | 60 | D1 |
| Salmons Rd., Chess. | 195 | G6 |
| Salomons Rd. E13 | 115 | J5 |
| *Chalk Rd.* | | |
| Salop Rd. E17 | 77 | G6 |
| Saltash Cl., Sutt. | 198 | C4 |
| Saltash Rd., Ilf. | 65 | G7 |
| Saltash Rd., Well. | 158 | C1 |
| Saltcoats Rd. W4 | 126 | E2 |
| Saltcroft Cl., Wem. | 88 | B1 |
| Salter Cl., Har. | 85 | F3 |
| Salter Rd. SE16 | 133 | G1 |
| Salter St. E14 | 114 | A7 |
| Salter St. NW10 | 107 | G3 |
| Salterford Rd. SW17 | 168 | A6 |
| **Salters Hall Ct. EC4** | **20** | **B5** |
| Salters Hill SE19 | 170 | A5 |
| Salters Rd. E17 | 78 | D4 |
| Salters Rd. W10 | 108 | A4 |
| Salterton Rd. N7 | 93 | E3 |
| Saltley Cl. E6 | 116 | B6 |
| *Dunnock Rd.* | | |
| Saltoun Rd. SW2 | 151 | G4 |
| Saltram Cl. N15 | 76 | C4 |
| Saltram Cres. W9 | 108 | C3 |
| Saltwell St. E14 | 114 | A7 |
| **Saltwood Gro. SE17** | **36** | **B4** |
| Salusbury Rd. NW6 | 108 | B1 |
| Salutation Rd. SE10 | 135 | E4 |
| Salvia Gdns., Grnf. | 104 | D2 |
| *Selborne Gdns.* | | |
| Salvin Rd. SW15 | 148 | A3 |
| Salway Cl., Wdf.Grn. | 63 | F7 |
| Salway Pl. E15 | 96/97 | E6 |
| *Broadway* | | |
| Salway Rd. E15 | 96 | D6 |
| Sam Bartram Cl. SE7 | 135 | J5 |
| Samantha Cl. E17 | 77 | J7 |
| Sambruck Ms. SE6 | 172 | B1 |
| Samels Ct. W6 | 127 | G5 |
| *South Black Lion La.* | | |
| **Samford St. NW8** | **7** | **F6** |
| Samford St. NW8 | 109 | G4 |
| Samos Rd. SE20 | 189 | E2 |
| Sampson Av., Barn. | 40 | A5 |
| Sampson Cl., Belv. | 138 | D3 |
| *Carrill Way* | | |
| **Sampson St. E1** | **29** | **J2** |
| Sampson St. E1 | 132 | D1 |
| Samson St. E13 | 115 | J2 |
| Samuel Cl. E8 | 112 | C1 |
| *Pownall Rd.* | | |
| Samuel Cl. SE14 | 133 | G6 |
| Samuel Cl. SE18 | 136 | B4 |
| Samuel Gray Gdns., Kings.T. | 181 | G1 |
| Samuel Johnson Cl. SW16 | 169 | G4 |
| *Curtis Fld. Rd.* | | |
| Samuel Lewis Trust Dws. E8 | 94 | D4 |
| *Amhurst Rd.* | | |
| Samuel Lewis Trust Dws. N1 | 93 | G7 |
| *Liverpool Rd.* | | |
| **Samuel Lewis Trust Dws. SW3** | **31** | **G2** |
| Samuel Lewis Trust Dws. SW6 | 128 | D7 |
| **Samuel St. SE15** | **37** | **F7** |
| Samuel St. SE15 | 132 | C7 |
| Samuel St. SE18 | 136 | C4 |
| Samuels Cl. W6 | 127 | G5 |
| *South Black Lion La.* | | |
| Sancroft Cl. NW2 | 89 | H3 |
| Sancroft Rd., Har. | 68 | C2 |
| **Sancroft St. SE11** | **34** | **D3** |
| Sancroft St. SE11 | 131 | F5 |
| **Sanctuary, The SW1** | **25** | **J4** |
| Sanctuary, The, Bex. | 158 | D6 |
| Sanctuary, The, Mord. | 184 | D6 |
| Sanctuary Rd., Houns. | 140 | D6 |
| **Sanctuary St. SE1** | **28** | **A4** |
| Sandal Rd. N18 | 60 | D5 |
| Sandal Rd., N.Mal. | 182 | D5 |
| Sandal St. E15 | 114 | E1 |
| Sandale Cl. N16 | 94 | A3 |
| *Stoke Newington Ch. St.* | | |
| Sandall Cl. W5 | 105 | H4 |
| Sandall Rd. NW5 | 92 | C6 |
| Sandall Rd. W5 | 105 | H4 |
| Sandalwood Cl. E1 | 113 | H4 |
| *Solebay St.* | | |
| Sandalwood Rd., Felt. | 160 | B3 |
| Sandbach Pl. SE18 | 137 | F4 |
| Sandbourne Av. SW19 | 184 | E3 |
| Sandbourne Rd. SE4 | 153 | H2 |
| Sandbrook Cl. NW7 | 54 | D6 |
| Sandbrook Rd. N16 | 94 | B3 |
| Sandby Grn. SE9 | 156 | B3 |
| Sandcroft Cl. N13 | 59 | H6 |
| **Sandell St. SE1** | **27** | **E3** |
| Sanders Cl., Hmptn. | 161 | J5 |
| Sanders La. NW7 | 56 | A7 |
| Sanders Way N19 | 92 | D1 |
| *Sussex Way* | | |
| Sanderson Cl. NW5 | 92 | B4 |
| Sanderstead Av. NW2 | 90 | B2 |
| Sanderstead Cl. SW12 | 150 | C7 |
| *Atkins Rd.* | | |
| Sanderstead Rd. E10 | 95 | H1 |
| Sanderstead Rd., S.Croy. | 202 | A7 |
| Sandfield Gdns., Th.Hth. | 187 | H3 |
| Sandfield Pas., Th.Hth. | 187 | J3 |
| Sandfield Rd., Th.Hth. | 187 | H3 |
| Sandford Av. N22 | 59 | J7 |
| Sandford Av., Loug. | 49 | F3 |
| Sandford Cl. E6 | 116 | C4 |
| Sandford Ct. N16 | 94 | B1 |
| Sandford La. N16 | 94 | C2 |
| *Lawrence Bldgs.* | | |
| Sandford Rd. E6 | 116 | B4 |
| Sandford Rd., Bexh. | 159 | E4 |
| Sandford Rd., Brom. | 191 | G4 |
| Sandford St. SW6 | 128/129 | E7 |
| *King's Rd.* | | |
| Sandgate La. SW18 | 167 | H1 |
| Sandgate Rd., Well. | 138 | C7 |
| Sandgate St. SE15 | 132 | E6 |
| Sandham Pt. SE18 | 136/137 | E4 |
| *Troy Ct.* | | |
| Sandhills, Wall. | 200 | D4 |
| Sandhurst Av., Har. | 67 | H6 |
| Sandhurst Av., Surb. | 182 | B7 |
| Sandhurst Cl. NW9 | 70 | A3 |
| Sandhurst Dr., Ilf. | 99 | J4 |
| Sandhurst Rd. N9 | 45 | F6 |
| Sandhurst Rd. NW9 | 70 | A3 |
| Sandhurst Rd. SE6 | 172 | D1 |
| Sandhurst Rd., Bex. | 158 | D5 |
| Sandhurst Rd., Sid. | 176 | J6 |
| Sandhurst Way, S.Croy. | 202 | B7 |
| Sandiford Rd., Sutt. | 198 | C2 |
| Sandiland Cres., Brom. | 205 | F2 |
| Sandilands, Croy. | 202 | D2 |
| Sandilands Rd. SW6 | 148 | E1 |
| Sandison St. SE15 | 152 | C3 |
| **Sandland St. WC1** | **18** | **D2** |
| Sandland St. WC1 | 111 | F5 |
| Sandling Ri. SE9 | 174 | D3 |
| Sandlings, The N22 | 75 | G2 |
| Sandlings Cl. SE15 | 152/153 | E2 |
| *Pilkington Rd.* | | |
| Sandmere Rd. SW4 | 150 | E4 |
| Sandon Cl., Esher | 180 | A7 |
| Sandow Cres., Hayes | 121 | J3 |
| Sandown Av., Dag. | 101 | J6 |
| Sandown Cl., Houns. | 142 | A1 |
| Sandown Rd. SE25 | 188 | E5 |
| Sandown Way, Nthlt. | 85 | E6 |
| Sandpiper Cl. E17 | 77 | G1 |
| Sandpiper Cl. SE16 | 133 | J2 |
| Sandpiper Rd., Sutt. | 198 | B2 |
| *Gander Grn. La.* | | |
| Sandpit Pl. SE7 | 136 | B5 |
| Sandpit Rd., Brom. | 172 | E5 |
| Sandpits Rd., Croy. | 203 | G4 |
| Sandpits Rd., Rich. | 163 | G2 |
| Sandra Cl. N22 | 75 | J1 |
| *New Rd.* | | |
| Sandra Cl., Houns. | 143 | H5 |
| Sandridge Cl., Har. | 68 | B4 |
| Sandridge Ct. N4 | 93 | J3 |
| *Queens Dr.* | | |
| Sandridge St. N19 | 92 | C2 |
| Sandringham Av. SW20 | 184 | B2 |
| Sandringham Cl. SW19 | 166 | A1 |
| Sandringham Cl., Enf. | 44 | B2 |
| Sandringham Cl., Ilf. | 81 | F3 |
| **Sandringham Ct. W9** | **6** | **D4** |
| Sandringham Cres., Har. | 85 | G2 |
| Sandringham Dr., Well. | 157 | H2 |
| Sandringham Gdns. N8 | 75 | E6 |
| Sandringham Gdns. N12 | 57 | G6 |
| Sandringham Gdns., Houns. | 142 | A1 |
| Sandringham Gdns., Ilf. | 81 | F3 |
| Sandringham Ms. W5 | 105 | G7 |
| *High St.* | | |
| Sandringham Rd. E7 | 97 | J5 |
| Sandringham Rd. E8 | 94 | C5 |
| Sandringham Rd. E10 | 78 | D6 |
| Sandringham Rd. N22 | 75 | J3 |
| Sandringham Rd. NW2 | 89 | H6 |
| Sandringham Rd. NW11 | 72 | B7 |
| Sandringham Rd., Bark. | 99 | J6 |
| Sandringham Rd., Brom. | 173 | G5 |
| Sandringham Rd., Houns. | 140 | B5 |
| Sandringham Rd., Nthlt. | 85 | G7 |
| Sandringham Rd., Th.Hth. | 187 | J5 |
| Sandringham Rd., Wor.Pk. | 197 | G3 |
| Sandrock Pl., Croy. | 203 | G4 |
| Sandrock Rd. SE13 | 154 | A3 |
| Sand's End La. SW6 | 149 | E1 |
| Sands Way, Wdf.Grn. | 64 | B6 |
| Sandstone Pl. N19 | 92 | B2 |
| Sandstone Rd. SE12 | 173 | H2 |
| Sandtoft Rd. SE7 | 135 | H6 |
| Sandwell Cres. NW6 | 90 | D6 |
| **Sandwich St. WC1** | **10** | **A4** |
| Sandwich St. WC1 | 110 | E3 |
| Sandwick Cl. NW7 | 55 | G7 |
| *Sebergham Gro.* | | |
| Sandy Bury, Orp. | 207 | G3 |
| Sandy Hill Av. SE18 | 136 | E5 |
| Sandy Hill Rd. SE18 | 136 | E5 |
| Sandy La., Har. | 69 | J6 |
| Sandy La., Kings.T. | 162 | D7 |
| Sandy La., Mitch. | 186 | A1 |
| Sandy La., Nthwd. | 50 | A5 |
| Sandy La., Rich. | 163 | F2 |
| Sandy La., Sid. | 176 | D7 |
| Sandy La., Sutt. | 198 | B7 |
| Sandy La., Tedd. | 162 | D7 |
| Sandy La., Wall. | 178 | B6 |
| Sandy La. Est., Rich. | 163 | G2 |
| Sandy La. N., Wall. | 200 | D5 |
| Sandy La. S., Wall. | 200 | D6 |
| Sandy Ridge, Chis. | 174 | D6 |
| Sandy Rd. NW3 | 90 | E3 |
| Sandy Way, Croy. | 203 | J3 |
| Sandycombe Rd., Felt. | 160 | A1 |
| Sandycombe Rd., Rich. | 146 | A3 |
| Sandycoombe Rd., Twick. | 145 | F6 |
| Sandycroft SE2 | 138 | A6 |
| Sandyhill Rd., Ilf. | 98 | E4 |
| Sandymount Av., Stan. | 53 | F5 |
| **Sandy's Row E1** | **21** | **E2** |
| Sandy's Row E1 | 112 | B5 |
| Sanford La. N16 | 94 | C2 |
| *Stoke Newington High St.* | | |
| Sanford St. SE14 | 133 | H6 |
| Sanford Ter. N16 | 94 | C3 |
| Sanford Wk. N16 | 94 | C2 |
| *Sanford Ter.* | | |
| Sanford Wk. SE14 | 133 | H6 |
| *Cold Blow La.* | | |
| Sanger Av., Chess. | 195 | H5 |
| Sangley Rd. SE6 | 154 | B7 |
| Sangley Rd. SE25 | 188 | B4 |
| Sangora Rd. SW11 | 149 | G4 |
| **Sans Wk. EC1** | **11** | **F5** |
| Sans Wk. EC1 | 111 | G4 |
| Sansom Rd. E11 | 97 | E2 |

Sansom St. SE5 132 A7
Santley St. SW4 151 F4
Santos Rd. SW18 148 D6
Santway, The, Stan. 52 B5
Sapcote Trd. Cen. 89 F5
NW10
**Saperton Wk. SE11 34 D1**
Saperton Wk. SE11 131 F4
Saphora Cl., Orp. 207 G5
*Oleander Cl.*
Sapphire Cl. E6 116 D6
Sapphire Cl., Dag. 100 C1
Sapphire Rd. SE8 133 H4
Sara Ct., Beck. 190 B1
*Albemarle Rd.*
Saracen Cl., Croy. 188 A6
Saracen St. E14 114 A6
**Saracen's Head Yd. 21 F4
EC3**
Sarah Ho. SW15 147 F4
**Sarah St. N1 12 E3**
Saratoga Rd. E5 95 F4
**Sardinia St. WC2 18 C4**
Sarita Cl., Har. 68 A2
Sarjant Path SW19 166 A2
*Queensmere Rd.*
Sark Cl., Houns. 123 G7
Sark Wk. E16 115 H6
Sarnesfield Ho. 132/133 E6
SE15
*Pencraig Way*
Sarnesfield Rd., Enf. 44 A3
*Church St.*
Sarre Rd. NW2 90 C5
Sarsen Av., Houns. 143 F2
Sarsfeld Rd. SW12 167 J1
Sarsfield Rd., Grnf. 105 E2
Sartor Rd. SE15 153 G4
Sarum Ter. E3 113 J4
Satanita Cl. E16 116 A6
*Fulmer Rd.*
Satchell Mead NW9 71 F1
**Satchwell Rd. E2 13 H4**
Satchwell Rd. E2 112 D3
Sauls Grn. E11 96/97 E3
*Napier Rd.*
Saunders Cl. E14 113 J7
*Limehouse Causeway*
Saunders Ness Rd. 134 C5
E14
Saunders Rd. SE18 137 J5
**Saunders St. SE11 34 E1**
Saunders St. SE11 131 G4
Saunders Way SE28 118 B7
*Oriole Way*
Saunderton Rd., 86 E5
Wem.
Saunton Av., Hayes 121 J7
Savage Gdns. E6 116 C6
**Savage Gdns. EC3 21 E5**
Savernake Rd. N9 44 D6
Savernake Rd. NW3 91 J4
Savery Dr., Surb. 181 F7
Savile Cl., N.Mal. 183 E5
Savile Cl., T.Ditt. 194 C1
Savile Gdns., Croy. 202 C2
**Savile Row W1 17 F5**
Savile Row W1 110 C7
Savill Gdns. SW20 183 G3
*Bodnant Gdns.*
Savill Row, Wdf.Grn. 63 F6
Saville Rd. E16 136 B1
Saville Rd. W4 126 D3
Saville Rd., Rom. 83 F6
Saville Rd., Twick. 162 C1
Savona Cl. SW19 166 B7
Savona Est. SW8 130 C7
Savona St. SW8 130 C7
Savoy Av., Hayes 121 H5
**Savoy Bldgs. WC2 18 C6**
Savoy Cl. E15 114/115 E1
*Arthingworth St.*
Savoy Cl., Edg. 54 A5
**Savoy Ct. WC2 18 B6**
**Savoy Hill WC2 18 C6**
**Savoy Pl. WC2 18 B6**
Savoy Pl. WC2 111 E7
**Savoy Row WC2 18 C5**
Savoy Steps WC2 111 F7
*Savoy St.*
**Savoy St. WC2 18 C5**
Savoy St. WC2 111 F7
**Savoy Way WC2 18 C6**
Sawbill Cl., Hayes 102 D5
Sawkins Cl. SW19 166 B2
Sawley Rd. W12 127 G1
Sawtry Cl., Cars. 185 H7
Sawyer Cl. N9 60 D2
*Lion Rd.*
**Sawyer St. SE1 27 J3**
Sawyer St. SE1 131 J2
Sawyers Cl., Dag. 101 J6

Sawyer's Hill, Rich. 146 B7
Sawyers Lawn W13 104 C6
Saxby Rd. SW2 150 E7
Saxham Rd., Bark. 117 J2
Saxlingham Rd. E4 62 D3
Saxon Av., Felt. 161 F2
Saxon Cl. E17 78 A7
Saxon Cl., Surb. 181 G6
Saxon Dr. W3 106 B6
Saxon Gdns., 102/103 E7
Sthl.
*Saxon Rd.*
Saxon Rd. E3 113 J2
Saxon Rd. E6 116 C4
Saxon Rd. N22 75 H1
Saxon Rd. SE25 188 A5
Saxon Rd., Brom. 173 F7
Saxon Rd., Ilf. 99 E6
Saxon Rd., Sthl. 123 E1
Saxon Rd., Wem. 88 C3
Saxon Wk., Sid. 176 C6
Saxon Way N14 42 D6
Saxonbury Av., Sun. 178 B3
Saxonbury Cl., 185 G3
Mitch.
Saxonbury Gdns., 195 F1
Surb.
Saxonfield Cl. SW2 151 F7
Saxton Cl. SE13 154 D3
Sayers Wk., Rich. 145 J7
*Stafford Pl.*
Sayes Ct. SE8 133 J5
*Sayes Ct. St.*
Sayes Ct. St. SE8 133 J6
Sayesbury La. N18 60 D5
Scadbury Pk., Chis. 175 J6
Scads Hill Cl., Orp. 193 J6
**Scala St. W1 17 G1**
Scala St. W1 110 C5
Scales Rd. N17 76 C3
Scampston Ms. W10 108 A6
Scampton Rd., 140 C6
Houns.
*Southampton Rd.*
Scandrett St. E1 132 E1
Scarba Wk. N1 94 A6
*Marquess Rd.*
Scarborough Rd. E11 96 D1
Scarborough Rd. N4 75 G7
Scarborough Rd. N9 45 F7
Scarborough Rd., 141 F6
Houns.
*Southern Perimeter Rd.*
**Scarborough St. E1 21 G4**
Scarbrook Rd., Croy. 201 J3
Scarle Rd., Wem. 87 G6
Scarlet Rd. SE6 172 E3
Scarlette Manor Way 151 G7
SW2
*Papworth Way*
Scarsbrook Rd. SE3 156 A3
**Scarsdale Pl. W8 22 A5**
Scarsdale Rd., Har. 85 J3
Scarsdale Vil. W8 128 D3
Scarth Rd. SW13 147 F3
Scawen Cl., Cars. 200 A4
Scawen Rd. SE8 133 H5
**Scawfell St. E2 13 G2**
Scawfell St. E2 112 C2
Scaynes Link N12 56 D5
Sceaux Est. SE5 152 B1
Sceaux Gdns. SE5 152 C1
Sceptre Rd. E2 113 F3
Schofield Wk. SE3 135 H7
*Dornberg Cl.*
Scholars Rd. E4 62 C1
Scholars Rd. SW12 168 C1
Scholefield Rd. N19 92 D1
Schonfeld Sq. N16 94 A2
School Ho. La., Tedd. 163 E7
School La. SE23 170 E2
School La., Kings.T. 181 F1
*School Rd.*
School La., Pnr. 66 E4
School La., Surb. 196 A1
School La., Well. 158 B3
School Pas., Kings.T. 181 J2
School Pas., Sthl. 123 F1
School Rd. E12 98 C4
School Rd. NW10 106 D4
School Rd., Chis. 193 F1
School Rd., Dag. 119 G1
School Rd., E.Mol. 180 A4
School Rd., Hmptn. 161 J6
School Rd., Houns. 143 J3
School Rd., Kings.T. 181 F1
School Rd., West Dr. 120 A4
School Rd. Av., 161 J6
Hmptn.
School Way N12 57 F4
*High Rd.*
School Way, Dag. 100 C3
Schoolbell Ms. E3 113 H2
*Arbery Rd.*

Schoolhouse Gdns., 48 E4
Loug.
Schoolhouse La. E1 113 G7
Schoolway N12 57 G6
Schooner Cl. E14 134 D3
Schooner Cl. SE16 133 G2
*Kinburn St.*
Schooner Cl., Bark. 117 H3
*Thames Rd.*
Schubert Rd. SW15 148 C5
**Sclater St. E1 13 F5**
Sclater St. E1 112 C4
Scoble Pl. N16 94 C4
*Amhurst Rd.*
Scoles Cres. SW2 169 G1
**Scoresby St. SE1 27 G2**
Scoresby St. SE1 131 H1
Scorton Av., Grnf. 104 D2
Scot Gro., Pnr. 50 D7
Scotch Common 104 D5
W13
Scoter Cl., Wdf.Grn. 63 H7
*Mallards Rd.*
Scotia Rd. SW2 151 G7
Scotland Grn. N17 76 D2
Scotland Grn. Rd., 45 G5
Enf.
Scotland Grn. Rd. N., 45 G4
Enf.
**Scotland Pl. SW1 26 A1**
Scotland Rd., Buck.H. 63 J1
Scotsdale Cl., Orp. 193 H4
Scotsdale Cl., Sutt. 198 B7
Scotsdale Rd. SE12 155 H5
**Scotswood St. EC1 11 F5**
Scotswood Wk. N17 60 D7
Scott Cl. SW16 187 F1
Scott Cl., Epsom 196 C5
Scott Cl., West Dr. 120 C4
Scott Ct. W3 126 C2
*Petersfield Rd.*
Scott Cres., Har. 85 H1
**Scott Ellis Gdns. 6 E4
NW8**
Scott Ellis Gdns. 109 G3
NW8
Scott Fm. Cl., T.Ditt. 194 E1
Scott Gdns., Houns. 122 D7
Scott Ho. N18 60 D5
**Scott Lidgett Cres. 29 H4
SE16**
Scott Lidgett Cres. 132 D2
SE16
Scott Russell Pl. E14 134 B5
*Westferry Rd.*
Scott St. E1 112 E4
Scott Trimmer Way, 143 E2
Houns.
Scottes La., Dag. 100 D1
*Valence Av.*
Scotts Av., Brom. 190 D2
Scotts Dr., Hmptn. 161 H7
Scotts Fm. Rd., 196 C6
Epsom
Scotts La., Brom. 190 D3
Scotts Rd. E10 96 C1
Scotts Rd. W12 127 H2
Scotts Rd., Brom. 173 G7
Scotts Rd., Sthl. 122 C3
**Scott's Yd. EC4 20 B5**
Scottwell Dr. NW9 71 F5
*Crossway*
Scoulding Rd. E16 115 F6
Scouler St. E14 114 D7
*Quixley St.*
Scout App. NW10 88 E4
Scout La. SW4 150 C3
*Old Town*
Scout Way NW7 54 D4
**Scovell Cres. SE1 27 J4**
**Scovell Rd. SE1 27 J4**
Scrattons Ter., Bark. 118 D2
Scriven St. E8 112 C1
Scrooby St. SE6 154 B6
Scrubs La. NW10 107 G3
Scrubs La. W10 107 G3
Scrutton Cl. SW12 150 D7
**Scrutton St. EC2 12 D6**
Scrutton St. EC2 112 B4
Scudamore La. NW9 70 C3
Scutari Rd. SE22 153 F5
Scylla Cres., Houns. 141 E7
Scylla Pl. SE15 152 E3
Scylla Rd., Houns. 141 E6
Seabright St. E2 112/113 E3
*Bethnal Grn. Rd.*
Seabrook Dr., 204 E2
W.Wick.
Seabrook Gdns., 83 G7
Rom.
Seabrook Rd., Dag. 100 D3
Seacole Cl. W3 106 D5
Seacourt Rd. SE2 138 D2
Seacroft Gdns., Wat. 50 D3

Seafield Rd. N11 58 D4
Seaford Rd. E17 78 B3
Seaford Rd. N15 76 A5
Seaford Rd. W13 124 E1
Seaford Rd., Enf. 44 B4
Seaford Rd., Houns. 140 A5
**Seaford St. WC1 10 B4**
Seaford St. WC1 111 E3
Seaforth Av., N.Mal. 183 H5
Seaforth Cres. N5 93 J5
Seaforth Gdns. N21 43 F7
Seaforth Gdns., 197 F4
Epsom
Seaforth Gdns., 63 J5
Wdf.Grn.
**Seaforth Pl. SW1 130 C3**
*Buckingham Gate*
Seagrave Rd. SW6 128 D6
Seagry Rd. E11 79 G6
Seagull Cl., Bark. 117 H3
*Thames Rd.*
Seal St. E8 94 C4
Sealand Rd., Houns. 140 B6
Sealand Wk., 102/103 E3
Nthlt.
*Wayfarer Rd.*
Searle Pl. N4 93 F1
*Evershot Rd.*
Searles Cl. SW11 129 H7
Searles Dr. E6 116 D5
*Winsor Ter.*
**Searles Rd. SE1 36 C1**
Searles Rd. SE1 132 A4
**Sears St. SE5 36 B7**
Sears St. SE5 132 A7
Seasprite Cl., Nthlt. 102 D3
Seaton Av., Ilf. 99 H5
Seaton Cl. E13 115 H4
**Seaton Cl. SE11 35 F3**
Seaton Cl. SE11 131 G5
Seaton Cl. SW15 165 H1
Seaton Cl., Twick. 144 A6
Seaton Gdns., Ruis. 84 A3
Seaton Pt. E5 94 D4
*Nolan Way*
Seaton Rd., Hayes 121 G4
Seaton Rd., Mitch. 185 H2
Seaton Rd., Twick. 143 J6
Seaton Rd., Well. 138 C7
Seaton Rd., Wem. 105 H2
Seaton St. N18 60 D5
**Sebastian St. EC1 11 H4**
Sebastian St. EC1 111 H3
Sebastopol Rd. N9 60 D4
Sebbon St. N1 93 H7
Sebergham Gro. NW7 55 G7
Sebert Rd. E7 97 H5
**Sebright Pas. E2 13 J2**
Sebright Rd., Barn. 40 A2
Secker Cres., Har. 67 J1
**Secker St. SE1 27 E2**
Second Av. E12 98 B4
Second Av. E13 115 G3
Second Av. E17 78 A5
Second Av. N18 61 F4
Second Av. NW4 72 A4
Second Av. SW14 146 E3
Second Av. W3 127 F1
Second Av. W10 108 B4
Second Av., Dag. 119 H1
Second Av., Enf. 44 C5
Second Av., Hayes 121 J1
Second Av., Rom. 82 C5
Second Av., Walt. 178 B6
Second Av., Wem. 87 G2
Second Cl., W.Mol. 179 J4
Second Cross Rd., 162 B2
Twick.
Second Way, Wem. 88 B4
**Sedan Way SE17 36 D3**
Sedcombe Cl., Sid. 176 B4
*Knoll Rd.*
Sedcote Rd., Enf. 45 F5
**Sedding St. SW1 32 B1**
Sedding St. SW1 130 A4
Seddon Rd., Mord. 185 G5
**Seddon St. WC1 10 D4**
Sedge Rd. N17 61 F7
Sedgebrook Rd. SE3 156 A2
Sedgecombe Av., 69 F5
Har.
Sedgeford Rd. W12 127 F1
Sedgehill Rd. SE6 172 A4
Sedgemere Av. N2 73 F3
Sedgemere Rd. SE2 138 C3
Sedgemoor Dr., Dag. 101 G4
Sedgeway SE6 173 F1
Sedgewood Cl., 191 F7
Brom.
Sedgmoor Pl. SE5 132 B7
Sedgwick Rd. E10 96 C2
Sedgwick St. E9 95 G5
Sedleigh Rd. SW18 148 C6

Sedlescombe Rd. SW6 128 C6
**Sedley Pl. W1 16 D4**
Sedley Ri., Loug. 48 C2
Sedum Cl. NW9 70 B5
Seeley Dr. SE21 170 B4
Seelig Av. NW9 71 G7
Seely Rd. SW17 168 A6
**Seething La. EC3 21 E6**
Seething La. EC3 112 B7
Seething Wells La., Surb. 181 F6
Sefton Av. NW7 54 D5
Sefton Av., Har. 68 A1
Sefton Cl., Orp. 193 J4
Sefton Rd., Croy. 202 D1
Sefton Rd., Orp. 193 J4
Sefton St. SW15 147 J2
Segal Cl. SE23 153 H7
**Sekforde St. EC1 11 G6**
Sekforde St. EC1 111 H4
Sekhon Ter., Felt. 161 G3
Selan Gdns., Hayes 102 B5
Selbie Av. NW10 89 F5
Selborne Av. E12 98 D4
*Walton Rd.*
Selborne Av., Bex. 176 E1
Selborne Gdns. NW4 71 G4
Selborne Gdns., Grnf. 104 D1
Selborne Rd. E17 77 J5
Selborne Rd. N14 58 E3
Selborne Rd. N22 75 F1
Selborne Rd. SE5 152 A2
*Denmark Hill*
Selborne Rd., Croy. 202 B3
Selborne Rd., Ilf. 98 D2
Selborne Rd., N.Mal. 182 E2
Selborne Rd., Sid. 176 B4
Selborne Wk. E17 77 J4
Selbourne Av., Surb. 195 J2
Selby Chase, Ruis. 84 B2
Selby Cl. E6 116 B5
*Linton Gdns.*
Selby Cl., Chess. 195 H7
Selby Cl., Chis. 174 D6
Selby Gdns., Sthl. 103 G4
Selby Grn., Cars. 185 H7
Selby Rd. E11 96 E3
Selby Rd. E13 115 H5
Selby Rd. N17 60 B6
Selby Rd. SE20 188 D2
Selby Rd. W5 105 E4
Selby Rd., Cars. 185 H7
**Selby St. E1 13 J6**
Selby St. E1 112 D4
Selden Rd. SE15 153 F2
Selden Wk. N7 93 F2
*Durham Rd.*
Selhurst Cl. SW19 166 A1
Selhurst New Rd. SE25 188 B6
Selhurst Pl. SE25 188 B6
Selhurst Rd. N9 60 A3
Selhurst Rd. SE25 188 B5
Selinas La., Dag. 83 E7
Selkirk Rd. SW17 167 H4
Selkirk Rd., Twick. 161 J2
Sellers Cl., Borwd. 38 C1
Sellers Hall Cl. N3 56 D7
Sellincourt Rd. SW17 167 H5
Sellindge Cl., Beck. 171 J7
**Sellon Ms. SE11 34 D2**
Sellons Av. NW10 107 F1
Sellwood Dr., Barn. 40 A5
Selsdon Av., S.Croy. 202 A6
*Selsdon Rd.*
Selsdon Cl., Rom. 83 J1
Selsdon Cl., Surb. 181 H5
Selsdon Rd. E11 79 G7
Selsdon Rd. E13 115 J1
Selsdon Rd. NW2 89 F2
Selsdon Rd. SE27 169 H3
Selsdon Rd., S.Croy. 202 A5
Selsdon Rd. Ind. Est., S.Croy. 202 A6
*Selsdon Rd.*
Selsdon Way E14 134 B3
Selsea Pl. N16 94 B5
*Crossway*
Selsey Cres., Well. 158 D1
Selsey St. E14 114 A5
Selvage La. NW7 54 D5
Selway Cl., Pnr. 66 B4
**Selwood Pl. SW7 30 E3**
Selwood Pl. SW7 129 G5
Selwood Rd., Chess. 195 G4
Selwood Rd., Croy. 202 E2
Selwood Rd., Sutt. 198 C1
**Selwood Ter. SW7 31 E3**
Selworthy Cl. E11 79 G5
Selworthy Rd. SE6 171 J3
Selwyn Av. E4 62 C6
Selwyn Av., Ilf. 81 H6
Selwyn Av., Rich. 145 H3
Selwyn Cl., Houns. 143 E4
Selwyn Ct. SE3 155 E3
Selwyn Ct., Edg. 54 B7
*Camrose Av.*
Selwyn Cres., Well. 158 B4
Selwyn Rd. E3 113 J2
Selwyn Rd. E13 115 H1
Selwyn Rd. NW10 88 D7
Selwyn Rd., N.Mal. 182 D5
Semley Gate E9 95 J6
*Eastway*
**Semley Pl. SW1 32 C2**
Semley Pl. SW1 130 A4
Semley Rd. SW16 187 E2
Senate St. SE15 153 F2
Senator Wk. SE28 137 G3
*Broadwater Rd.*
Seneca Rd., Th.Hth. 187 J4
Senga Rd., Wall. 200 A1
Senhouse Rd., Sutt. 198 A3
**Senior St. W2 14 A1**
Senior St. W2 108 E5
Senlac Rd. SE12 173 H1
Sennen Rd., Enf. 44 C7
Sennen Wk. SE9 174 B3
Senrab St. E1 113 G6
Sentinel Cl., Nthlt. 103 E4
Sentinel Sq. NW4 71 J4
September Way, Stan. 53 E6
Sequoia Cl., Bushey 52 A1
*Giant Tree Hill*
Sequoia Gdns., Orp. 193 J7
Sequoia Pk., Pnr. 51 H6
Serbin Cl. E10 78 C7
**Serjeants Inn EC4 19 F4**
**Serle St. WC2 18 D3**
Serle St. WC2 111 F6
**Sermon La. EC4 19 J4**
**Serpentine Rd. W2 23 J2**
Serpentine Rd. W2 129 J1
Serviden Dr., Brom. 192 A1
**Setchell Rd. SE1 37 F1**
**Setchell Way SE1 37 F1**
Seth St. SE16 133 F2
*Swan Rd.*
Seton Gdns., Dag. 100 C7
Settle Pt. E13 115 G2
*London Rd.*
Settle Rd. E13 115 G2
*London Rd.*
**Settles St. E1 21 J2**
Settles St. E1 112 D5
Settrington Rd. SW6 148 E2
Seven Acres, Cars. 199 H2
Seven Acres, Nthwd. 50 A6
Seven Kings Rd., Ilf. 99 J2
Seven Sisters Rd. N4 93 F3
Seven Sisters Rd. N7 93 F3
Seven Sisters Rd. N15 76 A6
Seven Stars Cor. W12 127 G3
*Goldhawk Rd.*
Sevenoaks Cl., Bexh. 159 J4
Sevenoaks Ho. SE25 188 D3
Sevenoaks Rd. SE4 153 H6
Sevenoaks Rd., Orp. 207 J4
Sevenoaks Rd. (Green St. Grn.), Orp. 207 J7
Sevenoaks Way, Orp. 176 C7
Sevenoaks Way, Sid. 176 C7
Seventh Av. E12 98 C4
Seventh Av., Hayes 122 A1
Severn Dr., Esher 194 D2
Severn Way NW10 89 F5
Severnake Cl. E14 134 A4
Severus Rd. SW11 149 H4
Seville Ms. N1 94 B7
**Seville St. SW1 24 A4**
Seville St. SW1 129 J2
Sevington Rd. NW4 71 H6
**Sevington St. W9 6 A6**
Sevington St. W9 108 E4
Seward Rd. W7 124 D2
Seward Rd., Beck. 189 G2
**Seward St. EC1 11 H5**
Seward St. EC1 111 J3
Sewardstone Gdns. E4 46 B5
Sewardstone Rd. E2 113 F2
Sewardstone Rd. E4 46 B7
Sewdley St. E5 95 G3
Sewell Rd. SE2 138 A3
Sewell St. E13 115 G3
Sextant Av. E14 134 D4
Seymour Av. N17 76 D2
Seymour Av., Mord. 184 A7
Seymour Cl., E.Mol. 179 J5
Seymour Cl., Loug. 48 B6
Seymour Cl., Pnr. 67 F1
Seymour Ct. E4 63 F2
Seymour Dr., Brom. 206 C1
Seymour Gdns. SE4 153 H3
Seymour Gdns., Felt. 160 C4
Seymour Gdns., Ilf. 98 C1
Seymour Gdns., Ruis. 84 D1
Seymour Gdns., Surb. 181 J5
Seymour Gdns., Twick. 144 E7
**Seymour Ms. W1 16 B3**
Seymour Ms. W1 110 A6
Seymour Pl. SE25 188 E4
**Seymour Pl. W1 15 J2**
Seymour Pl. W1 109 H5
Seymour Rd. E4 62 B1
Seymour Rd. E6 116 A2
Seymour Rd. E10 95 J1
Seymour Rd. N3 57 E7
Seymour Rd. N8 75 G5
Seymour Rd. N9 61 E2
Seymour Rd. SW18 148 C7
Seymour Rd. SW19 166 A2
Seymour Rd. W4 126 C4
Seymour Rd., Cars. 200 A5
Seymour Rd., E.Mol. 179 J5
Seymour Rd., Hmptn. 161 J5
Seymour Rd., Kings.T. 181 G1
Seymour Rd., Mitch. 186 A7
**Seymour St. W1 15 J4**
Seymour St. W1 109 J6
**Seymour St. W2 15 J4**
Seymour St. W2 109 J6
Seymour Ter. SE20 188 E1
Seymour Vil. SE20 188 E1
**Seymour Wk. SW10 30 C5**
Seymour Wk. SW10 129 F6
Seymours, The, Loug. 48 D1
Seyssel St. E14 134 C4
Shaa Rd. W3 106 D7
Shacklegate La., Tedd. 162 B4
Shackleton Cl. SE23 170/171 E2
*Featherstone Av.*
Shackleton Ct. E14 134 A5
*Napier Av.*
Shackleton Rd., Sthl. 103 F7
Shacklewell Grn. E8 94 C4
Shacklewell La. E8 94 C5
Shacklewell Rd. N16 94 C4
Shacklewell Row E8 94 C4
**Shacklewell St. E2 13 G5**
Shacklewell St. E2 112 C4
**Shad Thames SE1 29 F2**
Shad Thames SE1 132 C1
Shadbolt Av. E4 61 H5
Shadbolt Cl., Wor.Pk. 197 F2
Shadwell Ct., Nthlt. 103 F2
*Shadwell Dr.*
Shadwell Dr., Nthlt. 103 F3
Shadwell Gdns. E1 113 F6
*Martha St.*
Shadwell Pierhead E1 113 F7
*Glamis Rd.*
Shadwell Pl. E1 113 F7
*Sutton St.*
Shaef Way, Tedd. 162 D7
Shafter Rd., Dag. 101 J6
Shaftesbury, Loug. 48 A3
**Shaftesbury Av. W1 17 H5**
Shaftesbury Av. W1 110 D7
**Shaftesbury Av. WC2 17 H5**
Shaftesbury Av. WC2 110 D7
Shaftesbury Av., Barn. 41 F4
Shaftesbury Av., Enf. 45 G2
Shaftesbury Av., Felt. 142 A6
Shaftesbury Av., Har. 85 H1
Shaftesbury Av. (Kenton), Har. 69 G6
Shaftesbury Av., Sthl. 123 G4
Shaftesbury Circle, Har. 85 J1
*Shaftesbury Av.*
Shaftesbury Ct. N1 112 A2
*Shaftesbury St.*
Shaftesbury Gdns. NW10 107 E4
Shaftesbury Ms. SW4 150 C5
*Clapham Common S. Side*
Shaftesbury Ms. W8 128 D3
*Stratford Rd.*
Shaftesbury Pl. W14 128 C4
*Warwick Rd.*
Shaftesbury Pt. E13 115 H2
*High St.*
Shaftesbury Rd. E4 62 D1
Shaftesbury Rd. E7 97 J7
Shaftesbury Rd. E10 96 A1
Shaftesbury Rd. E17 78 B6
Shaftesbury Rd. N18 60 B6
Shaftesbury Rd. N19 92 E1
Shaftesbury Rd., Beck. 189 J2
Shaftesbury Rd., Cars. 185 G7
Shaftesbury Rd., Rich. 145 H3
**Shaftesbury St. N1 12 A2**
Shaftesbury St. N1 111 J2
Shaftesbury Way, Twick. 162 A3
Shaftesbury Waye, Hayes 102 B5
Shaftesburys, The, Bark. 98 D7
**Shafto Ms. SW1 23 J6**
Shafton Rd. E9 113 G1
Shakespeare Av. N11 58 C5
Shakespeare Av. NW10 106 D1
Shakespeare Av., Felt. 142 A6
Shakespeare Av., Hayes 102 B4
Shakespeare Cres. E12 98 C6
Shakespeare Cres. NW10 106 D1
Shakespeare Dr., Har. 70 A6
Shakespeare Gdns. N2 73 J4
Shakespeare Ho. N14 58 D2
*High St.*
Shakespeare Rd. E17 77 G2
Shakespeare Rd. N3 72 D1
*Popes Dr.*
Shakespeare Rd. NW7 55 F4
Shakespeare Rd. SE24 151 H5
Shakespeare Rd. W3 126 C1
Shakespeare Rd. W7 104 C7
Shakespeare Rd., Bexh. 158 E1
Shakespeare Sq., Ilf. 65 F6
Shakespeare Way, Felt. 160 C4
Shakspeare Ms. N16 94 B4
*Shakspeare Wk.*
Shakspeare Wk. N16 94 B4
**Shalcomb St. SW10 30 D6**
Shalcomb St. SW10 129 F6
Shaldon Dr., Mord. 184 B5
Shaldon Dr., Ruis. 84 C3
Shaldon Rd., Edg. 69 J1
Shalfleet Dr. W10 108 A7
Shalford Cl., Orp. 207 F4
Shalimar Gdns. W3 106 C7
Shalimar Rd. W3 106 C7
*Hereford Rd.*
Shallons Rd. SE9 174 E4
Shalston Vil., Surb. 181 J6
Shalstone Rd. SW14 146 B3
Shamrock Rd., Croy. 187 F6
Shamrock St. SW4 150 D3
Shamrock Way N14 58 B1
**Shand St. SE1 28 E3**
Shand St. SE1 132 B2
Shandon Rd. SW4 150 C6
Shandy St. E1 113 G5
Shanklin Gdns., Wat. 50 C4
Shanklin Rd. N8 74 D5
Shanklin Rd. N15 76 D4
Shanklin Way SE15 132 C7
*Pentridge St.*
Shannon Cl. NW2 90 A3
Shannon Cl., Sthl. 122 D5
Shannon Gro. SW9 151 F4
**Shannon Pl. NW8 7 H1**
Shannon Way, Beck. 172 B6
Shap Cres., Cars. 199 J1
Shapland Way N13 59 F5
Shardcroft Av. SE24 151 H5
Shardeloes Rd. SE14 153 J2
Sharland Cl., Th.Hth. 187 G6
*Dunheved Rd. N.*
Sharman Ct., Sid. 176 A4
Sharnbrooke Cl., Well. 158 C3
Sharon Cl., Surb. 195 G1
Sharon Gdns. E9 113 F1
Sharon Rd. W4 126 D5
Sharon Rd., Enf. 45 H2
Sharpe Cl. W7 104 C5
*Templeman Rd.*
Sharpleshall St. NW1 91 J7
Sharpness Cl., Hayes 102 E5
Sharratt St. SE15 133 F6
**Sharsted St. SE17 35 G4**
Sharsted St. SE17 131 H5
Sharvel La., Nthlt. 102 A1
**Shavers Pl. SW1 17 H6**
Shaw Av., Bark. 118 E2
Shaw Cl. SE28 138 B1
Shaw Cl., Bushey 52 B2

Shoreham Cl., Croy. 189 F6
Shoreham Rd. E., Houns. 140 B5
Shoreham Rd. W., Houns. 140 B5
Shoreham Way, Brom. 191 G6
**Shorncliffe Rd. SE1 37 F3**
Shorncliffe Rd. SE1 132 C5
Shorndean St. SE6 172 C1
Shorne Cl., Sid. 158 B6
Shornefield Cl., Brom. 192 D3
Shornells Way SE2 138 C5
*Willrose Cres.*
Shorrolds Rd. SW6 128 C7
Short Hedges, Houns. 143 H1
Short Hill, Har. 86 B1
*High St.*
Short Path SE18 136/137 E6
*Westdale Rd.*
Short Rd. E11 96 E2
Short Rd. E15 114 D1
Short Rd. W4 126 E6
Short Rd., Houns. 140 B6
Short St. NW4 71 J4
*New Brent St.*
**Short St. SE1 27 F3**
Short Wall E15 114 C3
Short Way SE9 156 B3
Short Way, Twick. 143 J7
Shortcroft Rd., Epsom 197 F7
Shortcrofts Rd., Dag. 101 F6
**Shorter St. E1 21 F5**
Shorter St. E1 112 C7
Shortgate N12 56 C4
Shortlands W6 128 A4
Shortlands, Hayes 121 G6
Shortlands Cl. N18 60 A3
Shortlands Cl., Belv. 139 F3
Shortlands Gdns., Brom. 191 E2
Shortlands Gro., Brom. 190 D3
Shortlands Rd. E10 78 B7
Shortlands Rd., Brom. 190 D3
Shortlands Rd., Kings.T. 163 J7
Shorts Cft. NW9 70 B4
**Shorts Gdns. WC2 18 A4**
Shorts Gdns. WC2 110 E6
Shorts Rd., Cars. 199 H4
Shortway N12 57 H6
Shotfield, Wall. 200 B6
Shott Cl., Sutt. 199 F5
*Turnpike La.*
Shottendane Rd. SW6 148 D1
Shottery Cl. SE9 174 B3
Shottfield Av. SW14 146 E4
Shoulder of Mutton All. E14 113 H7
*Narrow St.*
**Shouldham St. W1 15 H2**
Shouldham St. W1 109 H5
Showers Way, Hayes 122 A1
Shrapnel Cl. SE18 136 B7
Shrapnel Rd. SE9 156 C3
Shrewsbury Av. SW14 146 C4
Shrewsbury Av., Har. 69 H4
Shrewsbury Cl., Surb. 195 H2
Shrewsbury Ct. EC1 111 J4
*Whitecross St.*
Shrewsbury Cres. NW10 106 D1
Shrewsbury La. SE18 156 E1
Shrewsbury Ms. W2 108 D5
*Chepstow Rd.*
Shrewsbury Rd. E7 98 A5
Shrewsbury Rd. N11 58 C6
Shrewsbury Rd. W2 108 D6
Shrewsbury Rd., Beck. 189 H3
Shrewsbury Rd., Cars. 185 H6
Shrewsbury Rd., Felt. 141 G5
*Great South-West Rd.*
Shrewsbury Rd., Houns. 141 G5
*Great South-West Rd.*
Shrewsbury St. W10 107 J4
Shrewsbury Wk., Islw. 144 D3
*South St.*
Shrewton Rd. SW17 167 J7
Shroffold Rd., Brom. 173 E4
Shropshire Cl., Mitch. 187 E4
**Shropshire Pl. WC1 9 G6**
Shropshire Rd. N22 59 F7
**Shroton St. NW1 15 G1**
Shroton St. NW1 109 H5
Shrubberies, The E18 79 G2
Shrubberies, The, Chig. 65 F5
Shrubbery Cl. N1 111 J1
*St. Paul St.*
Shrubbery Gdns. N21 43 H7
Shrubbery Rd. N9 60 D3
Shrubbery Rd. SW16 168 E4
Shrubbery Rd., Sthl. 123 F1
Shrubland Gro., Wor.Pk. 197 J3
Shrubland Rd. E8 112 D1
Shrubland Rd. E10 78 A7
Shrubland Rd. E17 78 A5
Shrublands Av., Croy. 204 A4
Shrublands Cl. N20 57 G1
Shrublands Cl. SE26 171 F3
Shrublands Cl., Chig. 65 F6
Shrubsall Cl. SE9 174 B1
Shuna Wk. N1 94 A6
*St. Paul's Rd.*
Shurland Av., Barn. 41 G6
**Shurland Gdns. SE15 37 G7**
Shurlock Dr., Orp. 207 F4
Shuters Sq. W14 128 C5
*Sun Rd.*
Shuttle Cl., Sid. 157 J7
**Shuttle St. E1 13 H6**
Shuttlemead, Bex. 159 F7
Shuttleworth Rd. SW11 149 H2
Sibella Rd. SW4 150 D2
Sibley Cl., Bexh. 159 E5
Sibley Gro. E12 98 B7
Sibthorpe Rd. SE12 155 H6
Sibton Rd., Cars. 185 H7
**Sicilian Av. WC1 18 B2**
Sidbury St. SW6 148 B1
Sidcup Bypass, Chis. 174 E2
Sidcup Bypass, Orp. 176 D7
Sidcup Bypass, Sid. 175 H4
Sidcup High St., Sid. 176 A4
Sidcup Hill, Sid. 176 B4
Sidcup Hill Gdns., Sid. 176 C5
*Sidcup Hill*
Sidcup Pl., Sid. 176 A5
Sidcup Rd. SE9 156 A7
Sidcup Rd. SE12 155 H5
Sidcup Technology Cen., Sid. 176 D5
Siddeley Dr., Houns. 142 E3
**Siddons La. NW1 8 A6**
Siddons Rd. N17 76 D1
Siddons Rd. SE23 171 H2
Siddons Rd., Croy. 201 G3
Side Rd. E17 77 J5
Sidewood Rd. SE9 175 G1
**Sidford Pl. SE1 26 D6**
Sidings, The E11 96 C1
Sidings, The, Loug. 48 B6
Sidings Ms. N7 93 G3
Sidmouth Av., Islw. 144 B2
Sidmouth Cl., Wat. 50 B2
Sidmouth Dr., Ruis. 84 A3
Sidmouth Par. NW2 89 J7
*Sidmouth Rd.*
Sidmouth Rd. E10 96 C3
Sidmouth Rd. NW2 89 J7
Sidmouth Rd. SE15 152 C1
Sidmouth Rd., Well. 138 C7
**Sidmouth St. WC1 10 B4**
Sidmouth St. WC1 111 E3
Sidney Av. N13 59 F5
Sidney Elson Way E6 116 D2
*Edwin Av.*
Sidney Gdns., Brent. 125 F6
**Sidney Gro. EC1 11 G2**
Sidney Rd. E7 97 G3
Sidney Rd. N22 59 F7
Sidney Rd. SE25 188 D5
Sidney Rd. SW9 151 F2
Sidney Rd., Beck. 189 H2
Sidney Rd., Har. 67 J3
Sidney Rd., Twick. 144 D6
Sidney Rd., Walt. 178 A7
Sidney Sq. E1 113 F6
Sidney St. E1 113 E5
Sidworth St. E8 95 E7
Siebert Rd. SE3 135 G6
Siemens Rd. SE18 136 A3
Sigdon Rd. E8 94 D5
Sigers, The, Pnr. 66 B6
Signmakers Yd. NW1 110 B1
*Delancey St.*
Sigrist Sq., Kings.T. 181 H1
Silbury Av., Mitch. 185 H1
**Silbury St. N1 12 B3**
Silchester Rd. W10 108 A6
Silecroft Rd., Bexh. 159 G1
Silesia Bldgs. E8 94/95 E7
*London La.*
**Silex St. SE1 27 H4**
Silex St. SE1 131 H2
Silk Cl. SE12 155 G5
Silk Mills Path SE13 154 C2
*Lewisham Rd.*
**Silk St. EC2 20 A1**
Silk St. EC2 111 J5
Silkfield Rd. NW9 71 E5
Silkin Ho., Wat. 50 C3
Silkmills Sq. E9 95 J6
Silkstream Rd., Edg. 70 C1
Silsoe Rd. N22 75 F2
Silver Birch Av. E4 61 J6
Silver Birch Cl. N11 58 A6
Silver Birch Cl. SE28 138 A1
Silver Birch Gdns. E6 116 C4
Silver Birch Ms., Ilf. 65 F6
*Fencepiece Rd.*
Silver Cl. SE14 133 H7
*Southerngate Way*
Silver Cl., Har. 52 A7
Silver Cres. W4 126 B4
Silver Jubilee Way, Houns. 142 B2
Silver La., W.Wick. 204 D2
**Silver Pl. W1 17 G5**
Silver Rd. SE13 154 B3
*Elmira St.*
Silver Rd. W12 108 A7
Silver Spring Cl., Erith 139 H6
Silver St. N18 60 B4
Silver St., Enf. 44 A3
Silver Wk. SE16 133 J1
Silver Way, Rom. 83 H3
Silverbirch Wk. NW3 92 A6
*Queens Cres.*
Silvercliffe Gdns., Barn. 41 H4
Silverdale SE26 171 F4
Silverdale, Enf. 43 E4
Silverdale Av., Ilf. 81 H5
Silverdale Cl. W7 124 B1
Silverdale Cl., Nthlt. 85 F5
Silverdale Cl., Sutt. 198 C4
Silverdale Dr. SE9 174 B2
Silverdale Dr., Sun. 178 B2
Silverdale Gdns., Hayes 122 A2
Silverdale Rd. E4 62 D6
Silverdale Rd., Bexh. 159 H2
Silverdale Rd., Hayes 122 A2
Silverdale Rd. (Petts Wd.), Orp. 193 F4
Silverhall St., Islw. 144 D3
Silverholme Cl., Har. 69 G7
Silverland St. E16 136 C1
Silverleigh Rd., Th.Hth. 187 F4
Silvermere Rd. SE6 154 B6
Silverston Way, Stan. 53 F6
Silverthorn Gdns. E4 62 A2
Silverthorne Rd. SW8 150 B2
Silverton Rd. W6 128 A6
Silvertown Way E16 115 F6
Silvertree La., Grnf. 104 A3
*Cowgate Rd.*
Silverwood Cl., Beck. 172 A7
Silvester Rd. SE22 152 C5
**Silvester St. SE1 28 A4**
Silvocea Way E14 114 D6
Silwood Est. SE16 133 F4
Silwood St. SE16 133 F4
Simla Cl. SE14 133 H6
**Simla Ho. SE1 28 C4**
Simmil Rd., Esher 194 B5
Simmons Cl. N20 57 H1
Simmons Cl., Chess. 195 F7
Simmons La. E4 62 D2
Simmons Rd. SE18 136 E5
Simmons Way N20 57 H2
Simms Cl., Cars. 199 H2
Simms Gdns. N2 73 F2
*Tarling Rd.*
**Simms Rd. SE1 37 H2**
Simms Rd. SE1 132 D4
Simnel Rd. SE12 155 H7
Simon Cl. W11 108 C7
*Portobello Rd.*
Simonds Rd. E10 96 A2
Simone Cl., Brom. 192 A1
Simons Wk. E15 96 D5
*Waddington St.*
Simpson Cl. N21 42/43 E5
*Macleod Rd.*
Simpson Dr. W3 106 D6
Simpson Rd., Houns. 143 F6
Simpson Rd., Rich. 163 F4
Simpson St. SW11 149 G2
Simpsons Rd. E14 114 B7
Simpsons Rd., Brom. 191 G3
Simrose Ct. SW18 148 D5
*Wandsworth High St.*
Sims Wk. SE3 155 F4
Sinclair Ct., Beck. 172 A7
Sinclair Gdns. W14 128 A2
Sinclair Gro. NW11 72 A6
Sinclair Rd. E4 61 J5
Sinclair Rd. W14 128 A2
Sinclare Cl., Enf. 44 C1
Singapore Rd. W13 124 D1
**Singer St. EC2 12 C4**
Singleton Cl. SW17 167 J7
Singleton Cl., Croy. 187 J7
*St. Saviours Rd.*
Singleton Rd., Dag. 101 F5
Singleton Scarp N12 56 D5
Sinnott Rd. E17 77 G1
Sion Rd., Twick. 162 E1
Sipson Cl., West Dr. 120 D6
Sipson La., Hayes 120 D6
Sipson La., West Dr. 120 D6
Sipson Rd., West Dr. 120 D5
Sipson Way, West Dr. 120 D7
Sir Alexander Cl. W3 127 F1
Sir Alexander Rd. W3 127 F1
Sir Cyril Black Way SW19 166 D7
**Sir Thomas More Est. SW3 31 F6**
Sirdar Rd. N22 75 H3
Sirdar Rd. W11 108 A7
Sirdar Rd., Mitch. 168 A6
*Grenfell Rd.*
**Sirinham Pt. SW8 34 D6**
Sirinham Pt. SW8 131 F6
Sirius Rd., Nthwd. 50 A5
**Sise La. EC4 20 B4**
Siskin Cl., Borwd. 38 A4
Sisley Rd., Bark. 117 H1
Sispara Gdns. SW18 148 C6
Sissinghurst Rd., Croy. 188 D7
Sissulu Ct. E6 115 J1
*Redclyffe Rd.*
**Sister Mabel's Way SE15 37 H7**
Sisters Av. SW11 149 J4
Sistova Rd. SW12 168 B1
Sisulu Pl. SW9 151 G3
Sittingbourne Av., Enf. 44 A6
Sitwell Gro., Stan. 52 C5
Siverst Cl., Nthlt. 85 H6
**Sivill Ho. E2 13 G3**
Sivill Ho. E2 112 C3
Siviter Way, Dag. 101 H7
Siward Rd. N17 76 A1
Siward Rd. SW17 167 F3
Siward Rd., Brom. 191 H3
Six Acres Est. N4 93 G2
**Six Bridges Trd. Est. SE1 37 J4**
Six Bridges Trd. Est. SE1 132 D5
Sixth Av. E12 98 C4
Sixth Av. W10 108 B3
Sixth Av., Hayes 121 J1
Sixth Cross Rd., Twick. 161 J3
Skardu Rd. NW2 90 B5
Skeena Hill SW18 148 B7
Skeffington Rd. E6 116 C1
Skelbrook St. SW18 167 E2
Skelgill Rd. SW15 148 C4
Skelley Rd. E15 97 F7
Skelton Cl. E8 94 C6
*Buttermere Wk.*
Skelton Rd. E7 97 G6
Skeltons La. E10 78 B7
Skelwith Rd. W6 127 J6
Skenfrith Ho. SE15 132/133 E6
*Commercial Way*
Skerne Rd., Kings.T. 181 G1
Sketchley Gdns. SE16 133 G5
Sketty Rd., Enf. 44 B3
Skiers St. E15 114 E1
Skiffington Cl. SW2 169 G1
Skinner Ct. E2 112/113 E2
*Parmiter St.*
**Skinner Pl. SW1 32 B2**
**Skinner St. EC1 11 F4**
Skinner St. EC1 111 G3
**Skinners La. EC4 20 A5**
Skinners La., Houns. 143 H1
Skinner's Row SE10 154 B1
*Blackheath Rd.*
Skipsey Av. E6 116 C3
Skipton Cl. N11 58 A6
*Ribblesdale Av.*
Skipton Dr., Hayes 121 F3

Skipworth Rd. E9 — 113 F1
Skomer Wk. N1 — 93 J6
*Clephane Rd.*
Sky Peals Rd., — 78 D1
*Wdf.Grn.*
Skyport Dr., West Dr. — 120 A7
Slade, The SE18 — 137 H6
Slade Ho., Houns. — 143 F6
Slade Twr. E10 — 96 B2
**Slade Wk. SE17** — **35 H6**
Sladebrook Rd. SE3 — 156 A2
Sladedale Rd. SE18 — 137 H5
Slades Cl., Enf. — 43 G3
Slades Dr., Chis. — 175 F3
Slades Gdns., Enf. — 43 G2
Slades Hill, Enf. — 43 G3
Slades Ri., Enf. — 43 G3
Slagrove Pl. SE13 — 154 B5
**Slaidburn St. SW10** — **30 D6**
Slaidburn St. SW10 — 129 F6
Slaithwaite Rd. SE13 — 154 C4
Slaney Pl. N7 — 93 G5
*Hornsey Rd.*
Slater Cl. SE18 — 136 D5
*Woolwich New Rd.*
Slattery Rd., Felt. — 160 C1
Sleaford Grn., Wat. — 50 D3
**Sleaford St. SW8** — **33 F7**
Sleaford St. SW8 — 130 C7
Slievemore Cl. SW4 — 150 D3
*Voltaire Rd.*
**Slingsby Pl. WC2** — **18 A5**
Slippers Pl. SE16 — 133 E3
**Sloane Av. SW3** — **31 G2**
Sloane Av. SW3 — 129 H4
**Sloane Ct. E. SW3** — **32 B3**
**Sloane Ct. W. SW3** — **32 B3**
**Sloane Gdns. SW1** — **32 B2**
Sloane Gdns. SW1 — 130 A4
Sloane Gdns., Orp. — 207 F3
**Sloane Sq. SW1** — **32 B2**
Sloane Sq. SW1 — 129 J4
**Sloane St. SW1** — **24 A5**
Sloane St. SW1 — 129 J2
**Sloane Ter. SW1** — **32 A1**
Sloane Ter. SW1 — 129 J4
Sloane Wk., Croy. — 189 J6
Slocum Cl. SE28 — 118 C7
Slough La. NW9 — 70 C6
Sly St. E1 — 112/113 E6
*Cannon St. Rd.*
Smaldon Cl., West Dr. — 120 D3
*Walnut Av.*
Smallberry Av., — 144 C2
*Islw.*
**Smallbrook Ms. W2** — **14 E4**
Smalley Cl. N16 — 94 C3
Smalley Rd. Est. N16 — 94 C3
*Smalley Cl.*
Smallwood Rd. SW17 — 167 G4
Smardale Rd. SW18 — 149 F5
*Alma Rd.*
Smarden Cl., Belv. — 139 G5
*Essendon Rd.*
Smarden Gro. SE9 — 174 C2
Smart St. E2 — 113 G3
Smarts La., Loug. — 48 A4
Smarts Pl. N18 — 60 D5
*Fore St.*
**Smart's Pl. WC2** — **18 B3**
Smeaton Cl., Chess. — 195 G6
*Merritt Gdns.*
Smeaton Rd. SW18 — 148 D7
Smeaton Rd., — 64 C5
*Wdf.Grn.*
Smeaton St. E1 — 132 E1
Smedley St. SW4 — 150 D2
Smedley St. SW8 — 150 D2
Smeed Rd. E3 — 96 A7
Smiles Pl. SE13 — 154 C2
Smith Cl. SE16 — 133 G1
**Smith Sq. SW1** — **26 A6**
Smith Sq. SW1 — 130 E3
**Smith St. SW3** — **31 J3**
Smith St. SW3 — 129 J5
Smith St., Surb. — 181 J6
**Smith Ter. SW3** — **31 J4**
Smith Ter. SW3 — 129 J5
**Smithfield St. EC1** — **19 G2**
Smithies Ct. E15 — 96 C5
Smithies Rd. SE2 — 138 B4
**Smith's Ct. W1** — **17 G5**
Smiths Fm. Est., — 103 G2
*Nthlt.*
Smiths Rd. SW18 — 167 F2
*Summerley St.*
Smith's Yd., Croy. — 201 J3
*St. Georges Wk.*
Smithson Rd. N17 — 76 A1
Smithwood Cl. SW19 — 166 B1
Smithy St. E1 — 113 F5
Smock Wk., Croy. — 187 J6
**Smokehouse Yd. EC1** — **19 H1**

Smokehouse Yd. — 111 H5
EC1
Smugglers Way — 149 E4
SW18
**Smyrks Rd. SE17** — **36 E4**
Smyrks Rd. SE17 — 132 B5
Smyrna Rd. NW6 — 90 D7
Snakes La. E14 — 114 B7
Snakes La., Barn. — 42 B3
Snakes La. E., — 63 J6
*Wdf.Grn.*
Snakes La. W., — 63 G6
*Wdf.Grn.*
Snaresbrook Dr., Stan. — 53 G4
Snaresbrook Rd. E11 — 78 E4
Snarsgate St. W10 — 107 J5
Sneath Av. NW11 — 72 C7
Snells Pk. N18 — 60 C6
Sneyd Rd. NW2 — 89 J4
**Snow Hill EC1** — **19 G2**
Snow Hill EC1 — 111 H5
**Snow Hill Ct. EC1** — **19 H3**
Snowberry Cl. E15 — 96 D4
Snowbury Rd. SW6 — 149 E2
**Snowden St. EC2** — **12 D6**
Snowden St. EC2 — 112 B4
Snowdon Cres., — 121 F3
Hayes
Snowdon Dr. NW9 — 70 E6
Snowdon Rd., — 141 F5
Houns.
*Southern Perimeter Rd.*
Snowdown Cl. SE20 — 189 G1
Snowdrop Cl., — 161 G6
Hmptn.
*Gresham Rd.*
Snowman Ho. NW6 — 109 E1
**Snowsfields SE1** — **28 C3**
Snowsfields SE1 — 132 A2
Snowshill Rd. E12 — 98 B5
Snowy Fielder Waye, — 144 E2
Islw.
Soames St. SE15 — 152 C3
Soames Wk., N.Mal. — 182 E1
Socket La., Brom. — 191 H7
**Soho Sq. W1** — **17 H3**
Soho Sq. W1 — 110 D6
**Soho St. W1** — **17 H3**
Sojourner Truth Cl. — 94/95 E6
E8
*Richmond Rd.*
Solander Gdns. — 112/113 E7
E1
*Dellow St.*
Solebay St. E1 — 113 H4
Solent Ri. E13 — 115 G3
Solent Rd. NW6 — 90 D5
Solent Rd., Houns. — 140 C6
**Soley Ms. WC1** — **10 E3**
Solna Av. SW15 — 147 J5
Solna Rd. N21 — 60 A1
Solomon Av. N9 — 60 D4
Solomon's Pas. SE15 — 152 E4
Solon New Rd. SW4 — 150 E4
Solon New Rd. — 150/151 E4
Est. SW4
*Solon New Rd.*
Solon Rd. SW2 — 151 E4
Solway Cl. E8 — 94 C6
*Buttermere Wk.*
Solway Cl., Houns. — 143 E3
Solway Rd. N22 — 75 H1
Solway Rd. SE22 — 152 D4
Somaford Gro., Barn. — 41 G6
Somali Rd. NW2 — 90 C4
Somerby Rd., Bark. — 99 G7
Somercoates Cl., — 41 H3
Barn.
Somerfield Rd. N4 — 93 H2
Somerford Cl., Pnr. — 66 A4
Somerford Gro. N16 — 94 C4
Somerford Gro. N17 — 60 D7
Somerford Gro. Est. — 94 C4
N16
*Somerford Gro.*
Somerford St. E1 — 112 E4
Somerford Way SE16 — 133 H2
Somerhill Av., Sid. — 158 B7
Somerhill Rd., Well. — 158 B2
Somerleyton Pas. — 151 H4
SW9
Somerleyton Rd. SW9 — 151 G4
**Somers Cl. NW1** — **9 H1**
**Somers Cres. W2** — **15 G4**
Somers Cres. W2 — 109 H6
**Somers Ms. W2** — **15 G4**
Somers Pl. SW2 — 151 F7
Somers Rd. E17 — 77 J4
Somers Rd. SW2 — 151 F6
Somersby Gdns., Ilf. — 80 C5
Somerset Av. SW20 — 183 H2
Somerset Av., — 195 G4
Chess.
Somerset Av., Well. — 157 J5

Somerset Cl. N17 — 76 A2
Somerset Cl., N.Mal. — 183 E6
Somerset Cl., — 79 G1
*Wdf.Grn.*
Somerset Est. SW11 — 149 G1
Somerset Gdns. N6 — 74 A7
Somerset Gdns. N17 — 60 B7
Somerset Gdns. — 154 B2
SE13
Somerset Gdns. — 187 F3
SW16
Somerset Gdns., — 162 B5
Tedd.
Somerset Rd. E17 — 78 A5
Somerset Rd. N17 — 76 C3
Somerset Rd. N18 — 60 C5
Somerset Rd. NW4 — 71 J4
Somerset Rd. SW19 — 166 B4
Somerset Rd. W4 — 126 D3
Somerset Rd. W13 — 125 E1
Somerset Rd., Barn. — 41 E6
Somerset Rd., Brent. — 125 F6
Somerset Rd., Har. — 67 J5
Somerset Rd., — 181 J2
Kings.T.
Somerset Rd., Sthl. — 103 F5
Somerset Rd., Tedd. — 162 B5
Somerset Sq. W14 — 128 B2
Somerset Waye, — 122 E6
Houns.
Somersham Rd., — 159 E2
Bexh.
Somerton Av., Rich. — 146 B3
Somerton Rd. NW2 — 90 B3
Somerton Rd. SE15 — 153 E4
Somertrees Av. SE12 — 173 H2
Somervell Rd., Har. — 85 F5
Somerville Av. SW13 — 127 H6
Somerville Rd. SE20 — 171 G7
Somerville Rd., Rom. — 82 C6
Sonderburg Rd. N7 — 93 F2
**Sondes St. SE17** — **36 B5**
Sondes St. SE17 — 132 A6
Sonia Cl., Har. — 68 C6
Sonia Gdns. N12 — 57 F4
Sonia Gdns. NW10 — 89 F4
Sonia Gdns., Houns. — 123 G7
Sonning Gdns., — 161 E6
Hmptn.
Sonning Rd. SE25 — 188 D6
Soper Cl. E4 — 61 J5
Sophia Cl. N7 — 93 F6
*Mackenzie Rd.*
Sophia Rd. E10 — 96 B1
Sophia Rd. E16 — 115 H6
Sophia Sq. SE16 — 113 H7
*Rotherhithe St.*
Sopwith Av., Chess. — 195 H5
Sopwith Cl., Kings.T. — 163 J5
Sopwith Rd., Houns. — 122 C7
**Sopwith Way SW8** — **32 D7**
Sopwith Way SW8 — 130 B7
Sopwith Way, — 181 H1
Kings.T.
Sorrel Cl. SE28 — 138 A1
Sorrel Gdns. E6 — 116 B5
Sorrel La. E14 — 114 D6
Sorrell Cl. SE14 — 133 H7
*Southerngate Way*
Sorrento Rd., Sutt. — 198 E3
Sotheby Rd. N5 — 93 H3
Sotheran Cl. E8 — 112 D1
Sotheron Rd. SW6 — 129 E7
Soudan Rd. SW11 — 149 J1
Souldern Rd. W14 — 128 A3
South Access Rd. E17 — 77 H7
South Acre NW9 — 71 E2
South Africa Rd. W12 — 127 H1
**South Audley St. W1** — **16 C6**
South Audley St. W1 — 110 A7
South Av. E4 — 46 B7
South Av., Cars. — 199 J7
South Av., Rich. — 146 A2
*Sandycombe Rd.*
South Av., Sthl. — 103 F7
South Av. Gdns., — 103 F7
Sthl.
South Bank, Chis. — 175 F4
South Bank, Surb. — 181 H6
South Bank Ter., — 181 H6
Surb.
South Birkbeck Rd. — 96 D3
E11
South Black Lion La. — 127 G5
W6
**South Bolton Gdns.** — **30 B3**
**SW5**
South Bolton Gdns. — 129 E5
SW5
**South Carriage Dr.** — **23 J3**
**SW1**
South Carriage Dr. — 129 H2
SW1

**South Carriage Dr.** — **23 F4**
**SW7**
South Carriage Dr. — 129 H2
SW7
South Cl. N6 — 74 B6
South Cl., Barn. — 40 C3
South Cl., Bexh. — 158 D4
South Cl., Dag. — 119 G1
South Cl., Mord. — 184/185 E6
*Green La.*
South Cl., Pnr. — 67 F7
South Cl., Twick. — 161 G3
South Cl., West Dr. — 120 C3
South Colonnade E14 — 134 A1
South Countess Rd. — 77 J3
E17
South Cres. E16 — 114 D4
**South Cres. WC1** — **17 H2**
South Cres. WC1 — 110 D5
South Cross Rd., Ilf. — 81 F5
South Croxted Rd. — 170 A3
SE21
South Dene NW7 — 54 D3
South Dr., Orp. — 207 H5
South Ealing Rd. W5 — 125 G2
South Eastern Av. N9 — 60 C3
**South Eaton Pl. SW1** — **32 C1**
South Eaton Pl. SW1 — 130 A4
South Eden Pk. Rd., — 190 B6
Beck.
South Edwardes Sq. — 128 C3
W8
**South End W8** — **22 B5**
South End, Croy. — 201 J4
South End Cl. NW3 — 91 H4
South End Grn. NW3 — 91 H4
*South End Rd.*
South End Rd. NW3 — 91 H4
**South End Row W8** — **22 B5**
South End Row W8 — 129 E3
South Esk Rd. E7 — 97 J6
South Gdns. SW19 — 167 G7
South Gipsy Rd., — 158 D3
Well.
South Glade, The, — 177 F1
Bex.
South Grn. NW9 — 70/71 E1
*Clayton Fld.*
South Gro. E17 — 77 J5
South Gro. N6 — 92 A1
South Gro. N15 — 76 A5
South Gro. Ho. N6 — 92 A1
*Highgate W. Hill*
South Hill, Chis. — 174 C6
South Hill Av., Har. — 85 J3
South Hill Gro., Har. — 86 B4
South Hill Pk. NW3 — 91 H4
South Hill Pk. Gdns. — 91 H4
NW3
South Hill Rd., Brom. — 190 E3
South Huxley N18 — 60 A5
South Island Pl. SW9 — 131 F7
South Kensington — 129 G4
Sta. Arc. SW7
*Pelham St.*
**South Lambeth Pl.** — **34 B5**
**SW8**
South Lambeth Pl. — 131 E6
SW8
South Lambeth Rd. — 131 E7
SW8
South La., Kings.T. — 181 G3
South La., N.Mal. — 182 D4
South La. W., N.Mal. — 182 D4
South Lo. Av., — 186 E4
Mitch.
South Lo. Cres., Enf. — 42 D4
South Lo. Dr. N14 — 42 E5
South Mall N9 — 60 D3
*Plevna Rd.*
South Mead NW9 — 71 F1
South Mead, Epsom — 197 E7
South Meadows, — 87 J5
Wem.
**South Molton La. W1** — **16 D4**
South Molton La. W1 — 110 B6
South Molton Rd. E16 — 115 G6
**South Molton St. W1** — **16 D4**
South Molton St. W1 — 110 B6
South Norwood Hill — 188 B2
SE25
South Oak Rd. SW16 — 169 F4
**South Par. SW3** — **31 F3**
South Par. SW3 — 129 G5
South Par. W4 — 126 D4
South Pk. SW6 — 148 D2
South Pk. Cres. SE6 — 173 F1
South Pk. Cres., Ilf. — 99 G3
South Pk. Dr., Bark. — 99 H4
South Pk. Dr., Ilf. — 99 H4
South Pk. Gro., — 182 C4
N.Mal.
South Pk. Hill Rd., — 202 A5
S.Croy.

| Name | Pg | Grid |
|---|---|---|
| South Pk. Ms. SW6 | 148 | E3 |
| South Pk. Rd. SW19 | 166 | D6 |
| South Pk. Rd., Ilf. | 99 | G3 |
| South Pk. Ter., Ilf. | 99 | H3 |
| South Pk. Way, Ruis. | 84 | C6 |
| South Penge Pk. Est. SE20 | 188 | E2 |
| **South Pl. EC2** | 20 | C1 |
| South Pl. EC2 | 112 | A5 |
| South Pl., Enf. | 45 | F5 |
| South Pl., Surb. | 181 | J7 |
| **South Pl. Ms. EC2** | 20 | C2 |
| South Ri. Way SE18 | 137 | G5 |
| South Rd. N9 | 60 | D1 |
| South Rd. SE23 | 171 | G2 |
| South Rd. SW19 | 167 | F6 |
| South Rd. W5 | 125 | G4 |
| South Rd., Edg. | 70 | B1 |
| South Rd., Felt. | 160 | D5 |
| South Rd., Hmptn. | 161 | E6 |
| South Rd. (Chadwell Heath), Rom. | 82 | C5 |
| South Rd. (Little Heath), Rom. | 82 | E6 |
| South Rd., Sthl. | 123 | F2 |
| South Rd., Twick. | 162 | A3 |
| South Rd., West Dr. | 120 | D3 |
| South Row SE3 | 155 | F2 |
| South Sea St. SE16 | 133 | J3 |
| South Side W6 | 127 | F3 |
| South Sq. NW11 | 72 | E6 |
| **South Sq. WC1** | 18 | E2 |
| **South St. W1** | 24 | C1 |
| South St. W1 | 130 | A1 |
| South St., Brom. | 191 | G2 |
| South St., Enf. | 45 | G5 |
| South St., Islw. | 144 | D3 |
| South St., Rain. | 119 | J2 |
| **South Tenter St. E1** | 21 | G5 |
| South Tenter St. E1 | 112 | C7 |
| **South Ter. SW7** | 31 | G1 |
| South Ter. SW7 | 129 | H4 |
| South Ter., Surb. | 181 | H6 |
| South Vale SE19 | 170 | B6 |
| South Vale, Har. | 86 | B4 |
| South Vw., Brom. | 191 | H2 |
| South Vw. Dr. E18 | 79 | H3 |
| South Vw. Rd. N8 | 74 | D3 |
| South Vw. Rd., Loug. | 48 | C6 |
| South Vw. Rd., Pnr. | 50 | B6 |
| South Vil. NW1 | 92 | D6 |
| South Wk., W.Wick. | 204 | E3 |
| South Way N9 | 61 | F2 |
| South Way N11 | 58 | C6 |
| *Ringway* | | |
| South Way, Brom. | 191 | G7 |
| South Way, Croy. | 203 | H3 |
| South Way, Har. | 67 | G4 |
| South Way, Wem. | 88 | A5 |
| South W. India Dock Entrance E14 | 134 | C2 |
| *Prestons Rd.* | | |
| South Western Rd., Twick. | 144 | D6 |
| **South Wf. Rd. W2** | 15 | E1 |
| South Wf. Rd. W2 | 109 | G6 |
| South Woodford to Barking Relief Rd. E11 | 79 | J4 |
| South Woodford to Barking Relief Rd. E12 | 98 | D3 |
| South Woodford to Barking Relief Rd. E18 | 79 | J4 |
| South Woodford to Barking Relief Rd., Bark. | 98 | D3 |
| South Woodford to Barking Relief Rd., Ilf. | 98 | D3 |
| South Worple Av. SW14 | 146 | E3 |
| South Worple Way SW14 | 146 | B3 |
| Southacre Way, Pnr. | 66 | C1 |
| Southall La., Houns. | 122 | B6 |
| Southall La., Sthl. | 122 | C4 |
| **Southall Pl. SE1** | 28 | B4 |
| Southall Pl. SE1 | 132 | A2 |
| Southam St. W10 | 108 | B4 |
| **Southampton Bldgs. WC2** | 18 | E3 |
| Southampton Gdns. Mitch. | 186 | E5 |
| Southampton Ms. E16 | 135 | H1 |
| *Wesley Av.* | | |
| **Southampton Pl. WC1** | 18 | B2 |
| Southampton Pl. WC1 | 111 | E5 |
| Southampton Rd. NW5 | 91 | J5 |
| Southampton Rd., Houns. | 140 | D6 |
| **Southampton Row WC1** | 18 | B1 |
| Southampton Row WC1 | 111 | E5 |
| **Southampton St. WC2** | 18 | B5 |
| Southampton St. WC2 | 111 | E7 |
| **Southampton Way SE5** | 36 | C7 |
| Southampton Way SE5 | 132 | A7 |
| Southbank, T.Ditt. | 180 | E7 |
| Southborough Cl., Surb. | 195 | G1 |
| Southborough La., Brom. | 205 | B5 |
| Southborough Rd. E9 | 113 | F1 |
| Southborough Rd., Brom. | 192 | B3 |
| Southborough Rd., Surb. | 195 | H1 |
| Southbourne, Brom. | 191 | G7 |
| Southbourne Av. NW9 | 70 | C2 |
| Southbourne Cl., Pnr. | 67 | E7 |
| Southbourne Cres. NW4 | 72 | B4 |
| Southbourne Gdns. SE12 | 155 | H5 |
| Southbourne Gdns. Ilf. | 99 | F5 |
| Southbourne Gdns. Ruis. | 84 | B1 |
| Southbridge Pl., Croy. | 201 | J4 |
| Southbridge Rd., Croy. | 201 | J4 |
| Southbridge Way, Sthl. | 123 | E2 |
| Southbrook Ms. SE12 | 155 | F6 |
| Southbrook Rd. SE12 | 155 | F6 |
| Southbrook Rd. SW16 | 187 | E1 |
| Southbury Av., Enf. | 44 | D5 |
| Southbury Rd., Enf. | 44 | A3 |
| Southchurch Rd. E6 | 116 | C2 |
| Southcombe St. W14 | 128 | B4 |
| Southcote Av., Surb. | 182 | B7 |
| Southcote Rd. E17 | 77 | G5 |
| Southcote Rd. N19 | 92 | C4 |
| Southcote Rd. SE25 | 189 | E6 |
| Southcroft Av., Well. | 157 | H3 |
| Southcroft Av., W.Wick. | 204 | C2 |
| Southcroft Rd. SW16 | 168 | A6 |
| Southcroft Rd. SW17 | 168 | A6 |
| Southcroft Rd., Orp. | 207 | H3 |
| Southdale, Chig. | 65 | G6 |
| Southdean Gdns. SW19 | 166 | C2 |
| Southdown Av. W7 | 124 | D3 |
| Southdown Cres., Har. | 85 | H1 |
| Southdown Cres., Ilf. | 81 | H5 |
| Southdown Dr. SW20 | 166 | A7 |
| *Crescent Rd.* | | |
| Southdown Rd. SW20 | 184 | A1 |
| Southend Cl. SE9 | 156 | E6 |
| Southend Cres. SE9 | 156 | D6 |
| Southend La. SE6 | 171 | J4 |
| Southend La. SE26 | 171 | J4 |
| Southend Rd. E4 | 61 | H5 |
| Southend Rd. E6 | 98 | C7 |
| Southend Rd. E17 | 78 | B1 |
| Southend Rd. E18 | 79 | G1 |
| Southend Rd., Beck. | 172 | A7 |
| Southend Rd., Wdf.Grn. | 79 | J2 |
| Southern Av. SE25 | 188 | C3 |
| Southern Av., Felt. | 160 | A1 |
| Southern Dr., Loug. | 48 | C6 |
| Southern Gro. E3 | 113 | J3 |
| Southern Perimeter Rd., Houns. | 141 | G5 |
| Southern Rd. E13 | 115 | H2 |
| Southern Rd. N2 | 73 | J4 |
| Southern Row W10 | 108 | B4 |
| **Southern St. N1** | 10 | C1 |
| Southern St. N1 | 111 | F2 |
| Southern Way, Rom. | 83 | G6 |
| Southerngate Way SE14 | 133 | H7 |
| Southernhay, Loug. | 48 | A5 |
| Southerton Rd. W6 | 127 | J3 |
| Southey Ms. E16 | 135 | G1 |
| *Wesley Av.* | | |
| Southey Rd. N15 | 76 | B5 |
| Southey Rd. SW9 | 151 | G1 |
| Southey Rd. SW19 | 166 | D7 |
| Southey St. SE20 | 171 | G7 |
| Southfield, Barn. | 40 | A6 |
| Southfield Cotts. W7 | 124 | C2 |
| *Oaklands Rd.* | | |
| Southfield Gdns. Twick. | 162 | C4 |
| Southfield Pk., Har. | 67 | H4 |
| Southfield Rd. N17 | 76 | B2 |
| *The Av.* | | |
| Southfield Rd. W4 | 126 | E3 |
| Southfield Rd., Chis. | 193 | J3 |
| Southfield Rd., Enf. | 45 | E6 |
| Southfields NW4 | 71 | G2 |
| Southfields, E.Mol. | 180 | B6 |
| Southfields Ct. SW19 | 166 | B1 |
| Southfields Pas. SW18 | 148 | D6 |
| Southfields Rd. SW18 | 148 | D6 |
| Southfleet Rd., Orp. | 207 | H3 |
| Southgate Circ. N14 | 58 | D1 |
| *The Bourne* | | |
| Southgate Gro. N1 | 94 | A7 |
| Southgate Rd. N1 | 94 | A7 |
| Southholme Cl. SE19 | 188 | B1 |
| Southill La., Pnr. | 66 | A4 |
| Southill Rd., Chis. | 174 | B7 |
| Southill St. E14 | 114 | B6 |
| *Chrisp St.* | | |
| Southland Rd. SE18 | 137 | J7 |
| Southland Way, Houns. | 144 | A5 |
| Southlands Av., Orp. | 207 | G4 |
| Southlands Dr. SW19 | 166 | A2 |
| Southlands Gro. Brom. | 192 | B3 |
| Southlands Rd. Brom. | 191 | J4 |
| Southly Cl., Sutt. | 198 | D3 |
| Southmead Rd. SW19 | 166 | B1 |
| Southmont Rd., Esher | 194 | B2 |
| Southmoor Way E9 | 95 | J6 |
| Southold Ri. SE9 | 174 | C3 |
| Southolm St. SW11 | 150 | B1 |
| Southover N12 | 56 | D4 |
| Southover, Brom. | 173 | G5 |
| Southport Rd. SE18 | 137 | G4 |
| Southridge Pl. SW20 | 166 | A7 |
| Southsea Rd., Kings.T. | 181 | H4 |
| Southside Common SW19 | 165 | J6 |
| Southspring, Sid. | 157 | G7 |
| Southvale Rd. SE3 | 155 | E2 |
| Southview Av. NW10 | 89 | F5 |
| Southview Cl. SW17 | 168 | A5 |
| Southview Cl., Bex. | 159 | F6 |
| Southview Cres., Ilf. | 80 | E6 |
| Southview Gdns. Wall. | 200 | C7 |
| Southview Rd., Brom. | 172 | D4 |
| Southville SW8 | 150 | D1 |
| Southville Rd., T.Ditt. | 180 | E7 |
| **Southwark Br. EC4** | 28 | A1 |
| Southwark Br. EC4 | 131 | J1 |
| **Southwark Br. SE1** | 28 | A1 |
| Southwark Br. SE1 | 131 | J1 |
| **Southwark Br. Rd. SE1** | 27 | H5 |
| Southwark Br. Rd. SE1 | 131 | H3 |
| **Southwark Gro. SE1** | 27 | J2 |
| Southwark Pk. Est. SE16 | 133 | E4 |
| **Southwark Pk. Rd. SE16** | 37 | G1 |
| Southwark Pk. Rd. SE16 | 132 | C4 |
| Southwark Pl., Brom. | 192 | C3 |
| *St. Georges Rd.* | | |
| **Southwark St. SE1** | 27 | H1 |
| Southwark St. SE1 | 131 | H1 |
| Southwater Cl. E14 | 113 | J6 |
| Southwater Cl., Beck. | 172 | B7 |
| Southway N20 | 56 | D2 |
| Southway NW11 | 73 | E6 |
| Southway SW20 | 183 | J4 |
| Southway, Wall. | 200 | C4 |
| Southwell Av., Nthlt. | 85 | G6 |
| **Southwell Gdns. SW7** | 30 | C1 |
| Southwell Gdns. SW7 | 129 | F4 |
| Southwell Gro. Rd. E11 | 96 | E2 |
| Southwell Rd. SE5 | 151 | J3 |
| Southwell Rd., Croy. | 187 | G6 |
| Southwell Rd., Har. | 69 | G6 |
| Southwest Rd. E11 | 96 | D1 |
| **Southwick Ms. W2** | 15 | F3 |
| **Southwick Pl. W2** | 15 | G4 |
| **Southwick St. W2** | 15 | G3 |
| Southwick St. W2 | 109 | H6 |
| Southwold Dr., Bark. | 100 | A5 |
| Southwold Rd. E5 | 95 | E2 |
| Southwold Rd., Bex. | 159 | H6 |
| Southwood Av. N6 | 74 | B7 |
| Southwood Av., Kings.T. | 182 | C1 |
| Southwood Cl., Brom. | 192 | C4 |
| Southwood Cl., Wor.Pk. | 198 | A1 |
| Southwood Dr., Surb. | 182 | C7 |
| Southwood Gdns., Esher | 194 | D3 |
| Southwood Gdns., Ilf. | 80 | E4 |
| Southwood La. N6 | 74 | A7 |
| Southwood Lawn Rd. N6 | 74 | A7 |
| Southwood Rd. SE9 | 174 | E2 |
| Southwood Rd. SE28 | 138 | B1 |
| Southwood Smith St. N1 | 111 | G1 |
| *Barford St.* | | |
| Sovereign Cl. E1 | 113 | E7 |
| Sovereign Cl. W5 | 105 | F5 |
| Sovereign Ct., Brom. | 192 | C5 |
| Sovereign Ct., W.Mol. | 179 | F4 |
| Sovereign Cres. SE16 | 133 | H1 |
| *Rotherhithe St.* | | |
| Sovereign Gro., Wem. | 87 | G3 |
| **Sovereign Ms. E2** | 13 | F1 |
| Sovereign Pk. NW10 | 106 | B4 |
| Sovereign Rd., Bark. | 118 | C3 |
| Sowerby Cl. SE9 | 156 | B5 |
| Spa Cl. SE25 | 188 | B1 |
| **Spa Grn. Est. EC1** | 11 | F3 |
| Spa Grn. Est. EC1 | 111 | G3 |
| Spa Hill SE19 | 188 | A1 |
| **Spa Rd. SE16** | 29 | F6 |
| Spa Rd. SE16 | 132 | C3 |
| Space Waye, Felt. | 142 | A5 |
| **Spafield St. EC1** | 11 | E5 |
| Spalding Cl., Edg. | 54/55 | E7 |
| *Blundell Rd.* | | |
| Spalding Rd. NW4 | 71 | J6 |
| Spalding Rd. SW17 | 168 | B5 |
| Spanby Rd. E3 | 114 | A4 |
| Spaniards Cl. NW11 | 91 | G1 |
| Spaniards End NW3 | 91 | F1 |
| Spaniards Rd. NW3 | 91 | F2 |
| **Spanish Pl. W1** | 16 | C2 |
| Spanish Pl. W1 | 110 | A6 |
| Spanish Rd. SW18 | 149 | F6 |
| Sparleaze Hill, Loug. | 48 | C5 |
| Sparkbridge Rd., Har. | 68 | B4 |
| Sparks Cl. W3 | 106 | D6 |
| *Joseph Av.* | | |
| Sparks Cl., Dag. | 100 | D2 |
| Sparks Cl., Hmptn. | 160/161 | E6 |
| *Victors Dr.* | | |
| Sparrow Dr., Orp. | 207 | F1 |
| Sparrow Fm. Dr., Felt. | 142 | D7 |
| Sparrow Fm. Rd., Epsom | 197 | G4 |
| Sparrow Grn., Dag. | 101 | H3 |
| Sparrows La. SE9 | 157 | F7 |
| Sparsholt Rd. N19 | 93 | F1 |
| Sparsholt Rd., Bark. | 117 | H1 |
| Sparta St. SE10 | 154 | B1 |
| Spear Ms. SW5 | 128 | D4 |
| Spearman St. SE18 | 136 | D6 |
| Spearpoint Gdns., Ilf. | 81 | J4 |
| Spears Rd. N19 | 92 | E1 |
| Speart La., Houns. | 122 | E7 |
| Spedan Cl. NW3 | 91 | E3 |
| Speedwell St. SE8 | 134 | A7 |
| *Comet St.* | | |
| **Speedy Pl. WC1** | 10 | A4 |
| Speer Rd., T.Ditt. | 180 | C5 |
| Speirs Cl., N.Mal. | 183 | F6 |
| Speke Ho. SE5 | 131 | J7 |
| Speke Rd., Th.Hth. | 188 | A2 |
| Spekehill SE9 | 174 | C3 |
| Speldhurst Cl., Brom. | 191 | F5 |
| Speldhurst Rd. E9 | 95 | G7 |
| Speldhurst Rd. W4 | 126 | D3 |
| Spellbrook Wk. N1 | 111 | J1 |
| *Basire St.* | | |
| **Spelman St. E1** | 21 | H1 |
| Spelman St. E1 | 112 | D5 |
| *Vaughan St.* | | |
| Spencer Av. N13 | 59 | F6 |
| Spencer Av., Hayes | 102 | A5 |
| Spencer Cl. N3 | 72 | D2 |
| Spencer Cl. NW10 | 105 | J3 |
| Spencer Cl., Orp. | 207 | H2 |
| Spencer Cl., Wdf.Grn. | 63 | J5 |
| Spencer Dr. N2 | 73 | F6 |
| Spencer Gdns. SE9 | 156 | C5 |
| Spencer Gdns. SW14 | 146 | C5 |
| Spencer Hill SW19 | 166 | B6 |
| Spencer Hill Rd. SW19 | 166 | B7 |
| Spencer Ms. SW8 | 151 | F1 |
| *Lansdowne Way* | | |
| Spencer Ms. W6 | 128 | B6 |
| *Greyhound Rd.* | | |
| Spencer Pk. SW18 | 149 | G5 |
| Spencer Pas. E2 | 112/113 | E2 |
| *Pritchard's Rd.* | | |

Spencer Pl. N1 93 H7
*Canonbury La.*
Spencer Pl., Croy. 188 A7
*Gloucester Rd.*
Spencer Ri. NW5 92 B4
Spencer Rd. E6 116 A1
Spencer Rd. E17 78 C1
Spencer Rd. N8 75 F5
Spencer Rd. N11 58 B4
Spencer Rd. N17 76 D1
Spencer Rd. SW18 149 G4
Spencer Rd. SW20 183 H1
Spencer Rd. W3 126 C1
Spencer Rd. W4 126 C7
Spencer Rd., Brom. 173 E7
Spencer Rd., E.Mol. 179 J5
Spencer Rd., Har. 68 B2
Spencer Rd., Ilf. 99 J1
Spencer Rd., Islw. 144 A1
Spencer Rd., Mitch. 186 A3
Spencer Rd. (Beddington Cor.), Mitch. 186 A7
Spencer Rd., S.Croy. 202 B5
Spencer Rd., Twick. 162 B3
Spencer Rd., Wem. 87 F2
**Spencer St. EC1 11 G4**
Spencer St. EC1 111 H3
Spencer St., Sthl. 122 D2
Spencer Wk. NW3 91 F4
*Hampstead High St.*
Spencer Wk. SW15 148 A4
Spenser Gro. N16 94 B4
Spenser Ms. SE21 170 A1
*Croxted Rd.*
Spenser Rd. SE24 151 G5
**Spenser St. SW1 25 G5**
Spenser St. SW1 130 C3
Spensley Wk. N16 94 A3
*Clissold Rd.*
Speranza St. SE18 137 J5
Sperling Rd. N17 76 B2
Spert St. E14 113 H7
Spey St. E14 114 C5
Speyside N14 42 C6
Spezia Rd. NW10 107 G2
Spicer Cl. SW9 151 H2
Spicer Cl., Walt. 178 C6
Spice's Yd., Croy. 201 J4
Spigurnell Rd. N17 76 A1
Spikes Br. Rd., Sthl. 103 E6
Spilsby Cl. NW9 70/71 E2
*Kenley Av.*
Spindle Cl. SE18 136 B3
Spindlewood Gdns., Croy. 202 B4
Spindrift Av. E14 134 B4
Spinel Cl. SE18 137 J5
Spinnaker Cl., Bark. 117 H3
*Thames Rd.*
Spinnells Rd., Har. 85 F1
Spinney, The N21 43 G7
Spinney, The SW16 168 D3
Spinney, The, Barn. 41 E2
Spinney, The, Sid. 176 E5
Spinney, The, Stan. 53 H4
Spinney, The, Sun. 178 A1
Spinney, The, Sutt. 197 J4
Spinney, The, Wem. 86 D3
Spinney Cl., N.Mal. 182 E5
Spinney Cl., Wor.Pk. 197 F2
Spinney Dr., Felt. 141 F7
Spinney Gdns. SE19 170 C5
Spinney Gdns., Dag. 101 E5
Spinney Oak, Brom. 192 B2
Spinneys, The, Brom. 192 C2
**Spirit Quay E1 29 J1**
**Spital Sq. E1 21 E1**
Spital Sq. E1 112 B5
**Spital St. E1 21 H1**
Spital St. E1 112 D4
**Spital Yd. E1 21 E1**
Spitfire Est., Houns. 122 C5
Spitfire Way, Houns. 122 C5
Splendour Wk. SE16 133 F5
*Verney Rd.*
Spode Wk. NW6 90/91 E6
*Lymington Rd.*
Spondon Rd. N15 76 D4
Spoonbill Way, Hayes 102 D5
Spooner Wk., Wall. 200 D5
Spooners Ms. W3 126 D1
*Churchfield Rd.*
Sportsbank St. SE6 154 C7
Spottons Gro. N17 75 J1
*Gospatrick Rd.*
Spout Hill, Croy. 204 A5
Spratt Hall Rd. E11 79 G6
Spray La., Twick. 144 B6
Spray St. SE18 137 E4
Spreighton Rd., W.Mol. 179 H4
**Sprimont Pl. SW3 31 J3**
Sprimont Pl. SW3 129 J5
Spring Br. Ms. W5 105 G7
*Spring Br. Rd.*
Spring Br. Rd. W5 105 G7
Spring Cl., Barn. 40 A5
Spring Cl., Borwd. 38 A1
Spring Cl., Dag. 100 D1
Spring Cl. La., Sutt. 198 B6
Spring Cotts., Surb. 181 G5
*St. Leonard's Rd.*
Spring Ct., Sid. 176 A3
*Station Rd.*
Spring Dr., Pnr. 66 A6
*Eastcote Rd.*
Spring Gdns. N5 93 J5
*Grosvenor Av.*
**Spring Gdns. SW1 25 J1**
Spring Gdns., Rom. 83 J5
Spring Gdns., Wall. 200 C5
Spring Gdns., W.Mol. 179 J5
Spring Gdns., Wdf.Grn. 63 J7
Spring Gdns. Ind. Est., Rom. 83 J5
Spring Gro. SE19 170 C7
*Alma Pl.*
Spring Gro. W4 126 A5
Spring Gro., Hmptn. 179 H1
*Plevna Rd.*
Spring Gro., Loug. 48 A6
Spring Gro., Mitch. 186 A1
Spring Gro. Cres., Houns. 143 J1
Spring Gro. Rd., Houns. 143 J1
Spring Gro. Rd., Islw. 143 J1
Spring Gro. Rd., Rich. 145 J5
Spring Hill E5 76 D7
Spring Hill SE26 171 F4
Spring Lake, Stan. 52 E4
Spring La. E5 95 E1
Spring La. N10 74 A3
Spring La. SE25 188 E6
**Spring Ms. W1 16 A1**
Spring Pk. Av., Croy. 203 G2
Spring Pk. Dr. N4 93 J1
Spring Pk. Rd., Croy. 203 G2
Spring Pas. SW15 148 A3
*Embankment*
Spring Path NW3 91 G5
Spring Pl. NW5 92 B5
**Spring St. W2 15 E4**
Spring St. W2 109 G6
Spring Ter., Rich. 145 H5
Spring Vale, Bexh. 159 H4
Spring Vil. Rd., Edg. 54 A7
**Spring Wk. E1 21 H1**
Springall St. SE15 133 E7
Springbank N21 43 F6
Springbank Rd. SE13 154 D6
Springbank Wk. NW1 92 D7
*St. Paul's Cres.*
Springbourne Ct., Beck. 190 C1
Springcroft Av. N2 73 J4
Springdale Ms. N16 94 A4
*Springdale Rd.*
Springdale Rd. N16 94 A4
Springfield E5 94 E1
Springfield, Bushey 52 A1
Springfield Av. N10 74 C3
Springfield Av. SW20 184 C3
Springfield Av., Hmptn. 161 H6
Springfield Cl. N12 56 E5
Springfield Cl., Stan. 52 D3
Springfield Dr., Ilf. 81 F6
Springfield Gdns. E5 95 E1
Springfield Gdns. NW9 70 D5
Springfield Gdns., Brom. 192 C4
Springfield Gdns., Ruis. 84 B1
Springfield Gdns., W.Wick. 204 B2
Springfield Gdns., Wdf.Grn. 63 J7
Springfield Gro. SE7 135 J6
Springfield La. NW6 108 E1
Springfield Mt. NW9 70 E5
Springfield Pl., N.Mal. 182 C4
Springfield Ri. SE26 170 E3
Springfield Rd. E4 62 E1
Springfield Rd. E6 98 C7
Springfield Rd. E15 115 E3
Springfield Rd. E17 77 J6
Springfield Rd. N11 58 B5
Springfield Rd. N15 76 D4
Springfield Rd. NW8 109 F1
Springfield Rd. SE26 171 E5
Springfield Rd. SW19 166 C5
Springfield Rd. W7 124 B1
Springfield Rd., Bexh. 159 H3
Springfield Rd., Brom. 192 C4
Springfield Rd., Har. 68 B6
Springfield Rd., Hayes 122 C1
Springfield Rd., Kings.T. 181 H3
Springfield Rd., Tedd. 162 D5
Springfield Rd., Th.Hth. 187 J1
Springfield Rd., Twick. 161 G1
Springfield Rd., Wall. 200 B5
Springfield Rd., Well. 158 B3
Springfield Wk. NW6 108 E1
Springfield Wk., Orp. 207 G1
*Place Fm. Av.*
Springhill Cl. SE5 152 A3
Springhurst Cl., Croy. 203 J4
Springpark Dr., Beck. 190 C3
Springpond Rd., Dag. 101 E5
Springrice Rd. SE13 154 D6
Springvale Av., Brent. 125 G5
Springvale Est. W14 128 B3
*Blythe Rd.*
Springvale Ter. W14 128 A3
Springwater Cl. SE18 156 D1
Springway, Har. 68 A7
Springwell Av. NW10 107 F1
Springwell Cl. SW16 169 G4
*Etherstone Rd.*
Springwell Ct., Houns. 142 D2
Springwell Rd. SW16 169 G4
Springwell Rd., Houns. 142 D1
Springwood Cres., Edg. 54 B2
Sprowston Ms. E7 97 G6
Sprowston Rd. E7 97 G5
Spruce Ct. W5 125 H3
*Elderberry Rd.*
Spruce Hills Rd. E17 78 C2
Spruce Pk., Brom. 191 F4
*Cumberland Rd.*
Sprucedale Gdns., Croy. 203 G4
Sprules Rd. SE4 153 H2
Spur Rd. N15 76 A4
*Philip La.*
**Spur Rd. SE1 27 E3**
Spur Rd. SE1 131 G2
**Spur Rd. SW1 25 F4**
Spur Rd. SW1 130 C2
Spur Rd., Bark. 117 F3
Spur Rd., Edg. 53 H4
Spur Rd., Felt. 142 B5
Spur Rd., Islw. 124 E7
Spur Rd. Est., Edg. 53 J4
Spurfield, W.Mol. 179 H3
Spurgeon Av. SE19 188 A1
Spurgeon Rd. SE19 188 A1
**Spurgeon St. SE1 28 B6**
Spurgeon St. SE1 132 A3
Spurling Rd. SE22 152 C4
Spurling Rd., Dag. 101 F6
Spurstowe Rd. E8 94/95 E6
*Marcon Pl.*
Spurstowe Ter. E8 94 E5
Square, The W6 127 J5
Square, The, Cars. 200 A5
Square, The, Hayes 121 G1
Square, The, Ilf. 80 D7
Square, The, Rich. 145 G5
Square, The, Wdf.Grn. 63 G5
Square Rigger Row SW11 149 F3
*York Pl.*
Squarey St. SW17 167 F3
Squires Ct. SW19 166 D4
Squires La. N3 73 E2
Squires Mt. NW3 91 G3
*East Heath Rd.*
Squires Wd. Dr., Chis. 174 B7
Squirrel Cl., Houns. 142 C2
Squirrel Ms. W13 104 D7
Squirrels, The SE13 154 D3
*Belmont Hill*
Squirrels, The, Pnr. 67 F3
Squirrels Cl. N12 57 F4
*Woodside Av.*
Squirrels Grn., Wor.Pk. 197 F1
Squirrels La., Buck.H. 64 A3
Squirrels Trd. Est., The, Hayes 122 A3
**Squirries St. E2 13 J3**
Squirries St. E2 112 D3
Stable Cl., Nthlt. 103 G2
Stable Wk. N2 73 G1
*Old Fm. Rd.*
Stable Way W10 107 J6
*Latimer Rd.*
**Stable Yd. SW1 25 F3**
Stable Yd. SW9 151 F2
*Broomgrove Rd.*
Stable Yd. SW15 147 J3
*Danemere St.*
**Stable Yd. Rd. SW1 25 F2**
Stable Yd. Rd. SW1 130 C1
Stables, The, Buck.H. 47 J7
Stables End, Orp. 207 F3
Stables Ms. SE27 169 J5
**Stables Way SE11 35 E3**
Stables Way SE11 131 G5
Stacey Av. N18 61 F4
Stacey Cl. E10 78 D5
*Halford Rd.*
Stacey St. N7 93 G3
**Stacey St. WC2 17 J4**
Stacey St. WC2 110 D6
**Stackhouse St. SW3 23 J5**
Stacy Path SE5 132 B7
*Harris St.*
Stadium Rd. NW2 71 J7
Stadium Rd. SE18 136 C7
Stadium St. SW10 129 F7
Stadium Way, Wem. 87 J4
**Staff St. EC1 12 C4**
Staffa Rd. E10 95 H1
Stafford Cl. E17 77 J6
Stafford Cl. N14 42 C5
Stafford Cl. NW6 108 D3
Stafford Cl., Sutt. 198 B6
Stafford Ct. W8 128 D3
Stafford Cross, Croy. 201 F5
Stafford Gdns., Croy. 201 F5
**Stafford Pl. SW1 25 F5**
Stafford Pl. SW1 130 C3
Stafford Pl., Rich. 145 J7
Stafford Rd. E3 113 J2
Stafford Rd. E7 97 J7
Stafford Rd. NW6 108 D3
Stafford Rd., Croy. 201 G4
Stafford Rd., Har. 51 J7
Stafford Rd., N.Mal. 182 C3
Stafford Rd., Sid. 175 H4
Stafford Rd., Wall. 200 C6
**Stafford St. W1 25 F1**
Stafford St. W1 130 C1
Stafford Ter. W8 128 D3
Staffordshire St. SE15 152 D1
Stag Cl., Edg. 70 C2
Stag La. NW9 70 B2
Stag La. SW15 165 F2
Stag La., Buck.H. 63 H2
Stag La., Edg. 70 B2
**Stag Pl. SW1 25 F5**
Stag Pl. SW1 130 C3
Stag Ride SW19 165 F3
Staggart Grn., Chig. 65 J6
Stags Way, Islw. 124 C6
Stainbank Rd., Mitch. 186 B3
Stainby Cl., West Dr. 120 B3
Stainby Rd. N15 76 C4
**Stainer St. SE1 28 C2**
Stainer St. SE1 132 A1
Staines Av., Sutt. 198 A2
Staines Rd., Felt. 141 G7
Staines Rd., Houns. 143 H3
Staines Rd., Ilf. 99 G4
Staines Rd., Twick. 161 G3
Staines Rd. E., Sun. 160 A7
Staines Wk., Sid. 176 C6
*Evry Rd.*
Stainforth Rd. E17 78 A4
Stainforth Rd., Ilf. 81 G7
**Staining La. EC2 20 A3**
Staining La. EC2 111 J6
Stainmore Cl., Chis. 193 G1
Stainsbury St. E2 113 F2
*Royston St.*
Stainsby Pl. E14 114 A6
*Stainsby Rd.*
Stainsby Rd. E14 114 A6
Stainton Rd. SE6 154 D6
Stainton Rd., Enf. 45 F1
**Stalbridge St. NW1 15 H1**
Stalham St. SE16 133 E3
Stambourne Way SE19 170 B7
Stambourne Way, W.Wick. 204 C3
Stamford Brook Av. W6 127 F3
Stamford Brook Rd. W6 127 F3
Stamford Cl. N15 76 D4
Stamford Cl. NW3 91 F4
*Heath St.*
Stamford Cl., Har. 52 B7
Stamford Cl., Sthl. 103 G7

Stamford Cotts. SW10 128/129 E7
*Billing St.*
Stamford Ct. W6 127 F4
*Goldhawk Rd.*
Stamford Dr., Brom. 191 F4
Stamford Gdns., Dag. 100 C7
Stamford Gro. E. N16 94 D1
*Oldhill St.*
Stamford Gro. W. N16 94 D1
*Oldhill St.*
Stamford Hill N16 94 C2
Stamford Hill Est. N16 94 C1
Stamford Rd. E6 116 B1
Stamford Rd. N1 94 B7
Stamford Rd. N15 76 D5
Stamford Rd., Dag. 118 B1
**Stamford St. SE1 27 E2**
Stamford St. SE1 131 G1
**Stamp Pl. E2 13 F3**
Stamp Pl. E2 112 C3
Stanard Cl. N16 76 B7
Stanborough Cl., Hmptn. 161 F6
Stanborough Pas. E8 94 C6
*Abbot St.*
Stanborough Rd., Houns. 144 A3
Stanbridge Pl. N21 59 H2
Stanbridge Rd. SW15 147 J3
Stanbrook Rd. SE2 138 B2
Stanbury Rd. SE15 153 E1
Stancroft NW9 70 E4
Standard Ind. Est. E16 136 C2
**Standard Pl. EC2 12 E4**
Standard Rd. NW10 106 C4
Standard Rd., Belv. 139 G5
Standard Rd., Bexh. 159 E4
Standard Rd., Houns. 143 E3
Standen Rd. SW18 148 C7
Standfield Gdns., Dag. 101 G6
*Standfield Rd.*
Standfield Rd., Dag. 101 G5
Standish Rd. W6 127 G4
Standlake Pt. SE23 171 G3
Stane Cl. SW19 184/185 E1
*Hayward Cl.*
Stane Way SE18 136 A7
Stanfield Rd. E3 113 H2
Stanford Cl., Hmptn. 161 F6
Stanford Cl., Rom. 83 H6
Stanford Cl., Wdf.Grn. 64 B5
Stanford Ho., Bark. 118 B2
**Stanford Pl. SE17 36 D2**
Stanford Rd. N11 57 J5
Stanford Rd. SW16 186 D2
**Stanford Rd. W8 22 B5**
Stanford Rd. W8 129 E3
**Stanford St. SW1 33 H2**
Stanford Way SW16 186 D2
Stangate Cres., Borwd. 38 E5
Stangate Gdns., Stan. 53 E4
Stanger Rd. SE25 188 D4
Stanhope Av. N3 72 C3
Stanhope Av., Brom. 205 F1
Stanhope Av., Har. 68 A1
Stanhope Cl. SE16 133 G2
*Middleton Dr.*
Stanhope Gdns. N4 75 H6
Stanhope Gdns. N6 74 B6
Stanhope Gdns. NW7 55 F5
**Stanhope Gdns. SW7 30 D1**
Stanhope Gdns. SW7 129 F4
Stanhope Gdns., Dag. 101 F3
Stanhope Gdns., Ilf. 98 C1
**Stanhope Gate W1 24 C1**
Stanhope Gate W1 130 A1
Stanhope Gro., Beck. 189 J5
**Stanhope Ms. E. SW7 30 D1**
Stanhope Ms. E. SW7 129 F4
**Stanhope Ms. S. SW7 30 D2**
**Stanhope Ms. W. SW7 30 D1**
Stanhope Ms. W. SW7 129 F4
**Stanhope Par. NW1 9 F3**
Stanhope Pk. Rd., Grnf. 103 J4
**Stanhope Pl. W2 15 J4**
Stanhope Pl. W2 109 J6
Stanhope Rd. E17 78 B5
Stanhope Rd. N6 74 C6
Stanhope Rd. N12 57 F5
Stanhope Rd., Barn. 39 J6
Stanhope Rd., Bexh. 159 E2
Stanhope Rd., Cars. 200 A7
Stanhope Rd., Croy. 202 B3
Stanhope Rd., Dag. 101 F2
Stanhope Rd., Grnf. 103 J5
Stanhope Rd., Sid. 176 A4
**Stanhope Row W1 24 D2**
**Stanhope St. NW1 9 F4**
Stanhope St. NW1 110 C3
**Stanhope Ter. W2 15 F5**
Stanhope Ter. W2 109 G7
Stanier Cl. W14 128 C5
*Aisgill Av.*
Stanlake Ms. W12 127 J1
Stanlake Rd. W12 127 H1
Stanlake Vil. W12 127 H1
Stanley Av., Bark. 117 J2
Stanley Av., Beck. 190 C2
Stanley Av., Dag. 101 F1
Stanley Av., Grnf. 103 J1
Stanley Av., N.Mal. 183 G5
Stanley Av., Wem. 87 H7
**Stanley Cl. SW8 34 C6**
Stanley Cl. SW8 131 F6
Stanley Cl., Wem. 87 H7
Stanley Cres. W11 108 C7
Stanley Gdns. NW2 89 J5
Stanley Gdns. W3 126 E1
Stanley Gdns. W11 108 C7
Stanley Gdns., Mitch. 168 A6
*Ashbourne Rd.*
Stanley Gdns., Wall. 200 C6
Stanley Gdns. Ms. W11 108 C7
*Stanley Cres.*
Stanley Gdns. Rd., Tedd. 162 B5
Stanley Gro. SW8 150 A2
Stanley Gro., Croy. 187 G6
Stanley Pk. Dr., Wem. 87 J7
Stanley Pk. Rd., Cars. 199 J7
Stanley Pk. Rd., Wall. 200 B6
**Stanley Pas. NW1 10 A2**
Stanley Rd. E4 62 D1
Stanley Rd. E10 78 B6
Stanley Rd. E12 98 B5
Stanley Rd. E15 114 D1
Stanley Rd. E18 79 F1
Stanley Rd. N2 73 G3
Stanley Rd. N9 60 C1
Stanley Rd. N10 58 B7
Stanley Rd. N11 58 D6
Stanley Rd. N15 75 H4
Stanley Rd. NW9 71 G7
*West Hendon Bdy.*
Stanley Rd. SW14 146 B4
Stanley Rd. SW19 166 D7
Stanley Rd. W3 126 C3
Stanley Rd., Brom. 191 H4
Stanley Rd., Cars. 200 A7
Stanley Rd., Croy. 187 G7
Stanley Rd., Enf. 44 B3
Stanley Rd., Har. 85 J2
Stanley Rd., Houns. 143 J4
Stanley Rd., Ilf. 99 G2
Stanley Rd., Mitch. 168 A7
Stanley Rd., Mord. 184 D4
Stanley Rd., Nthwd. 66 A1
Stanley Rd., Sid. 176 A3
Stanley Rd., Sthl. 102 E7
Stanley Rd., Sutt. 198 E6
Stanley Rd., Tedd. 162 B4
Stanley Rd., Twick. 162 A3
Stanley Rd., Wem. 87 J6
Stanley St. SE8 133 J7
Stanley Ter. N19 92 E2
Stanleycroft Cl., Islw. 144 B1
Stanmer St. SW11 149 H1
Stanmore Gdns., Rich. 145 J3
Stanmore Gdns., Sutt. 199 F3
Stanmore Hall, Stan. 52 E3
Stanmore Hill, Stan. 52 D3
Stanmore Pk., Stan. 52 E5
Stanmore Pl. NW1 110 B1
*Arlington Rd.*
Stanmore Rd. E11 97 F1
Stanmore Rd. N15 75 H4
Stanmore Rd., Belv. 139 J4
Stanmore Rd., Rich. 145 J3
Stanmore St. N1 111 F1
*Caledonian Rd.*
Stanmore Ter., Beck. 190 A2
Stanmore Way, Loug. 48 D1
Stannard Ms. E8 94 D6
Stannard Rd. E8 94 D6
**Stannary Pl. SE11 35 F4**
Stannary Pl. SE11 131 G5
**Stannary St. SE11 35 F5**
Stannary St. SE11 131 G6
Stannet Way, Wall. 200 C4
Stannington Path, Borwd. 38 A1
Stansfeld Rd. E6 116 A5
Stansfield Rd. SW9 151 F3
Stansfield Rd., Houns. 142 B2
Stansgate Rd., Dag. 101 G2
Stanstead Cl., Brom. 191 F5
Stanstead Gro. SE6 171 J1
*Catford Hill*
Stanstead Manor, Sutt. 198 D6
Stanstead Rd. E11 79 H5
Stanstead Rd. SE6 171 G1
Stanstead Rd. SE23 171 G1
Stanstead Rd., Houns. 140 C6
Stansted Cres., Bex. 176 D1
Stanswood Gdns. SE5 132 B7
*Sedgmoor Pl.*
Stanthorpe Cl. SW16 168/169 E5
*Stanthorpe Rd.*
Stanthorpe Rd. SW16 168 E5
Stanton Av., Tedd. 162 B5
Stanton Cl., Epsom 196 B5
Stanton Cl., Wor.Pk. 198 A1
Stanton Rd. SE26 171 J4
*Stanton Way*
Stanton Rd. SW13 147 F2
Stanton Rd. SW20 184 A2
Stanton Rd., Croy. 187 J7
Stanton Sq. SE26 171 J4
*Stanton Way*
Stanton Way SE26 171 J4
Stanway Cl., Chig. 65 H5
Stanway Ct. N1 112 B2
*Hoxton St.*
Stanway Gdns. W3 126 A1
Stanway Gdns., Edg. 54 C5
**Stanway St. N1 12 E1**
Stanway St. N1 112 B2
Stanwell Cl., Stai. 140 A6
Stanwell Gdns., Stai. 140 A6
Stanwell Rd., Felt. 141 F7
Stanwick Rd. W14 128 C4
**Stanworth St. SE1 29 F4**
Stanworth St. SE1 132 C2
Stanwyck Dr., Chig. 65 F5
Stapenhill Rd., Wem. 86 E3
**Staple Inn WC1 19 E2**
**Staple Inn Bldgs. WC1 18 E2**
Staple Inn Bldgs. WC1 111 G5
**Staple St. SE1 28 C4**
Staple St. SE1 132 A2
Staplefield Cl. SW2 169 E1
Staplefield Cl., Pnr. 50 E7
Stapleford Av., Ilf. 81 H5
Stapleford Cl. E4 62 C3
Stapleford Cl. SW19 148 B7
Stapleford Cl., Kings.T. 182 A3
Stapleford Rd., Wem. 87 G7
Stapleford Way, Bark. 118 B3
Staplehurst Rd. SE13 154 E5
Staplehurst Rd., Cars. 199 H7
Staples Cl. SE16 133 H1
Staples Cor. NW2 89 H1
Staples Cor. Business Pk. NW2 89 H1
Staples Rd., Loug. 48 B3
Stapleton Gdns., Croy. 201 G5
Stapleton Hall Rd. N4 75 F7
Stapleton Rd. SW17 168 A3
Stapleton Rd., Bexh. 139 F7
Stapleton Rd., Orp. 207 J3
Stapley Rd., Belv. 139 G5
Stapylton Rd., Barn. 40 B3
Star & Garter Hill, Rich. 163 H1
Star La. E16 115 E4
Star Path, Nthlt. 103 G2
*Brabazon Rd.*
**Star Pl. E1 21 G6**
Star Rd. W14 128 C6
Star Rd., Islw. 144 A2
Star St. E16 115 F5
**Star St. W2 15 F3**
Star St. W2 109 H5
**Star Yd. WC2 18 E3**
Starboard Way E14 134 A3
Starch Ho. La., Ilf. 81 G2
**Starcross St. NW1 9 G4**
Starcross St. NW1 110 C3
Starfield Rd. W12 127 G2
Starling Cl., Buck.H. 63 G1
Starling Cl., Pnr. 66 C3
Starling Ms. SE28 137 G2
*Whinchat Rd.*
Starling Wk., Hmptn. 160/161 E6
*Oak Av.*
Starmans Cl., Dag. 119 E1
Starts Cl., Orp. 206 D3
Starts Hill Av., Orp. 207 E4
Starts Hill Rd., Orp. 206 D3
Starveall Cl., West Dr. 120 C3
State Fm. Av., Orp. 207 E4
Staten Gdns., Twick. 162 C1
*Lion Rd.*
Statham Gro. N16 93 J4
*Green Las.*
Statham Gro. N18 60 B5
Station App. E7 97 H4
*Woodford Rd.*
Station App. (Snaresbrook) E11 79 G5
*High St.*
Station App. N11 58 B5
*Friern Barnet Rd.*
Station App. N12 56/57 E5
*Holden Rd.*
Station App. (Woodside Pk.) N12 56 E4
Station App. (Stoke Newington) N16 94 C2
*Stamford Hill*
Station App. NW10 107 F3
*Station Rd.*
**Station App. SE1 26 D4**
Station App. SE1 131 G2
Station App. SE3 155 H3
*Kidbrooke Pk. Rd.*
Station App. (Mottingham) SE9 174 C1
Station App. (Lower Sydenham) SE26 171 J5
*Worsley Br. Rd.*
Station App. (Sydenham) SE26 171 F4
*Sydenham Rd.*
Station App. SW6 148 B3
Station App. SW16 168 D5
Station App. W7 124 B1
Station App., Barn. 41 F4
Station App., Bex. 159 G7
*Bexley High St.*
Station App., Bexh. 158/159 E2
*Avenue Rd.*
Station App. (Barnehurst), Bexh. 159 J2
Station App., Brom. 205 G1
Station App., Buck.H. 64 A4
*Cherry Tree Ri.*
Station App., Chis. 192 D1
Station App. (Elmstead Wds.), Chis. 174 B6
Station App. (Stoneleigh), Epsom 197 G5
Station App. (Hinchley Wd.), Esher 194 C3
Station App., Grnf. 86 A7
Station App., Hmptn. 179 G1
*Milton Rd.*
Station App., Har. 68 B7
Station App., Hayes 121 J2
Station App., Kings.T. 182 A1
Station App., Loug. 48 B5
Station App. (Debden), Loug. 49 F4
Station App., Orp. 207 J2
Station App., Pnr. 66 E3
Station App. (Hatch End), Pnr. 51 G7
*Uxbridge Rd.*
Station App., Rich. 146 A1
Station App., Ruis. 84 B5
Station App., Sun. 178 A1
Station App. (Cheam), Sutt. 198 B7
Station App. (Carpenders Pk.), Wat. 50 D3
*Prestwick Rd.*
Station App., Well. 157 J2
Station App., Wem. 87 E6
Station App., West Dr. 120 B1
Station App. N., Sid. 176 A2
Station App. Rd. W4 126 C7
Station Av. SW9 151 H3
*Coldharbour La.*
Station Av., N.Mal. 183 E3
Station Av., Rich. 146 A1
*Station Par.*
Station Cl. N3 72 D1
Station Cl. (Woodside Pk.) N12 56 E4
Station Cl., Hmptn. 179 H1
Station Cres. N15 76 A4
Station Cres. SE3 135 G5
Station Cres., Wem. 87 E6
Station Est., Beck. 189 G4
*Elmers End Rd.*
Station Est. Rd., Felt. 160 B1
Station Garage Ms. SW16 168 D6
*Estreham Rd.*
Station Gdns. W4 126 C7
Station Gro., Wem. 87 H6
Station Hill, Brom. 205 G2

Talbot Rd., Sthl. 123 E4
Talbot Rd., Th.Hth. 188 A4
Talbot Rd., Twick. 162 B1
Talbot Rd., Wem. 87 G5
**Talbot Sq. W2 15 F4**
Talbot Sq. W2 109 G6
Talbot Wk. NW10 88/89 E6
*Garnet Rd.*
Talbot Wk. W11 108 B6
**Talbot Yd. SE1 28 B2**
Talfourd Pl. SE15 152 C1
Talfourd Rd. SE15 152 C1
Talgarth Rd. W6 128 B5
Talgarth Rd. W14 128 B5
Talgarth Wk. NW9 70 E5
Talisman Cl., Ilf. 100 B1
Talisman Sq. SE26 170 D4
Talisman Way, Wem. 87 J3
Tall Elms Cl., Brom. 191 F5
Tall Trees SW16 187 F3
Tallack Cl., Har. 52 B7
*College Hill Rd.*
Tallack Rd. E10 95 J1
Tallis Cl. E16 115 H6
Tallis Gro. SE7 135 H6
**Tallis St. EC4 19 F5**
Tallis St. EC4 111 G7
Tallis Vw. NW10 88 D6
Tally Ho Cor. N12 57 F5
Talma Gdns., Twick. 144 B6
Talma Rd. SW2 151 G4
Talmage Cl. SE23 153 F7
*Tyson Rd.*
Talman Gro., Stan. 53 G6
Talwin St. E3 114 B3
Tamar Cl. E3 113 J1
*Lefevre Wk.*
Tamar Sq., Wdf.Grn. 63 H6
Tamar St. SE7 136 B3
*Woolwich Rd.*
Tamar Way N17 76 D3
**Tamarind Yd. E1 29 J1**
Tamarisk Sq. W12 107 F7
Tamesis Gdns., Wor.Pk. 196 E1
Tamian Way, Houns. 142 C4
Tamworth Av., Wdf.Grn. 63 E6
Tamworth La., Mitch. 186 B2
Tamworth Pk., Mitch. 186 B4
Tamworth Pl., Croy. 201 J2
Tamworth Rd., Croy. 201 H2
Tamworth St. SW6 128 D6
Tancred Rd. N4 75 H6
Tandridge Dr., Orp. 207 G1
Tandridge Pl., Orp. 193 G7
*Tandridge Dr.*
Tanfield Av. NW2 89 F4
Tanfield Rd., Croy. 201 J4
Tangier Rd., Rich. 146 B3
Tangle Tree Cl. N3 73 E2
Tanglebury Cl., Brom. 192 C4
Tanglewood Cl., Croy. 203 F3
Tanglewood Cl., Stan. 52 B2
Tanglewood Way, Felt. 160 B3
Tangley Gro. SW15 147 F6
Tangley Pk. Rd., Hmptn. 161 F6
Tangmere Gdns., Nthlt. 102 C2
Tangmere Gro., Kings.T. 163 G5
Tangmere Way NW9 71 E2
Tanhurst Wk. SE2 138 D3
*Alsike Rd.*
Tankerton Rd., Surb. 195 J2
**Tankerton St. WC1 10 B4**
Tankerville Rd. SW16 168 D6
Tankridge Rd. NW2 89 H2
**Tanner St. SE1 28 E4**
Tanner St. SE1 132 B2
Tanner St., Bark. 99 F6
Tanners Cl., Walt. 178 B6
Tanners End La. N18 60 B4
Tanners Hill SE8 153 J1
Tanners La., Ilf. 81 F3
Tannery Cl., Beck. 189 G5
Tannery Cl., Dag. 101 H3
Tannington Ter. N5 93 G3
Tannsfeld Rd. SE26 171 G5
Tansley Cl. N7 92 D5
*Hilldrop Rd.*
**Tanswell Est. SE1 27 F4**
**Tanswell St. SE1 27 E4**
Tansy Cl. E6 116 D6
Tant Av. E16 115 F6
Tantallon Rd. SW12 168 A1
Tantony Gro., Rom. 82 D3
Tanworth Gdns., Pnr. 66 B2
Tanyard La., Bex. 159 G7
*Bexley High St.*
Tanza Rd. NW3 91 J4
Tapestry Cl., Sutt. 198 E7
Taplow NW3 91 G7
**Taplow SE17 36 D4**
Taplow Rd. N13 59 J4
**Taplow St. N1 12 A2**
Taplow St. N1 111 J2
Tapp St. E1 113 E4
Tappesfield Rd. SE15 153 F3
Tapster St., Barn. 40 C4
Taransay Wk. N1 94 A6
*Marquess Rd.*
Tarbert Rd. SE22 152 B5
Tarbert Wk. E1 113 F7
*Juniper St.*
Target Cl., Felt. 141 H6
Tariff Cres. SE8 133 J4
Tariff Rd. N17 60 D6
Tarleton Gdns. SE23 171 E1
Tarling Cl., Sid. 176 B3
Tarling Rd. E16 115 F6
Tarling Rd. N2 73 F2
Tarling St. E1 113 E6
Tarling St. Est. E1 113 F6
**Tarn St. SE1 27 J6**
Tarnbank, Enf. 43 E5
Tarnwood Pk. SE9 174 C1
Tarquin Ho. SE26 170 D4
Tarragon Cl. SE14 133 H7
Tarragon Gro. SE26 171 G6
**Tarrant Pl. W1 15 J2**
Tarrington Cl. SW16 168 D3
Tarry La. SE8 133 H4
**Tarver Rd. SE17 35 H4**
Tarver Rd. SE17 131 H5
Tarves Way SE10 134 B7
Tash Pl. N11 58 B5
*Woodland Rd.*
Tasker Cl., Hayes 121 F7
Tasker Ho., Bark. 117 G2
*Dovehouse Mead*
Tasker Rd. NW3 91 J5
Tasman Rd. SW9 151 E3
Tasman Wk. E16 116 A6
*Royal Rd.*
Tasmania Ter. N18 59 J6
Tasso Rd. W6 128 B6
Tatam Rd. NW10 88 C7
Tate & Lyle Jetty E16 136 B2
Tate Rd. E16 136 C1
*Newland St.*
Tate Rd., Sutt. 198 D5
Tatnell Rd. SE23 153 H6
Tattersall Cl. SE9 156 B5
Tatton Cres. N16 76 C7
*Clapton Common*
**Tatum St. SE17 36 C2**
Tatum St. SE17 132 A4
Tauheed Cl. N4 93 J2
Taunton Av. SW20 183 H2
Taunton Av., Houns. 143 J2
Taunton Cl., Ilf. 65 J6
Taunton Cl., Sutt. 198 D1
Taunton Dr. N2 73 F2
Taunton Dr., Enf. 43 G3
**Taunton Ms. NW1 7 J6**
**Taunton Pl. NW1 7 J5**
Taunton Pl. NW1 109 J4
Taunton Rd. SE12 155 E5
Taunton Rd., Grnf. 103 H1
Taunton Way, Stan. 69 H3
Tavern Cl., Cars. 185 H7
Tavern La. SW9 151 G2
Taverner Sq. N5 93 J4
*Highbury Gra.*
Taverners Cl. W11 128 B1
*Addison Av.*
Taverners Way E4 62/63 E1
*Douglas Rd.*
Tavistock Av. E17 77 H3
Tavistock Av., Grnf. 104 D2
Tavistock Cl. N16 94 B5
*Crossway*
Tavistock Cres. W11 108 C5
Tavistock Cres., Mitch. 186 E4
Tavistock Gdns., Ilf. 99 H4
Tavistock Gate, Croy. 202 A1
Tavistock Gro., Croy. 188 A7
Tavistock Ms. E18 79 G4
*Avon Way*
Tavistock Ms. W11 108 C6
*Lancaster Rd.*
Tavistock Pl. E18 79 G3
*Avon Way*
Tavistock Pl. N14 42 B7
*Chase Side*
**Tavistock Pl. WC1 9 J5**
Tavistock Pl. WC1 110 E4
Tavistock Rd. E7 97 F4
Tavistock Rd. E15 97 F6
Tavistock Rd. E18 79 G3
Tavistock Rd. N4 76 A6
Tavistock Rd. NW10 107 F2
Tavistock Rd. W11 108 C5
Tavistock Rd., Brom. 191 F4
Tavistock Rd., Cars. 199 G1
Tavistock Rd., Croy. 202 A1
Tavistock Rd., Edg. 70 A1
Tavistock Rd., Well. 158 C1
Tavistock Rd., West Dr. 120 A1
**Tavistock Sq. WC1 9 J5**
Tavistock Sq. WC1 110 D4
**Tavistock St. WC2 18 B5**
Tavistock St. WC2 111 E7
Tavistock Ter. N19 92 D3
Tavistock Wk., Cars. 199 G1
*Tavistock Rd.*
**Taviton St. WC1 9 H5**
Taviton St. WC1 110 D4
**Tavy Cl. SE11 35 F3**
Tavy Cl. SE11 131 G5
Tawney Rd. SE28 118 B7
Tawny Cl. W13 124 E1
Tawny Cl., Felt. 160 A3
*Chervil Cl.*
Tawny Way SE16 133 G4
Tayben Av., Twick. 144 B6
Taybridge Rd. SW11 150 A3
Tayburn Cl. E14 114 C6
Taylor Av., Rich. 146 B2
Taylor Cl. N17 60 D7
Taylor Cl., Hmptn. 161 J5
Taylor Cl., Houns. 143 J1
Taylor Cl., Orp. 207 J4
Taylor Ct. E15 96 C5
*Clays La.*
Taylor Rd., Mitch. 167 H7
Taylor Rd., Wall. 200 B5
Taylors Bldgs. SE18 136/137 E4
*Spray St.*
Taylors Cl., Sid. 175 J4
Taylors Grn. W3 106/107 E6
*Long Dr.*
Taylors La. NW10 88 E7
Taylors La. SE26 170 E4
Taylors La., Barn. 40 C1
Taymount Ri. SE23 171 F2
Tayport Cl. N1 93 E7
Tayside Dr., Edg. 54 B3
Taywood Rd., Nthlt. 103 F3
Teak Cl. SE16 133 H1
Teal Cl. E16 116 A5
*Fulmer Rd.*
Teal Pl., Sutt. 198 B2
*Gander Grn. La.*
**Teale St. E2 13 J1**
Teale St. E2 112 D2
Tealing Dr., Epsom 196 D4
Teasel Cl., Croy. 203 G1
Teasel Way E15 114 E3
Tebworth Rd. N17 60 C7
Teck Cl., Islw. 144 D2
Tedder Cl., Chess. 195 F5
Tedder Cl., Ruis. 84 B5
*West End Rd.*
Tedder Rd., S.Croy. 203 F7
Teddington Lock, Tedd. 162 E4
Teddington Pk., Tedd. 162 C5
Teddington Pk. Rd., Tedd. 162 C4
**Tedworth Gdns. SW3 31 J4**
**Tedworth Sq. SW3 31 J4**
Tedworth Sq. SW3 129 J5
Tee, The W3 106 E6
Tees Av., Grnf. 104 B2
Teesdale Av., Islw. 144 D1
**Teesdale Cl. E2 13 J2**
Teesdale Cl. E2 112 E2
Teesdale Gdns. SE25 188 B2
Teesdale Gdns., Islw. 144 D1
Teesdale Rd. E11 79 F6
Teesdale St. E2 112 E2
**Teesdale Yd. E2 13 J1**
Teeswater Ct., Erith 138 D3
*Middle Way*
Teevan Cl., Croy. 188 D7
Teevan Rd., Croy. 188 D7
Teignmouth Cl. SW4 150 D4
Teignmouth Cl., Edg. 69 J2
Teignmouth Gdns., Grnf. 104 D2
Teignmouth Rd. NW2 90 A5
Teignmouth Rd., Well. 158 C2
Telcote Way, Ruis. 66 C7
*Woodlands Av.*
Telegraph Hill NW3 90 E3
Telegraph La., Esher 194 C6
Telegraph Ms., Ilf. 100 A1
Telegraph Pl. E14 134 B4
Telegraph Rd. SW15 147 H7
**Telegraph St. EC2 20 B3**
Telemann Sq. SE3 155 H3
Telephone Pl. SW6 128 C6
*Lillie Rd.*
Telfer Cl. W3 126 C2
*Church Rd.*
Telferscot Rd. SW12 168 D1
Telford Av. SW2 168 E1
Telford Cl. E17 77 H7
Telford Cl. SE19 170 C6
*St. Aubyn's Rd.*
Telford Cl. W3 126 C2
*Church Rd.*
Telford Dr., Walt. 178 C7
Telford Rd. N11 58 C6
Telford Rd. NW9 71 G6
*West Hendon Bdy.*
Telford Rd. SE9 175 G2
Telford Rd. W10 108 B5
Telford Rd., Sthl. 103 H7
Telford Rd., Twick. 143 G7
**Telford Ter. SW1 33 F5**
Telford Ter. SW1 130 C6
Telford Way W3 106 E5
Telford Way, Hayes 102 E5
**Telfords Yd. E1 21 J6**
Telham Rd. E6 116 D2
Tell Gro. SE22 152 C4
Tellson Av. SE18 156 A1
Telscombe Cl., Orp. 207 H2
Temeraire St. SE16 133 F2
*Albion St.*
Temperley Rd. SW12 150 A7
Templar Dr. SE28 118 D6
Templar Ho. NW2 90 C6
*Shoot Up Hill*
Templar Pl., Hmptn. 161 G7
Templar St. SE5 151 H2
Templars Av. NW11 72 C6
Templars Cres. N3 72 D2
Templars Dr., Har. 52 A6
Temple EC4 111 G7
**Temple Av. EC4 19 F5**
Temple Av. EC4 111 G7
Temple Av. N20 41 G7
Temple Av., Croy. 203 J2
Temple Av., Dag. 101 G1
Temple Cl. E11 78/79 E7
*Wadley Rd.*
Temple Cl. N3 72 C2
*Cyprus Rd.*
Temple Cl. SE28 137 F3
Temple Ct. E1 113 G5
*Rectory Sq.*
Temple Fortune Hill NW11 72 D5
Temple Fortune La. NW11 72 D6
Temple Fortune Par. NW11 72 C5
*Finchley Rd.*
Temple Gdns. N21 59 H2
*Barrowell Grn.*
Temple Gdns. NW11 72 C6
Temple Gdns., Dag. 100 D3
Temple Gro. NW11 72 D6
Temple Gro., Enf. 43 H3
**Temple La. EC4 19 F4**
Temple Mead Cl., Stan. 52 E6
Temple Mill La. E15 96 B4
**Temple Pl. WC2 18 D5**
Temple Pl. WC2 111 F7
Temple Rd. E6 116 B1
Temple Rd. N8 75 F4
Temple Rd. NW2 89 J4
Temple Rd. W4 126 C3
Temple Rd. W5 125 G3
Temple Rd., Croy. 202 A4
Temple Rd., Houns. 143 H4
Temple Rd., Rich. 145 J3
Temple Sheen SW14 146 C5
Temple Sheen Rd. SW14 146 B4
Temple St. E2 112 E2
Temple Way, Sutt. 199 G3
**Temple W. Ms. SE11 27 G6**
Temple W. Ms. SE11 131 H3
Templecombe Rd. E9 113 F1
Templecombe Way, Mord. 184 B5
Templehof Av. NW2 71 J7
Templeman Rd. W7 104 C5
Templemead Cl. W3 106 E6
Templeton Av. E4 62 A4
Templeton Cl. N16 94 B5
*Truman's Rd.*
Templeton Cl. SE19 188 A1
Templeton Pl. SW5 128 D4
Templeton Rd. N15 76 A6
Templewood W13 105 E5
Templewood Av. NW3 90 E3
Templewood Gdns. NW3 91 E3
Tempsford Av., Borwd. 38 D4
Tempsford Cl., Enf. 43 J3
*Gladbeck Way*
Temsford Cl., Har. 67 J2

Thornfield Av. NW7 72 B1
Thornfield Rd. W12 127 H2
Thornford Rd. SE13 154 C5
Thorngate Rd. W9 108 D4
Thorngrove Rd. E13 115 H1
Thornham Gro. E15 96 D5
Thornham St. SE10 134 B6
**Thornhaugh Ms. WC1 9 J6**
**Thornhaugh St. WC1 17 J1**
Thornhaugh St. WC1 110 D4
Thornhill Av. SE18 137 H7
Thornhill Av., Surb. 195 H2
Thornhill Br. Wf. N1 111 F1
*Caledonian Rd.*
Thornhill Cres. N1 93 F7
Thornhill Gdns. E10 96 B2
Thornhill Gdns., Bark. 99 H7
Thornhill Gro. N1 93 F7
*Lofting Rd.*
Thornhill Ho. N1 93 G7
*Thornhill Rd.*
Thornhill Rd. E10 96 B2
Thornhill Rd. N1 93 G7
Thornhill Rd., Croy. 187 J7
Thornhill Rd., Surb. 195 H2
Thornhill Sq. N1 93 F7
Thornlaw Rd. SE27 169 G4
Thornley Cl. N17 60 D7
Thornley Dr., Har. 85 H2
Thornley Pl. SE10 134/135 E5
*Caradoc St.*
Thornsbeach Rd. SE6 172 C1
Thornsett Pl. SE20 188 E2
Thornsett Rd. SE20 188 E2
Thornsett Rd. SW18 167 E2
Thornside, Edg. 54 A6
*High St.*
Thornton Av. SW2 168 D1
Thornton Av. W4 127 E4
Thornton Av., Croy. 187 F6
Thornton Av., West Dr. 120 C3
Thornton Cl., West Dr. 120 C3
Thornton Ct. SW20 184 A5
Thornton Dene, Beck. 190 A2
Thornton Gdns. SW12 168 D1
Thornton Gro., Pnr. 51 G6
Thornton Hill SW19 166 B7
**Thornton Pl. W1 16 A1**
Thornton Pl. W1 109 J5
Thornton Rd. E11 96 D2
Thornton Rd. N18 61 F3
Thornton Rd. SW12 150 D7
Thornton Rd. SW14 146 D3
Thornton Rd. SW19 166 A6
Thornton Rd., Barn. 40 B3
Thornton Rd., Belv. 139 H4
Thornton Rd., Brom. 173 G5
Thornton Rd., Cars. 199 G1
Thornton Rd., Croy. 187 F7
Thornton Rd., Ilf. 98 E4
Thornton Rd., Th.Hth. 187 F7
Thornton Rd. E. SW19 166 A6
*Thornton Rd.*
Thornton Rd. Retail Pk., Croy. 187 F6
Thornton Row, Th.Hth. 187 G5
*London Rd.*
Thornton St. SW9 151 G2
Thornton Way NW11 73 E5
Thorntree Rd. SE7 136 A5
Thornville Gro., Mitch. 185 F2
Thornville St. SE8 154 A1
Thornwood Cl. E18 79 H2
Thornwood Rd. SE13 154 E5
Thorogood Gdns. E15 97 E5
Thorold Rd. N22 59 E7
Thorold Rd., Ilf. 98 E2
Thorparch Rd. SW8 150 D1
Thorpe Cl. W10 108 B6
*Cambridge Gdns.*
Thorpe Cl., Orp. 207 H2
Thorpe Cres. E17 77 J2
Thorpe Hall Rd. E17 78 C1
Thorpe Rd. E6 116 C1
Thorpe Rd. E7 97 F4
Thorpe Rd. E17 78 C2
Thorpe Rd. N15 76 B6
Thorpe Rd., Bark. 99 G7
Thorpe Rd., Kings.T. 163 H7
Thorpebank Rd. W12 127 G1
Thorpedale Gdns., Ilf. 80 D4
Thorpedale Rd. N4 93 E1
Thorpewood Av. SE26 171 E2
Thorsden Way SE19 170 B4
*Oaks Av.*
Thorverton Rd. NW2 90 B3
Thoydon Rd. E3 113 H2
Thrale Rd. SW16 168 C5
**Thrale St. SE1 28 A2**
Thrale St. SE1 131 J1
Thrasher Cl. E8 112 C1
*Stean St.*
**Thrawl St. E1 21 G2**
Thrawl St. E1 112 C5
**Threadneedle St. EC2 20 C4**
Threadneedle St. EC2 112 A6
**Three Barrels Wk. EC4 20 A5**
Three Colt St. E14 113 J7
**Three Colts Cor. E2 13 H5**
Three Colts La. E2 113 E4
Three Cors., Bexh. 159 H2
**Three Cups Yd. WC1 18 D2**
Three Kings Rd., Mitch. 186 A3
**Three Kings Yd. W1 16 D5**
Three Kings Yd. W1 110 B7
Three Mill La. E3 114 C3
**Three Oak La. SE1 29 F3**
Threshers Pl. W11 108 B7
Thriffwood SE26 171 F3
Thrift Fm. La., Borwd. 38 B2
Thrigby Rd., Chess. 195 J6
Throckmorten Rd. E16 115 H6
**Throgmorton Av. EC2 20 C3**
Throgmorton Av. EC2 112 A6
**Throgmorton St. EC2 20 C3**
Throgmorton St. EC2 112 A6
Throwley Cl. SE2 138 C3
Throwley Rd., Sutt. 199 E5
Throwley Way, Sutt. 199 E4
Thrupp Cl., Mitch. 186 B2
Thrush Grn., Har. 67 G4
**Thrush St. SE17 35 J3**
**Thruxton Way SE15 37 G7**
Thunderer Rd., Dag. 118 E4
Thurbarn Rd. SE6 172 B5
**Thurland Rd. SE16 29 H5**
Thurland Rd. SE16 132 D3
Thurlby Cl., Har. 68 D6
*Gayton Rd.*
Thurlby Cl., Wdf.Grn. 64 C5
Thurlby Rd. SE27 169 G4
Thurlby Rd., Wem. 87 G6
Thurleigh Av. SW12 150 A6
Thurleigh Rd. SW12 150 A6
Thurleston Av., Mord. 184 B5
Thurlestone Av. N12 57 J6
Thurlestone Av., Ilf. 99 J4
Thurlestone Rd. SE27 169 G3
**Thurloe Cl. SW7 31 G1**
Thurloe Cl. SW7 129 H3
**Thurloe Pl. SW7 31 F1**
Thurloe Pl. SW7 129 G4
**Thurloe Pl. Ms. SW7 31 F1**
**Thurloe Sq. SW7 31 G1**
Thurloe Sq. SW7 129 H4
**Thurloe St. SW7 31 F1**
Thurloe St. SW7 129 G4
Thurlow Cl. E4 62 B6
*Higham Sta. Av.*
Thurlow Gdns., Ilf. 65 G6
Thurlow Gdns., Wem. 87 G5
Thurlow Hill SE21 169 J1
Thurlow Pk. Rd. SE21 169 H1
Thurlow Rd. NW3 91 G5
Thurlow Rd. W7 124 D2
**Thurlow St. SE17 36 C3**
Thurlow St. SE17 132 A5
Thurlow Ter. NW5 92 A5
Thurlstone Rd., Ruis. 84 A3
Thurnby Ct., Twick. 162 B3
Thursland Rd., Sid. 176 E5
Thursley Cres., Croy. 204 D7
Thursley Gdns. SW19 166 A2
Thursley Rd. SE9 174 C3
Thurso St. SW17 167 G4
Thurstan Rd. SW20 165 H7
Thurston Rd. SE13 154 B2
Thurston Rd., Sthl. 103 F6
Thurtle Rd. E2 112 C1
Thwaite Cl., Erith 139 J6
Thyer Cl., Orp. 207 F4
*Isabella Dr.*
Thyra Gro. N12 57 E6
Tibbatts Rd. E3 114 B4
Tibbenham Wk. E13 115 F2
Tibberton Sq. N1 93 J7
*Popham Rd.*
Tibbets Cl. SW19 166 A1
Tibbet's Cor. SW15 148 A7
Tibbet's Cor. Underpass SW15 148 A7
*West Hill*
Tibbet's Ride SW15 148 A7
Tiber Gdns. N1 111 F1
*Treaty St.*
Ticehurst Cl., Orp. 176 A7
*Grovelands Rd.*
Ticehurst Rd. SE23 171 H2
Tickford Cl. SE2 138 C2
*Ampleforth Rd.*
Tidal Basin Rd. E16 115 F7
Tidenham Gdns., Croy. 202 B3
Tideswell Rd. SW15 147 J5
Tideswell Rd., Croy. 204 A3
Tideway Cl., Rich. 162/163 E4
*Locksmeade Rd.*
Tidey St. E3 114 A5
Tidford Rd., Well. 157 J2
Tidworth Rd. E3 114 A4
Tiepigs La., Brom. 205 E2
Tiepigs La., W.Wick. 205 E2
Tierney Rd. SW2 168 E1
Tiger La., Brom. 191 H4
Tiger Way E5 94 E4
Tilbrook Rd. SE3 155 J3
**Tilbury Cl. SE15 37 G7**
Tilbury Rd. E6 116 C2
Tilbury Rd. E10 78 C7
Tildesley Rd. SW15 147 J6
Tile Fm. Rd., Orp. 207 G3
Tile Kiln La. N6 92 B1
*Winchester Rd.*
Tile Kiln La. N13 59 J5
Tile Kiln La., Bex. 177 J2
Tile Yd. E14 113 J6
*Commercial Rd.*
Tilehurst Pt. SE2 138 C2
*Yarnton Way*
Tilehurst Rd. SW18 167 G1
Tilehurst Rd., Sutt. 198 B5
Tileyard Rd. N7 92 E7
Tilford Gdns. SW19 166 A2
Tilia Cl., Sutt. 198 C5
Tilia Rd. E5 94/95 E4
*Clarence Rd.*
Tilia Wk. SW9 151 H4
*Moorland Rd.*
Tiller Rd. E14 134 A3
Tillett Cl. NW10 88 C6
Tillett Sq. SE16 133 H2
*Howland Way*
**Tillett Way E2 13 H3**
Tilling Rd. NW2 89 J1
Tilling Way, Wem. 87 G2
Tillingbourne Gdns. N3 72 C3
Tillingbourne Way N3 72 C3
*Tillingbourne Gdns.*
Tillingham Way N12 56 D4
Tillman St. E1 112/113 E6
*Bigland St.*
Tilloch St. N1 93 F7
*Carnoustie Dr.*
Tillotson Rd. N9 60 C2
Tillotson Rd., Har. 51 H7
Tillotson Rd., Ilf. 80 D7
**Tilney Ct. EC1 12 A5**
Tilney Dr., Buck.H. 63 G2
Tilney Gdns. N1 94 A6
Tilney Rd., Dag. 101 F6
Tilney Rd., Sthl. 122 C4
**Tilney St. W1 24 C1**
Tilney St. W1 130 A1
Tilson Gdns. SW2 150 E7
Tilson Ho. SW2 150/151 E7
*Tilson Gdns.*
Tilson Rd. N17 76 D1
Tilt Yd. App. SE9 156 C6
Tilton St. SW6 128 B6
Tiltwood, The W3 106 C7
*Acacia Rd.*
Timber Cl., Chis. 192 D2
Timber Mill Way SW4 150 D3
Timber Pond Rd. SE16 133 G2
**Timber St. EC1 11 J5**
Timbercroft, Epsom 196 E4
Timbercroft La. SE18 137 H6
Timberdene NW4 72 A2
Timberdene Av., Ilf. 81 E1
Timberland Rd. E1 113 E6
Timberwharf Rd. N16 76 D6
Timbrell Pl. SE16 133 J1
*Silver Wk.*
Time Sq. E8 94 C5
Times Sq., Sutt. 199 E5
Timothy Cl. SW4 150 C5
*Elms Rd.*
Timothy Cl., Bexh. 158 E5
Timothy Ho., Erith 138/139 E2
*Kale Rd.*
Timothy Rd. E3 113 J5
Timsbury Wk. SW15 165 G1
Tindal St. SW9 151 H1
Tinderbox All. SW14 146 D3
Tine Rd., Chig. 65 H5
Tinniswood Cl. N5 93 G5
*Drayton Pk.*
Tinsley Rd. E1 113 F5
Tintagel Cres. SE22 152 C4
Tintagel Dr., Stan. 53 G4
Tintagel Gdns. SE22 152 C4
*Oxonian St.*
Tintern Av. NW9 70 B3
Tintern Cl. SW15 148 B5
Tintern Cl. SW19 167 F7
Tintern Gdns. N14 43 E7
Tintern Path NW9 70/71 E6
*Ruthin Cl.*
Tintern Rd. N22 75 J1
Tintern Rd., Cars. 199 G1
Tintern St. SW4 151 E4
Tintern Way, Har. 85 H1
Tinto Rd. E16 115 G4
Tinwell Ms., Borwd. 38 C5
*Cranes Way*
**Tinworth St. SE11 34 B3**
Tinworth St. SE11 131 F5
Tippetts Cl., Enf. 43 J1
Tipthorpe Rd. SW11 150 A3
Tipton Dr., Croy. 202 B4
Tiptree Cl. E4 62 C3
*Mapleton Rd.*
Tiptree Cres., Ilf. 80 D3
Tiptree Dr., Enf. 44 A4
Tiptree Est., Ilf. 80 D3
Tiptree Rd., Ruis. 84 B4
Tirlemont Rd., S.Croy. 201 J7
Tirrell Rd., Croy. 187 J6
Tisbury Ct. W1 110 D7
*Rupert St.*
Tisbury Rd. SW16 186 E2
**Tisdall Pl. SE17 36 C2**
Tisdall Pl. SE17 132 A4
**Titchborne Row W2 15 H4**
Titchfield Rd. NW8 109 J1
Titchfield Rd., Cars. 199 G1
Titchfield Wk., Cars. 185 G7
*Titchfield Rd.*
Titchwell Rd. SW18 149 G7
**Tite St. SW3 31 J4**
Tite St. SW3 129 J5
Tithe Barn Cl., Kings.T. 181 J1
Tithe Barn Way, Nthlt. 102 B3
Tithe Cl. NW7 71 G1
Tithe Cl., Walt. 178 B6
Tithe Fm. Av., Har. 85 G3
Tithe Fm. Cl., Har. 85 G3
Tithe Wk. NW7 71 G1
Titley Cl. E4 62 A5
Titmuss Av. SE28 118 B7
Titmuss St. W12 127 H2
Tiverton Av., Ilf. 80 D3
Tiverton Dr. SE9 175 F1
Tiverton Rd. N15 76 A6
Tiverton Rd. N18 60 B5
Tiverton Rd. NW10 108 A1
Tiverton Rd., Edg. 69 J2
Tiverton Rd., Houns. 143 J2
Tiverton Rd., Ruis. 84 A3
Tiverton Rd., Th.Hth. 187 G5
*Willett Rd.*
Tiverton Rd., Wem. 105 H2
**Tiverton St. SE1 27 J6**
Tiverton St. SE1 131 J3
Tiverton Way, Chess. 195 F5
Tivoli Ct. SE16 133 J2
Tivoli Gdns. SE18 136 B4
Tivoli Rd. N8 74 D5
Tivoli Rd. SE27 169 J5
Tivoli Rd., Houns. 142 E4
Toad La., Houns. 143 F4
Tobacco Quay E1 112/113 E7
*Wapping La.*
Tobago St. E14 134 A2
*Manilla St.*
Tobin Cl. NW3 91 H7
Toby La. E1 113 H4
Toby Way, Surb. 196 B2
Todds Wk. N7 93 F2
*Andover Rd.*
Token Yd. SW15 148 B4
*Montserrat Rd.*
**Tokenhouse Yd. EC2 20 B3**
Tokyngton Av., Wem. 88 A6
Toland Sq. SW15 147 G5
Tolcarne Dr., Pnr. 66 B3
Toley Av., Wem. 69 H7
Tollbridge Cl. W10 108 B4
*Kensal Rd.*
Tollesbury Gdns., Ilf. 81 G3
Tollet St. E1 113 G4
Tollgate Dr. SE21 170 B2
Tollgate Dr., Hayes 102 D7
*Delamere Rd.*
**Tollgate Gdns. NW6 6 A1**
Tollgate Gdns. NW6 108 E2
Tollgate Rd. E6 116 A5

Tollgate Rd. E16 115 J5
Tollhouse Way N19 92 C2
Tollington Pk. N4 93 F2
Tollington Pl. N4 93 F2
Tollington Rd. N7 93 F4
Tollington Way N7 92 E3
**Tolmers Sq. NW1 9 G5**
Tolpuddle Av. E13 115 J1
*Rochester Av.*
**Tolpuddle St. N1 10 E1**
Tolpuddle St. N1 111 G2
Tolsford Rd. E5 95 E5
Tolson Rd., Islw. 144 D3
Tolverne Rd. SW20 183 J1
Tolworth Cl., Surb. 196 B1
Tolworth Gdns., Rom. 82 D5
Tolworth Pk. Rd., Surb. 195 J2
Tolworth Ri. N., Surb. 182 C7
*Elmbridge Av.*
Tolworth Ri. S., Surb. 196 C1
*Warren Dr. S.*
Tolworth Rd., Surb. 195 H2
Tolworth Twr., Surb. 196 B2
Tom Coombs Cl. SE9 156 B4
*Well Hall Rd.*
Tom Cribb Rd. SE28 137 F3
Tom Gros. Cl. E15 96 D5
*Maryland St.*
Tom Hood Cl. E15 96 D5
*Maryland St.*
Tom Jenkinson Rd. E16 135 G1
Tom Mann Cl., Bark. 117 H1
Tom Nolan Cl. E15 114 E2
Tom Smith Cl. SE10 134/135 E6
*Maze Hill*
Tom Thumbs Arch E3 114 A2
*Malmesbury Rd.*
Tomahawk Gdns., Nthlt. 102 D3
*Javelin Way*
Tomlins Gro. E3 114 A3
Tomlins Orchard, Bark. 117 F1
Tomlins Ter. E14 113 J5
*Rhodeswell Rd.*
Tomlins Wk. N7 93 F2
*Briset Way*
**Tomlinson Cl. E2 13 G4**
Tomlinson Cl. E2 112 C3
Tomlinson Cl. W4 126 B5
*Oxford Rd. N.*
**Tompion St. EC1 11 G4**
Tomswood Ct., Ilf. 81 F1
Tomswood Hill, Ilf. 65 E7
Tomswood Rd., Chig. 64 D6
Tonbridge Cres., Har. 69 H4
Tonbridge Ho. SE25 188 D3
Tonbridge Rd., W.Mol. 179 E4
**Tonbridge St. WC1 10 A3**
Tonbridge St. WC1 110 E3
Tonbridge Wk. WC1 110/111 E3
*Tonbridge St.*
Tonfield Rd., Sutt. 198 C1
Tonge Cl., Beck. 190 A5
Tonsley Hill SW18 149 E5
Tonsley Pl. SW18 149 E5
Tonsley Rd. SW18 149 E5
Tonsley St. SW18 149 E5
Tonstall Rd., Mitch. 186 A2
Tony Cannell Ms. E3 113 J3
*Maplin St.*
Tooke Cl., Pnr. 66 E1
**Took's Ct. EC4 19 E3**
**Tooley St. SE1 28 C1**
Tooley St. SE1 132 A1
Toorack Rd., Har. 68 A2
Tooting Bec Gdns. SW16 168 D4
Tooting Bec Rd. SW16 168 A3
Tooting Bec Rd. SW17 168 A3
Tooting Gro. SW17 167 H5
Tooting High St. SW17 167 H6
Tootswood Rd., Brom. 190 E5
Top Ho. Ri. E4 46 C7
*Parkhill Rd.*
Top Pk., Beck. 190 E5
Topaz Wk. NW2 72 A7
*Marble Dr.*
Topcliffe Dr., Orp. 207 G4
Topham Sq. N17 75 J1
**Topham St. EC1 11 E5**
Topiary Sq., Rich. 145 J3
Topley St. SE9 156 A4
Topmast Pt. E14 134 A2
Topp Wk. NW2 89 J2
Topsfield Cl. N8 74 D5
*Wolseley Rd.*
Topsfield Par. N8 74/75 E5
*Tottenham La.*
Topsfield Rd. N8 74 E5
Topsham Rd. SW17 167 J3
Tor Gdns. W8 128 D2
Tor Rd., Well. 158 C1
Torbay Rd. NW6 90 C7
Torbay Rd., Har. 84 E2
Torbay St. NW1 92 B7
*Hawley Rd.*
Torbitt Way, Ilf. 81 J5
Torbridge Cl., Edg. 53 H7
Torbrook Cl., Bex. 159 E6
Torcross Dr. SE23 171 F2
Torcross Rd., Ruis. 84 B3
Tormead Cl., Sutt. 198 D6
Tormount Rd. SE18 137 H6
Toronto Av. E12 98 C4
Toronto Rd. E11 96 D4
Toronto Rd., Ilf. 99 E1
Torquay Gdns., Ilf. 80 A4
**Torquay St. W2 14 A2**
Torr Rd. SE20 171 G7
Torre Wk., Cars. 199 H1
Torrens Rd. E15 97 F6
Torrens Rd. SW2 151 F5
Torrens Sq. E15 97 E6
**Torrens St. EC1 11 F2**
Torrens St. EC1 111 G2
Torres Sq. E14 134 A5
*Napier Av.*
Torriano Av. NW5 92 D5
Torriano Cotts. NW5 92 C5
*Torriano Av.*
Torriano Ms. NW5 92 D5
*Torriano Av.*
Torridge Gdns. SE15 153 F4
Torridge Rd., Th.Hth. 187 H5
Torridon Rd. SE6 172 D1
Torridon Rd. SE13 154 D7
Torrington Av. N12 57 G5
Torrington Cl. N12 57 G4
Torrington Cl., Esher 194 B6
Torrington Dr., Har. 85 H4
Torrington Dr., Loug. 49 F4
Torrington Gdns. N11 58 C6
Torrington Gdns., Grnf. 87 F7
Torrington Gdns., Loug. 49 F4
Torrington Gro. N12 57 H5
Torrington Pk. N12 57 G5
**Torrington Pl. E1 29 J2**
Torrington Pl. E1 132 D1
**Torrington Pl. WC1 17 H1**
Torrington Pl. WC1 110 D5
Torrington Rd. E18 79 G3
Torrington Rd., Dag. 101 F1
Torrington Rd., Esher 194 B6
Torrington Rd., Grnf. 105 F1
**Torrington Sq. WC1 9 J6**
Torrington Sq. WC1 110 D4
Torrington Sq., Croy. 188 A7
*Tavistock Gro.*
Torrington Way, Mord. 184 D6
Torver Rd., Har. 68 B4
Torver Way, Orp. 207 G3
Torwood Rd. SW15 147 G5
**Tothill St. SW1 25 H4**
Tothill St. SW1 130 D2
Totnes Rd., Well. 138 B7
Totnes Wk. N2 73 G4
Tottan Ter. E1 113 G6
Tottenhall Rd. N13 59 G6
**Tottenham Ct. Rd. W1 9 G6**
Tottenham Ct. Rd. W1 110 C4
Tottenham Grn. E. N15 76 C4
Tottenham La. N8 74 E5
**Tottenham Ms. W1 17 G1**
Tottenham Rd. N1 94 B6
**Tottenham St. W1 17 G2**
Tottenham St. W1 110 C5
Totterdown St. SW17 167 J4
Totteridge Common N20 55 G2
Totteridge Grn. N20 56 D2
Totteridge La. N20 56 D2
Totteridge Village N20 56 B1
Totternhoe Cl., Har. 69 F5
Totton Rd., Th.Hth. 187 G3
**Toulmin St. SE1 27 J4**
Toulmin St. SE1 131 J2
**Toulon St. SE5 35 J7**
Toulon St. SE5 131 J7
Tournay Rd. SW6 128 C7
**Toussaint Wk. SE16 29 J5**
Tovil Cl. SE20 188 D2
Towcester Rd. E3 114 B4
**Tower Br. E1 29 F2**
Tower Br. E1 132 C1
**Tower Br. SE1 29 F2**
Tower Br. SE1 132 C1
**Tower Br. App. E1 29 F1**
Tower Br. App. E1 132 C1
Tower Br. Piazza SE1 132 C1
*Horselydown La.*
**Tower Br. Rd. SE1 28 D6**
Tower Br. Rd. SE1 132 B3
Tower Cl. NW3 91 G5
*Lyndhurst Rd.*
Tower Cl. SE20 170 E7
Tower Cl., Ilf. 65 E6
Tower Cl., Orp. 207 J2
**Tower Ct. WC2 18 A4**
Tower Gdns., Esher 194 D7
Tower Gdns. Rd. N17 75 J1
Tower Hamlets Rd. E7 97 F4
Tower Hamlets Rd. E17 78 A3
**Tower Hill EC3 21 E6**
Tower Hill EC3 112 B7
Tower Hill Ter. EC3 112 B7
*Byward St.*
Tower La., Wem. 87 G3
*Main Dr.*
Tower Ms. E17 78 A4
**Tower Mill Rd. SE15 36 D6**
**Tower Pier EC3 29 E1**
Tower Pier EC3 132 C1
**Tower Pl. EC3 20 E6**
Tower Pt., Enf. 44 A4
Tower Ri., Rich. 145 H3
*Jocelyn Rd.*
Tower Rd. NW10 89 G7
Tower Rd., Belv. 139 J4
Tower Rd., Bexh. 159 H4
Tower Rd., Orp. 207 J2
Tower Rd., Twick. 162 C3
**Tower Royal EC4 20 A5**
**Tower St. WC2 17 J4**
Tower St. WC2 110 D6
Tower Ter. N22 75 F2
*Mayes Rd.*
Tower Vw., Croy. 189 G7
Towers Pl., Rich. 145 H5
*Eton St.*
Towers Rd., Pnr. 66 E1
Towers Rd., Sthl. 103 G4
Towfield Rd., Felt. 161 F2
**Towing Path Wk. N1 10 A1**
Town, The, Enf. 44 A3
Town Ct. Path N4 93 J1
Town Fm. Way, Stai. 140 A7
*Town La.*
Town Fld. Way, Islw. 144 D2
Town Hall App. N16 94 B4
*Milton Gro.*
Town Hall App. Rd. N15 76 C4
Town Hall Av. W4 126 D5
Town Hall Rd. SW11 149 J3
Town La., Stai. 140 A6
Town Meadow, Brent. 125 G7
Town Quay, Bark. 117 E1
Town Rd. N9 61 E2
Towncourt Cres., Orp. 193 F5
Towncourt La., Orp. 193 G6
Towney Mead, Nthlt. 103 F2
Towney Mead Ct., Nthlt. 103 F2
*Towney Mead*
Townfield Rd., Hayes 121 J1
Townholm Cres. W7 124 C3
Townley Ct. E15 97 F6
Townley Rd. SE22 152 B5
Townley Rd., Bexh. 159 F5
**Townley St. SE17 36 B3**
Townmead Rd. SW6 149 F2
Townmead Rd., Rich. 146 B2
Townsend Av. N14 58 D4
Townsend Ind. Est. NW10 106 D2
Townsend La. NW9 70 D7
Townsend Rd. N15 76 C5
Townsend Rd., Sthl. 122 E1
**Townsend St. SE17 36 C2**
Townsend St. SE17 132 A4
Townsend Yd. N6 92 B1
Townshend Cl., Sid. 176 B6
**Townshend Est. NW8 7 G1**
Townshend Est. NW8 109 H2
Townshend Rd. NW8 109 H1
Townshend Rd., Chis. 174 E5
Townshend Rd., Rich. 145 J4
Townshend Ter., Rich. 145 J4
Townson Av., Nthlt. 102 A3
Townson Way, Nthlt. 102 A2
*Townson Av.*
Towpath Wk. E9 95 J5
Towpath Way, Croy. 188 C6
Towton Rd. SE27 169 J2
Toynbec Cl., Chis. 174/175 E4
*Beechwood Ri.*
Toynbee Rd. SW20 184 B1
**Toynbee St. E1 21 F2**
Toynbee St. E1 112 C5
Toyne Way N6 73 J6
*Gaskell Rd.*
Tracey Av. NW2 89 J5
Tracy Ct., Stan. 53 F7
Trade Cl. N13 59 G4
Trader Rd. E6 116 E6
Tradescant Rd. SW8 131 E7
Trading Est. Rd. NW10 106 C4
Trafalgar Av. N17 60 B6
**Trafalgar Av. SE15 37 G4**
Trafalgar Av. SE15 132 C5
Trafalgar Av., Wor.Pk. 198 A1
Trafalgar Business Cen., Bark. 117 J4
Trafalgar Cl. SE16 133 H4
*Greenland Quay*
Trafalgar Gdns. E1 113 G5
**Trafalgar Gdns. W8 22 B5**
Trafalgar Gro. SE10 134 D6
Trafalgar Pl. E11 79 G4
Trafalgar Pl. N18 60 D5
Trafalgar Rd. SE10 134 D6
Trafalgar Rd. SW19 167 E7
Trafalgar Rd., Twick. 162 A2
**Trafalgar Sq. SW1 25 J1**
Trafalgar Sq. SW1 130 D1
**Trafalgar Sq. WC2 25 J1**
Trafalgar Sq. WC2 130 D1
**Trafalgar St. SE17 36 B3**
Trafalgar St. SE17 132 A5
Trafalgar Ter., Har. 86 B1
*Nelson Rd.*
Trafalgar Way E14 134 C1
Trafalgar Way, Croy. 201 F2
Trafford Cl. E15 96 B5
Trafford Cl., Ilf. 65 J6
Trafford Rd., Th.Hth. 187 F5
Tralee Ct. SE16 132/133 E5
*Masters Dr.*
Tramway Av. E15 96 E7
Tramway Av. N9 45 E7
Tramway Path, Mitch. 185 J5
Tranby Pl. E9 95 G5
*Homerton High St.*
Tranley Ms. NW3 91 H4
*Fleet Rd.*
Tranmere Rd. N9 44 C7
Tranmere Rd. SW18 167 F2
Tranmere Rd., Twick. 143 H7
Tranquil Pas. SE3 155 F2
*Tranquil Vale*
Tranquil Vale SE3 155 E2
Transay Wk. N1 94 A6
*Marquess Rd.*
**Transept St. NW1 15 G2**
Transept St. NW1 109 H5
Transmere Cl., Orp. 193 F6
Transmere Rd., Orp. 193 F6
Transom Cl. SE16 133 H4
*Plough Way*
Transom Sq. E14 134 B5
Transport Av., Brent. 124 E5
**Tranton Rd. SE16 29 J5**
Tranton Rd. SE16 132 D3
Traps Hill, Loug. 48 C3
Traps La., N.Mal. 182 E1
Travellers Way, Houns. 142 C2
Travers Cl. E17 77 G1
Travers Rd. N7 93 G3
Treacy Cl., Bushey 51 J2
Treadgold St. W11 108 A7
Treadway St. E2 112 E2
Treaty Rd., Houns. 143 H3
*Hanworth Rd.*
Treaty St. N1 111 F1
**Trebeck St. W1 24 D1**
Trebovir Rd. SW5 128 D5
Treby St. E3 113 J4
Trecastle Way N7 92 D4
*Carleton Rd.*
Tredegar Ms. E3 113 J3
*Tredegar Ter.*
Tredegar Rd. E3 113 J2
Tredegar Rd. N11 58 D7
Tredegar Sq. E3 113 J3
Tredegar Ter. E3 113 J3
Trederwen Rd. E8 112 D1
Tredown Rd. SE26 171 F5
Tredwell Cl. SW2 169 F2
*Hillside Rd.*
Tredwell Cl., Brom. 192 B4
Tredwell Rd. SE27 169 H4
Tree Cl., Rich. 163 G1
Tree Rd. E16 115 J6
Treen Av. SW13 147 F3

Treeside Cl., West Dr. 120 A4
Treetops Cl. SE2 139 E5
Treetops Vw., Loug. 47 J6
*High Rd.*
Treeview Cl. SE19 188 B1
Treewall Gdns., Brom. 173 H4
Trefgarne Rd., Dag. 101 G2
Trefil Wk. N7 93 E4
Trefoil Ho., Erith 138/139 E2
*Kale Rd.*
Trefoil Rd. SW18 149 F5
Tregaron Av. N8 75 E6
Tregaron Gdns., N.Mal. 182/183 E4
*Avenue Rd.*
Tregarvon Rd. SW11 150 A4
Tregenna Av., Har. 85 F4
Tregenna Cl. N14 42 C5
Tregenna Ct., Har. 85 G4
Trego Rd. E9 96 A7
Tregothnan Rd. SW9 151 E3
**Tregunter Rd. SW10 30 C5**
Tregunter Rd. SW10 129 F6
Trehearn Rd., Ilf. 65 G7
Trehern Rd. SW14 146 D3
Treherne Ct. SW9 151 G1
*Eythorne Rd.*
Treherne Ct. SW17 168 A4
Trehurst St. E5 95 H5
Trelawn Rd. E10 96 C3
Trelawn Rd. SW2 151 G5
Trelawney Cl. E17 78 B4
*Orford Rd.*
Trelawney Est. E9 95 F6
Trelawney Rd., Ilf. 65 G7
Trellick Twr. W10 108 C4
Trellis Sq. E3 113 J3
*Malmesbury Rd.*
Treloar Gdns. SE19 170 A6
*Hancock Rd.*
Tremadoc Rd. SW4 150 D4
Tremaine Cl. SE4 154 A2
Tremaine Rd. SE20 189 E2
Trematon Pl., Tedd. 163 F7
Tremlett Gro. N19 92 C3
Tremlett Ms. N19 92 C3
Trenance Gdns., Ilf. 100 A3
Trench Yd. Ct., Mord. 184/185 E6
*Green La.*
Trenchard Av., Ruis. 84 B4
Trenchard Cl. NW9 70/71 E1
*Fulbeck Dr.*
Trenchard Cl., Stan. 52 D6
Trenchard Ct., Mord. 184/185 E6
*Green La.*
Trenchard St. SE10 134 D5
**Trenchold St. SW8 34 A6**
Trenchold St. SW8 130 E6
Trenholme Cl. SE20 171 E7
Trenholme Rd. SE20 170 E7
Trenholme Ter. SE20 170 E7
Trenmar Gdns. NW10 107 H3
Trent Av. W5 125 F3
Trent Gdns. N14 42 B6
Trent Rd. SW2 151 F5
Trent Rd., Buck.H. 63 H1
Trent Way, Wor.Pk. 197 J3
Trentbridge Cl., Ilf. 65 J6
Trentham St. SW18 166 D1
Trentwood Side, Enf. 43 F3
Treport St. SW18 149 E7
Tresco Cl., Brom. 172 E6
Tresco Gdns., Ilf. 100 A2
Tresco Rd. SE15 153 E4
Trescoe Gdns., Har. 67 E7
**Tresham Cres. NW8 7 G5**
Tresham Cres. NW8 109 H4
Tresham Rd., Bark. 99 J7
Tresham Wk. E9 95 F5
*Churchill Wk.*
Tresilian Av. N21 43 F5
Tressell Cl. N1 93 H7
*Sebbon St.*
Tressillian Cres. SE4 154 A3
Tressillian Rd. SE4 153 J4
Trestis Cl., Hayes 102/103 E5
*Jollys La.*
Treswell Rd., Dag. 119 E1
Tretawn Gdns. NW7 55 E4
Tretawn Pk. NW7 55 E4
Trevanion Rd. W14 128 B5
Treve Av., Har. 67 J7
Trevelyan Av. E12 98 C4
Trevelyan Cres., Har. 69 G7
Trevelyan Gdns. NW10 107 J1
Trevelyan Rd. E15 97 F4
Trevelyan Rd. SW17 167 H5
**Treveris St. SE1 27 G2**
Treverton St. W10 108 A4
Treves Cl. N21 43 F5
Treville St. SW15 147 H7
Treviso Rd. SE23 171 G2
*Farren Rd.*
Trevithick St. SE8 134 A5
Trevone Gdns., Pnr. 67 E6
Trevor Cl., Barn. 41 G5
Trevor Cl., Brom. 191 F7
Trevor Cl., Har. 52 C7
*Kenton La.*
Trevor Cl., Islw. 144 C5
Trevor Cl., Nthlt. 102 C2
Trevor Gdns., Edg. 70 D1
Trevor Gdns., Nthlt. 102 C2
**Trevor Pl. SW7 23 H4**
Trevor Pl. SW7 129 H2
Trevor Rd. SW19 166 B7
Trevor Rd., Edg. 70 D1
Trevor Rd., Hayes 121 H2
Trevor Rd., Wdf.Grn. 63 G7
**Trevor Sq. SW7 23 J4**
Trevor Sq. SW7 129 J2
**Trevor St. SW7 23 H4**
Trevor St. SW7 129 H2
Trevose Rd. E17 78 D1
Trevose Way, Wat. 50 C3
Trewenna Dr., Chess. 195 G5
Trewince Rd. SW20 183 J1
Trewint St. SW18 167 F2
Trewsbury Ho. SE2 138 D2
*Hartslock Dr.*
Trewsbury Rd. SE26 171 G5
Triandra Way, Hayes 102 D5
Triangle, The EC1 111 H4
*Goswell Rd.*
Triangle, The N13 59 G4
*Lodge Dr.*
Triangle, The, Bark. 99 F6
*Tanner St.*
Triangle, The, Hmptn. 179 J1
*High St.*
Triangle, The, Kings.T. 182 C2
*Kenley Rd.*
Triangle Ct. E16 116 A5
*Tollgate Rd.*
Triangle Pas., Barn. 41 F4
Triangle Pl. SW4 150 D4
Triangle Rd. E8 112 E1
Trident Gdns., Nthlt. 102 D3
*Jetstar Way*
Trident St. SE16 133 G4
Trident Way, Sthl. 122 B3
**Trig La. EC4 19 J5**
**Trigon Rd. SW8 34 D7**
Trigon Rd. SW8 131 F7
Trilby Rd. SE23 171 G2
Trim St. SE14 133 J6
Trimmer Wk., Brent. 125 H6
Trinder Gdns. N19 92/93 E1
*Trinder Rd.*
Trinder Rd. N19 93 E1
Trinder Rd., Barn. 39 J5
Tring Av. W5 125 J1
Tring Av., Sthl. 103 F6
Tring Av., Wem. 88 A6
Tring Cl., Ilf. 81 F5
Trinidad St. E14 113 J7
Trinity Av. N2 73 G3
Trinity Av., Enf. 44 C6
Trinity Buoy Wf. E14 115 F7
Trinity Ch. Pas. SW13 127 H6
Trinity Ch. Rd. SW13 127 H6
**Trinity Ch. Sq. SE1 28 A5**
Trinity Ch. Sq. SE1 131 J3
Trinity Cl. E8 94 C6
Trinity Cl. E11 97 E2
Trinity Cl. NW3 91 G4
*Hampstead High St.*
Trinity Cl. SE13 154 D4
*Wisteria Rd.*
Trinity Cl., Brom. 206 B1
Trinity Cl., Houns. 143 E4
Trinity Cotts., Rich. 145 J3
*Trinity Rd.*
Trinity Ct. N1 94 B7
*Downham Rd.*
Trinity Ct. SE7 136 A4
*Charlton La.*
Trinity Cres. SW17 167 J2
Trinity Gdns. E16 115 F4
*Cliff Wk.*
Trinity Gdns. SW9 151 F4
Trinity Gro. SE10 154 C1
Trinity Ms. SE20 189 E1
Trinity Ms. W10 108 A6
*Cambridge Gdns.*
Trinity Path SE26 171 F3
Trinity Pl., Bexh. 159 F4
Trinity Ri. SW2 169 G1
Trinity Rd. N2 73 G3
Trinity Rd. N22 75 E1
Trinity Rd. SW17 167 J2
Trinity Rd. SW18 149 G5
Trinity Rd. SW19 166 D6
Trinity Rd., Ilf. 81 F3
Trinity Rd., Rich. 145 J3
Trinity Rd., Sthl. 122 E1
**Trinity Sq. EC3 21 E6**
Trinity Sq. EC3 112 D7
Trinity St. E16 115 G5
*Vincent St.*
**Trinity St. SE1 28 A4**
Trinity St. SE1 131 J2
Trinity St., Enf. 43 J2
Trinity Wk. NW3 91 F6
Trinity Way E4 61 J6
Trinity Way W3 107 E7
**Trio Pl. SE1 28 A4**
Tristan Sq. SE3 155 E3
Tristram Cl. E17 78 D3
Tristram Rd., Brom. 173 F4
**Triton Sq. NW1 9 F5**
Triton Sq. NW1 110 C4
Tritton Av., Croy. 201 E4
Tritton Rd. SE21 170 A3
Triumph Cl., Hayes 121 F7
Triumph Ho., Bark. 118 B3
Triumph Rd. E6 116 C6
Trojan Ct. NW6 90 B7
*Willesden La.*
Trojan Way, Croy. 201 F3
Troon Cl. SE16 132/133 E5
*Masters Dr.*
Troon St. E1 113 H6
Trosley Rd., Belv. 139 G6
Trossachs Rd. SE22 152 B5
**Trothy Rd. SE1 37 J1**
Trott Rd. N10 57 J7
Trott St. SW11 149 H1
Trotwood, Chig. 65 G6
Troughton Rd. SE7 135 H5
Trout Rd., West Dr. 120 A1
Troutbeck Rd. SE14 153 H1
Trouville Rd. SW4 150 C6
Trowbridge Est. E9 95 J6
*Osborne Rd.*
Trowbridge Rd. E9 95 J6
Trowlock Av., Tedd. 163 F6
Trowlock Island, Tedd. 163 G5
Trowlock Way, Tedd. 163 G6
Troy Ct. SE18 137 E4
Troy Rd. SE19 170 A6
Troy Town SE15 152 D3
Trubshaw Rd., Sthl. 123 H3
*Havelock Rd.*
Truesdale Rd. E6 116 C6
Trulock Ct. N17 60 D7
Trulock Rd. N17 60 D7
Truman Cl., Edg. 54 B7
*Pavilion Way*
Truman's Rd. N16 94 B5
**Trump St. EC2 20 A4**
Trumpers Way W7 124 B3
Trumpington Rd. E7 97 F4
**Trundle St. SE1 27 J3**
Trundlers Way, Bushey 52 B1
Trundleys Rd. SE8 133 G5
Trundleys Ter. SE8 133 G4
Truro Gdns., Ilf. 80 B7
Truro Rd. E17 77 J4
Truro Rd. N22 59 E7
Truro St. NW5 92 A6
Truslove Rd. SE27 169 G5
Trussley Rd. W6 127 J3
Trust Wk. SE21 169 H1
*Peabody Hill*
Tryfan Cl., Ilf. 80 A5
**Tryon St. SW3 31 J3**
Tryon St. SW3 129 J5
Trystings Cl., Esher 194 D6
Tuam Rd. SE18 137 G6
Tubbenden Cl., Orp. 207 H2
Tubbenden Dr., Orp. 207 G4
Tubbenden La., Orp. 207 H3
Tubbenden La. S., Orp. 207 G5
Tubbs Rd. NW10 107 F2
Tudor Av., Hmptn. 161 G6
Tudor Av., Wor.Pk. 197 H3
Tudor Cl. N6 74 C7
Tudor Cl. NW3 91 H5
Tudor Cl. NW7 55 G6
Tudor Cl. NW9 88 C2
Tudor Cl. SW2 151 F6
*Elm Pk.*
Tudor Cl., Chess. 195 H5
Tudor Cl., Chig. 64 D4
Tudor Cl., Chis. 192 C1
Tudor Cl., Pnr. 66 A5
Tudor Cl., Sutt. 198 A5
Tudor Cl., Wall. 200 C7
Tudor Cl., Wdf.Grn. 63 H5
Tudor Ct. E17 77 H7
Tudor Ct., Felt. 160 C4
Tudor Ct. N., Wem. 88 A5
Tudor Ct. S., Wem. 88 A5
Tudor Cres., Enf. 43 H1
Tudor Cres., Ilf. 65 E6
Tudor Dr., Kings.T. 163 H5
Tudor Dr., Mord. 184 A6
Tudor Est. NW10 106 B2
Tudor Gdns. NW9 88 C2
Tudor Gdns. SW13 146/147 E3
*Treen Av.*
Tudor Gdns. W3 106 A6
Tudor Gdns., Har. 68 A2
*Tudor Rd.*
Tudor Gdns., Twick. 162 C1
Tudor Gdns., W.Wick. 204 C3
Tudor Gro. E9 95 F7
Tudor Gro. N20 57 H3
*Church Cres.*
**Tudor Pl. W1 17 H3**
Tudor Pl., Mitch. 167 H7
Tudor Rd. E4 62 B6
Tudor Rd. E6 115 J1
Tudor Rd. E9 113 E1
Tudor Rd. N9 45 E7
Tudor Rd. SE19 170 C7
Tudor Rd. SE25 189 E5
Tudor Rd., Bark. 117 J1
Tudor Rd., Barn. 40 D3
Tudor Rd., Beck. 190 B3
Tudor Rd., Hmptn. 161 G7
Tudor Rd., Har. 68 A2
Tudor Rd., Houns. 144 A4
Tudor Rd., Kings.T. 164 A7
Tudor Rd., Pnr. 66 C2
Tudor Rd., Sthl. 102 E7
**Tudor St. EC4 19 F5**
Tudor St. EC4 111 G7
Tudor Wk., Bex. 159 E6
Tudor Way N14 58 D1
Tudor Way W3 126 A2
Tudor Way, Orp. 193 G6
Tudor Well Cl., Stan. 53 E5
Tudway Rd. SE3 155 H3
Tufnell Pk. Rd. N7 92 C4
Tufnell Pk. Rd. N19 92 C4
Tufter Rd., Chig. 65 J5
Tufton Gdns., W.Mol. 179 H2
Tufton Rd. E4 62 A4
**Tufton St. SW1 25 J5**
Tufton St. SW1 130 D3
Tugboat St. SE28 137 H2
Tugela Rd., Croy. 188 A6
Tugela St. SE6 171 J2
Tugmutton Cl., Orp. 206/207 E4
*Acorn Way*
**Tuilerie St. E2 13 H1**
Tuilerie St. E2 112 D2
Tulip Cl. E6 116 C5
*Bradley Stone Rd.*
Tulip Cl., Croy. 203 G1
Tulip Cl., Hmptn. 161 F6
*Partridge Rd.*
Tulip Cl., Sthl. 123 J2
*Chevy Rd.*
Tulip Ct., Pnr. 66 C3
Tulip Gdns., Ilf. 98 E6
Tulip Way, West Dr. 120 A3
*Wise La.*
Tull St., Mitch. 185 J7
Tulse Cl., Beck. 190 C3
Tulse Hill SW2 151 G6
Tulse Hill Est. SW2 151 G6
Tulsemere Rd. SE27 169 J2
Tumbling Bay, Walt. 178 A6
Tummons Gdns. SE25 188 B2
Tun Yd. SW8 150 B2
*Peardon St.*
Tuncombe Rd. N18 60 B4
Tunis Rd. W12 127 H1
Tunley Grn. E14 113 J5
*Burdett Rd.*
Tunley Rd. NW10 106 E1
Tunley Rd. SW17 168 A1
Tunmarsh La. E13 115 J3
Tunnan Leys E6 116 D6
Tunnel Av. SE10 134 D2
Tunnel Gdns. N11 58 C7
Tunnel Rd. SE16 133 F2
*St. Marychurch St.*
Tunstall Cl., Orp. 207 H4
Tunstall Rd. SW9 151 F4
Tunstall Rd., Croy. 202 B1
Tunstall Wk., Brent. 125 H6
Tunstock Way, Belv. 139 E3
Tunworth Cl. NW9 70 C6
Tunworth Cres. SW15 147 F6
Tupelo Rd. E10 96 B2
Turenne Cl. SW18 149 F4
Turin Rd. N9 45 F7
**Turin St. E2 13 H4**
Turin St. E2 112 D3
Turkey Oak Cl. SE19 188 B1
**Turk's Head Yd. EC1 19 G1**
**Turks Row SW3 32 A3**
Turks Row SW3 129 J5

Turle Rd. N4 93 F1
Turle Rd. SW16 186 E2
Turlewray Cl. N4 93 F1
Turley Cl. E15 115 E1
**Turnagain La. EC4 19 G3**
Turnage Rd., Dag. 100 E1
Turnberry Cl. NW4 72 A2
Turnberry Cl. SE16 132/133 E5
*Ryder Dr.*
Turnberry Ct., Wat. 50 C3
Turnberry Quay E14 134 B3
*Pepper St.*
Turnberry Way, Orp. 207 G1
Turnbury Cl. SE28 118 D6
Turnchapel Ms. SW4 150 B3
*Cedars Rd.*
Turner Av. N15 76 B4
Turner Av., Mitch. 185 J1
Turner Av., Twick. 161 J3
Turner Cl. NW11 72 E6
Turner Cl. SW9 151 H1
*Langton Rd.*
Turner Cl., Wem. 87 G5
Turner Dr. NW11 72 E6
Turner Rd. E17 78 C3
Turner Rd., Edg. 69 J3
Turner Rd., N.Mal. 182 D7
Turner St. E1 112 E5
Turner St. E16 115 F6
Turners Meadow Way, Beck. 189 J1
Turners Rd. E3 113 J5
Turners Way, Croy. 201 G2
Turners Wd. NW11 73 F7
Turneville Rd. W14 128 C6
Turney Rd. SE21 152 A7
Turnham Grn. Ter. W4 126 E4
Turnham Grn. Ter. Ms. W4 126/127 E4
*Turnham Grn. Ter.*
Turnham Rd. SE4 153 H5
**Turnmill St. EC1 11 F6**
Turnmill St. EC1 111 G4
Turnpike Cl. SE8 133 J7
*Amersham Vale*
**Turnpike Ho. EC1 11 H4**
Turnpike Ho. EC1 111 H3
Turnpike La. N8 75 F4
Turnpike La., Sutt. 199 F5
Turnpike Link, Croy. 202 B2
Turnpike Way, Islw. 144 D1
Turnpin La. SE10 134 C6
Turnstone Cl. E13 115 G3
Turnstone Cl. NW9 70/71 E2
*Kestrel Cl.*
**Turpentine La. SW1 32 E3**
Turpin Rd., Felt. 141 J6
*Staines Rd.*
Turpin Way N19 92 D2
*Elthorne Rd.*
Turpin Way, Wall. 200 B7
Turpington Cl., Brom. 192 B6
Turpington La., Brom. 192 B7
Turpins La., Wdf.Grn. 64 C5
**Turquand St. SE17 36 A2**
Turret Gro. SW4 150 C3
Turton Rd., Wem. 87 H5
**Turville St. E2 13 F5**
Tuscan Rd. SE18 137 G5
Tuskar St. SE10 134 E5
Tustin Est. SE15 133 F6
Tuttlebee La., Buck.H. 63 G2
Tweedale Ct. E15 96 C5
Tweeddale Rd., Cars. 199 G1
Tweedmouth Rd. E13 115 H2
Tweedy Cl., Enf. 44 C5
Tweedy Rd., Brom. 191 G1
**Tweezer's All. WC2 18 E5**
Twelvetrees Cres. E3 114 C4
Twentyman Cl., Wdf.Grn. 63 G5
Twickenham Br., Rich. 145 F5
Twickenham Br., Twick. 145 F5
Twickenham Cl., Croy. 201 F3
Twickenham Gdns., Grnf. 86 D5
Twickenham Gdns., Har. 52 B7
Twickenham Rd. E11 96 D2
Twickenham Rd., Felt. 161 F3
Twickenham Rd., Islw. 144 D3
Twickenham Rd., Rich. 145 F4
Twickenham Rd., Tedd. 162 D5
Twickenham Trd. Est., Twick. 144 C6
Twig Folly Cl. E2 113 G2
*Roman Rd.*
Twilley St. SW18 148 E7
Twin Tumps Way SE28 118 A7
Twine Cl., Bark. 118 B3
*Thames Rd.*
Twine Ct. E1 113 F7
Twine Ter. E3 113 J4
*Ropery St.*
Twineham Grn. N12 56 D4
*Tillingham Way*
Twining Av., Twick. 161 J3
Twinn Rd. NW7 56 B6
Twisden Rd. NW5 92 B4
Twybridge Way NW10 88 C7
Twycross Ms. SE10 134/135 E4
*Blackwall La.*
Twyford Abbey Rd. NW10 105 J3
Twyford Av. N2 73 J3
Twyford Av. W3 106 A7
Twyford Cres. W3 126 A1
**Twyford Pl. WC2 18 C3**
Twyford Rd., Cars. 199 G1
Twyford Rd., Har. 85 H1
Twyford Rd., Ilf. 99 F5
Twyford St. N1 111 F1
Tyas Rd. E16 115 F4
Tybenham Rd. SW19 184 D3
Tyberry Rd., Enf. 45 E3
Tyburn La., Har. 68 B7
**Tyburn Way W1 16 A5**
Tyburn Way W1 109 J7
Tycehurst Hill, Loug. 48 C4
Tye La., Orp. 207 F5
**Tyers Est. SE1 28 D3**
Tyers Est. SE1 132 B2
**Tyers Gate SE1 28 D3**
**Tyers St. SE11 34 C3**
Tyers St. SE11 131 F5
**Tyers Ter. SE11 34 C4**
Tyers Ter. SE11 131 F5
Tyeshurst Cl. SE2 139 E5
Tylecroft Rd. SW16 186 E2
Tylehurst Gdns., Ilf. 99 F5
**Tyler Cl. E2 13 F1**
Tyler Cl. E2 112 C2
Tyler St. SE10 135 E5
Tylers Cl., Loug. 48 B7
**Tyler's Ct. W1 17 H4**
Tylers Gate, Har. 69 H6
Tylers Path, Cars. 199 J4
*Rochester Rd.*
Tylney Av. SE19 170 C5
Tylney Rd. E7 97 J4
Tylney Rd., Brom. 192 A2
Tynan Cl., Felt. 160 A1
*Sandycombe Rd.*
Tyndale Ct. E14 134 B4
Tyndale La. N1 93 H7
*Upper St.*
Tyndale Ter. N1 93 H7
*Canonbury La.*
Tyndall Rd. E10 96 C2
Tyndall Rd., Well. 157 J3
**Tyne St. E1 21 G3**
Tyneham Rd. SW11 150 A2
Tynemouth Cl. E6 116/117 E6
*Covelees Wall*
Tynemouth Rd. N15 76 C4
Tynemouth Rd. SE18 137 J5
Tynemouth Rd., Mitch. 168 A7
Tynemouth St. SW6 149 F2
Type St. E2 113 G2
Tyrawley Rd. SW6 148 E1
Tyrell Cl., Har. 86 B4
Tyrell Ct., Cars. 199 J4
Tyrols Rd. SE23 171 G1
*Wastdale Rd.*
Tyron Way, Sid. 175 H4
Tyrone Rd. E6 116 C2
Tyrrel Way NW9 71 F7
Tyrrell Av., Well. 158 A5
Tyrrell Rd. SE22 152 D4
Tyrrell Sq., Mitch. 185 H1
Tyrwhitt Rd. SE4 154 A3
**Tysoe St. EC1 11 E4**
Tyson Rd. SE23 153 F7
Tyssen Pas. E8 94 C6
Tyssen Rd. N16 94 C3
Tyssen St. E8 94 C6
**Tyssen St. N1 12 E2**
Tytherton Rd. N19 92 D3

## U

Uamvar St. E14 114 B5
Uckfield Gro., Mitch. 186 A1
**Udall St. SW1 33 G2**
Udney Pk. Rd., Tedd. 162 D5
Uffington Rd. NW10 107 G1
Uffington Rd. SE27 169 G4
Ufford Cl., Har. 51 H7
*Ufford Rd.*
Ufford Rd., Har. 51 H7
**Ufford St. SE1 27 F3**
Ufford St. SE1 131 G2
Ufton Gro. N1 94 A7
Ufton Rd. N1 94 B7
Uhura Sq. N16 94 B3
Ujima Ct. SW16 168/169 E4
*Sunnyhill Rd.*
Ullathorne Rd. SW16 168 C4
Ulleswater Rd. N14 59 E4
Ullin St. E14 114 C5
*St. Leonards Rd.*
Ullswater Cl. SW15 164 D4
Ullswater Cl., Brom. 173 E6
Ullswater Ct., Har. 67 G7
*Oakington Av.*
Ullswater Cres. SW15 164 D4
Ullswater Rd. SE27 169 H2
Ullswater Rd. SW13 127 G7
Ulster Gdns. N13 59 J4
**Ulster Pl. NW1 8 D6**
**Ulster Ter. NW1 8 D5**
Ulundi Rd. SE3 135 E6
Ulva Rd. SW15 148 A5
*Ravenna Rd.*
Ulverscroft Rd. SE22 152 C5
Ulverston Rd. E17 78 D2
Ulverstone Rd. SE27 169 H2
Ulysses Rd. NW6 90 C5
Umberston St. E1 112/113 E6
*Hessel St.*
Umbria St. SW15 147 G6
Umfreville Rd. N4 75 H6
Undercliff Rd. SE13 154 A3
Underhill, Barn. 40 D5
Underhill Pas. NW1 110 B1
*Camden High St.*
Underhill Rd. SE22 152 E6
Underhill St. NW1 110 B1
*Camden High St.*
Underne Av. N14 58 B2
**Undershaft EC3 20 D4**
Undershaft EC3 112 B6
Undershaw Rd., Brom. 173 E3
Underwood, Croy. 204 C5
Underwood, The SE9 174 C2
**Underwood Rd. E1 13 H6**
Underwood Rd. E1 112 D4
Underwood Rd. E4 62 B5
Underwood Rd., Wdf.Grn. 64 A7
**Underwood Row N1 12 A3**
Underwood Row N1 111 J3
**Underwood St. N1 12 A3**
Underwood St. N1 111 J3
Undine Rd. E14 134 B4
Undine St. SW17 167 J5
Uneeda Dr., Grnf. 104 A1
Union Cl. E11 96 D4
Union Cotts. E15 96/97 E7
*Welfare Rd.*
**Union Ct. EC2 20 D3**
Union Ct., Rich. 145 H5
*Eton St.*
Union Dr. E1 113 H4
*Canal Cl.*
Union Gro. SW8 150 D2
Union Pk. NW10 106 C3
*Acton La.*
Union Rd. N11 58 D6
Union Rd. SW4 150 D2
Union Rd. SW8 150 D2
Union Rd., Brom. 192 A5
Union Rd., Croy. 187 J7
Union Rd., Nthlt. 103 G2
Union Rd., Wem. 87 H6
Union Sq. N1 111 J1
Union St. E15 114 C1
**Union St. SE1 27 H2**
Union St. SE1 131 H1
Union St., Barn. 40 B4
Union St., Kings.T. 181 G2
**Union Wk. E2 13 E3**
Unity Cl. NW10 89 G6
Unity Cl. SE19 169 J5
*Crown Dale*
Unity Way SE18 136 A3
**Unity Wf. SE1 29 G3**
University Cl. NW7 55 F7
University Gdns., Bex. 159 F7
University Pl., Erith 139 H7
*Belmont Rd.*
University Rd. SW19 167 G6
**University St. WC1 9 G6**
University St. WC1 110 C4
University Way E16 116 D7
Unwin Av., Felt. 141 H5
**Unwin Cl. SE15 37 H6**
Unwin Cl. SE15 132 D6
**Unwin Rd. SW7 23 F5**
Unwin Rd., Islw. 144 B3
**Upbrook Ms. W2 14 D4**
Upcerne Rd. SW10 129 F7
Upchurch Cl. SE20 171 E7
Upcroft Av., Edg. 54 C5
Updale Rd., Sid. 175 J4
Upfield, Croy. 203 E2
Upfield Rd. W7 104 C4
Upgrove Manor Way SW2 151 G7
*Trinity Ri.*
Uphall Rd., Ilf. 99 E5
Upham Pk. Rd. W4 127 E4
Uphill Dr. NW7 55 E5
Uphill Dr. NW9 70 C5
Uphill Gro. NW7 55 E4
Uphill Rd. NW7 54 E4
Upland Ms. SE22 152 D5
*Upland Rd.*
Upland Rd. E13 115 F4
*Sutton Rd.*
Upland Rd. SE22 152 D5
Upland Rd., Bexh. 159 F3
Upland Rd., S.Croy. 202 A5
Upland Rd., Sutt. 199 G7
Uplands, Beck. 190 A2
Uplands, The, Loug. 48 C3
Uplands, The, Ruis. 84 A1
Uplands Av. E17 77 G2
*Blackhorse La.*
Uplands Business Pk. E17 77 G2
Uplands Cl. SW14 146 B5
*Monroe Dr.*
Uplands End, Wdf.Grn. 64 B7
Uplands Pk. Rd., Enf. 43 G3
Uplands Rd. N8 75 F5
Uplands Rd., Barn. 58 A1
Uplands Rd., Rom. 82 D3
Uplands Rd., Wdf.Grn. 64 B7
Uplands Way N21 43 G5
Upney La., Bark. 99 H6
**Upnor Way SE17 37 E3**
Uppark Dr., Ilf. 81 F6
Upper Abbey Rd., Belv. 139 F4
Upper Addison Gdns. W14 128 B2
Upper Bardsey Wk. N1 93 J6
*Clephane Rd.*
**Upper Belgrave St. SW1 24 C5**
Upper Belgrave St. SW1 130 A3
**Upper Berkeley St. W1 15 J4**
Upper Berkeley St. W1 109 J6
Upper Beulah Hill SE19 188 B1
Upper Brighton Rd., Surb. 181 G6
Upper Brockley Rd. SE4 153 J2
**Upper Brook St. W1 16 B6**
Upper Brook St. W1 110 A7
Upper Butts, Brent. 125 F6
Upper Caldy Wk. N1 93 J6
*Clephane Rd.*
Upper Camelford Wk. W11 108 B6
*Lancaster Rd.*
Upper Cavendish Av. N3 72 D3
**Upper Cheyne Row SW3 31 G6**
Upper Cheyne Row SW3 129 H6
Upper Clapton Rd. E5 94 E1
Upper Clarendon Wk. W11 108 B6
*Lancaster Rd.*
Upper Dengie Wk. N1 111 J1
*Popham Rd.*
Upper Elmers End Rd., Beck. 189 H4
Upper Fm. Rd., W.Mol. 179 F4
Upper Fosters NW4 71 J5
*New Brent St.*
Upper Grn. E., Mitch. 185 J3
Upper Grn. W., Mitch. 185 J3
*London Rd.*
Upper Grenfell Wk. W11 108 A7
*Whitchurch Rd.*
**Upper Grosvenor St. W1 16 B6**
Upper Grosvenor St. W1 110 A7
Upper Grotto Rd., Twick. 162 C2
**Upper Grd. SE1 26 E1**

Vine Gdns., Ilf. 99 F5
**Vine Hill EC1 10 E6**
**Vine La. SE1 28 E2**
Vine Pl. W5 125 H1
*The Common*
Vine Pl., Houns. 143 H4
Vine Rd. E15 97 F7
Vine Rd. SW13 147 F3
Vine Rd., E.Mol. 179 J4
Vine Rd., Orp. 207 J6
Vine Sq. W14 128 C5
**Vine St. EC3 21 F5**
**Vine St. W1 17 G6**
Vine St., Rom. 83 J5
**Vine St. Br. EC1 11 F6**
Vine St. Br. EC1 111 G4
**Vine Yd. SE1 28 A3**
Vinegar All. E17 78 B4
Vinegar St. E1 132/133 E1
*Reardon St.*
**Vinegar Yd. SE1 28 D3**
Viner Cl., Walt. 178 C6
Vineries, The N14 42 C6
Vineries, The, Enf. 44 B3
Vineries Bank NW7 55 H5
Vineries Cl., Dag. 101 G6
*Heathway*
Vineries Cl., West Dr. 120 D6
Vines Av. N3 72 E1
Viney Rd. SE13 154 B3
Vineyard, The, Rich. 145 H5
Vineyard Av. NW7 56 B7
Vineyard Cl. SE6 172 A1
Vineyard Cl., Kings.T. 181 J3
Vineyard Gro. N3 73 E1
Vineyard Hill Rd. SW19 166 D4
Vineyard Pas., Rich. 145 H5
*Paradise Rd.*
Vineyard Path SW14 146 D3
Vineyard Rd., Felt. 160 A3
Vineyard Row, Kings.T. 181 F1
**Vineyard Wk. EC1 11 E5**
Vineyard Wk. EC1 111 G4
Vining St. SW9 151 G4
Vintry Ms. E17 78 A4
*Cleveland Pk. Cres.*
Viola Av. SE2 138 B4
Viola Av., Felt. 142 C6
Viola Sq. W12 107 F7
Violet Cl. E16 115 E4
Violet Cl., Wall. 200 B1
Violet Gdns., Croy. 201 H5
**Violet Hill NW8 6 C2**
Violet Hill NW8 109 F2
Violet La., Croy. 201 H5
Violet Rd. E3 114 B4
Violet Rd. E17 78 A6
Violet Rd. E18 79 H2
Violet St. E2 112/113 E4
*Three Colts La.*
**Virgil Pl. W1 15 J2**
**Virgil St. SE1 26 D5**
Virgil St. SE1 131 F3
Virginia Cl., N.Mal. 182 C4
*Willow Rd.*
Virginia Gdns., Ilf. 81 F2
**Virginia Rd. E2 13 F4**
Virginia Rd. E2 112 C3
Virginia Rd., Th.Hth. 187 H1
**Virginia St. E1 21 J6**
Virginia St. E1 112 D7
Virginia Wk. SW2 151 F6
Viscount Cl. N11 58 B5
Viscount Dr. E6 116 C5
Viscount Gro., Nthlt. 102 D3
*Wayfarer Rd.*
**Viscount St. EC1 11 J6**
Viscount Way, Houns. 141 H4
Vista, The SE9 156 A6
Vista, The, Sid. 175 J5
*Langdon Shaw*
Vista Av., Enf. 45 G2
Vista Dr., Ilf. 80 A5
Vista Way, Har. 69 H6
Viveash Cl., Hayes 121 J3
Vivian Av. NW4 71 H5
Vivian Av., Wem. 88 A5
Vivian Cl., Wat. 50 A1
Vivian Gdns., Wat. 50 A1
Vivian Gdns., Wem. 88 A5
Vivian Rd. E3 113 H2
Vivian Sq. SE15 152/153 E3
*Scylla Rd.*
Vivian Way N2 73 G5
Vivien Cl., Chess. 195 H7
Vivienne Cl., Twick. 145 F6
Voce Rd. SE18 137 G7
Voewood Cl., N.Mal. 183 F6
Volta Way, Croy. 201 F1
Voltaire Rd. SW4 150 D3
Voluntary Pl. E11 79 G6
Vorley Rd. N19 92 C2
Voss Ct. SW16 169 E6
**Voss St. E2 13 J4**
Voss St. E2 112 D3
Voyagers Cl. SE28 118 C6
Vulcan Cl., Wall. 201 F7
Vulcan Gate, Enf. 43 G2
Vulcan Rd. SE4 153 J2
Vulcan Sq. E14 134 A4
*Britannia Rd.*
Vulcan Ter. SE4 153 J2
Vulcan Way N7 93 F6
Vyne, The, Bexh. 159 H3
Vyner Rd. W3 106 D7
Vyner St. E2 113 E1
Vyse Cl., Barn. 39 J4


## W


Wadbrook St., Kings.T. 53 G7
*High St.*
**Wadding St. SE17 36 B2**
Wadding St. SE17 132 A4
Waddington Cl., Enf. 44 B4
Waddington Rd. E15 96 D5
Waddington St. E15 96 D6
Waddington Way SE19 169 J7
Waddon Cl., Croy. 201 G3
Waddon Ct. Rd., Croy. 201 G4
Waddon Marsh Way, Croy. 201 F1
Waddon New Rd., Croy. 201 H3
Waddon Pk. Av., Croy. 201 G3
Waddon Rd., Croy. 201 G3
Waddon Way, Croy. 201 G6
Wades Gro. N21 43 G7
Wades Hill N21 43 G6
Wades La., Tedd. 162 D5
*High St.*
Wades Ms. N21 43 G7
*Wades Hill*
Wades Pl. E14 114 B7
Wadeson St. E2 113 E2
Wadeville Av., Rom. 83 F7
Wadeville Cl., Belv. 139 G6
Wadham Av. E17 62 B7
Wadham Gdns. NW3 109 H1
Wadham Gdns., Grnf. 86 A6
Wadham Rd. E17 78 B1
Wadham Rd. SW15 148 B4
Wadhurst Cl. SE20 188 E2
Wadhurst Rd. SW8 150 C1
Wadhurst Rd. W4 126 D3
Wadley Rd. E11 78 E7
Wadsworth Business Cen., Grnf. 105 F2
Wadsworth Cl., Enf. 45 G5
Wadsworth Cl., Grnf. 105 F2
Wadsworth Rd., Grnf. 105 E2
Wager St. E3 113 J4
Waggon Ms. N14 58 C1
*Chase Side*
Waghorn Rd. E13 115 J1
Waghorn Rd., Har. 69 G3
Waghorn St. SE15 152 D3
Wagner St. SE15 133 F7
Wagstaff Gdns., Dag. 100 C7
*Ellerton Rd.*
Wagtail Cl. NW9 70/71 E2
*Swan Dr.*
Waights Ct., Kings.T. 181 H1
Wainfleet Av., Rom. 83 J2
Wainford Cl. SW19 166 A1
*Windlesham Gro.*
Wainwright Gro., Islw. 144 A4
Waite Davies Rd. SE12 155 F7
**Waite St. SE15 37 F5**
Waite St. SE15 132 C6
**Waithman St. EC4 19 G4**
Wakefield Gdns. SE19 170 B7
Wakefield Gdns., Ilf. 80 B6
**Wakefield Ms. WC1 10 B4**
Wakefield Rd. N11 58 D5
Wakefield Rd. N15 76 C5
Wakefield Rd., Rich. 145 G5
Wakefield St. E6 116 A1
Wakefield St. N18 60 D5
**Wakefield St. WC1 10 B5**
Wakefield St. WC1 111 E3
Wakeham St. N1 94 A6
Wakehams Hill, Pnr. 67 F3
Wakehurst Rd. SW11 149 H5
Wakelin Rd. E15 114 E2
Wakeling Rd. W7 104 C5
Wakeling St. E14 113 H6
Wakeman Rd. NW10 107 J3
Wakemans Hill Av. NW9 70 D5
Wakering Rd., Bark. 99 F6
Wakerley Cl. E6 116 C6
*Truesdale Rd.*
**Wakley St. EC1 11 G3**
Wakley St. EC1 111 H2
Walberswick St. SW8 131 E7
**Walbrook EC4 20 B5**
Walbrook EC4 112 A7
Walbrook Ho. N9 61 F1
Walbrook Wf. EC4 111 J7
*Upper Thames St.*
Walburgh St. E1 112/113 E6
*Bigland St.*
**Walcorde Av. SE17 36 A2**
Walcot Rd., Enf. 45 J2
**Walcot Sq. SE11 35 F1**
Walcot Sq. SE11 131 G4
**Walcott St. SW1 33 G1**
Waldair Ct. E16 136/137 E2
*Barge Ho. Rd.*
Waldair Wf. E16 136 E2
Waldeck Gro. SE27 169 H3
Waldeck Rd. N15 75 H4
Waldeck Rd. SW14 146 C3
*Lower Richmond Rd.*
Waldeck Rd. W4 126 A6
Waldeck Rd. W13 105 E6
Waldeck Ter. SW14 146 C3
*Lower Richmond Rd.*
Waldegrave Av., Tedd. 162 C5
*Waldegrave Rd.*
Waldegrave Gdns., Twick. 162 C2
Waldegrave Pk., Twick. 162 C4
Waldegrave Rd. N8 75 G3
Waldegrave Rd. SE19 170 C7
Waldegrave Rd. W5 105 J6
Waldegrave Rd., Brom. 192 B4
Waldegrave Rd., Dag. 100 C2
Waldegrave Rd., Tedd. 162 C4
Waldegrave Rd., Twick. 162 C4
Waldegrove, Croy. 202 C3
Waldemar Av. SW6 148 B1
Waldemar Av. W13 125 F1
Waldemar Rd. SW19 166 D5
Walden Av. N13 59 J4
Walden Av., Chis. 174 C4
Walden Cl., Belv. 139 F5
Walden Gdns., Th.Hth. 187 F3
Walden Rd. N17 76 A1
Walden Rd., Chis. 174 C6
Walden St. E1 112 E6
Walden Way NW7 56 A6
Walden Way, Ilf. 65 H7
Waldenshaw Rd. SE23 171 F1
Waldo Cl. SW4 150 C5
Waldo Pl., Mitch. 167 H7
Waldo Rd. NW10 107 G3
Waldo Rd., Brom. 192 A3
Waldram Cres. SE23 171 F1
Waldram Pk. Rd. SE23 171 G1
Waldram Pl. SE23 171 F1
*Waldram Cres.*
Waldrist Way, Erith 139 F2
Waldron Gdns., Brom. 190 D3
**Waldron Ms. SW3 31 F5**
Waldron Rd. SW18 167 F3
Waldron Rd., Har. 86 B1
Waldronhyrst, S.Croy. 201 H4
Waldrons, The, Croy. 201 H4
Waldrons Path, S.Croy. 201 J4
Waldstock Rd. SE28 118 A7
Waleran Cl., Stan. 52 C6
*Chenduit Way*
Waleran Flats SE1 132 B4
*Old Kent Rd.*
Walerand Rd. SE13 154 C2
Wales Av., Cars. 199 J5
Wales Cl. SE15 132 E7
Wales Fm. Rd. W3 106 D5
Waley St. E1 113 G5
Walfield Av. N20 41 E7
Walford Rd. N16 94 B4
Walfrey Gdns., Dag. 101 E7
Walham Grn. Ct. SW6 128/129 E7
*Waterford Rd.*
Walham Gro. SW6 128 D7
Walham Ri. SW19 166 B6
Walham Yd. SW6 128 D7
*Walham Gro.*
Walkden Rd., Chis. 174 D5
Walker Cl. N11 58 C4
Walker Cl. SE18 137 F4
Walker Cl. W7 124 B1
Walker Cl., Hmptn. 161 F6
*Fearnley Cres.*
Walkers Ct. E8 94 D6
*Wilton Way*
**Walkers Ct. W1 17 H5**
Walkers Pl. SW15 148 B3
*Felsham Rd.*
Walkerscroft Mead SE21 169 J1
**Walkford Way SE15 37 F7**
Walks, The N2 73 G3
Wall End Rd. E6 98 D7
Wall St. N1 94 A6
Wallace Cl. SE28 118 D7
*Haldane Rd.*
Wallace Cres., Cars. 199 J5
Wallace Rd. N1 93 J6
Wallace Way N19 92 D2
*Giesbach Rd.*
Wallbutton Rd. SE4 153 H2
Wallcote Av. NW2 90 A1
Waller Dr., Nthwd. 66 A2
Waller Rd. SE14 153 G1
Wallers Cl., Dag. 119 E1
Wallers Cl., Wdf.Grn. 64 C6
Wallers Hoppit, Loug. 48 B2
Wallflower St. W12 107 F7
**Wallgrave Rd. SW5 30 A1**
Wallgrave Rd. SW5 128 E4
Wallingford Av. W10 108 A5
Wallington Cor., Wall. 200 B4
*Manor Rd. N.*
Wallington Rd., Ilf. 81 J7
Wallington Sq., Wall. 200 B6
*Woodcote Rd.*
**Wallis All. SE1 28 A4**
Wallis Cl. SW11 149 G3
Wallis Ms. N22 75 G3
*Brampton Pk. Rd.*
Wallis Rd. E9 95 J6
Wallis Rd., Sthl. 103 H6
Wallis's Cotts. SW2 150 E7
Wallman Pl. N22 75 F1
*Bounds Grn. Rd.*
Wallorton Gdns. SW14 146 D4
Wallwood Rd. E11 78 D7
Wallwood St. E14 113 J5
Walm La. NW2 90 A5
Walmar Cl., Barn. 41 G1
Walmer Cl. E4 62 B2
Walmer Cl., Orp. 207 G4
*Tubbenden La. S.*
Walmer Cl., Rom. 83 H2
Walmer Gdns. W13 124 D2
Walmer Ho. N9 44 C7
**Walmer Pl. W1 15 J1**
Walmer Rd. W10 107 J6
*Latimer Rd.*
Walmer Rd. W11 108 B7
**Walmer St. W1 15 J1**
Walmer Ter. SE18 137 F4
Walmgate Rd., Grnf. 104 E1
Walmington Fold N12 56 D6
Walney Wk. N1 93 J6
*St. Paul's Rd.*
Walnut Av., West Dr. 120 D3
Walnut Cl. SE8 133 J6
*Clyde St.*
Walnut Cl., Cars. 199 J5
Walnut Cl., Ilf. 81 F4
*Civic Way*
Walnut Ct. W5 125 H2
*Rowan Cl.*
Walnut Gdns. E15 96/97 E4
*Burgess Rd.*
Walnut Gro., Enf. 44 A5
Walnut Ms., Sutt. 199 F7
Walnut Rd. E10 96 A2
Walnut Tree Av., Mitch. 185 H3
*De'Arn Gdns.*
Walnut Tree Cl. SW13 147 F1
Walnut Tree Cl., Chis. 193 F1
Walnut Tree Cotts. SW19 166 B4
*Church Rd.*
Walnut Tree Rd. SE10 135 E5
Walnut Tree Rd., Brent. 125 H6
Walnut Tree Rd., Dag. 100 D2
Walnut Tree Rd., Houns. 123 F6
**Walnut Tree Wk. SE11 34 E1**
Walnut Tree Wk. SE11 131 G4
Walnut Way, Buck.H. 64 A3
Walnut Way, Ruis. 84 C6
Walpole Av., Rich. 145 J2
Walpole Cl. W13 125 F2
Walpole Cl., Pnr. 51 G6
Walpole Cres., Tedd. 162 C5
Walpole Gdns. W4 126 C5
Walpole Gdns., Twick. 162 B2

**Wedgwood Ms. W1** 17 J4
Wedgwood Way SE19 169 J7
Wedlake St. W10 108 B4 *Kensal Rd.*
Wedmore Av., Ilf. 80 D1
Wedmore Gdns. N19 92 D2
Wedmore Ms. N19 92 D3 *Wedmore St.*
Wedmore Rd., Grnf. 104 A3
Wedmore St. N19 92 D3
Weech Rd. NW6 90 D4
Weedington Rd. NW5 92 A5
Weekley Sq. SW11 149 G3 *Thomas Baines Rd.*
Weigall Rd. SE12 155 G4
**Weighhouse St. W1** 16 C4
Weighhouse St. W1 110 A6
Weighton Rd. SE20 188 E2
Weighton Rd., Har. 68 A1
Weihurst Gdns., Sutt. 199 G5
Weimar St. SW15 148 B3
Weir Est. SW12 150 C7
Weir Hall Av. N18 60 A6
Weir Hall Gdns. N18 60 A5
Weir Hall Rd. N17 60 A5
Weir Hall Rd. N18 60 A5
Weir Rd. SW12 150 C7
Weir Rd. SW19 167 E3
Weir Rd., Bex. 159 H7
Weir Rd., Walt. 178 A6
Weirdale Av. N20 57 J2
**Weir's Pas. NW1** 9 J3
Weir's Pas. NW1 110 D3
Weirside Gdns., West Dr. 120 A1
Weiss Rd. SW15 148 A3
Welbeck Av., Brom. 173 G4
Welbeck Av., Hayes 102 B4
Welbeck Av., Sid. 176 A1
Welbeck Cl. N12 57 G5 *Torrington Pk.*
Welbeck Cl., Borwd. 38 A3
Welbeck Cl., Epsom 197 G7
Welbeck Cl., N.Mal. 183 F5
Welbeck Rd. E6 116 A3
Welbeck Rd., Barn. 41 G6
Welbeck Rd., Cars. 199 H1
Welbeck Rd., Har. 85 H1
Welbeck Rd., Sutt. 199 G2
**Welbeck St. W1** 16 D3
Welbeck St. W1 110 A5
Welbeck Wk., Cars. 199 H1 *Welbeck Rd.*
**Welbeck Way W1** 16 D3
Welbeck Way W1 110 B6
Welby St. SE5 151 H1
Welch Pl., Pnr. 66 C1
Weld Pl. N11 58 B5
Weldon Cl., Ruis. 84 B6
Weldon Dr., W.Mol. 179 F4
Welfare Rd. E15 97 E7
Welford Cl. E5 95 G3 *Denton Way*
Welford Pl. SW19 166 B4
Welham Rd. SW16 168 A5
Welham Rd. SW17 168 A5
Welhouse Rd., Cars. 199 H1
Well App., Barn. 39 J5
Well Cl. SW16 169 F4
Well Cl., Ruis. 84/85 E3 *Parkfield Cres.*
Well Cottage Cl. E11 79 J7
**Well Ct. EC4** 20 A4
Well Ct. SW16 169 F4
Well Gro. N20 41 F7
Well Hall Par. SE9 156 C4 *Well Hall Rd.*
Well Hall Rd. SE9 156 C3
Well La. SW14 146 C5
Well Pas. NW3 91 G3
Well Rd. NW3 91 G3
Well Rd., Barn. 39 J5
Well St. E9 95 F7
Well St. E15 96 E6
Well Wk. NW3 91 G4
Wellacre Rd., Har. 69 E6
Wellan Cl., Sid. 158 B5
Welland Gdns., Grnf. 104 C2
**Welland Ms. E1** 29 J1
Welland St. SE10 134 C6
Wellands Cl., Brom. 192 C2
Wellbrook Rd., Orp. 206 D4
**Wellclose Sq. E1** 21 J5
Wellclose Sq. E1 112 D7
**Wellclose St. E1** 21 J6
Welldon Cres., Har. 68 B6
**Weller St. SE1** 27 J3
**Weller's Ct. N1** 10 A2
Wellesley Av. W6 127 H3
**Wellesley Ct. W9** 6 C3
Wellesley Ct. Rd., Croy. 202 A2
Wellesley Cres., Twick. 162 B2
Wellesley Gro., Croy. 202 A2
Wellesley Pk. Ms., Enf. 43 H2
**Wellesley Pl. NW1** 9 H4
Wellesley Rd. E11 79 G5
Wellesley Rd. E17 78 A6
Wellesley Rd. N22 75 G2
Wellesley Rd. NW5 92 A5
Wellesley Rd. W4 126 A5
Wellesley Rd., Croy. 201 J1
Wellesley Rd., Har. 68 B5
Wellesley Rd., Ilf. 98 E2
Wellesley Rd., Sutt. 199 F6
Wellesley Rd., Twick. 162 B3
Wellesley St. E1 113 G5
**Wellesley Ter. N1** 12 A3
Wellesley Ter. N1 111 J3
Wellfield Av. N10 74 B3
Wellfield Rd. SW16 169 E4
Wellfield Wk. SW16 169 F5
Wellfields, Loug. 48 D3
Wellfit St. SE24 151 H3 *Hinton Rd.*
Wellgarth, Grnf. 86 E6
Wellgarth Rd. NW11 91 E1
Wellhouse La., Barn. 39 J4
Wellhouse Rd., Beck. 189 J4
Welling High St., Well. 158 B3
Welling Way SE9 157 G3
Welling Way, Well. 157 G3
Wellings Ho., Hayes 122 B1
Wellington Av. E4 62 A2
Wellington Av. N9 61 E3
Wellington Av. N15 76 C6
Wellington Av., Houns. 143 G5
Wellington Av., Pnr. 67 F1
Wellington Av., Sid. 158 A6
Wellington Av., Wor.Pk. 197 J4
**Wellington Bldgs. SW1** 32 C4
Wellington Cl. SE14 153 G1 *Rutts Ter.*
Wellington Cl. W11 108 D6 *Ledbury Rd.*
Wellington Cl., Dag. 101 J7
Wellington Cl., Wat. 51 F3 *Highfield*
**Wellington Ct. NW8** 7 E2
Wellington Ct., Stai. 140 B7 *Clare Rd.*
Wellington Cres., N.Mal. 182 C3
Wellington Dr., Dag. 101 J7
Wellington Gdns. SE7 135 J6
Wellington Gdns., Twick. 162 A4
Wellington Gro. SE10 134 D7 *Crooms Hill*
Wellington Ms. SE7 135 J6
Wellington Ms. SE22 152 D4 *Peckham Rye*
Wellington Pk. Est. NW2 89 G2
Wellington Pas. E11 79 G5 *Wellington Rd.*
Wellington Pl. N2 73 H5 *Great N. Rd.*
**Wellington Pl. NW8** 7 G2
Wellington Pl. NW8 109 H2
Wellington Rd. E6 116 C2
Wellington Rd. E7 97 F4
Wellington Rd. E10 95 H1
Wellington Rd. E11 79 G5
Wellington Rd. E17 77 H4
**Wellington Rd. NW8** 7 F1
Wellington Rd. NW8 109 G2
Wellington Rd. NW10 108 A3
Wellington Rd. SW19 166 D2
Wellington Rd. W5 125 F3
Wellington Rd., Belv. 139 F5
Wellington Rd., Bex. 158 D5
Wellington Rd., Brom. 191 J4
Wellington Rd., Croy. 187 H7
Wellington Rd., Enf. 44 B5
Wellington Rd., Felt. 141 H5
Wellington Rd., Hmptn. 162 A5
Wellington Rd., Har. 68 B3
Wellington Rd., Pnr. 67 F1
Wellington Rd., Twick. 162 A5
Wellington Rd. N., Houns. 143 F3
Wellington Rd. S., Houns. 143 F4
**Wellington Row E2** 13 G3
Wellington Row E2 112 C3
**Wellington Sq. SW3** 31 J3
Wellington Sq. SW3 129 J5
Wellington St. SE18 136 D4
**Wellington St. WC2** 18 B5
Wellington St. WC2 111 E7
Wellington St., Bark. 117 F1 *Axe St.*
Wellington Ter. E1 132 E1
Wellington Ter. N8 75 G3 *Turnpike La.*
Wellington Ter., Har. 86 A1 *West St.*
Wellington Way E3 114 A3
Wellmeadow Rd. SE6 155 E7
Wellmeadow Rd. SE13 154 E6
Wellmeadow Rd. W7 124 D4
Wellow Wk., Cars. 199 G1
Wells, The N14 42 D7
Wells Cl., Nthlt. 102 C3 *Yeading La.*
Wells Dr. NW9 88 D1
Wells Gdns., Dag. 101 H5
Wells Gdns., Ilf. 80 B7
Wells Ho. Rd. NW10 106 E5
**Wells Ms. W1** 17 G3
Wells Pk. Rd. SE26 170 D3
Wells Ri. NW8 109 J1
Wells Rd. W12 127 J2
Wells Rd., Brom. 192 C2
**Wells Sq. WC1** 10 C4
**Wells St. W1** 17 F2
Wells St. W1 110 C6
Wells Ter. N4 93 G2
**Wells Way SE5** 36 C5
Wells Way SE5 132 B6
**Wells Way SW7** 22 E5
Wells Way SW7 129 G3
Wells Yd. N7 93 G5 *Holloway Rd.*
Wellside Cl., Barn. 39 J4
Wellside Gdns. SW14 146 C5 *Well La.*
Wellsmoor Gdns., Brom. 192 D3
Wellsprings Cres., Wem. 88 B3
Wellstead Av. N9 45 G7
Wellstead Rd. E6 116 D2
Wellwood Rd., Ilf. 100 A1
**Welsford St. SE1** 37 H3
Welsford St. SE1 132 D5
Welsh Cl. E13 115 G3
Welshpool Ho. E8 112 D1 *Benjamin Cl.*
Welshpool St. E8 112/113 E1 *Broadway Mkt.*
Welshside Wk. NW9 70/71 E6 *Fryent Gro.*
Welstead Way W4 126/127 E5 *Bath Rd.*
Weltje Rd. W6 127 G4
Welton Rd. SE18 137 H7
Welwyn Av., Felt. 141 J6
Welwyn St. E2 113 F3 *Globe Rd.*
Wembley Commercial Cen., Wem. 87 G2
Wembley Hill Rd., Wem. 87 J5
Wembley Pk. Business Cen., Wem. 88 B3
Wembley Pk. Dr., Wem. 87 J3
Wembley Pt., Wem. 88 B7
Wembley Rd., Hmptn. 161 G7
Wembley Way, Wem. 88 B6
Wemborough Rd., Stan. 53 F7
Wembury Rd. N6 74 B7
Wemyss Rd. SE3 155 F2
Wendela Ct., Har. 86 B3
Wendell Rd. W12 127 F2
**Wendle Ct. SW8** 34 A6
Wendle Ct. SW8 130 E6
Wendling Rd., Sutt. 199 G1
Wendon St. E3 113 J1
**Wendover SE17** 36 D4
Wendover SE17 132 B5
Wendover Cl., Hayes 102/103 E4 *Kingsash Dr.*
Wendover Dr., N.Mal. 183 F6
Wendover Rd. NW10 107 F2
Wendover Rd. SE9 156 A3
Wendover Rd., Brom. 191 H3
Wendover Way, Well. 158 A5
Wendy Cl., Enf. 44 C6
Wendy Way, Wem. 105 H1
**Wenlock Ct. N1** 12 C2
Wenlock Gdns. NW4 71 G4 *Rickard Cl.*
**Wenlock Rd. N1** 11 J2
Wenlock Rd. N1 111 J2
Wenlock Rd., Edg. 54 B7
**Wenlock St. N1** 12 A2
Wenlock St. N1 111 J2
Wennington Rd. E3 113 G2
Wensley Av., Wdf.Grn. 63 F7
Wensley Cl. SE9 156 C6
Wensley Rd. N18 60 E6
Wensleydale Av., Ilf. 80 B2
Wensleydale Gdns., Hmptn. 161 H7
Wensleydale Pas., Hmptn. 179 G1
Wensleydale Rd., Hmptn. 161 G6
Wentland Cl. SE6 172 D2
Wentland Rd. SE6 172 D2
Wentworth Av. N3 56 D7
Wentworth Cl. N3 56 E7
Wentworth Cl. SE28 118 D6
Wentworth Cl., Brom. 205 G2 *Hillside La.*
Wentworth Cl., Mord. 184 D7
Wentworth Cl., Orp. 207 H5
Wentworth Cl., Surb. 195 G2
Wentworth Cres. SE15 132 D7
Wentworth Cres., Hayes 121 G3
Wentworth Dr., Pnr. 66 A5
Wentworth Gdns. N13 59 H4
Wentworth Hill, Wem. 87 J1
Wentworth Ms. E3 113 J4 *Eric St.*
Wentworth Pk. N3 56 D7
Wentworth Pl., Stan. 52/53 E6 *Greenacres Dr.*
Wentworth Rd. E12 98 A4
Wentworth Rd. NW11 72 C6
Wentworth Rd., Barn. 40 A3
Wentworth Rd., Croy. 187 G7
Wentworth Rd., Sthl. 122 C4
**Wentworth St. E1** 21 F3
Wentworth St. E1 112 C6
Wentworth Way, Pnr. 66 E4
Wenvoe Av., Bexh. 159 H2
Wernbrook St. SE18 137 F6
Werndee Rd. SE25 188 D4
Werneth Hall Rd., Ilf. 80 C3
**Werrington St. NW1** 9 G2
Werrington St. NW1 110 C2
Werter Rd. SW15 148 B4
Wesley Av. E16 135 G1
Wesley Av. NW10 106 D3
Wesley Av., Houns. 143 E2
Wesley Cl. N7 93 F2
**Wesley Cl. SE17** 35 H2
Wesley Cl. SE17 131 H4
Wesley Cl., Har. 85 J2
Wesley Rd. E10 78 C7
Wesley Rd. NW10 106 C1
Wesley Rd., Hayes 102 A7
Wesley Sq. W11 108 B6 *Bartle Rd.*
**Wesley St. W1** 16 C2
Wesleyan Pl. NW5 92 B4 *Gordon Ho. Rd.*
Wessex Av. SW19 184 D2
Wessex Cl., Ilf. 81 H6
Wessex Cl., Kings.T. 182 B1 *Gloucester Rd.*
Wessex Dr., Pnr. 51 E7
Wessex Gdns. NW11 90 B1
Wessex La., Grnf. 104 A2
Wessex Rd., Houns. 140 A2
Wessex St. E2 113 F3
Wessex Way NW11 90 B1
West App., Orp. 193 F5
West Arbour St. E1 113 G6
West Av. E17 78 B4
West Av. N3 56 D6
West Av. NW4 72 A5
West Av., Pnr. 67 F6
West Av., Sthl. 103 F7
West Av., Wall. 201 E5
West Av. Rd. E17 78 A4
West Bank N16 76 B7
West Bank, Bark. 116/117 E1 *Highbridge Rd.*
West Bank, Enf. 43 J2
West Barnes La. SW20 183 H2
West Barnes La., N.Mal. 183 H3
**West Carriage Dr. W2** 23 F2
West Carriage Dr. W2 109 G7
**West Cen. St. WC1** 18 A3
West Cen. Av. W10 107 H3 *Harrow Rd.*
West Chantry, Har. 67 H1 *Chantry Rd.*
West Cl. N9 60 C3
West Cl., Barn. 39 H5
West Cl. (Cockfosters), Barn. 42 A4
West Cl., Grnf. 103 J2
West Cl., Hmptn. 160/161 E6 *Oak Av.*

William IV St. WC2 110 E7
William Gdns. SW15 147 H5
William Guy Gdns. E3 114 B3
*Talwin St.*
William Margrie Cl. SE15 152 D2
*Moncrieff St.*
**William Ms. SW1 24 A4**
William Morley Cl. E6 116 A1
William Morris Cl. E17 77 J3
William Morris Way SW6 149 F3
William Pl. E3 113 J2
*Roman Rd.*
**William Rd. NW1 9 E4**
William Rd. NW1 110 B3
William Rd. SW19 166 B7
William Rd., Sutt. 199 F5
William Saville Ho. NW6 108 C2
William Sq. SE16 113 H7
*Rotherhithe St.*
William St. E10 78 B6
William St. N17 60 C7
**William St. SW1 24 A4**
William St. SW1 129 J2
William St., Bark. 99 F7
William St., Cars. 199 H3
Williams Av. E17 77 J1
Williams Bldgs. E2 113 F4
Williams Cl. N8 74 D6
*Coolhurst Rd.*
Williams Gro. N22 75 G1
Williams Gro., Surb. 181 F6
William's La. SW14 146 C2
Williams La., Mord. 185 F5
Williams Rd. W13 104 D7
Williams Rd., Sthl. 122 E4
Williams Ter., Croy. 201 G6
Williamson Cl. SE10 135 F4
*Lenthorp Rd.*
Williamson Rd. N4 75 H6
Williamson St. N7 93 E4
Williamson Way NW7 56 B6
Willifield Way NW11 72 C5
Willingale Cl., Loug. 49 F2
*Willingale Rd.*
Willingale Cl., Wdf.Grn. 64 A6
Willingale Rd., Loug. 49 F3
Willingdon Rd. N22 75 H2
Willingham Cl. NW5 92 C5
*Leighton Rd.*
Willingham Ter. NW5 92 C5
*Leighton Rd.*
Willingham Way, Kings.T. 182 A3
Willington Ct. E5 95 H3
*Mandeville St.*
Willington Rd. SW9 150 E3
Willis Av., Sutt. 199 H6
Willis Rd. E15 115 F1
Willis Rd., Croy. 187 J7
Willis Rd., Erith 139 J4
Willis St. E14 114 B6
Willmore End SW19 184 E1
Willoughby Av., Croy. 201 F4
Willoughby Gro. N17 60 E7
Willoughby La. N17 61 E7
Willoughby Ms. SW4 150 B4
*Wixs La.*
Willoughby Pk. Rd. N17 60 E7
Willoughby Pas. E14 134 A1
Willoughby Rd. N8 75 G3
Willoughby Rd. NW3 91 G4
Willoughby Rd., Kings.T. 181 J1
Willoughby Rd., Twick. 145 G6
**Willoughby St. WC1 18 A2**
Willoughby Way SE7 135 H4
Willoughbys, The SW14 146/147 E4
*Upper Richmond Rd. W.*
Willow Av. SW13 147 F2
Willow Av., Sid. 158 A6
Willow Bank SW6 148 B3
Willow Bank, Rich. 163 E3
Willow Br. Rd. N1 93 J6
Willow Business Cen., Mitch. 185 J5
Willow Cl., Bex. 159 F6
Willow Cl., Brent. 125 F6
Willow Cl., Brom. 192 C5
Willow Cl., Buck.H. 64 A3
Willow Cl., Th.Hth. 187 H6
Willow Cotts., Mitch. 186 C3
Willow Cotts., Rich. 126 A6
*Kew Grn.*
**Willow Ct. EC2 12 D5**
Willow Ct., Edg. 53 H4
Willow Dene, Pnr. 66 D2
Willow Dr., Barn. 40 B4
Willow End N20 56 D2
Willow End, Nthwd. 50 A6
Willow End, Surb. 195 H1
Willow Fm. La. SW15 147 H3
*Queens Ride*
Willow Gdns., Houns. 143 G1
Willow Grn. NW9 70/71 E1
*Clayton Fld.*
Willow Grn., Borwd. 38 D5
Willow Gro. E13 115 G2
*Libra Rd.*
Willow Gro., Chis. 174 D6
Willow La., Mitch. 185 J5
Willow Mt., Croy. 202 B3
*Langton Way*
**Willow Pl. SW1 33 G1**
Willow Pl. SW1 130 C4
Willow Rd. NW3 91 G4
Willow Rd. W5 125 H2
Willow Rd., Enf. 44 B3
Willow Rd., N.Mal. 182 C4
Willow Rd., Rom. 83 E6
Willow Rd., Wall. 200 B7
Willow St. E4 46 D7
**Willow St. EC2 12 D5**
Willow St. EC2 112 B4
Willow St., Rom. 83 J4
Willow Tree Cl. E3 113 J1
*Birdsfield La.*
Willow Tree Cl. SW18 166/167 E1
*Cargill Rd.*
Willow Tree Cl., Hayes 102 C4
Willow Tree La., Hayes 102 C4
Willow Tree Wk., Brom. 191 H1
Willow Vale W12 127 G1
Willow Vale, Chis. 174 E6
Willow Vw. SW19 185 G1
Willow Wk. E17 77 J5
Willow Wk. N2 73 G2
Willow Wk. N15 75 H4
Willow Wk. N21 43 F6
**Willow Wk. SE1 37 E1**
Willow Wk. SE1 132 B4
Willow Wk., Orp. 206 E3
Willow Wk., Sutt. 198 C3
Willow Way N3 56 E7
Willow Way SE26 171 E3
Willow Way W11 128 A1
*Freston Rd.*
Willow Way, Epsom 196 D6
Willow Way, Sun. 178 A4
Willow Way, Twick. 161 H2
Willow Way, Wem. 86 D3
Willow Wd. Cres. SE25 188 B6
Willowbrook Est. SE15 132 C7
*Sumner Rd.*
**Willowbrook Rd. SE15 37 G6**
Willowbrook Rd. SE15 132 C6
Willowbrook Rd., Sthl. 123 G3
Willowcourt Av., Har. 69 E5
Willowdene N6 73 J7
*Denewood Rd.*
Willowdene Cl., Twick. 143 J7
Willowfield Cl. SE18 58/59 E3
*Conway Rd.*
Willowhayne Dr., Walt. 178 B7
Willowhayne Gdns., Wor.Pk. 197 J3
Willowmead Cl. W5 105 G5
Willows, The, Buck.H. 64 A3
Willows, The, Esher 194 B6
*Albany Cres.*
Willows Av., Mord. 185 E5
Willows Cl., Pnr. 66 C2
Willowtree Way, Th.Hth. 187 G1
*Kensington Av.*
Willrose Cres. SE2 138 C5
Wills Cres., Houns. 143 H6
Wills Gro. NW7 55 G5
Wilman Gro. E8 94 D7
Wilmar Gdns., W.Wick. 204 B1
**Wilmcote Ho. W2 14 A1**
Wilmcote Ho. W2 108 E5
Wilmer Cl., Kings.T. 163 J5
Wilmer Cres., Kings.T. 163 J5
Wilmer Gdns. N1 112 B1
Wilmer Lea Cl. E15 96 D7
Wilmer Pl. N16 94 C2
*Stoke Newington Ch. St.*
Wilmer Way N14 58 D5
Wilmington Av. W4 126 D7
Wilmington Gdns., Bark. 99 G6
**Wilmington Sq. WC1 11 E4**
Wilmington Sq. WC1 111 G3
**Wilmington St. WC1 11 E4**
Wilmington St. WC1 111 G3
Wilmot Cl. N2 73 F2
Wilmot Cl. SE15 132 D7
Wilmot Pl. NW1 92 C7
Wilmot Pl. W7 124 B1
*Boston Rd.*
Wilmot Rd. E10 96 B2
Wilmot Rd. N17 76 A3
Wilmot Rd., Cars. 199 J5
Wilmot St. E2 112 E4
Wilmount St. SE18 136 E4
Wilna Rd. SW18 149 F7
Wilsham St. W11 128 A1
Wilshaw St. SE14 154 A1
Wilsmere Dr., Har. 52 C7
Wilsmere Dr., Nthlt. 85 E6
Wilson Av., Mitch. 167 H7
Wilson Cl., S.Croy. 202 A5
*Bartlett St.*
Wilson Cl., Wem. 69 J7
Wilson Cl., West Dr. 120 A6
*Hatch La.*
Wilson Dr., Wem. 69 J7
Wilson Gdns., Har. 67 J7
Wilson Gro. SE16 132 E2
Wilson Rd. E6 116 A3
Wilson Rd. SE5 152 B1
Wilson Rd., Chess. 195 J6
Wilson Rd., Ilf. 80 C7
Wilson St. E17 78 C5
**Wilson St. EC2 20 C1**
Wilson St. EC2 112 A5
Wilson St. N21 43 G7
Wilsons Pl. E14 113 J6
*Salmon La.*
Wilsons Rd. W6 128 A5
Wilstone Cl., Hayes 102/103 E4
*Kingsash Dr.*
Wilthorne Gdns., Dag. 101 H7
*Acre Rd.*
Wilton Av. W4 127 E5
Wilton Cl., West Dr. 120 A6
*Hatch La.*
**Wilton Cres. SW1 24 B4**
Wilton Cres. SW1 130 A2
Wilton Cres. SW19 184 C1
Wilton Gdns., W.Mol. 179 G3
Wilton Gro. SW19 184 C1
Wilton Gro., N.Mal. 183 F6
**Wilton Ms. SW1 24 C5**
Wilton Ms. SW1 130 A3
Wilton Par., Felt. 160 A2
*Highfield Rd.*
Wilton Pk. Ct. SE18 156 D1
*Prince Imperial Rd.*
**Wilton Pl. SW1 24 B4**
Wilton Pl. SW1 130 A2
Wilton Rd. N10 74 A2
Wilton Rd. SE2 138 C3
**Wilton Rd. SW1 25 E6**
Wilton Rd. SW1 130 C3
Wilton Rd. SW19 167 H7
Wilton Rd., Barn. 41 J4
Wilton Rd., Houns. 142 D3
Wilton Rd., Ilf. 98/99 E3
*Ilford La.*
**Wilton Row SW1 24 B4**
Wilton Row SW1 130 A2
Wilton Sq. N1 112 A1
**Wilton St. SW1 24 D5**
Wilton St. SW1 130 B3
**Wilton Ter. SW1 24 B5**
Wilton Ter. SW1 130 A3
Wilton Vil. N1 112 A1
Wilton Way E8 94 D6
Wiltshire Cl. NW7 55 F5
**Wiltshire Cl. SW3 31 J1**
Wiltshire Gdns. N4 75 J6
Wiltshire Gdns., Twick. 161 J1
Wiltshire Rd. SW9 151 G3
Wiltshire Rd., Th.Hth. 187 G3
Wiltshire Row N1 112 A1
Wilverley Cres., N.Mal. 183 E6
Wimbart Rd. SW2 151 F7
Wimbledon Br. SW19 166 C6
Wimbledon Common SW19 165 G4
Wimbledon Hill Rd. SW19 166 B6
Wimbledon Pk. SW19 166 C2
Wimbledon Pk. Est. SW19 166 B1
Wimbledon Pk. Rd. SW18 148 C7
Wimbledon Pk. Rd. SW19 166 C1
Wimbledon Pk. Side SW19 166 A2
Wimbledon Rd. SW17 167 F4
Wimbledon Sta. SW19 166 C6
*The Bdy.*
**Wimbolt St. E2 13 H3**
Wimbolt St. E2 112 D3
Wimborne Av., Hayes 102 B6
Wimborne Av., Sthl. 123 G4
Wimborne Cl. SE12 155 F5
Wimborne Cl., Buck.H. 63 H2
Wimborne Cl., Wor.Pk. 197 J1
Wimborne Dr. NW9 70 A3
Wimborne Dr., Pnr. 66 D7
Wimborne Gdns. W13 105 E6
Wimborne Rd. N9 60 D2
Wimborne Rd. N17 76 B2
Wimborne Way, Beck. 189 G3
Wimbourne Av., Orp. 193 J4
Wimbourne Ct. N1 112 A2
*Wimbourne St.*
**Wimbourne St. N1 12 B1**
Wimbourne St. N1 112 A2
Wimpole Cl., Brom. 191 J4
*Stanley Rd.*
Wimpole Cl., Kings.T. 181 J2
**Wimpole Ms. W1 16 D1**
Wimpole Ms. W1 110 B5
Wimpole Rd., West Dr. 120 A1
**Wimpole St. W1 16 D3**
Wimpole St. W1 110 B6
Wimshurst Cl., Croy. 201 E1
Winans Wk. SW9 151 G2
Wincanton Cres., Nthlt. 85 G5
Wincanton Gdns., Ilf. 80 E2
Wincanton Rd. SW18 148 C7
Winchcomb Gdns. SE9 156 A3
Winchcombe Rd., Cars. 185 G7
Winchelsea Av., Bexh. 139 F7
Winchelsea Cl. SW15 148 A5
Winchelsea Rd. E7 97 G4
Winchelsea Rd. N17 76 B3
Winchelsea Rd. NW10 106 D1
Winchelsey Ri., S.Croy. 202 C6
Winchendon Rd. SW6 128 C7
Winchendon Rd., Tedd. 162 A4
Winchester Av. NW6 108 B1
Winchester Av. NW9 70 A3
Winchester Av., Houns. 123 F6
Winchester Cl. E6 116 B6
*Boultwood Rd.*
**Winchester Cl. SE17 35 H2**
Winchester Cl. SE17 131 H4
Winchester Cl., Brom. 191 F3
Winchester Cl., Enf. 44 B5
Winchester Cl., Kings.T. 164 B7
Winchester Ct. E17 77 G1
*Billet Rd.*
Winchester Dr., Pnr. 66 D5
Winchester Ho. SE18 136 A7
*Shooter's Hill Rd.*
Winchester Ms. NW3 91 G7
*Winchester Rd.*
Winchester Pk., Brom. 191 F3
Winchester Pl. E8 94 C5
*Kingsland High St.*
Winchester Pl. N6 92 B1
Winchester Pl. W3 126 C2
*Avenue Rd.*
Winchester Rd. E4 62 C7
Winchester Rd. N6 74 B7
Winchester Rd. N9 60 D1
Winchester Rd. NW3 91 G7
Winchester Rd., Bexh. 158 D2
Winchester Rd., Brom. 191 F3
Winchester Rd., Felt. 161 F3
Winchester Rd., Har. 69 H4

| | | |
|---|---|---|
| Woodman St. E16 | 136 | D1 |
| Woodmans Gro., NW10 | 89 | F6 |
| Woodmans Ms. W12 | 107 | H5 |
| Woodmansterne Rd. SW16 | 168 | D7 |
| Woodmere SE9 | 174 | C1 |
| Woodmere Av., Croy. | 189 | G7 |
| Woodmere Cl. SW11 Lavender Hill | 150 | A3 |
| Woodmere Cl., Croy. | 189 | G7 |
| Woodmere Gdns., Croy. | 189 | G7 |
| Woodmere Way, Beck. | 190 | D5 |
| Woodnook Rd. SW16 | 168 | B5 |
| Woodpecker Cl. N9 | 44 | E6 |
| Woodpecker Cl., Bushey | 51 | J1 |
| Woodpecker Cl., Har. | 68 | C1 |
| Woodpecker Rd. SE14 | 133 | H6 |
| Woodpecker Rd. SE28 | 118 | C7 |
| Woodquest Av. SE24 | 151 | J5 |
| Woodridge Cl., Enf. | 43 | G1 |
| Woodridings Av., Pnr. | 67 | F1 |
| Woodridings Cl., Pnr. | 51 | E7 |
| Woodriffe Rd. E11 | 78 | D7 |
| Woodrow SE18 | 136 | C4 |
| Woodrow Cl., Grnf. | 87 | E7 |
| Woodrow Ct. N17 Heybourne Rd. | 60/61 | E7 |
| Woodrush Cl. SE14 Southengate Way | 133 | H7 |
| Woodrush Way, Rom. | 82 | D4 |
| Woods, The, Nthwd. | 50 | A5 |
| Woods Cl. SE19 Woodland Hill | 170 | B6 |
| **Woods Ms. W1** | **16** | **A5** |
| Woods Ms. W1 | 110 | A7 |
| **Woods Pl. SE1** | **28** | **E6** |
| Woods Rd. SE15 | 152 | E1 |
| **Woodseer St. E1** | **21** | **G1** |
| Woodseer St. E1 | 112 | C5 |
| **Woodsford SE17** | **36** | **C4** |
| Woodsford Sq. W14 | 128 | B2 |
| Woodshire Rd., Dag. | 101 | H3 |
| Woodside NW11 | 72 | D5 |
| Woodside SW19 | 166 | C6 |
| Woodside, Buck.H. | 63 | J2 |
| Woodside Av. N6 | 73 | J5 |
| Woodside Av. N10 | 73 | J5 |
| Woodside Av. N12 | 57 | F4 |
| Woodside Av. SE25 | 188 | E6 |
| Woodside Av., Chis. | 175 | F5 |
| Woodside Av., Esher | 180 | B2 |
| Woodside Av., Wem. | 105 | H1 |
| Woodside Cl., Stan. | 52 | E5 |
| Woodside Cl., Surb. | 182 | C7 |
| Woodside Cl., Wem. | 105 | H1 |
| Woodside Ct. N12 Woodside Av. | 57 | F4 |
| Woodside Ct. Rd., Croy. | 188 | D7 |
| Woodside Cres., Sid. | 175 | H3 |
| Woodside End, Wem. | 105 | H1 |
| Woodside Gdns. E4 | 62 | B5 |
| Woodside Gdns. N17 | 76 | B2 |
| Woodside Gra. Rd. N12 | 57 | E4 |
| Woodside Grn. SE25 | 188 | E6 |
| Woodside Gro. N12 | 57 | F3 |
| Woodside La. N12 | 57 | E3 |
| Woodside La., Bex. | 158 | D6 |
| Woodside Ms. SE22 Heber Rd. | 152 | C6 |
| Woodside Pk. SE25 | 188 | D5 |
| Woodside Pk. Av. E17 | 78 | D4 |
| Woodside Pk. Rd. N12 | 57 | E4 |
| Woodside Pl., Wem. | 105 | H1 |
| Woodside Rd. E13 | 115 | J4 |
| Woodside Rd. N22 | 59 | F7 |
| Woodside Rd. SE25 | 188 | E6 |
| Woodside Rd., Brom. | 192 | B5 |
| Woodside Rd., Kings.T. | 163 | H7 |
| Woodside Rd., N.Mal. | 182 | D2 |
| Woodside Rd., Sid. | 175 | H3 |
| Woodside Rd., Sutt. | 199 | F3 |
| Woodside Rd., Wdf.Grn. | 63 | G4 |
| Woodside Way, Croy. | 189 | G6 |
| Woodside Way, Mitch. | 186 | B1 |
| Woodsome Rd. NW5 | 92 | A3 |
| Woodspring Rd. SW19 | 166 | B2 |
| Woodstead Gro., Edg. | 53 | H6 |

| | | |
|---|---|---|
| Woodstock Av. NW11 | 72 | B7 |
| Woodstock Av. W13 | 124 | D3 |
| Woodstock Av., Islw. | 144 | D5 |
| Woodstock Av., Sthl. | 103 | F3 |
| Woodstock Av., Sutt. | 184 | C7 |
| Woodstock Cl., Bex. | 177 | F1 |
| Woodstock Cl., Stan. | 69 | H2 |
| Woodstock Ct. SE12 | 155 | G6 |
| Woodstock Cres. N9 | 44 | E6 |
| Woodstock Gdns., Beck. | 190 | B1 |
| Woodstock Gdns., Ilf. | 100 | A2 |
| Woodstock Gro. W12 | 128 | A2 |
| Woodstock La. N., Surb. | 195 | F2 |
| Woodstock La. S., Chess. | 195 | F4 |
| Woodstock La. S., Esher | 194 | E5 |
| **Woodstock Ms. W1** | **16** | **C2** |
| Woodstock Ri., Sutt. | 184 | C7 |
| Woodstock Rd. E7 | 97 | J7 |
| Woodstock Rd. E17 | 78 | D2 |
| Woodstock Rd. N4 | 93 | G1 |
| Woodstock Rd. NW11 | 72 | C7 |
| Woodstock Rd. W4 | 127 | E3 |
| Woodstock Rd., Cars. | 200 | A5 |
| Woodstock Rd., Croy. | 202 | A3 |
| Woodstock Rd., Wem. | 87 | J7 |
| Woodstock St. E16 Victoria Dock Rd. | 114/115 | E6 |
| **Woodstock St. W1** | **16** | **D4** |
| Woodstock Ter. E14 | 114 | B7 |
| Woodstock Way, Mitch. | 186 | B2 |
| Woodstone Av., Epsom | 197 | G5 |
| Woodsyre SE26 | 170 | C4 |
| Woodthorpe Rd. SW15 | 147 | H4 |
| Woodtree Cl. NW4 Ashley La. | 71 | J2 |
| Woodvale Av. SE25 | 188 | C3 |
| Woodvale Wk. SE27 Elder Rd. | 169 | J5 |
| Woodvale Way NW11 The Vale | 90 | A3 |
| Woodview Av. E4 | 62 | C4 |
| Woodview Cl. N4 | 75 | H7 |
| Woodview Cl. SW15 | 164 | D4 |
| Woodview Cl., Orp. Crofton Rd. | 207 | F2 |
| Woodville SE3 | 155 | H1 |
| Woodville Cl. SE12 | 155 | G5 |
| Woodville Cl., Tedd. | 162 | D4 |
| Woodville Gdns. NW11 | 72 | A7 |
| Woodville Gdns. W5 | 105 | H6 |
| Woodville Gdns., Ilf. | 80 | E3 |
| Woodville Gro., Well. | 158 | A3 |
| Woodville Rd. E11 | 97 | F1 |
| Woodville Rd. E17 | 77 | H4 |
| Woodville Rd. E18 | 79 | H2 |
| Woodville Rd. N16 | 94 | B5 |
| Woodville Rd. NW6 | 108 | C2 |
| Woodville Rd. NW11 | 72 | A7 |
| Woodville Rd. W5 | 105 | G6 |
| Woodville Rd., Barn. | 40 | E3 |
| Woodville Rd., Mord. | 184 | D4 |
| Woodville Rd., Rich. | 163 | E3 |
| Woodville Rd., Th.Hth. | 187 | J4 |
| Woodville St. SE18 Woodhill | 136 | B4 |
| Woodward Av. NW4 | 71 | G5 |
| Woodward Cl., Esher | 194 | C6 |
| Woodward Gdns., Dag. Woodward Rd. | 100 | C7 |
| Woodward Gdns., Stan. | 52 | C7 |
| Woodward Rd., Dag. | 100 | B7 |
| Woodwarde Rd. SE22 | 152 | B6 |
| Woodway Cres., Har. | 68 | D6 |
| Woodwell St. SW18 Huguenot Pl. | 149 | F5 |
| Woodyard Cl. NW5 Gillies St. | 92 | A5 |
| Woodyard La. SE21 | 152 | B7 |
| Woodyates Rd. SE12 | 155 | G6 |
| Wool Rd. SW20 | 165 | H6 |
| Woolacombe Rd. SE3 | 155 | J1 |
| Woolacombe Way, Hayes | 121 | H4 |

| | | |
|---|---|---|
| Woolmer Rd. N18 | 60 | D5 |
| Woolmore St. E14 | 114 | C7 |
| Woolneigh St. SW6 | 148 | E3 |
| **Woolstaplers Way SE16** | **29** | **H6** |
| Woolstaplers Way SE16 | 132 | D4 |
| Woolston Cl. E17 Riverhead Cl. | 77 | G2 |
| Woolstone Rd. SE23 | 171 | H2 |
| Woolwich Ch. St. SE18 | 136 | B3 |
| Woolwich Common SE18 | 136 | D6 |
| Woolwich Ferry Pier E16 | 136 | D2 |
| Woolwich Foot Tunnel E16 | 136 | D2 |
| Woolwich Foot Tunnel SE18 | 136 | D2 |
| Woolwich Garrison SE18 | 136 | C6 |
| Woolwich High St. SE18 | 136 | D3 |
| Woolwich Ind. Est. SE28 Hadden Rd. | 137 | H3 |
| Woolwich Manor Way E6 | 116 | E6 |
| Woolwich Manor Way E16 | 136 | E2 |
| Woolwich New Rd. SE18 | 136 | D5 |
| Woolwich Rd. SE2 | 138 | D6 |
| Woolwich Rd. SE7 | 135 | G5 |
| Woolwich Rd. SE10 | 135 | F5 |
| Woolwich Rd., Belv. | 138 | D6 |
| Woolwich Rd., Bexh. | 159 | G4 |
| Wooster Gdns. E14 | 114 | D6 |
| Wooster Ms., Har. | 67 | J3 |
| Fairfield Dr. | | |
| **Wooster Pl. SE1** | **36** | **C1** |
| Wootton Gro. N3 | 72 | D1 |
| **Wootton St. SE1** | **27** | **F3** |
| Wootton St. SE1 | 131 | G1 |
| Worbeck Rd. SE20 | 189 | E2 |
| Worcester Av. N17 | 60 | D7 |
| Worcester Cl. NW2 Newfield Rd. | 89 | H3 |
| Worcester Cl., Croy. | 203 | J2 |
| Worcester Cl., Mitch. | 186 | B3 |
| Worcester Cres. NW7 | 54 | E3 |
| Worcester Cres., Wdf.Grn. | 63 | H5 |
| Worcester Dr. W4 | 127 | E2 |
| Worcester Gdns. SW11 Grandison Rd. | 149 | J5 |
| Worcester Gdns., Grnf. | 85 | J6 |
| Worcester Gdns., Ilf. | 80 | B7 |
| Worcester Gdns., Wor.Pk. | 197 | E3 |
| Worcester Ms. NW6 Lymington Rd. | 90/91 | E6 |
| Worcester Pk. Rd., Wor.Pk. | 196 | C3 |
| Worcester Rd. E12 | 98 | C4 |
| Worcester Rd. E17 | 77 | G2 |
| Worcester Rd. SW19 | 166 | C5 |
| Worcester Rd., Sutt. | 199 | E6 |
| Wordsworth Av. E12 | 98 | B6 |
| Wordsworth Av. E18 | 79 | F3 |
| Wordsworth Av., Grnf. | 104 | A2 |
| Wordsworth Dr., Sutt. | 197 | J4 |
| Wordsworth Rd. N16 | 94 | B4 |
| **Wordsworth Rd. SE1** | **37** | **F2** |
| Wordsworth Rd. SE20 | 171 | G7 |
| Wordsworth Rd., Hmptn. | 161 | F4 |
| Wordsworth Rd., Wall. | 200 | C6 |
| Wordsworth Rd., Well. | 157 | H1 |
| Wordsworth Wk. NW11 | 72 | D4 |
| Wordsworth Way, West Dr. | 120 | B4 |
| Worfield St. SW11 | 129 | H7 |
| **Worgan St. SE11** | **34** | **C3** |
| Worgan St. SE11 | 131 | F5 |
| Worgan St. SE16 | 133 | G3 |
| Worland Rd. E15 | 97 | E7 |
| **World's End Est. SW10** | **30** | **E7** |
| World's End Est. SW10 | 129 | G7 |
| World's End La. N21 | 43 | F5 |
| World's End La., Enf. | 43 | F5 |
| World's End La., Orp. | 207 | J6 |

| | | |
|---|---|---|
| **World's End Pas. SW10** | **30** | **E7** |
| Worlidge St. W6 | 127 | J5 |
| Worlingham Rd. SE22 | 152 | C4 |
| Wormholt Rd. W12 | 107 | G7 |
| **Wormwood St. EC2** | **20** | **D3** |
| Wormwood St. EC2 | 112 | B6 |
| Wornington Rd. W10 | 108 | B5 |
| Woronzow Rd. NW8 | 109 | G1 |
| Worple Av. SW19 | 166 | A7 |
| Worple Av., Islw. | 144 | D5 |
| Worple Cl., Har. | 85 | F1 |
| Worple Rd. SW19 | 166 | B7 |
| Worple Rd. SW20 | 183 | J2 |
| Worple Rd., Islw. | 144 | D4 |
| Worple Rd. Ms. SW19 | 166 | C6 |
| Worple St. SW14 | 146 | D3 |
| Worple Way, Har. | 85 | F1 |
| Worple Way, Rich. | 145 | H5 |
| **Worship St. EC2** | **12** | **C6** |
| Worship St. EC2 | 112 | A4 |
| Worslade Rd. SW17 | 167 | G4 |
| Worsley Br. Rd. SE26 | 171 | J4 |
| Worsley Br. Rd., Beck. | 171 | J5 |
| Worsley Rd. E11 | 96 | E4 |
| Worsopp Dr. SW4 | 150 | C5 |
| Worth Cl., Orp. | 207 | H4 |
| **Worth Gro. SE17** | **36** | **B4** |
| Worthfield Cl., Epsom | 196 | D7 |
| Worthing Cl. E15 Mitre Rd. | 114/115 | E2 |
| Worthing Rd., Houns. | 123 | F6 |
| Worthington Cl., Mitch. | 186 | B3 |
| Worthington Rd., Surb. | 195 | J1 |
| Worthy Down Ct. SE18 Prince Imperial Rd. | 156 | D1 |
| Wortley Rd. E6 | 98 | A7 |
| Wortley Rd., Croy. | 187 | G7 |
| Worton Gdns., Islw. | 144 | A2 |
| Worton Hall Ind. Est., Islw. | 144 | B4 |
| Worton Rd., Islw. | 144 | B3 |
| Worton Way, Houns. | 144 | A2 |
| Worton Way, Islw. | 144 | A2 |
| Wotton Rd. NW2 | 89 | J4 |
| Wotton Rd. SE8 | 133 | J6 |
| Wouldham Rd. E16 | 115 | F6 |
| Wragby Rd. E11 | 97 | E3 |
| Wrampling Pl. N9 | 60 | D1 |
| Wrangthorn Wk., Croy. Epsom Rd. | 201 | G4 |
| Wray Av., Ilf. | 80 | D3 |
| Wray Cres. N4 | 93 | E2 |
| Wrayfield Rd., Sutt. | 198 | A3 |
| Wraysbury Cl., Houns. Dorney Way | 142/143 | E5 |
| Wrekin Rd. SE18 | 137 | F7 |
| Wren Av. NW2 | 89 | J5 |
| Wren Av., Sthl. | 123 | F4 |
| Wren Cl. E16 | 115 | F6 |
| Wren Cl. N9 Chaffinch Cl. | 61 | G1 |
| Wren Cres., Bushey | 51 | J1 |
| Wren Dr., West Dr. | 120 | A3 |
| Wren Gdns., Dag. | 100 | D5 |
| Wren Landing E14 Cabot Sq. | 134 | A1 |
| Wren Path SE28 | 137 | G3 |
| Wren Rd. SE5 | 152 | A1 |
| Wren Rd., Dag. | 100 | D5 |
| Wren Rd., Sid. | 176 | C4 |
| **Wren St. WC1** | **10** | **D5** |
| Wren St. WC1 | 111 | F4 |
| Wrentham Av. NW10 | 108 | A2 |
| Wrenthorpe Rd., BR1 Brom. | 172 | E4 |
| Wrenwood Way, Pnr. | 66 | B4 |
| Wrestlers Ct. EC3 Camomile St. | 112 | B6 |
| Wrexham Rd. E3 | 114 | A2 |
| Wricklemarsh Rd. SE3 | 155 | H1 |
| Wrigglesworth St. SE14 | 133 | G7 |
| Wright Rd. N1 Burder Cl. | 94 | B6 |
| Wright Rd., Houns. | 122 | C7 |
| Wrights All. SW19 | 165 | J6 |
| Wrights Cl. SE13 Wisteria Rd. | 154 | D4 |
| Wrights Cl., Dag. | 101 | H3 |
| Wrights Grn. SW4 Nelson's Row | 150 | D4 |
| **Wrights La. W8** | **22** | **A5** |
| Wrights La. W8 | 128 | E3 |